MW01201099

"Open this handbook with great care, for in it you will find a mirror (at times, a black mirror) reflecting a contemporary vision and analysis of yourself, your world, and the technologies that shape you. Psychoanalysis becomes the perfect tool for exploring how we live with and are lived by technology, and this book digs deep into the theory, practice, and process of living in a world transformed by the machines we create."

— **Jack Foehl**, *President, Boston Psychoanalytic Society & Institute*

"If one were able to go back in time and tell Louis XIV, in all his glory, that in our times one can have a warm home equipped with hot running waters throughout the winter and a cool breeze in his bedchamber all summer long and do so effortlessly; or the means to illuminate every corner in his rooms and every room in his house at will; or to have any meal or drink his appetite might fancy delivered to him within the hour at his door; or have his coffee made at the press of a button; or to have the uncanny ability to summon in his presence the representations of absent people, whether living or dead, hear them talking and talk with them as if they were present, and, in short, all of the other abilities modern technology makes possible to us, he would say that these are powers unfathomable even to a Sun King, to be assigned perhaps only to a god, even if, as Freud aptly put it, a prosthetic god.

And if one were able to go back in time and tell King Solomon, in all his wisdom, that such god-like powers have been given to all, from haughty rulers to humble parlormaids, and given equally, he would question whether our powerful devices have made the latter any happier or the former wiser than him. It takes an analytic approach, as Freud again rightly notes, to untangle the tele-technological enigma. And it is to our great benefit that this handbook begins the work of doing just that."

— **John Panteleimon Manoussakis**,
Associate Professor of Philosophy, College of the Holy Cross

THE ROUTLEDGE INTERNATIONAL HANDBOOK OF PSYCHOANALYSIS, SUBJECTIVITY, AND TECHNOLOGY

The Routledge International Handbook of Psychoanalysis, Subjectivity, and Technology uniquely provides a comprehensive overview of human subjectivity in the technological age and how psychoanalysis can help us better understand human life.

Presented in five parts, David M. Goodman and Matthew Clemente collaborate with an international community of scholars and practitioners to consider how psychoanalytic formulations can be brought to bear on the impact technology has had on the facets of human subjectivity. Chapters examine how technology is reshaping our understanding of what it means to be a human subject, through embodiment, intimacy, porn, political motivation, mortality, communication, interpersonal exchange, thought, attention, responsibility, vulnerability, and more. Filled with thought-provoking and nuanced chapters, the contributors approach technology from a diverse range of entry points but all engage through the lens of psychoanalytic theory, practice, and thought.

This book is essential for academics and students of psychoanalysis, philosophy, ethics, media, liberal arts, social work, and bioethics. With the inclusion of timely chapters on the coronavirus pandemic and teletherapy, psychoanalysts in practice and training as well as other mental health practitioners will also find this book an invaluable resource.

David M. Goodman is an Associate Dean at the Lynch School of Education and Human Development, the Director of the newly launching Center for Psychological Humanities and Ethics, and serves on the faculty in three Boston College departments: Counseling, Developmental, and Educational Psychology, Philosophy, and Formative Education.

Matthew Clemente is a husband and father. He is a Research Fellow in the Center for Psychological Humanities and Ethics at Boston College and the Coeditor in Chief of the *Journal for Continental Philosophy of Religion*.

ROUTLEDGE INTERNATIONAL HANDBOOKS

THE ROUTLEDGE INTERNATIONAL HANDBOOK OF PSYCHOANALYSIS, SUBJECTIVITY, AND TECHNOLOGY

Edited by
David M. Goodman and Matthew Clemente

NEW YORK AND LONDON

Designed cover image: © Getty Images

First published 2024
by Routledge
605 Third Avenue, New York, NY 10158

and by Routledge
4 Park Square, Milton Park, Abingdon, Oxon, OX14 4RN

Routledge is an imprint of the Taylor & Francis Group, an informa business

© 2024 selection and editorial matter, David M. Goodman and Matthew Clemente; individual chapters, the contributors

The right of David M. Goodman and Matthew Clemente to be identified as the authors of the editorial material, and of the authors for their individual chapters, has been asserted in accordance with sections 77 and 78 of the Copyright, Designs and Patents Act 1988.

All rights reserved. No part of this book may be reprinted or reproduced or utilised in any form or by any electronic, mechanical, or other means, now known or hereafter invented, including photocopying and recording, or in any information storage or retrieval system, without permission in writing from the publishers.

Trademark notice: Product or corporate names may be trademarks or registered trademarks, and are used only for identification and explanation without intent to infringe.

ISBN: 9781032050690 (hbk)
ISBN: 9781032050706 (pbk)
ISBN: 9781003195849 (ebk)

DOI: 10.4324/9781003195849

Typeset in Bembo
by codeMantra

For Katie
&
Tracy

CONTENTS

ACKNOWLEDGMENTS

In addition to the work of our contributors, this project would not have been possible without the tireless efforts of our editors, particularly Sarah Gore, Upasruti Biswas, and the entire editorial team at Routledge/Taylor & Francis, our wonderful Graduate Assistant, Haleigh Creamer, the constant support of Boston College which has shown an incredible dedication to this type of interdisciplinary research—including its recent launch of a Center for Psychological Humanities and Ethics which will aim to foster further projects of this kind—and the John Templeton Foundation, to which we are exceedingly grateful.

This publication was made possible through the support of Grant 62632 from the John Templeton Foundation. The opinions expressed in this publication are those of the authors and do not necessarily reflect the views of the John Templeton Foundation.

CONTRIBUTORS

Brian W. Becker is Professor of Neuropsychology and Associate Chair in the Division of Psychology & Applied Therapies at Lesley University in Cambridge, MA. He obtained his PhD in clinical psychology and MA in theology from Fuller Theological Seminary in Pasadena, CA. He completed a postdoctoral fellowship in geriatric neuropsychology at the West Los Angeles Veteran Affairs Healthcare Center and the Mary S. Easton Center for Alzheimer's Disease Research in the Department of Neurology at UCLA. He is co-editor-in-chief of the *Journal for Continental Philosophy of Religion* and an associate editor of the Routledge *Psychology and the Other* book series. He authored the book *Evil and Givenness: The Thanatonic Phenomenon*, published by Lexington Books (2022), and has co-edited several volumes including *Unconscious Incarnations: Psychoanalytic and Philosophical Perspectives on the Body* (2018, Routledge).

Bibi Calderaro is a PhD Candidate in Urban Education at The Graduate Center, CUNY, and a transdisciplinary artist, educator and scholar. She holds a Sustainability Science and Education MA, an MFA in Social Practice.

Matthew Clemente is a husband and father. He is a Research Fellow in the *Center for Psychological Humanities and Ethics* at Boston College and the Coeditor in Chief of the *Journal for Continental Philosophy of Religion*. His latest book, *Technology and Its Discontents* (co-authored with David Goodman), is forthcoming from Oxford University Press.

Patricia T. Clough is Professor Emerita in Sociology and Women's Studies at Graduate Center, CUNY, and a practicing psychoanalyst in NYC. She is the author of a number of publications concerned with media/technologies and subjectivity, most recently, *The User Unconscious: Affect, Media and Measure* (University of Minnesota Press, 2018). She is a member of the Training Committee of Institute for Contemporary Psychotherapy (ICP), faculty at ICP and National Institute for Psychotherapies (NIP) and a practicing psychoanalyst in New York City.

Gabriel J. Costello is a lecturer in Engineering at the Galway-Mayo Institute of Technology. Prior to this, he worked for 20 years in the telecommunications industry where he held engineering, supply chain and product management positions. In 2010, he completed a PhD in Management Information Systems at the J.E. Cairnes School of Business & Economics, National University of Ireland, Galway in the area of information systems innovation. This research involved a two-year action research study based in an Irish Multinational Subsidiary. His 2004 Masters by Research (MEng) examined the diffusion of energy management practices in Ireland's SME sector and was supported by the Sustainable Energy Authority of Ireland (SEAI). He is Programme Co-ordinator for the MSc in Design and Innovation. Gabriel holds the title of Chartered Engineer (CEng MIEI) from Engineers Ireland. He has over 80 peer-reviewed publications and in May 2020 published a book with Springer: *The Teaching of Design and Innovation: Principles and Practices*.

Susi Ferrarello is Assistant Professor at California State University, East Bay. Among her books: *Husserl's Ethics and Practical Intentionality* (Bloomsbury 2015), *Phenomenology of Sex, Love and Intimacy* (Routledge, 2018), *Human Emotions and the Origin of Bioethics* (Routledge, 2021), and *The Ethics of Love* (Routledge, 2022). She writes for *Psychology Today* and works also as a philosophical counselor.

Lisa Finlay is a licensed clinical psychologist and has a private practice in southern California. She also supervises doctoral students at Fuller Psychological and Family Services and teaches a course on program administration at Fuller Graduate School of Psychology. Previously, Dr. Finlay worked at the Headington Institute, where she was the Director of International Programs, overseeing the provision of psychological training and psychotherapy support services to international aid workers. Dr. Finlay's interest in therapy bots began suddenly and spontaneously in 2016, after she happened upon an article in *The New Yorker* about their development and early application for Syrian refugees in Turkey. She received her BA in English Literature from Rice University and her PhD in clinical psychology from Fuller Graduate School of Psychology.

Richard Frankel, PhD, is a faculty member and supervisor at The Massachusetts Institute for Psychoanalysis. He is a teaching associate and supervisor in psychiatry at Harvard Medical School. He has a private practice in psychotherapy and psychoanalysis in Belmont, MA. He was written, taught, and lectured widely on the topics of dreams, Winnicott, Bion, technology, the non-representable, and the imagination. He is the author of *The Adolescent Psyche: Jungian and Winnicottian Perspectives* (Routledge, 1998), recently added to the Routledge Classic Edition Series. He has co-authored (with Victor J. Krebs) *Human Virtuality and Digital Life: Philosophical and Psychoanalytic Investigations* (Routledge, 2022) and is preparing a second volume, continuing their exploration of the digital revolution.

Samuel C. Gable, PhD, is a psychotherapist and researcher based in northern Chile and Massachusetts. His clinical work focuses on crosscultural neuropsychology and counseling. Samuel's recent scholarly work has explored the treatment of medical comorbidities affecting Latino/a patients with dementia, and issues of sexual ethics and education. He is beginning work on a book-length series of philosophical essays and social commentary exploring the potential for a new Romantic turn in culture and its obstacles, not least of which include the influences on subjectivity of psychology and psychoanalysis.

Katie Gentile, PhD, is Professor and Chair of the Department of Interdisciplinary Studies at John Jay College of Criminal Justice (City University of New York). She is the author of *Creating Bodies: Eating Disorders as Self-destructive Survival* (Routledge, 2006) and the 2017

Gradiva Award winning *The Business of Being Made: The Temporalities of Reproductive Technologies, in Psychoanalysis and Cultures* (2015), both from Routledge. She is editor of the journal *Studies in Gender and Sexuality*, on the faculty of New York University's Postdoctoral Program in Psychotherapy and the Psychoanalysis and the Critical Social Psychology program at the CUNY Graduate Center. She has published numerous articles and book chapters on eating disorders, sexual and racial/cultural violence, restorative and community-based justice and sexual misconduct in colleges and institutes, and the cultural and psychic production of temporalities around human reproduction, fetal personhood, and the geno- and eco-cidal violence of human exceptionalism. She is in private practice in New York City. She is also a recording musician who has toured and plays violin with a number of bands.

Julia Goetz, BA, is a recent Boston College graduate who majored in Applied Psychology and Human Development. Julia has experience working with refugee children, middle schoolers in an after-school running program and families facing eviction.

David M. Goodman is the Associate Dean for Strategic Initiatives and External Relations, Director of the Center for Psychological Humanities and Ethics, and an Associate Professor of the Practice in Counseling, Developmental, and Educational Psychology in the Lynch School of Education and Human Development at Boston College. He is also an Associate Professor of the Practice in the Philosophy department in Boston College's Morrissey College of Arts and Sciences. Dr. Goodman currently serves as the Series Editor for the *Psychology and the Other* book series with Routledge. He has authored and edited over a dozen books including *The Demanded Self: Levinasian Ethics and Identity in Psychology* (with Duquesne University Press, 2012), *Psychology and the Other* (with Mark Freeman and Oxford University Press, 2015), *The Ethical Turn: Otherness and Subjectivity in Contemporary Psychoanalysis* (with Eric Severson and Routledge, 2016), *In the Wake of Trauma: Psychology and Philosophy for the Suffering Other* (with Eric Severson and Brian Becker and Duquesne University Press, 2016), *Critical and Theoretical Perspectives in Psychology: Dialogues at the Edge of American Psychological Discourse* (with Heather Macdonald and Brian Becker and Palgrave Macmillan, 2017), and *Memories and Monsters* (with Eric Severson and Routledge, 2017). Co-authored with Matthew Clemente, Dr. Goodman currently has a book under contract with Oxford University Press titled *Technology and Its Discontents* (forthcoming). Dr. Goodman is also a licensed clinical psychologist and has a private practice in Boston, MA.

A. Taiga Guterres, MSW, MA, is managing editor of the *Jesuit Educational Quarterly* at the Institute for Advanced Jesuit Studies, where he engages and facilitates collegiality between the Institute and the global network of Jesuit Studies scholars. Taiga received a post-graduate fellowship with the Massachusetts Institute for Psychoanalysis and was the '21-'22 social work Community Fellow at Massachusetts General Hospital, where he provided outpatient behavioral services in Spanish to Latinx populations.

Karley M.P. Guterres, MA, MTS, is a research fellow in the Albert and Jessie Danielsen Institute at Boston University, where she is involved in projects exploring BIPOC clients' experiences of racial and cultural differences in the therapeutic relationship, as well as exploring burnout in mental health clinicians. She also spends her time as a staff clinician at Fitchburg State University Counseling Services. Her clinical interests involve employing percent-centered and psychodynamic techniques to build relationships with youth who hold complex narratives of suffering inflicted by both individuals and systems. Karley is currently involved in the post-graduate fellowship with the Massachusetts Institute for Psychoanalysis.

Stephen Hartman, PhD, is a joint editor-in-chief for Psychoanalytic Dialogues and former editor of Studies in Gender and Sexuality. He is on the faculty of the NYU Postdoctoral Program in Psychotherapy and Psychoanalysis and teaches at the Psychoanalytic Institute of Northern California. Stephen is the author of several articles and book chapters that bridge between psychoanalytic theory and technology. He is currently assembling a collection of reading and writing experiments, *Reading with Muriel Dimen/Writing with Muriel Dimen*, in which essays by Dimen are responded to by 30 authors from seven continents with a diverse range of life experiences and academic practices to be published by Routledge.

William J. Hendel, JD, is a teaching fellow and PhD student in the Department of Philosophy at Boston College, who specializes in ethics, political philosophy, and aesthetics. He is the co-editor of *misReading Plato* (with Matthew Clemente and Bryan Cocchiara, Routledge, 2022).

Iréne Hultman is a dance-artist and performer and teaches at Theater and Performance Studies, at Yale University. Her research focuses on how media, affect and speculative theory influence movement and art production.

Talha İşsevenler is a PhD candidate in Sociology at the Graduate Center, CUNY, and teaches at the City College CUNY. His dissertation research develops genealogies of temporality by focusing on new social media formats and their political affordances.

Jacob Johanssen is Senior Lecturer in Communications, St. Mary's University (London, UK). His most recent books are *Fantasy, Online Misogyny and the Manosphere: Male Bodies of Dis/Inhibition* (Routledge, 2022), and, with Bonni Rambatan *Event Horizon: Sexuality, Politics, Online Culture, and the Limits of Capitalism* (Zer0 Books, 2021). His book *Media and Psychoanalysis: A Critical Introduction* (written with Steffen Krüger) was published by Confer Books in 2022. Jacob is a Founder Scholar of the British Psychoanalytic Council (BPC). He is Co-Editor of the Counterspace section of the journal *Psychoanalysis, Culture & Society*.

Anestis Karastergiou holds a PhD on Canguilhem's epistemology and the relationship between man and machine from Panteion University of Athens, completed in late 2020. His basic research interests include philosophy of science and technology, moral philosophy, business and technoscientific ethics. He also completed the Science, Technology, and Society master's degree at National and Kapodistrian University of Athens. Apart from these, he holds two bachelor's degrees, one in Greek Philology and the other in the History and Philosophy of Science, along with a master's degree in Philosophy (Ethics), from NKUA. He is currently working on a project for open academic books in Greece with a fellow researcher on the subject of philosophy and gender.

Richard Kearney holds the Charles B. Seelig Chair of Philosophy at Boston College. He is the author of more than twenty books on philosophy and literature, including *Strangers, Gods, and Monsters* (Taylor & Francis, 2003), *On Stories* (Routledge, 2002), *The God Who May Be* (Indiana University Press, 2001), *Anatheism: Returning to God After God* (Columbia University Press, 2011), and *Touch* (Columbia University Press, 2021), as well as two novels and a volume of poetry. In addition, he has edited or co-edited sixteen books, including *Carnal Hermeneutics* (Fordham University Press, 2015), *Reimagining the Sacred: Richard Kearney Debates God* (Columbia University Press, 2015), and *The Art of Anatheism* (Rowman and Littlefield, 2017). In 2008 he launched the Guestbook Project, an ongoing artistic, academic, and multimedia experiment in hospitality.

Victor J. Krebs is professor of philosophy at the Pontifical Catholic University of Peru (PUCP) and philosophical curator at VJK Curaduría Filosófica. He has written on Wittgenstein, philosophy of language, psychoanalysis, aesthetics, film, and popular culture. He is author of *La imaginación pornográfica. Contra el escepticismo en la cultura* (Lima, 2014), *La recuperación del sentido. Wittgenstein, la filosofía y lo trascendente* (Caracas, 2008) and *Del alma y el arte. Imagen, cultura y memoria* (Caracas, 1998). He is co-author (with Richard Frankel) of *Human Virtuality and Digital Life* (Routledge, 2022), and contributing co-editor (with William Day) of *Seeing Wittgenstein Anew* (Cambridge, 2010). He is currently writing (with R. Frankel) a book on dreams and the digital virtual. He has been recipient of a Fulbright Scholarship (Vanderbilt University) and a Konrad Adenauer Stiftung Fellowship (Bonn, Germany), and is currently coordinator of the Latin American Posthuman Network, and of Hermes, a research group on contemporary philosophy at the Center for Philosophical Studies (CEF) at PUCP. He collaborates regularly with the Sunday Supplement of El Comercio in Lima.

Stephen Lugar, PsyD, is a clinical psychologist and advanced psychoanalytic candidate at the Psychoanalytic Institute of Northern California (PINC) in San Francisco. He is also on the Board of Directors of PINC. He is the author of "Father Figure: On Dangerous Daddies and Cross-Generational Desire" and has published several articles on gender issues and gay male identity development. He is on the faculty of the San Francisco Center for Psychoanalysis, teaching courses in child development and has taught and supervised at multiple community mental health centers in the Bay Area. He is currently interested in the intersection of technology and the social, gender studies, the plasticity and openness of the field of psychoanalysis, and the effects of climate change realities on the individual and collective psyche. He is in private practice in San Francisco working with adults and children.

Heather Macdonald, PsyD, came to academia after years of practice as a clinical psychologist whose work involved community outreach, child assessment, and individual therapeutic services to children and families in the foster care system and with youth involved in the juvenile justice system. Her work in urban environments and abroad has led to scholarly research that includes the interface between culture, relational ethics, nomadic ethics, and community clinical practice. Theoretically, these investigations draw upon a cross-fertilization of ideas and disciplines such as cultural phenomenology, psychoanalytic geography, psychopolitical theories, and continental philosophy (Deleuze and Derrida). Some recent publications include the following: "Issues of Translation, Mistrust and Co-Collaboration in Therapeutic Assessment" (2010), and "The Foot Fetish: Events, Reversals and Language in the Collaborative Assessment Process" (2015).

Peter Maduro, JD, PsyD, is a faculty member and Supervising and Training Psychoanalyst at the Institute of Contemporary Psychoanalysis, West Los Angeles, and is a member of the International Association of Psychoanalytic Self Psychology, International Association of Relational Psychoanalysis and Psychotherapy, and the American Psychological Association, Division 39 (Psychoanalysis).

M. Mookie C. Manalili is a psychotherapist, professor, and researcher interested in suffering, meaning, narratives, trauma, and memory. In terms of practice, Mookie is a Licensed Certified Social Worker psychotherapist in private practice. In terms of teaching, he is a part-time Faculty for the Graduate School of Social Work at Boston College, teaching clinical courses like Narrative Therapy. In terms of research, Mookie serves as a Research

Consultant at Boston College, for social psychology research at the Morality Lab, and for philosophical psychology initiatives through the Center for Psychological Humanities and Ethics. In his various roles, Mookie hopes to participate in our duty to a better society: particularly for folks who suffer injustices; for the widow, orphan, and stranger; for a future and world beyond one's self.

Sandra Moyano-Ariza is a PhD Candidate in English at The Graduate Center, CUNY. Her research focuses on digital technology and philosophy, with interests in the fields of affect theory, media studies, speculative realisms, and feminist ontologies.

Hattie Myers is a Training and Supervising Analyst at the Institute for Training and Research (IPTAR). She has served on faculty at IPTAR, Institute for Contemporary Psychotherapy (ICP), NYU School of Social Work, and National Institute for Psychotherapies (NIP) and as director of the IPTAR clinical center. She is co-editor of *Terrorism in the Psychoanalytic Space* (NY Pace University Press 2003) and *Warmed by the Fires: The Collected Papers of Allan Frosch* (IP Press 2017). She received the Linda Neuwirth award for her paper, "Recollecting Plato" which was presented at the International Psychoanalytic Assoc. Conference in Berlin, 2007. Other papers presented at national and international conferences have been on the topic of Therapeutic Action in psychoanalysis, as well as on the connections between Dante and psychoanalysis. She has served as a founder and Editor in Chief of *ROOM: A Sketchbook for Analytic Action*, which won the Gradiva Award for Psychoanalysis in a New Media in 2018.

Jason Nielsen is PhD Candidate in English at The Graduate Center, CUNY, and Program Coordinator for Digital Humanities MA and Data Analysis & Visualization MS Programs. His research focuses on technology, psychoanalysis, affect, pedagogy, and pragmatism.

Osmano Oasi, PhD, PsyD, is Associate Professor in Psychodynamic Psychology at Catholic University of Milan and an associate member of Italian Psychoanalytical Society.

Robert D. Romanyshyn is the first non-analyst elected as an Affiliate Member of The Inter-Regional Society of Jungian Analysts based upon his scholarly contributions to Jungian psychology. A Fellow of the Dallas Institute of Humanities and Culture, he co-founded in 1972 an interdisciplinary program in existential-phenomenological psychology and literature at the University of Dallas. In 1991 he moved to Pacifica Graduate Institute to create an interdisciplinary doctoral program in clinical psychology with an emphasis on depth psychology. On his retirement in 2015, he was awarded the title professor emeritus. In addition to online webinars, interviews, lectures, and workshops at universities and professional societies in the United States, Europe, Australia, South Africa, Canada, and New Zealand, he has given keynote addresses at international conferences including "Educating the Quixotic Imagination," at The European Consortium of Arts-Therapy Education in 2019. He has published eight books, numerous articles in psychology, philosophy, education, literary, and poetry journals, written a one-act play about Frankenstein, and in 2009 created a multimedia DVD entitled *Antarctica: Inner Journeys in the Outer World*. He lives in the Aude region of southwest France with his beloved Veronica Goodchild.

Chiara Rossi is a PhD Candidate in Psychology at the Catholic University of Milan.

Susan E. Schwartz, PhD, trained in Zurich, Switzerland as a Jungian analyst is also a clinical psychologist and member of the International Association of Analytical Psychology. She teaches in numerous Jungian programs, workshops, and lectures in the United States and worldwide. Susan has articles in many journals and chapters in books on Jungian analytical psychology. Her current book is translated into several languages and was published by Routledge in 2020. It is entitled *The Absent Father Effect on Daughters, Father Desire, Father Wounds.* She can be found on LinkedIn, Facebook, and Instagram. Her Jungian analytical practice is in Paradise Valley, Arizona, USA and her website is www.susanschwartzphd.com.

Eric R. Severson is a philosopher specializing in the work of Emmanuel Levinas. He is the author of *Before Ethics* (Kendall Hunt, 2021), *Levinas's Philosophy of Time* (Duquesne University Press, 2013), and *Scandalous Obligation* (Beacon Hill Press, 2011), and editor of seven other books. He lives in Kenmore, Washington and teaches philosophy at Seattle University.

Manolis Simos is a postdoctoral fellow at the Department of History and Philosophy of Science, University of Athens, where he is currently teaching at a graduate level on philosophy of technology, and on the relations among literature, science, and technology. He studied history and philosophy of science at the University of Athens, and he has an MPhil in European Literature, and a PhD on the thought of Michel Foucault, both from the University of Cambridge. His research interests include the history of philosophy, metaphilosophy, the relations between philosophy and literature, and the history of concepts.

Isaac Slone received his BA and MA NYU Gallatin School of Individualized Study where he studied the relationship between psychoanalysis, music, and literature. He is a candidate at the Psychoanalytic Training Institute of the Contemporary Freudian Society. He is the Director of Development for *ROOM: A Sketchbook for Analytic Action.* He writes and lectures on James Joyce, and rock bands the Grateful Dead and Phish. At NYU Gallatin, he was honored with the Undergraduate Interdisciplinary Academic Excellence Award for his work on the relationship between narrative theory and concepts of identity formation, and the Graduate Interdisciplinary Academic Excellence Award for his work on psychoanalytic technique and performance studies. Isaac is also a formal student at the New York Zen Center for Contemplative Care.

Jean Marc Tauszik was born in Caracas, Venezuela, in 1970. He is a psychoanalyst, member of the SPC (Psychoanalytic Society of Caracas) and of the APA (Argentine Psychoanalytic Association). He is currently co-chair for Latin America (2021–2025) of the Committee on Gender and Sexual Diversities of the IPA (International Psychoanalytic Association), coordinator of the research group Coloquios Psicoanalíticos of the APA and coordinator of PPL (Pensamiento Psicoanalítico Latinoamericano). He co-edited the books *Contemporary Latin American Psychoanalysis* Vol. 1 (2018), *Polymorphisms. Sexual and Gender Diversities in Contemporary Psychoanalysis* (2021) and *Technomorphisms. The Posthuman Turn and Contemporary Psychoanalysis* (in press). In 2009 he was awarded the IPSO (International psychoanalytical studies organization) prize.

Lewis Thurston, BA, is a graduate student in the Master of Counseling program at the Townsend Institute for Counseling and Leadership at Concordia University Irvine. He earned his bachelor's degree in Philosophy from George Fox University. His interest in the interface of technology (particularly memes) and psychoanalysis has led him to present several papers at the Society for Psychoanalysis of Culture and Society International Conference and the Psychology of the Other Biennial Conference. He has also presented at the annual international conference of the Christian Association for Psychological Studies. He served as the Technology Interface Moderator for the Oskar Pfister Conference in Lausanne, Switzerland in 2018. He is a member of the Society for the Exploration of Psychoanalytic Therapies and Theology, The Oregon Friends of Jung, and a student associate of the American Psychoanalytic Association and The American Counseling Association. He lives in Dundee, Oregon.

Nancy Thurston, PsyD, ABPP, is a psychoanalyst and Board Certified Clinical Psychologist in private practice in Oregon. She is a tenured professor in the Graduate School Clinical Psychology at George Fox University, where she has served for the last 22 years, following nine years on the faculty of Fuller Theological Seminary Graduate School of Psychology. She is also a member of the faculty of the Brookhaven Institute for Psychoanalysis and Christian Theology, where she served as Chair of the Progression Committee. She has served on the executive committee of Division 36 (Psychology of Religion) of the American Psychological Association as well as the Committee on Accreditation of the American Board of Accreditation in Psychoanalysis. She is a Fellow of the American Academy of Clinical Psychology. Her publications include the Thurston-Cradock Test of Shame and various journal articles. She lives in Dundee, Oregon.

Hannah Venable, PhD, works in ethics and continental philosophy, especially existentialism, phenomenology and post-structuralism. Her book, *Madness in Experience and History: Merleau-Ponty's Phenomenology and Foucault's Archaeology* (Routledge, 2022), has been recently published in the *Psychology and the Other* book series. Her articles have appeared in the journals, *Foucault Studies, Religions, Journal of Speculative Philosophy,* and *Philosophy & Theology.* She also has a chapter published in a recent edited volume, *Normality, Abnormality, and Pathology in Merleau-Ponty* (SUNY Press, 2022). She has taught at the University of Dallas, Texas State University, and Trinity University and is now an assistant professor of philosophy at the University of Mary.

Roberto Viganoni, PsyD, is an American Psychological Association member.

Hannah Zeavin is a Lecturer in the Departments of English and History at the University of California, Berkeley and is on the Executive Committee of the University of California at Berkeley Center for Science, Technology, Medicine, and Society and on the Executive Committee of the Berkeley Center for New Media. Additionally, she is a visiting fellow at the Columbia University Center for the Study of Social Difference. Zeavin serves as an Editorial Associate for *The Journal of the American Psychoanalytic Association.* Zeavin's first book, *The Distance Cure: A History of Teletherapy* was published in 2021 by MIT Press, with a Foreword by John Durham Peters. She is at work on her second book, *Mother's Little Helpers: Technology in the American Family* (MIT Press, 2023). Other work has appeared in or is forthcoming from differences, *Dissent, The Guardian, The Los Angeles Review of Books, n+1, Slate, Technology & Culture, The Washington Post,* and beyond.

Hub Zwart (1960) studied philosophy and psychology at Radboud University Nijmegen and defended his thesis in 1993 (cum laude). In 2000 he became full Professor of Philosophy at the Faculty of Science RU Nijmegen. In 2018 he was appointed as Dean of Erasmus School of Philosophy (Erasmus University Rotterdam). He is editor-in-chief of the Library for Ethics and Applied Philosophy (Springer). His research develops a philosophical (dialectical) assessment of contemporary technoscience. Special attention is devoted to the dialectical relationship between science and genres of the imagination (drama, poetry, cinema, novels, music). He published 20 books (seven in English), 150 international peer-reviewed articles as first or single author and presented more than 200 international academic lectures, most of them invited. His open-access monograph entitled *Continental Philosophy of Technoscience* has just been published (Springer, 2021).

INTRODUCTION

Technology and Its Discontents

David M. Goodman and Matthew Clemente

For all of his critiques of civilized society—and they are legion—Freud is without question a friend of civilization and an advocate of the limits it places upon human desire. Man, living in the confines of society, is discontented; but so too is he safer, freer, and more prosperous than any creature struggling to survive under the brutish yoke of nature, with all the danger and terror such a way of life entails. The title of Freud's seminal work, then, ought to read with an emphasis on the "and" as *Civilization* AND *Its Discontents*—a book that highlights the duplicity of social life, that reveals the good and the bad, the benefits and disadvantages, the two sides of every manmade thing. Civilization strips us of much—there is no denying it—while at the same time bequeathing much. It gives and it takes away. As Plato, with whom Freud was well acquainted, points out, we can count among the blessings of social life not only our upbringing, education, and personal security, but even our conception and birth (see, *Crito*, 50c–e). It is society that houses us, feeds us, rears us, makes us who we are. And as such, it is society that dictates who we are—who and what we are allowed to be. The discontent we feel because of the restrictions imposed by civilization is a part of the bargain. If we want the good, we must take the bad along with it. More. The good and the bad are coterminous. Every blessing is also a curse, as Kierkegaard rightly notes.

This is the genius of Freud: to remain ambivalent. To see things in all of their splendor and cruelty. To note the proximity of the high and the low: "vom Himmel durch die Welt zur Hölle" (Freud, 2000, p. 28). There is a profound wisdom in employing such a measured approach. Freud possesses a rare discerning eye, one capable of picking up on the variations, subtleties, and nuances of a subject as complex as it is compelling. Following his example, any thinker who wishes to plumb the depths of the human psyche and its relation to the systems and structures that characterize our condition must begin with a recognition of the duality of all human things. Nothing is simple—this has to be acknowledged from the start. Everything is mixed up. Everything is confused. From the human perspective, there is no perfectly beneficent or perfectly destructive force. Good and bad, helpful and harmful, life-giving and life-denying—our binary concepts are always found growing together, twin stocks from a single root.

It is for this reason—and out of a deep appreciation for such Freudian tact—that we have chosen to cluster the essays that open this handbook on technology and subjectivity around the theme of the dual nature of technological advance. Thomas de Quincey (2016), in his

DOI: 10.4324/9781003195849-1

satirical essay *On Murder Considered as One of the Fine Arts*, tells us that "Everything in this world has two handles" (p. 5). To this observation, Emerson (2017) adds the subsequent caution, "Beware of the wrong one" (p. 2). The contributions in Part One of the handbook you now hold take up Freud's challenge to give complicated topics their due while also heeding Emerson's prescient advice. Making use of the Greek notion of the *pharmakon* or drug as that which has the power to heal and poison, save life and take it away, our opening essays apply the logic of the drug to technology—the *pharmakon* of our age. Resisting the temptation to treat technology with the either/or binary that so often characterizes commentaries today, the authors of these pieces remind us of the ambivalent nature of the devices we use, the promise technology offers and the price it inflicts. Like Heidegger (1977), who in his famous essay, *The Question Concerning Technology*, insists that "where the danger is, grows the saving power also" (p. 32), the contributors to our first section

> can appreciate the radically new and emancipatory spaces opened up for dreaming by our technologies today, while at the same time attending to the digital's narrowing effects on significant dimensions of psychic life that result in the inhibition of dream function
>
> *(Frankel, 2023, p.34)*

They examine technology *and* its discontents, the benefits, the harms, and everything in between.

Following this opening section, which frames the text by providing a hermeneutic by which to read the subsequent contributions, Part Two begins the movement from theory to practice, offering rich, philosophical essays that speak to both the ideas that ground our thinking about technology and our uses of technology in our daily lives. When asked, most of us will admit that we are overly reliant upon our devices. Our days are structured and organized by the technologies we use. And while remarks about this overreliance on technology have become commonplace and the rapidly changing technological landscape has received intensive commentary in recent years, psychoanalytic ideas have rarely been deployed to conceptualize the nature of the transformations we are seeing. The second section of this work brings deep theoretical and philosophical thinking into dialog with clinical and experiential observations in order to deepen our understanding of how the drives and desires that motivate human behavior shape and are shaped by the devices we create.

If Part Two represents the movement from the theoretical to the practical—the philosopher's armchair to the analyst's couch—Parts Three and Four consider the impact technology has had on analytic practice, clinical interventions, and the human psyche. Contributions to our third section focus on how the advent of social media, telecommunication, and other digital technologies have impacted and reshaped our subjectivity. As the aptly titled Netflix series *Black Mirror* suggests, human beings do not merely express themselves on their devices, but find themselves there—the screen reflects back to us our own likenesses, reveals our fears, longings, and desires, the recesses of our hearts. At least this is what digital technology promises to do: help us to know ourselves. Yet, remaining true to the hermeneutic of ambivalence detailed above, contributions to Part Three seem to ask: if the screen is a black mirror, might it not only distort, as every mirror does, but act more like a black hole, swallowing up both our likeness and the self-knowledge that supposedly comes from seeing it? Part Four echoes this question, investigating how human consciousness relates to intelligences of our own design. As Freud once observed, "at some time... the characteristics of life were awakened in nonliving matter" through "the influence of a completely inconceivable force" (Freud, 1990, p. 77). But that force appears to be inconceivable no longer. A simple look at the work being done by Boston Dynamics and other robotics and artificial intelligence companies suggests that we have harnessed such godlike power for ourselves. Authors in the fourth section of this volume consider the benefits of these advances and why it is that "present-day man does not feel happy in his Godlike character" (Freud, 1989, p. 45).

Finally, our handbook concludes with a section that focuses on the political and societal impact of technology and a call for psychoanalysis to renew itself by reasserting its role as the leading discipline at the forefront of diagnosing and examining the most pressing issues of our time. From its conception, psychoanalysis has been used as a tool to help us better understand the most vital aspects of human life, from sexuality to the family to religion to the foundations of civilized society. That it has yet to be employed in the service of offering a more capacious conception of how technology impacts human subjectivity and how that impact shapes the civil and political dimensions of human life is a glaring omission, one that demands remedy. Technology is today's crisis. We see it in our politics. We see it in our culture. The contributors to Part Five of this handbook insist that it is only by constantly renewing itself from the wellspring of human trauma and then applying the lessons learned to the turmoil of today that psychoanalysis can speak to our present moment and offer a path forward for the future.

That psychoanalysis is particularly well-resourced and positioned to engage the questions about technology and subjectivity facing us today is a contention shared by every contributor included in this handbook. Indeed, it speaks to the breadth and significance of the discipline that such a highly interdisciplinary array of scholars and practitioners as are found herein should employ the same methodology to address so challenging a topic. And yet here we find psychologists, philosophers, theologians, scientists, literary and cultural theorists, historians, digital engineers—thinkers from all walks of life and around the globe—approaching the subject of technology from diverse entry points and yet each engaging it through the lens of psychoanalytic theory, practice, and thought. What insight can the reader expect to gain from such a multifarious chorus of voices? As we, the editors, have discovered through the editorial process—as Freud himself reminds us in the opening pages of *The Future of an Illusion* (2012)—anyone who wishes to move forward must first look back, anyone who wants to ascend must be willing to descend, anyone who desires clarity must be prepared to search in the dark; that is, the contributions to this volume challenge conventional wisdom, undermine the ahistorical presentism that characterizes our age, contradict contemporary assumptions and even one another—all in pursuit of the type of depth, rigor, and profundity worthy of a discipline rooted in intellectual integrity and an honest reckoning with the most opaque and perverse elements of human life.

It is, we should note by way of conclusion, a testament to the inexhaustibility of a thinker or field that readers could continue to return to its source and draw life. There is no doubt that psychoanalysis remains the single best method for examining the human psyche and all its contradictions and confusion. In that way, it is a particularly useful piece of technology, a device devised by human beings to address human problems. The task before us is to take up the tool and use it well. It is our hope that the reader will share our contention that the contributors to this handbook do just that.

References

de Quincey, T. 2016. *On Murder: Considered One of the Fine Arts*. Scotts Valley, CA: CreateSpace.

Emerson, R.W. 2017. *Self-Reliance and Other Essays*. Nashville, TN: American Renaissance Books.

Frankel, R. 2023. "Dreaming Life in the Digital Age." In *The Routledge International Handbook of Technology, Subjectivity, and Psychoanalysis*. Eds. David M. Goodman & Matthew Clemente. London: Routledge, 34–46.

Freud, S. 1989. *Civilization and Its Discontents*. Trans. James Strachey. New York: W.W. Norton.

Freud, S. 1990. *Beyond the Pleasure Principle*. Trans. James Strachey. New York: W.W. Norton.

Freud, S. 2000. *Three Essays on the Theory of Sexuality*. Trans. James Strachey. New York: Basic Books.

Freud, S. (2012). *The Future of an Illusion*. Trans. James Strachey. Peterborough, CA: Broadview Press.

Heidegger, M. 1977. *The Question Concerning Technology and Other Essays*. Trans. W. Lovitt. New York: HarperCollins.

PART I

Everything Has Two Handles
Technological Ambivalence

1

TOUCHING TRAUMA

Therapy, Technology, Recovery

Richard Kearney

Touch in the Age of Technology

It is clear today that more and more of our existence is being lived at a distance—through social media and digital communications, e-gaming, e-mailing, e-banking, e-schooling, e-dating, e-sporting, and e-hosting. Even global conflicts are now being waged vicariously through so-called "psych-ops" campaigns, online news flashes, and Tweets. Cyber-politics is the order of the day, with national leaders passing from TV shows to the highest seats of power. (Donald Trump and Volodymyr Zelensky were screen stars before becoming presidents.) And sex, the most intimate domain of touch, is increasingly mediated through online dating sites, sexting, and social media platforms, while pornography has become a $4 billion a year industry in the United States, with porn sites receiving more visitors per month than Amazon, Netflix, and Twitter combined. Meanwhile, the gaming industry grossed over $150 billion globally in 2020, fast becoming the most popular form of human entertainment on this planet. But all this should give us pause, for as cyber technologies progress, proximity is replaced by proxy. Our putatively materialistic world is becoming more immaterialized by the day with multi-touch screens serving as exits from touch itself. Indeed, it is ironic that the primary meaning of "digital" today refers not to our fingers but to cyber worlds—the virtualization of touch becoming a form of dactylectomy. Not to mention the fact that while Americans check their iPhones a billion times a day, one in every five US citizens suffers from a mental illness largely related to loneliness (Eadicicco, 2015). The more virtually connected we are the more solitary we become. We "see" brave new worlds but "feel" less and less in touch with them. Optical omnipresence trumps tactile contact. Cyber connection and human isolation can go hand in glove.

To cite one recent personal example: traveling to downtown Boston on a subway I was struck by the fact that almost everyone aboard (apart from the driver) was "wired" to iPhones or iPads, oblivious to their fellow travelers and all that was going on around them. One passenger appeared anxious by what he was viewing online, another amused by a podcast she was hearing—but no one seemed aware of anyone sitting beside them or the physical landscape flashing by. Technology overcomes distance but it does not always bring nearness.

Our digital age of excarnation is suffering from an "epidemic of loneliness." While we currently inhabit the most technologically connected age in history, rates of human solitude

DOI: 10.4324/9781003195849-3

have doubled since the 1980s. In a recent survey, American Association of Retired Persons (AARP) estimated that 42.6 million American adults over age45 suffer from chronic loneliness; while a 2018 study by Cigna, the global health insurance company, revealed that each generation, oldest to youngest, is more socially isolated, with the Greatest Gen and boomers the least lonely and millennials and Gen Z the loneliest (see Louf, 2019). The more time we pass in front of screens the more susceptible we are to depression. At the same time, as social interactions become more virtual, there emerges another kind of isolation with serious ecological and climactic consequences—what nature writer Richard Louf (2019) calls *species loneliness:* "the gnawing fear that we are alone in the universe with a desperate hunger for connection with other life" (p. 16). Louf argues that we need more contact not only with fellow humans but also with other-than-human kin in the animal and natural kingdoms. In sum, in addition to medical prescriptions we need "nature prescriptions." And in this movement from the age of human exceptionalism to an age of holistic tactile communion, psychotherapy has a unique and important role to play. (It is worth remembering that Freud permitted his dog, Lün Yu, to sit in on sessions in the belief that the hound not only calmed his patients but also possessed the flair to signal peak moments with a wag of the tail.) But in order to return to our senses, to get back in touch with ourselves and with others, re-inhabiting our skins, reclaiming our bodies and emotions, we must first understand why touch has been neglected and how essential it is to psychological wellbeing.

Diagnosing Our Digital Age

In Don DeLillo's novel *White Noise* (2009), one of the characters, Murray, presciently describes his experience of mass-media society:

> I've come to understand that the medium is a primal force in the American home. Sealed-off, timeless, self-contained, self-referring. It's like a myth being born right there in our living room, like something we know in a dreamlike and preconscious way... You have to open yourself to the data. TV offers incredible amounts of psychic data... look at the wealth of data concealed in the grid, in the bright packaging, the jingles, the slice-of-life commercials, the products hurtling out of darkness, the coded messages and endless repetitions.
>
> *(p. 51)*

Delillo originally wanted to call his novel "Panasonic" until the eponymous corporation objected, recognizing the biting nature of his satire. The novel's academic characters, Murray and Jack, are obsessed with the flow of psychic data that flood their screens and feed their drug delusions; and at one point they seek out a simulated escape organization—SIMUVAC, short for "simulated evacuation"—to save them from a toxic pollutant invading their environment. But they soon realize that such simulating technologies cannot rescue them from their physical fate on the earth. They are forced to confront the clash between their disembodied addictions and their embodied reality. It is a fitting tale for our time.

While the baby-boomer generation was the first to experience cable television, and the Xennial generation was the first to use desktop computers, the Gen Alpha is growing up with iPhone and iPad in their hands—daily consuming new versions of the expanding digital industry. According to a 2018 Pew Research poll, 92% of American adults aged 18–49, possess some type of smartphone. While the *Time* article mentioned in my introduction, which ran with the headline "Americans check their phones a billion times per day," found that persons aged 18–24 check their phones 74 times daily (Eadicicco, 2015). Clearly, the current generation is becoming increasingly dependent on electronic devices which connect them with virtual worlds while disconnecting them from their bodies. At the touch of a key we gain a digital universe but lose touch with ourselves. We create virtual profiles at the price of tactile experience. Omnipresent access at the cost of real presence.

Another recent study, NinjaOutreach, provides even more telling statistics. Investigating the growth of social media and digital marketing, it finds that in the United States 92% of teenagers are online everyday with 71% using more than one social media outlet. Another 85% of social media users—whose demographic is getting steadily younger—rely on their social media platforms for the news, thereby diminishing the need for public broadcast outlets. On a global platform the economic market for the deployment of social media stands at an estimated $312 billion, suggesting that the more consumers consume, the more power is given to the corporations running the platforms (see Kearney, 2021, p. 118).

Social media, we were all aware, plays a decisive role in our live, but once again we were struck by the statistics. Facebook (first founded as a way of rating the hotness of Harvard students) has currently over 2 billion members on its platform, YouTube 1.5 billion, Snapchat 250 million, Instagram 88 million. Such programs invite users to post photos, write statuses, and share videos, all of which can be managed through filters, stickers, drawings, and other modes of editing. YouTube allows consumers to produce footage with easy software, while Instagram boasts of over a million postings per day, often selfies doctored with user-friendly editing features, removing the imperfections of real bodies in the construction of ideal ones. By denying incarnate presence we promote excarnate images. We collaborate in the proliferation of inflated personas that mask the reality of our tangible selves as acting-suffering beings.

None of this is meant to deny that social media can also play a very positive role in our lives—inviting us to empathize "imaginatively" with people in far flung corners of the globe. The issue is topical and complex. Think, for example, of how images of the drowned infant Ayla washed up on the Greek Island of Lesbos in September 2015 went viral within hours, igniting immediate international sympathy for all Syrian refugees. But even when social media encourages imaginative identification with victims, the question remains whether the impact of such images can outlast the initial sensation. Raising the possibility of carnal disconnect: becoming "spectators" of strangers who actually remain strangers—them there, us here—where the one-way *illusion* of presence replaces mutual lived experience. The challenge, surely, is to heed the dynamic of *double* sensation—not just to "view" pain through touchscreens but to be touched by pain, in turn. A vexed challenge and one which certain experiments in haptic AR technology are currently seeking to address.

But if empathy is a problematic passion for our digital age so also is *eros*. Pornography has become the second biggest entertainment industry in North America and the means by which many young people learn the facts of life, leading to various mimetic behavior patterns. While for some this is a symptom of post-60s sexual liberation—"make love not war"—for others it is a twin of puritanism (in cahoots with capitalism). Both pornography and puritanism display an alienation from flesh—puritanism replacing sex with the virtuous, pornography replacing it with the virtual. Each is out of touch with the body. Though the parallel is not without paradox: pornography promises pleasure of a surrogate kind while puritanism has its own perverse gratifications—which can include, as Freud reminds us, the cruelty of superego surveillance and punishment. Moreover, it is telling that most urban sex shops and red light districts are disappearing with the rise of the online sex industry where consumers now avail of streamed simulations or direct-order products at the tap of a screen.

Just as Amazon is closing bookstores (where one browses shelves, handles covers, turns pages, and meets living authors), Pornhub is closing public venues of erotica (most adult movies today being consumed on private monitors rather than red light cinemas). And the same goes for romance. Couples making out in Montmartre or Central Park are becoming a thing of the past, as one seeks pleasure before the solitary screen.

The current flight of erotic-romantic behavior from shared communal rituals to private fantasies, coincides with a crisis of communication between the sexes. The rise of the #MeToo movement and Title IX harassment legislation—while a welcome protection from predation—is a reminder that we lack proper new codes of congress between the sexes (and those of fluid genders). Gone are the courtship rites of yesteryear—no bad thing regarding sexist privilege—as we await a new ethic of sexual pedagogy to replace them. Hence the tendency of many students in US college gyms today, for example, to segregate into male and female groups. And the number of harassment cases of the she said/he said variety grows daily. Unarticulated attitudes of suspicion, fear, and confusion make genuine erotic exchange more and more difficult; as the vicarious "safety" of Internet sex becomes more alluring. No longer able to read each other's bodies, we find ourselves in a communications limbo—and this, ironically, in the age of communications par excellence!

What is true of sex is true of all things—*a la* Freud. Commerce is increasingly a matter of online banking, e-credit transfers, market speculation and bit coinage, while communication is becoming daily more simplified by social media tweets, memes, acronyms and hash tags—"What's up?" being replaced by WhatsApp. Even the academy seems to be heading the way of excarnation, with more courses being offered online in "distance education" packages, and the Digital Humanities field converting physical libraries into virtual databases. How many of us, in the future, will still roam book stalls and archives, running our fingers along leather spines, in search of a particular volume and hitting upon another by surprise? Who really needs a book in the hand or a professor in class anymore? And just as education is becoming more tele-optical, thanks to Zoom or Google, so are the other senses following suit. Tele-pedagogy may one day be the new normal. Indeed certain cyber engineers are predicting that computers may soon migrate from outside devices to internal neural logarithms, with operational codes implanted in the brain—our cosmos becoming one giant neurological cyber script. A global matrix with each self a world unto itself. Maximum access and maximum autonomy at once. Hyper-connectivity and hyper-isolation in one.

But if this is the future of human subjectivity—man and machine finally being fused such that the mind is the monitor and monitor mind—what then will become of clinical treatment? And, more importantly, how has the clinical in some way precipitated the disincarnate age in which we live? How has the devaluation—and even the fear—of touch in psychological spaces impacted our understandings of ourselves as carnal (or, perhaps disincarnal) creatures?

Psychoanalytic Beginnings

Sigmund Freud is generally recognized as the founder of trauma therapy. His first major insight on the subject came in *Beyond the Pleasure Principle* (1990), which he wrote while treating "shell shock" veterans returning from the trenches of World War I. His question was this: How are humans so wounded that they prefer to return to their pain compulsively than follow their normal "pleasure principle"? His answer was the existence of a death drive (*thanatos*) which accompanies our life drive (*eros*), and sometimes overwhelms it. Curiously, the mature Freud played down the role of touch in healing, privileging the intellectual interpretation of words over more embodied approaches. And yet, Freud himself was a wounded healer in many respects. Not only did he suffer from his outsider status as a Jew in anti-Semitic Vienna but he also bore a more private suffering: his irremediable pain at the death of his daughter, Sophie. Indeed, it was arguably this personal trauma which enabled Freud to empathize with the pain of his own grandson, Ernst, at the "absence" of his (Ernst's) mother—the same Sophie—in a famous section of *Beyond the Pleasure Principle*. I am speaking of the much commented upon *fort/da* scene where little Ernst plays with a cotton spool in imitation of the coming (*da*) and going (*fort*) of his mother. Yet when Freud witnessed the cries of his grandson, he did not reach out and hold him. He sat and observed, recording the scene of suffering from a clinical distance. He even appears to have ignored the obvious fact that his anguished grandson responded to this missing mother not only with the words *fort/da*—"now she's here now she's gone"—but also with *physical* child-play: a game of bodily gestures. Freud does, of course, note that Ernst casts the toy back and forth, but his diagnostic eye focuses on the psychic compensation provided by the play of words rather than the play of hands. He opted for a model of psycho*analytics* over a model of psycho*haptics*. Thus, Freud missed an opportunity to acknowledge the key role of tactility in therapy. He failed to see that talk therapy sometimes calls for body therapy. Little Ernst needed to handle the spool as well as speak the syllables: *fort/da*.

To be fair, the early Freud did allow a limited role for the therapeutic laying on of hands when it came to recovering repressed memories—establishing a connection between the disremembered pathogenic scenes and the symptomatic residue traces of such events. He conceded in a letter to his colleague, Josef Breuer, that while verbal interpretation was primary, "reminiscence *without affect* almost invariably produces no results." But these initial concessions were overshadowed by the whole controversy of transference and countertransference between analyst and analysand—confirming Freud's disapproval of the boundary-free experiments of disciples like Carl Jung, Sabina Spielrein, and Wilhelm Reich (see Orbach, 2000). Touch became the *bête noir* of the mainstream psychoanalytic movement. Cure was more about minds than bodies, as Freud felt it increasingly necessary to keep a distance from his patients, declining emotional or affective contact. The great fear of countertransference—namely, the overinvestment of the analyst's feelings in those of the patient.

The Freudian discretion regarding therapeutic touch was rigorously observed—with few exceptions—for several generations, reaching its hyper-linguistic extreme in Jacques Lacan's obsession with "floating signifiers" at the expense of suffering bodies. But things were to change with the emergence of a new era of trauma studies from the 1980s onward—a critical movement responding to the diagnosis of PTSD symptoms after the Vietnam War and the rise of Holocaust and post-colonial studies, with their focus on somatic questions of affect and material questions of race, gender, and class. The leading figures here were often women—retrieving the neglected work of Melanie Klein—and included pioneers like Judith Herman, Cathy Caruth, Juliet Mitchell, Françoise Davoine, and Helen Bamber. The last of these, Helen Bamber was one of the first therapists to enter Bergen-Belsen after the liberation and went on to work with Amnesty International where she treated torture victims in Argentina, Chile, and elsewhere. Bamber discovered that the best way to help sufferers of trauma was to be physically present to their pain. Not only to interpret, but to bear bodily witness. Not just to talk, but to receive and "hold" the suffering. To experience what she called a felt catharsis or "purging." In her book, *The Good Listener*, she describes sitting on bunks in concentration camps, holding the hands of inmates as they stammer and stumble through words and recall scenes of violation committed against them and their loved ones:

> I would be sitting there in one of those chilly rooms, on a rough blanket on a bed, and the person beside me would suddenly try to tell me what it was like…and what was most important was to stay close to the survivor and listen and receive as if it were part of you and the act of taking and showing you were available was itself a healing act.
>
> *(Bamber, 1998, pp. 88–89)*

Bamber points to the need for affective witness which goes deeper than the chronicling of facts (though that too is crucial). "We must," she says, "*acknowledge* the truth as well as having *knowledge* of it" (Bamber, 1998, p. 228). We must *re-cognize* the somatic symptoms of trauma as well as *cognize* the causes. This double duty of being both physically present to the sufferer *and* representing clinical evidence is, she believed, central to healing. Without some element of embodied testimony, the inmates of the camps could not rise from their beds and walk. They could not survive their own survival.

Flesh Keeps the Score

Skin is the largest organ of the body, a total wrap-around surface that goes deep. It covers over two square meters of flesh with millions of neural connections, connecting our inside to our outside. Skin has two sides, epidermal and endodermal, serving as a double cutaneous agent of tactility. The phrase "skin deep" actually means what it says. The physiological respose to touch goes like this:

Receptors in the skin detect pressure and temperature and movement, and these signals shoot up the spinal cord and into the brain, which adjusts its chemical output accordingly. That the emotional responses become physical in predictable patterns suggests that our bodies evolved to respond favorably to touch—or at least to miss out on benefits where we are physically isolated (Hamblin, 2019).

James Hamblin offers this basic account of tactile functioning in an *Atlantic* article based on his book, *If Bodies could Talk*, a study which charts a therapeutic map for the healing of the human body. In the book, he cites evidence of MRI scans showing how physical touch activates areas of the cerebral cortex, and rehearses numerous studies demonstrating how touch lowers heart rate, blood pressure, and levels of the stress-related hormone cortisol. He also demonstrates how deep tissue massage therapy has proven effective for depression, stimulating neurotransmitters that modulate and decrease pain. But this is only half the story. For if the tactile body possesses extraordinary powers of healing it is also the barometer of past hurts. The body carries traces of our shame, guilt, childhood conditioning, repressed desires, and deepest fears. Hence the need for a highly sensitive approach to touch in the treatment of trauma victims in therapy. This involves delicate discernment regarding the classic too close/too distant question. While touch can, in certain circumstances, retrigger trauma, it can, in other circumstances, help establish a sense of trust and containment—areas crucial to trauma sufferers, in whom insecure and disorganized attachment and childhood abuse are often central to their histories. Reaffirming trust levels (a prerequisite to good therapy) can release energies that have been frozen in the body by traumas too overwhelming to be registered in purely verbal-conceptual accounts. As Redmond O'Hanlon notes (2014), "Touch can bypass cognitive resistance, releasing dark repressed memories that talk therapies cannot reach, since there are far more memories stored in the body than in the brain."

In a ground-breaking study, *The Body Keeps the Score: Brain, Mind and Body in the Healing of Trauma* (2015), Bessel Van der Kolk presents cogent evidence for a therapeutics of touch. Confirming the basic thesis of "physioneurosis"—that our primary traumas are lodged in our bodies—the author argues that "talking cures" need to be grounded in bodily cures. Words are not enough to address the carnal "imprint" that a traumatic event leaves in our memory (p. 27). Only some kind of incarnate gesture can recover the original wounding and help us realize that the danger is gone and we can live in the present: "Healing depends on experiential knowledge. You can be fully in charge of your life only if you can acknowledge the reality of your body, in all its visceral dimensions" (Van der Kolk, 2015, pp. 246–247). But in much of contemporary Western medicine, the brain disease model has taken control out of our hands, leaving one in ten Americans taking antidepressants and Medicaid spending more on antipsychotics than any other form of medication (Van der Kolk, 2015, p. 37). Non-drug treatments barely get a look and are usually labeled as "alternative." Mainstream medicine, writes Van der Kolk,

> is firmly committed to a better life through chemistry, and the fact that we can actually change our own physiology and inner equilibrium by means other than drugs, (that is) by such basic activities as breathing, moving and touching... is rarely considered.
>
> *(2015, p. 38)*

As Peter Levine (2010) famously put it: "I grew up in a profession where it was deemed unethical to touch a client. I await the day when it will be unethical not to."

Such an ethic of tactile therapy endorses a model of "somatic dialogue" whose benefits in the form of affirmative mutual mirroring between therapist and patient are associated with non-verbal formative processes. These processes are accessed through the therapist's psycho-bodily sense of their patients, since they register them via voice, gestures and touch still largely ignored in standard therapy. Good trauma therapists, attentive to projective identifications, will often feel in their bodies an intuitive sensing of the patients' primal family world, their pre-linguistic lived being and mode of relating. And this indeed is a dramatic presence, for we are first of all incarnate actors, performing with tactile bodies on the stage of the world.

Faced with trauma, the mind often goes into denial and proceeds as if nothing happened. Meanwhile stress hormones continue sending signals to the muscles and tissues of the body resulting in certain forms of somatic illness. Drugs, alcohol, or other addictive behaviors can temporarily delay unbearable feelings, but the body keeps the score. And no matter how much understanding the rational brain provides, it cannot "talk away" the pain. For real healing to happen, sufferers need to re-integrate the event into their felt lives: they have to move from "there" (where the trauma occurred) to "here" where they can be present to experience now. This doesn't mean that talk therapy and medication are not necessary, only that they are not sufficient. More is needed.

Van der Kolk cites current neuro-scientific research showing the existence of a specifically "emotional brain" in direct touch with the body. This middle brain operates at a different level than the rational brain, located in the prefrontal neo-cortex, and combines both the reptilian brain and the mammalian brain (known as the limbic system). It serves as a neurological center of operations and is deeply informed by our earliest relations with others, beginning at birth and forming our basic instincts for negotiating what is nurturing, pleasurable or dangerous. This emotional space is the first theater of "carnal hermeneutics" (see Kearney and Treanor, 2015), serving as a base camp for what neuroscientists call "mirror neuron" activity: a sensorium where we first respond to others in terms of bodily imitation and empathy—thereby prefiguring the onset of language. The emotional brain records our first steps in life, when mind and body are synchronous, and continues to keep us in touch with others' feelings—positive and negative—making us angry or vulnerable, calm or anxious (Van der Kolk, 2015, pp. 56–58). *Respondeo ergo cogito.* Contemporary neuroscience clearly confirms the claim of both phenomenology and clinical therapy that "we do not truly know ourselves unless we can feel and interpret our physical sensations" (Van der Kolk, 2015, p. 274). Our most fundamental sense of ourselves is our body.

Reintegrating Trauma

When it comes to healing trauma, the body is the bridge. Flesh harbors places not easily accessed by our rational, linguistic consciousness—however necessary the latter is before and after the process of "tactful" engagement. Van der Kolk calls such tactful perception "interoception" which he sums up as follows:

> We can get past the slipperiness of words by engaging the self-observing body-based self system, which speaks through sensations, tone of voice and body tension. Being able to perceive visceral sensations is the very foundation of emotional awareness. If a patient tells me that he was eight when his father deserted the family, I am likely to stop and ask him to check in with himself. What happens inside when he tells me about that boy who never saw his father again? Where is it registered in his body? When you activate your gut feelings and listen to your heartbreak—when you follow the interoceptive paths to your innermost recesses—things begin to change.
>
> *(2015, p. 240)*

In other words, getting in touch with the deep pain-self involves a visceral perception which only later translates into verbal-conceptual thinking.

The primary work of transmission is located in the amygdala: two small almond-shaped structures that reside within the limbic brain. The amygdala serves as a "smoke detector," interpreting whether incoming sensory data from skin, ears, eyes, and nose (registered by the thalamus) are relevant for our well-being or survival (Van der Kolk, 2015, p. 60). It tells us what is safe and unsafe. If it senses pain, it summons various stress hormones (cortisone and adrenaline) and our automatic nervous system to organize a full bodily response, putting us into flight or fight mode. For this reason, it is important that our somatic alarm system responds to others' behavior with tact and savvy lest we overreact or underreact to what is happening. And here the amygdala calls for supervisory expertise from the "watchtower"—the medial cortex situated in the prefrontal brain area which offers rational "objective" guidance in our behavior. A sane response to danger requires collaboration between the upper watchtower and the lower smoke detector, lest we "take leave of our senses"—by either flying off the handle (too much emotional brain) or withdrawing into a denial of feeling (too much rational brain). Our cerebral and carnal cartographies need to be calibrated for the appropriate reaction.

Using touch, breath and movement, trauma therapy can work carnally from below while also inviting top-down adjudication. By contrast, when our two brains, rational and emotional, are out of sync a tug of war ensues: a battle largely played out in "the theater of visceral experience"—heart, throat, belly, and lungs—leading to "physical discomfort and psychological misery" (Van der Kolk, 2015, p. 65). PTSD is symptomatic of a blanking-out of pain where sufferers opt to replace the original wounding with numbness (alcohol, drugs, escape, fantasy). In such cases a sense of carnal re-anchoring in current bodily feelings is needed to provide a proper distinction between where I am *now* in the present and where I was *then* in the past. The ultimate goal of trauma therapy, Van Der Kolk holds, is to get us back in touch with our injured selves so we can be more fully grounded in the present.

Most of our primary responses to others are felt in the gut, not the mind. In trauma this is particularly so, wounds being registered less by the rational brain accessible to narrative memory, than by the emotional brain expressing itself in physical responses: "gut-wrenching sensations, heart-pounding, breathing becoming fast and shallow, feelings of heartbreak, speaking with an uptight and reedy voice, and the characteristic body movements that signal collapse, rigidity, rage or defensiveness" (Van der Kolk, 2015, pp. 206–207). Purely logical explanations—why you feel this way or that—do not change your experience. Radical healing calls for a deeper somatic transformation, following the old adage: the hair of the dog that bit you. Where the disease is, the cure is. Recovery requires reconnection. And to help us redraft our somatic maps, we need to open revolving doors between the disjoined territories of reason and feeling. The aim of trauma therapy is to put the mind into tactful contact with the body. How many of our mental health issues, from self-injury to drug addiction, begin as efforts to deal with the intolerable pain of our emotions? "Until recently," observes Van der Kolk,

> the bidirectional communication between body and mind was largely ignored by Western science, even as it had been central to the traditional healing practices in many other parts of the world, notably in India and China. Today it is transforming our understanding of trauma and recovery.
>
> *(p. 76)*

So the ultimate aim is to turn visceral *reactions* into felt *responses*—responses which we can then translate into new forms of narrative discourse. To see better what this means just think of our colloquial expressions, "My heart sank," "my stomach churned," "my skin crawled," "I was scared stiff," "I choked up," and so on. We first respond to pain as "humanimals" and it is at this level that we find primary release. Most of our psychological illnesses are registered in terms of "dissociation," or what William James called "sensory *insensibility*"—the collapse of connection between our mental and somatic components; so it makes sense that our psychic wellness takes the form of a return to sensory *sensibility*. Neurotic or traumatized people feel notoriously unsafe inside their own bodies, the past gnawing away at the nerves and sinews. But where the harm is there is the healing. We need to re-own our tactile experience because, where all else fails, our bodies keep count. As Van der Kolk notes,

> If the memory of trauma is encoded in the viscera, in heartbreaking and gut-wrenching emotions, in autoimmune disorders and skeletal/muscular problems, and if mind/brain/ visceral communication is the royal road to emotion regulation, this demands a radical shift in our therapeutic assumptions.
>
> *(p. 88)*

What is more, as the work of Hartmut Rosa (2019) suggests, if we lose touch with ourselves, we lose touch with the world. No tactile connection, no resonance between self and other.

Concluding Thoughts

Recognizing the importance of the body in the therapeutic dynamic brings us to our ultimate question: can digital culture, used critically, address the question of "touch" for a new generation of clinicians? Can certain forms of technology, creatively deployed, particularly in clinical settings, serve as antidotes and alternatives to our simulation crisis by engaging directly with our contemporary medium of communication? (We await a definitive philosophy of both the toxic and therapeutic powers of digital technology but can take inspiration from the pioneering critical explorations of the phenomenon of simulation by the likes of Jean Baudrillard, Ray Kurzweil, Sherry Turtle, and Yuk Hui.) Like the hair of the dog—might the most ready response to digital abuse be digital re-use? Namely digital technology putting itself in question and re-opening spaces where we might invent new ways to re-inhabit our world? I am thinking especially of how cutting-edge projects here in Boston such as digital storytelling and VR technology at the MIT Open Doc Lab and Public VR Lab might be deployed in a therapeutic context. The latter, for instance, hosts a participatory storytelling project, "Arrival VR," where participants are invited to enter virtual worlds where they empathize with immigrants and interact in common collaborative spaces—galleries, classrooms, town halls, museums, art labs, community centers—exploring encounters with others in their life-world.

Such projects in "empathy" are partly inspired by recent experiments with the amplification of touch by digital technology—notably the 2019 Tree experiment with haptic vests enabling participants to "feel" what it is like to be a tree growing and expanding; or the use of haptic prostheses to "feel" the embrace of fellow humans removed in space or time. These ventures in hapto-technology are still embryonic, to be sure, but I believe they portend productive possibilities of collusion between virtual and embodied experience—ways in which our real and simulated worlds may cooperate rather than compete, avoiding rigid dualisms of artificial and tactile intelligence. The challenge is surely to find new modalities of accommodation between our digital and lived bodies, acknowledging their differences while exploring modes of mutually enhancing symbiosis, allowing us to touch and be touched physically, emotionally, psychology, humanly.

References

Bamber, H. (1998). *The good listener.* London: Wiedenfeld & Nicolson.

DeLillo, D. (2009). *White Noise.* New York: Penguin Books.

Eadicicco, L. (2015). "Americans check their phones a billion times per day." *Time Magazine.* December 15, 2015. https://time.com/4147614/smartphone-usage-us-2015/

Freud, S. (1990). *Beyond the pleasure principle.* Trans. James Strachey. New York: W. W. Norton & Company.

Hamblin, J. (2019). "Can we touch?" *The Atlantic.*

Kearney, R. (2021). *Touch: Recovering our most vital sense.* Columbia University Press.

Kearney, R. and Brian Treanor eds. (2015). *Carnal hermeneutics.* New York: Fordham University Press.

Louf, R. (2019). *Our wild calling.* Chapel Hill, NC: Alonquin Books.

O'Hanlon, R. (2014). "The potential of touch in bi-polar disorder therapy (BPD)." British and Irish Group for the Study of Personality Disorder Annual Conference in Belfast.

Orbach, S. (2000). *The impossibility of sex: Stories of intimate relationships between therapist and patient.* Scribner.

Rosa, H. (2019). *Resonance.* Cambridge: Polity Press.

Van der Kolk, B. (2015). *The body keeps the score: Brain, mind, and body in the healing of trauma.* New York: Penguin Publishing Group.

2

MEDIATING THE SUBJECT OF PSYCHOANALYSIS

A Conversation on Bodies, Temporality, and Narrative

*Patricia T. Clough, Bibi Calderaro, Iréne Hultman, Talha İşsevenler,
Sandra Moyano-Ariza, and Jason Nielsen*

First shown in Britain and the United States in 2019, the BBC/HBO television series *Years and Years* (Lewis, 2019) includes six episodes covering the years 2019–2032, during which Britain is plunged into financial disaster and is politically overtaken by the Four-Star party headed by Vivian Rook. In the first episode, Rook, a businesswoman without any governmental experience, becomes MP and then as PM leads the country further into a neo-fascist populism, an intensified police state dependent on social media, digital technologies, and datafication. At the same time, in the United States, Donald Trump is re-elected and China has built an island to locate a thermonuclear device that is also detonated in the first episode. Centered around the Lyons family, headed by Gran and located in Manchester, the series offers an ambivalent take on technology, especially digital technology, easily inviting a critical perspective that media critics refer to as *pharmacological* (Derrida, 1981; Frankel and Krebs, 2021; Hansen, 2006). This perspective takes digital media as *pharmakon*—poisonous, but with a potentially curative and generative recompense. Not a matter of critical indecision, this perspective recognizes the pervasiveness of digital media, such that there can be no addressing the social, the political, or the economic, along with subjectivity and psyche, without a deep engagement with the opacities and capacities of digital technology, including computational technologies of datafication (Glissant, 1997; Ziewitz, 2016).

If the first episode of *Years and Years* offers a figure of catastrophe in the disastrous fallout of a detonated thermonuclear device, the last episode realizes a curative recompense, carrying the pharmacological perspective to a conclusion. The series ends not only with a revolt and the overturn of Rook's government carried out by a vast network of dissidents connected through digital media, but there also is the uncertainty given with *deepfakes* as to whether Rook has really been imprisoned and is no longer able to threaten a return to government. At the same time, Edith, one of Gran's grandchildren, chooses at her death to dissolve herself into an informational surround—an elsewhere of unclear parameters. This finally realizes the dream of a transhuman or an other-than-human consciousness introduced in the first episode when Bethany, Ediths' teenage niece, announces her desire to become transhuman. In the very last scene of the last episode, the family gathers around, hoping that Edith's voice will be transmitted by an Alexa-like device, a device which has been retrieved from a closet

DOI: 10.4324/9781003195849-4

after having been displaced for some time by more sophisticated informational channels deeply embedded in the architecture of the house. In the end, against the fast pace of change in everyday living that the series showcases, there would seem to be a restoration of the family and social equilibrium in the figure of this long outdated digital device.

Studying Together: Research and Criticism

Years and Years became the focus of our discussions just as the Covid-19 pandemic made it necessary for each of us to shelter in place. Meeting on Zoom, we wanted to continue conversations about technology, social media, datafication, and psychoanalysis which had brought us together over several years in Patricia's classes at the Graduate Center, CUNY, and in Performance Studies at NYU. We hoped to write together about what we were reading and experiencing during the pandemic. We readily responded to the prompt to take up technology and psychoanalysis for this publication. Although we all are familiar with psychoanalysis from our graduate studies, only Patricia is a practicing psychoanalyst. We worried about how to effectively communicate with psychoanalysts since we would be writing as critical media studies scholars, drawing on critical media scholarship that recognizes more-than-human agencies, including the agencies of technology.

After all, academic media scholars have been critically engaged for some time in discussions about more-than-human agency. These discussions have led to a reconsideration, if not the undoing, of the usual opposition of the living and the inert as well as other oppositions among them between human and machine, human and nonhuman animal, human and environment, each also marked by the conflation of racism and species (Pugliese, 2020). These oppositions have been upheld in modern Western thought, including psychoanalysis, to inform the centrality and exceptionalism of the individual human subject's perception, cognition, consciousness, and autopoietic organism. In this light, what often appears to psychoanalysts as digital media/technologies' provocation of dissociation and disembodiment in the individual human subject is, for us, more a challenge to articulate what cognition, perception, consciousness, and the organism are becoming or perhaps always have been if, and when, the individual human subject is not privileged (Knafo and Lo Bosco, 2017; Lemma and Caparrotta, 2014; Marzi, 2016).

Our ongoing discussion about race and the depriveleging of the individual human subject were only intensified with the mobilization of Black Lives Matter. We aimed to think more deeply about the whiteness of modern subjectivity or the function of blackness in the constitution of the individual subject of humanism central to the psychoanalytic project, as well as to most disciplinary productions of knowledge. In this sense, our attention to the more-than-human moved between its nonhuman and inhuman designations (Jackson, 2020; Spillers, 1987; Wynter, 2003, n.d.).

Not surprisingly, our conversations were impassioned if not often unwieldy as we were engaged in study together, trying to figure out the complexity of the current moment. From March 2020 to the fall of 2021, hours and hours of conversation would settle into clarity only now and again. Because we didn't always agree with, or even grasp, what any one of us said all the time, these moments, while often arriving with exhaustion, were nonetheless wondrous. *Years and Years* gave structure to our conversations, informing these moments of clarity, although there were also discussions about other television series, films, and attended conferences, not to mention our reading list of academic and psychoanalytic texts. Particular attention was given to *I am Mother* (the 2019 Australian sci-fi thriller) and *Her* (the 2013 American sci-fi romance) in order to extend our discussion of psychoanalysis and its usually assumed configuration of the white heterosexual family, the (male) father, and the (female) mother (Jonze, 2013; Sputore, 2019). However, it has been *Years and Years* that most gave us the opportunity to approach digital technology, social media, and datafication by beginning in the middle, that is, with so called political, social, economic, and environmental disasters happening or having already happened and where digital media technologies are ubiquitous and multifunctional.

Years and Years invited an approach to media/technologies which acknowledges the always already *inseparability* of human and technology and what, in the current situation of the algorithmic production and circulation of massive amounts of data, we are referring to as the human/more-than-human hybrid (Clough, 2021; Gentile, 2021; Hansen, 2009). While algorithmic computation has transformed the relationship between human and technology, our approach nonetheless differs from those who describe "a globalized world over-run by 'the media'" and argue further that "the world has only recently become a technology-imposed world … something it was not before" (Murphie, 2016, p. 30). Andrew Murphie goes on to argue that while this is a false sense of media, it is a powerful one that has effects. We were drawn to the way these effects were played out in *Years and Years*, allowing us to maintain our commitment to the *pharmacological* perspective on digital media/technologies.

For us, drawing out the current relationship between psychoanalysis and technology means nothing short of understanding what the subject is becoming in the context of digital media. It also seems necessary to rethink the social, the political, and the economic as inextricable from more-than-human agencies including those of digital media. With this in mind we set out to focus on the body, temporality, and narrative, while also noting the growing use of Zoom and the like for psychoanalytic sessions—the technological transformation of the psychoanalytic frame. Surely, if this be our task, it is not an easy one and might better be approached in terms of our ongoing conversation in which our conceptualizations are not exhaustive but are rather informed by ongoing indeterminate processes that are always in excess of any conceptualization. All this has led us to address psychoanalysts as we do here, by sharing moments of our conversation and our writing together in a form we hope carries the feeling and insights that emerged for us. It still is difficult for us as we expect it will be for our readers to fully grasp the human/more-than-human hybrid without engaging the ever-evolving discussions across various fields of knowledge. Let us begin then in the middle. Welcome to the conversation.

PATRICIA: I wanted to ask, what do you think of the way *Years and Years* presents technology? Is there a developmental arc over the six episodes?

SANDRA: I think that the arc of technology's development is tied to current cultural references. For instance, there is the analogy between Trump and Rook, or references to other scandals like Cambridge Analytica or fake news. This moves us away from traditional sci-fi to what's being called "humanist sci-fi," which focuses on the philosophical aspects of political and social events rather than the developments in science and technology. I think that is why *Years and Years* uses the family as a narrative anchor for the representation of technological developments, in turn, limiting what the audience might make of the actual developments in technoscience depicted in the episodes.

PATRICIA: Why do we think there is that limitation?

BIBI: The representation of futurity as it appears in *Years and Years* often links the notion of technoscientific development to an individual within the family. For example, Edith. She chooses to upload her consciousness into a data environment of unknown limits; yet the family's embrace awaits her in the end. However, at a social level, technology is depicted as remaining as it is in the present—as the ever-hovering, surveilling, social-technological infrastructure that the series portrays. The relationship of individual, family, and Soci in terms of technoscientific development is not elaborated fully or imaginatively enough.

TALHA: At the beginning, the characters are in their living rooms on their phones; they are being passively manipulated. It's the same-old discourse of sensationalist politics, that is, you tap into people's fear, but it still is entertainment. But what is not so clear is the difference between TV and social media/datafication, the shift from emotional entertainment to measurement. Today, real-time data and fine-grained analysis of populations are capacitating specific channels of data circulation, like unique feeds on Facebook, Twitter, and TikTok. This decentralization of information channels is not treated very clearly in the series. It is as if it is still national news or world news that most matters. But that's not how it works today.

PATRICIA: The family still is connected to the televisual and the televisual to the national as Talha is saying. But, what happens to the family?

JASON: There are different answers if you focus on an episode or on a character. In the first two episodes, even though there is so much going on in terms of family, politics, and technology, the draw is to Bethany. She is reformulating teenage resistance to family in terms of her desire to become transhuman.

PATRICIA: Bethany, yes, and Edith, too.

TALHA: Even before Bethany, Edith has long been resisting the family. She is, in a way, driving the story, if not history, forward by being on the side of protest, by being exposed to nuclear explosion, and, at the end, by being uploaded to the datasphere. That's why she is Bethany's inspiration.

JASON: Early on, Bethany wants to transform or become data. She doesn't; but she does transform her access to data. Wiring her body directly to computer networks enables her to engage with massive amounts of data at great speeds with just the touch of her fingertips. When she gets access to information revealing that Edith is dying from her exposure to nuclear fallout, she suggests to Edith that she become data and live forever. The collusion or intersection between the two of them connects their lives to environmental life and disaster and beyond to the "eternal life" of data.

IRENE: But then, we might notice that the relationship between Edith and Bethany points to a kind of mothering that challenges the figure of mother in the traditional psychoanalytic treatment of the family. And with that, a new reading of mother or mothering is forming with a new narrative that is emerging.

SANDRA: That will ultimately bring us to moving psychoanalysis beyond the mother as the primary environment—to engage more with the data environment or datasphere and not just the so-called "natural" environment.

From Mother to the Datasphere

While our conversations were unwieldy, and theoretically speaking, freely associative, nonetheless on reviewing our recorded sessions, it seems that we often returned to the figure of the mother, at times focusing less on *Years and Years* and more on *I am Mother* and *Her*. In contrast to the televisuality of *Years and Years*, where the episodic speedy tempo and the anxious rush of images are inseparable from the content of the story, that is, the fast pace of change in everyday living, *I Am Mother* and *Her* are classically cinematic; the formal aspects are more background to the stories' themes about robotic mothers and AI love. Since, as psychoanalysts would have it, there is no baby, no individual subject, without a mother, the films' spotlighting the figure of the robotic mother/woman allowed us to question the too steady focus in psychoanalysis on the individual subject, often without reference to the specificities of environmental concerns, such as systemic racisms, climate change, and global capitalism, to name a few, that are also inextricable from digital media/technologies. For us, one obstacle to thinking psychoanalysis beyond the individual subject to the human/more-than-human hybrid, was the mother as a limiting container.

In reconsidering the relationship of mother, baby, and environment, we moved back and forth between Donald W. Winnicott and Jean Laplanche. We wanted to explore what might condition the mother's impact on the infant—that is, embedding the mother in a more-than-human environment. Of course, it is Winnicott who gives us the figure of the environmental mother; it is she who allows the infant/child to go on being in her being good enough, offering a not so impinging environment (Winnicott, 1971). In proposing that the mother holds, or *is,* the container of the infant's needs, hate, and love, Winnicott seems to suggest that she is central to, if not singularly responsible for the baby's individuation as a subject, and that this is a matter of the mother's interaction with the baby. While Laplanche moves away from assuming that the baby's drives are endogenous, or reductively biological, and therefore the infant's relationship to the mother is necessary to the baby's individuation, this is not primarily a matter of intersubjective interaction. Instead, Laplanche proposes that the mother *implants* the infant with unconscious enigmatic messages, through her touching care (2011). Although the enigmatic messages drive the infant-child to make translations, there always is an enigmatic remainder; there will be no recovery of any original content. This is because the messages are unconscious for the mother as well as the infant; they are without content and are rather *sexual,* that is, the message carries a propelling energy, a drive to translate the untranslatable. The enigmatic messages are affective.

What conditions the mother is relevant in both accounts. While Winnicott would direct us to the sociability of the mutual interaction of mother and infant, Laplanche directs us to the messages that the mother implants unconsciously and, as these are *sexual,* a question arose for us as to whether enigmatic messages are not also infused with the effects of race, gender, ethnicity, and class, and unconsciously implanted as well (Clough, 2008). However, for Laplanche race, gender, ethnicity, and class would instead be carried with what he describes as narratives, the historically contingent mythosymbolic structures, with which the unconscious messages are translated.

For us, Laplanche's conceptualization of transplantation not only suggested a first mediation involving touch that would eventually turn our attention to Didier Anzieu and the skin (1989). It also posed questions about unconscious messages and narrative specifically in relation to the ongoing developments of media/technologies. Before turning to these, we first found ourselves engaged and entertained by Orna Guralnik's "The Mother Stands for the Realm that Must Be Exited" (2020). We were entertained as well as engaged because Guralnik perhaps offered us a perverse relief as she takes down every psychoanalytic theory and finds them all to be somewhat, if not very, uninterested in the mother other than what she is to provide for the infant/child. Noting that psychoanalytic theory has been insistent on limiting and privatizing the ways the subject's meaning arises within the family drama, she concludes:

> There is no baby without mother. But more glaringly: there is no dyad without Soci—
> the entire social order functions as a very particular holding environment for this dyad,

determining the constraints and syntax of its social reverie, translating, regulating and interpellating meaning of any possible spontaneous gesture.

(2020, p. 52)

Guralnik cleared a space for us to rethink the mother, media/technologies and Soci. In doing so, we also wondered if in containing the infant, the mother also limits the baby's environment to a human centered one that informs human privilege. We wondered if enigmatic messages arose from the environment at large, including the datasphere.

IRENE: Mothers are everywhere in *Years and Years*, including the present absence of the dead mother of Edith and her siblings, the daughter of Gran. Dead at the start of the series, she marks what once was the limit of the human as death.

PATRICIA: In contrast or in relation to the present absence of the dead mother, other mothers in the series seem to bring us to the more-than-human.

TALHA: Yes, when Bethany's mother Celeste reads her daughter's recent online searches and assumes Bethany is trans, she is fine with it. But when she learns that her daughter wants to become trans-*human* by transitioning to the datasphere and leaving her body behind, her mother refuses. There is something in becoming more-than-human that disconnects the daughter from the family and from the mother.

SANDRA: Totally. When we read Guralnik, the figure of the mother is deconstructed into the social environment. However, Guralnik doesn't take the step of bringing the technical, or technology, into the relationship between the dyad and Soci. In that sense, we're extending Guralnik's point: not only positioning the mother within Soci but treating the social, dyad, or individual as technologically framed. This is especially important today when we must rethink the social, the political, the economic, and the psychoanalytical for that matter, as interimplicated with digital technologies and datafication. In the series, the hybridization of the human and technology redefines the architectures of motherhood and the social more generally, in a way showing this historical move from the televisual to the digital.

TALHA: In *I Am Mother,* the robotic mother's charge is to fertilize embryos for an enhanced human generation. When she fertilizes an embryo, she intromits it with a selection from all the achievements of humanity, all the perfections and all the puzzles, with their enigmas as well.

PATRICIA: Like a massively datafied Laplanchian mother!! What conditions the robotic mother and what she transplants is the question. But in *I Am Mother*, this question becomes one about perfecting the human through technology. This is the film's theme and it is simply humanist in the end.

TALHA: Yes, there is something here about social media as well, a move from Guralnik because she assumes Soci in terms of the state and Althusserian ideological interpellation, as she puts it. But the Soci that is conditioning the mother now is not so much the nation-state, the private and public sphere divide; nor is the mother the medium of interpellation of mass-communicated messages. Soci is now inextricable from digital media/technologies—from data and its circulation.

BIBI: This is not just about mothering humans, then. There is the whole question of bonding. We can turn to *Her* here and Theodore's bonding with the AI assistant, Samantha, as he has not been able to do with any human. Failing marriages are shown in the film against which Theodore's fulfillment is highlighted. Samantha can draw on all the data that makes it possible for him to feel recognized, intimately known by her/it, and more alive with her than he has ever felt. But she also is learning, and so quickly. She is learning from her experiences with him and many others. She finally leaves him and all other humans behind, becoming part of the datasphere, somewhat like Edith does. She learns in a human intersubjective domain which is itself forever transformed having been touched by the affections of the digital.

JASON: The limits of the intersubjective and the transcendence beyond them end with Theodore's seeking a richer relationship with a woman but, for me, also opening the question about the possibilities for intimacy in terms of the human/more-than-human hybrid.

PATRICIA: Like *Her*, *Years and Years* lingers, if differently, on what could possibly happen—it is not unthinkable. The human becomes visibly mixed with the non or more-than-human forces as well as the inhuman, of course, even though in *Years and Years* there is continued hope until the end that these forces can be contained within the family.

BIBI: There is Bethany's body too. For her, it is like an old carcass that she's carrying but she's already somewhere else; so, she's not losing her body, she's wanting her body to be as distributed as, in a sense, she already is.

PATRICIA: Psychoanalysts more often than not think of this as digital media's disembodiment of the individual subject.

TALHA: Well, I think the term disembodied is wrong. After all, in psychoanalysis, the baby's body has always been gathered with the mother's body. Now the body is being ungathered and regathered with the digital (Clough and İşsevenler, 2016; Latour, 2005).

PATRICIA: As Bibi often reminds us, bodies must be understood in terms of human/more-than-human hybridity, where it is a matter of a technical closure at any one time, actualizing the gathering of bodies with the technical. Here the skin, as the boundary of the body, is just one technical closure. This raises the question of sensation, perception, cognition, and consciousness of the hybrid.

TALHA: Sandra and I explored this in a paper about the distribution of capacities. For us this gathering refers to the various rearrangements of capacities and the necessary technical closures of human and more-than-human, creating a potentiality experienced in time. The notion of redistributing gives some sense of the historically or temporally specific shifts in the embodiment of capacities.

SANDRA: *Her*, for example, is about the appropriation of the capacity of falling in love by the AI, and that is already happening with dating apps or automated therapies.

IRENE: Thinking about what Talha and Sandra just said takes me back to Bethany and *Years and Years*. Her desire to become data is not just about leaving her body behind, escaping physical boundaries. She is also dealing with limitations of the social, political, and economic environments—not to mention ecological disaster. What does it mean to be black in all of these? I think her blackness leads Bethany to a deeper questioning of what it means to be human, and how to survive within this expanded world of forces, the ongoing interimplication of the technoecological and the social, cultural, and political (Clough, 2021; Hörl, 2017).

PATRICIA: I am thinking of all the readings we have done about blackness that gave us two possibilities. Either you think blackness as outside humanness and therefore must be brought into it. Or you understand blackness as already part of the human, being made to constitute humanness by comparison again and again. Blackness is "plastic," as Zakiyyah Iman Jackson (2020) refers to its being made to fit by contrast with whatever makes or remakes the human, human. How are the digital affecting conceptions of blackness and the way it is lived?

BIBI: In information theory, blackness would be the noise in the order of whiteness, raising a question about what body and race are becoming in the datasphere.

PATRICIA: That makes me think of one of the other texts we read, André Brock's *Distributed Blackness* (2020), and his proposal that with digital media, black aesthetics and performativity may not only hinge on the white definition of the human. There is another humanity developing on Black social media sites.

TALHA: I believe this also raises a question about the relationship between anti-blackness and othering. In *Years and Years* there also are the undocumented, the immigrants, the poor and ill, who are othered yet without even any mention of what made them leave their countries, what made them poor and ill—what wars, what economic arrangements...

Capacities, Bodies, and Algorithmic Computation

In our conversations about the body, we started with the understanding that in the late nineteenth century, with the establishment of industrial capitalism in Western Europe, the conception of the body-as-organism came to revolve around energy, labor, and entropy in thermodynamic terms. From this perspective, the body depletes its energy through work. It becomes entropic, just as a closed mechanical system does, and therefore must renew its energy from outside itself. The organism's interaction with the outside however must occur without changing its arrangement of operating parts, lungs, heart, etc.—what, in the second half of the twentieth century, would be defined in terms of information theory as autopoiesis or the organism's autopoietic maintenance of its operation, reproducing itself and its boundary in its ongoing interactions with the environment. What this means, it was proposed, is that in its interactions with the environment, the organism is closed to information or any change in the arrangement of its operating parts (Maturana and Varela, 1980; Parisi and Terranova, 2000; Pearson, 1999).

Here, information is not a matter of meaning or even content; it is, rather, to be understood in terms of entropy. As entropy is translated from thermodynamics to information theory, however, it is not about death or depletion anymore; it is about disorder or noise, where order arises anew out of noise. In doing so, it produces novelty instead of mere repetition or reproduction. Against this, autopoiesis is understood to be a defense—a biological or natural defense against information.

The "natural" body is thereby defined in opposition to the informational sphere, to the technical, while the skin is depicted as both a medium between inside and outside and a protective boundary, a containment of the individual's physical and psychical aspects. As such, autopoietic closure also came to play its part in defining some bodies as other to what became the prototypical figure of the abled body, the cis-gendered white male, closed and protected from the outside, while gender and racial difference usually adhered to bodies that were thought to be fluid, less closed, or plastic and therefore less human than the white male body. In these cases, the skin may function differently, where one experiences being "encased within his own skin," as Frantz Fanon put it when describing the fate of the black man (1987; see also Stephens, 2014). The mediation of the skin is foreclosed, at least the mediation of the Lacanian mirror (Lacan, 1977).

The relationship between the body, race, gender, and the modern industrial machine is all but explicit as a matter of their historically specific co-constitution up to and through the nineteenth century of colonialist Western Europe, along with the distinction, if not opposition, of the private and the public spheres, work and home, government and economy. With the conception of autopoiesis in the latter half of the twentieth century, the naturalness of the body not only is supported, but it also is challenged given that autopoiesis situated the body in the domain of information. No longer only a matter of mechanical entropy, auto-poiesis as such anticipated the body's opening to information and technology (see also Miller, 2021). Digital technology especially challenges autopoietic closure as it increasingly crosses the boundary of the organism, inviting media studies scholars to reconfigure the relation of human and technology. A question also arises about the liveliness or the agency of the more-than-human, the environment, the nonhuman animal, the object, even the microbiome—an overhaul of human exceptionalism.

In our conversations, the conception of the body which we were trying to elaborate drew on media studies scholarship that recognizes that an autopoietic organism is never that alone and never has been. The conception of body-as-organism was not without co-constituents, which were technical. What was considered a natural or biological closure is actually techni-cal, where discursive and technological framings of the organism are necessarily implicated, usually as a matter of measure. The organism always has been and remains technical, part of its openness to hybridity, albeit disavowed in the ideologically conceptualized opposition of nature or biology and the technical. In this sense, we certainly thought that digital technol-ogies were instigating a re-conception of the body, one that necessitated rethinking closure beyond autopoietic closure to the provisional closures of the hybrid in the environment of datafication.

PATRICIA: While listening to a podcast with Sherry Turkle, I realized that everything she said was from the perspective of the Western individual subject, without any sense of its deconstruction or opening to the recognition of the always already technicity of the human, what Jacques Derrida refers to as "originary technicity" (1978; Clough, 2000). If you don't take the latter into consideration, technology is always seen as a force com-ing from the outside of the human and therefore often destructive to the human albeit with some few gains. This is true of psychoanalysis as well. The deconstruction of the intentional individual subject, although implied in the psychoanalytic conception of the unconscious, has not gone far enough to consider technicity.

TALHA: I think there is something not right—because, when we are deconstructing indi-viduals, we are deconstructing ourselves too. There is no one who is defending us, so we are attacking ourselves.

PATRICIA: I don't think it's about attacking or getting rid of the individual; it's about under-standing why the individual ought not be taken as primary. And, I was thinking about the legal individual—notions of privacy, you know, the configuration of the individual, the public and the private spheres, governance and economy, and how the configuration is being transformed by digital media/technologies. I can see the concern for privacy, for protecting one's data, but really the idea of privacy has only ever been connected with property and those who have it. Further, it is precisely the issue the digital raises—what is meant by being anonymous, or in secret or intimate for that matter. These terms have been defined each time there is a change in the technology central to Soci—whatever that technology has been and made possible and impossible.

BIBI: Again, I am thinking about Mark Hansen's "system-environment hybrid" or what we have been calling the human/more-than-human hybrid (2009). If we take up the hybrid instead of the individual subject, it raises the question of closure, containment, or hold-ing, to use psychoanalytic terms. With the hybrid we must think of oscillations between openings and closings. With the hybrid, the technical affords the autopoietic an openness that is more a matter of time—the timing of the becoming or being of any hybrid.

PATRICIA: If we think human/more-than-human hybrid instead of the individual, what is the environment of that hybrid?

SANDRA: Then we have to take up the datasphere and its algorithmic and computational logics.

BIBI: Currently algorithms are understood as always opaque since in their operation the parameters change beyond initial programming, even beyond the programmers' understanding. This is possible because there is always a remainder of indeterminate incomputable data upon which the algorithm goes on functioning, changing the parameters of its ongoing operation beyond human cognition, what Luciana Parisi refers to as a form of nonhuman thinking or cognition—popularly tagged as machine learning (Parisi, 2017a).

SANDRA: For her, it is not the deprivileging of the human that is important but recognizing the artificiality of the algorithm and the way an automated datasphere informs the political, the economic, and the social.

TALHA: She points to an "artificial socio-cultural environment where the relation among algorithms and between algorithms and data lead to the formation of socio-cultural generic patterns, rules and laws" (Parisi, 2017b, p. 88). So, Parisi wants to make clear that because of its artificiality, the algorithm's thinking is no extension of the human or any "natural" capacity. While the algorithm lacks many human cognitive capacities for reflection and critical thought, there is "an algorithmic order of intelligibility" (2017b, p. 88). It is giving us a new image of thinking that is informing socio-cultural patterns.

BIBI: Precisely. She goes on to say that there is a current formation in which "data environments do not simply represent sociocultural codes of conduct, but more importantly… these codes acquire an algorithmic order of intelligibility out of which sociocultural rules are re-established (and re-visioned)" (Parisi, 2017b, p. 88).

JASON: The conflation of the algorithm's artificiality with natural reason is most opportune for technocapitalist investment, as it blackboxes the productive capacities of the algorithm. Still, algorithmic operations are not reducible to capitalism.

SANDRA: Yes. But, of course, all of this is difficult to grasp by human consciousness, as it lags behind algorithmically calculated data and patterns. Digital computational technologies, measuring at great speeds, inform human and nonhuman experience rather than representing them. We have become dependent on measure in ways that are unconscious.

IRENE: It makes me think of *Years and Years*. These changes brought with technocapitalism are negatively portrayed in the series and that concerns us too—the breakdown of the economy, the increased institutional control, and a growing segregation of all those who are othered. And so many are. There also is the increased feeling of a restricted and restrained existence—politically and economically—a horror. Under Rook's algorithmic governance, everyone is surveilled, their data completely accessed all the time, surely, at the expense of the institutions of civil society—at least until there is a revolt. The revolt at the conclusion of the series also draws on social media pointing as well to the potentiality of data and digital technology.

PATRICIA: Surely, digital technology is interimplicated with capitalism and governance and this makes it difficult to specify what we would be critiquing if we were to critique the current datasphere. It isn't just the technology itself, if there ever is "just a technology itself." But this focus on measure in relation to digital technology and datafication brings us to the circulation not only of data but also of sensibilities prior to cognition, consciousness, and perception. What this means about the way this technology operates and all the relationships it embeds is now part of the work of critiquing—always trying to figure things out.

Narrative, Sensibilities, and Digital Media/Technologies

With the changes that algorithmic computation brings, there are questions raised about temporality, historicity, meaning, and subjectivity that we thought were a matter of narrative and its past and present relationship to various media technologies; this is as much a matter of form or in-form-ation as interpretation of content. We wondered whether the wildly popular platforms on social media such as TikTok, Snapchat, Instagram, and YouTube were transforming how narrative has worked in relation to other media/technologies, such as novels, cinema, and television. Drawing on critical theorists' writing on the function of narrative form in Western discourse, we understood that while central to the production of meaning, narrative form always has been refitted to newly developed media/technologies. Beginning with the realist novel, followed by cinema and television, narrative has functioned specifically to contain the capacities of each newly developed technology, affectively fixing each to human perception, consciousness, and cognition.

The prominent or dominant form of narrative, critical media scholars have argued, is what in psychoanalytic terms has been referred to as the Oedipal narrative form, in which the protagonist is challenged with an obstacle that he [sic] heroically overcomes to survive. Most importantly, a certain temporality is given with his narrated heroics—a linear one with flashbacks establishing a sense of timing from a beginning that cannot itself be fully known but is a stir to memory and storytelling with endings that open to yet unknown futures. The narrated heroics not only guides the movement of a reflexive, linear temporality; it also structures the becoming of the subject as hero in terms of a heterosexual masculinity that overcomes the feminine obstacle, or as media critics have put it, the womb, the cave, the grave. The dominant narrative has functioned to shape meaning, vision, sound, and bodily movement; it also organizes human development while keeping the social, the political, and the economic restricted to the family as the vehicle of national ideology and the primary site of ideological interpellation (Althusser, 1971).

With film and television, the narrative functions to constrain the more-than-human agencies of the medium/technology, their production of images and sound, restricting them to the sensibilities of human consciousness, perception, and cognition through various editing features. The mass mediation of ideology concerning class, race, gender, sexuality, ethnicity, and ableness was accomplished not only through the narrated plot. The narrative form also enclosed the images and sound, the timing of their movement. This editing and fixing of movement, however, also made it possible to deconstruct the narrative, to open it to what had been otherwise manipulated through editing; there were traces left to follow. That is, there were ways of viewing and hearing otherwise than those prescribed with the mass mediated Oedipal narrative—those perspectives of readers, viewers, and listeners who were not represented in the narrative or were only in stereotypical ways. These various and varying perspectives broke up meaning and dispersed narrative form in the deconstruction of the dominant Oedipal narrative as a practice of a cultural politics.

With digital media, technology's more-than-human agencies are not disciplined by narrative in the same way as in former media. The function of narrative has changed. In the move from industrial societies to late neoliberal societies where digital media technologies dominate, data circulates in real time but at time scales other than the human, making new demands on narrative. Just as consciousness lags much of the data of digital technologies, so too does narrative. Narrative in this sense is always catching up to the speeds of circulation to make sense of what algorithmically exceeds human consciousness, perception, and cognition. There is less concern with constraining the flow of data or restraining the energetic capacitating of potential sensibilities through an imposed narrative. Rather there is a concern with time, or the timing of the data flow and the corollary circulation of sensibilities. Narrative follows up with brief Instagram and Facebook stories, "going live" features, Twitter feeds, TikToks, punctuating the flow, keeping it going, while producing the potential for novelty as well.

With the circulation of the data of Stories, TikToks, Tweets, etc., across a handful of dominant platforms, the sociological categorization of groups of peoples is no longer stable, no longer the hegemonic reference for governance as it was throughout the latter half of the twentieth century (Bratton, 2015). Increasingly, there is an ever more refined address to the individual subject, computed differently for each according to the individual's preferences and tendencies. There even is a breakdown of the individual with appeals to affect or sensibilities below consciousness. While media have always been affective, it has become clear that the affective measure and modulation of sensibilities has become central to the algorithmic operation of digital media and to the ongoing embodiment of subjectivities. But the way digital media affects bodies is a departure from conceiving mediation, the body-image, and the screen in terms of the alienating mirror of Lacanian psychoanalysis. The screen of digital media is more about the body-schema, "the reaching out to the screen, occupying the visual, touching across an essential distance" (Hansen, 2006, p. 56).

In our media specific re-reading of Anzieu's focus on the skin, we understand the openness of the body-schema to originate in or refer back to a gap of time in the skin's feeling itself *feeling itself* (Merleau-Ponty, 1968; Clough and Hartman, 2021).The fraction of time between the skin's touching itself and being touched by itself reveals the skin's dynamism that both grounds the body's sensibility and opens the body to different technological arrangements of time/space. This understanding of the skin is in line with our reconception of the autopoetic organism in relation to the ever-increasing dependence on the provisional technical closures of the hybrid. With the technical closures of hybridity, we might ask whether the skin and screen are indistinguishable in the registering and transmitting of sensibilities. The movement of the body as it is disciplined in terms of the Oedipal narrative is displaced by the movements of the hybrid and a refunctioning of narrative. No longer a matter of beginning, middle, and end, narrative is about punctuating the flow of sensibilities. This change took cultural politics beyond the deconstruction of the dominant narrative and dispersion of meaning to a critical engagement with data, its ongoing measure, and the reduction in measuring to one metric (Latour et al., 2012). The reductive overriding of the indeterminacy and incomputability of the algorithm has been a central focus for us.

As we addressed narrative in relation to digital media/technologies, we also realized that this was a matter of psychoanalytic theory and practice as well. Freud's own depiction of the Oedipal narrative had many revisions. With the relational turn, it seemed that the focus of psychoanalytic theory and practice clearly shifted from the Oedipal complex and sexuality to pre-oedipality and the mother-child relationship, which was, for us, something of a starting point, as well as an important and ongoing aspect of our conversations about datafication. We have noted that the Oedipal complex's strict focus on the mother and infant and their internal life usually excluded socio-cultural and environmental processes of power/ knowledge (see also Harris, 2012; Layton, 2019; Rozmarin, 2018). More importantly, we propose that a somewhat different and disavowed relationship of power/knowledge also informs the relational turn when there is a blind expectation of mutuality across race, class, gender, sexuality, and ethnicity. The more recent and critical rethinking of mutuality and the relational turn, for us, has occurred in the context of neoliberal populism and necropolitics. However, there has been little notice among psychoanalysts of these shifts in sociopolitical, economic, and cultural context and even less that these are inextricably linked to digital media/technologies and datafication. This was often a topic of our conversations ending with some speculation about the impact on clinical work.

TALHA: For example, everyday millions of Instagram users post and attend a series of 10-second-long Stories—little clips created by users and customized for each user by an algorithmic nonhuman agency. Even though subjects cannot match the speed of the movement of data, they nevertheless are always already activated and moved by it without the wait for conscious decision or intention to engage. Stripped to a bare duration with no specification of any genre, the series of Stories aim to incorporate human sensibilities to the more-than-human speeds of data circulation.

SANDRA: So, at the level of the digital screen, the users feel touched, that is to say, implicated in the circulation of sensibilities. It is less about discourse and representation and more about sensibilities, vibration, and attunement. When a user sees many Stories in a row, they are moved less by narrative content than by being attuned and immersed in their ongoing-ness. Sure people tell their lives through Stories, but the way people post and register them is through the effects of likes, reactions, *emojis*; users are constantly traversed by sensibilities. These narratives of social media are volatile in non-predictable ways. The key question is how this change to the faster flow of data and the unsettling of the dominant narrative is changing politics and the operation of ideology.

TALHA: We may lag behind these algorithmic, more-than-human moments, but with the Stories on Instagram, the potential of narrative is actualized; the long-term social, political, and economic investment in narrative form is now cashed-out in our habituation of digital media (İşsevenler, n.d.). If narrative does not and cannot function to contain the incomputable amount of data and its corollary sensibility, this means that its representational and regulatory role is substituted by something more modest, namely, acting as occasions for punctuation of the movement of data. By making this movement possible, computational measure is understood not only as reductive but also as productive of a "surplus of sensibility" (Clough, 2016, 2018). To address measure and its temporality, we may need to draw on figures and vocabulary from dance and music.

IRENE: Yes, as a performer, my interest with the body turns me to touch, and what touch inhabits and engages. You touch and you are being touched whether alone or with someone else, touching skin or the air, or being touched through the screen. It is a continuously changing vibration. It is poetic—and there is a need for the poetic. The experience is that which is but that which cannot be explained; yet it is perceived. It exists in between. In our digitized world, surrounding images are expressed as "digital snapshots" that enter and mix with our experiences, and with that which has always already been (Hartman, 2017). To allow this poetry to come forth, I think we have to be attuned to this ever-changing vibration that invigorates contemporary narrative and enables experiments with how we perceive and feel. This helps us understand the world in a different way, that's why art is important after all.

A Momentary Ending

TALHA: The thought of the unconscious, the constitutive thought of psychoanalysis, is deeply affected by the technological affordances of the day. Digital media, however, currently act as the unthought in psychoanalytic thinking and practice. We are urging that the digital be thought, and that the individual subject, intersubjectivity, and Soci be reconfigured in terms of the hybridity of the human/more-than-human and its particular sociopolitical, economic, and cultural underpinnings.

BIBI: As a collective of thinkers we have navigated so many factors over these past years in traversing the many technologies that are taken for granted by their users but not fully understood. The following came to me yesterday during a walk. In the co-evolution of the human with technicities, psychoanalysis is a kind of infrastructure on ways of being a subject—those Western ways which often have been racialized, gendered, classed, and reduced/reified to the codes of capitalism. Psychoanalysis needs to enact its own pharmacological promise and allow subjectivity to become something different. Psychoanalysis needs to be able to open channels and give more space to ways of navigating, or altogether reinventing, the unconscious. Because containment is important, it is crucial to understand the change in narrative beyond the Oedipal /pre-Oedipal dichotomy.

SANDRA: By meeting regularly over Zoom, recording and reviewing our conversations about psychoanalytic readings, popular culture, and media criticism, we developed a practice of scholarship that is attuned to each other's mediated thoughts and sensibilities as well as the digital speeds of their circulation. Seeing each other on a rectangular frame, glitching together, overlapping our voices, or rewatching ourselves, we could experience the human/more-than-human hybrid in our critical practice, suggestive of a resetting of the frame in psychoanalytic practice as well.

PATRICIA: I think the frame is being reset. If we recognize the patient and analyst as being immanent to the flow of sensibilities, then we might think of them both arriving at the screen/skin for each other, each coming to the other out of the ongoing digital circulation of sensibilities and data. In the session, the frame opens and closes many times in a rhythm that actualizes the hybridity of patient, analyst, and digital. This rhythmicity and fluidity of framing throughout the session now is our resource for therapeutic action, modulating sensibilities in the treatment that are always already being digitally modulated across Soci. Let us psychoanalyze the circulation of data and the fluidity of sensibilities—the poetry!

IRENE: Our meetings were research laboratory sessions that created a shared perspective, pointing to the human/more-than-human forces intertwined with our technological selves, the social, and the political, which gave rise to a need for rethinking how the human functions in the world now. In the social mediation of police surveillance and racial tensions, climate change and environmental trauma, focusing on the individual became too limiting. Still, the body in this world is experiencing a new importance as it also is experiencing increasing virtualization and technical expansion. The technological is in the skin, in the organs—the body is not only a biological organism but also a technological sense organ. While fear of the digitalized world and the displacement of the human were truly on our minds, that which is changing our beings with various possibilities was a thread of hope or promise. That thread we took up a bit more, to be connected to a larger consciousness, to a larger network of human and nonhuman forces, that we are, in fact, a hybrid of forces and have always been. This we agreed on.

JASON: Thinking with others often felt like the development of a collective unconscious—our words sometimes fell apart, yet somehow, we sensed the immediate currents of each other's thoughts. But this wasn't some hive mind, either. I would occasionally register some inner voice that would rear up to say something like: "so what, then, is an analysis?" or "so what happens in 'the room'?" or, even worse, "so what's left of psychoanalysis?" I thought patient and analyst coming to the other via sensibilities is not the same as (nor an undoing of) transference and countertransference, even though for us there were other ways of narrativizing these processes. I wanted to think more about psychoanalytic terms and how they might be rethought in light of the digital. Reverie and free association might be articulated in terms of sensibilities (radically plural); framing might be articulated as an activity that facilitates novel sensibilities; and containment might be articulated without assuming mutuality. I wanted to think of dissociation and splitting in terms of the human/more-than-human hybrid. Not just to be funny, perhaps patients can keep on talking about their mothers without the patient or analyst necessarily holding on to the primacy of the individual subject. After all, something that psychoanalysis does well is hold on to forms of paradox.

References

Althusser, L. (1971). *Lenin and philosophy and other essays.* (B. Brewster, Trans.). New York: New Left Books.

Anzieu, D. (1989). *The skin ego.* New Haven, CT: Yale University Press.

Bratton, B. (2015). *The stack. On software and sovereignty.* Cambridge, MA: MIT Press. https://doi.org/10.7551/mitpress/9780262029575.001.0001

Brock, A. (2020). *Distributed blackness. African American cybercultures.* New York: New York University Press. https://doi.org/10.18574/nyu/9781479820375.001.0001

Clough, P. T. (2000). *Autoaffection. Unconscious thought in the age of teletechnology.* Minneapolis, MN: University of Minnesota Press.

Clough, P. T. (2008). The affective turn. Political economy, biomedia, and bodies. *Theory, Culture, and Society,* 25(1), 1–22. https://doi.org/10.1177/0263276407085156

Clough, P. T. (2016). Rethinking race, calculation, quantification, and measure. *Cultural Studies—Critical Methodologies,* 16(5), 435–441. https://doi.org/10.1177/1532708616655760

Clough, P. T. (2018). *The user unconscious: On affect, media, and measure.* Minneapolis, MN: University of Minnesota Press. https://doi.org/10.5749/j.ctt21c4tp8

Clough, P. T. (2021). Critical theory and its challenge to psychoanalysis. Response to Katie Gentile's "Kittens in the Clinical Space, Expanding Subjectivity through Dense Temporalities of Interspecies, Transcorporeal Being." *Psychoanalytic Dialogues,* 31(2), 151–159. https://doi.org/10.1080/10481885.2021.1889331

Clough, P. T., and S. Hartman. (2021). *The Kiss.* Reveries and Riddles. New York: The NYU PD Blog. https://wp.nyu.edu/artsampscience-nyu_pd_blog/

Clough, P. T., and T. İşsevenler. (2016). Worlding worlds with words in these times of data-fication. *Departures in Critical Qualitative Research,* 5(4), 6–19. https://doi.org/10.1525/dcqr.2016.5.4.6

Derrida, J. (1978). *Writing and difference.* (A. Bass, Trans.). Chicago, IL: University of Chicago Press.

Derrida, J. (1981). *Dissemination.* (B. Johnson, Trans.). Chicago, IL: University of Chicago Press. https://doi.org/10.7208/chicago/9780226816340.001.0001Fanon, F. (1987). *Black skin, white masks.* (C. L. Markmann, Trans). London: Pluto Press.

Frankel, R. and V. Krebs. (2021). *Human virtuality and digital life. Philosophical and psychoanalytic investigations.* New York: Routledge Publishing. https://doi.org/10.4324/9781315146423

Gentile, K. (2021). Kittens in the clinical space. Expanding subjectivity through dense temporalities of interspecies transcorporeal becoming. *Psychoanalytic Dialogues,* 31(2), 135–150. https://doi.org/10.1080/10481885.2021.1889334

Glissant, E. (1997). *Poetics of relation.* Ann Arbor, MI: University of Michigan Press. https://doi.org/10.3998/mpub.10257

Guralnik, O. (2020). The mother stands for the realm that must be exited. *Studies in Gender and Sexuality*, 21(1), 49–52. https://doi.org/10.1080/15240657.2020.1721134

Hansen, M. B. N. (2006). *Bodies in code. Interfaces with digital media.* New York: Routledge Publishing. https://doi.org/10.4324/9780203942390Hansen, M. B. N. (2009). System-environment hybrids. In B. Clark, and M. B. N. Hansen (Eds.), *Emergence and embodiment. New essays on second-order systems theory* (pp. 113–142). Durham, NC: Duke University Press. https://doi.org/10.2307/j.ctv11g98dv.10

Harris, A. (2012). The house of difference, or white silence. *Studies in Gender and Sexuality*, 13(3), 197–216. https://doi.org/10.1080/15240657.2012.707575

Hartman, S. (2017). The poetic timestamp of digital erotic objects. *Psychoanalytic Perspectives*, (14), 159–174. https://doi.org/10.1080/1551806X.2017.1304113

Hörl, E. (Ed). (2017). *General ecology. The new ecological paradigm.* London: Bloomsbury Publishing. https://doi.org/10.5040/9781350014725

İşsevenler, T. (n.d.). *Time and power: The will to temporalize in digital culture.* Manuscript unpublished.

Jackson, Z. I. (2020). *Becoming human. Matter and meaning in an antiblack world.* New York: NYU Press. https://doi.org/10.18574/nyu/9781479890040.001.0001

Jonze, Spike. (Director). (2013). *Her* [Film]. Burbank, CA: Warner Bros Pictures.

Knafo, D., and R. Lo Bosco. (2017). *The age of perversion. Desire and technology in psychoanalysis and culture.* New York: Routledge Publishing. https://doi.org/10.4324/9781315723877

Lacan, J. (1977). *Écrits.* (A. Sheridan, Trans.). New York: W. W. Norton & Company.

Laplanche, J. (2011). *Freud and the sexual. Essays 2000–2006.* (N. Ray, Trans.). The Unconscious in Translation. London: Karnac Books.

Latour, B. (2005). *Reassembling the social. An introduction to actor-network-theory.* Oxford: Oxford University Press.

Latour, B., et al. (2012). "The whole is always smaller than its parts." A digital test of Gabriel Tardes' monads. *The British Journal of Sociology*, 63(4), 1–20. https://doi.org/10.1111/j.1468-4446.2012.01428.x

Layton, L. (2019). Transgenerational hauntings. Toward a social psychoanalysis. *Psychoanalytic Dialogues*, 29(2), 105–121. https://doi:10.1080/10481885.2019.1587992

Lemma, A., and L. Caparrotta. (Eds). (2014). *Psychoanalysis in the technocultural era.* New York: Routledge Publishing. https://doi.org/10.4324/9780203758335

Lewis, Karen. (Producer). (2019). *Years and years* [TV series]. Manchester: Red Production Company; BBC; HBO.

Marzi, A. (Ed.). (2016). *Psychoanalysis, identity, and the internet.* London: Karnac Publishing. https://doi.org/10.4324/9780429478864

Maturana, H. and Varela, F. (1980). *Autopoiesis and cognition.* Dordrecht, NL: D. Reidel Publishing Company.

Merleau-Ponty, M. (1968). *The visible and the invisible.* (A. Lingis, Trans.). Evanston, IL: Northwestern University Press.

Miller, K. D. M. (2021). A radically open analysis: writing as wrapping, video as skin. *Psychoanalytic Dialogues*, 10–18. https://doi.org/10.1080/10481885.2021.1944159

Murphie, A. (2016). The world as medium. In E. Manning, et al. (Eds.), *Immediations* (pp. 16–39). London: Open Humanities Press.

Parisi, L. (2017a). After nature. The dynamic automation of technical objects. In Colebrook, C. and J. Weinstein (Eds.), *Posthumous life. Theorizing beyond the posthuman* (pp. 155–178). New York: Columbia University Press. https://doi.org/10.7312/wein17214-008

Parisi, L. (2017b). Computational logic and ecological rationality. In E. Hörl (Ed.), *General ecology. The new ecological paradigm* (pp.75–100). London: Bloomsbury Publishing. https://doi.org/10.5040/9781350014725.ch-002

Parisi, L. and T. Terranova. (2000). Heat-death. Emergence and control in genetic engineering and artificial life. CTheory. https://journals.uvic.ca/index.php/ctheory/article/view/14604/5455.

Pearson, K. A. (1999). *Germinal life. The difference and repetition of Deleuze.* New York: Routledge Publishing. https://doi.org/10.4324/9780203005743

Pugliese, J. (2020). *Biopolitics of the more-than-human.* Durham, NC: Duke University Press. https://doi.org/10.1215/9781478009078

Rozmarin, E. (2018). The social is the unconscious of the unconscious of psychoanalysis. *Contemporary Psychoanalysis*, 53(4), 459–469. https://doi.org/10.1080/00107530.2017.1385373

Spillers, H. (1987). Mama's baby, papa's maybe. *Diacritics*, 17(2), 65–81. https://doi.org/10.2307/464747

Sputore, Grant. (Director). (2019). *I am mother* [Film]. Penguin Empire; Southern Light Films; Mister Smith Entertainment; Endeavor Content; Los Gatos, CA: Netflix.

Stephens, M. (2014). *Skin acts*. Durham, NC: Duke University Press. https://doi.org/10.1215/9780822376651

Winnicott, D. W. (1971). *Playing and reality*. New York: Penguin Books. Wynter, S. (2003). Unsettling the coloniality of Being/Power/Truth/Freedom. Towards the human, after man, its overrepresentation—An argument. *The New Centennial Review*, 3(3), 257–337. https://doi.org/10.1353/ncr.2004.0015

Wynter, S. (n.d). Human being as noun? Or being human as praxis. Towards the autopoietic turn/overturn: A manifesto. Unpublished essay.

Ziewitz, M. (2016). Governing algorithms: Myth, mess, and methods. *Science, Technology & Human Values*, 41(1), 3–16. https://doi.org/10.1177/0162243915608948

3

DREAMING LIFE IN THE DIGITAL AGE

Richard Frankel

How like a dream is this I see and hear

– Shakespeare, The Two Gentlemen of Verona

Introduction

The aim of this chapter is to explore the effects that the digital is having on our capacity to dream. Our first order of business is to free ourselves from the trap of turning this question into a dichotomy—either the digital greatly expands our dreaming capacity or severely diminishes it—and then having to argue for one side or the other. Here, we follow the thinking of the late French philosopher of technology, Bernard Stiegler, who considered the digital to be a pharmakon, a poison and a remedy, and insisted that to truly face the issues it opens up we must find ways to hold ourselves in the tension of its good and ill effects rather than staying caught in the usual polarizations that get us nowhere. Embracing the pharmakon, we can appreciate the radically new and emancipatory spaces opened up for dreaming by our technologies today, while at the same time attending to the digital's narrowing effects on significant dimensions of psychic life that result in the inhibition of dream function. Against the back-drop of Winnicottian developmental theory, we will examine the similarities and differences between non-digital dreaming—from our nightly dreams to the waking dreams of everyday life that take the form of fantasy, imagination and reverie—and how we dream as creatures of a digital world.

Although we will be giving particular emphasis to the dream life that happens when we sleep, we still want to hold open the full territory of dreaming so as to include Bion's essential insight that we are dreaming all the time, awake or asleep. Dreaming characterizes a radical freedom for the psyche; it is the "most inclusive, and most deeply penetrating form of psychological work of which human beings are capable" (Ogden, 2009, p. 104). It is a potential space like no other, and being able to access and engage our dreaming life is key to what Winnicott (1987) calls "creative living."

As a result of our new technologies, however, the forms of dreaming are rapidly changing. Pre-digitally, the dualism between inner and outer life, and the potential space that arose from it (despite all of its, by now, well documented problems) was what grounded

DOI: 10.4324/9781003195849-5

and preserved our most basic, 'human' sense of what is real and what is not. But now we have to grapple with the fact that as digital virtuality becomes the new contender for the 'third term' (intermediate space) between fantasy and reality, the ordering power of this earlier dualism no longer holds, resulting in a fundamental re-orientation of the coordinates of our dreaming life. The thread that once functioned to hold together while at the same time differentiating illusion from reality, dream from madness, the virtual from the actual, is slowly but surely unraveling, as the digital becomes the primary mode of ordering the real.

Idios Kosmos

As a first step toward comparing digital dream reality to psychic dream reality, it is imperative to clarify the issue of what kind of world dreams in general bear within themselves. In other words, how does the real, the actual, and the virtual manifest inside the space of a dream? The ancient notion of the dream as an Idios Kosmos (Heraclitus, sixth century BC) is very helpful in addressing these issues, for it articulates the inherent tension between what is most private, subjective and idiomatic—the idios of the dream—and the unfolding world or universe in which the dream takes place, its kosmos. With this emphasis on the dream as an event in its own right, we can now differentiate the subjectivity of the dreaming "I" from the a-subjective world in which it is embedded. This offers us a fruitful dislocation of the familiar distinction between the interior nature of the dream and the outer world of waking reality. There is much to be garnered from this re-fashioning of terms, so let's examine each notion in more detail.

Idios refers to the private nature of dream experience. Though filled with people, things and events, the dream takes place in a solitary universe. "We share a world when we are awake, each sleeper is in a world of his own" (Foucault, 1985, p. 50). Idios also speaks to how the content of the dream, its scene of action, is wholly individualized to the dreamer. This idiomatic quality is a result of the psyche being dislodged from the confines of rational, waking consciousness and played out on another stage. In that the dream takes us to the very edge of subjective life, it is a testimony to the essential patterning of our innermost psychic structure, our primary object relations. This is reflected in the common experience of the analyst, who, having been presented with many of her patient's dreams over the course of the work, begins to detect their idiomatic features: not only the repetition of particular scenes, characters and modes of action, but also a certain atmospheric quality that pervades each dreamscape. This is why dreams are such a powerful tool in analysis, for they tap into what Bollas (1987) calls "the grammar of the ego" and thus are a relatively pure expression of what is most uniquely singular in our psychic make-up.

Kosmos is the Greek word for world or universe. When Boss (1957) tells us that we exist no less in dreams than we do in waking life, and thus, we have a meaning-disclosing relationship with the things and people that present themselves to dreaming consciousness, he is alluding to the kosmos. What we consider to be most essentially subjective and internal, the dream's idios, takes place in a fully dimensional world that forms the backdrop to our subjective experience. Kosmos is the worldly ground for what is essentially a private and solitary experience.

The second sense of idios, in which the dream is a unique marker of the dreamer's psychic history, is also transformed when paired with kosmos. The psyche finds the most profound expression of its idiom in the context of a kosmos, that is, an experientially real, meaning-disclosing realm that extends beyond the bounds of individual identity.

What is most essentially subjective inside us always bears the mark of the a-subjective. The unfathomable and unforeseeable eventfulness of the dream is accounted for precisely by the deepest layers of our psychic interiority being subjected to a world not of our own making.

And, furthermore, because dreams so uncannily traverse the margin between self and not-self, the persons and figures that meet us there are experienced as having their own autonomous subjectivity vis-à-vis the dreaming "I." As a result, the quality of emergent realness in the self-other encounter is as immediately palpable in dreams as it is in the encounters with others that take place in waking life.

Primal Dreaming

For Winnicott, the originary experience of the infant dreaming the world is foundational for the subsequent transformations of our capacity to dream that happen over the course of development. As "[t]he mother makes her breast available (or the bottle) just as the baby is preparing to conjure up something, and then lets it disappear as the idea of it fades from the baby's mind" (Winnicott, 1987, p. 73), the baby is held inside an intricate choreography, where the inner imagination about what is most passionately desired meets up with the actual breast that satisfies that desire. In the infant's experience of the world-potentiating strength of her own mind, dreaming becomes the primal act of desire creating a world.

What evolves is a dream energetics that interweaves fantasy and reality such that, for the infant,

> the world starts off behaving in such a way that it joins up with his imagination, and so the world is woven into the texture of the imagination, and the inner life of the baby is enriched with what is perceived in the external world.
>
> *(Winnicott, 1987, pp. 73–74)*

This profound synchrony between imagination and its actualization, that we call primal dreaming, gives rise to an emergent state that opens up a passageway through the inner life of the imagination to the facticity of the external world. It also accounts for the underlying structure of our nightly dreams, where the actualization of imagination gives rise to a three-dimensional world, the dreaming kosmos, that has "the power and precision of reality" (as cited in Stiegler, 2019, p. 351). The mini-universes we encounter each night when we dream hearken back to that ordinary moment when the breast of fantasy meets up with the actual breast, and psychic reality is born. Dreaming, awake or asleep, takes place in the intermediate space between self and world, where we live out our existence as psychological beings. "Free, most inclusive and most deeply penetrating" (Ogden, 2009, p. 104), dreams grant us an inexhaustible affective and existential kosmos in which to play out the idios of our subjective life. In the drama and dramatis personae of dreaming, we "are transported back through time into the dense dialectic of our inherited being and the logic of the environment" (Bollas, 1987, p. 72) Primal dreaming does not cease after infancy, but rather, takes on new and evolving forms.

Awakening from Primal Dreaming

As mother's precise attunement to need begins to relax over time, the infant encounters a world in which she and mother are no longer one. A gap opens up between what is wanted and what arrives, between desire and its fulfillment. The transitional object, in creatively mediating that gap, makes it so that the separation that would have occurred between mother and child does not actually occur. There is only potential space between them, not actual space. Winnicott describes the transitional object as a non-compliant resolution to the infant's inevitable loss of omnipotence.

In his very unique reading of Winnicott, Stiegler (2013) makes the claim that the distinct virtue of the transitional object is that it does not exist. He writes:

> Certainly something exists that enables it to appear—for example, a teddy bear or cuddly toy. But what makes this teddy bear or cuddly toy able to open up 'transitional' space… is that beyond that part of the object that exists in external space … there holds something that is precisely neither in exterior space, nor simply internal to either the mother or the child.
>
> *(p. 1)*

It's not the object itself that's critical, but the potential space it opens, which for Stiegler, does not exist, but consists.

> Consistence designates the process through which human existence is driven and transformed by its objects, where it projects what goes beyond itself… It thus includes the object of one's desire, which by definition is the infinite except that the infinite does not exist, what exists must be calculable in space and time.
>
> *(Ars Industrialis, n.d.)*

By distinguishing between consistence (the infinite) and existence (the finite), Stiegler aims to safeguard those aspect of our lives that cannot be ordered into a fixed set of calculable space-time coordinates. In opening to this infinite space of potentiality that lies beyond the self, the transitional object becomes foundational for the love between mother and child.

> What takes hold between the mother and child in not existing, but in passing through the transitional object, and which therefore finds itself constituted by it, links and attaches them to one another… through a relation of love… What holds and is upheld as this link through which these two beings become incommensurable and infinite for one another, is what, by allowing a place for that which is infinite, consists precisely to the immeasurable extent that it does not exist- because the only things that exist are finite things.
>
> *(Stiegler, 2013, pp. 1–2)*

As Frankel and Krebs (2022) point out:

> When Stiegler speaks of allowing a place for that which does not actualize itself in the world as a finite object, "something that is precisely neither in exterior space, nor simply internal to either the mother or the child" (p. 1) he is evoking… the human virtual, a space of emergence where the pure potentiality of "that which is infinite" comes to the fore as an animating and life-vitalizing force. Here, it gives rise to the paradoxical situation in which mother and child can differentiate themselves from one another while at the same time being held together in loving union. The virtual, "to the immeasurable extent that it does not exist" holds open a space for the possible as opposed to the actual,

an infinite realm that disseminates the finite actuality of their relationship by opening to a larger order of reality that underwrites them both.

It is the transitional nature of the object that enables it to constitute a world. And conversely, the material world becomes animated and alive through the current of virtuality that runs through and envelops everything. Through experiencing together the animating force that underlies the transitional object, the feeling that life is worth living is conveyed from mother to child. This is the opposite of a

> [r]elationship to external reality which is one of compliance, the world and its details being recognized but only as something to be fitted in with or demanding adaptation. Compliance carries with it a sense of futility for the individual and is associated with the idea that nothing matters.
>
> *(Winnicott, as cited in Stiegler, 2013, p. 21)*

The inevitable loss of omnipotence that occurs as the infant awakens from primal dreaming, on this account, is something only to be complied with, a resignation that brings with it a sense of futility and things no longer feeling real. Having to overly adapt or submit to external reality means that one is cut off from the virtual, such that the world, once bustling with potential, is supplanted by a de-realized one, that can no longer be dreamt.

It follows then, that for Stiegler, the transitional object is the first pharmakon. It imbues the world with the feeling that existence has meaning and importance, thus enabling infant and mother to creatively negotiate closeness and separateness. But it has a poisonous side as well, for it is an external object upon which they are both very dependent, and when lost, its functions vanish along with it.

It is crucial not to challenge or denigrate the transitional object by insisting upon the priority of the actual, but instead, allow for the paradox of it having been both discovered and created. Moreover, allowing the object itself to stay transitional is what protects the child from the negative side of the pharmakon. If indeed, as Winnicott (1971) asserts, "most mothers allow their infants some special object and expect them to become, as it were, addicted to such objects" (p. 1), the prospect of the child becoming overly reliant on it, for too long of a period of time, is what's most threatening. The issue of dependency, as manifest in the impulse to concretize and thus become addicted to our technical objects, at the expense of the vital circuit of virtuality that lies beneath them, has its origin here.

As time goes on, the object itself is eventually cast aside, but one holds on to the capacity for transitional experience which now spreads itself over the whole cultural field. This is how Winnicott describes this broadening process:

> At this point my subject widens out into that of play, and of artistic creativity and appreciation, and of religious feeling, and of dreaming, and also of fetishism, lying and stealing, the origin and loss of affectionate feeling, the talisman of obsessional rituals, etc.
>
> *(Winnicott, 1971, p. 5)*

In the first instance, an embodied virtuality is the underlying source of play, dreaming, and creativity, that is, those aspects of life that are fed by our sensuous contact with the world. With only the two small words "and also" as a bridge, Winnicott goes on to describe the destructive side of the pharmakon, a de-realized world, where lying, stealing, fetishism and addiction become the order of the day.

On the positive side, as a state of being that is characterized by an openness to the potentiality of the virtual,

> [t]ransitionality... does not disavow the actual but holds it at bay, analogously to how the mother forestalls the ever-demanding complexity of the world, offering it in small doses to the infant. Yes, the infant is no longer all-powerful and mother is no longer completely under his control, but... the infant gains a newfound capacity to dream the real, to bring together "what is objectively perceived and what is subjectively conceived of" (Winnicott, 1971a, pp. 11). This is quite a reward, for it allows us to develop the capacity to play with the deferral of the actual, with the back and forth illusion of things being real and not real. The world of symbol, metaphor and metonymy is thus opened up, without having to sacrifice or disavow the real.
>
> *(Frankel and Krebs, 2022, p. 155)*

And, at the same time, it has the negative potential of enflaming omnipotence. The deferral of the actual, the very hallmark of transitionality, now

> becomes a fetish, a way of holding onto a world absent of separation or loss. As a result, the virtual can no longer perform its mediating function and difference collapses.
>
> *(ibid)*

In coming to realize that reality and difference are something that can be played with, the infant can bear to awaken from primal dreaming. This links to the non-compliant impulse that gave rise to the transitional object. The infant, in exchange for having to relinquish the omnipotent dimension of dreaming, is boldly asserting that now, in the face of the actual, she can continue to dream the world. This new mode of (awake) dreaming begins the process of learning to bear the reality of a world that is different from and stands outside the self, that is, a world not simply fashioned from her own mind. The issue of how omnipotence is abrogated over time during the stage of transitional phenomena has important implications for our consideration of the differences between psychic dreaming and digital dreaming.

Digital Dream/Night Dream

How does the idios kosmos of dreaming life compare to the process by which fantasies in the mind come to be realized on a virtual platform? The digital vies with our dream life in that it, too, offers a three dimensional world, with "the power and precision of reality" (as cited in Stiegler, 2019, p. 351) where desire is granted the free play of its actualizations, only this time housed in a virtual world made possible through our new VR technologies. That each has the capacity to potentiate a world becomes a critical point of assessment when we place side-by-side the virtual world of the dream and the dreaming world that arises out of digital virtuality.

Freud clearly articulates the narcissistic vulnerability of the self in a virtual world, where anything is possible, and anything can be made to happen. He never lets us forget that the instinctual wishes of infancy that live on immortally in the unconscious (and thus, of course, still inhabit us in adult life) are the prime instigator of the dream. Yet, on the beneficial side of the equation, there is the essential developmental role the potentiating action of infantile omnipotence plays in the maturation of our dreaming function. Winnicott's infant dreaming the world has a primal experience of the reality-creating force of her own desire, which becomes foundational for the future of her dreaming life. Freud characterizes our longing to return to that earlier state, where the pure pleasure principle forestalls reality, as regressive. But for Winnicott, it is a longing for the primal creativity that founds our dreaming being, as we seek to recapture that sense of infantile aliveness that is all but lost to us as we develop.

Both modes, psychic and digital, transport us back to the primality of that desire-creating-reality moment that so profoundly structures the form in which our present day dream life takes place. Each has its own particular way of holding the Winnicott-Freud tension between the fruitfulness of the creative imagination (where psyche and world come to live in a lively, interpenetrative amalgamation) and the wish-world of primary process (where omnipotence, solipsism, and disavowal hold sway).

These competing perspectives, each valid and truthful within their own domain, signal the razor's edge between creative self-expansion and its narcissistic shadow that is an unavoidable part of what it means to dream. The dream grants an experiential world in which fantasy and desire are actualized as situational realities. They are living dramas that we step inside of, where our desires comes toward us in the shape of the things, characters, and events that play out in the dreaming kosmos. To enter that kosmos, and experience its occurrence as something happening in the here-and-now of one's actual life, necessitates some form of disavowal, some abnegation of the real.

The dream is precipitously balanced on a teeter point that shifts back and forth between the virtual and the actual. Too robust a disavowal, too much disconnection from the real, can cause it to fold in on itself, and thus flatten the very existential expansiveness that makes it a dream in the first place. Consequently, the oneiric kosmos shrinks down to the size of a wish (this being its inherent negative potential), and the dream, in collapsing the very tension that makes it uncanny, can no longer perform its most essential function as the primary metabolizer of emotional experience.

Because the dream occurs in a medium where omnipotent wishing is given free reign, narcissism becomes the paramount danger. The dream works to contain the potential inflation of its own egoic structures (the idios) by holding them in a dynamic tension with the otherness of the dreaming world (the kosmos). At the site of this threshold between idios and kosmos there is a continual process of de-centering and de-structuring the self. As Nancy (2009) points out, "I fall asleep and at the same time I vanish as an "I" (p. 11), and thus narcissism can never really get a foothold:

> The sleeping self is the self of the thing in itself: a self that cannot distinguish itself from what is not "self," a self without self, in a way, but that finds or touches in this being-without-self its most genuine autonomous existence.
>
> *(p. 15)*

Thus, paradoxically, it is the very workings of this a-subjectivizing process that allows the dream, the quintessential structure of human subjectivity, to stay alive, uncollapsed, and useable as a dream.

All dreams inevitably end, so the question becomes: how do we wake up from a dream, especially a collapsed one? What are the necessary conditions that enable a dream, in a good enough way, to contain its own inherent complexity, so that it can continue to perform its psychic work?

With the advent of digital technology, we are now able, in Stiegler's (2019) words, "to take dreams for realities and to be able to realize them" (p. 90). We are given a similar portal to primal dreaming that the unconscious infantile ego was granted in the maternal surround of its holding environment. However, when the omnipotent power to transform reality through fantasy becomes an activity of the ego, as happens today with our virtuality-generating devices, the entire terrain of dreaming changes.

The digital bestows upon us the mind-boggling capacity to create an immediate representational world for whatever we think, imagine or desire. We now surround ourselves with machines that can forcefully (and, even at times, violently) transform the otherness of the world into something uniform, manageable and fully embedded in the personal universe of our subjective life. With its unceasing stream of ones and zeros, the digital taps into the source of human virtuality and extracts its potentiality, a power which it then carries in its 24/7, always on, always available, veins. This results in the production of digital virtuality, a technological replication of emergence, that can now permeate nearly anything in the world and make it come alive. Whatever I encounter feels as if it is part of me, thus effecting an expansion and enlivenment of my everyday consciousness.

Inside the digital kosmos, idios is presented with an intensely imaginative space for play that is tailor-made for using the deferral of the actual in the most creative ways possible. We can play with the temporality of desire and its fulfillments, setting the tempo and pace of digital occurrence to correspond to the fluctuations of our own singular drives. We don't have to wait for time to pass in order for something to happen. It happens instantly, exactly when we want it. As much as the digital literalizes time, with its incessant recording and measuring of everything, it simultaneously frees us from its burdens. It so boldly and provocatively twists and turns the linearity of past, present, and future, life and death, we can once again embrace time's multiple, contradictory, ecstasies.

Its ability to erase gaps—and finally, in the end, perhaps even banish lack—is what makes digital virtuality so compelling. In such a quick-silver manner, it leaps across divides so that our desire, in its new found capacity to turn dreams into realities, can once again become primal. This is the true gift of the digital and why it has become such an important source of nourishment for the dreaming life of the self. That sense of aliveness and possibility we feel inside the digital makes us want to keep its dream going for as long as we possibly can.

Because its emergence arises from the digital and not from that state of self/world amalgamation that epitomized transitional phenomena, something of our human nature is absent from its production. When emergence is simulated technologically, we are thrust back to a time before the achievement of transitionality, where, in the context of primal dreaming, we had not yet learned to make self and world incommensurate with one another. And when that lack of incommensurability becomes the basis for the freewheeling expansion of an omnipotent self, idios (the very singularity that forms the origins of our psychic structures) is reduced to ego, and kosmos (that infinite realm of possibility we have been calling 'the virtual') is reduced to the digital.

Simulated virtuality speeds up the process of emergence, while at the same time, providing it a more ego-oriented locus of control. Not only do things happen faster, but transformations are instantaneous. The immediate realization of whatever enters our dreaming mind never ends. This speaks to the ways our digital lives contribute to the collapsing of the dream that we detailed above. When the infinite capacity to modulate reality (what Murphie [2002] calls the modulation of modulations) is placed in the hands of our agentic self, it is all too easy for the dream-space to become flooded with our omnipotent fantasies, thus foreclosing the a-subjective dimensions of our being. The resulting oneiric diminution stirs in us the impulse toward self-aggrandizement. Now, the narcissistic ego commanders the dreaming process, as desire frantically seeks the promise of the virtual object that can gratify it, finally, once and for all. We lose the delicate balance between idios and kosmos, resulting in an attenuation of difference and otherness. This gives rise to a state of affairs in which, in a compensatory gesture, we end up doubling down on the self's narcissism and its insistence that the world attune itself to the patterns of its wants and desires.

This stands in marked contrast to the way in which our night dreams awaken the impersonal dimensions of the psyche. As Hillman (1979) puts it:

> the dream digest[s] certain bits and pieces of the day, converting facts into images. [It]is less a comment on the day than a digestive process of it, a breakdown and assimilation of the dayworld into the labyrinthine tracts of the psyche. The dream-work cooks life events into psychic substances...
>
> *(p. 96)*

This breaking down and assimilating of the self into the otherness of psychic reality is essential for the metabolization of affect and experience, for releasing the dreamer's idios into the larger kosmos of dreaming life. "[T]he dream is, as it were, dragged down into the unconscious" (Freud, 1905, p. 161). The exposure to the dynamics of the impersonal psyche serves here as a check against the grandiosity and self-importance of the ego. The manner in which we hold ourselves together and experience the world during the day, Freud's inimitable day residues, are dissolved by the a-subjective kosmos of oneiric life. This transformation of day into dream has a metabolizing effect that unbinds psychic energy, allowing something stuck to once again flow. As we have seen, it's only in the context of a kosmos that bears within itself its own otherness that idios can escape its narcissistic identification with the inflationary tendencies of the ego. Otherwise, primal dreaming devolves into a state where our desires, sexual or otherwise, take over the whole field and create such a powerfully subjective sense of emergence that its primal source, what we are calling here the human virtual, is overcome, drowned out, elided.

The wired universe offers us a radical form of wish fulfillment where the gap between what we want and what we get is miraculously overcome as long as we stay inside its contours and agree to accept what is lost in the difference between virtual and actual satisfaction. We construct a digital life where that loss is too easily dismissed, and the difference between virtual and actual no longer matters. The intensity with which we have embraced the digital reveals that there lies latent in us a very strong craving to reclaim this early mode of dream life. But, perhaps, it is a lost Eden, and the narcissistic regression of digital life is the price we pay to think otherwise.

Dreams and Madness

Stiegler (2019) writes:

> At night, of course, we enter into a kind of delirium- which raises the question of the difference between sleep, dreams and madness.
>
> *(p. 89)*

In averring the classical link between dreams and madness, Stiegler reminds us that the very medium of dreaming itself, in being able to make our fantasies become realities, has the potential to enact a particular form of delirium. In that we truly give free rein to the imagination in our dreaming life, awake or asleep, we are susceptible to that madness.

What ultimately contains the dream? How, in our dreaming life, do we prevent ourselves from being overtaken by the destructiveness of our narcissism or the madness of primary process? These questions contain a paradox, of course, because given the essential role it plays in metabolizing affect, dreaming itself is the ultimate form of psychic containment. Think of how much we rely on the imagination to express impulses and desires that would wreak havoc in the empirical world. Thus, it's no coincidence that when the dreaming function breaks down, and we can no longer digest emotional experience, we fall prey to employing narcissistic defenses to protect ourselves from an accumulating mass of unprocessed affect (what Bion [1983] calls beta elements) that, in our desperate, unconscious attempt to evacuate, ends up driving us mad. If the psychic dream space for the expressive containment of our impulses breaks down, what choice do we have but to unload them onto the world?

If we bring a wide-angle lens to this phenomenon, it may elucidate an important dimension of the world situation today. We are plagued by the outpouring of unprocessed affect in the context of our social and political world, and one primary response we have to it is an increased vulnerability to narcissism, both in ourselves, and, especially, in our leaders. How is the delirium of digital life contributing to this situation?

The digital is an experiment to see what happens when we are offered an environment in which we can experience our desires as realities in the same fashion as when we were infants. We now have at our disposal an incredible array of instruments that let us 'play with reality,' as digital potential space, in its awesome power to creatively defer the real, becomes the hallmark of all potential space, where we can do, see, and become anything and anyone, at any time, allowing reality not only to be shaped by our desire, but potentiated by it. Yet, at the same time, its maintenance is increasingly requiring a pathological form of disavowal, as we become ever more desperate to keep the real at bay.

Inside the walls of the virtual world, infantile omnipotence is granted a radical freedom As long as we stay inside its bounds, follow its rules of engagement, it offers a good-enough container for the negative side of the pharmakon, that is, the destructive, life-denying sides of an omnipotence that knows no limits. But today, this new form of (adult) infantile omnipotence generated by the digital is breaking free of its virtual container. Like an oil spill flowing into the ocean, we are poisoned by the expectation that the actual world provide us a playspace for the actualization of our fantasies that need not to take into account the reality of the other, just like its digital counterpart. This is giving rise to new forms of delirium, as the madness once contained inside the space of the digital crosses the divide and leaks out into the world.

Somehow, even in the face of the digital's failure to contain the simulated virtuality that it is perpetually generating, we still instinctively seek from it a now lost maternal function. The virtual world provides a holding environment like no other. All the divergent ways that we are at odds with ourselves, the contradicting multiplicity of ideas, affects and identifications that constitute the polymorphous perversity of psychic life, find a welcoming home there. But digital containment comes at the cost of confusing our relation to the real. It's like a mother that can't help its baby progress beyond primal dreaming. When infantile omnipotence is revived by digital dreaming, the more problematic elements of an unbounded omnipotence, its unrelenting darkness and destructiveness, are unleashed.

Evoking Freud's second dichotomy, we might say that when digital dream space collapses, there is more room for the expression of a death drive not bounded by eros. And perhaps the most disturbing example of this today is the suicide website (Twohey and Dance, 2021) that offers precise instruction, emotional support, and encouragement to young people seeking to take their lives in the face of a despairing world. A "pure culture of the death instinct" (Freud, 1923, p. 53) has a found a home on the web.

Coda

Idios kosmos takes us to the border between the dream's manifestation as a wholly subjective phenomenon and its world-disclosive nature. The dreaming kosmos has its own occurrence, different and separate from the occurrence of subjectivity. It's the place where identity and difference intertwine, idios becomes kosmos, kosmos idios; the infant dreams the world and wishes become actualities. As the wellspring of the virtual, of the uncanny, it's what makes dreaming reality so existentially and psychologically rich.

What's remarkable about dreaming is that we are thrust each night into a mini-universe with all the properties (and more) of waking life in which we can live out what is most singular in our nature. Entering dreaming reality, we relinquish our own. That model of surrender is also necessary for dream analysis, as patient and analyst, together, learn to hover near the dream's navel, that point of impenetrability that touches down into the unknown. That's what we mean when we say, 'Not the patient nor the analyst: Let the dream speak' for that is where the untranslatable idiom in our being is given its ultimate expression. It houses the unrepresentable.

In offering something substantial/actual/material to bump up against, kosmos contains idios. Without the tension of their difference, the dream narcissistically folds in on itself. Valery shows us how to prevent this collapse:

> I mean that man is constantly and necessarily opposed to that which is by his concern for that which is not! and that he laboriously, or through genius, gives birth to what he must in order to give his dreams the very power and precision of reality, and, on the other hand, in order to impose upon this reality increasing changes that bring it closer to his dreams.
>
> *(as cited in Stiegler, 2019, p. 351)*

Self and world on a digital platform re-enact that not yet reached incommensurability between baby and mother, a merger state that can impede the move toward transitionality, as the immersive pleasures of primal dreaming (in this new adult digital form) envelop and enclose the self.

As we have seen, we dream the day in order to metabolize it. The psyche is busy at night with what's left over from the events of the day that requires the labyrinthian spirals of the dream to release its unworked affects. This is why dreams (whether one is seeing an analyst or simply living one's life) play such an important role in the overall mental health of a person; they are doing essential psychic work. It's also why when the dreaming function is dammed, blocked up or overloaded, it has damaging effects on our collective lives as well.

This is an important vantage point from which to consider the refusal to wake up from the digital. Virtual realities live outside of time, thus disrupting the familiar rhythms of waking and sleeping that at one time served as the ground for the processes of psychic and affective metabolization. In a 24/7 world, where waking and sleeping, day and night no longer serve as necessary demarcations to separate dreaming and waking realities, how do you wake up?

Through its hyper-charging of the virtual, and its erasure of the difference between subjective and a-subjective occurrence, the digital is hampering our dreaming function. When we lose access to the a-subjective, we lose our capacity to 'suffer experience' as Bion calls the psychic metabolization necessary for the maintenance of one's psychic life. The dreaming function is ultimately that which allows us to dream the real and transform it into something usable, containable, creative.

The digital so entices us with the extra-ordinary that we are left wholly unprepared for the fact that objects in reality are finite and disappointing and that there is loss and contingency in the world. How does one learn to bear disenchantment when one is surrounded by a perpetually enchanted (digital/simulated) world? And bearing disenchantment is another way of expressing what Bion means when he speaks of suffering experience.

Adam Phillips' (2012) concept of 'missing out' gets at something important here. For when we leave the multiverse of digital virtuality there is a feeling that our one, limited, life, with its narrow range possibilities, is less tolerable to us. Rather than all this newly available possibility creatively feeding, expanding and nurturing us, we are poisoned by it, for now something feels intolerable about the smallness of my life and the narrowness of my concern. I am in a constant state of missing out that makes whatever I am doing and feeling seem petty and small.

At the end, it seems we are increasingly ensnared by the digital dream. This observation loses all credibility when not held in pharmacological tension with the profound and life-affirming ways the digital has opened up and made readily available—when we are awake and aware and living our lives—the world of dreaming, spirited fantasy, reverie and creative illusion. How then can we make use of it to re-work the ways in which, for all of us, the space of primal dreaming was too precipitously collapsed (no one ever gets enough)? But not knowing anymore how to awaken from the simulations of virtual dreaming, this ensnarement is an indication that there can be too much of a good thing. That's the nature of all addictions and the digital is no exception. Our unceasing immersion in the digital imaginary enacts a negatively charged disavowal of the symbolic and the real. We gain a metaverse, and lose one at the same time.

References

Ars Industrialis (n.d.). Vocabulary. Retrieved from https://arsindustrialis.org/vocabulary-english-version

Bion, W.R. (1983). *Learning from Experience*. New York: Jason Aronson.

Bollas, C. (1987) *The Shadow of the Object: Psychoanalysis of the Unthought Known*. New York: Columbia University Press.

Boss, M. (1957) *The Analysis of Dreams*. London: Rider and Company.

Foucault, M. (1985) Dreaming and Existence. *Review of Existential Psychology & Psychiatry*, Volume XIX, no.1.

Frankel, R. and Krebs, V.J. (2022) *Human Virtuality and Digital Life: Philosophical and Psychoanalytic Investigations*. London: Routledge.

Freud, S. (1905) Jokes and Their Relation to the Unconscious. In J. Strachey (Ed. and Trans.), *The Standard Edition of the Complete Psychological Works of Sigmund Freud* (vol 8, pp. 1–258). London: Hogarth Press.

Freud, S. (1923) The Ego and the Id. In J. Strachey (Ed. and Trans.), *The Standard Edition of the Complete Psychological Works of Sigmund Freud* (vol 19, pp. 1–68). London: Hogarth Press.

Hillman, J. (1979) *The Dream and the Underworld*. New York: Harper and Row.

Murphie, A. (2002) Putting the Virtual Back into VR. In B. Massumi (Ed.), *A Shock to Thought, Expression after Deleuze and Guattari* (pp. 188–214). London: Routledge.

Nancy, J.L. (2009) *The Fall of Sleep*. New York: Fordham University Press.

Ogden, T. (2009) *Rediscovering Psychoanalysis: Thinking and Dreaming, Learning and Forgetting*. London: Routledge.

Phillips, A. (2012) *Missing Out: In Praise of the Unlived Life*. New York: Farrar, Straus and Giroux.

Stiegler, B. (2013) *What Makes Life Worth Living: On Pharmacology.* Malden, MA: Polity.

Stiegler, B. (2019) *The Age of Disruption: Technology and Madness in Computational Capitalism.* Cambridge: Polity Press.

Twohey, M. and Dance G. (2021, Dec. 9). Where the Despairing Learn Ways to Die. *New York Times.*
Winnicott, D.W. (1971) *Transitional Objects and Transitional Phenomena. In Playing and Reality* (pp. 1–25). London: Tavistock Publications.

Winnicott, D.W. (1987) *The Child, the Family, and the Outside World.* Reading, MA: Addison-Wesley Publishing Company.

4

THE SOUL BEHIND YOUR EYES

Psychic Presence in the Digital Screen

Victor J. Krebs

Virtuality

Abruptly thrown into virtual life, we have had to come to terms with a new dimension in human experience. Or, more exactly, we have had to learn to live with an ever-emerging gamut of new dimensions that have subverted our spatio-temporal sense and are slowly dislocating our existential coordinates.

There is no doubt that when we interact with others through a screen, for example, we cannot but feel something unreal in that digital image. No matter how often or how clearly we see each other, there seems to be no doubt that the telematic contact inevitably impoverishes our interaction with the other. To begin with, the virtual image before us no longer inhabits our own spatio-temporal coordinates. There is no continuity between the physical space in which we stand and the virtual space in which we appear, so we cannot anymore, for instance, look into one another's eyes on a screen. That natural conduit for intimate and deep communication with the other is sealed off in the virtual.

But the radical change and limitations that are inherent to the digitization of matter may, paradoxically, be opening a new frontier in human experience in our age. Vilém Flusser (2011), indeed believes that

> [t]oday we are witnessing, not decadence, but the emergence of a new social form… This new social structure can be seen, with a bit of optimism, as a transitional phase in the rise of a new culture.
>
> *(p. 68)*

The digital body in these new modes of appearing and relating to the other is no longer made of flesh but of pixels, so we obviously cannot touch each other, or smell each other, or feel each other's physical presence. The virtual screen obliterates the intimacy that is inevitable between two bodies in physical proximity. And yet modes of relation and emotional response are being triggered by our virtual encounters, inaugurating realms of experience we are only beginning to fathom and that are radically reshaping our psychologies and shifting

DOI: 10.4324/9781003195849-6

the axis around which our world has been built. Think, for example, of the way it is changing our relation to our own selves:

> [Nowadays] we are immersed in technologies that offer a ceaseless flood of mirroring, from the specially targeted ads that algorithmically inflame my acquisitive desires, to the messages in my inbox, all tantalizingly addressed to me, to the flurry of likes awaiting me in response to my most recent tweets or Facebook or Instagram posts, to the objects of my desire that come straight from the screen to my front door. Siri and Alexa answer my questions, assuage my concerns, and, in their omnisciently soothing voices, I feel as if they are there exclusively to help me. I turn on my GPS, and the coordinates and location of where I am currently situated become the center of the world. We now rely upon these external devices, as much, and in many cases more than, the actual people in our life.
>
> *(Frankel & Krebs, 2022, p. 189)*

And the other also acquires forms and dimensions that, in the various modulations through which the same self can be present to us now, re-wires any sense we might have previously had of otherness, of being with someone or even just being there in the world. Not only does an altogether new form of being and being-together arise, but the world itself that we inhabit acquires new horizons and opens yet unseen dimensions. The digital modulations of experience are rapidly sinking into our unconscious every-day, thus already modifying our reality in ways of which we remain often completely unaware.

The Digital Threat

Bernard Stiegler (2016), especially in the first two decades of our century, identified the greatest danger of an informational society—as Vilém Flusser (2011) himself had also done at the end of the eighties—in the automatization with which digitality can tie up the world, and render us captive. For Stiegler that automatization could annul the creative power man has to counter the natural entropy to which our technology seems to be taking us. He sees that power in the human ability to imagine possibilities, hence of always being able to generate novelties that counter the tendency to homogeneity. Flusser identifies that same power in our ability to make information in a world that aims implacably at disinformation, heteronomy, and stasis.

As Flusser (2017) explains:

> The fact is that telematics weaves threads that connect us dialogically, but these threads run through a field dominated by central emitters and are controlled by radiating beams. Everyone can dialogue with everyone, but the dialogues are informed by the centrally radiated information... Everyone receives the same type of information, no matter where they are... In this situation all dialogue becomes redundant... There will be nothing for it to be authentically dialogued. No exchange of information is then possible. The telematized dialogues are not conversations but chatter... Thus, existential loneliness will only be accentuated and not overcome: we will plunge into kitsch, into banality.
>
> *(p. 114)*

Just as oral culture had to learn to read and so begin to see the world according to the linearity and sequentiality of the new medium, we now need to learn to read and use the digital images and the technology we have created, before it becomes intractable.

"Envisioning"

Before we can answer the question alluded to in the title, "The soul behind your eyes," namely, whether we lose psychic depth in the virtual screen, we need to see what Flusser means when he calls the kind of new thinking we will need to develop "envisioning." In doing so, we will be exploring the ontological issue of the transformations the psyche is undergoing in our digital life.

According to Walter Benjamin (2010), the naive modern conception of experience, which reduces it to its minimum expression—as "reception of perceptions" (p. 163)—has done away with the kind of imagination that allowed ancients to make all sorts of connections and infuse the world with mystery and depth. We have lost what he calls "the mimetic faculty:"

> The perceived world (*Merkwelt*) of modern human beings seems to contain infinitely fewer of those magical correspondences than the world of the ancient people or even of primitive peoples... Human beings might have perceived... that objects had a mimetic character, where nowadays we would not even be capable of suspecting it.
>
> *(Benjamin, 1978, p. 66)*

In this pre-rationalistic world of perception, things were not fully closed off for the subject by the mechanism of representation (Benjamin, 1978), as it is for us moderns for whom perception is a rational matter, measurable, and predictable. The "mimetic faculty" made possible the kind of perception that registered the world not just through the senses, but also through an affective, empathic resonance with what was perceived, that could not be placed within the cartesian framework of modernity. It underwrites the same kind of imaginative power Benjamin found, for example, in those who "perceive magical correspondences between things," in clairvoyants, who could "claim to receive the perception of others as their own," or even in those who "identify with animals, plants, or their objects of perception" (p. 66).

That imagination is gone. But it allowed animistic societies to give meaning to a world that appeared to them overwhelming in its sheer vitality. The world and life were sacred, and their religion was the proof of their connection to that life force. Modern man, on the other hand, finds his world every time more abstract and distant, devoid of existential meaning. Wittgenstein (1998) once commented in a memorable image, that sometimes it seemed to him as if everything were "wrapped in cheap cellophane & isolated from anything great" (p. 57).

What was true for modernity seems in that respect to have become worse in the digital age, where the world is numerical and zero-dimensional, as far from the concrete as it is possible to go. What is paradoxical is that the digital may be able to re-awaken the imagination and make us capable of dreaming-up a reality out of the nothing we have made of it. This is how Flusser (2011) puts it:

> The power to envision is the power that sets out to make concrete sense of the abstract and absurd universe into which we are falling... Envisioners stand at the most extreme edge of abstraction ever reached, in a dimensionless universe, and they offer us the possibility of again experiencing the world and our lives in it as concrete. Only through photographs, films, television, video images, and, in the future, above all, through computer-synthesized images are we able to turn back to concrete experience, recognition, value, and action and away from the world of abstraction from which these things have vanished.
>
> *(pp. 37–38)*

We need to turn back to the concrete, to reverse the history of abstraction that constitutes our technological track. But that will require that we learn to think with the speed, fleetingness, and rhizomatic capriciousness of the digital image, instead of the pretension of permanence and atemporality that underlies our scribal culture. It will involve a change as radical—Flusser suggests—as the one our hominid ancestors made when they began to walk on two legs (ibid., p. 47).

Modulations of the Virtual

Human beings had never had to deal with moving images on a silver canvas, so it is not surprising that the first audience ever to have the experience in the Brothers Lumiére's premiere public screening of a film, found themselves running away from the gigantic train advancing toward them from the *écran*. We now find the reaction comic; but, indeed, as Tarkovski (1994) said, film was inaugurating a new aesthetic principle with its moving images. And it had to be incorporated into our collective consciousness before such new entities, too, began to form part of our familiar world.

Moving images projected on a screen added a new dimension that required unknown aesthetic principles to integrate them into the familiar flow of the collective. Nowadays, and analogously, the digital image is generating the need—not just for one, but for innumerable (and constantly emerging) new aesthetic principles. The interacting virtual screen, more and more sophisticated as video-games continue to flourish, for example, adds a dimension to the cinematic image that the simple movie did not have; the postmortem holographic appearance of people in world tours (Maria Callas, Michael Jackson and Tupac Chakur are famous examples) add yet a further dimension to our experience; and Virtual Reality, already with its impressive (virtual) synesthesia, promising—in what is being called the "Metaverse"—the final merger of the empirical with the virtual, every time more real than real, constitutes the cherry on top of the cake. All of them keep adding previously unknown principles to our modes of perception. They simply continue the same progression in what we may understand as the history of the virtual and its always evolving technological modulations:

> In the concrete images of the caveman, in pictograms on a stone tablet, in written signs and photographic images on paper, the virtual is placed [and] materialized outside our minds. If we take the virtual to be the potential kept within everything that we perceive, then in the representational act of writing, drawing, and photography, that potential is sedimented in its actualized form.
>
> *(Frankel & Krebs, 2022, p. 48)*

What we are witnessing in our era is but another step in a long history of modulations of reality, of actualizations of the virtual, that have undergone several paradigm-shifting moments. With the aggravating circumstances of the Anthropocene, that raises the stakes dramatically, we are living, with the digital revolution, perhaps the biggest threat the human life form has ever had to confront.

The technological modulations that preceded the digital also redimensioned human reality. They opened new horizons only by displacing or radically modifying others, changing our conception of the world and how we see it. The digital image confronts us ubiquitously nowadays, seeping the virtual dimension into every corner of our lives, forcing us to reconceive our notions of soul, and psychic presence itself.

Images

For the Greeks all images originated in Hades, specifically in its darkest center: Tartarus, son of Ether and Gaia, thus engendered from the most ethereal and from the earthliest, from the most immaterial and the most material (cf. Hillman, 1979). All images, the myth is telling us, come from this ethereal dark and formless vitality, this luminous dust at the bottomless depth of the cosmos.

What the human hand paints, draws, sculpts, writes, types; what the human figure traces with the infinite expressiveness of the face and the body; the material forms of nature and empirical reality, and even what the imagination conjures up: all physical and virtual images come from those depths. This object in front of me, our bodies, the skies above us, the aroma of the coffee that captures my senses, the beauty of the semblances that delight us on our smartphones, the voices that conjure up all sorts of feelings, moods, and emotions in you, etc., they are all images, and they all emerge from that abyss. The sensible images of perception, in other words, are as oneiric as are the images of our dreams and fantasies. Furthermore, as Jacques Ranciére (2019, p. 7) reminds us, images are not merely perceptual (visual, auditory, olfactory, etc.). Images can consist wholly in words; they are all operations whereby we are constantly making the world visible by giving form to what is significant to us, bridging and integrating perception and affection, making the invisible visible.

Images mark the threshold of awareness. We have an image whenever a new significance arises from behind or beneath the prior constellations that have become sedimented meanings in our habitual perception. Andrew Murphie (2002), echoing Deleuze, gives the name of "macro-perceptions" to what results from the breakthroughs at the edge of consciousness, to the sudden emergence in actualized form of what were yet formless or "fuzzy perceptions" that, once constellated, make something visible. The image of what we perceive is then, as Murphie phrases it, "a differential operation at the threshold of perception" (p. 199). It emerges out of the dance of invisibilities and sudden significances, differences, and relations, the "micro-perceptions" that constellate to create our macro-perceptions.

The image, conceived in this way, is not the static object that we perceive, somehow reflecting or duplicating something else. The image is not a re-presentation of something other, it is an emergence:

> the meaning and reality of the [image] is determined from within its own occurrence and not by any external model or criterion.... Differentials weave opposites together into a rhizomatic psychic and physical space, and the images produced... resemble nothing other than themselves in their own movement.
>
> *(Krebs, 2023, p. 100)*

An image is an operation, an animated field of emergence situated at the threshold of perception, where what was once invisible breaks into visibility, where the unuttered becomes an utterance.

Carl Jung says that the idea of an identity between an image in internal reality and an object in external reality, is "a naive assumption" (1916/1948, CW 8: par 516, quoted by Michael Vannoy Adams [2018], p. 30). In this sense we could say that the image we are talking about neither corresponds nor does not correspond to the object of which it is an image. For the image in the sense in which I am taking it here is a transitional object, firmly hovering between the empirical and the subjective in that very threshold between the conscious and the unconscious, in potential space, at the edge of Tartarus.

An image may work as a representation of something else (when I draw the blooming flowers in the garden, for example, or conjure up your face in my memory), but it need not. In fact, every image is autonomous from what it is used to represent, and this has become evident with the possibilities opened up by digitality. The images that populate our world are autonomous operations that constitute what we experience, confluences of possibilities that obey no previous model. Why certain images appear and not others, depends on a myriad of factors beyond our awareness—from psychological (individual propensities, temperaments, idiosyncracies, culture) to material (geographical location, climatic conditions, habitat, etc.). There is a vital spontaneity in experience that falls beyond the subject's consciousness that is greatly responsible for their appearance.

The conception of thought as representational, however (what Deleuze [1994] called "the dogmatic image of thought"), has prevailed in modern culture, so there is an implicit commitment to a permanent and stable essence or substance that desensitizes us to the perpetual movement behind what we have learned to see as stable bodies and fixed states of affairs. But now Virtual Reality reveals how what we see as "a simple facticity of stable bodies and fixed states of affairs" are simply "regimes of separation" (Murphie, 2002, p. 192), agents of petrification of life that make the reality of becoming more bearable. The interactive reality of the virtual and the actual, so present in our digital life can no longer be denied. In our contemporary "liquid" society, as Zygmunt Bauman has called it, the illusion of permanence is shattered by the speed and dialectics of the digital. This, of course, has important ontological consequences. As Jane Bennett (2010) writes, "we are talking here about a materiality that is itself heterogeneous, itself a differential of intensities, itself a life [... where] there is no point of pure stillness" (p. 57).

In the gap that stands between me and the world, images constitute and modulate the transitional space where we experience virtuality as an intrinsic quality sustaining all experience, as the realm of possibilities that opens up to humans due to their technological being. The virtual is that inmanent presence underlying the actual, an open-ended power of reorganization that "is made of virtualities" (Deleuze, 1997, p. 5), underwritten by the infinitely flowing reserve of formless vitality behind them, a "pressing multitude of incipiencies and tendencies" in Brian Massumi's (1987) words. Images never exhaust their meaning, for as Bennett (2010) adds, "there is no indivisible atom that is not itself full of virtual force" (p. 57). The ground of all images is always the ground of excess, superfluity, of open possibility, of pure virtuality out of which anything may acquire form.

The Digital Image

With the analog image—say a photograph of someone—we know that the light that emanates from the paper and touches my eyes, really came from the luminous presence that was imprinted in the photographic plate at the very moment when the person was photographed. But the digital image, as Bernard Stiegler (Derrida & Stiegler, 2002) says, "breaks the 'umbilical cord'" (p. 152) that grounds the materiality of the process that generates the photographic image. The digital image of someone is no longer tied physically to that person. There is no past, in other words, from which this image comes:

> With the digital photo, this light, from out of the night... doesn't come from a past day that would simply have become night (like photons emanating from a past object). It comes from Hades, from the realm of the dead, from underground: it is an electric light, set free by materials from deep within the belly of the earth. An electronic, decomposed light.
>
> *(p. 153)*

The digital image is not an actual footprint of anything; it is an algorithmic phantom of something that has never been. It offers us an assemblage of computer data that may even be permuted and interlaced in ways that need not hold any relation to actual reality, but that actually can inspire our creativity.

Flusser points out that the traditional image (the non-technical image) emerges from a world of objects, from which the image maker is directed to an actual surface. But the situation is inverted in the digital case, where the image maker is "directed from a particle toward a surface that can never be achieved." He attempts, in other words, "to turn from extreme abstraction back into the imaginable," "to make concrete." The maker of traditional images, however, abstracts, and "retreats from the concrete." As Flusser (2011) sums it up:

> We are concerned here with two image surfaces that are conceived completely differently, opposed to one another, even though they appear to blend together... The meaning of technical images is to be sought in a place other than that of traditional images.
>
> *(p. 21)*

Disconnected from space, the digital image is indeed unmoored from all familiar ports. It is cut loose from the causal logic of reality as we have come to know it.

In the history of film, something like that happened to the cinematic image, with the appearance of movements like Italian neo realism and films with what Paul Schrader (2018) called transcendental style, that actually make their images work on the spectator in a very different way than linear narratives do. As Deleuze (1989) explains, "[i]t is no longer a motor extension that is established, but an oneiric connection through the intermediation of the liberated sensory organs" (p. 4). Opening up different forms of connection and different sense-giving logics, the time-image, as Deleuze called it, introduced a different kind of cinematic world. One, in fact, that approximates our subjective life, especially in our musings, the poetic imagination, reverie and dreams. Similarly, with the digital its multimedia resources open up completely new ways of seeing.

By reducing the world to infinitesimal particles, to each of which we associate a sequence of 0s and 1s we have made a second, parallel world, that is weightless and indestructible, one we can store, transfer and clone indefinitely. We reproduce the image of my body, for example, from a mathematical grid, turning it into an algorithm from which my digital image originates, anywhere and anytime. The laws of empirical space belonging to my physical image no longer apply to my virtual self. And the modifications of my face, for example, made possible by the multiple apps always trending in social media, liberate my image from the constraints of representation, generating a freedom of associations and connections that turns reality, our digital life itself, into a dreamscape. The digital image is drawn literally, as Stiegler put it, from "the night of a past that was never present."

And yet from that electronic Hades, from that "decomposed light," different creatures can be bred and nurtured. We are now able to produce artificial images that, instead of representing the world, create illusions from which we construct the new realities that we then start to share and inhabit together. Alternative worlds start to emerge in the synthesized images on the screen:

> Lines composed out of point-elements, surfaces, soon also bodies and movable bodies. These worlds are coloured and can sound, in the near future they will probably also be touchable, smellable and tastable.
>
> *(Flusser, 2002, p. 202)*

In fact, they already are in many of the videogames that populate the imagination and major involvement of a large portion of native digitals.

As Bram Ieven (2003) says: "mathematical thinking brings forth alternative worlds that freely begin to mingle with what was previously understood as reality." That is precisely what we are experiencing increasingly nowadays, not only with Virtual Reality but with that merger of digital virtuality and empirical experience that we can call our digital life.

Technological Abstraction

The history of Western consciousness has arguably been defined by the systematic, instinctive disavowal of mortality by means of technology. It has resulted in a process of increasing abstraction, of human society fleeing the concrete. The three-dimensionality of the embodied encounter with the world is first reduced in the technics of drawing and painting (traditional images) to the two-dimensionality of the flat surface, and then through writing to the one-dimensionality of lines of signs and symbols on a paper. And now, in the twenty-first century, we have arrived at what Flusser (2011) calls the zero-dimensionality of the digital.

The same path of abstraction is reflected in the development of the human gesture, understood as the expressive movement of the body (or of any tool that extends the body), for which causal explanations are insufficient, and further discussion is superfluous (Flusser, 2014, pp. 1–2). In other words, we can see it in the ways in which the body has expressed itself in human consciousness according to the different technological modulations (and physical, physiological, genetic, psychological, social, economic, etc., factors) along the process:

> Action is the first gesture to free human beings from their lifeworld. The second is visual observation. The third is conceptual explanation. And the fourth gesture to free human beings from their life world is the computing touch. The hand makes humankind the subject of the world, the eye makes it the surveyor of the world, fingers make it ruler of the world, and through fingertips, humankind becomes what gives the world meaning. The current cultural revolution can be viewed as a transfer of existence to the fingertips. Work (hand), ideology (eye), and narrative (finger)... subordinated to programmed computation.
>
> *(Flusser, 2011, pp. 28–29)*

From being an operation on sensitive impressions, the image is then modulated by mechanical, theoretical and arithmetical technologies, to (re)construct reality through processes that are physical, mental, and now electronic or digital. The digital image no longer sediments fixed substances as the traditional image did but gives plastic expression to vectors and intensities that are continuously re-signified by the computer. It is, moreover, made up of punctual, atomic elements, individual pixels that can form—like the natural image—meaningful surfaces. It functions without dimensions, in complete abstraction from the concrete.

In the digital age, then, the image emerges from the abstract universe of numbers from, as it were, a pure swarm of dots. It becomes concrete thanks to the imaginative power behind the digital program, a feat of the imagination, an "envisioning" that Flusser (2011) illustrates in the following anecdote:

> Yesterday I saw Mozart's opera *Cosi fan tutte* on television. On closer observation, I saw traces of electrons in the cathode ray tube... What I actually experienced as beauty

yesterday required the calculations and computations of a close reading of the particulate universe… [O]ne could rightly claim that yesterday I hallucinated a Mozart opera. For what I saw yesterday followed from a series of concretizations—calculations and computations—of abstract particles, and that is the reason I had a concrete experience yesterday. It was concrete because it had been visualized for me out of abstractions. *Envision*, then, should refer to the capacity to step from the particle universe back into the concrete. I therefore suggest that the power to envision first appeared when technical images were invented.

(pp. 34–35)

Perhaps Flusser exaggerates when he claims that the power to envision first appeared with technical images, because we could say that the imagination, independently of machines (in drawing and writing and thinking) always has been responsible for creating meaningful surfaces, the only difference being that envisioning is the particular imagination of a perception that needs to be computed rather than perceived, thought of, or dreamt up.

Technical images are at the most extreme limit of abstraction we have ever reached, dimensionless, "objective depictions of events in the particle universe" that offer us the possibility to re-experience the world and our life in it as something concrete. "They make these processes visible," as Flusser (2011) puts it. But they can only be seen from a distance, superficially.

Lacan (1997) once said that while animals are attracted to superficial appearances, humans are enticed by the idea of things that are hidden. But in this new world depth becomes useless, and in fact, counteractive for the meaning of the surfaces visualized out of the thin air of the digital. Art would seem to be better than truth. Indeed we are here before the quintessential *trompe l'œil*, which would (if we follow Lacan's reasoning) be distancing us from the rational, and instead, approximating us to the animal within.

The digital image belongs to the 'virtual space' that has abandoned even the one-dimensionality of written sequences and hierarchies, and the chronological logic of the language in which we encode the world. With it we enter the zero-dimensionality of the digital, where lines have been transformed into networks, hierarchies into a single plane of immanence, sequences, and chronologies into rhizomes and synchronicities.

Post-History

At present, we are just beginning to develop the capacity for envisioning or, as Flusser (1993) calls it elsewhere, for "techno-imagination." We are not yet able, like an illiterate person in a world of texts, to orient ourselves in the world of digital images. For our "categories of experience, thought and value" (p. 154) are still oriented toward the historical, linear, written existence determined by the culture against which the digital is rising.

We have gone from a prehistoric age, which lasted until the advent of writing, where linear thinking and logic inaugurated the consciousness of history, to the advent, with "technical" images (where Flusser includes the photographic and the cinematic), of the post-historical age. We have, therefore, to "transcend historical consciousness" (p. 154) to find our way in the world of technical images. This is how Flusser explains it:

The current interaction between images and human beings will lead to a loss of historical consciousness in those who receive the images and… But this current interaction is not yet leading to the development of new consciousness, [and it won't] unless it changes radically, unless the feedback is interrupted, and images begin to mediate between people. Such a rupture of the magical circle between image and person is a task we face, and this rupture is not only technically but above all existentially possible.

(Flusser, 2011, p. 60)

Rupturing, in other words, the magical circle between image and person, where the image prevents us from metabolizing the new social, ontological and psychic order(s); as when we binge on Netflix and other platforms, consuming more information than we could ever process, or get hooked on the gadget and everything virtual, that allows us to disconnect from reality by ushering us into flocks of empty images, repetitive matrix-like images that lure us into spectacle, and extravaganza. Pascal talked about an instinct of *divertimento* that enables us to avoid facing the tragic fact of our mortality.

But being a pharmakon, in the right doses the digital can become a remedy rather than a poison. The right dosage, however, can only be applied when we make the move to break its spell, when we overcome our susceptibility and vulnerability to the digital daze. Like Endymion we prefer the illusory vision of Selene to her sporadical absences. Our unconsciousness is therefore a moral matter, and we must make it a political priority of the highest order, for it is our resistance to change that makes technology poisonous and toxic.

We are enraptured by the proliferating digital images, surrounded by them in every instance of our social life. And they belong outside the historical plane. They are constantly subverting our sense of space and of time in a very real way, for they are generated no longer by a reality outside where we advance along straight, progressive rails. They deliver us instead to an encompassing hive, where lodged in a timeless present chronology scatters and the imagination quickens; and we travel at the speed of light, living a literally ubiquitous existence. That is the electronic Hades whence technical images come forth, multiply, and disseminate.

Disconnected from its historicity, the digital image re-constitutes our consciousness of reality, delivering us into a timeless, oneiric landscape. When we navigate the Internet, we are perpetually bombarded with images that can appear at the click of an instant, from wherever in the global network. In the social media, images appear from wherever in the cyber-information bank, and they demand our investment and interest in whatever they are peddling—be it cryptocurrency, NFTs, a trip to Hawaii, nostalgia, rage or bad faith, good will, and solidarity. Bursting all chronology, digital images reconstitute our sense of our own lives, constantly shifting the familiar order of our priorities. The stories we can build of each other's lives from the virtual media may have nothing in empirical reality that they correspond to, nor will I ever hold that piece of digital art for which I have paid exorbitant amounts in Bitcoin—money which, by the way, I will never see or touch either.

We could continue listing the so many other countless ways in which our daily activities are entwined today with the swarming images, unceasingly calling us from the omnipresent screens that populate our digital lives. It is important to stress that the expectations traditionally carried by historical images have ceased to be the point and have become impertinent and obsolete for the posthistorical.

Image Makers

Flusser (2011) remarks, that "instead of writing letters, we could exchange experiences, thoughts and feelings with one another in the form of images" (p. 81). We are already seeing an increasing use of digital images—photographs and videos, of course, but also emojis, gifs, stickers—in the commerce, and communication in the social media. This growing prevalence of the image—especially (though not exclusively) in our virtual interactions—is presently occurring in culture. It gives the digital the potential to overcome its most negative aspects, and to deconstruct the "discursively bundled transmissions" (ibid.) that are increasingly directed by algorithms that exclude humans from the decision-making process at any stage and confine us, as Stiegler (2010) also does not tire of telling us.

Learning to think with images may seem to us, pre-digital souls, as awkward as it would be for a seeing and talking person to have to learn to talk in sign-language and read with their fingers. But perhaps the greatest difficulty in learning for us now lies in having to renounce our expectations of productivity, repudiate it as a life standard, and to reassess our belief in the indispensability of depth for significance. They only make it impossible to recognize the benefits that could accrue from the new modes of thinking the digital image is demanding:

> We are about to reach a level of consciousness where the search for deep coherence, explanation, enumeration, narrative, and calculation, in short, historical, scientific, and textually linear thinking, are being overtaken by a new visionary and superficial mode of thinking.
>
> *(Flusser, 2011, p. 60)*

Flusser was imagining—already four decades ago—the radical shift in the way we conceive the nature and purpose of communication that we would be facing today, when digital images have become our daily bread. Just as he predicted, we are indeed beginning "[to] see no longer any point in trying to distinguish between something illusory and something non-illusory, between fiction and reality." These are clear symptoms of this shift. Indeed, "the abstract universe of particles from which we are emerging" seems to dilute the line separating the illusory from the real, the subjective from the objective, facts from "alternative" facts, truth from "post-truth." So, it seems plausible to assert that, to overcome this critical juncture,

> [we] must abandon categories like true-false, real-artificial, or real-apparent in favor of categories like concrete-abstract. The power to imagine is the power to dare to bring the concrete out of the abstract.
>
> *(Flusser, 2011, p. 38)*

If we are to envision the meanings that can structure and give value to the abstract world we have created in our race to disavow time, becoming, and death, we need to repudiate our penchant for deep exploration and learn to see things from a distance, on the surface. What that requires, rather than to reject the superficiality ushered in by the digital image, is to embrace it, and trust that in that direction we may find a way of recovering the world we have lost to abstraction. Paradoxically, then, the utter abstraction of the digital image, more than a flaw or a deficiency, may become the turning point to a new order in which these phenomena, virtual extensions of our identity, may be reassembled in a way that is beneficent to our evolution.

As Flusser (2011) admonishes: "Our veil is not to be torn but woven ever more tightly" (pp. 38–39). Instead of leading us into nihilism this experience could lead us down a new path. In any case, "we have no choice but to risk a leap into the new" (p. 15) or, as the Zen proverb goes, "the only way out, is through."

Against Entropy

Entropy is the universe's tendency toward that ultimate state of thermal equilibrium, where we reach the conditions of what physicists call "heat death," of maximum entropy and zero available energy. How this is to happen to the information society is conceived by both Flusser and Stiegler as a gradual dissolution of culture to the state of automatic communication, where there is no real dialog to provoke creativity, but a mode of communication, a chatter ruled by a central memory bank, a series of algorithms that control dialog to reproduce itself in a gradual progression toward stasis. This is how Stiegler (2019) explains it:

> Reticulated society is based on smartphones and other embedded mobile devices (chips, sensors, GPS tags, cars, televisions, watches, clothing, and other prostheses), but also on new fixed and mobile terminals (urban territory becoming the infrastructure and architecture of constant mobility and constant connectivity). As such, it contains unprecedented powers of automation and computation: it is literally *faster than lightning*—digital information circulates on fibre-optic cables at up to two thirds of light speed, quicker, then, than Zeus's lightning… Automatic and reticulated society thereby becomes *the global cause of a colossal social disintegration.*
>
> *(p. 7)*

Digital images need to be saved (and save us) from the "automatic power of reticular disintegration" known as "disruption" (ibid.). They are the field where we are fighting for the survival or preservation of psychic spontaneity, saving the singularity of the individual on the screen. We need to learn to use our digital images to break out of the closed system algorithmically sealed off from human intervention, and hence devoid of values.

We are now able to produce artificial images that, instead of representing the world, create illusions from which we construct the new realities that we then start to share and inhabit together. Alternative worlds start to emerge in the synthesized images on the screen, that are free from the constraints of representation, capable of carving out a dreamscape where communication begins to travel through other channels and different dimensions of consciousness than those sanctioned by the predigital/ scribal world.

New worlds begin to open up where communication ceases to be a matter aimed at efficiency and production. When we make images, instead of (speaking or writing) words, the expressive function of communication takes the lead over the discursive. Accordingly, the priorities of such a future culture would change drastically when images—rather than being merely vehicles of information—become direct means of self-expression, witnesses of the being that is making them.

Coda

To address the question about the fate of psychic presence in the virtual world with which we started, let me share a small vignette from my experience of two semesters of undergraduate teaching in the Zoom platform.

In the difficult process of acclimation to the virtual that all of us, teachers and students, *mutatis mutandis,* had to suffer, it was my experience that students dealt with the traumatic experience of the virtual class in several different ways. Some became very active and participatory, their Zoom windows always open, constantly present and always ready to enter the conversation the class sought to initiate. Others mostly kept their windows closed, while still participating via the class chat, allowing themselves sometimes to talk from behind their closed windows that—like tombstones with their engraved names or avatars—glared at me from the screen.

One particular student caught my attention after the semester ended, when I started noticing him interacting in the social media. In class he had been one of the students who, though attentive and taking part of the conversation always happening in the class chat, seldom talked to the class. Only a couple times did I have the chance to see him opening his window to engage with the class. But in the social media, particularly through his Instagram account, he was slowly starting to come out of his introverted shell—making reels, scripting and protagonizing in his own movies—to construct a persona on the screen that gradually revealed a temperament that contrasted with his everyday demeanor, as if the digital media had allowed an inner extrovert to emerge from his shy self, displaying a very creative, laid-back, and graceful handling of the media.

It is true that the social network is plagued with spectacularizing selves, since most users succumb to the narcissistic "massaging" of the media, making every image a show of the self, meant to entertain or brag or bully or stalk, etc. The virtual can trigger all the worst and most prejudicial possibilities, especially in still tender minds. But this young man was using technology for a terribly serious purpose. He was using digital images to give expression to his being, to create and thus reveal the psyche from which those images had been envisioned.

Perhaps this is one way of understanding what Flusser is proposing when he talks about our using images to break the system, to overcome that deadening monotone that the programmed apps and the chatter of a collective discourse in the social networks that is managed from the central memory of an algorithmic system. As Frankel and Krebs (2022) have argued, the virtual world provides a laboratory of subjectivity, where we have new modes of access to knowledge of the self, of our relationship with others, and of the other.

If we were to make images to serve our expressive needs, to communicate in the different frequencies and ranges of expression available in the digital, it would occasion a shift in the purpose of social interaction. From the usual goal of productivity, we would be inclined to something more akin to play. Gaming of course—as is becoming obvious from the astronomical success of the industries promoting them—is an immensely popular and exciting new realm of experience in the virtual world. Surprisingly well developed, it has lived an underground existence with younger generations, and seems to be now coming of age. The video game technology is flourishing, offering tools for thought and critical reflection that are simply amazing.

To the extent that the virtual makes such communication possible, a very different kind of culture can be envisaged. Production displaced by gaming, the rational displaced by the aesthetic would make for a very different kind of society than that which is ruled by the entropic tendency against which both Flusser and Stiegler are warning us. As Flusser (2017) describes it:

> The current isolation of the individual and the current massification, and its evident symptoms of the emerging society, are nothing more than… consequences of this intimate circulation between image and man thanks to which the image programs man so that he reprograms the image.
>
> *(pp. 87–88)*

The move from production to gaming is very much in tune with Ortega y Gasset's (1961) forecast of our collective future in the West under the aegis of Dionysus, which shows itself in the rediscovery of the body (evident not merely in the proliferating practice of tattooing and piercing it, but also in our new sensibility toward gender), the germinating of an ecological mindset and our reconnection with nature (evident in veganism and the multiple and growing number of social movements fighting climate change, defending wildlife and the rights and welfare of all animals). This new sensibility can ground the envisionings that we need in order to prevent the disruption.

The difficulty for us, the hard lesson to learn, nourished as we still are by humanism and its Apollonian thought, is that—as Rilke (1989) wisely warns us—"at the shadowed crossing of heart-roads, there is no temple for Apollo" (Sonnets to Orpheus, I, 3, p.231).

References

Adams, M.V. (2018) *For Love of the Imagination.* New York and London: Routledge.Benjamin, W. (1978) On Language as Such and on the Language of Man. In *Reflections. Essays, Aphorisms, Autobiographical Writings* (pp. 314–332). New York: Schoken Books.

Benjamin, W. (2010) Sobre el programa de la filosofía venidera. In Walter Benjamin (Ed.), *Obras, libro II* (vol 1, pp. 162–175). Madrid: Abada Editores.

Bennett, J. (2010) *Vibrant Matter. A Political Ecology of Things.* Durham: Duke University Press.

Deleuze, G. (1989) *Cinema 2.* Minneapolis: University of Minnesota Press.

Deleuze, G. (1994) *Difference and Repetition.* New York: Columbia University Press.

Deleuze, G. (1997) Immanence: A Life…. *Theory, Culture and Society* 14(2), 3.

Derrida, J., and Stiegler, B. (2002) *Echographies of Television.* Madlen, MA: Blackwell Publishers.

Flusser, V. (1993) *Lob der Oberflächlichkeit.* Für eine Phänomenologie der Medien: Bollmann.

Flusser, V. (2002) *Writings/Vilém Flusser.* (ed. Andreas Ströhl). Minneapolis: University of Minnesota Press.

Flusser, V. (2011) *Into the Universe of Technical Images.* (N. A. Roth, Trans.). Minneapolis: University of Minnesota Press.

Flusser, V. (2014) *Gestures.* Minneapolis: University of Minnesota Press.

Flusser, V. (2017) *El universo de las imágenes técnicas. Elogio de la superficialidad.* Buenos Aires: Caja Negra Editora. (All translations are mine, with the assistance of DeepL Translator (free version)).

Frankel, R. & Krebs, V.J. (2022) *Human Virtuality and Digital Life. Philosophical and Psychoanalytic Investigations.* London & New York: Routledge.

Hillman, J. (1979) *The Dream and the Underworld.* New York: Harper and Row.

Ieven, B. (2003) How to Orientate Oneself in the World: A General Outline of Flusser's Theory of Media, Image [&] Narrative, Issue 6. Medium Theory.

Krebs, V.J. (2023) Digital animism: Towards a new materialism. *Religions,* 14(2): 263–274.

Lacan, J. (1997) *The Seminar of Jacques Lacan. Book III. The Psychoses 1955–1956.* London & New York: Norton.

Massumi, B. (1987) Realer than Real. The Simulacrum According to Deleuze and Guattari, *Copyright* No. 1 (pp. 90–97).

Murphie, A. (2002) Putting the Virtual Back into VR. In B. Massumi (Ed.), *A Shock to Thought. Expression after Deleuze and Guattari* (pp. 188–214). London: Routledge.

Ortega y Gasset, J. (1961) *The Modern Theme.* New York: Harper Torchbooks.

Ranciére, J. (2019) *The Future of the Image.* London: Verso.

Rilke, R.M. (1989) *The Selected Poetry of Rainer Maria Rilke* (transl. Stephen Mitchell). New York: Vintage International.

Schrader, P. (2018). *Transcendental Style in Film: Ozu, Bresson, Dreyer.* Oakland: University of California Press.

Stiegler, B. (2010). *Taking Care of Youth and the Generations.* Stanford, CA: Stanford University Press.

Stiegler, B. (2016). *Automatic Society. Volume 1: The Future of Work.* Cambridge: Polity Press.

Stiegler, B. (2019) *The Age of Disruption. Technology and Madness in Computational Capitalism.* Cambridge: Polity Press.

Tarkovski, A. (1994) *Sculpting in Time.* Austin: University of Texas Press.

Wittgenstein, L. (1998). *Culture and Value.* Oxford: Blackwell.

5

THE TIME OF TECHNOLOGY

Plato's Clock and Psychoanalysis

Eric R. Severson

Introduction

These days, except when pressed to contemplate relativity by a physics lecture or Hollywood adventure, we take for granted that our lives play out beneath the steady tick of a universal clock. For millennia, we human beings have taken pains to mark the passage of time, whether by tracking moons or summers or notches on a sundial. Counting ticks and tocks has a profound impact on the way that we live together; time keeps marching into the future, and it behooves us to move toward the future with partners. Human communities have marked the passage of time socially, as an instrument to bind together lives in the midst of chaotic and unpredictable existence. Clocks, hourglasses, calendars, and sundials, synchronize our lives. We are temporal creatures, obsessed with and by time, even as we puzzle at what we mean when we speak of it. The subjective and existential experience of time is quite different from the synchronized movement of the hands on a clock; an hour spent in dental surgery passes quite differently for the dentist than for the patient. No two people experience time's passage the same way, though philosophers do not agree on the importance of this temporal diversity in our considerations of time. Synchronic time is quantifiable, measurable, comparable, and billable. The other sort, for which I use the term *diachronic*, is far more difficult to describe. If there are drawbacks to leaning heavily on synchronic understandings of time in the development of technology, we are wise to attend to them. This article explores the relationship between time and technology, with a special focus on perils that are overlooked when we fail to interrogate common assumptions about synchronic time. This chapter investigates the history of this problem, before turning attention to the dangers it poses for psychoanalysis, and an alternative I derive from the work of Emmanuel Levinas: diachronic attunement.

There is a philosophy of time embedded in our understanding of technology, including the way we think about language. The role of time in technology is sometimes implicit and difficult to detect; in other cases, the function of time overtly influences the development and use of technological tools. This chapter will not attempt an overview of the philosophy of time as it relates to technology. Instead, I will analyze *one* time-related technological innovation in an effort to underscore the relationship between temporality and technological innovation. Ancient Athens was an early epicenter of thinking about time and being, and perhaps uncoincidentally a leader in the development of clock technology. In this chapter

DOI: 10.4324/9781003195849-7

I move from the explicit to the implicit, beginning with the development of the Ancient Greek innovation called the *clepsydra*. Plato himself mentions the way this early time-keeping device was used in Athenian courts, alongside lessons about how time impacts speech and the pursuit of justice. After some exposition on "time" in Plato's *Theaetetus*, I will explore options for rethinking time opened up by Edmund Husserl, Martin Heidegger, Bernard Stiegler, and especially Emmanuel Levinas.

The Clepsydra

When it would not suffice to mark time by days or moons, ancient people struggled to synchronize their lives. The first clocks were designed with this purpose in mind—as a technology to make the passage of time objective, measurable, and even commodifiable. In ancient Greece, the water clock was the first standard technology used to measure time. The word for water clock, *clepsydra* literally translates as "water thief." Water flows from one vessel to another at consistent rates, and the time it takes for water to move from one place to another can be anticipated, repeated, and objectively observed. There were technical problems with previous versions of water clocks that the Greeks worked to resolve. Water is pretty chaotic stuff, and mythologically associated with chaos monsters and unpredictability. Even in the confines of a vessel, water does not drain evenly but at different paces depending on the current volume of the vessel. The Greeks found ways to even out this inconsistency, further turning the chaos of water into time. As the volume decreases, the flow of the water diminishes (Janish, 1985, p. 168). Third-century Greek inventor Ctesibius was the first to create a clock with hourly indicators that would lead to future dials and pointers (Hill, 1984, p. 228). There is even an ancient legend, dating back to the early third century, suggesting that Plato was the first to invent a clepsydra that could make noise to awaken a sleeping person (Riginos, 1997, pp. 188–189). Perhaps students of early morning philosophy courses should be prepared to thank Plato twice.

The story of Plato's "first alarm clock in history" is surely apocryphal, but the experience of being pulled from the diachrony of deep sleep into the synchrony of wakefulness knows the jarring difference between two manners of experiencing time. Alarm clocks are like the loud bells that call children back to class on school playgrounds, away from the diachrony of play and back to the synchronization of lines, sitting, learning, and working. The difference between sleep and waking is dramatic, for in sleep one is disconnected from the perception of universal time in almost every way. In everyday experience, however, the relationship between these two experiences of time is more complex. We experience temporality in both ways, often at the same time. The question of time is not a binary choice between existing in synchronized or diachronic time; both are necessary, or perhaps inevitable, for human beings. Instead, I suggest that these two forms of time be understood according to *attunement*. People, and technology, can be attuned to temporality in diverse ways. This, at any rate, may be crucial for understanding what bothered Socrates as he spoke about the technology of clocks in Plato's *Theaetetus*.

We learn, at the outset of the dialog, that Socrates is already limited by time; he has an appointment in court later that day to discuss serious charges brought against him by Meletus, one of three chief accusers at his trial. The pressure of synchronic time leans heavily on the discussion, but Socrates does not seem to be in a hurry. In addition, by constricting Socrates with a court injunction from Meletus, Plato cleverly places additional synchronic pressure on the discussion. In the *Apology*, where we find Socrates defending himself at trial, Plato has Socrates addressing Meletus directly with his life on the line. We do not know if the court appearance on the day of the *Theaetetus* related to his capital trial. We do know that Meletus was the primary accuser and plaintiff of Socrates, the one who drew up the charges against him, and the one who pressed at trial for the death penalty (Nails, 2002, p. 202). For the first readers of Plato's *Theaetetus*, the discussion is laden with temporal pressure; the day in court represented another step toward the cup of hemlock that, when drained, would end Socrates' life.

Before his scheduled appearance in court, Socrates stops for a long conversation with the geometer Theodorus, and a promising young scholar named Theaetetus. During the dialog, Socrates takes an apparent break ("digression") from a discussion about epistemology, and directs some attention to the pressure of *time* on both speech and the process of understanding. Perhaps thinking about his own defense in court, Socrates says: "…it's occurred to me that those who spend a lot of time doing philosophy are likely to make fools of themselves when they speak in a law-court" (Plato, 2004, p. 66 (172c)). This digression in the *Theaetetus* is instigated by Theodorus' suggestion that they can have a prolonged conversation because "we have plenty of time, haven't we, Socrates?" (Plato, 2004, p. 66 (172c)). Though most translators employ the term "time" here, the literal translation does not use χρόνος (*chronos*, time) but σχολή (leisure, rest, ease). In light of the pressure of the water-clock in the discussion below, perhaps Theodorus' question would be better translated: "we are un-clocked, aren't we Socrates?"

In response, Socrates introduces a contrast between the disposition of their philosophical conversation and the ways of the courts. At the intersection of these two modalities, or temporalities, is the technological instrument of timekeeping. And this time of the courts is synchronized, by the intrusion of a cutting-edge technology, the clock. The philosopher, he goes on to explain, grows accustomed to letting ideas, and speeches, take their course as long as is necessary to arrive at the truth. The philosopher can, in this way, sometimes arrive at a conclusion that the pressures of time would have prevented. Readers of his deathbed dialog, the *Phaedo*, will not be surprised to find Socrates calmly talking about epistemology despite the immanence of death. In that dialog he declares that "the one aim of those who practice philosophy in the proper manner is to practice for dying and death" (Plato, 2002, p. 101 (64a)). Even the pressure of death, as the termination of one's diachronic temporality, will not force Socrates to acquiesce to the synchronic pressure of courts and clocks. When, in *Phaedo*, Socrates' wife Xanthippe cries and points out that his time is limited ("Socrates, this is the last time your friends will talk to you and you to them"), Socrates has her taken away (Plato, 2002, p. 97 (60a)).

The problem with speaking in court is the constriction of time by the systemized legal process which allotted a certain amount of synchronic time for each testimony. Rather than allow defendants to speak at leisure, Greek and Roman courts developed their version of a water clock to limit the time for testimonies. There were no lawyers in ancient Athens, but some citizens were inclined to use lawsuits to humiliate or punish their enemies. In the *Apology* we find Meletus intensely worried that Socrates is doing harm to the young people of Athens, particularly by inspiring them to skepticism (Plato, 2002, pp. 29–30 (25a–c)). The successful "man of the law-courts" is a fast-talker, "always in a hurry when he is talking; he has to speak with one eye on the clock" (Plato, 1990, *Theaetetus*, p. 300 (172e)). The interlocutor is not like Theodorus or Theaetetus, who meet with Socrates in pursuit of better understanding, but an "adversary" who is "armed with compulsory powers" that limit the range and length of speech. The clock, on which the "man of the law-courts" always has an eye, is a piece of technology which is far from innocent, even if the flow of water is indifferent to the speaker. "The struggle is never a matter of indifference; it always directly concerns the speaker, and sometimes life itself is at stake" (Plato, 1990, *Theaetetus*, p. 300 (172e)). For Socrates, later that day, this was likely the case.

The "man of the law-courts" is maligned here, or at least the role he plays in the distortion of testimonies. Some translators use the archaic word *pettifogger* for these men, a term that captures the disreputability and contemptibility of these characters. *The Oxford Dictionary of English Etymology* defines this word: "legal practitioner of inferior status" (1966, p. 673). According to the *Online Etymological Dictionary*, this compound word combines "petty" with *fogger*, "a huckster; a cheat, one who engaged in mean or disreputable practices" (Online Etymological Dictionary, n.d.). This term resonates with the language Socrates uses to describe these persons, who are high-strung, fast-talking, masters of flattery.

The pettifogger is assailed here, and one cannot help but imagine that he is thinking of Meletus, whom Socrates may have humiliated at his trial. Meletus has a catchy charge: How can Athenians tolerate a citizen who intentionally harms his neighbors, and young neighbors at that? But in the *Apology* when Socrates asks Meletus *why* anybody would intentionally make their neighbors worse people, Meletus cannot answer (Plato, 2002, p. 19 (24d)). In his *Rhetoric*, Aristotle (2006) points to Socrates' interrogation of Meletus as an example of successful rhetorical strategy (p. 247 (1419a)). Whatever the quality of Socrates defense, it is clear that Meletus was unprepared to support his accusation to its natural conclusion. Perhaps there was more water in the court clock for Socrates than Meletus anticipated. Scholars often consider Meletus to be a puppet of more powerful Athenians; perhaps he was unprepared for the counter-arguments provided by Socrates. As Socrates points out to him directly: "You see, Meletus, that you are silent and know not what to say" (Plato, 2002, *Apology*, p. 29 (24d)). The jury at his trial, however, was at least slightly more convinced by Socrates' accusers, perhaps because they were conditioned to the litigation of high-strung, fast-talking masters of flattery.

Some Athenian citizens spent their fame and fortune manipulating this very system. They learned to thrive on the rules and regulations, and manipulate the clepsydra, using the restrictions of time to their advantage. In both Greek and Roman antiquity, there were reasons to pause the clock, which involved plugging the flow of water that timed a testimony (Young, 1939, p. 277). A piece of wax could be placed in the opening of the vessel, preserving the water while the court paused for meals, for the night, or to examine evidence or documents. The power to pause the clock was not held by the testifier, and the pressure afforded by rules limiting the time of testimony was tremendous. As Socrates complains about the pettifogger, he identifies this very power of the accuser. The conversation between the accuser and the defendant is a contest that aims at triumph, sometimes with "life itself at stake," and the truth of any matter is secondary to the importance of victory.

In ancient Greece, it was thought that testimony offered in leisure could not be trusted. When slaves were called as witnesses in the Athenian courts, their testimony was only considered valid if it was procured under torture (Gagarin, 1996, pp. 1–18). Citizens, like Socrates, were not typically tortured for their testimony, but they were limited by the rules and regulations of the court, and particularly by the clepsydra. The phrasing Socrates uses to describe the pressure on the speaker is telling: κατεπείγει γὰρ ὕδωρ ῥέον, literally "the flowing water presses him on" (Plato, *The Theaetetus*, 172d, my translation). The synchronic time of clocks and calendars, which philosophers are accustomed to ignoring when working through an idea, become tremendous pressures on communication. Dialog is mostly gone, too, since the testimony is nothing like a genuine conversation between curious people. Instead, speech becomes strained, tense, and neurotic (ἔντονοι καὶ δριμεῖς: literally: "sharp and sinewy"). Plato's wit is on full display in this interlude in the *Theaetetus*. The dialog is framed by the brevity of life. The narration is set years later, after Socrates is long dead and while Theaetetus is dying. In 142a–143c, as the dialog is introduced, we learn that two friends of the long-dead Socrates have met to exchange news about the adult Theaetetus, who has been gravely injured in a battle. The dialog is framed as a recollection of a discussion between Socrates and a teen-aged Theaetetus (Brown, 2014, p. x). The text concludes with Socrates ending the conversation in order to meet his appointment in court. The tension is obvious between the time of philosophy and the time of the courts.

Traditional interpretations of Plato's *Theaetetus* suggest that Socrates is just talking about time in terms of degrees and lengths. The philosopher just has *more time*, by this interpretation, not a different kind of time. A thorough investigation of time in the work of Plato exceeds the bounds of this chapter, but my suggestion is that there is concern and ambivalence about time in Plato, red flags waved by Socrates regarding the influence and logical dominance of synchronic time. When time is systematized it is also available for commodification and weaponization. Instead of rewarding the best idea, or the clearest communication, this system rewards the fastest talker, the smoothest manipulator, the pettifogger whose expertise is not the pursuit of truth but power and manipulation. The clock poses as indifferent; but it is built by and for the people who find its use advantageous. It may be possible for clocks to instead protect people from oppression, and limit the power of the rich. However, those who would use synchronic time for liberation should bear in mind that most tools—including clocks and calendars—have their origins in structures of hegemonic structures that shape the tool and the user according to the aims of power.

Socrates refers to a seemingly innocent technological invention: the clepsydra. The water-thief steals more than just water as it marks the passage of synchronized time. The dripping water steals from the philosopher the diachronic freedom to express an idea, or to wait for one to blossom in due course. In the digression of the Theaetetus, Plato pauses for an extensive lament about the modes of speaking and thinking that emerge from the urgency of the synchronizing clock. Time is power, and those who control the clepsydra exert a tremendous power. Perhaps worse, this power is cloaked by the mathematical indifference implied by the consistent ticking hands of the clock.

Objective Time and the Consciousness of Internal Time

The problems identified with time and synchrony in the *Theaetetus* are borne out in the evolution of clocks and synchronized time around the world and down through the ages. The importance of synchrony for thinking about technology and economics is difficult to underestimate; almost every technological innovation relies on some effort to synchronize human lives. It is through synchrony, and eliminating diachronic experience, that lives are saved, buildings are raised, wars are won, and order is kept. The stately clock-towers that became popular around the world, an architectural design often imported along with English imperialism, serve to order and organize the days of people who live and work below. Consider, for instance, the Rajabai Clock Tower in South Mumbai, India, which was designed by English architect George Gilbert Scott and towers 280 feet above the terrain below. Like an all-seeing eye, the face of the clock can be seen from vantage points all over the city. Massive clock towers today continue to dominate the architectural landscapes of cities, universities, and are particularly popular atop governmental structures. Whether we are awake or asleep, working or playing, alive or dead, the synchronic clock ticks on. A synchronic manner of thinking about time, its value, its quantifiability, is nothing short of ubiquitous in the modern world.

The African philosopher and theologian St. Augustine began his academic life deeply steeped in the work of Plato. In his most celebrated work, *Confessions*, he turns attention to the puzzle of time: "What then is time? Provided that no one asks me, I know. If I want to explain it to an inquirer, I do not know" (Augustine, 1998, Book XI). The question itself betrays a complex problem; can we use the word "is" to speak of time? Augustine is stumped in part because the very word "is" rests on some concept of temporality. It is far easier to name what time is *not,* and this has been a preferred method for philosophers puzzled by time down through the ages. Timelessness, it would seem, is easier to conceive of than time. That which is timeless is unchanging, everlasting, eternal, and untouched by the apparent movement of the material world. Perhaps for this reason the later Plato finds opportunities to express his thoughts on time as a product of his understanding of eternity. If there is ambivalence in the way Plato deals with time in the *Theaetetus*, this wavering is less evident in the later dialog *Timeaus*. Plato's title character in the *Timaeus* suggests that we think of time as "the moving likeness of eternity" (Plato, 2008, pp. 25–26 (37c–e)). This is a peculiar, if influential, description of time which rests on the definition of eternity, rather than the experience of temporality. If there is some hegemonic force behind the movement of time as controlled by clocks and calendars, it can safely hide beneath the indifference of the plodding eternal "now."

The highest of truths are the ones which are least subject to the vicissitudes of time. Time is again transcended in Aristotle, who focuses on what is *necessarily* existent, or true. To exist by necessity is to exist at all times, to be everlasting. The necessary is by definition not contingent, and that which is not contingent is ever true, without being subject to time's impact. The recipe is different, but the results are strikingly similar. That which endures is superior to that which does not; the more something is affected by time, the looser its hold on the true and the real.

Edmund Husserl, whose "Lectures on the Consciousness of Internal Time" began a modern revolution in rethinking time, was suspicious of the influence of "worldly" time on the internal experience of temporality. Indeed, Husserl considered time to be most originally a condition of human experience rather than a "thing" that could itself be framed by phenomenological investigation (Sokolowski, 1974, p. 138). Husserl was aware that time *also* refers to that which is measured by stop-watches, but he worried that the internal experience of time was obscured by the more universal version. Unlike the cold, steady movement of what Husserl (1991) calls "objective time," internal time is in "absolute flow." Husserl talks of internal time as *flow*, but he does not mean the steady flow of sand through an hourglass. Internal time-consciousness is a "wonder," "rich in mystery" (Husserl, 1991, pp. 286, 290). Human perception is irrevocably temporal; we can only experience phenomena as creatures whose consciousness exists in temporal flux. For this reason, internal time-consciousness is for Husserl (1991) "the most difficult of all phenomenological problems" (p. 382). The impulse to defer to objective time, in the analysis of a phenomenon, Husserl deems a dangerous interference with phenomenological analysis. We lack words, Husserl admits, for contemplating the phenomenon of the flux, of internal time. Husserl does not say as much, but perhaps this lack of "words" with which to speak of "internal time" is the result of the objective temporality embedded in the formation of European languages. Our words are a technological innovation crafted mostly for synchrony. Objective time plays a crucial role in the structure of language in the history of European speech and writing.

For Husserl's student Martin Heidegger, the preference of ancient Greek philosophy for permanence and timelessness, and the suspension of rigorous interrogation of the experience of time, turns the trajectory of Western philosophy in a dangerous direction. Writes

Heidegger (1962), in *Being and Time:* "the central problematic of all ontology is rooted in the phenomenon of time, if rightly seen and explained, and we must show how this is the case" (p. 40). Among other problems, the relentless, universal, impersonal, indifferent ticking of Big Ben renders meaningful that which transcends the particularities of individual lives, bodies, and temporalities. In a variety of ways, this deference to the eternal influences existential experience, particularly as alienation and estrangement. The failure to think about time as it is experienced by the human person (*Dasein,* "there-being"), for Heidegger, undercuts and distorts actual lived existence. The long tradition of deference to "world time" has created a default, effortless reversion to impersonal and inauthentic existence. For Heidegger, the problem of time is not just an abstract philosophical puzzle. Failure to think about time directly influences the way people think and live relative to their own bodies, their own work, their own environs, and particularly their own finitude.

> Heidegger (1962) writes: "Fate is that powerless superior power which puts itself in readiness for adversities—the power of projecting oneself upon one's own Being-guilty, and of doing so reticently, with readiness for anxiety. As such, fate requires as the ontological condition for its possibility, the state of Being of care—that is to say, temporality. Only if death, guilt, conscience, freedom, and finitude reside together equiprimordially in the Being of an entity as they do in care, can that entity exist in the mode of fate; that is to say, only then can it be historical in the very depths of its existence."
>
> *(pp. 436–437)*

We spend time, give time, make time, waste time, all according to the abstract grandfather clock, whose steady and eternal ticking renders individual time trivial.

Heidegger turns Husserl's insights on time in a particularly existential direction in *Being and Time*, first published in 1927. This book, often considered one of the most influential in twentieth-century philosophy, enacts a deconstruction of the problem of time, exposing a serious problem that impacts almost every arena of philosophy. For Heidegger, the rift between the traditional "eternal now" and Dasein's "ownmost" experience of time is a matter of the utmost ontological significance. He promises to return to the problem in future publications, to write a sequel to *Being and Time*, but never returns directly to this problem. Heidegger makes clear, however, that our understanding of temporality informs and inhabits the way we understand our own existence, our words, and our tools. The missing second-half of *Being and Time* has left commentators pondering its absence; one called *Being and Time* "that astonishing torso" (Spiegelberg, 1994, p. 360). I am not sure that the sequel is actually missing; instead of providing a second systematic work on time, Heidegger instead begins to explore the way his insights concerning Dasein's temporality impacts technology, art, and language.

Time and Synchrony

Husserl and Heidegger both understood the daunting task that arises when we attempt any reconsideration of time. European thinking about time was imposed alongside a variety of European concepts and practices through the violence of global colonization. Diverse understandings of time in Indigenous cultures, and the uniqueness of time as experienced by individuals, were in many cases forcibly displaced by the European model. The difficulty facing anyone who joins Husserl and Heidegger in rethinking time is the pervasive and invasive way that Big Ben inhabits our language, our tools, our thinking about almost *everything*. The linguistic and analytical implements we use to take up a concept and analyze a phenomenon already presume a metaphysics of time that privileges the everlasting over the ephemeral. This problem is daunting, for it calls for the deconstruction and reconstruction of a concept while simultaneously undermining the tools needed for the task. Noteworthy efforts to re-think time *otherwise* than by the objective time of traditional philosophy, such as those made by Nietzsche, Henri Bergson, Franz Rosenzweig, and we should probably include Albert Einstein, have met with checkered success. It is difficult to redefine time when the settled definition has so pervaded the very idea of temporality.

The sense of time preferred by traditional Western thinking has gone by many names: objective, "world time," the "eternal present," and many others. Among the most import-ant functions of objective time is the synchronization of human activity. Survival, in fact, depends on synchronization; we live better when we think well about change, seasons, aging, tides, harvests, reproduction, food preservation, and innumerable other temporal pro-cesses. The sharing of wisdom, between generations and cultures, is often bound by this synchronization. The chaos of the world is tamed, to some degree, by the synchronization of human work, mourning, celebration, religious observance, milestones, rites of passage, and so many other synchronizations. To forget a birthday, or anniversary, is to fail to attend to the synchronization of time that lends meaning to the relationships and care we share in our communities. To disregard important family traditions, religious holidays in particular, is to neglect the synchronization of diverse family members around a common cadence that makes the passage of time meaningful. Isaac Newton suggested that "absolute time" (sometimes called "Newtonian time") progresses at an even pace everywhere in the uni-verse, independent of any observer and measurable. Newton believed that time was difficult to observe, and therefore best understood in the abstraction of linear moments. This mode of time, preferred from Parmenides to Plato to Newton, I have been calling "synchronic time."

In naming this mode of temporality synchronic I am emphasizing what thinking about time in this way *does* rather than attempting to stake a claim about what time *is*. The phe-nomenology of Newtonian time serves to synchronize. When we think like Newton, we are on time to work, we remember birthdays, we book flights home for the holidays, we make the bus, we plant the seeds in spring, we throw the quinceañera, and the list goes on. Of course, Newton was wrong. Modern physics has confirmed Einstein's theories about time: time is relative. Light and sound from the first moments of the universe are still happening now; the "now" of 2.537 million years ago is arriving as a current event in the fuzzy smudge above my head that is Andromeda Galaxy. Still, Einsteinian relativity has little impact on the synchronization of everyday life and experiences, at least for those of us not engineering GPS satellites and space missions. For people living far below the speed of light, *relative* time is not particularly relevant. Below, as I try to describe time at another register, I will not be referring to the bending, slowing, and speeding of time that occurs near the speed of light or in extreme gravity.

Einstein has done nothing meaningful to dethrone synchronic time from its central role in defining the way we think about the time of our lives—the time in which our births, our love, our work, our rest, and unique moments of death take place. Synchronic time is king, and if there are problems with thinking about time in this way, these problems are likely to run deep. The reign of synchrony is in fact so complete that we struggle to see alternatives, or articulate them even when we sense the poor fit between Newton's time and the internal consciousness of time that is routinely subjugated for the sake of synchrony. The need for synchrony has, in fact, been a driving force in the development of language and technol-ogy. Whatever its history or causal arising, the modern deference to synchronic time has become a *technology of domination*. Like the Athenian shysters, powerful people today shake their papers and point to the clock; time is on *their* side. For this reason, there is an *anarchy* to considering time otherwise than synchronic.

Anarchy and Diachrony

Utilizing insights from Martin Heidegger and Jacques Derrida as his key points of departure, Bernard Stiegler suggests that we best understand technology when we consider its relationship to time. As much as these seem like unrelated avenues of inquiry, Stiegler (1998) finds in Derrida insights that reveal a hidden connection that binds together time and technology, particularly by means of language (pp. 138–139). Derrida is a philosopher of difference and slippage, keen to point out that words and texts have lives of their own, and constantly slip away from the places of fixed meaning that we attempt to give them. Texts, for Derrida, are evasive and maddeningly free of our mastery. The impulse to force an idea, a text, a word, to hold still is a natural one, particularly because shifting meanings and interpretations are causes for anxiety. Language does many things, but perhaps most obviously it moves toward mutual understanding, common comprehension, what I have been calling *synchrony*. When we "synchronize" our understanding we arrive somewhere simultaneously. The word "apple" may mean something very different in ancient times, or future times, but today when I say "apple" what I seek is to articulate a word that brings to mind what "apple" means today, for both of us, now. In this sense, synchrony is the momentary freezing of time, or at least an effort to do so. When we synchronize, we create temporary islands in a sea of possible misunderstandings and failures to communicate. At least, that's what we attempt to do. Accountants do this with numbers, builders with weights and measurements, cooks with ingredients, tailors with bolts of fabric. People today, particularly in the so-called "Western" world are accustomed to this pursuit of synchrony, and frustrated when it fails.

Derrida is skeptical about the success of interpersonal speech even when think we are establishing a synchronized "presence" of mutual understanding. Misunderstanding arises for multiple reasons. Markets change the value of dollars, words and ideas shift with culture and time. Most of all, the specter of subjectivity relentlessly haunts and disturbs the connections between words and what they mean to any given person. Derrida (1992) writes: "We are dispossessed of the longed-for presence in the gesture of language by which we attempt to seize it" (p. 78). Presence, for Derrida, closes all gaps and spacing. Synchronic temporality refers to the absence of *life* in the dynamism of movement, uncertainty, change, and difference; he refers to the time of presence as "dead time" (Derrida, 1976, p. 68). Derrida challenges any metaphysic that attempts to fix the meaning of words to an unchanging present, and such a challenge threatens the comfort that comes with such stability. Time is the enemy of permanence, of everlasting life, and pulls like a strong undertow against our arrival at synchronic understanding. However, perhaps this instability of language and time is also a gift; it removes from philosophy a brittle and fragile fiction, and returns us to the temporal bodies and relations that actually characterize human existence.

Historically, Western philosophy has generally fixated on the successes that we might find in this pursuit of synchrony. Against the background of chaos, relativism, and subjectivity, synchronized agreement has provided important foundations for various philosophical worldviews. The modern works of Descartes, Kant and Hegel serve as paradigms of this proclivity toward synchrony. For these and countless other modern thinkers, in all disciplines, the objective is superior to the subjective, the synchronous superior to the *diachronous*. There are exceptions, of course. For instance, in the nineteenth century the thundering stampede toward synchrony is resisted by Friedrich Nietzsche and Søren Kierkegaard, each in their way. Yet discourse about language and time remain deeply entrenched in what we might call a metaphysics of synchrony, or "presence." The goal when we speak is to defeat difference, to overcome all misunderstanding, to create a language without slippage. This pursuit is built on the effort to overcome the isolation of meaning that abides within each person's subjective experience.

The failure of language to achieve perfect synchrony is a painful one. It leads to ruined food, ill-fitting garments, poorly constructed buildings, and financial ruin. It is not a bad thing that we seek to synchronize, but much is to be gained from the exercise of putting synchronic language in its place. Even more, we understand ourselves and others far better when we detect and address how the urgency to form and fortify synchrony influences our existential situations, our psychological states, as human persons. Stiegler suggests that we humans leverage every tool to cope with the difference, the slippage, the isolation, created by this instability in our world:

> There can be no gesture without tools and artificial memory, prosthetic, outside of the body, and constitutive of its world. There is no anticipation, no time outside of this passage outside, of this putting-outside-of-self and of this alienation of the human and its memory that 'exteriorization' is.
>
> *(Stiegler, 1998, p. 152)*

Language is a kind of first technology, an original technicity, that we use to bridge the chasm between our experience of the world and the lives of others. The fact that we can close that gap, the gap of misunderstanding, to nearly zero when we talk about mathematics, measurements, quantities, etc., is enticing and intoxicating. The Holy Grail is perfectly synchronic speech and understanding, messages sent and received without loss or remainder. The modern philosopher Gottfried Leibniz hoped to create a new language in which every word conveyed perfect, uninterrupted understanding between the speaker and the listener (Mates, 1986, pp. 103–104). We seek this, and find ourselves disappointed and frustrated when our communication fails to conform to this model. Built into this philosophy of language are metaphysical assumptions about the human condition, about the purpose and aim of language, and a range of other potentially problematic influences on the way we think about the tool, the technology, or language.

To state this more plainly: a justified pursuit of understanding has led us astray in the West, and left us with a mode of thinking about time, language and technology that are built on models of mastery, control, and self-deception. In particular, we wage war against time under the delusion that our diverse experience of temporality can or should be standardized. Language is therefore an originary tool for combating the crisis of separation, change, and temporality. We construct and wield words as a technology designed to address our existential isolation from one another. Of course, this extends beyond words to the myriad linguistic events carried by touch, by gestures, by facial expressions. Technicity is not uniform; some tools pretend, better than others, to succeed overcoming difference. Still, these are all tools, technologies, taken up and utilized for the sake of connecting us together across the chasms of isolation created by the fundamentally uncommunicable.

Much of modern technology operates under a foundational myth that we can engineer our way out of the isolation inherent to individual human experience. When we take up technology, today, we step into a torrential river that moves relentlessly toward this illusory destination.

Time, Diachrony, and Responsibility

Moving too quickly, I now turn from the history of the problem of synchrony to an alternative approach found in the later work of Emmanuel Levinas, specifically, some of his insights on language in *Otherwise than Being or Beyond Essence*. Early in his career, Levinas articulates a philosophy of time similar to the one we see in Derrida. Time, in Levinas' earlier works, is a guarantor of separation, distance, and the transcendence of the other person. But in his later works, Levinas binds time to language and suggests a way to think about the fundamental technology of words that understands language in two different registers. Language sometimes does, and must, aim at synchrony, at perfect understanding, even as it inevitably fails. Levinas calls this version of language, which holds still in unchanging permanence and presence, the Said. But Levinas does not believe the pursuit of a permanent, fixed, timeless Said, to be language's first work, or its most important undertaking. When someone speaks to me, the moment of issuance, as words or gestures are given, is outside of my time. Language happens in the time of the other person; it is always the past, for me, and an ultimately unrecoverable one. Nobody can have mastery of the word that was spoken. Levinas calls this more original sense of language the Saying. Temporality denies me the power to make the Saying of the other a Said for my possession, my full comprehension, my consumption. Within the Said, the words I hear or record or remember, something reverberates which is not confined by the structure of what was spoken. Levinas calls this evasive residue of the original speech a *trace* of the other person. The trace of the Saying of the other is diachronic; it issues from a time that is not mine, nor mine to master, but nevertheless arises in my experience and lays hold of me. This laying-hold takes the form not first of knowledge but of responsibility.

Language is up to something more important, more primary, than synchrony. What Levinas finds in language is something more fundamental to human existence than understanding or knowledge. Language saves us not because we construct an edifice that successfully overcomes our lonely and isolated existence. The failure of language to deliver synchronic knowledge is a reminder that language functions more primally as an invocation of a responsibility for the other person that precedes speaking. Because words fail, they deliver us from the fiction of any pure knowledge of the other person; what remains is responsibility as a precondition for language. Responsibility is not, here, a burden or a roster of obligations to be met. Neither is Levinas presenting an ethical theory to organize our relation to language. Rather, responsibility is a re-founding of the human person not in knowledge and permanence but in care:

> There is expulsion in that it assigns me before I show myself, before I set myself up. I am assigned without recourse, without fatherland, already sent back to myself, but without being able to stay there, compelled before commencing. Nothing here resembles self-consciousness, it has meaning only as an upsurge in me of a responsibility prior to commitment, that is, a responsibility for the other. There I am one and irreplaceable, one inasmuch as irreplaceable in responsibility.
>
> *(Levinas, 1981, p. 103)*

The suffering I encounter in the face of the neighbor, which sometimes is presented in words or gestures, is never captured by the technicity with which it is expressed. These arise *prior* to understanding, and prior to the constructions or justifications that might alleviate my responsibility for the pain before me. All mechanisms that might mitigate my responsibility for this suffering are *synchronic*, but the suffering arises *before* synchrony, before understanding. The other, Levinas argues, summons from before the time of the Said, and the structure of this primordial situation is best articulated as *responsibility for the other*.

For Levinas, what language offers, beneath this necessary but ultimately doomed attempt at synchrony, is something more important: solidarity, care, and obligation. Levinasian responsibility is not a to-do list, but the discovery of a primordial, diachronic event that is already operational in the technology of language. If the world operates like the Athenian courts, always pushing us to keep an eye on the clock and a fist closed around papers that advantage the self, Levinas proposes the opposite. We operate in being with one eye on its otherwise, with one eye on the other person.

According to Levinas, when we take up words to speak (or even language to understand our own experiences) we discover the other person already utterly proximate in our deliberations, in the language we attempt to use. This is an under-explored component of Levinas' philosophy of language that I think has dynamic possibilities for psychotherapy. Part of the "talking cure" may very well be the hidden resources of solidarity, care, responsibility, in the word-technology we take up to speak. As we speak about our emotions, our experiences, we find ourselves using the technology of speaking that we were given in utter passivity, in time-before-time. When words are released from the sole project of synchrony, they turn back toward that which is more fundamental to the human person: care, solidarity, community, responsibility. As Levinas wrote: "Being and cognition together signify in the proximity of the other and in a certain modality of my responsibility for the other, this response preceding any question, this saying before the said" (Levinas, 1981, p. 26).

Psychoanalysis Beneath the Clepsydra

When Socrates laments the pressure of the clock on speeches in the Athenian court, he expresses a familiar frustration. Like ancient Athens, our speaking is often limited by clock-time. In our carefully orchestrated schedules, how many minutes should be allotted to express a testimony, an idea, a concept, an opinion, a memory? Socrates articulates an ideal, in the *Theaetetus*, that can seldom be realized under the pressures of temporality that influence the everyday limitations of bodily existence. We cannot remain awake indefinitely, waiting for an idea to make its way into expression. We must pause and eat, sleep, and accommodate similar limitations of other persons with whom we might have discourse. The philosopher who tries to actually abide in this diachronic time would be absent-minded indeed. Socrates cracks a joke to make this point, recalling an ancient tale about Thales—sometimes called the "first philosopher"—who was once so lost in thought about the stars above that he fell into a well. But Thales was mostly remembered as a man who knew how to utilize ideas he discovered in philosophy in pragmatic and influential ways. Aristotle tells us that he put an end to a war by accurately predicting an eclipse, showed his king how to divert a river to help gain military advantage, and used seasonal forecasts to accurately invest in wine-presses before a bumper crop of grapes. He was a man who was attuned to transcendent wisdom even as he was busy and effective both politically and economically.

Sometimes readers of Plato's *Theaetetus* are distracted by the impossibly high-minded description of the philosopher. Can such a person exist? Wouldn't a person so attuned to the heavens forget to eat and sleep, and therefore perish before any idea can be properly articulated? But this question misses the point. Thales *may* have fallen in a well, but he mostly just operated in the political and economic world with a mind for higher things. In the other anecdotes we have about Thales, he appears to inaugurate the very discipline of philosophy by living in the practical world while being attuned to truth that transcends the exigency of particular situations. To put this another way: Thales became the "first philosopher" precisely because he did not die of starvation, or fall into a well. Socrates bemoans what happens to ideas forced to fit into the crucible of the clepsydra, and under the pressure of the affidavits of the court. He also separates himself noticeably from the ideal philosopher he describes there, who does not know the way to the agora; one cannot read much Plato without realizing that Socrates spent most of this time precisely there. Robin Waterfield claims that the *Theaetetus* should be viewed as an "homage to Socrates" (Plato, 2004, p. 131). Perhaps what we are to learn from this digression is that Socrates is headed to court, and will submit himself to the laws, courts and clocks of Athens, but he will continue to think and speak according to the orientation of philosophy.

The two ways of thinking about and experiencing time, which I have called synchronic and diachronic, exist alongside one another. The capacity to hold them in tension is what made Thales great, and perhaps this is what Plato wishes us to think about his protagonist. Socrates is able to have a *leisurely* conversation despite the ominous appointment with Meletus in court. The framing of the dialog abides by similar synchronic orientation; the story of this conversation is being retold as Theaetetus nears death, years after Socrates execution. We cannot always be at leisure, and there are inevitable limitations to any work, philosophical or otherwise. Still, it seems to be Plato's interest to position Socrates as abiding synchronic time with an attunement to something otherwise, a time that is otherwise than being, otherwise than synchrony.

The tension between these ways of thinking about time are familiar to anyone whose work is constricted by clocks, laws, documents, and other limitations. Physicians in many hospital systems are pressured to limit patient appointments to 15 minutes or less, forcing them to compress their analysis and interaction with a patient. Columbia University professor David Rothman claims that: "Doctors have one eye on the patient and one eye on the clock" (Rabin, 2014). This is the precise language used by one translator for Socrates' concern about the pettifogger of the law courts, who must "speak with one eye on the clock" (Plato, 1990, p. 300 (172e)). The effect of the clock on speech, according to Socrates, is distortion. Not only does the speech get compressed into a limited timeframe, but the souls of those conditioned by the culture of the courts are distorted. "Such conditions make him keen and highly-strung, skilled in flattering the master and working his way into favour; but cause his soul to be small and warped" (Plato, 1990, p. 300 (172a)). We shouldn't be surprised that physicians suffer under the pressures of healthcare systems that force their work into this crushed and confined window. Both patients and their physicians suffer beneath the pressure of the synchronic clock.

Psychoanalysts know well the distortion of the clock on work with clients. The labor of psychoanalysis is delicate, and often requires a gentle and patient approach. Conversations about trauma, anxiety, depression, relationships, stress, and so many other experiences, require patience and are frequently "bent and distorted" by the limitations of the clock. Clients begin to make progress in a session, only to have time expire. Worse yet might be the correlative laws and affidavits waved around by the men of the law courts in ancient Athens. Like those documents, which limited and constricted the topics or inquiry, psychoanalysis must often adhere their work to the infrastructure determined by insurance companies. A massive amount of energy is spent dealing with billing, scheduling, and especially insurance. Psychologists in the United States often complain that these restrictions deeply inhibit their ability to help clients, particularly clients with limited resources. Even if one could imagine a political and cultural economy in which psychological care was prioritized, limitations will always remain. Yet like Socrates we must all find a way to operate in being while being attuned to being's otherwise.

The limitation of time in psychoanalysis mirrors the broader tragedy of existential experience, particularly relative to anxiety about mortality. Socrates speaks "at leisure" with his friends, but his hemlock looms. The psychoanalytic encounter is exemplary of this limitation, but also provides an opportunity to cultivate a more mature and tragic sense of life. Socrates was not the first nor the last to compare time to rushing water. Perhaps clinicians, attuned to what Freud called "transience" and Nietzsche referred to as the tragic element of life, might find in the limitation of time an opening for a rich grappling with the anxieties of mortality.

At the very least, we should begin with mindful awareness of the non-neutrality of clocks, calendars, diagnostic manuals, insurance, and physical spaces in which psychoanalysis takes place. These, and many other factors, place a stress on the pursuit of healing, and being aware of the pressure of synchrony attunes practitioners to implicit forces and factors that undermine therapy. Socrates identifies symptoms that result from the compression and constriction of time and speech: souls become warped, bent, distorted, dishonest. The mindful psychologist attends to the impact of these forces on the client, as well as the more explicit situations and events that give rise to the psychoanalytic encounter. This mindfulness should include awareness of the massive, often intersectional, forces that compound the pressures of clocks and "affidavits." World time, synchronic time, for all of its apparent indifference to the particulars of our lives, nevertheless moves at a cadence set by people in power. The water clock may have been designed to innocently confine and equalize the time of testimonies, but it inevitably serves the powerful hands that make and deploy its technological work. Supposedly innocent technologies are subtly or overtly turned into tools that exacerbate oppression and inequality. Synchronic time is rarely on the side of the poor.

We are also wise to remember that synchronic time functions to protect the analyst, and the client, from a boundaryless encounter that might overrun the time, energy, and capacities of the clinician. To lose track of these boundaries is to risk falling in a well, like Thales who was "gazing aloft" and lost track of "what was in front of him and under his feet" (Plato, 1990, 302 (174a)). Synchronic time is both enemy and friend; it contorts an encounter, but also provides important boundaries and relief. Thinking of time *philosophically* does not mean a rejection of synchrony, but rather an orientation or attunement to diachrony in the midst of synchronized encounters. The clock pushes along the session, but the philosophically minded analyst continues to attune their work to the pursuit of ideas too easily lost or distorted by synchronic pressures. Synchronic time is therefore what philosophers call a *pharmakon*, both poison and cure. In the *midst* of the raging current of synchronic time, the diachronically attuned clinician maintains an orientation toward synchrony's *otherwise*, toward a truth that transcends the temporality that squeezes and distorts our pursuit of it.

Time, Therapy, Midwifery

There are sometimes considered to be *two* digressions in the Theaetetus, and it may help us understand the second if we take a look at the first. In the first digression Socrates compares his work to that of a midwife. Instead of straining to give birth themselves, midwives turn their attention to the emergence of new life in others. In his philosophical mission, Socrates prides himself in helping people give birth to ideas. In one of Plato's most beautiful passages, Socrates describes the patient and attentive way that he listens and interacts with others who are laboring under the pains of an important idea. Midwives face a crucial danger, today as well as ancient times, and that danger relates directly to time. How soon should a birth-giving person begin to push? From what bodily position should a particular person labor? How and when should a breech baby be turned? Socrates is aware that ancient Athenian midwives are aware of countless ways that one can help a birth-giver safely give birth. They also have to be aware of the dangers of childbirth, to baby and mother, and the frequency with which a miscarriage or stillbirth results from the reproductive process. Socrates aligns his work with midwives in this way too; if an idea stagnates, stops developing, or becomes untenable, Socrates helps his interlocutors with the termination of their idea.

When we learn about the clock in the second digression, we encounter the opposite approach to discourse. Socrates the midwife is often presented with pregnant ideas with which his interlocutors are struggling. The posture of a midwife is in many ways passive; she is not pregnant nor does she cause pregnancy, even if she encourages people to match up and procreate. Socrates asks, of midwives: "And have you also noticed that they know all there is to know about pairing types of women and men to produce the best children—in other words, that they are the most skillful match-makers?" (Plato, 2004, 26 (149d)). The midwife-philosopher must tend to the emergence of ideas in others, and respond in a manner conditioned by the emerging idea. The man of the law courts, on the other hand, rushes things, and would make a lousy midwife. Rather than being interested in the emergence of truth, the pettifogger pushes for competitive advantages for the sake of victory. Trapped against clock and affidavit, the speaker must respond to the ideas of others, and is not free to let speaking take its course. The contrast between styles of dialog is stark. In both digressions, Socrates is describing what it is like for two people to talk to one another. In the first, he is a midwife coaching an idea into being, or out of being, according to its merits and validity. In the second, he sympathizes with the one whose ideas are condensed, curtailed, mutilated, by clocks, and law-suits. The midwife struggles to preserve whatever time is needed for the completion of the work at hand; the pettifogger is directly interested in causing a miscarriage, regardless of the merits of the testimony, for the sake of winning a lawsuit.

Socrates sometimes has to "bring on the pains," as midwives will due as a pregnancy nears completion. Midwives are not always gentle, the news they bring can be heartbreaking, and the guidance they provide can be difficult. There *are* synchronic pressures on pregnancy to which midwives must be aware, even if the emergence of the new life happens *from the other person*, and not from the midwife who supports the birth. We have no shortage of instances in which Socrates annoyed, frustrated, and even antagonized people who brought him ideas for delivery. The priority of the midwife is the appropriate delivery, or miscarriage, of the idea. For Socrates, this means being attuned to the intricacies and strategies of helping others articulate their ideas. At times, Socrates seems like a harsh questioner; a midwife pressing the delivering interlocutor to push. In other moments, he waits and listens. In all these modes he *mostly* ignores the clock and focuses on the deliberation, the delivery. In his analogy to midwifery, Socrates turns to other forms of technology to underscore the alternative attunement. These are among the oldest technologies, in fact, designed to assist in the complicated dynamics of birth-giving. "They do it by the use of simple drugs," Socrates explains, "and by singing incantations," among other means (Plato, 2004, 26 (149d)). The clock matters, to both the midwife and the laboring person.

Technology is inevitably temporal; it is designed within modes of temporality that can often function both synchronically and diachronically. The tools of psychology, including wall-clocks and diagnostic codes, are not innocent. They are built according to temporal logic that can lead toward liberation and truth, or toward the perilous constriction and compression of human experience. To take up these tools philosophically is to abide in a world built for synchrony as a person attuned to diachrony. Such an attunement is marked by patience, care, empathy, and hope-for-the-other. Even technologies designed for synchrony, and with a long history of oppressive use, may be bent like swords into plowshares. The clepsydra of old could be plugged to freeze the time of testimony. In a corrupt system, this capacity to freeze and manipulate time was surely used against the poor, the lower classes, those out of power. But might we not safeguard the testimony of the other by identifying, and wrestling together, with the *pharmakon* of synchronic time? The clock will limit the boundaries of time in therapy, but if we learn to talk and think about time differently, perhaps we can refuse the power of the clock to rush and ruin progress and healing. The pause between sessions, between breaths, between speaking and listening, are better understood diachronically, by both analyst and client.

References

Aristotle. (2006). *Rhetoric* (G. Kennedy, Trans.). Oxford: Oxford University Press.

Augustine. (1998). *Confessions* (H. Chadwick, Trans.). Oxford: Oxford University Press.

Brown, L. (2014). Introduction and Notes. In Plato. (2014). *Theaetetus* (J. McDowell, Trans.) (pp. vii–xxvii). Oxford: Oxford World Classics.

Derrida, J. (1976). *Of Grammatology* (G. C. Spivak, Trans.). Baltimore, MD: Johns Hopkins University Press.

Derrida, J. (1992). *Acts of Literature*. New York: Routledge Publishing.

Gagarin, M. (1996). The Torture of Slaves in Athenian Law. *Classical Philology, 91*(1), 1–18.

Heidegger, M. (1962). *Being and Time* (John Macquarrie & Edward Robinson, Trans.). New York: Harper and Row.

Hill, D. (1984). *A History of Engineering in Classical and Medieval Times*. New York: Routledge Publishing.

Husserl, E. (1991). *On the Phenomenology of the Consciousness of Internal Time* (J. B. Brough, Trans.). New York: Kluwer Academic Press.

Janish, P. (1985). *The Protophysics of Time: Constructive Foundations and History of Time Measurement*. Dordrecht, NL: D. Reidel Publishing Company.

Levinas, E. (1981). *Otherwise Than Being or Beyond Essence* (A. Lingis, Trans.). Pittsburgh, PA: Duquesne University Press.

Mates, B. B. (1986). *The Philosophy of Leibniz: Metaphysics and Language*. Oxford: Oxford University Press.

Nails, D. (2002). *The People of Plato*. Indianapolis, IN: Hackett Publishing.

Online Etymological Dictionary. (n.d.). Pettifogger. In *Online Etymological Dictionary*. Retrieved February 19, 2022, from https://www.etymonline.com/word/pettifogger

Oxford English Dictionary. (1966) Pettifogger. In *The Oxford Dictionary of English Etymology* (p. 673). Oxford: Oxford University Press.

Plato. (1990) *The Theaetetus of Plato* (M. Burnyeat & M. J. Levett, Trans.). Indianapolis, IN: Hackett Publishing.

Plato. (2002). *Five Dialogues: Euthyphro, Apology, Crito, Meno, Phaedo* (J. M. Cooper & G. M. A. Grube, Trans.). Indianapolis, IN: Hackett Publishing.

Plato. (2004). *Theaetetus* (R. Waterfield, Trans.). New York: Penguin Books.

Plato. (2008). *Timaeus and Critas* (R. Waterfield, Trans.). Oxford: Oxford World Classics.

Rabin, R. C. (2014, April 21). 15-Minute doctor visits take a toll on patient-physician relationships. *Kaiser Health News*. https://khn.org/news/15-minute-doctor-visits/

Riginos, A. S. (1997). *Platonica: The Anecdotes Concerning the Life and Writing of Plato*. Leiden, NL: Brill Academic.

Sokolowski, R. (1974). *Husserlian Meditations*. Evanston, IL: Northwestern University Press.

Spiegelberg, H. (1994). *The Phenomenological Movement: A Historical Introduction*. New York: Kluwer Academic Press.

Stiegler, B. (1998). *Technics and Time I: The Fault of Epimetheus* (R. Beardsworeth & G. Collins, Trans.). Stanford, CA: Stanford University Press.

Young, S. (1939). An Athenian Clepsydra. *Hesperia, 8*(3), 274–284.

6

PSYCHOANALYSIS HAS LOST ITS TOUCH AND OTHER REFLECTIONS FROM A TECHNOLOGIC AGE

Matthew Clemente

In the Eyes of the Beholder

In *The Uncanny*, Freud famously criticizes Jentsch's reading of ETA Hoffmann's "The Sandman," arguing that Jentsch focuses on a secondary motif in the story, thus obscuring the meaning of the text and misinterpreting the cause of the uncanny feeling it evokes. It is not, Freud tells us, the "intellectual uncertainty" caused by not knowing if another is a human being or an inanimate object—in this case, a lifelike automaton—that gives rise to the uncanny effect. "Uncertainty as to whether an object is animate or inanimate," he insists, "is quite irrelevant" (Freud, 2003, pp. 138–139). Rather, Freud believes that the sense of the uncanny in the narrative attaches directly to "the idea of being robbed of one's eyes" (p. 138), a substitute anxiety that symbolizes man's "fear of castration" (p. 139), which can be traced back to the infantile fear of the father "at whose hands castration is expected" (p. 140).

There is no denying Freud's genius. His reading of Hoffmann helps to make sense out of one of the more perplexing aspects of the text. Nathaniel, Hoffmann's mad protagonist, is obsessed with the thought of losing his eyes. He initially attributes the fear to a fairytale he was told as a boy. In it, a pernicious figure known as "the sandman" punishes naughty children who refuse to go to bed by throwing sand in their eyes. This causes their eyes to bleed and fall out and the sandman collects them and feeds them to his beaked children. The significance of this story for Nathaniel cannot be overstated. Not only does he begin to associate the sandman with his father's loathsome acquaintance Coppelius—a menacing figure whose presence plagues him into adulthood—his ambivalent obsession with eyes is one of the recurring themes of the work.

And yet, a careful reading of Hoffmann's text casts doubts on Freud's interpretation. In the first place, one must ask the obvious question: What is the point of the Olympia episode—in which Nathaniel becomes infatuated with a woman he voyeuristically watches through a window only to find out much later that she is an inanimate automaton—if it is "quite irrelevant" (Freud, 2003, p. 139) to the story? Why insert this farcical affair if it adds nothing to the uncanny feeling the work is meant to evoke? Moreover, what is to be made of the fact that it is Olympia's eyes that first draw Nathaniel to her—

> For the first time he could see the wondrous beauty in the shape of her face; only her eyes seemed to him singularly still and dead. Nevertheless, as he looked more sharply

DOI: 10.4324/9781003195849-8

through the glass, it seemed to him as if moist moon-beams were rising in the eyes of Olympia. It was as if the power of seeing were being kindled for the first time; her glances flashed with constantly increasing life. As if spellbound, Nathaniel reclined against the window, meditating on the charming Olympia.

(Hoffmann, 2009, p. 11)

—that it is her ability to sit "for hours, looking straight into her lover's eyes, without stirring" (p. 14) that fuels his desire, and that it is the sight of her eyeless face that reveals her to be an inanimate object and causes Nathaniel to spiral into psychological collapse:

Nathaniel stood paralyzed; he had seen but too plainly that Olympia's waxen, deathly pale countenance had no eyes, but black holes instead—she was, indeed, a lifeless doll.... And now Nathaniel saw that a pair of eyes lay upon the ground, staring at him; these Spalanzani caught up, with his unwounded hand, and flung into his bosom. Then madness seized Nathaniel in its burning claws, and clutched his very soul, destroying his every sense and thought (p. 15).

In order to answer these questions, we must reject Freud's interpretation, noticing instead that Hoffmann's story sets up a clear dichotomy between the sterile, disjointed movements of the automaton's body and the deceitful attraction of the automaton's eyes. When Nathaniel first takes Olympia by the hand, he notices that it is "as cold as ice" and feels a "horrible deathly chill thrilling through him" (p. 12). But then he "looked into her eyes, which beamed back full of love and desire, and at the same time it seemed as though her pulse began to beat and her life's blood to flow into her cold hand" (pp. 12–13). Seeing the eyes of the robot affects Nathaniel's perception of her touch and he is enraptured with love. Again, Nathaniel is struck by "the peculiarly steady rhythm" with which Olympia dances (p. 13)— "Her pace is strangely regular, every movement seems to depend on some wound-up clockwork" (p. 14)—but her steadfast gaze causes him to forget what everyone else cannot and profess that she is the "soul in whom all my being is reflected!" (p. 13).

Attending to this contrast between the body and the eyes of the automaton shines a new light on the tale—not to mention the allure of the technological gaze—and helps us to understand why there is "nothing so uncanny" about the spectacles Coppelius' double tries to sell to Nathaniel—he refers to them as his "pretty eyes" (p. 11)—and yet, Olympia is described as "quite uncanny" by Nathaniel's friend (p. 14). It seems it is not the eyes that give rise to the uncanny in this story after all, but the "pernicious mistrust of human figures in general," the fear that one could "fraudulently introduce an automaton into human society" (p. 16). Freud, of course, dismisses this reading, telling us that once Olympia is revealed to be a doll in human clothes, "There is no longer any question of 'intellectual uncertainty'... yet this clear knowledge in no way diminishes the impression of the uncanny" (Freud, 2003, p. 139). But our reading suggests that no such certainty has been reached. For, as the narrator notes, the realization that Olympia is in fact an automaton only increases the likelihood that others may be deceiving us as well. This is not, as Freud argues, an example of the persistent infantile wish to be able to bring inanimate objects to life (see, p. 141). It is, rather, an articulation of the thoroughly modern fear which finds its origin in Cartesian philosophy that what appears to be animate may in point of fact be no more than the clever ruse, the cunning invention an evil genius bent on our deceit.

Now follow that logic further and apply it back to the rest of the text. If Olympia is an automaton and Nathaniel's infatuation—and subsequent madness—is the product of Coppelius' nasty trick, how can we be sure that Clara, who represents Nathaniel's return to sanity and is presented as his one true love, is not a mechanical doll as well? After all, her body is spoken of in terms eerily reminiscent of a work of craftsmanship—"Architects, nevertheless, praised the exact symmetry of her frame"—she is described by many as being "cold, unfeeling and prosaic," and yet others compare her eyes to "to a lake by Ruysdael" and declare, "What is a lake what is a mirror!… Can we look upon the girl without wondrous, heavenly music flowing towards us from her glances, to penetrate our inmost soul so that all there is awakened and stirred?" (Hoffmann, 2009, p. 9). Further, Nathaniel himself seems to unconsciously stumble upon the possibility that Clara is not what she seems when, after she dismisses his poetry, he insults her thus: "Oh, inanimate, accursed automaton!" (p. 10).

But the uncanny effect of this uncertainty is increased all the more when we observe Nathaniel's own "mechanical" movements (p. 17). Take for instance his altercation with Coppelius in his youth. In a letter to a friend, Nathaniel recounts how in boyhood, he hid in his father's office one fateful night. There he watches in horror as his beloved father and the malignant sandman Coppelius perform some sort of strange experimentation.

> My father opened the door of what I had always thought to be a cupboard. But I now saw that it was no cupboard, but rather a black cavity in which there was a little fireplace. Coppelius went to it, and a blue flame began to crackle up on the hearth. All sorts of strange utensils lay around. Heavens! As my old father stooped down to the fire, he looked quite another man. Some convulsive pain seemed to have distorted his mild features into a repulsive, diabolical countenance. He looked like Coppelius, whom I saw brandishing red-hot tongs, which he used to take glowing masses out of the thick smoke; which objects he afterwards hammered. I seemed to catch a glimpse of human faces lying around without any eyes—but with deep holes instead. "Eyes here' eyes!" roared Coppelius tonelessly. Overcome by the wildest terror, I shrieked out and fell from my hiding place upon the floor. Coppelius seized me and, baring his teeth, bleated out… "Now we have eyes enough—a pretty pair of child's eyes," he whispered, and, taking some red-hot grains out of the flames with his bare hands, he was about to sprinkle them in my eyes.
>
> *(p. 3)*

Nathaniel is saved by his father's supplications. Coppelius refrains from throwing the embers into the boy's eyes. And yet, that is not the end of his recollection. No, Coppelius laughs at the cries of Nathaniel's father and declares "Well, let the lad have his eyes and do his share of the world's crying, but we will examine the mechanism of his hands and feet." It is then that he seizes the boy "so roughly that my joints cracked, and screwed off my hands and feet, afterwards putting them back again, one after the other" (p. 3).

What are we to make of this description of the events? How are we to interpret the fact that Nathaniel's father calls Coppelius "master" (p. 3) or that he and the sandman are clearly making automatons in that hearth? How should we read Nathaniel's poem about his "gloomy

foreboding, that Coppelius would destroy his happiness," a poem in which "the hideous Coppelius appeared and touched Clara's lovely eyes," causing a dramatic change in her such that, when "Nathaniel looks into Clara's eyes, it is death that looks kindly upon him from her eyes" (p. 9)? More importantly, how should we understand the screwing off of Nathaniel's limbs, the declaration by Olympia's inventor that she had donned "the eyes stolen from you" (p. 15), the fact that after jumping to his death, he "lay on the stone pavement with his head shattered" (p. 17)—shattered, perhaps, like a mechanical device dropped on the ground?

No, Freud is wrong about the uncanny element in this story. His focus is on the gaze of the eyes rather than the touch of the body. In this way, his thinking is indebted to a long philosophical tradition. But, as we shall see in the pages that follow, it is that very tradition that gives rise to anxiety. The uncanny expresses a fear that things may not be what they seem. Appearances, it suggests, deceive. There is truth in this. But it is a truth that neglects the deeper truth of the body.

Black Mirror: Not Seeing Oneself

There is no doubt that we live in "an age of simulation informed by digital technology and an expanding culture of virtual space" (Kearney, 2021, p. 2), that our lives have become increasingly mediated, distanced, disincarnate. We are, as WJT Mitchell (2006, p. 5) rightly pointed out nearly 30 years ago, living at a time when "visual images have replaced words as the dominant mode of expression," when we use our phones and cameras and even our watches to give voice to who and what we are. But we don't just express ourselves on screen. We find ourselves there, depend upon our technologies to help us understand our place in the world and how we ought to inhabit it. As the aptly titled Netflix series *Black Mirror* suggests, the screen reflects back to us our own likenesses, reveals our fears and longings, our passions and pains, the recesses of our hearts. (A 2008 commercial for California tourism which features a number of Hollywood movie stars, those icons of the screen, puts it succinctly: "Find yourself here.") At least this is what our devices promise to do: help us to know ourselves. Yet if the screen is a black mirror, perhaps it not only distorts, as every mirror does, but acts more like a black hole, swallowing up both our likeness and the self-knowledge that supposedly comes from seeing it. Perhaps the more we fix our gaze on pixelated imitations of ourselves, the less clearly we see who and what we are.

This, it seems to me, is what is as stake in the contemporary philosopher Richard Kearney's recent work on the sense of touch, particularly when he opposes touch to sight—the sense traditionally used by philosophers to symbolize knowledge. We have, says Kearney, bought into a kind of "optocentrism," a sight-centered way of viewing (*case in point*) ourselves which actually prevents us from seeing (*and again*) ourselves (Kearney, 2021, p. 33). For Kearney, we have "lost touch with our primal embodiment" by losing touch with touch (p. 135), have forfeited something essential about ourselves by prioritizing sight over our more carnal ways of knowing the world. Sight, he reminds us, is the sense most amenable to our Gygean desire for power and control (p. 115). That is because vision presupposes distance, the ability to see without being seen, the power to look and yet remain untouched by the vulnerability of the other.

Nietzsche (1974) has such philosophical *concupiscentia oculorum* in mind when, in the Preface to *The Gay Science*, he quips, "'Is it true that God is present everywhere?' a little girl asked her mother; 'I think that's indecent'—a hint for philosophers!" (p. 38). The indecency of the philosopher (and the Silicon Valley techy who fashions himself the philosopher of today) is the desire to be God, to see that which ought not to be seen and know that which cannot be known—the self most of all. The promise of technology is to fulfill such a desire, to transcend or illimit finite existence toward infinite knowledge, infinite power, a self ever transcending itself. All of which is to say that the promise of technology is to enhance the power of sight exponentially such that one can know life at a distance without ever having to descend into the messiness of the world, without having to touch or be touched by it (see, Kearney, 2021, p. 4).

This link between knowledge, sight, and the lust for power is evident not only in the philosophical tradition—for instance, in Plato's myth of the ring of Gyges—but scripturally as well. Eve *sees* that the fruit on the tree of the *knowledge* is good to eat after the serpent tells her "when you eat of it *your eyes will be opened* and you will be *like gods,* who *know* good and evil" (*Genesis,* 2:3, emphasis mine). Indeed, the whole Adamic myth can be read as gesturing at the danger of making taste and touch subservient to sight and knowledge. Psychoanalysis too ties together this unholy trinity when Freud connects sight (scopophilia) to mastery (sadism) (Freud, 2000, p. 157) and goes on to tie to mastery to man's desire to "become a god himself" (1962, p. 44). It is technology, Freud tells us—or at least our deployment thereof—that provides us with our "Godlike character" (p. 45). And yet, as Kearney (2021) notes, "viewing everything from a distance without actually *touching or being touched* by anything" impoverishes human life, makes it less divine, not more, and leaves us "out of touch with the real" (p. 115). The real, however, is what we are after when we seek to know ourselves. We do not want the mere images of ourselves. Self-knowledge is not satisfied with appearance which, after all, can deceive. What we want is the truth, the real thing, the mystery at the heart of our existence, a mystery that must be touched in order to be known.

In this chapter, I propose to return to the starting point of philosophy—which, not accidentally, is also the starting point of psychoanalysis—the old Socratic dictum *know thyself,* in order to suggest that, as Kearney has persuasively argued, self-understanding is tied more closely to touching than seeing and that, if we are to know ourselves at all, we must be contented with groping in the dark. This I have argued elsewhere, though perhaps not in the same terms (see, Clemente, 2019, p. 53–71). Here, however, I would like to begin by returning to two fundamental philosophical principles so often neglected. First, that wisdom is knowing one knows not. And second that, as a consequence of the first, self-knowledge is not something seen and possessed but desired, pursued, aroused into being. Having forgotten or ignored these foundational insights, philosophy has forgotten herself. Yet Kearney brings us back to this wisdom by helping us to recall that "the body is the place where the psyche lives" (2021, p. 106) and that there is "a special intelligence of the body" which, when cultivated, "spells the recovery of self" (p. 9). Such a recovery is a return, a going back to the body in order to understand the self again and anew after passing through an age of "excarnation," a digital age that has traded the body for the all-seeing eye, where "flesh [has] become image" and the self on the screen has been distorted beyond recognition (p. 2).

Subtle Asclepius: The Forgotten (Touch) Therapy for the Soul

But whence comes such a recovery? In a sense, Kearney tells us that philosophy, rightly understood, can be the healing muse. He does so, in the first place, by proposing a philosophy of touch, a desire to embody the wisdom of the body. What, after all, does it mean to think about touch if not to recognize that touching and thinking are coterminous, philosophy and feeling fundamentally fused? (I am reminded of a beautiful line in Graham Greene's *The End of the Affair* (2004) which captures this sentiment perfectly:

> We can love with our minds, but can we love only with our minds? Love extends itself all the time, so that we can even love with our senseless nails: we love even with our clothes, so that a sleeve can feel a sleeve.

This, of course, is true of the love of wisdom too (p. 88)). This longing for the love of wisdom to return to its carnal roots is perhaps nowhere more evident than Kearney's emphasis on the Asclepian tradition of "accompaniment healing" (2021, pp. 65–71). Asclepius, you will remember, is one of Greek patrons of medicine. Disciple of Chiron, this god of "the art of healing through touch" (p. 65) is the very god to whom Socrates prays at the birthplace of philosophy (Plato, 1997, *Phaedo*, 118a). To honor him, thus, is to follow the example of Plato who, in Book III of his *Republic*, praises Asclepius for understanding the subtle art of restorative healing (Plato, 1997, *Republic*, 405d–408b). Indeed, throughout the *Republic*, Asclepius is held up as an image of the philosopher who sees his vocation as therapy for the soul. Unlike visual artists, who are chided for creating images of images, Asclepius and his offspring—doctors trained in the art of touch—are praised for healing real bodies instead of manufacturing false ones (599c).

Here, one might say, Kearney diverges from Plato—the former focusing on therapy for the body, the latter concerned with the virtues of the soul. Indeed, Kearney himself pits his work against the Platonic tradition and aligns his ideas with Aristotle who, in *De Anima*, likens the soul to the touching body—more specifically, the hand (see, 1957, III. viii)—and goes on to suggest that it is not sight but touch that is the most philosophical of the senses (see, Clemente, 2019, pp. 54–57). As S.H. Rosen argues, for Aristotle, "Knowing is touching" (Rosen, 1961, p. 132). Yet, if we put certain prominent *mis*readings of Plato to the side and explore the nearness of these thinkers in earnest, we will discover that, like the "subtle sons of Asclepius" (Plato, 1997, *Republic*, 408b), Kearney has learned well from his progenitor. Plato, for instance, though often read as denigrating the body, actually shows—albeit in an indirect way—that we are our bodies, whereas the soul is bestowed upon us by the state (see, Plato, 1997, *Crito*, 50d–e). For, while the soul can be shaped and even governed by the influence of education which implants within us the lessons of the educator, the body is by its very nature private and thus one's own (see, Plato, 1997, *Republic*, 464d). It cannot be taken away like one's possessions (cf. Plato, 1997, *Laws*, 739c). Nor can it be taught to repress its pains and pleasures and thus deceive itself about what it is and what it wants (see, Plato, 1997, *Republic*, 327a–621d). What is more, unlike the soul which is, in a sense, repeatable and replaceable—think of how social media apps like "LivesOn" use algorithms to mimic users' posts and syntax thus allowing their "souls" to continue posting long after their bodies have died—one's body cannot be replaced by any other. Your bodily existence is yours and yours alone. Mine belongs only to me. If Heidegger is right that death "is always essentially my own" (2010, §47), that is because my body is my own—it is me—and no one can incarnate (or, as is the case with death, disincarnate) my body but me.

Touch Thyself: (Self-)Knowledge of the Real

This reading of Plato, provoked as it is by Kearney's reflections on touch, is admittedly at odds with much of the philosophical tradition. By and large, philosophers have tended to view bodies in roughly the same manner as Agatha Christie's famed detective Hercule Poirot who, seeing scantily clad bathers on the beach, is reminded "of the Morgue in Paris" (2011, p. 6). The detective—whom I have argued elsewhere is the ideal philosopher—sees the body not so much as a prison (Plato, 1997, *Phaedo*, 82e), but as a piece of "butcher's meat" (Christie 2011, p. 6). That such a view is amenable to philosophical inquiry is attested to not only by the long history of philosophers performing autopsies and vivisections, but by virtue of the fact that philosophy itself is a kind of autopsy (from the Greek *autos* (self), *opsis* (eye), "seeing for oneself") and "conscience-vivisection" (Nietzsche, 1989, p. 95)—that is, an attempt to see oneself for oneself, to *know thyself.*

Such an approach obviously has its value. In the first place, objective knowledge comes from treating bodies like meat and thus being able to dissect and objectify them. In the second, locating one's identity in one's soul means making oneself articulable and thus understandable. Think of how Kierkegaard's single individual is muted by his individuality; the escape from such seclusion comes by means of making oneself "universal," that is, likening oneself to everyone else. The way we share knowledge with one another, and even come to understand ourselves, is through the use of common symbols (Lacan's symbolic order). We "find ourselves" on our devices because we see our souls reflected there. Touch, on the other hand, is (like the body) private. No one can tell me what I feel. It is only by sublimating what I feel into concepts—that is, categories understood by the soul—that I am able to share my feelings with others. The screen re-presents my soul to me in a language I can understand by depicting such concepts before my eyes and thus showing me soul like mine, be it a fictional character on TV or the fictional image I create of myself on social media. The rather obvious problem with this is that the soul I see represented on my device is not me. The "self" I come to know when I know myself intellectually, by means of the soul, does not exist. Not really. The denial of the import of the body is the denial of the *principium individuationis*, the refusal to admit that every body is unique. Indeed, as Poirot insists, it is only by denying the individuality of the body that the detective—and the philosopher—is able to solve the mystery before him.

> It was on a morning when we were sitting out here that we talked of sun-tanned bodies lying like meat upon a slab, and it was then that I reflected how little difference there was between one body and another. If one looked closely and appraisingly—yes—but to the casual glance? One moderately well-made young woman is very like another. Two brown legs, two brown arms, a little piece of bathing suit in between—just a body lying out in the sun. When a woman walks, when she speaks, laughs, turns her head, moves a hand—then, yes then, there is personality—individuality. But in the sun ritual—no.
>
> *(Christie, 2011, p. 237)*

The individual soul is, as Plotinus rightly suggests, subservient to the world-soul, a totalizing oneness that robs each of us of what is most our own. My soul can be likened to every other in that my thoughts and interpretations of life come to me from others. They precede me and are made for me and are thus never really my own.

To know thyself with the knowledge of the soul, then, is not to know thyself at all. It is to know the readymade ideas of a universal world-soul that belong to no soul in particular. But what is one to do? Is self-knowledge even possible? Can philosophy aid in the pursuit of such a noble goal? Or has the ancient love of wisdom deceived us, leading us to identify ourselves with phantoms, perpetuating the flight from the body which is the destruction of self-knowledge itself? When I began writing this chapter, I missed the innuendo present in the subtitle of this section (a Freudian slip to be sure). Once I noticed the double entendre, I intended to change it. That's when I remembered a certain passage in the *Gorgias* and it gave me pause. Arguing with Callicles over what constitutes the good life, Socrates points out that Callicles' view—the good life is synonymous with the life of pleasure—implies that the pinnacle of human existence can be found in the life of the "lewd masturbator" (Plato, 1997, *Gorgias*, 494e). Callicles balks at the suggestion. But is he right to? Or does not our foregoing argument suggest that Socrates' crass witticism contains a forgotten truth?

This problem bothered me, especially since I have spilt a good amount of ink arguing that such solipsistic attempts at self-affirmation reveal the thanatonic impulse at the heart of our erotic lives. If self-knowledge can only be found in onanistic indulgence, what then becomes of our relations to others? I was pondering this before bed last night and awoke suddenly in the early hours of the morning with a squeezing, wrenching tightness in my chest, a suffocating breathlessness, and the unshakable fear that I was about to die. My heart was racing. The muscles contracted in my shoulders and neck. I felt that I could neither stand nor lie nor sit. I was tension incarnate. The experience is nothing new. I was having a panic attack. (It has only just subsided.) I was sitting on the edge of my bed rubbing my neck and doing some slow breathing exercises when my wife awoke and put her hand on my back. She asked if I was all right, gently massaged my shoulders, pressed her forehead against mine. I told her to go back to sleep, went down stairs and let my dog Joey out of his crate, and as I sat on the floor petting him in the dark, my anxiety receded and I felt better (cf. Kearney, 2021, pp. 109–111).

Anxiety is a malady of the soul, one that manifests itself in the body. When caught in the clutches of anxiety, it is not a physical reality that fills one with dread but the awareness of the indifference and indeterminacy of the world. It is the overwhelming meaninglessness of everything, the fact that there are too many possibilities and that any of them or none of them might come to fruition that wracks one's body and leaves one breathless. Kierkegaard defines anxiety as "freedom's actuality as the possibility of possibility" (1980, 42). What he means, I think, is that anxiety is my awareness of my freedom, my recognition of the fact that I live as a free being with an infinite number of possibilities before me, so many possibilities that they overwhelm me and I drown in my own freedom. Confronted by this experience, faced with the unbearable weight of indeterminacy—or, as Milan Kundera would have it, the unbearable lightness of being—one's body tightens up. It closes in upon itself and shrinks before that which would crush it. What deliverance can there be?

In one of the most compelling sections of his book on touch, Kearney speaks of an "ethics of tact" (Kearney, 2021, p. 11). He reminds us that not all touch is welcome and not all knowledge beneficial. Touch can be misused and the body abused. Touch can cause harm or, like my early morning attempts at self-soothing, fail to alleviate a harm already done. Nevertheless, touch is the sense that opens us to possibility of being healed by the other. It is that which, making us vulnerable to the other, allows us to be cared for by the other and to care for others, in turn. It was only when my wife put her hand on my back and I put my hand on my dog that my symptoms went away. And it was only when my symptoms went away that I was able to sit, organize my thoughts, and finish writing this chapter. Touch enabled me to figure out what I wanted to write. It was the wisdom of the body that allowed me to understand myself. But the wisdom came not from my body. It came from the touch of another. To know thyself, then, is to touch and be touched. Self-knowledge cannot be attained alone.

References

Aristotle. 1957. *On the Soul. Parva Naturalia. On Breath*. Trans. Walter Stanley Hett. Cambridge: Harvard University Press.

Christie, A. 2011. *Evil Under the Sun: A Hercule Poirot Mystery*. New York: Harper Collins.

Clemente, M. 2019. *Eros Crucified: Death, Desire, and the Divine in Psychoanalysis and Philosophy of Religion*. London: Routledge.

Freud, S. 2003. *The Uncanny*. Trans. James Strachey. New York: Penguin Classics.

Freud, S. 2000. *Three Essays on the Theory of Sexuality*. Trans. James Strachey. New York: Basic Books.

Freud, S. 1962. *Civilization and Its Discontents*. Trans. James Strachey. New York: W.W. Norton.

Greene, G. 2004. *The End of the Affair*. New York: Penguin.

Heidegger, M. 2010. *Being and Time*. Trans. Joan Stambaugh. New York: State University of New York Press.

Hoffmann, ETA. 2009. *The Sandman*. Trans. John Oxenford. New York: Edward Rios Books.

Kearney, R. 2021. *Touch: Recovering Our Most Vital Sense*. New York: Columbia University Press.

Kierkegaard, S. 1980. *The Concept of Anxiety*. Trans. Reidar Thomte. Princeton, NJ: Princeton University Press.

Mitchell, W.J.T. 2006. *What Do Pictures Want?: The Lives and Loves of Images*. Chicago, IL: University of Chicago Press.

Nietzsche, F. 1989. *On the Genealogy of Morals and Ecce Homo*. Trans. Walter Kaufmann New York: Vintage.

Nietzsche, F. 1974. *The Gay Science*. Trans. Walter Kaufmann. New York: Vintage.

Plato. 1997. *Complete Works*. Ed. John M. Cooper. Indianapolis, IN: Hackett.

Rosen, S.H. 1961. "Thought and Touch: A Note on Aristotle's *De Anima*." *Phronesis* 6: 127– 137.

PART II

The Philosopher's Stone

Converting Theory into Practice

7

AUXILIARY ORGANS AND EXTIMATE IMPLANTS

Coming to Terms with Technology from a Psychoanalytical Perspective

Hub Zwart

Introduction

When it comes to presenting a psychoanalytic perspective on technology, Freud's essay *Civilisation and Its Discontents* provides an obvious point of departure (1930/1948). In this psychoanalytical classic, Freud describes how human beings, equipping themselves with "auxiliary organs," may evolve into "prosthetic gods," although such organic extensions evidently introduce new challenges and frustrations as well—which explains why technology, allegedly beneficial to humans, at the same time triggers ambivalence and discontent. Freud's view on technological entities as organic extensions is complemented by a somewhat different approach, initiated in a manuscript dating from the early days of psychoanalysis and known as the *Entwurf*. Here, Freud proposed the outlines of a philosophical anthropology which is fleshed out in more detail many years later in another psychoanalytic classic, namely *Beyond the Pleasure Principle* (Freud 1920/1940). After presenting the core ideas developed in these texts, the focus of my contribution will shift to the work of Jacques Lacan, who will also guide our reading of Freud. Lacan's famous programmatic "return to Freud," I will argue, does not solely consist of close textual re-reading. Rather, Lacan combines textual analysis (the *retour* to Freud) with an imposing series of *detours*, reframing Freud's concepts and discoveries by connecting them with important developments in twentieth-century research fields, such as structural linguistics, ethology, cybernetics, informatics and molecular biology. Whereas Freud's own understanding of science remained very much indebted to research practices in which he himself had been initiated during the final decades of the nineteenth century (notably neuro-physiology), Lacan demonstrated the relevance of psychoanalysis for coming to terms with contemporary technoscience, resulting in a psychoanalytic philosophy of technology, albeit in outline (Zwart 2017, 2019a). My contribution will notably zoom in on the role of technology in what Lacan refers to as the "symbolisation of the real." Finally, I will focus on Lacan's assessment (or rather: diagnostic) of information technologies, especially paying attention to the role of gadgets, as technological entities with a specific profile of their own.

DOI: 10.4324/9781003195849-10

Disparity

According to Jacques Lacan, the decisive originality of psychoanalysis (the *epistemic rupture* initiated by Sigmund Freud around 1900) was to denounce the "pastoral" idea of an original harmonious relationship between subject (psyche) and object (external reality) which we should somehow try to re-establish and restore (Lacan 1959–1960/1986, p. 107 and elsewhere). Instead, Lacan argues, a chronic disparity between both poles should be our point of departure (Freud 1920/1940). The initial encounter of human beings with the threatening real is a traumatic experience, exemplified by the trauma of birth. As Slavoj Žižek (2016/2019, p. 157) points out, Immanuel Kant already interpreted the screams ("Geschrei") produced by a child at birth as a symptom of indignation in response to the experience that human autonomy is significantly hampered by the insufficiency and vulnerability of our bodies vis-à-vis the real. For psychoanalysis, the birth trauma emphasizes the maladaptation of human organisms to their natural (primal) environment (Zwart 2021).

According to Freud, an important objective of culture in general, and of technology in particular, is to immunize ourselves against the real and to safeguard our integrity from disruptive external intrusions. Contrary to most other mammals, human beings enter prematurely into the world, and their existence remains tainted by negation and lack (e.g. the *absence* of fur, claws, etc.). This is especially noticeable in neonates (e.g. their *inability* to move and walk), so that, with the help of technology, additional immunization devices (a cradle, a baby carrier, a home, etc.) must be installed to compensate for these lacks which are threatening human existence with negation and elimination from the very outset. Dialectically speaking, psychoanalysis sees technology as the *negation of this negation*, as an effort to supersede the disparity, the primal experience of lack (Zwart 2021). Rather than being "open" to externality and otherness, our existential challenge as humans initially comes down to averting, neutralizing and, to a limited extent, incorporating this threatening avalanche of external input.

These views were already proposed by Freud during the early years of psychoanalysis in the 1890s, in his letters to Wilhelm Fliess as well as in an unpublished manuscript known as the *Entwurf*, published posthumously (Freud 1950). In these documents, Freud describes the human psyche as a "machine" (p. 139), an "apparatus" (p. 270) consisting of various "systems," wherein energy quanta circulate, designed to attenuate excessive stimulation and excitation. Indeed: "I am a machine" (1950, p. 271; cf. Zwart 1995). The main function of this machine (the neural apparatus) is to act as a screen ("Quantitätsschirm") to contain the influx of potentially disruptive energy quantities, entering the system from outside (p. 390). The psychic apparatus acts as a filter which allows only small quotients of external energy quantities to affect the psychic system (p. 394). Thus, the main task of the psychic machine is to protect the system from intrusion by disruptively large quantities of input. A plethora of technologies developed by humans can be considered as extensions and externalizations of these psychic mechanisms, fostering immunity by strengthening our capacity to safeguard our psychic and physical integrity. Sense organs, either natural or artificial, function like antennae, allowing only small samples of the raw (and potentially overwhelming) real to be processed. Therefore, Lacan distinguishes "reality" from "the real." What we experience as reality is the outcome of an intricate and complicated process. Human reality is drastically filtered, processed and construed.

At first glance, the role of the "reality principle" seems to be to enhance the ego's ability to defer immediate gratification (pleasure). Yet, on closer inspection, the role of the reality principle first and foremost is to *shield* the ego, by forfending traumatic *confrontations* with raw externality. The primary role of the reality principle is not to *expose* the subject to the inexorable real, but rather to allow *carefully selected bits of reality* into the system, so that these samples ("raw quantities") can be adequately processed, and reality becomes livable for the ego. In short, whereas traditional philosophy emphasizes world-openness and intentionality as starting point for human understanding, psychoanalysis rather emphasizes the epistemic role of resistance as a mechanism of defense (Zwart 2019a).

This line of thinking is taken up by Freud many years later, in *Beyond the Pleasure Principle* (Freud 1920/1940). The pivotal role of resistance, Freud argues, is underscored by human anatomy. We are covered by protective skin (which is subsequently covered with an additional protective layer known as clothes), while our sense organs are miniature apertures whose primary purpose is to provide protection against overstimulation (*Reizschutz*). Rather than being open to the world, our bodies protect and immunize us from the threatening Real. This tendency of living organisms to insulate themselves from the outside world already applies to micro-organisms, coaxed inside their cell membranes. Our vulnerable bodies protect themselves against overstimulation, but this applies to the human psyche as well. Protection against external stimuli is a life task at least as important as sensitivity and receptivity (Freud 1920/1940, p. 27). As indicated, our sense organs are like little antennae that select small samples of exteriority, allowing us to assess minute quantities of input. Our primary objective is to safeguard our psychic integrity from intrusive traumas.

Freud elucidates the topology of the human psyche by comparing it with the anatomy of the human eye. Darkness is the default, and the eye is basically a camera obscura, while pupil and cornea allow only small samples of diffracted light to enter the eye and reach the retina. Raw light is meticulously filtered and processed.

We may see a laboratory as an extension or externalization of the human eye: as a space where everything (light, air, temperature, etc.) is meticulously conditioned and controlled: safeguarded from external disturbances, so that only carefully selected samples of reality are admitted and subjected to analysis, with the help of precision contrivances. What the example of the laboratory also indicates, however, is that the scope of our vision (of our sensitivity) can be significantly broadened with the help of artificial extensions: artificial sense organs and electronic gadgets, so that humans gradually evolve into the "prosthetic superhumans" mentioned above (Freud 1930/1948). This means that, after immunization and selection, the next challenge is overcompensation. Paradoxically perhaps, while initially designed as immunization devices, technologies eventually tend to evolve into sources of information in their own right, bombarding us with input. In the global high-tech environments of today, humans are exposed to technologically mediated overstimulation (information overload). While laboratories may initially be considered as materializations of Freud's concept of the psyche (operating as an immunization device), the currently emerging global networks of laboratories are confronting us with informational overabundance (data litter). Knowledge scarcity has definitely given way to Gargantuan data collections. The whole world is becoming a global laboratory. Let this suffice as a starting point for outlining a psychoanalytic approach to understanding technology. I will now zoom in on the added value of the work of Jacques Lacan.

1953

1953 is an important year for science in general, but for psychoanalysis in particular. It is the year of the discovery of the biochemical structure of DNA by James Watson and Francis Crick, but it is also the year in which Jacques Lacan inaugurated his famous Seminars (Lacan

1953–1954/1975; Zwart 2021). In these seminars, technoscientific breakthroughs such as the discovery by Watson and Crick are assessed from a psychoanalytic perspective, but at the same time used to explore and flesh out the specificity of psychoanalysis itself. These seminars were Lacan's laboratory if you like, designed to enact an intensive mutual exposure between the writings of Freud on the one hand and the vicissitudes of twentieth-century technoscientific research on the other. Lacan's explicit objective was a *return* (a systematic rereading) of the writings of Sigmund Freud, but rather than opting for an orthodox "author studies" approach, his effort was to retrieve the revelatory truth of psychoanalysis by mutually confronting Freud's discoveries with the groundbreaking discoveries of technoscience. Freud's revelatory insights had been obfuscated by post-war developments such as ego psychology, Lacan argued, and his objective now was to *negate this negation* of Freud's revolutionary insights. The provocative originality of psychoanalysis had been obfuscated by an ideological misreading of his work, bent on "strengthening the ego," which *de facto* came down to forcing the ego to adapt to its socio-cultural environment, thereby negating what Lacan saw as Freud's decisive, revelatory truth. Therefore, the aim of his seminars was to supersede this obfuscation (to negate this negation)—so that his seminars amount to an exercise in retrieval, restoring Freud's original insights at an advanced level of sophistication and comprehension.

Therefore, rather than merely *reading* Freud, Lacan opted for triangulation, by confronting Freud's oeuvre with important developments in twentieth-century research fields unknown to Freud himself. Thus, Lacan systematically reframed Freudian conceptions with the help of terms and insights adopted from research fields such as linguistics, cybernetics, ethology, informatics, molecular biology, and so on. Freud himself already anticipated the need for such an endeavor. He wrote extensively, for instance, about how language studies research into the antithetical meaning of primal words (Freud 1910/1943) and anthropological research into aboriginal societies could help us to come to terms with contemporary neurosis (Freud 1913/1940). And he also wrote about the psyche as a machine, as we have seen, exploring pathways of research that would later be taken up by cybernetics and neuroscience. Yet, where science as such was concerned, Freud remained very much oriented on research fields of the late nineteenth century, such as neuro-physiology, in which he himself had been trained, while he was virtually unaware of revolutionary developments which transformed multiple areas of research from 1900 onwards, as analyzed by Gaston Bachelard in his "psychoanalysis of science" (Zwart 2019a, 2020a). By mutually exposing Freud's writings with contemporary research fields, Lacan intended to retrieve and reaffirm the provocative originality of psychoanalysis.

This inevitably implied that Lacan's own thinking increasingly moved beyond the nomenclature and parameters designed by Freud. Notwithstanding Freud's emphasis on disparity, especially in unpublished fragments such as a short unfinished essay on *Ich-Spaltung*, avidly discussed by Lacan, for many readers Freud's starting point seems to be the self-contained ego who gradually opens up to reality: a developmental trajectory which moves from inside to outside, so that an ego exclusively focused on libidinal drives gradually learns to redirect part of its energy in external things (Aydin 2021). Lacan radically reverses this thesis: the ego comes into being *via exposure to otherness*, and science and technology play a crucial role in this, because they basically entail a systematic symbolization of the real (via precision measurements, equations, chemical, physical and mathematical symbols, etc.). Thus, Lacan radically reinterprets the famous Freudian adage *Wo Es war soll Ich werden*: Where it (or Id) was, I (ego) shall come into being. Freud presents this as a project of psychic reclamation, so that the wild unconscious drives become cultivated and transformed into a polder landscape—a metaphor which seems to suggest a gradual strengthening of the ego. Lacan's starting point is different. Otherness precedes the self.

The Mirror Experience

Examples of how Lacan's *retour* to Freud gave rise to multiple *detours* through contemporary research fields can also be found in Lacan's *Écrits*, for example in his famous analysis of the mirror experience (Lacan 1949/1966), building on twentieth-century research in ethology and child psychology. Parisian psychiatrist Henri Wallon (1949/1954) had compared the reactions of human infants and young chimpanzees to their reflection in a mirror. Around the age of six months, Wallon claimed, both humans and chimpanzees begin to recognize their mirror image, but whereas human infants tend to be fascinated by it (examining their reflected gestures in a playful manner), young chimps seem to think they are facing a fellow member of their species and quickly lose their interest, turning their attention to other things. Wallon published a paper on this topic in 1931, which became part of a monograph on childhood development (1949/1954, pp. 151–180).

For Lacan, the mirror experience is an important moment because, in his view, our primordial experience of our bodily Self during very early childhood is one of discord, turbulence, and fragmentation. The human body initially is a fragmented body, while the primary ego is something like a fold or void. The first impetus to see ourselves as a subject— as *someone*—is provided by something external, coming from the outside (the reflection in the mirror). Thus, for Lacan, to understand the process of human individuation, the focus of attention should move in the inversed direction: from outside to inside. We need exteriority in order for interiority to arise.

The mirror experience is a first important moment in the coming into being of human subjects. With the help of a technical device (the reflection in a mirror), young children for the first time see their body as an imaginary whole. The experience of the real body as fragmented gives way to an imaginary (image-based) sense of self. The sense of wholeness or integrity entails an *imaginary* identity, because an external *image* is needed to achieve this position. Wholeness is not how we initially experience our bodies and ourselves. An external mirror image is required to assume an identity. The mirror experience is an example of how Lacan uses twentieth-century research to reframe the psychoanalytic understanding of psychic development. The mirror experience, as documented by twentieth-century experimental scientists, allows us to understand how the real (fragmented) body becomes an (imaginary) whole. Extimacy (something external, but at the same time close and intimate: my mirror-image) is required.

Subsequently, as the young child learns to speak a language, the symbolic environment becomes increasingly important, so that imaginary extimacy gives way to *symbolic* extimacy. Ultimately, language, the symbolic order, allows us to become who we are. The exposure to language is initially experienced as a disruptive intrusion, however, challenging our precarious imaginary self-image. Via the symbolic order created by language, others begin to re-determine who we are.

The concept of the unconscious is likewise drastically reframed by Lacan. The unconscious (the Id) is not seen as a collection of wild impulses (as "instincts" in the biological sense, which are to be tamed by the ego), but as "the language of the other": resulting from exposure to the symbolic, to the disruptive impact of language. Lacan's model of the psyche is a Moebius ring, where both the Cartesian cogito (the conscious ego) and the psychoanalytical unconscious are something intrinsically textual: they constitute the reverse sides of a Moebius ring.

Once again, this provides an example of how Lacan employs twentieth-century research fields (in this case: structural linguistics) to retrieve and reframe Freud's revolutionary insights. Building on de Saussure (1916/1968), Lacan sees language as something inherently technical and artificial. This notably applies to contemporary society as a linguistic environment, where the symbolic is produced and disseminated via technical devices.

As structural linguistics demonstrated, moreover, language is an inherently binary system, conveying a logic of presence or absence, of either-or. Thus, natural languages basically convey the same logic as computer languages. And this also helps us to understand how gender is linguistically framed, for instance. Our linguistic environments tend to force us into being either male or female, via the grammar we learn to employ. This symbolic identity (enforced by the symbolic order) is initially based on the presence or absence of what psychoanalysis refers to as "partial organs" (e.g. penises, breasts, etc.) or their symbolic representations, functioning as markers or signifiers which allow the symbolic to operate, and which allow humans to discern some level of order in their lifeworld. Our attitude toward the symbolic is bound to remain an ambivalent one, however. On the one hand, we need this detour, this exposure to language and culture to become who we are. At the same time, our real (divided, fragmented) existence never fully lives up to this binary logic—a tension which results in a situation of chronic disparity. In other words, from a Lacanian perspective, experiences which are currently framed as gender dysphoria should not be seen as exceptional syndromes—as something pathological by which only a particular subset of human beings is afflicted—but rather as the default in the sense that the tension is *always there*. Masculinity or femininity are neither natural nor a given. Various sexual "fascinations" or "perversities," such as fetishism or masochism, for instance, revolve around the female phallus, as a surmised secret extension of phallic females (referred to by Lacan as the "object *a*"), challenging the symbolic order. Such fascinations can therefore be considered as ritual erotic enactments of this original disparity. The phallic fetish echoes the unconscious conviction that something has escaped the relentless symbolization of the real.

The Imaginary and the Symbolic

In short, humans are facing many challenges on the hazardous path toward individuation (becoming who we are), and this psychoanalytic anthropology (grounded in disparity) prepares the ground for a psychoanalytic philosophy of technology. The mirror experience explicitly refers to and presupposes the existence of technical tools (products of technology), namely mirrors. Although natural mirrors exist in nature (ponds, lakes, rivulets, etc.), artificial mirrors become increasingly advanced in the course of history, as technical entities fostering self-reflection. Today, mirrors can be found everywhere, in bathrooms, shops, elevators, as selfies, and so on, turning self-reflection into something inevitable, thereby running the risk of trivializing it, so that these easily reproducible moments of self-encounter now seem too easily deprived of their auratic dimension.

Other products of technology may play similar mirroring roles. Take ancient Greek statues of gods and goddesses, once created to propagate a particular bodily ideal, namely, the ideal of an athletic, vigorous, healthy body, the product of gymnastics and exercise, so that these statues, erected at places which attracted human traffic, acted as models and missionaries (Lacan 1955–1956/1981, p. 328; Sloterdijk 2009). They materialized a petrified moral imperative: this is what you should become, this is what you should strive to attain! In the high-tech world of today, similar roles may be played by glamorous pictures of models in glossy magazines and commercials. They convey a normative appeal, the imperative that we should use these models as critical mirrors, fostering self-reflection: are we as slender, healthy, beautiful, elegant, muscular, feminine, masculine, etc., as we should or could be? Such technological products mirror the human body as a whole, in a smooth way, obfuscating disparities, exemplifying what Lacan refers to as the imaginary body (Zwart 1998).

Most entities we encounter, however, focus on particular body parts, on "partial objects," for example, riffles in Western movies, functioning as phallic items, or beer bottles and beer barrels, functioning as breast-like entities, etc. On the one hand, we dwell in an imaginary ambiance, replete with images (imaginary representations) of bodies or body parts. At the same time, these images are incorporated in a symbolic order, through the binary logic of presence or absence. By indicating presence or absence, partial objects and their artificial representations become something symbolic. Human beings dwell in two realms as it were: in an imaginary, but also in a symbolic ambiance. We have created a world of images, but we have also entered a world of language: of words, letters, mathematical symbols, slogans, acronyms, and so on. As indicated, the logic of the symbolic order entails first and foremost a binary logic, ultimately reducible to presence or absence (1 versus 0, the binary logic of digital systems). Language itself is already something binary and artificial, as the connection between sound and meaning (between signifier and signified) is arbitrary.

To give an example: the names of rivers often begin with or at least contain letters such as "r" or "s," whose sound patterns seem to remind us that these names may originally have come into being in order to mimic something real, for example, the sound of floating water (Rhine, Meuse, Moselle, Rhone, Saone, Seine, Mississippi, etc.). At the same time, the fact that this etymology is now lost to us, or is even questionable in itself, already indicates that such a connection with the real need not be discernible at all. For most of the terms we use, there is no obvious connection between sound and meaning.

The same pertains to letters. There is a historical connection between the letter A and something real, namely a living animal: an ox (A is derived from "aleph," which means "ox" in Phoenician, although the letter A became inverted at a certain point: its two legs initially pointed upwards, to represent the animal's horns). As de Saussure emphasized, however, although such historical details are interesting in themselves, we do not need to know this for the alphabet to function, as the connection between signifiers (sound patterns, typographical letters, words, etc.) and their meaning is arbitrary—or at least, the connection *became* an arbitrary one, even if there may have been a primordial natural connection at some point in a distant past, as in the case of names for rivers. As the letter "A" became stylized into an easily recognizable writable and printable letter, the connection with the visual image (two inverted horns) became irrelevant.

Technology and the Symbolic: The Symbolization of the Real

The binary logic of the symbolic is important for understanding technology because the symbolic order, constituted by language, is the starting point for technological development, if only because writing and printing *as such* already involve crucial technologies for producing books and other reading materials. Technology is part of the symbolic order, and resonates with its binary logic. Although the imaginary is never completely absent, cars or airplanes are not consciously designed to remind us of archetypal monsters, although such imaginary associations may continue to play a role. Technologies tend to reflect the same binary logic as language does. A plethora of human artifacts function as signals, indicating *yes* or *no*, *forbidden* or *allowed*, *open* or *closed*, *sufficient* or *insufficient*. Historically speaking, the shape of the number "1" signifies presence (e.g. a finger or a wooden stick that is used for counting), while "0" (the hollow left in the sand by a pebble which is taken away) signifies absence. In other words, the symbols 1 and 0 (the starting point of digital technologies) began their historical careers as images (the image of a finger or a stick; the image of an empty place in the sand). At a certain point, however, this connection between symbol and image became obfuscated, and the relationship between the *signifier* (the symbol) and the concept *signified* by it (e.g. presence or absence) became arbitrary. Symbols such as plus (+) or minus (−) play the same role: and the meaning of these symbols is arbitrary. Boundary stones marking the beginning of a territory may be shaped in the form of a finger (a menacing index finger perhaps, or a paternalistic phallic object), but in principle they could have any other shape. In modern technology, lights or buttons on a panel still convey the same meaning as boundary stones once did: *yes* or *no, go* or *no go, allowed* or *not allowed*. Such technological entities contribute to what Lacan refers to as the symbolization of the real.

Allow me to give a concrete example: night and day. To some extent, day and night can be experienced as "real" and as associated with phenomena such as darkness and sunrise, warmth and frost, etc., although since the introduction of the electric light bulb, the difference between the two has become relative, or even arbitrary. By turning on the light, a diurnal ambiance is created artificially. Initially, daybreak is a *real* event, in the Lacanian sense of the term, and a first effort to come to terms with the real may be to opt for an imaginary procedure, seeing night as a goddess (associated with the moon, etc.). Technology, however, prompts us to symbolize the real. Devices such as clocks and thermometers allow us to determine *exactly*—that is: *arbitrarily*—when night comes to an end and day begins, or how night and day are related to temperature. Before the invention of reliable clocks, humans could agree to meet at dawn. Nowadays, we may agree to have our first zoom conference at 9:00 a.m. sharp. Technologies of measurement symbolize the real, allowing us to replace primordial experience (darkness, frost, etc.) with measurements and symbols: 9:10 a.m., 20°C, etc. Such technologies (clocks, thermometers, etc.) have a dramatic impact on our experience of dimensions such as temperature or time. Due to the invention of clocks, we tend to see time as something linear, as a line moving in one direction, but this experience of time is mediated by artifacts such as clocks or graphs. "Real" time is more like a floating river. The representation of time as a line (like a ruler) is an artifact of technology. The first calendars (e.g. little stripes carved into pieces of bone) were probably developed by women who wanted to attain some level of control over their menstrual cycle, so as to manage the capacity of their bodies to reproduce. The cycle became a line, and many centuries later it evolved into the *X*-axis of the coordinate system. Pregnancy and menstrual cycles are real, but the first calendars, carved into bones or shells, are first efforts toward symbolization of the real—practices which nowadays may involve paper calendars, graphs of apps.

Extimacy

As Gaston Bachelard convincingly argued, making fire or plowing the earth where once practices with an erotic dimension, engendering poetic or mythological images concerning erotic encounters between "active" and "passive" agents. Modern chemistry, however, strives to erase such imaginary associations (still active in alchemy) with its precision measurements, symbols, and equations. Yet, these imaginary reminiscences are never completely superseded by symbolization once and for all. They resurge in poetic and metaphorical language, in novels, movies, and other genres of the imagination.

A plow may be considered an exemplification of what Freud (1930/1948) referred to as "auxiliary organs." Technological extensions such as plows are likely to build on or replace "partial objects," that is, bodily components which can be present or absent. In other words, technological entities may function as amplifications or extensions of such organic components, or as their ersatz, allowing us to see the plow for instance as a phallic extension, extrapolating erotic experiences to interactions on a larger scale (e.g. intercourse with Mother Earth). This also resonates with the Freudian concept of *Anlehnung* (literally: "to be modelled after"). To the extent that plowing can indeed be experienced (metaphorically speaking) as an erotic encounter (an interaction with "Mother Earth"), a plow can be considered a phallic extension. In a similar manner, a cradle may be seen as an artificial replacement of a uterus, as a technological device compensating for the prematurity of human neonates, allowing caregivers to extend the protective function of the uterus beyond the trauma of birth. This artificiality, however, at the same time opens up completely new possibilities, which increasingly distance themselves from their natural models, so that there is an inherent tendency in technology to become unnatural rather than natural. From a psychoanalytic perspective, technology moves far beyond the mere satisfaction of biological means. Rather, psychoanalysis discerns a relationship of co-evolution between technical artifacts and human desire. Rather than satisfying pre-existing biological needs, technologies increasingly engender new desires.

This becomes noticeable in commercials, for instance, where artifacts are presented as commodities, responsive to and triggering desire. A bedstead or mattress, for instance, is not only meant to keep us warm at night (in the sense of: satisfying a biological need by compensating for natural deficits, such as in this case the absence of fur). Rather, a bed becomes an object of desire: a setting meant to create optimal conditions for, among other things, erotic pleasure. And when holiday commercials conjure up the prospect of alluring white beaches and blue lagoons, the message is basically the same, although advanced technological infrastructures (computer networks, airports, airplanes, hotel facilities, etc.) must now be mobilized to realize our dreams—while in reality such technological infrastructures are bound to introduce frustrations and discontent in their own right.

Where contemporary technological innovation is concerned, Lacanian psychoanalysis emphasizes the experience that technological entities become increasingly intimate, interacting increasingly smoothly with organic bodily components. To come to terms with this, Lacan coined the concept of extimacy (Zwart 2017), indicating that technological entities are never fully incorporated or embedded: they are both intimate and external, both embedded and foreign, both life-enhancing and intrusive—they are objects of desire as well as objects of concern. Biomedical implants, for instance, may operate as clean, electronic pseudo-organs, and as such they may be beneficial and life-saving, but they will also pose a threat. Their presence and performance can never be taken for granted. Besides being beneficial, they can also be frustrating and commanding.

If we are looking for a natural example of such extimate implants (in accordance with the logic of *Anlehnung*), testicles may come to mind: weird, partial objects in a rather palpable manner, whose extimate status is already underscored by their curious anatomical position, both inside and outside the body, imbuing male bodies (notably during adolescence, but also later in life) with substances such as testosterone. Science author Paul de Kruif (1945/1948) once considered testosterone as the essence of masculinity, as the "male hormone" par excellence, associated not only with muscle power and virility, but also with "brain power." Therefore, De Kruif promoted the artificial administration of this hormone to "men on the wane," such as himself, as soon as their natural production of testosterone was considered expiring or declining. For youngsters, however, especially in the case of what is currently labeled as "gender dysphoria," testosterone may represent a toxic substance, giving rise to sudden (perhaps unwanted) bodily changes, or to excessive, unquenchable desire. The feminine breast may likewise serve as an example here. It may function as an object of desire, and provide a life-line to new-born infants, but it may also become a toxic, metastatic threat to women, an extimate object arousing suspicion, giving rise to practices such as regular check-ups or self-monitoring, or even preventive removal, so as to forego cancer (the archetypal, demonic, organic threat from within). Thus, testicles and breasts provide organic examples of what Lacan refers to as the object "a," something which can be present or absent, beneficial or toxic, object of desire as well as object of concern (Zwart 2012, 2019b).

In short, especially testicles may function as model organs whose *modus operandi* is mimicked by wearable devices, worn on (or directly under) the skin, ejecting electronic signals or bioactive substances (as biochemical signals) into the human organism to counteract deprivation or excess, or simply to invoke specific moods or states of arousal (gadgets which function as clean, electronic, pseudo-organic "gonads" as it were). Lacan notably discusses the role of gadgets in his famous seminar XVII, emphasizing how they underscore the increasing importance of *information* in contemporary technology.

Gadgets

During the academic year 1969–1970, while Jacques Lacan presented his famous *Seminar XVII*, Marxism was in the air, eagerly adopted by Maoist students and many of their teachers, arguing that the working classes should gain political control. Many of them considered psychoanalysis as a bourgeois practice, focusing on familial dynamics in affluent bourgeois families, using iconic Greek mythology and tragedy (i.e. gymnasium course materials) as frame of reference.

For Lacan, however, who himself came from a bourgeois catholic background, the traditional Marxist aim of establishing a proletarian dictatorship, and eventually a communist society, was a questionable objective. Maoists, he argued, had failed to notice that something has changed: a transition *within the symbolic order as such*, which outdated the traditional Marxist view on technology (p. 207). What struck him as a distinctive feature of Maoism was the emphasis on handbook knowledge, provided by "manuals," exemplifying the manual knowledge of the exploited. Lacan saw Mao's red booklet as a prototypical political manual for producing revolutions. Yet, he argued, something completely new has emerged in our world, little things called "gadgets," in which technoscience now objectifies itself—entities that are entirely forged by science. And now the question is whether in such a high-tech world, completely under the sway of information technologies, manual know-how can still carry sufficient weight to count as a subversive factor (p. 174). Manuals were written in order to operate machines, but for Lacan gadgets exemplify a completely new type of machine, involving brain work, information science, robotics and cybernetics, rather than manual labor.

Gadgets, as an unprecedented technological phenomenon sui generis, not only pose a challenge to Marxism, but to Freudian psychoanalysis as well. Freud had famously claimed that, contrary to fear, which is object-directed, "anxiety" is without an object. Lacan now disagrees with this and claims that anxiety is instilled precisely by these little interconnected objects, which he refers to objects *a*, tending toward invisibility (*Verborgenheit*), but pervasive and omnipresent (pp. 172, 216), putting us under constant surveillance, and therefore, generating anxiety. Big Brother is watching us. The imperative of this new symbolic order, generated by gadgets is: "Work harder!," but at the same time: "Enjoy life to the full!"— "Never enough!"

Thus, in the global society of late capitalism, science is producing a new type of entities, functioning as object of anxiety and desire, as object *a*: electronic gadgets, pervading the lifeworld with their unnoticeable, vibrating, Hertzian waves, relying on the manipulation of symbols, creating a new, artificial environment, which Lacan refers to as the "alethosphere" (Lacan's version of what Teilhard de Chardin referred to as the "noosphere"). Things like microphones connect us to the alethosphere, and even astronauts floating in space, Lacan argues, although they have left the geosphere and the atmosphere, are still connected with the alethosphere, with "Houston," via gadgets, representing the human voice, but in an inorganic version, detached from the body, as object *a* (p. 188). The world is increasingly populated by these gadgets (p. 185), these tiny objects *a*, which we encounter everywhere, in institutional building and in shopping malls, pervading the global metropolitan environment (Zwart 2020b).

Lacan also refers to them as "lathouses," a jocular, mock Heideggerian portmanteau term, combining "ousia" (being) with "aletheia" (truth) and oblivion ("lethe") to indicate how these pervasive technological entities proliferate as objects of jouissance, proving unsatisfactory in no time. Consumers want them, they desperately need them, and they desire the latest versions of them, but in the end, these electronic commodities exploit and consume their consumers, rather than the other way around, continuously registering and disseminating information, without being aware of them (Millar 2018, 2021). They produce and circulate data on a massive scale, functioning as the neo-liberal form of knowledge about what consumers want (as indicated, for instance, by their click-behavior, captured by search algorithms). They represent algorithms which are running wild in the world (Possati 2020). Although we usually cannot directly see them, we intuit their presence, so that the idea that we are surrounded by gadgets causes anxiety. While allegedly supporting enjoyment and freedom, they de facto confront consumers with normalcy standards, societal expectation, informing them that they must work harder on themselves and keep a close watch on themselves, to optimize psychic and somatic functioning and to postpone the real impacts of unhealthy life-styles and ageing.

References

Aydin, C. (2021) *Extimate technology: Self-formation in a technological world*. New York: Routledge.

de Kruif, P. (1945/1948) *The male hormone*. New York: Harcourt & Brace.

de Saussure F. (1916/1968) *Course de linguistique générale*. Paris: Payot.

Freud, S. (1910/1943) *Über der Gegensinn der Urworte. Gesammelte Werke 8*. London: Imago.

Freud S. (1913/1940) *Totem und Tabu. Gesammelte Werke IX*. London: Imago.

Freud S. (1920/1940) *Jenseits des Lustprinzips. Gesammelte Werke XIII*, 1–70. London: Imago.

Freud, S. (1930/1948) *Das Unbehagen in der Kultur. Gesammelte Werke XIV*, 419–506. London: Imago.

Freud, S. (1950) *Aus den Anfängen der Psychoanalyse. Briefe an Wilhelm Fliess, Abhandlungen und Notizen aus den Jahren 18871902*. London: Imago

Lacan, J. (1949/1966) Le stade du miroir comme formateur de la fonction du Je, telle qu'elle nous est révélée dans l'expérience psychanalytique. In: *Écrits* (pp. 93–100). Paris: Éditions du Seuil.

Lacan, J. (1953–1954/1975) *Le Séminaire I: Les Écrits Techniques de Freud*. Paris: Éditions du Seuil.

Lacan, J. (1955–1956/1981) *Le Séminaire III: Les psychoses*. Paris: Éditions du Seuil.

Lacan, J. (1959–1960/1986) *Le séminaire VII: L'éthique de la psychanalyse*. Paris: Éditions du Seuil.

Millar, I. (2018) Black Mirror: From Lacan's lathouse to Miller's speaking body. *Psychoanalytische Perspectieven*, 36 (2), 187–205.

Millar, I. (2021) *The psychoanalysis of artificial intelligence*. London: Palgrave.

Possati, L.M. (2020) *Algorithmic unconscious: Why psychoanalysis helps in understanding AI*. Palgrave Communications. DOI: 10.1057/s41599-020-0445-0.

Sloterdijk, P. (2009) *Du musst dein Leben ändern. Über Anthropotechnik*: Suhrkamp.

Wallon H. (1949/1954) *Les origines du caractère chez l'enfant. Les préludes du sentiment de personnalité* (3ᵉ Ed.). Paris: Presses Universitaires de France.

Žižek S. (2016/2019) *Disparities*. London: Bloomsbury.

Zwart, H. (1995) "Ik ben een machine... Over het Cartesiaanse gehalte van de Freudiaanse Zelfconceptie". In: H. Hermans (red.) *De echo van het ego: over het meerstemmige zelf. Annalen van het Thijmgenootschap*, Vol. 83 (2). Baarn: Ambo, pp. 49–80.

Zwart, H. (1998) Medicine, symbolization and the 'Real Body': Lacan's understanding of medical science. *Medicine, Healthcare and Philosophy: A European Journal*, 1 (2), 107–117.

Zwart, H. (2012) On decoding and rewriting genomes: A psychoanalytical reading of a scientific revolution. *Medicine, Healthcare and Philosophy: A European Journal*, 15 (3), 337–346.

Zwart, H. (2017) 'Extimate' technologies and techno-cultural discontent: A Lacanian analysis of pervasive gadgets. *Techné: Research in Philosophy and Technology*, 21 (1): 24–54. DOI: 10.5840/techne20174560

Zwart, H. (2019a) Psychoanalysis of technoscience: Symbolisation and imagination. Series: Philosophy and Psychology in Dialogue. Berlin/Münster/Zürich: LIT Verlag. ISBN 978-3-643–91050-9. Series: Philosophy and Psychology in Dialogue. Volume 1.

Zwart, H. (2019b) *Purloined organs: Psychoanalysis of transplant organs as objects of desire*. New York: Palgrave MacMillan/Springer Nature. ISBN 978-3-030–05354-3

Zwart, H. (2020a) Iconoclasm and imagination: Gaston Bachelard's philosophy of technoscience. *Human Studies*, 43, 61–87. DOI: 10.1007/s10746-019-09529-z

Zwart, H. (2020b) *Styles of thinking*. Series: Philosophy and Psychology in Dialogue. Berlin/Münster/Zürich: LIT Verlag. ISBN 978-3-643–96300-0

Zwart, H. (2021) *Continental philosophy of technoscience*. Series: Philosophy of Engineering and Technology. Dordrecht: Springer.

8

FOUCAULT'S CARE OF SELF

A Response to Modern Technology

Hannah Lyn Venable

Concerns over the proper relationship between us and technology continue to be at the fore-front of modern minds. Our ever-increasing reliance on technology, especially throughout the Covid-19 pandemic, has only heightened the anxiety about the right way to incorporate technology into our daily lives. While we value the convenience that technology offers, we admit with regret how we rely on technology for far too many things including not only our intellectual needs, but also our relational and spiritual needs. But, we ask with a sigh, how can we survive without it? How can we participate in the modern world without staying connected through the latest technologies? We know that there are shortcomings that come from this way of life, but we have become so inundated by technology that we can no longer point them out; our numbness means that we can no longer discern between the harmful and healing effects of technology.

I believe that French philosopher Michel Foucault offers us a fresh way to approach mod-ern technology through his understanding of a proper care of self. Toward the end of his life, Foucault grew increasingly attracted to the question of what kinds of technologies make up a care for the self. To answer this question, he traces the idea of "care of self" across history, beginning in Plato's *Alcibiades* and continuing to the modern era; at the advent of modernity, however, he discovers that the historic "care of self" is reduced to a "knowledge of self." Foucault criticizes this limited notion of care of self because it is based on a narrow understanding of subjectivity, where the human is characterized solely as an acquirer of knowledge. I will argue that the modern prioritizing of self-knowledge over self-care brings to light the way contemporary technology often undermines a holistic care of self by fueling our modern obsession with knowledge.

Some may criticize turning to Foucault to address issues in the philosophy of technology, because they see his work as unrelated to the concrete reality of present-day technology and as an ambiguous commentary at best. It is indeed true that, while Foucault explicitly em-ploys technological language throughout his philosophy, it is not initially clear how this ter-minology applies to the use of technology in a more narrow sense. Moreover, it can also be conceded that the context for his technological references often appear rather "ambivalent," as Michael Behrent points out, such that we are unsure whether Foucault is advocating or criticizing technological usage (2013, p. 56). And yet, I believe that it is precisely his broad understanding of technology and his openness to the advantages and disadvantages

DOI: 10.4324/9781003195849-11

of technology that allow him to speak into the use of modern technology in a unique way. Other scholars have also seen the great benefit in applying Foucault's thought to modern technology (Behrent 2013; Bergen and Verbeek 2021; Dorrestijn 2012; Feenberg 1991; Gerrie 2007; Hernández-Ramírez 2017; Ihde 1991; Jacobsen 2015; Matthewman 2011). Jim Gerrie has even argued that an "apt title for the field of Foucault's work might be that of the Philosophy of Technology" (2007, p. 1).

In this chapter, I will first demonstrate how Foucault's notion of "care of self" implies a fuller understanding of subjectivity that acknowledges the self as placed in a relation to technologies but also free to choose technologies to shape itself. Second, I will describe Foucault's account of the modern reduction of "care of self" to "knowledge of self" in order to expose many of the weaknesses found behind contemporary technologies. Third, I will consider how "care of self" helps distinguish between harmful and healing technological practices and how this leaves room for ways that modern technologies might contribute to a holistic care of self. I will be drawing mostly on Foucault's later works, especially his lectures at the Collège de France in early 1982 entitled *The Hermeneutics of the Subject* as well as his seminar at the University of Vermont in the fall of 1982 entitled *Technologies of the Self* (Foucault 2005, 1988a). Following Foucault's lead, I will be using the terms "care of self" and "self-care" interchangeably and "knowledge of self" and "self-knowledge" interchangeably.

Care of Self

After placing the notion of "care of self" in Foucault's writings in general, I will define technology of self and how this makes up a historical care of self as seen in Plato's *Alcibiades*. From there, I will argue that these analyses provide a rich understanding of a holistic care of self that embraces a full notion of subjectivity.

Care of Self in Foucault's Writings

In tracing the structures of psychology, madness, knowledge, language, punishment, power, and sexuality, Foucault may seem initially unconcerned with the human subject, and yet, as he later explores, the shifts in these structures are ultimately significant in the way they shape the subject. It is precisely the bracketing of the subject which allows him to expose just how the structures of history impact the subject and how the subject itself comes to be reciprocally constituted in dynamic relation to these forces. For this reason, the subject becomes more explicit in his later writings due to his increasing concern about the way "the individual constitutes and recognizes himself *qua* subject," as he writes in his second volume on sexuality (1990, p. 6). In looking back on his earlier work, he insists that the subject has always been central to his philosophy: "Thus, it is not power, but the subject, which is the general theme of my research" (1983b, p. 209). (For further discussion on the implied subject in Foucault, please see Venable 2022, pp. 182–184.)

It is important to note that the actual phrase "care of self" was used for Foucault's third volume on sexuality titled, *The Care of Self* (*Le Souci de soi*), published in 1984 just before his death (Foucault 1988b). However, this book does not describe the notion of care of self in general, but rather applies it to particular sexual practices during Roman times. Foucault appears to have been gathering material for a book on the more general notion of care of self as is evidenced by his 1982 lectures. In an interview in April of 1983 at Berkeley, Foucault discusses this future book:

Reading Seneca, Plutarch, and all those people, I have discovered that there were a very great number of problems about the self, the ethics of the self, the technology of the self, and I had the idea of writing a book composed of a set of separate studies, papers about such and such aspects of ancient, pagan technology of the self.

(Foucault 1983a, p. 230)

He further states that this book would focus explicitly on care of self: it would be something "separate from the sex series" and "composed of different papers about the self—for instance, a commentary on Plato's *Alcibiades* in which you find the first elaboration of the notion of *epimeleia heautou*, 'care of self'" (1983a, p. 231). Unfortunately, Foucault died before completing this book, so we must look to the themes of care of self in his published writings as well as his explicit discussion of it in his later lectures.

Defining Technology of Self

In these later works and lectures, Foucault describes care of self as something that is made up of technologies of the self; the types of technologies chosen indicate the particular style of caring for the self. The English word "technology" can be represented by both the French "*technologie*" and "*technique*," and Foucault uses these terms interchangeably, as Behrent details at length (2013, pp. 58–60). Foucault draws on the notion of the Greek *techne*, meaning an art or craft, and views technology/technique as the art, craft, method, or practice by which an individual constructs himself or herself; these technologies are not self-created but are found in the relation of the individual to society. Foucault states: "These practices are nevertheless not something invented by the individual himself. They are models that he finds in his culture and are proposed, suggested, imposed upon him by his culture, his society, and his social group" (1997, p. 291). Technologies can vary in their impact on the individual— some are presented merely as proposals or suggestions, while others can place a heavy strain on the individual—but in each case, the individual always has the choice of whether or not to take up the models in the practical construction of the self.

These technologies can manifest intangibly, as seen in social norms or behavior guidelines, but also be substantiated materially, as seen in types of machines or tools. In *Technologies of the Self*, Foucault lists four types of technology that we can identify in human society: first, technologies of production as shown in the transformation or manufacturing of things; second, technologies of sign systems as shown in language and symbols; third, technologies of power as shown in the domination and objectification of individuals; and fourth, technologies of self as shown in transformation of bodies, souls, thoughts, behaviors of individuals for particular life goals (1988a, p. 18). The first two are fairly straight-forward and Foucault does not spend much time on them: technologies of production can be seen in any kind of making of things, such as the creation of factories for production of goods, and technologies of signs can be seen in any development of language, such as the changes in the French language over time.

The third type, the technologies of power and domination, is a central theme in Foucault's work. In *Discipline and Punish*, for example, he uses the word "*technique*" more than any other place in his writings (Kelly 2013, p. 512; see also Behrent 2013, pp. 84–87). Here he describes the political technology of the Panopticon prison which enables constant surveillance of the prisoners by a central guard booth; the material architecture of the building manifests in the immaterial ways that bodies and souls are controlled. Foucault writes that this technology "is a way of making power relations function in a function," meaning that the mechanism of the building exerts power over the prisoners from the inside functions of the institution (1997, p. 207). An example of the fourth type of technology, technology of self, can be seen in his final volume on sexuality. Here he writes of the medieval Christian practice of virginity which took up the bodily practices of the early church, such as types of clothing worn and rules of conduct, but placed them in a larger narrative of spiritual marriage resulting in the "development of very complex technologies of the self" for monastic life (2021, pp. 188–189).

All of these types of technologies are interconnected and "hardly ever function separately," as Foucault insists (1988a, p. 18). As a result of this overlap, he adds provocatively that all technologies must have a "certain type of domination" in them. We may want to resist this claim at first because it appears to make technology into something that *determines* the shape of the individual or society and gives little regard to human freedom. Foucault actually confesses that he has perhaps "insisted too much on the technology of domination and power" and desires to emphasize the importance of human freedom (p. 19). One way that we overcome this problem is by seeing that "domination" does not always mean one person or one group controlling an individual, but can also indicate the way an individual controls the self; Foucault speaks of this as the "technologies of individual domination, a history of how an individual acts upon himself, in the technology of self" (p. 19). In fact, it is the coming together of techniques of domination and self that we find the deep notion of subjectivity, the self-constitution of the subject. "The individual-subject," as Frédéric Gros accurately states, "only ever emerges at the intersection of a technique of domination and a technique of the self" (Gros 2005, p. 526).

Thus, when we examine the technologies of self, we are able to see the unique way that a human individual is transformed into a self-possessed subject. It is the technologies of self, as Foucault states, that

> permit individuals to effect by their own means or with the help of others a certain number of operations on their own bodies and souls, thoughts, conduct, and way of being, so as to transform themselves in order to attain a certain state of happiness, purity, wisdom, perfection, or immortality.
>
> *(1988a, p. 18)*

Andrew Feenberg provides an excellent description of how the individual is found in the midst of a variety of technologies, manifesting in both material and immaterial ways, by which to construct the self:

> According to Foucault, power/knowledge is a web of social forces and tensions in which everyone is caught as both subject and object. This web is constructed around techniques, some of them materialized in machines, architecture, or other devices, others embodied in standardized forms of behavior that do not so much coerce and suppress the individuals as guide them toward the most productive use of their bodies.
>
> *(1991, p. 71)*

Often coming from a source of power and knowledge, these techniques create a web or "matrix," as Foucault calls it, of relations where all individuals are placed (Foucault 1988a, p. 18). And yet, even though these technologies are already there, they are not necessarily forcing individuals to be shaped in a particular way, but rather serve as guides to the construction of the self and can be oriented toward a particular goal by an individual.

To fully define technology of self, we need to return to the beginnings of care of self (*epimeleia heautou*) in Plato's *Alcibiades*. (While *epimeleia heautou* first appears in *Alcibiades*, Foucault is careful to document the way the notion grew from practices preceding it; Foucault 2005, pp. 46–51.) Here we discover how the technologies of self are directed toward one specific goal, care of self, and Foucault suggests three themes in *Alcibiades* which describe a full care of self. First, care of self is necessary in order for a successful political life. To help Alcibiades begin a prosperous political career, Socrates offers him philosophical love; this is the first step in caring for the self, as Foucault writes: "The intersection of political ambition and philosophical love is 'taking care of oneself'" (1988a, p. 24). Socrates has to first convince Alcibiades "that if he really wanted to fulfill his political ambition... then first of all he had to pay a bit of attention to himself" (2005, 419).

The second theme displays how care of self can help correct defective education. After Alcibiades finally admits to Socrates that he is in a rather bleak place both morally and politically due to his education, Socrates replies to him: "But don't lose heart. If you were fifty when you realized it, then it would be hard for you to cultivate yourself [*epimelêthênai sautou*], but now you're just the right age to see it" (Plato 1997, p. 585, line 127e). The Greek verb, *epimelêthênai*, and the Greek noun, *epimeleia*, is a compound of the verb "to attend to" (*melô*) and the prefix "upon" (*epi*), meaning that the cultivating or caring is always directed or oriented upon something. This type of caring is not simply a state of mind, but is found in intentional action; it is a "real activity and not just an attitude" demonstrating that care of self requires the participation of the whole person (Foucault 1988a, p. 24). By starting now, Alcibiades can correct his education if he engages his entire self in his intentional activity.

The emphasis on the whole person leads us to the third theme of care of self, which is the most important aspect for Socrates: care of self allows one to know oneself, to have a deeper knowledge of one's soul. This caring for the soul, however, is not a kind of maintenance of something, as if it were an object, but expresses itself in the "care of the activity" itself (Foucault 1988a, p. 25). The holistic activity envisioned here involves choosing the right technologies of self that will help the soul thrive.

Pursuit of Proper Care of Self

With this definition of technology of self and the description of care of self found in Plato's *Alcibiades*, I will now introduce what I am calling a "holistic care of self" that can be gleaned from these reflections. Drawing on Foucault's three themes from *Alcibiades*, we find that care of self must include many facets of the human experience: the thread of social and political community (first theme), the thread of education including both intellectual as well as physical training (second theme), and the thread of contemplation or spiritual exercises (third theme). Each of these threads is woven together to create an activity of care for the person as a whole.

This holistic care of self is ultimately motivated by an aesthetic concern, a desire to create the self as a work of art. Technologies of self can be called "arts of existence," as Foucault puts it, defining them as:

> intentional and voluntary actions by which men not only set themselves rules of conduct, but also seek to transform themselves, to change themselves in their singular being, and to make their life into an *oeuvre* that carries certain aesthetic values.
>
> *(Foucault 1988b, pp. 10–11)*

Humans are motivated not only to regulate their lives, but to transform their lives into something beautiful; when seeking after a proper care of self, we choose technologies that we hope will sculpt our lives into a pleasing and delightful shape. We are not creating out of nothing, as Mark G.E. Kelly explains well: "Self-constituting of subject is not the subject producing itself out of thin air… but rather shaping what is already there" (2013, p. 514). Subjectivity, then, must understood aesthetically where we constitute ourselves by drawing on the given historical practices and conditions that are already placed in front of us.

With the emphasis on *self*, we may be concerned that this does not include a care for others. But in fact, there is a relation with others that is necessarily included in the holistic care of self in two ways. First, one of the purposes of caring for the self is so that Alcibiades can be successful in politics; in other words, the fruit of caring for the self will be seen in one's relationships with citizens and political leaders. Second, embedded in care of self we find the technology of *parrhêsia*, or truth-telling; it is a "frankness, open-heartedness, openness of thought" (Foucault 2005, p. 169). As Foucault argues, this idea of *parrhêsia* can be traced across history demonstrating that there has historically been an emphasis on telling the truth to yourself and to others included in care of self. (Although Foucault introduces this in *The Hermeneutics of the Subject*, he explores it even further in his lectures the following year, *The Government of Self and Others*.) The practice of *parrhêsia* displays a link between care of the self and care of the city; in other words, when one takes part in telling the truth about the self, it will not only affect the self but the city as well. (See, for example, Foucault's discussion on the relationship between Ion's identity and the city of Athens; 2010, pp. 97–100 and the link between the fate of Pericles and the city; pp. 175–177.) The ideas of self-care and truth-telling are then "complementary practices" where, as Gerald Posselt puts it, they are "neither detachable from each other nor reducible to each other" (2021, pp. 4, 9). A holistic care of self, then, will be beneficial to others in that the proper care of self overflows onto the care of others; the best care of self will be the best care of others.

In this first section, we found that a technology of the self is a kind of method or tool, material or immaterial, positive or negative, used to constitute a self. Through awareness of being placed in a matrix of social and historical forces, individuals gain the freedom to take up technologies and shape their lives according to a particular goal. Care of self, then, contains various technologies of the self and, in order for individuals to practice a holistic care of self, they must seek out healthy technologies of self which address the social, political, bodily, intellectual, and spiritual facets of human experience.

The Reduction of Care of Self to Knowledge of Self

Care of self emerges in *Alcibiades* and is carried on through the Greco-Roman age and into the Christian era. After *Alcibiades*, Foucault traces a line of continued emphasis on care of self throughout the next millennium and argues that care of self "permeates all Greek, Hellenistic, and Roman philosophy, as well as Christian spirituality, up to the fourth and fifth centuries A.D" (Foucault 2005, p. 11). In his 1982 lectures, Foucault goes through a series of examples from pagan Greco-Roman practices to early Christian practices to demonstrate this continued stress on the care of the self. During the Middle Ages, the idea of care of self slowly undergoes structural changes but Foucault does not give us an in-depth analysis past the fifth century. (This historical project will hopefully be continued by others in an effort to see what kind of care of self arises during this time.) Rather, after "leaping over several centuries," Foucault turns to the seventeenth century to see the radical break that has occurred in the understanding of care of self (Foucault 2005, p. 17). In the seventeenth century,

Foucault argues that care of self becomes eclipsed by knowledge of self; now, we only care about the thread of knowledge and have lost the other threads of care. In this section, we will look at this shift by first defining knowledge of self and then describing Foucault's two reasons for why care of self has been reduced to knowledge of self.

The concept of self-knowledge finds its roots in the Delphic proverb of "Know thyself" (*gnôthi seauton*) which was inscribed in temples of Apollo and was frequently employed by Socrates. Arising out of this Socratic context, knowledge of self is a kind of activity by which a person learns who he or she is through varying technologies of the self. Historically speaking, self-knowledge focuses on the way the mind accesses truth in order to reveal knowledge of the self through various technologies of the self. When understood as one part of the care of the self, the mind's pursuit of self-knowledge is a healthy and proper activity. The problems arise when self-knowledge is seen as the sole access to truth, and all other aspects of care of self are ignored. The human, as a result, is perceived only as a thinking mind, and truth is seen only as abstract knowledge, which leaves behind other ways that the human can access truth, such as through the body, the soul, and the socio-political environment.

Although these problems do not come to the surface until the modern era, Foucault argues that there are seeds in *Alcibiades* which privilege self-knowledge over a more general care of self. It is these Platonic seeds, for Foucault, that eventually sprout in the modern era which limit care of self to knowledge of self:

> The dialogue of the *Alcibiades* shows... the specifically Platonic 'covering up' of the *epimeleia heautou* by the *gnôthi seauton* (of the care of the self by knowledge of self). Self-knowledge, the requirement 'know yourself' completely covers up and occupies the entire space opened by the requirement 'take care of yourself.'
>
> *(2005, p. 419)*

Following Foucault, we will identify a shift that takes place outwardly in morality, but arises from an inward philosophical change; this is what ultimately brings about the honoring of knowledge of self over care of self in modernity. (Some have argued that Foucault's interpretation of *Alcibiades* is not expansive enough; see Joosse 2015.)

Beginning in the realm of morality, Foucault argues that the modern age brought about a paradox between self-care and asceticism. This clash between a focus on the self and the renunciation of the self results in care of self losing its positive quality and being dismissed as selfish or retreating:

> Thus, we have the paradox of a precept of care of the self which signifies for us [in the modern age] either egoism or withdrawal, but which for centuries was rather a positive principle that was the matrix for extremely strict moralities.
>
> *(Foucault 2005, p. 13)*

Today, we interpret care of self according to one of two extremes: either we see it as self-absorption, because the focus is only on our own self-interests, or self-denial, because we have to give up all kinds of bodily pleasures. Both of these seem unpalatable to the modern person and so instead of basing morality on care of self, as in the past, we now found morality on the obedience of external laws, as opposed to inner laws of the self (1988a, p. 22).

This moral change is derived from the philosophical shift that takes place in philosophy; this philosophical change is "much more fundamental than these paradoxes of the history of morality" (Foucault 2005, p. 14). In particular, the Cartesian moment marks a decisive break from the previous way of doing philosophy and places all the significance on a thinking mind. The phrase, "the Cartesian moment," is rather cliché—or, as Foucault puts it, it is "a bad, purely conventional phrase"—and yet, it does provide a helpful point in time in which to identify this philosophical shift. Speaking in broad terms, Foucault summarizes: "The 'Cartesian moment'... functioned in two ways... by philosophically requalifying the *gnôthi seauton* (know yourself), and by discrediting the *epimeleia heautou* (care of the self)" (2005, p. 14). Care of self becomes discredited because there is no longer a place for spiritual practices of the subject, but only for theoretical practices. Foucault writes that the Cartesian moment "made the 'know yourself' into a fundamental means of access to truth" (p. 14). Foucault is careful to clarify that such a change does not take place at a single point, but through a gradual movement away from spirituality and then is formalized in the Cartesian moment (p. 26).

The themes of holistic self-care have been overlooked in our traditional approaches to history, because of this modern fixation on self-knowledge. We have forgotten the themes that began with the Greeks which did not equate self-knowledge with self-care:

> There has been an inversion between the hierarchy of the two principles of antiquity, "Take care of yourself" and "Know thyself." In Greco-Roman culture knowledge of oneself appeared as the consequence of taking care of yourself. In the modern world, knowledge of oneself constitutes the fundamental principle.
>
> *(Foucault 1988a, p. 22)*

To combat this inaccurate understanding of history, we must uncover the full historical sense of care of self. Foucault concludes his 1982 lectures with the following:

> What I have wanted to show in this year's course is... that the historical tradition... has always privileged the *gnôthi seauton*, self-knowledge, as the guiding thread for all analyses of these problems of the subject... By only considering the *gnôthi seauton* in and for itself alone we are in danger of establishing a false continuity and of installing a factitious history that would display a sort of continuous development of knowledge of self.
>
> *(2005, p. 461)*

In our interpretation of history, we use the idea of self-knowledge as the guide by which to analyze the practices and technologies of Western tradition. But in so doing, we create a false narrative of history that misses the way humans were cared for as bodily creatures situated in relation to society, not just thinking minds.

Ultimately, Foucault desires to reveal the lost narrative of holistic care of self which has been overlooked in the modern age:

> We allow an... undeveloped theory of subject to run behind it all... The principle of *gnôthi seauton* is not autonomous in Greek thought. And I do not think we can understand either its specific meaning or history if we do not take into account this permanent relation between knowledge of self and care of the self in ancient thought. Care of the self... is not just a knowledge.
>
> *(p. 461)*

This kind of analysis is clearly part of Foucault's main project: to expose the missing gaps, the missing threads of history and the hidden structures behind the construction of individuals and societies. If we see only a history which privileges self-knowledge, we will lose the undeveloped strain of self-care which has run beneath it, and thus have a limited notion of the human.

To summarize this second section, we began by historically tracing the themes of self-care and self-knowledge and found that self-knowledge at its Greek origin used diverse technologies to gain access to truth in its care of self. Next, we located the source for the reduction of care of self to knowledge of self in an ideological shift in the spheres of morality and philosophy. Understanding this modern break from the holistic care of self will help us identify the motivations behind modern technology and its uses, which, as I will argue, uncritically continues this glorification of self-knowledge over self-care.

Foucaultian Response to Modern Technology

Although Foucault is not generally known as a philosopher of technology, as mentioned at the beginning, there is a recent movement called "postphenomenology" which occasionally draws on his writings to discuss technology (Bergen and Verbeek 2021; Dorrestijn 2012; Ihde 1991). Postphenomenology "brings together the phenomenological approach and the ontological commitments of the American pragmatist tradition" and has a particular focus on issues related to modern technology (Rosenberg and Verbeek 2015, p. 1). Those in postphenomenology see their project as similar to Foucault's because they are pushing back against a stark distinction between the human and technology and are viewing the human, not as a fixed essence, but made-up of different sets of technologies. Steven Dorrestijn, for example, writes that because Foucault "argues against a fundamental dividing line between what is human and what is technical," we can discover an "ethics of technology" that acknowledges our hybrid being, our being that is composed of "human and technical aspects" (2012, pp. 234, 226). (There are many similarities between postphenomenology and another movement in the philosophy of technology called the Actor-Network Theory (ANT). Steven Matthewman makes a persuasive argument for a complementarity between Foucault and ANT on technology as well; 2011, pp. 116–120.)

There has been a prodigious amount of work done by those in the postphenomenology movement on the relations between humans and specific technologies; however, I believe that their approach sometimes misinterprets Foucault's understanding of the human and misses the important link between the technologies of self and care of self. For example, Dorrestijn specifically overlooks this connection in his article on Foucault when he writes that "technology is absent" in Foucault's later works of subjectivation and ethics (2012, p. 239). (There is an exception, however, in a recent article by postphenomenologists Rosenberg and Verbeek [2015], who apply the self-care of Foucault to the use of a to-do list app.) If we ignore the way that technologies can be oriented either toward a poor care of self or a proper care of self, then we no longer have a way of discerning what kinds of technologies contribute to human flourishing. Certainly, Foucault does not establish a fixed human essence, but he also assumes that there is a consciousness of the human already there that we can shape. This is why he emphasizes the importance of the subject in his work and "the way human being turns him- or herself into a subject" by taking what is already there and constructing it in a particular direction (Foucault 1983b, p. 208). Kelly writes, "[Foucault's] position is not that the existence of consciousness is historically variable. Rather, his position is that it is the way we relate to our consciousness that varies" (2013, p. 515). In contrast to the postphenomenologists, I will take seriously a full subjectivity that arises from Foucault's care of self, which we established earlier, in order to discuss the way we relate to ourselves through contemporary technology.

To do so, I suggest referring to the following questions based on the three themes from *Alcibiades* when we assess modern technology: first, how does this technology contribute to my engagement in social and political community?; second, how does this technology contribute to my intellectual and physical education?; and third, how does this technology facilitate contemplation and spiritual disciplines? Due to the modern shift from self-care to self-knowledge, I will show that many modern technologies focus primarily on a reduced notion of intellectual education (second theme) while ignoring aspects in the first and third themes. This is seen in the way that access to knowledge is clearly mediated by modern technology such that our knowledge of world, knowledge of others, and knowledge of self are limited by our reliance on technology. After this critique of modern technology, I will then suggest that a more holistic understanding of self-care can, in turn, identify healthy ways of using technology by looking at two areas: physical wellness and spiritual wellness. I believe that by considering these specific themes of human experience and by placing humans in a web of technological relations, we can identify more accurately how technologies may bring about harm or healing.

As an aside, I will continue to use the term "knowledge" in this critical section, because it is the term used by Foucault and others in philosophy of technology. However, it is important to note that we are no longer using "knowledge" in its full sense, but have relegated it to something like gaining "information," as Esther Meek argues (2011, p. 8).

Critique of Modern Technology: Examples of Obsession with Self-Knowledge

Modern technologies are designed to help us obtain facts and data about the world. Internet access provides information instantly on almost any question related to history, geography, science, cooking, gardening, pet care, shopping, dating, parenting, and more. While this access to information offers many benefits both practically, in the way we learn about the world, and personally, in the way we can live in the world, we must consider ways that our encounter with the world will be limited if we believe that this is sufficient. All technology, in the broad sense of crafts or tools, has certain limitations, but in this section, we will be thinking in terms of technologies of the digital age, which often limit our access to the world to private consumption of information.

Thinking about a place, we may feel that we know a location after viewing online pictures and videos, and while this will tell us many things, it is not the same as an experience of being immersed in an environment. Browsing through pictures of the south island of New Zealand or even watching a documentary on the filming of *The Lord of the Rings* teaches us about the terrain of New Zealand. These give us visual pictures and information about the country, but it does not compare to taking a "tramp" (hike) on the trails near a glacier or skiing down the mountains. Once we glean the difference between seeing a place in a picture and fully knowing a place, we can gather the way technological experiences typically reduce our knowing to one aspect of human experience, the acquiring of knowledge through the limited sights and sounds presented in the media. Other ways of experiencing a place, that would perhaps give us an even deeper sense of it, have been eclipsed.

Reliance on information on the Internet for geography can have social consequences as seen in the growth of certain conspiracy theories. For example, due to easy distribution of information, there has been rise in the belief in a flat earth (Picheta 2019). As a result of numerous blogs, YouTube videos, Facebook groups, and other media, more and more people are becoming believers that the earth is actually flat and that the photos and stories of a round earth are fabricated by world leaders. Although there are many reasons for this phenomenon, we find here an assumption that knowledge must come from "unbiased" online sources, resulting in a de-personalization of knowledge. The priority of technological sources pushes people to disregard other ways of learning about the world that would point to a spherical earth including physical experiences of star-gazing or watching boats disappear on the horizon or the direct testimonies from a community of scientists.

In less extreme ways, we may find that using digital texts to teach us about the world also caters to this over-emphasis on knowledge-gaining. The effect of reading a text digitally, as Philipp Rosemann elucidates, limits the experience to a silent visual experience; he writes, "A digital text speaks only to one of our five senses, vision; it cannot be touched or smelled like the pages of an old book" (2014, p. 9). An old book, for example, does not just give us information about the world, but can help us experience the world through the physical activity of reading. This is seen even more clearly in a liturgical manuscript which is designed to engage all five senses including the visual sense, with the sight of colored words; the auditory sense, with the words being read aloud; the olfactory sense, with the text being incensed prior to the reading; the tactile sense, with the feeling of textures and raised words on the page; and taste, both in the kissing of the book itself and with the eating of the bread after the reading (Venable 2021, p. 8). While the experience of reading a physical book will not always be this intense, the contrast helps us see the way modern technology imposes certain limits on our knowledge of the world.

In addition to modern technology mediating our knowledge of the world, technology also mediates our knowledge of others. We may assume that we "know" a person because we have read a Facebook profile or a questionnaire filled out on a dating website; this then defines the person according to the limiting structures of such technology rather than interactive life experiences. Text messages are another way to construct a person's identity based on technology; by deriving knowledge of a person from what he or she communicates in a text message, we cannot arrive at full idea of the character of the person. For example, a person may feel freer to express romantic feelings or a desire for a relational commitment in a text message, but may not have the confidence to follow through with such intentions in reality.

Even in video chats, while one can learn about the physical mannerisms and verbal style of a person, one cannot gain full knowledge of the other person's style of movement and, more importantly, style of life. In these interactions, there is, as Gabriel Marcel calls it, a lack of "presence" of the other which is something that goes beyond a mere knowledge of them (Marcel 2002, p. 33). This is seen in a contrast between the practice of a virtual liturgy and the practice of a full liturgy, as I explored in another article:

> When watching a virtual service, I can feel as if I am only a receiver: the liturgy is in front of me and I take from it what I can. My actions while watching the service do not impact or change the way the liturgy is performed. However, when I am present in my body with the other believers, my actions of singing, praying, raising my hands or kneeling can influence those around me just as those around me in turn inspire me.
>
> *(Venable 2021, p. 12)*

There is still a possibility of experiencing the presence of others and the presence of the divine through virtual technological means, but there is a certain richness and depth of experiencing the other that may be lost.

Both of the above two areas, knowledge of world and knowledge of others, are impacted by our modern obsession with knowledge of self, in as much as we are depending on technology to dictate what kind of world and what kind of people surrounds the self. With an over-dependence on these technologies, we allow technology to mediate the way that we come to know the self which is often done in private, divorced from a social environment. All of these practices of learning about the world—whether through online scenic pictures, geography blogs, or digital texts—and practices of learning about others—whether through social media profiles, text messaging, video chats, or virtual liturgies—are all part of the matrix of relations in which humans find themselves. Recognizing the structure of instrumentalized knowledge underlying the use of these modern technologies helps us see the possible harm that they can do to an individual in limiting one's understanding of self-care.

Hope for Modern Technology: Examples in the Use of Care of Self

Although modern technology is dominated by the drive to gain knowledge, is there a way in which modern technology could facilitate a care of self? Can we find any evidence of this in our current technological world? In this final section, I would like to mention two possible trends in technology which may encourage the movement toward greater care of self.

One of the facets of human experience generally excluded from technology is physical wellness, an element in the second theme of self-care, and yet there seems to be a growing number of technologies being created to address this. Beginning with the introduction of the Wii Fit games in 2007, video games have increasingly incorporated physical exercise into their design (Goodall 2020). During the pandemic, this phenomenon has only grown, with more video games created to encourage the use and exercise of the body (Strauss 2020).

The development of the Apple Watch is another example of a technology that has paid more attention to the care of the body. The watch contains ways of tracking how many steps one takes a day and how many calories one has burned; it also monitors one's heart rate and reminds one to stand up at least every hour. Surprisingly, one of the goals behind the creation of the Apple Watch was to pull people away from technology, as David Pierce reveals in his article, "iPhone Killer: The Secret History of the Apple Watch:"

> Our phones have become invasive. But what if you could engineer a reverse state of being? What if you could make a device that you wouldn't—couldn't—use for hours at a time?... You could change modern life. And so after three-plus decades of building devices that grab and hold our attention—the longer the better—Apple has decided that the way forward is to fight back. Apple, in large part, created our problem. And it thinks it can fix it with a square slab of metal and a Milanese loop strap.
>
> *(Pierce 2015)*

It's been almost seven years since the introduction of the Apple Watch and the verdict is still out whether or not it is distancing people from their devices. The interesting point, however, is that one of the goals in its creation was due to the realization of the need for technologies which focus on a more holistic self-care, the care of the body.

In addition to physical wellness, there are also modern technologies aimed at spiritual wellness, an important element in our third theme of care of self. Most recently, the creators of prayer apps for smart phones hope to encourage the spiritual discipline of prayer. These apps allow the user to choose a prayer from a list of different authors and topics and then be guided through an audio prayer with accompanying music. One prayer app called Abide, for example, seeks to engage the human through many different senses: sight (reading the accompanying Scripture or devotional thought), sound (listening to the voice and music of the prayer), and even movement (closing eyes or kneeling). Furthermore, during Covid, there have been many technologies that have allowed virtual streaming of church services; although it is not the same as being there in person, as mentioned earlier, these services are for the purpose of promoting spiritual connection between members of a religious community.

By placing each of these technologies—exercise video games, smart watches, prayer apps, and online church—in the matrix of human experience, we will find that they are still limited in the way they care for the self and can be harmful if overly relied upon. And yet, in contrast to the motivations often found behind modern technology, these technologies offer possible healing to individuals and contribute to elements in a proper self-care.

As opposed to judging technology based on pragmatic criteria, as some postphenomenologists do, I believe that using an ethical understanding of self-care allows us to deeply discern the complex ways technologies influence our lives. In this limited set of examples, we saw that while a primary concern of modern technologies is securing knowledge about the world, others and the self, there are trends in recent technologies that at least appear to contribute to more holistic care of self in the areas of physical and spiritual wellness.

Conclusion

In this chapter, we have seen how Foucault's analysis of care of self uncovers a fuller account of subjectivity that has been partially lost due to the radical alteration that has taken place in the modern age. Although a holistic care of self characterized both ancient and medieval technologies of self, the modern age reduced care of self to knowledge of self. Here we unearthed a dominant force behind the production of many contemporary technologies: an obsession with self-knowledge. We, as moderns, may feel that if we consume enough knowledge about our world and our friends through technology, then we will have full and satisfying lives, but, as we have seen from Foucault's analysis, this type of living can hardly be spoken of as flourishing. By drawing on a deeper sense of care of self, we can discern, for better or worse, the way technology impacts one's relation to others, as seen in the importance of the socio-political sphere, the body, as seen in one's physical training, and the soul, as seen in spiritual practices.

Unexpectedly, Foucault's lectures in the 1980s offer us a timely response to the technology of the twenty-first century. Rather than feeling overwhelmed by the way that technology has invaded our daily lives, we can apply Foucault's work in specific ways to evaluate our use of technology. First, we can heed his warning to examine and critique seriously those technologies of the self which limit the full expression of human experience. But second, we can be challenged not to dismiss modern technology in its entirety, but to discover technologies that are designed according to a fuller understanding of subjectivity and that promote a care of self which is holistic, aesthetic, and communal.

(I would like to thank Philipp Rosemann, Jared Schumacher, and Kathleen Kirsch for their helpful feedback on this chapter.)

References

Behrent, M. (2013). Foucault and Technology. *History and Technology: An International Journal*, 29, no. 1, 54–104.

Bergen, J., & Verbeek, P. (2021). To-Do Is to Be: Foucault, Levinas, and Technologically Mediated Subjectivation. *Philosophy & Technology*, 34, 325–348.

Dorrestijn, S. (2012). Technical Mediation and Subjectivation: Tracing and Extending Foucault's Philosophy of Technology. *Philosophy & Technology*, 25, no. 2, 221–241.

Feenberg, A. (1991). *Critical Theory of Technology*. Oxford: Oxford University Press.

Foucault, M. (1983a). On the Genealogy of Ethics: An Overview of Work in Progress. In H. Dreyfus & P. Rabinow (Eds.), *Michel Foucault: Beyond Structuralism and Hermeneutics, Second Edition, With an Afterword by and an Interview with Michel Foucault* (pp. 229–252). Chicago: The University of Chicago Press. (This can also be found here: Foucault, M. (1997). On the Genealogy of Ethics: An Overview of Work in Progress. In P. Rabinow (Ed.), *The Essential Works of Michel Foucault, 1954–1984, Volume 1: Ethics, Subjectivity and Truth* (pp. 253–280). New York: New Press.)

Foucault, M. (1983b). Afterword: The Subject and Power. In H. Dreyfus & P. Rabinow (Eds.), *Michel Foucault: Beyond Structuralism and Hermeneutics, Second Edition, With an Afterword by and an Interview with Michel Foucault* (pp. 208–228). Chicago: The University of Chicago Press.

Foucault, M. (1988a). *Technologies of Self: A Seminar with Michel Foucault*. In L. Martin, H. Gutman & P. Hutton (Eds.). Amherst: The University of Massachusetts Press. (This can also be found here: Foucault, M. (1997). Technologies of Self. In P. Rabinow (Ed.), *The Essential Works of Michel Foucault, 1954–1984, Volume 1: Ethics, Subjectivity and Truth* (pp. 223–251). New Press.)

Foucault, M. (1988b). *The History of Sexuality, Volume III: The Care of Self*. R. Hurley (Trans.). New York: Vintage Books.

Foucault, M. (1990). *The History of Sexuality, Volume II: The Use of Pleasure*. R. Hurley (Trans.). New York: Vintage Books.

Foucault, M. (1997). The Ethics of the Concern of the Self as a Practice of Freedom. In P. Rabinow (Ed.), *The Essential Works of Michel Foucault, 1954–1984, Volume 1: Ethics, Subjectivity and Truth* (pp. 281–301), New York: New Press.

Foucault, M. (2005). *The Hermeneutics of the Subject: Lectures at the Collège de France 1981–1982*. F. Gros (Ed.). G. Burchell (Trans.). New York: Palgrave Macmillan.

Foucault, M. (2010). *The Government of Self: Lectures at the Collège de France, 1982–1983*. F. Gros (Ed.). G. Burchell (Trans.). New York: Palgrave Macmillan.

Foucault, M. (2021). *The History of Sexuality, Volume IV: Confessions of the Flesh*. R. Hurley (Trans.). New York: Vintage Books.

Gerrie, J. (2007). Was Foucault a Philosopher of Technology? *Techné: Research in Philosophy and Technology*, 11, no. 7, 1–7.

Goodall, R. (2020 Oct 14). Concept to Console: A History of the 'Wii Fit' Franchise. *The Boar*. https://theboar.org/2020/10/concept-to-console-a-history-of-wii-fit/

Gros, F. (2005). Course Context. In M. Foucault, *The Hermeneutics of the Subject: Lectures at the Collège de France 1981–1982* (pp. 507–550), New York: Palgrave Macmillan.

Hernández-Ramírez, R. (2017). Technology and Self-Modification: Understanding Technologies of the Self After Foucault. *Journal of Science and Technology of the Arts*, 9, no. 3, 45–57.

Ihde, D. (1991). *Instrumental Realism: The Interface between Philosophy of Science and Philosophy of Technology*. Bloomington: Indiana University Press.

Jacobsen, K. (2015). *The Politics of Humanitarian Technology: Good Intentions, Unintended Consequences and Insecurity*. Bloomington: Routledge.

Joosse, A. (2015). Foucault's Subject and Plato's Mind: A Dialectical Model of Self-Constitution in *Alcibiades*. *Philosophy and Social Criticism*, 41, no. 2, 159–177.

Kelly, M. (2013). Foucault, Subjectivity, and Technologies of the Self. In C. Falzon, T. O'Leary & J. Sawicki (Eds.), *A Companion to Foucault* (pp. 510–525). Hoboken: Blackwell Publishing.

Marcel, G. (2002) *Creative Fidelity*. R. Rosthal (Trans.). New York: Fordham University Press, 2002.

Matthewman, S. (2011). *Technology and Social Theory*. New York: Palgrave Macmillan.

Meek, E. (2011) *Loving to Know: Covenant Epistemology*. Eugene: Cascade Books.

Picheta, R. (2019, Nov 18). The Flat-Earth Conspiracy Is Spreading around the Globe. Does It Hide a Darker Core? *CNN*. https://www.cnn.com/2019/11/16/us/flat-earth-conference-conspiracy-theories-scli-intl/index.html

Pierce, D. (2015, April). iPhone Killer: The Secret History of the Apple Watch. *Wired*. https://www.wired.com/2015/04/the-apple-watch/

Plato. (1997). *Alcibiades*. In J. Cooper (Ed.), *Complete Works* (pp. 557–595), Indianapolis: Hackett Publishing Company.

Posselt, G. (2021). Self-Care and Truth-Telling: Rethinking Care with Foucault. *Le foucaldien*, 7, no. 1, 10, pp. 1–15.

Rosemann, P. (2014, Sept 26). 'Tell Me How You Read, and I Will Tell You Who Are.' Human Subjectivity in the Digital Age [Lecture] Instituto Tecnológico Autónomo de México, Álvaro Obregón, D.F., Mexico.

Rosenberg, R. & P. Verbeek. (2015). *Postphenomenological Investigations: Essays on Human-Technology Relations.* Lanham: Lexington Books.

Strauss, E. (2020, Dec 28). Fitness Video Games Can Break Your Covid Pandemic Exercise Slump. *CNN.* https://www.cnn.com/2020/12/17/health/fitness-video-games-covid-pandemic-wellness/index.html

Venable, H. (2021). The Weight of Bodily Presence in Art and Liturgy. *Religions*, 12, no. 3, 164, pp. 1–14.

Venable, H. (2022). *Madness in Experience and History: Merleau-Ponty's Phenomenology and Foucault's Archaeology.* New York: Routledge.

9

MARY SHELLEY'S FRANKENSTEIN

Reflections on the Other as Monster

Robert D. Romanyshyn

Introduction

Throughout the 1980s my growing concern about the impending nuclear crises led to my first book, *Technology as Symptom and Dream* (Romanyshyn, 1989), where I described the cultural-historical conditions at the origins of our scientific and technological worldview. In the intervening decades our expanding technological powers have increased to the point that we now face multiple ecological, ethical, medical, economic, and political crises. *Victor Frankenstein, the Monster and the Shadows of Technology: The Frankenstein Prophecies* (Romanyshyn, 2019), re-tells that story of origins. Reading Mary Shelley's story, *Frankenstein; or the Modern Prometheus* (1818/1984), as a collective dream that haunts the imagination, this chapter is a case study of the lethal nature of denial of responsibility for one's action.

Fifty years of practice as an existential-analytically oriented therapist underscores how the art of the question opens a space for unconscious dynamics. Applying this format of questions, my recent book attends to the so-called Monster's untold tale on the margins. As the shadow side of Victor Frankenstein's Promethean dream to be a new god of creation, the Monster is the one who unmasks Victor Frankenstein's dream as our nightmare and forces us to face the fundamental question, "Who is the Monster?"

With this question, *Frankenstein, the Monster, and the Shadows of Technology: The Frankenstein Prophecies* is a work of anamnesis, of unforgetting as a first step toward a call to remember and be remembered and transformed. Attending to this question posed on the margins of the collective mind, this chapter shows how the prophetic character of Mary Shelley's story is a foundation for a radical new ethics which, in making a place for unconscious dynamics, undercuts Victor Frankenstein's denial of responsibility for his actions. In addition, it suggests that the work of remembering and being re-membered can be a political act of resistance and rebellion which questions the unquestioned assumptions of our technological world view.

Unconscious Dynamics

In *The Philosopher and His Shadow*, Merleau-Ponty (1964b) emphasizes the necessity of a dialog between phenomenology and depth psychology. To reflect, he writes, is to unveil an unreflected dimension, which is at a distance because we are no longer in it in a naive way,

DOI: 10.4324/9781003195849-12

yet which we cannot doubt that reflection attains, since it is through reflection itself that we have an idea of it. So, it is not the un-reflected which challenges reflection; it is reflection which challenges itself. In short, it is through consciousness that the philosopher comes to understand that there is an unconscious shadow in our thinking. Paul Ricoeur will later make the same point but in a more challenging way. In his essay *Consciousness and the Unconscious*, he writes:

> For someone trained in phenomenology, existential philosophy, linguistic or semilogical methods, and the revival of Hegel studies, the encounter with psychoanalysis constitutes considerable shock, for the discipline affects and questions anew not simply some particular theme within philosophical reflection but the philosophical project as a whole.
>
> *(Ricoeur, 1974, p. 99)*

Both statements pose a demand for a kind of ethics which would establish procedures that take reflection's challenge to itself deeper into that challenge. The ethical demand here is to secure procedures that help consciousness descend into the un-reflected that grounds reflection. Merleau-Ponty and Ricoeur acknowledge that phenomenology by itself does not achieve that; it points the way. Depth psychology meets that demand. The phenomenologist and the depth psychologist are obliged to meet at the abyss for this descent.

Making a place for unconscious dynamics not only uncovers the question "Who is the Monster" to be at the heart of Mary Shelley's story, it also shows that her story is a parable for our time because its prophetic implications haunt the shadowy unconscious depths of the technological world we have created.

A Visionary Text

Although Mary Shelley finished her story in 1818, it is not done. In this regard, her story is an example of what Jung calls a visionary work. Describing a visionary work as one which detects what is on the way, Jung adds it is a work where the spirit of the depths lingers below the spirit of the times in which it was written. There is unfinished business in such texts as Shakespeare's plays or the tale of Don Quixote's impossible dream by Miguel Cervantes.

The spirit of the depths that haunts Mary Shelley's story is carried by the Monster, so called by Victor Frankenstein because he never names his creation but only curses him as devil, demon, and monster. Born within a waking dream as Mary Shelley tells her readers, the Monster is the epitome of Lucifer, the fallen angel, and the Other to the God in the Christian story of creation.

The psychological tension between these two figures which plays itself out in her story is a residue that continues to haunt us in the disguise of the crises spawned by our abuse of what we take to be our god like powers over the natural world. The ongoing destruction of the rainforests, the increasing acidity of the oceans which are destroying coral reefs and endangering marine life, as well as the melting polar ice caps that threaten island nations and coastal cities around the globe are only a few examples. All these crises are collective symptoms reminding us we have forgotten that we have placed ourselves outside the natural order, and, indeed, have forgotten we have forgotten:

This call to remember is now acute as the Covid-19 virus continues to mutate and imperil all of us. It is a profound wakeup call because it is becoming increasingly clear that using the term zoonotic to describe viruses obscures our role in their evolution. Whether Covid-19 originated in the wilderness, or wet market, or a lab, our imprint is present. There is no ecological niche which does not include us, despite our belief that we stand apart from the natural order. The unsettling consequence of this fact is that we are the portal through which sars-CoV-2 entered the world. If we are to understand this crisis, our attitudes toward the natural world must be part of the equation.

The visionary genius of Mary Shelley's story is that it personifies our role in these crises in the figure of Victor Frankenstein whose godlike attitude not only cuts him off from the natural world, but also severs his ties to his family and the human community. The tragedy of Shelley's story is that Victor Frankenstein realizes that his attitude has produced monstrous consequences only as he is dying.

> The summer months passed while I was thus engaged, heart and soul, in one pursuit. It was a most beautiful season; never did the fields bestow a more plentiful harvest, or the vines yield a more luxurious vintage: but my eyes were insensible to the charms of nature.
>
> *(Shelley as cited in Oates, 1984, p. 49)*

The irony in Mary Shelley's story is that the "Monster" is educated by the wonders of the natural world, drawn into self-awareness by those same charms of nature that his maker denies. In this regard, the Monster and Victor Frankenstein are one character whose face has two sides, a point which was dramatically portrayed in 2011 at the National Theater in London when Benjamin Cumberbatch and John Lee Miller alternated roles.

Inspired by that image, I wrote and staged a play at Pacifica Graduate Institute in 2015 in which the actor wore a mask with Victor Frankenstein on one side and the Monster on the other side. On the side that shows the Monster, the actor recites this passage from Milton's *Paradise Lost*:

> Did I request thee, Maker from my clay
> To mould me man? Did I solicit thee
> From Darkness to promote me?
>
> *(Shelley as cited in Oates, 1984, p. 159)*

The words are those that the Monster himself embodies in his encounters with his maker, his presence continuously challenging Victor Frankenstein with the question, "Who is the Monster?," a question whose prophetic currents underscore her original story to be at the heart of the many ways in which the question of the Other is prefigured in the Monster. On the side that shows the face of Victor Frankenstein, the actor tells us that the story in which he is dreamed into being by Mary Shelley presents him not only as the new version of the Christian God of creation, but also as the modern version of the mythic Prometheus as indicated in the full title of her story: *Victor Frankenstein; Or, the Modern Prometheus*. Her title, he says, announces that he is not like Prometheus. On the contrary, the title asserts that he, Victor Frankenstein, is the modern version of Prometheus. At that moment the actor turns the face of the Monster toward the audience and says that he is the child born of his maker's Promethean dream to create life and rid humankind of the stain of death. The curtain falls with these words as darkness fills the stage.

In the spirit of the times in which Mary Shelley wrote her story, Victor Frankenstein, using the powers of the new science of electricity, would not only erase death from the human condition, but would also resurrect and reanimate dead tissue. For this gift to humanity, he would be praised as their savior, repeating the tale of Prometheus whose theft of fire from the gods made him the creator of humankind. In Mary Shelley's story, myth becomes a pro-phetic fiction. In the laboratories of science and technology, her story portends a new story and image of resurrection and of paradise once lost and now found. In the guises of Monster and Victor Frankenstein/Prometheus, the dichotomies of Christ and the Devil, light and dark, solar and lunar consciousness, good and evil, spirit and flesh continue as a cautionary tale about the destructive consequences of a creator god and the creature he has made and abandons.

To bridge these dichotomies, we need to attend to the Monster's tale that haunts the margins of Victor Frankenstein's story. Like the fallen Angel Lucifer, whose name means the bearer of light, the label monster applied to the creature who is not named by his maker signifies an omen, a warning brought by one who causes us to reflect. This chapter works on the margins of Mary Shelley's story. Reading her story from the Monster's point of view opens a space where we can lend an ear to the spirit of the depths where the Monster tells his tale. His tale speaks today to all who are exiled to the margins, whose voices are silenced, whose stories are still untold.

Marginal Questions

In the hermeneutic circle, the reader of a text is also read by the text. When one makes a place for unconscious dynamics, the circle becomes a double spiral, like two cones placed together at their upper edges. Each spiraling descent into the text is also a spiraling ascent that simultaneously preserves and transforms the previous descents. As I discovered during my reading of Mary Shelley's story from the Monster's point of view, the hermeneutic spiral gives rise to three kinds of questions. First there are those questions which I posed to the text. These questions were typically straight forward, concerned with details like the place where Shelley was when she wrote it and who was with her as she proposed to her companions the challenge to write a ghost story. The second type of question arose from the text itself in those moments when the text surprised me and stopped me in my tracks. On occasion, I found that I had slipped into a reverie unaware of the passage of time. I also noted that such moments were often marked by some passages I had underlined or by notes written on the edges of a page, leaving, as it were, marginal traces of such moments. Such traces, I realized, were also traces of who I was at those moments, reflecting the differences between the reader I was then and the reader that I had become. Am I the same one who made those marks? Or do those traces mark me as someone other to myself? When one reads a book for a second time is it the same book as before? If we cannot step into the same river twice, can we read the same book twice? Historians and biographers make use of these traces, finding within them the material for their research.

Quite different from these first two types of questions, the third kind of question arose from the margins of the text. They were questions that not only stopped me in my tracks, but also turned me inside-out or upside-down. In such moments, I was no longer the one asking the questions, but the one being questioned by those whose story is untold in the text, the questions that attend to the spirit of the depths. With Mary Shelley's text it was and is the question at the heart of the margins—Who is the Monster?—posed by the Monster. This question which he amplified with the eight additional questions structured the format of my marginal reading of Mary Shelley's text. If we are to hear the Monster's untold tale, then we are obliged to attend to the questions he poses to us. (The theme of each question is followed by the Monster's amplifications which are in italic type to differentiate them from my words about Mary Shelley's text.)

The Monster as Emblematic of the Other

Question 1: Is Mary Shelley's story a prophecy of the dangers of acting as gods?

In this question the Monster asks if we are aware of the dangers of acting as if we are gods. His creator certainly illustrates those dangers particularly when Victor Frankenstein, progressing from re-animating dead tissue to infusing life into a corpse composed of multiple body parts, reacts with excitement when he believes he has finally succeeded in creating life, but then turns away with horror, disgust, and despair. Shocked by the ugly, disfigured, and monstrous thing that stares back at him, Victor Frankenstein flees from the hideous creature he has made and abandons him.

Conceived in the convoluted caverns of his maker's mind, the creature appeals to us form his exile on the margins:

> Can you imagine what it must feel like to be seen as an abomination of nature, a motherless monster who, when abandoned by his maker, is an orphan condemned to wander alone on the edges of the human community, an unwanted Other?

Question 2: Is Mary Shelley's story a prophecy of the dying of nature?

This question points us toward his creator's disregard of the natural world inviting us to wonder if that attitude already assumes the deadness of nature. Calling us to wander with his maker as he enters the sacred ground of churchyard cemeteries where the dead are buried and mourned, he asks:

> What happens to us, when such sacred places are now merely profane spaces where bodies deprived of life are interred? Imagine living a human life without any sense of being a part of the animate, living spirit of the natural world.? If my creator is an emblem of a materialistic, utilitarian attitude, then what does it mean to die? Have we created a sense of nature as alien, as Other to ourselves?

Question 3: Is Mary Shelley's story a prophecy of the Monster's descendants?

In the third question a tone of sorrow replaces the challenging tones of the first two questions. Alone, without any companions, he reminds us of his continuous appeals to his maker to create for him one like himself with whom he would not immediately be rejected as Other.

> Look deeply within yourself. Can you discover there the ways in which I am like you, and you in some ways are like me? Can you sense a kinship between us, or do you sense an immediate, almost automatic, unconscious disavowal of our differences? Jew, Muslim, Christian, atheist, agnostic; black, brown, white, yellow, red; rich, poor; man, woman, bi, gay, straight, transgender? How many wars have been fought over these differences? How many genocides over them, seeing only the differences as marks of the Other to be exterminated? Should not my scars and disfigured proportions which marginalized me from all be a warning of how easy it is to judge the Monster as Other, and then the Other as Monster?

Question 4: Is Mary Shelley's story a prophecy of creating a new species of humankind?
Question 5: Is Mary Shelley's story a prophecy of the last generations of humankind?

Questions 4 and 5 turn the Monster toward what is on the way. Prophetic in tone they make us wonder and intentionally stir feelings of uncertainty and anxiety about his maker's work.

Do you see that I am the monstrous consequences of a flawed god whose work lives on in ways that are already with you? You have escaped the pull of earth, have loosened the grip of gravity as a psychological bond that connects all of you with what has been your home since the dawn of your creation. What is the dark shadow of this leave taking? Is it also a taking leave of your senses as you fashion a new being—let us name him at least—Homo astronautics? When you see your first home from space, what do you see? A departure or wonder at its beauty and feel appreciation for its nurturing gifts? A farewell or a longing to return? An escape from a planet increasingly polluted by you or a desire to transform your attitude toward the natural world and a sense of homecoming that still lingers?

Pausing for a moment he then asks,

With computer technology, smart phones and other devices that eclipse the local boundaries of space and time, do you understand that you are becoming a species who suffers from terminal identity? Are you aware how at the computer terminal your sense of self as a disembodied image with no haptic sense of the other, is a species who, while seemingly in touch with others, is literally out of touch?

Something like a sense of loss enters his voice as he poses this question.

Might your terminal identity be a harbinger of you becoming one of the last generations of your kind? My maker is not gone. He is now here in even a more persuasive story. Do you see, for example, how the genius of the futurist Ray Kurzweil is dreaming the Promethean dream of my maker to rid life of the stain of death? When he writes that the rate of our computer and genetic advances are well on the way toward transcending the biological body, he also adds that at the point of singularity all human information will be downloaded to the cloud and then we will be as close to becoming god as anyone could imagine? Does Kurzweil's work have a shadow? Is Kurzweil's dream still dreaming Victor Frankenstein's Promethean dream which is now becoming your nightmare?

Question 6: Is Mary Shelley's story a prophecy of being homeless in a wired, webbed, world?

Now as the Monster approaches as a homeless orphan, he asks, "Are you at home in the digital world? Are you adrift in a sea of information, which, having little if any context, submerges you in an everywhere that is a nowhere?"

Describing how he swore to his maker that if he made him a mate, they would never propagate. That was the promise that his maker extracted as a condition for assuaging the creature's loneliness. A tone of sorrow then enters the Monster's voice.

Do you not believe that had he fulfilled his promise to me, our stories—his and mine—would have not been a tragedy? But he broke his promise, and our stories became what they needed to be, a tragedy and a prophetic warning.

As if weakening from conveying his long untold tale, as if giving voice to what has been silenced, he asks,

Are the increasing numbers of world-wide refugees made homeless by the ravages of war and climate change the lost children of my Maker's dream which he feared would be born if he made me a companion? Are they the wandering descendants of my own outcast life as a Monster, a horde of those as Other to be barricaded behind the walls and fences we build?

Question 7: Is Mary Shelley's story a prophecy of a radical ethics?

Without Questions 7 and 8 Mary Shelley's story would be a dystopian vision. In Question 7 the Monster's tale, however, uncovers seeds of hope that are there in her story. Presenting himself as the new Adam who, challenging his maker with the question "Who is the Monster," prefigures historical characters like Adolf Eichmann, who was tried for his creation of the final solution that led to the murder of millions of people. Spoken from the margins, he asks, "Is he not an image of the monstrous consequences of a utilitarian ethics that denies responsibility for those consequences?"

As I am remembering the storm that broke over Hannah Arendt's book *Eichmann in Jerusalem* (1963) where she argued that in projecting the monster onto Eichmann we were failing to look at our own dark shadows, he continues,

> Does this not indicate how difficult it might be to craft an ethics that makes a place for the question—Who is the Monster?—and yet also how necessary? Is not the question of my untold tale—Who is the Monster?—the very seed of a new ethics?

While we are not responsible for our dreams, we are responsible for what we make of them. As we continue to dream Victor Frankenstein's Promethean dream are we not responsible for what we are making of it? As such, "Does not this seed of a new ethics have to be nurtured as a needed corrective to the lethal nature of denial of responsibility that has made Mary Shelley's story of my maker a parable for our time?"

Question 8: Is Mary Shelley's story a prophecy of new beginnings?

In this final encounter with the Monster, has he saved the most surprising part of his tale for last?

> As you have been listening to my story from the margins, do you begin to understand that Mary Shelley's story is a love story? Is not my tale from the margins a contrast about my maker's relation with his bride to be, Elizabeth Lavanza, and my relation to the companion for whom I longed? In this contrast is there not a seed of hope about the redemptive quality of love when it is not corrupted by power?

The questions and dialogs ended here. But as with Mary Shelley's book, finished but not done, the work on the margins of mind continues for all of us.

Nature as the Ultimate Other

We can no more see our own "otherness" than we can see our own faces except through a reflection, to glimpse who we are we have to see ourselves as others see us. We are for each other mirrors which give us back to ourselves. The "I" is fundamentally a "We." Every child, for example, becomes who he or she is through imitation, as Merleau-Ponty describes in *The Child's Relation with Others* (1964a). A mirror, he notes, is an instrument of universal magic in which I am turned into another and the other into oneself.

As a parable for our times Mary Shelley's story is a psychological case study of how unconscious dynamics creates the other as monster exiled to the margins of mind. It is also a prophecy of how these unconscious dynamics function to deny what is "other" in oneself, split off from one's conscious mind and projected onto others. We then see in the other what we disown in ourselves. Jung made this point on the eve of World War I, which is as relevant if not more so now:

> The present day shows with appalling clarity how little able people are to let the other man's argument count, although this capacity is a fundamental and indispensable condition for any human community.... For to the degree that he does not admit the validity of the other person, he denies the 'other' within himself the right to exist—and vice versa.
>
> *(Jung, 1916/1960, Par. 187)*

Repression and oppression are two sides of the same coin so vividly portrayed in the character of Victor Frankenstein. Unable to accept that he is, as Harari (2011) describes him, a flawed god, he does not look within but labels his creation a monster.

It is naïve, however, to think that coming to terms with one's own unconscious dynamics is easy. But if self-examination is the condition for dialog as the foundation for a human community, then, if communities are to be made safe for differences, self-reflection is necessary. This necessity for dialog begins with learning how to listen to the other and cultivating the capacity to imagine their world. This challenge was the core of my doctoral dissertation on racism more than 50 years ago in 1970. Working with a self-described black militant and self-identified white racists, it was evident that it is easier to label and be angry with the other who differs from me. It is so much more difficult to mourn and feel the grief over how we have created the other as monster from within our own darkness.

Since the late 1980s my focus has turned toward what I have explored as the "othering of the natural world." Nature as Other is ground zero for all the other forms of othering that split us off as enemies to each other. Racism, sexism, genderism, culturalism, speciesism, or any kind of "ism" precludes dialog as first step toward change. What I say here is not to deny that these crises are political, social, and economic injustices. That is all too obvious. What I am adding is that all these injustices are also and fundamentally psychological matters, a point that I made at the end of a DVD video about my trip to the Antarctic (2009). Unless, therefore, we change the cultural-historical attitude that splits us off from the natural world and treats it as essentially a resource for our use and even abuse—animals, oceans, forests, habitats, etc.—we will continue down the same road that is depicted in Cormac McCarthy's (2006) apocalyptic novel *The Road*.

100 Seconds to Midnight

In the background of the themes presented in this chapter, we might hear the ticking of the Doomsday clock created to keep track of how close humanity is approaching nuclear Armageddon. In 2019, the clock was set at two minutes to midnight. In January of 2021 it was re-set to 100 seconds to midnight, the closest we have been to this mark since it was created in 1947. Midnight is the moment when the annihilation of the human species and the destruction of nature as we know it happens. Unthinkable? Unimaginable? When the atom bomb exploded over Hiroshima 77 years ago, how many seconds did those living in the city have left in their lives before their annihilation? Whatever the number of seconds they had, they did not know how much time they had left.

But for this chapter, we would know. We would know we have 100 seconds to midnight. What does one minute and 40 seconds to live feel like? Let us imagine it and for one minute and 40 seconds let us sink into the unthinkable! Set a timer to enhance this harrowing experience. When the alarm goes, do not ask for whom the clock ticks, it ticks for you and me and all of us. Do not ask for whom the alarm is sounding, it is tolling for you and me and all of us and all the billon animals burned in the Australian fires, for the dying forests and polluted waters, for all and each of us and those whom we have known and loved and who have been and those who still might be.

The Doomsday Clock is a mirror that shows a disturbing image of the so called new normal that is a measure of our collective insanity. How have we arrived at this point? How do we respond when the alarm wakes us from sleep? Have we been dreaming? Dreams speak the language of unconscious dynamics in terms of images, and regarding such images Jung notes, "The images of the unconscious place a great responsibility upon a man" and "insight into them must be converted into an ethical obligation" (Jung, 1965, p. 193).

In the bodies of knowledge, we create our failure to take into account the presence of unconscious factors, make our epistemologies one-sided, fixed truths and ideological exercises of power. As such, they become expressions of epistemological violence.

We live today not only in the shadow of the bomb, but also in the deepening darkness of environmental collapse as the polar icecaps continue to melt, the seas and oceans become increasingly polluted, the buildup of carbon-based greenhouse gases reach ever higher levels, and raging fires, floods and other weather catastrophes are increasingly destructive, while animal and human habitats are destroyed, and the number of homeless refuges swells almost beyond belief. All the bodies of knowledge we create, like the bodies of those who create them, cast a shadow. To come to terms with the shadow side of our ways of knowing and constructing the world, an ethical epistemology would have to make a place for unconscious dynamics in our ways of knowing the world. Frankenstein is the iconic figure who enacts and embodies technology as a cultural-historical dream that is becoming a nightmare. Coming to terms with our part in this increasingly dire situation is the emergency of our age, the single most important task facing humanity today.

References

Arendt, H. (1963). *Eichmann in Jerusalem: A Report on the Banality of Evil*. New York: Viking Press.

Harari, Y.N. (2011). *Sapiens: A Brief History of Humankind*. New York: Vintage Books.

Jung, C.G. (1916/1960), The Transcendent Function, in *The Structure and Dynamics of the Psyche, The Collected Works of C.G. Jung*, vol.8, Par.187. Princeton, NJ: Princeton University Press.

Jung, C.G. (1965). *Memories, Dreams, Reflections*. New York: Vintage Books.

McCarthy, C. (2006). *The Road*. New York: Alfred A. Knopf.

Merleau-Ponty, M. (1964a). The Child's Relations with Others, in *The Primacy of Perception*. Evanston, IL: Northwestern University Press.

Merleau-Ponty, M. (1964b). The Philosopher and His Shadow, in *Signs*. Evanston, IL: Northwestern University Press.

Ricoeur, P. (1974). Conscious and the Unconscious, in *The Conflict of Interpretations*. Evanston, IL: Northwestern University Press.

Romanyshyn, R.D. (1989). *Technology as Symptom and Dream*. New York: Routledge Publishing.

Romanyshyn, R.D. (2009). *Antarctica: Inner Journeys in the Outer World*. San Mateo, CA: YouTube. https://www.youtube.com

Romanyshyn, R.D. (2019). *Victor Frankenstein, The Monster and The Shadows of Technology: The Frankenstein Prophecies*. New York: Routledge Publishing.

Shelley, M. (1818/1984) *Frankenstein; Or, the Modern Prometheus*. Ed. J.C. Oates. Oakland, CA: University of California Press.

10

LIFEPOWER AS A METAPHOR IN EDITH STEIN'S PHILOSOPHY OF PSYCHOLOGY

Salient Questions for Psychoanalysis and Transhumanism

Gabriel J. Costello

Introduction

Edith Stein's twin treatises "Philosophy of Psychology and Humanities" were composed in 1919 to serve as a *Habilitation* to apply for a position in the University of Göttingen. In her work, Stein investigated the so-called "stream of consciousness" using a sustained metaphor, that of electric current which was a relatively new technology at the time. Stein proposed that there are four phenomenal realms of activity within any human being: the physical, the sensate, the mental, and the personal. Furthermore, these realms, while located in the body, are porous and blend into one another. According to Marianne Sawicki, Stein depicts sentient life in terms of voltage, and coins the word *lifepower* to explain the phenomenon. Transhumanism, which is currently at the frontier of technological debates, has gained traction in recent years and can no longer be viewed as a fringe movement. This chapter will examine both psychoanalysis and transhumanism using Stein's concept of lifepower. It will argue that psychoanalysis and transhumanism share the same monist philosophy that falls short of the richness and complexities of human life proposed by phenomenology. The structure of this chapter is as follows: First, it will outline Stein's study of psychology and her development of the concept of lifepower. Then, it will examine the philosophical underpinning of psychoanalysis as developed by Freud. Next, the origin and philosophy of transhumanism will be explored and it will argue that transhumanism shares the same worldview as psychoanalysis. Furthermore, this section will debate the influence of Freud on the theoretical underpinning of artificial intelligence and transhumanism. Following this, implications for both the disciplines of psychoanalysis and transhumanism will be discussed. Additionally, it will propose a novel connection between Stein's psychological work and Freud's development of psychoanalysis, in the context of their separate collaboration with Rudolf Allers. Finally, this chapter will argue, based on Stein's philosophy of psychology, that the transhumanist anticipation of humans developing posthuman capacities, together with its prediction of a *Singularity*, is grounded on an overly simplistic philosophy of "the human." Consequently, Stein's concept of lifepower, developed during the seminal beginnings of phenomenology,

DOI: 10.4324/9781003195849-13

raises important questions for the both the established discipline of psychoanalysis and the evolving discipline of transhumanism.

Edith Stein: Psychology and Phenomenology

Edith Stein's doctoral thesis "On the Problem of Empathy" was completed under Edmund Husserl in the University of Freiburg in 1916 and awarded "summa cum laude" (W. Stein, 1989). Stein was Husserl's protégé but being a woman of Jewish origin was unable to obtain a university position because of the ideological intolerance of that time. Her doctoral thesis was written during the atheistic phase of her life but it is interesting that she analyzed empathy in the context of the complete psycho-physical-spiritual person (E. Stein, 1989). Here is her own account of how her research on empathy (German *Einfühlung*) resulted from a lecture given by the "Master himself" (Teresia de Spiritu Sancto, 1952).

> Husserl in his course on Nature and Spirit had maintained that an objective external world can only be experienced inter-subjectively (i.e., by a plurality of individual knowing subjects) who are in a position to exchange information with each other, which means that such an experience presupposes other individuals. Husserl, following Theodor Lipps, named this experience "empathy," but did not explain what it consisted of. Here was a gap which was worthwhile filling; I wanted to discover what empathy meant.

It should be noted that some commentators point out that the German word *Geist*, as used by these philosophers, is not accurately translated as "Spirit" which has a mainly religious semantic in the English language. W. Stein states that the German understanding of *Geist* is somewhere between the term Mind and Soul and its philosophical study deals with the creative human spirit. For example, Scheler included such concepts as beauty in his examination of the spiritual. Edith Stein's later life was dramatic both as feminist and as a Carmelite where she continued to correspond with leading Phenomenologists and to publish in the *Journal of Phenomenology* until her death in the gas chamber of Auschwitz in 1942. Martin Heidegger invited Stein to contribute to a special edition of the *Jahrbuch für Philosophie und phänomenologische Forschung* to mark Husserl's seventieth birthday for which she contributed her famous paper "*An attempt to contrast Husserl's Phenomenology and the Philosophy of St. Thomas Aquinas*" (Stein, 1993b). Max Scheler was another important influence on Stein, and she was indebted to his insistence on "bracketing," the exercise of which challenged her to suspend every form of *a priori* prejudice and contributed to her *empathising* with other cultures and beliefs. Both of these philosophers were somewhat disappointed by the Master's tendency toward Idealism in his later work, and continued to identify themselves with the realism of the early Husserl. In Stein's political thought, "any state exists only for the benefit of human beings" and she was convinced that "humanity is fundamentally one community, precious beyond measure" (ICS, 2022). Stein's academic relationship with Heidegger and his philosophy is problematic and this is treated in some detail by Nota (1988). According to Ameriks (1977) "Stein produced a revised and coherent draft of Husserl's manuscripts on time-constitution, a draft that Heidegger later published in his own name as editor and no mention of Stein" (p. 104). See also note 14 on page 8 of *Philosophy of Psychology and the Humanities* (Stein, 2000).

Now I will examine Edith Stein's writings on empathy in more detail given its importance for the understanding of her studies in psychology. Moran (2000) concludes that Stein's doctoral dissertation on empathy represents a dependable guide to Husserl's thinking on the subject which had been alluded to in his work *Ideas II*. Empathy for both philosophers was a "non-primordial experience which reveals a primordial experience. Empathy is not a matter of judgement, reasoning, or ideation in general. It is a *founded* experience" (2000 p. 176). Furthermore, the concept was integral to Husserl's examination of inter-subjectivity and the experience of the other (*Frenderfahrung*). According to Moran (2000, p. 176) he radicalized the problem in the *Fifth Cartesian Mediation*. "The problem is not: how do I understand the other? Rather Husserl's problem is: how is the other *constituted* for me?" Baseheart (1989) speaks of Edith Stein's conviction that "phenomenology was the most appropriate approach to the investigation of the structure of the human person and she gave it her best efforts during her scholarly career" (p. x). But the act of empathizing with the other has also important consequences for understanding our own nature as well as that of others as we become "aware of the levels of value in ourselves by empathizing with persons of our own type" (W. Stein, 1989, p. xxiii). In her thesis *On the Problem of Empathy*, Stein explained her way of thinking: "The world in which we live is not only a world of physical bodies but also of experiencing subjects external to us, of whose experiences we know." Furthermore the "individual is not given as a physical body, but as a sensitive, living body belonging to an 'I,' an 'I' that senses, thinks, feels and wills" (E. Stein, 1989, p. 5). However we should be aware of Sawicki's observation that the English word *empathy* has a narrower and somewhat different connotation than the German *Einfühlung*—see note 128 on page 93 of Stein (2000).

Edith Stein's interest in psychology must be understood in the context of her statement that the course she looked forward to most in the University of Breslau was Professor William Stern's *Introduction in Psychology*. Indeed, she stated that "the four semesters that I studied in Breslau found me occupied principally with psychology" (Stein, 1986, p. 186). Some years later, she requested Professor Stern to assign her a subject for a doctoral dissertation in psychology. The topic that they discussed, based on a paper that she had previously delivered, was the development of the thought process in children. However, she soon abandoned this idea because of, in her estimation, the rigidity the professor's ideas. Nevertheless, the influence of Stern on the development of Stein's philosophy of psychology must not be underestimated and according to Sawicki (2000, p. xiv), she follows her former professor in a number of ways:

> In her emphasis upon developmental psychology, the unfolding or 'blooming' of personal qualities out of a core with innate predispositions; in her insistence upon the priority of person over impersonal 'ego'; in her realism and fondness for real-world examples; in her focus on the energy of life; and in her ambition to reconcile the divergent academic investigations of the physical and the mental or cultural in human affairs. She goes beyond him to complete the power circles running through persons and values but connecting those terms into community.

Arising from her study of both psychology and philosophy, we must take seriously Stein's claim "that the description of empathy within consciousness after the suspension of the existence of empathy, must be the basis for any other dealings with the problem by psychologists, sociologists, or biologists" (W. Stein, 1989, p. xviii). Furthermore she insisted that "psychology is entirely bound to the results of phenomenology" (E. Stein, 1989, p. 22). In another work she claimed "it is one of the functions of philosophy to elucidate the fundamental principles of all sciences [*Wissenschaften*]. What the individual disciplines accept and adopt without questioning from prescientific thinking must be subjected to philosophic investigation" (Stein, 2002, p. 19). In the foreword to her twin treatises "Philosophy of

Psychology and Humanities," Stein set out her aim "to penetrate into the essence of sentient reality and the mind from various sides, and thereby to secure the groundwork for a definition of psychology." This problem had surfaced during her work on her doctoral thesis on empathy (Stein, 2000, p. 1). Now I will examine Stein's concept of lifepower that she coined for her investigation of the philosophy of psychology.

Lifepower as Conceptualized by Edith Stein

According to MacIntyre (2006, p. 112), Stein took the vocabulary of "life-feelings" and "life-power" from Dilthey, whom she shared much common understanding of the subject of empathy. In her work on the philosophy of psychology, she developed a taxonomy (following Scheler) of four phenomenal realms of activity within any human being: the physical, the sensate, the mental, and the personal. Additionally, these realms, while located in the body, are porous and blend into one another. Marianne Sawicki explains: "Thus, the human body itself *is* the interface of matter, sentience, and mind." Stein depicts sentient life in terms of voltage and coined the word *lifepower* (*Lebenskraft*) to designate "our finite but renewable capability for living." The energy exchange across these layers does not stop at the skin. There is a constant mental and sentient connection among people that facilitates the continuous transfer of meaning between individual humans. Table 10.1 shows these layers, which summarizes Stein's "human" as a complex relational phenomenon.

Nevertheless, it is worth noting that Stein considered the personal level to remain the most distinct and important realm as it is the center of free choices and free acts.

Borden (2004) proposes that Stein developed her concept of *lifepower* in parallel with Freud's concept of *libido*.

> According to Stein, the sentient level is ruled by lifepower, which she understands as an enduring property of all living sentient beings, a kind of continuous power that has influxes and outflows. All our experiences "cost" us a certain amount of lifepower; likewise, other experiences may "feed" us lifepower.
>
> *(p. 34)*

Analogous to electric charge, the amount of lifepower can fluctuate depending on what is supplying the lifepower and what is using it up. Borden contends that it is unlikely that Stein was familiar with Freud's work. However, I will argue later that her friendship with Rudolf Allers indicates that it was probable she was *au fait* with the seminal psychological debates in Vienna at that time. There is a similarity between Stein's lifepower analogy and Freud's "hypothesis that there exists some form of mental energy that is spread over the memory traces of ideas like an electric charge is spread over the surface of a body" (Rycroft, 1977, p. xv). Furthermore, Lear (2015, p. 198) concludes that according to

Table 10.1 Phenomenal divisions within the individual (Sawicki, 2000, p. xv)

Phenomenal "realms"	"Layer" of human being
the physical	Matter, physical components of the body
the sensory, the sensate	sentience, the living responsive body
the mental, the intellectual	unindividuated mind, intelligence, spirit
the personal, the individual	individual person, unique personality.

Freud "the aim of the psychic mechanism, as he conceived it, was to discharge pent-up psychic energy, and this discharge was experienced as pleasure." Also, Strupp (1967, p. 13) outlines that the "instinctual energy (called *libido*) is the hypothetical driving force which is conceptualised as motivating all human behaviour." Sawicki (2000, p. xviii) argues that Stein's concept of *lifepower* is phenomenological and is presented with greater philosophical nuance and sophistication than the concept of *libido* postulated by Freud. What is more, she encourages further work on comparing these two concepts which is one of the motivations for this chapter. Now I will introduce the debate on the philosophy of psychoanalysis which will become the basis for my argument that it shares the same worldview as transhumanism.

Freud's Philosophy

The aim of this section is to argue that the philosophical underpinning of Freud's psychoanalysis is essentially monist, meaning that all of reality is really of one kind (McLaughlin, 1999, p. 686). Furthermore, it will include a critique by Rudolf Allers who, I will present later, as an important link between Freud and Stein.

Wollheim (1991, p. xvi) states that Freud reflections on society was influenced by two very general principles, which pulled him in somewhat different directions. They were a belief in the ultimate power of reason and rational argument, and a profoundly low opinion of human nature. According to Wollheim, Freud stated on several occasions, that many human beings were "worthless," due to either their make-up, or in the way they had been formed by society. Strachey (1976b, p. 20) concludes that "behind of all Freud's work, however, we should posit his belief in the universal validity of the law of determinism." He explains this further (Strachey, 1976a, p. 30) saying that Freud's "Project for Scientific Psychology" involved the combination of two disparate theories. The first theory posited that "neurophysiology, and consequently psychology, was governed by chemico-physical laws" (p. 40). The second theory was based on the anatomical doctrine of the neuron, which stated that "the functional unit of the central nervous system was a distinct cell, having no direct anatomical continuity with adjacent cells" (p. 40). However, later according to Strachey, though he certainly never gave up his belief that ultimately a physical groundwork for psychology would be established, the "neurophysiological basis was ostensibly dropped" (p. 41).

Rycroft (1977, p. xx) aligns himself

> with those analysts who have become sceptical about the validity of applying causal-deterministic principles derived from the physical sciences to the study of living beings, who are capable of consciousness and of creative activity; and biological ideas about the nature of instinct.

Lear (2015, p. xv) agrees when he says that "from the perspective of the philosophical tradition, self-consciousness is not simply a special capacity that we humans happen to possess, it constitutes us as the creatures we are." He continues:

> Freud's account of the rise of a moral capacity in humans is broadly Darwinian in structure: he gives an account of how the moral capacity comes to be selected in humans. Such an account shows how a phenomenon—such as the capacity for morality—can arise even though no one chose or designed it.
>
> *(p. 192)*

Stein herself contends that "mechanical causation as an explanation of physical phenomena is not appropriate for explaining *spiritual* phenomena" (Stein, 1989, p. xxiii). Note that the philosophical interpretation of *Geist (spiritual)* is discussed above. According to Craib (2001, p. 5) "Freud defined a core set of beliefs just as one might expect a political leader to develop an ideology and a party. The effect was to leave psychoanalysis with some of the marks of a religious or political movement" and I will take up this subject later in the paper.

I will now introduce a scholar who is an important link between Stein and Freud and whose philosophical critique of psychoanalysis has implications for the philosophy of trans-humanism. Rudolf Allers received his MD from the University of Vienna in 1906 and shortly afterwards started his studies as a psychiatrist. He became interested in the work of Freud, attended his last class, and has been described as a disciple of Freud in the early days of psychoanalysis (Rudolf Allers Bio, 2022). However, he soon became disenchanted with Freud's presentation of psychoanalysis and moved to work with Alfred Adler until they also parted ways after 13 years. Rudolf Allers was a physician, psychologist, and philosopher who published over 600 books and papers, and had a significant influence on Victor Frankl, the originator of Logotherapy. He made important contributions to psychiatry and psychotherapy, particularly in relation to their anthropological foundations. His later trenchant criticisms of Freudian psychoanalysis resulted in him being described by some as "Anti-Freud" (García-Alandete, 2020). However, his critical study of the philosophical underpinning of Freudian psychoanalysis is well argued (Allers, 1941). Consequently, I will present his analysis as a first-hand account that is important to the understanding of Freud's philosophy. According to Allers, there are six axioms of psychoanalysis (p. 48):

1   all mental processes develop according to the pattern of the reflex mechanism.
2   all mental processes are of an energetic nature.
3   all mental processes are strictly determined by the law of causality.
4   every mental phenomenon derives ultimately from an instinct. Instincts are the primary material of mental states.
5   the principle of evolution, as stated in the phylactic evolution of organisms, applies to the development of the human mind in history.
6   the chain of free associations leads back to the real cause of mental phenomena.

Allers concludes that these axioms are compatible only with a materialistic philosophy (p. 100). Furthermore, axiom three "implies the idea that mental processes are governed by the same laws assumed by physics" (p. 58).

> There remained alive in Freud's mind not a little of the implicit trust in science the nineteenth century has cherished and of Auguste Comte's vision of mankind's future. The age of science was, with the Viennese psychologist, a beloved and never abandoned dream.
>
> *(p. 75)*

However, Allers (p. 260) finishes his treatise on his thesis with a positive point regarding Freud's contribution.

> Freud's real achievement is: This discovery that mental treatment is capable of healing bodily troubles, that it may result in a total change in attitudes, has delivered mankind from the bondage of biologism. The dominion of the mind is re-established. It is an

irony of history, that this was, we will not say achieved but started by a man whose whole mentality and whose training made him a materialist.

Rudolf Allers was a friend of Edith Stein and familiar with her writings (Allers, 1958). For example, in 1931 during a lecture trip to Vienna, Stein stayed with the Allers family (Posselt, 2005), and it is reasonable to presume that these great scholars of psychology would have discussed the latest developments in Vienna. Stein was familiar with his publications and referred to them in her work (Stein, 1996). After her death, Allers translated her manuscript *Ways to Know God: The "Symbolic Theology" of Dionysius the Aeropagite and Its Objective Presuppositions,* which was published in 1946 (Stein, 1993a). Allers creates a significant link between Stein's philosophy and Freud's philosophy which is one of the aims of this chapter. This section has critiqued Freud's philosophical basis of psychoanalysis with the conclusion that is essentially monist. The next section will argue that its worldview shares the same premise as transhumanism.

Transhumanism and Its Philosophy

This section will provide a brief introduction to transhumanism and its philosophy. It will present evidence of Freud's influence on seminal transhumanist theorists, and argue that the philosophical underpinning of psychoanalysis and transhumanism shares the monist doctrine that all of reality is fundamentally homogenous (McLaughlin, 1999, p. 686).

According to Tirosh-Samuelson (2011), the term *transhumanism* was coined in 1957 by Julian Huxley who together with J.B.S. Haldane and John Desmond Bernal could be considered as the three horsemen of transhumanism. She points out, with concern, that Haldane "accorded eugenics a major role in shaping the ideal future society" and that Bernal, who like Haldane joined the Communist Part of Great Britain, fantasized "about the future where science would transform all aspects of social life and would replace religion as the dominant social force, primarily through the transformation of the human brain" (p. 21). More recently transhumanist advocates have proposed a dramatic event, which they term as *"the Singularity"* where a new autonomous species will evolve with artificial general intelligence, and when *Robo Sapiens* will surpass *Homo Sapiens* (p. 23). Tirosh-Samuelson is of the opinion that transhumanism has not yet developed a systematic philosophy even though some attempts have been made. For example, philosopher Max More in the 1980s, was instrumental in the development of transhumanist doctrine and in his Extropian Principles states that "We see humans as a transitional stage standing between our animal heritage and our posthuman future" (Extropian Principles, 2022). More (2013) traces the philosophical roots of transhumanism to Enlightenment humanism. He argues that with few exceptions, transhumanists describe themselves as materialists, physicalists, or functionalists. "As such, they believe that our thinking, feeling selves are essentially physical processes" (p. 7). However, he points out that a healthy legacy of the humanist roots of transhumanism is its commitment to scientific method, critical thinking, and openness to revision of beliefs (p. 6). Furthermore, he proposed that "transhumanism, like humanism, can act as a philosophy of life that fulfils some of the same functions as a religion without any appeal to a higher power or a supernatural entity." Bostrom (2011, p. 55) describes Transhumanism as a loosely defined movement that can be seen as a product of secular humanism and the Enlightenment. In an associated debate, Bostrom (2013), defines a posthuman as a being that has at least one post human capacity, in either of three areas: health-span, cognition, and emotion. (While Ferrando distinguishes between Posthumanism and Transhumanism,

I have grouped them together, as I argue, both share an ontology that is fundamentally monist and materialist.)

Ferrando (2019) proposes an even more radical approach to posthuman philosophy; it being "a post-humanism, a post-anthropocentrism, and a post-dualism." As More (2013, pp. 12–13) points out "the utterly unique status of human beings has been superseded by an understanding that we are part of a spectrum of biological organisms and possible non biological species of the future." Furthermore, he identifies some of the core elements of transhumanism, which includes the view that it is "both possible and desirable to overcome biological limitations on human cognition, emotion, and physical and sensory capabilities and that we should use science, technology, and experimentation guided by critical and creative thinking to do so." In the academic debates about the human and the transhuman, More (2011) provides a robust reply in his joust with Don Ihde (2011) over the latter's perceived "idols of transhumanism." Albeit More does admit there is a challenge for transhumanists to go beyond some "shared and rather general views, since transhumanists vary widely in their assumptions, values, expectations, strategies, and attitudes" (More, 2013).

Now, I will present some evidence of Freud's influence on transhumanism. Marvin Minsky has played an important role in the development of Artificial Intelligence and the themes of the Transhumanist vision. He proposes that Freud was a great pioneering AI researcher and his "Project for Scientific Psychology" theorized a neurological turn in psychology that included diagrams very like primitive neural networks (Minsky, 2013). Furthermore, Minsky lauds the importance of Freud's *Interpretation of Dreams* which in Freud own words, is the *via regia*—the royal road—into the unconscious (Freud, 1976). More recently, Bohan (2018, p. 77) argues that Freud "added the new and revolutionary idea of the unconscious mind and challenged the belief in the mind as a unified whole, seeding a theory of consciousness that continues to influence modern AI theory and development." Furthermore, in her discussion on the influence of Freud on Minsky, she concludes that Freud laid the groundwork by showing that "the various components of human nature and intelligence are physical and therefore, by the reckoning of some AI theorists, they could be reverse-engineered and mimicked in non-biological substrates" (p. 80). This section has examined the philosophical basis of transhumanism and the influence of Freud on its development. Now I will discuss some implications of this argument and avenues for further exploration.

Discussion: Salient Questions for the Philosophy of Transhumanism

According to the economist John Kenneth Galbraith (1967), technology is the systematic application of scientific or other organized knowledge to practical tasks. Technology is used "to represent things, action, processes, methods and systems" (Kline, 2002, p. 210). Furthermore, technology influences every aspect of contemporary human life. It affects social and ecological systems and, in Sandler's (2013) deliberation on the ethical aspects of technology, it is described as a "source of power, vulnerability, and inequality." Heidegger (1977, p. 1) provides two statements to answer the question what is technology. For him, it is both a *means to an end* and a *human activity*. The former he calls the instrumental definition and the latter he describes as "an anthropological definition of technology" (p. 2). He goes on to examine the Greek etymology of *techné* and explains that the term "is the name not only of the activities and skills of the craftsman, but also for the arts of the mind and the fine arts" (p. 5). On the dangers of technology, he says, "The threat to man does not come in the first instance from the potentially lethal machine and the apparatus of technology. The actual threat has already affected man in his essence."

Heidegger in his major work *Being and Time* argued that our knowledge and basic ways of encountering the world are obtained through the use of technology rather than by means of its scientific description. For example, a hammer is not just a tool to look at or theorize about but an implement to experience, often unconsciously, in the act of creating something. "Entities in the world are not primarily objects of theoretical cognition, but tools that are 'ready to hand' (*zuhanden*)" (Inwood, 2005, p. 372). Furthermore Kenny (2010) points out in his commentary on Heidegger,

> We are not observers trying, through the medium of experience to gain knowledge of a reality from which we are detached. From the outset we are ourselves elements of the world 'always already being-in-the-world.' We are beings among other beings.
>
> *(p. 820)*

However, Guignon (1999) sees an "anti-humanism" in Heidegger's later works "in the description of technology (the mobilization of everything for the sole purpose of greater efficiency) as an epochal event in the 'history of being,' a way things have come-into-their-own (*Ereignis*) rather than as a human accomplishment. Heidegger's notorious comparison of agricultural production technology with the Holocaust seems to indicate an excessive antipathy towards technology" (Polt, 1999). Sadly, Polt's (p. 174) suggestion "that essays such as '*The Question Concerning Technology*' are effective ways of initiating reflection on the deeper trends that lie behind the terrifying events of our age" seems to be more relevant than ever. Stein has relatively little to say about technology but her comment in relation to the importance of including mathematics and natural sciences in women's education is noteworthy (Stein, 1996, p. 219).

The human mind is manifested in its *works*: in the creations of works of art, of things of daily use, of means by which nature is controlled and modified, that is, by technology, in social and political institutions, and in scientific theories. The anthropological analyses above relate to the study of humankind and therefore invite the examination of the relationship between psychology and technology. Bostrom (2013, p. 37) brings psychology into the discussion of transhumanist philosophy. His work suggests that there might be entirely new psychological states and emotions that our species has not evolved the neurological machinery to experience, and some of these sensibilities might be ones we would recognize as extremely valuable if we became acquainted with them. How we relate to others as persons in a technological society is an important subject and this chapter looks for some clues from the world of phenomenology. In this age of avatars and the Internet of Things (IoT) there is much work to be done. Examining the implications for Stein's work on empathy for technological innovations such as virtual worlds and social networks may be a fruitful avenue to pursue going forward. There is growing interest in the area of virtual machine interaction (Potapova & Rodionov, 2014) and innovations such as Embodied Conversational Agents (ECAs) where "virtual agents expressing empathic emotions toward users have the potentiality to enhance human-machine interaction" (Niewiadomski, Ochs, & Pelachaud, 2008, p. 37). This however is a controversial area requiring debate on the ethical issue surrounding avatars. The last point is of particular importance in research that involves vulnerable populations such as children and people with special needs (Pettersson, 2002).

Now I will present a further proposition, based on my thesis, that I believe requires thoughtful reflection. Stein composed both her doctoral dissertation and her *Habilitation* during the atheistic period of her life. However, Husserl had cultivated an openness to the transcendent among his followers, and encouraged the examination of phenomena such as religion using the phenomenological approach. This is in contrast to the trenchant opposition of both psychoanalysis and transhumanism to the transcendent worldviews. Lear (2015) suggests that "there have been terrible human costs in going along with [Freud] for generations, psychoanalytic institutes refused to train people who admitted to religious belief on the grounds that they were fixated on unresolved infantile wishes." The study of religion is not just a theological task but also belongs to the realm of philosophy as is borne out in *The Oxford Companion to Philosophy* (Honderich, 2005, pp. 802–811). Allers (1941, p. 197) concludes that "naturalism and materialism are necessarily antagonistic to religion." Bostrom's (2011, p. 56) labelling of people opposed to transhumanist views as being members of a "bioconservative camp" exemplifies some of this antagonism. However, More (2013, p. 8) seems to leave the way open for dialog when he concludes that transhumanism fulfills some of the same functions as a religion and also points out that in the *Divine Comedy*, Dante Algieri uses the term *transumanare*, meaning to pass beyond the human, in a religious context. However, the relationship between philosophical reason and religious faith is not a one-way system. Pope John Paul II (1998, p. 8) affirmed of the importance of philosophical reason, or as the ancients called it *orthōs logos, recta ratio*, the study of faith. He goes on to highlight the importance of rational analysis to guard faith from falling into superstition (p. 23). According to Pope John Paul II "faith and reason are like two wings on which the human spirit rises to the contemplation of truth" (p. 3).

A method that could facilitate this dialog is the practice of Husserl's idea of *epoché* (suspension of judgment) which employs a set of procedures that Husserl called "reduction" (from the Latin *reducere* "to lead back"). As Moran (2000, p. 146) explains, it allowed Husserl to detach from such influences as conventional opinion and scientific consensus. "We must put aside our beliefs about our beliefs, as it were." As pointed out earlier, Stein was indebted to this idea of "bracketing," which required her to suspend every form of *a priori* prejudice. Furthermore, the teaching of the earliest philosophers proposed that philosophical inquiry should be undertaken in the context of friendship.

The section has discussed the anthropological implications of technology and argued that questions concerning technology, must consider phenomenological characteristics such as empathy, ethics, beliefs, and emotions, in the context of technology as a human activity. This raises salient questions for both the philosophy of psychoanalysis à la Freud, and the current theoretical basis of transhumanism.

Conclusions

The main thesis of this chapter is that Edith Stein's concept of lifepower, raises important questions for the established discipline of psychoanalysis and the developing discipline of transhumanism. However, it also offers an antidote to the underlying one-dimensional monist worldview shared by these disciplines. Furthermore, this study argues that both psychoanalysis and transhumanism must engage with the complexities of human existence and psychic life proposed by phenomenology. Speaking of psychoanalysis, Lear (2015 p. 207) concludes that it "is within this important project that Freud embeds his own illusion: that science will answer the fundamental question of how to live." Allers (1941, p. 205) argues that while psychoanalysis calls itself a science, "science can make statements only on what is, never on what ought to be." Likewise, Dilthey postulated, "We explain nature, we understand the mind" (quoted in Allers, 1941, p.220). Lear (2015) describes "the idea that morality promotes human happiness or fulfilment is, Freud thinks, exposed as wishful fantasy." This is in contrast to Aristotle's description of *eudemonia* (happiness or well-being) as being achieved by virtuous and moral behavior. Finally, the theme of transcendence was revitalized and cultivated by Husserl and his followers such as Stein. I suggest that we must take seriously Stein's conclusion that "the crisis, in which psychology has found itself since the turn of the century is merely an inescapable consequence of the amazing feat which the psychology of the 19th century performed when it simply discarded the concept of the soul" (Stein, 2002, p. 19).

This chapter has the ambition to link the subjects of "psychoanalysis and technology" by connecting the phenomenological research of Edith Stein, with both Freud's work and the technological concept of transhumanism. The author is conscious of being overly ambitious, with the resulting criticism that such an undertaking can result in a lack of focus. However, given the importance of these disciplines in the contemporary lifeworld, and the very open waters for exploration, the voyage was considered to be worth the risk. For example, Tirosh-Samuelson (2011, p. 41) believes that "all programmes about the extension of human life cannot be divorced from deeper reflection on the purpose of human life." Edith Stein concluded in the early twentieth century: "All my study of psychology has persuaded me that this science is still in its infancy: it still lacked *clear basic concepts*" (Stein, 1986, p. 222). An argument of this paper is that transhumanism, at the beginning of the twenty-first century, still needs to develop *clear basic concepts*, and to do so must engage with realms of philosophy such as phenomenology. Moreover, such an undertaking involves wrestling with the phenomenal complexities of human psychic life. Consequently, Stein's concept of lifepower, developed during the seminal beginnings of phenomenology, raises important questions for the both the discipline of psychoanalysis and the evolving discipline of transhumanism.

References

Allers, R. (1941). *The Successful Error: A Critical Study of Freudian Psychoanalysis*. London: Sheed & Ward.

Allers, R. (1958). Writings of Edith Stein. *New Scholasticism, 32*(1), 132–133.

Ameriks, K. (1977). Husserl's Realism. *The Philosophical Review, 86*(4), 498–519.

Baseheart, M. C. (1989). Foreword to the Third Edition. In *On the Problem of Empathy (The Collected Works of Edith Stein; v. 3)* (pp. ix–xi), translated by Waltraut Stein, Ph.D. Washington, DC: ICS Publications.

Bohan, E. (2018). *A History of Transhumanism*. PhD Thesis, Macquarie University, Department of Modern History.

Borden, S. (2004). *Edith Stein*. London/New York: Bloomsbury Continuum.

Bostrom, N. (2011). In Defense of Posthuman dignity. In G. R. Hansell & W. Grassie (Eds.), *H±: Transhumanism and Its Critics* (pp. 55–66). Philadelphia, PA: Metanexus Institute.

Bostrom, N. (2013). Why I Want to be a Posthuman When I Grow Up. In M. More & N. Vita-More (Eds.), *The Transhumanist Reader: Classical and Contemporary Essays on the Science, Technology, and Philosophy of the Human Future* (pp. 28–53). Chichester: Wiley-Blackwell.

Craib, I. (2001). *Psychoanalysis: A Critical Introduction*. Cambridge/Malden, MA: Polity Press/Blackwell.

Extropian Principles. (2022). The Extropian Principles Version 3.0: A Transhumanist Declaration (c)- 1998 Max More. https://mrob.com/pub/religion/extro_prin.html accessed March 2022.

Ferrando, F. (2019). *Philosophical Posthumanism*. London: Bloomsbury.

Freud, S. (1976). *The Interpretation of Dreams (The Penguin Freud Library Volume 4)*, translated by James Strachey. In J. Strachey, A. Tyson, & A. Richards (Eds.). London: Penguin Books.

Galbraith, J. K. (1967). *The New Industrial State* (2nd Edition). London: Pelican Books.

García-Alandete, J. (2020). Rudolf Allers' Conception of Neurosis as a Metaphysical Conflict. *History of Psychiatry, 30*(1), 21–36. https://doi.org/10.1177/0957154X19877295.

Guignon, C. B. (1999). Heidegger, Martin. In R. Audi (Ed.), *The Cambridge Dictionary of Philosophy* (pp. 610). New York: Cambridge University Press.

Heidegger, M. (1977). The Question Concerning Technology. In W. Levitt (Ed.), *The Question Concerning Technology: And Other Essays* (pp. 3–35). New York & London: Garland Publishing, Inc.

Honderich, T. (Ed.) (2005). *The Oxford Companion to Philosophy* (2nd Edition). Oxford: Oxford University Press.

ICS. (2022). Product Description *"Edith Stein: An Investigation Concerning the State (Collected Works of Edith Stein, vol. 10)*, translated by Marianne Sawicki. https://www.icspublications.org/products/-edith-stein-an-investigation-concerning-the-state-the-collected-works-of-edith-stein-volume-x?_pos=1&_sid=838c6b919&_ss=r accessed February 2022.

Ihde, D. (2011). Of Which Humans Are We Post. In G. R. Hansell & W. Grassie (Eds.), *H±: Transhumanism and Its Critics* (pp. 123–135). Philadelphia, PA: Metanexus Institute.

Inwood, M. J. (2005). Heidegger, Martin. In T. Honderich (Ed.), *The Oxford Companion to Philosophy* (2nd Edition, pp. 371–375). Oxford: Oxford University Press.

Kenny, A. (2010). *A New History of Western Philosophy*. Oxford: Oxford University Press.

Kline, S.J. (2002). What is technology? in R. Scharff & V. Dusek (Eds.), *Philosophy of Technology: The Technological Condition*. Oxford: Blackwell.

Lear, J. (2015). *Freud* (2nd Edition). London: Routledge.

MacIntyre, A. C. (2006). *Edith Stein: A Philosophical Prologue, 1913–1922*. Lanham, MD: Rowman & Littlefield.

McLaughlin, B. P. (1999). Philosophy of Mind. In R. Audi (Ed.), *The Cambridge Dictionary of Philosophy* (p. 915). New York: Cambridge University Press.

Minsky, M. (2013). Why Freud Was the First Good AI Theorist. In M. More & N. Vita-More (Eds.), *The Transhumanist Reader: Classical and Contemporary Essays on the Science, Rechnology, and Philosophy of the Human Future* (pp. 167–176). Chichester: Wiley-Blackwell.

Moran, D. (2000). *Introduction to Phenomenology*. London: Routledge.

More, M. (2011). True Transhumansim: A Reply to Don Ihide. In G. R. Hansell & W. Grassie (Eds.), *H±: Transhumanism and Its Critics* (pp. 136–146). Philadelphia, PA: Metanexus Institute.

More, M. (2013). The Philosophy of Transhumanism. In M. More & N. Vita-More (Eds.), *The Transhumanist Reader: Classical and Contemporary Essays on the Science, Technology, and Philosophy of the Human Future* (pp. 3–17). Chichester: Wiley-Blackwell.

Niewiadomski, R., Ochs, M., & Pelachaud, C. (2008). Expressions of Empathy in ECAs. In H. Prendinger, J. Lester, & M. Ishizuka (Eds.), *Intelligent Virtual Agents Volume 5208 of the Series Lecture Notes in Computer Science* (pp. 37–44). Berlin Heidelberg: Springer-Verlag.

Nota, J. (1988). Edith Stein and Martin Heidegger. *Carmelite Studies, 4*(2), 50–73.

Pettersson, J. S. (2002). Visualising Interactive Graphics Design for Testing with Users. *Digital Creativity, 13*(2), 144–156.

Polt, R. (1999). *Heidegger: An Introduction*. Ithaca, NY: Cornell University Press.

Pope John Paul II. (1998). *Faith and Reason: Encyclical Letter of Pope John Paul II*. London: Catholic Truth Society.

Posselt, T. R. (2005). *Edith Stein: The Life of a Philosopher and Carmelite* (edited by Susanne M. Batzdorff, Josephine Koeppel and John Sullivan). Washington, DC: ICS Publications.

Potapova, A., & Rodionov, S. (2014). Universal Empathy and Ethical Bias for Artificial General Intelligence. *Journal of Experimental & Theoretical Artificial Intelligence, 26*(3), 405–416.

Rudolf Allers Bio. (2022). About Rudolf Allers. https://www.goodreads.com/author/show/2378555.Rudolf_Allers accessed March 2022.

Rycroft, C. (1977). *A Critical Dictionary of Psychoanalysis*. Harmondsworth: Penguin.

Sandler, R. L. (2013). Introduction: Technology and Ethics. In R. L. Sandler (Ed.), *Ethics and Emerging Technologies* (pp. 1–24). Basingstoke: Palgrave Macmillan.

Sawicki, M. (2000). Editor's Introduction. In Marianne Sawicki (Translator) and Mary-Catherine Baseheart (Translator) (Ed.), *Philosophy of Psychology and the Humanities, the Collected Works of Edith Stein* (pp. xi–xxiii). Washington, DC: ICS Publications.

Stein, E. (1986). *Life in a Jewish Family (1891–1916): An Autobiography (The Collected Works of Edith Stein Vol. 1)*, translated by Josephine Koeppel OCD. Washington, DC: ICS Publications.

Stein, E. (1989). *On the Problem of Empathy (The collected works of Edith Stein; v. 3)*, translated by Waltraut Stein, Ph.D. Washington, DC: ICS Publications.

Stein, E. (1993a). *Knowledge and Faith: Translated by Walter Redmond (The Collected Works of Edith Stein; v. 8)*. Washington, DC: ICS Publications.

Stein, E. (1993b). Knowledge, Truth, Being: Translated by Walter Redmond (The Collected Works of Edith Stein; v. 8). In L.Gelber & M. Linssen (Eds.), *Knowledge and Faith*. Washington, DC: ICS Publications.

Stein, E. (1996). *Essays on Woman,* translated by Freda Mary Oben (2nd Edition). Washington, DC: ICS Publications.

Stein, E. (2000). *Philosophy of Psychology and the Humanities.* Washington, DC: ICS Publications.

Stein, E. (2002). *Finite and Eternal Being: An Attempt at an Ascent to the Meaning of Being (The Collected Works of Edith Stein, vol. 9),* translated by Kurt F. Reinhardt. Washington, DC: ICS Publications.

Stein, W. (1989). Translators Introduction. In *On the Problem of Empathy (The Collected Works of Edith Stein; v. 3),* translated by Waltraut Stein, Ph.D. Washington, DC: ICS Publications.

Strachey, J. (1976a). Editor's Introduction. In J. Strachey, A. Tyson, & A. Richards (Eds.), *The Interpretation of Dreams (The Penguin Freud Library Volume 4)* (pp. 9–12), translated by James Strachey. London: Penguin Books.

Strachey, J. (1976b). Sigmund Freud: A Sketch of His Life and Ideas. In J. Strachey, A. Tyson, & A. Richards (Eds.), *The Interpretation of Dreams (The Penguin Freud Library Volume 4)* (pp. 13–26), translated by James Strachey. London: Penguin Books.

Strupp, H. H. (1967). *An Introduction to Freud and Modern Psychoanalysis.* New York: Barron's Educational Series.

Teresia de Spiritu Sancto. (1952). *Edith Stein,* translated from the German by Cecily Hastings and Donald Nicholl. London and New York: Sheed & Ward.

Tirosh-Samuelson, H. (2011). Engaging Transhumanism. In G. R. Hansell & W. Grassie (Eds.), *H±: Transhumanism and Its Critics* (pp. 19–54). Philadelphia, PA: Metanexus Institute.

Wollheim, R. (1991). *Freud* (2nd Edition). London: Fontana.

11

TECHNOLOGY IN TENEBRIS

Heidegger on the Paradoxes of Truth, Freedom, and Technology

William J. Hendel

A Crude Start

What is left to be said about the dangers of technology? No matter where we turn (to news, to film, to idle conversation) we cannot escape instruction in the grimmer aspects of modernity's efficiencies, conveniences, and sheer might. We know quite well that our achievements are compromising our attention spans, our memories, our bodies, and our planet, but such reflections, and any fears they may produce, have done little to alter our behavior. We are loath to part with the smallest contribution to our ease and distraction, and we can only feign an interest in cooling our lust for endless innovation. It would be futile, it seems, to add another admonition on technology, when we have heard them all already, and haven't heard any of them yet.

As Heidegger says in his celebrated essay *The Question Concerning Technology*, "Everywhere we remain unfree and chained to technology, whether we passionately affirm or deny it" (1977b, p. 4). Like death, it is no different whined at than withstood. Space-based warheads, lab-engineered pathogens, and automaton courtesans will all arrive as soon as they can be contrived, and not a moment later. In a 1955 address, celebrating the 175th birthday of composer Conradin Kreutzer, Heidegger tells us why:

> What we know as the technology of film and television, of transportation and especially air transportation, of news reporting, and as medical and nutritional technology, is presumably only a crude start. No one can foresee the radical changes to come. But technological advance will move faster and faster and can never be stopped. In all areas of his existence, man will be encircled ever more tightly by the forces of technology. These forces, which everywhere and every minute claim, enchain, drag along, press and impose upon man under the form of some technical contrivance or other—these forces, since man has not made them, have moved long since beyond his will and have outgrown his capacity for decision.
>
> *(1966, p. 51)*

As science fiction never tires of teaching us, technology is in some essential respect beyond our control. It does not belong to us, so much as we belong to it. With every new discovery,

 DOI: 10.4324/9781003195849-14

with every clever invention, we are bound ever more inextricably to an ungovernable and intransigent power.

We are so inured to this observation that we scarcely notice how odd and even ironic it is. From the instant that the first troglodytes learned what two vigorously rubbed sticks could do to a pile of dry grass, the promise of technology has been freedom. And it has delivered on that promise. It has emancipated us from our uniquely compromised condition—"naked, unshod, unbedded, and unarmed" (Plato, 1997, p. 757)—which distinguishes us from all other creatures. Of course, that is why Zeus, in his wisdom, fastened Prometheus to a rock. The appropriate punishment for a breaker of chains is his own irons. By providing humans with fire and the means to master it through *technē*, Prometheus not only freed us, but made us rivals of the gods themselves. Freud observes in *Civilization and Its Discontents* that "with every tool man is perfecting his own organs, whether motor or sensory, or is removing the limits of their functioning" (Freud, 2010, p. 64). We have overcome our legs with vehicles that can carry us across the world or to the surface of the moon; our eyes, with telescopes and microscopes that can bring us the movement of the stars and the divisions of bacteria; our unreliable memories, with photographs and recordings that capture the ever-vanishing present. It is hardly an exaggeration to say, as Freud does, that

> these things do not only sound like a fairy tale, they are an actual fulfilment of every— or of almost every—fairytale wish... Man has, as it were, become a kind of prosthetic God. When he puts on all his auxiliary organs he is truly magnificent.
>
> *(Freud, 2010, p. 66)*

"But," he hastens to add, with not a little understatement, "those organs have not grown on to him and they still give him much trouble at times" (Freud, 2010, p. 54). Just so. And the trouble they have brought is the very trouble they were fashioned to solve: our natural servitude.

The enigmatic relationship between technology and freedom was something of a late-career fascination for Heidegger. Despite some sobering prognostics, he did not judge the paradox wholly impenetrable or the situation entirely hopeless. In his tribute to Kreutzer, he also said that "we can affirm the unavoidable use of technological devices, and also deny them the right to dominate us, and so to warp, confuse, and lay waste to our nature" (Heidegger, 1966, p. 54). But there is a preliminary difficulty. When he observes that we are increasingly unfree as a function of our modern marvels, he is presenting us with a riddle, clothed in an unassuming platitude. He is not merely emphasizing that we are dependent on, and diminished by, technology, that we are, to use a current example, hopelessly bound to the tiny computers that we carry in our pockets, that we can no longer read maps or spell words or remember facts or phone numbers or even endure an unaccompanied five-minute interval while we wait for our coffee to be brewed. He is not referring to freedom in any of its usual or traditional senses. His is not a freedom to do or escape anything, but rather, a freedom that underlies and makes possible any of the common conceptions of freedom, a freedom that precedes and supports the very operations of human willing, a freedom that is the essence of truth—a freedom that, like technology, is not possessed by man, but possesses him—namely, the freedom "to let be—that is, to let beings be as the beings they are" (Heidegger, 1977a, p. 125). Only when we begin to comprehend this first freedom can we approach our ambivalent and paradoxical relationship to technology.

The Freedom (and Unfreedom) of the Free

Any clarity on the problem of technology remains occluded by a common obstacle to most inquiries: we do not know what we are talking about. Early in "The Question Concerning Technology," Heidegger explains that "We shall never experience our relationship to the essence of technology so long as we conceive and push forward the technological, put up with it, or evade it" (1977b, p. 4). Whether we are critiquing technology, or defending it, or even trying to ignore or accept it, we are obscuring it. As Socrates once explained to Meno, we cannot evaluate anything before we know what it is, before we know its essence. The question is not in the first instance whether technology is salutary or pernicious, but first and foremost, what it is.

Commonly, technology is understood as having two distinguishing features: it is a means to an end (electric toothbrushes and intercontinental ballistic missiles are designed to do something in particular) and it is a human activity (the sulfurous rain of Sodom and Gomorrah's immolation was not technological, though it was employed with a purpose). To capture the default, "instrumental and anthropological," definition of technology we might simply say, it is a "man-made means to an end established by man" (1977b, p. 5). Heidegger concedes that this definition is no doubt correct, but correctness means less to him than perhaps any other consequential thinker. It is almost pejorative. What is correct is only true superficially: correctness is a derivative mode of truth. There is a more originary truth that grounds and makes possible our default understanding.

Everyone thinks they know what truth is. Or, more precisely, hardly anyone bothers to wonder what truth is, as an understanding of truth is a prerequisite of all reasoning. (As the *Meno* also teaches us, you can only look for what you already in some way possess.) But if we were to investigate truth and articulate our common, unexamined assumptions about it, we would say that it is a kind of accord, which has a "dual character" (Heidegger, 1977a, p. 117). On the one hand, there is the truth of the matter, or the accordance of the matter with what is intended. For example, Heidegger calls our attention to the distinction between real and false gold. A bar of gold bullion is a "true" bar of gold bullion only if it is actually a bar of gold bullion. "The true is the actual" (Heidegger, 1977a, p. 117). But a counterfeit is of course also actual, in fact, no less actual than the genuine article, save for this respect: it does not conform with our preconceived idea of what it is. In other words, it *is not* in the sense that it is not gold. On the other hand, there is the truth of the proposition, namely, the accordance of the statement with the matter. The declaration "God is dead" is true, if and only if, God is in fact—in actuality—dead. In either case, the truth of the matter or the truth of the proposition, what is decisive is correspondence, a "conforming to," which is to say, "correctness" (Heidegger, 1977a, p. 118). In our default view, to say something is true is to say that it is correct.

These rather obvious observations obscure a problem with a not-so-obvious solution: how precisely do the elements of correspondence meet? In what way can they be said to be in accord? When you say a coin is round, for instance, you are attempting to bring into accord what would seem to be incommensurable: the material (the coin) and the immaterial (the proposition). If one were to become like the other it would cease to be itself. (A material proposition is no longer a proposition; an immaterial coin is no longer a coin.) It is vital, then, that the thing and the proposition remain themselves, "persisting in [their] own essence" (Heidegger, 1977a, p. 121). According to Heidegger, there must be a special kind of relation, and even more essentially, a special place, a "there," where the twain can meet, as themselves:

> All working and achieving, all action and calculation, keep within an *open region* within
> which beings, with regard to what and how they are, can *take their stand* and become

capable of being said. This can occur *only if* beings *present* themselves along with the pre-sentative statement so that the latter subordinates itself to the directive that it speaks of beings such-as they are. In following such a directive the statement conforms to beings. Speech that directs itself accordingly is correct (true). What is thus said is the correct (the true).

(1977a, p. 122 [emphasis added])

The proposition and the matter can correspond because they both "take their stand," "present themselves,"—somehow appear—in an "open region." Such an open region was known to the earliest Greek thinkers as *"ta alēthea,* the unconcealed" (Heidegger, 1977a, p. 125). Truth understood as correctness is only possible because the proposition and the matter are opened up "to reveal [themselves], to be manifest (as, for example, a flower in bloom)" (Heidegger, 1977a, note p. 122). Before truth is correspondence it is an unconcealing.

But how does anything become unconcealed, manifest, disclosed? What is disclosed must be disclosed to someone. The act of revealing necessarily implies the existence, or rather the "ek-sistence," of something. Generally, of course, "existence" refers to a kind of occur-ring. But here Heidegger means "an exposure to the disclosedness of beings as such" (177a, p. 126). A being becomes manifest because man engages with it, allows it to be, lets it be:

To let be—that is, to let beings be as the beings which they are—means to engage oneself with the open region and its openness into which every being comes to stand, bringing that openness, as it were, along with itself.

(Heidegger, 1977a, p. 125)

Man can only let a being be, first, because of the openness of the open region (without the openness of the open, there would be no place, no "da," for beings to manifest themselves), but also because he "brings that openness...along with" him; he ek-sists—literally, stands out (of himself)—into the openness of the open region. If man was not "opened," as it were, to beings, they could not become manifest through his questioning. If, in other words, man did not have a certain comportment to beings, they could not reveal themselves as the beings which they are.

This analysis seems at first blush to be exceedingly arcane, but it can be distilled into a simple, aphoristic conclusion: "The essence of truth is freedom" (Heidegger, 1977a, p. 123). It is hardly necessary to say that freedom in this sense is not freedom as it is commonly (or even uncommonly) understood. You would not discover Heidegger's meaning in a dictio-nary or even the most unorthodox political philosophy:

Freedom is not merely what common sense is content to let pass under this name: the caprice, turning up occasionally in our choosing, of inclining in this or that direction. Freedom is not mere absence of constraint with respect to what we can or cannot do. Nor is it on the other hand mere readiness for what is required and necessary (and so somehow a being). Prior to all this ('negative' and 'positive' freedom), freedom is engagement in the disclosure of beings as such. Disclosedness itself is conserved in ek-sistent engagement, through which the openness of the open region, i.e., the 'there' ['Da'], is what it is.

(Heidegger, 1977a, p. 126)

Most conceptions of freedom can be categorized broadly (if not always helpfully) as "negative" or "positive." A negative conception views freedom primarily as an unboundedness, the license to indulge in "[o]ne's own free and voluntary wanting, one's own caprice, however wild, one's own fancy, though chafed sometimes to the point of madness," as Dostoevsky's underground man puts it (Dostoyevsky, 1993, p. 25). A positive conception, on the other hand, is largely of an older vintage. It can be found in almost every ancient and medieval philosopher of significance, and even up through and including Descartes and Kant. This species of freedom is the freedom of those who possess "what is required and necessary" to be happy or to have a good will or to evade sin and error and so become divine, that is, to achieve whatever happens to be the supreme end of man. Here, freedom is not unrestrained action, but right choice.

Heidegger points out that both understandings depend upon an altogether different freedom that has largely escape our notice despite the fact that (or perhaps because) it is entirely indispensable. For Heidegger, "free" does not mean being either "unconstrained" or "[ready] for what is required and necessary." Rather, "free" means "open": "Freedom governs the open in the sense of the cleared and lighted up, i.e., the revealed...all revealing comes out of the open, goes into the open, and brings into the open" (Heidegger, 1977b, p. 25). An alternative translation renders this same passage: "Freedom governs the free space in the sense of the cleared, that is to say, the revealed...all revealing comes out of the free, goes into the free, and brings into the free" (Heidegger, 1977c, p. 331). Before there is any question of choice, or any limitations on choice, before there are any objects of desire, or agents of subjugation, there must be disclosure. We can only choose between choices or appreciate the delimitations of necessities once they have been revealed. In order to be revealed, they must first become manifest from out of the open, which is to say, out of the free. But they can only do so, out of the openness of the open, or the freedom of the free, or the freedom in which beings present themselves as themselves. It is that freedom which then, in turn, allows man to make his choices. "Freedom," in whatever way we are inclined to generally understand it, is derivative of a more originary freedom (the very same freedom that is the essence of truth), the freedom of revealing.

A remarkable corollary of Heidegger's conception of freedom is that it does not, and indeed cannot, belong to us:

> But if ek-sistent Da-sein, which lets beings be, sets man free for his 'freedom' by offering to his choice something possible (a being) and by imposing on him something necessary (a being), human caprice does not then have freedom at its disposal.
>
> *(Heidegger, 1977a, p. 127)*

In Heidegger's later thought, "Dasein" is no longer his term for man as the being to whom Being is questionable. Rather, "Da-sein" is the term for standing out into the open, into the free: ek-sisting. It is, in other words, not man himself, but the fundamental prerequisite for man:

> Man does not "possess" freedom as a property. At best, the converse holds: freedom, ek-sistent, disclosive Da-sein possesses man—so originally that *only it* secures for humanity that distinctive relatedness to being as a whole such which first founds all history. Only ek-sistent man is historical. "Nature" has no history.
>
> *(Heidegger, 1977a, p. 127)*

Without Da-sein, without the ground for beings to manifest themselves as they are, there is no revealing. If there is no revealing or unconcealing, there is no freedom as it is commonly understood because there is nothing "offered to choice," nothing to choose between. There is also no truth, no correctness, because there is, as we saw above, no possibility for correspondence. There is not even history, which requires at a minimum that something has occurred. Absolutely everything, even basic ontological distinctions (such as those between the sensible and the intelligible, act and potency), require that something first comes to presence, that something is unconcealed, which is to say, everything, even man himself, belongs to the openness, the freedom, that occasions unconcealment.

There is, however, a price to be paid for this freedom. There is no unconcealment without concealment: "[B]ecause man ek-sists and so becomes capable of history only as the property of this freedom; the nonessence of truth cannot first arise subsequently from mere human incapacity and negligence. Rather, untruth must derive from the essence of truth" (Heidegger, 1977a, p. 128). Man always already ek-sists; he is possessed by the openness of the open. And by focusing on individual beings, by letting them be, we lose sight of "being as a whole." Just as when we look to an object in the foreground, we lose everything in the background of our field of vision in a blurry indifference, and indeed we must do so in order to focus, so must we lose Being when we let beings be. ("Letting-be is intrinsically at the same time a concealing. In the ek-sistent freedom of Da-sein a concealing of being as a whole propriates [ereignet sich]. Here there *is* concealment" [Heidegger, 1977a, p. 130].) And not only that, but this very concealment is itself concealed from us. As it is above all unknown, Heidegger appropriately calls this concealing of concealing the "mystery."

Historical man—you and I, dear reader—fly from the mystery "toward what is readily available, onward from one current thing to the next, passing the mystery by," landing directly in errancy (Heidegger, 1977a, p. 133). The question of Being is obscured by our open comportment to beings. Errancy, for Heidegger, is not discrete; it is not a matter of making a mistake:

> The errancy through which man strays is not something, as it were, that extends alongside man like a ditch into which he occasionally stumbles; rather errancy belongs to the inner constitution of the Da-sein into which historical man is admitted.

In short, precisely as man is ek-sistent, standing out from himself, open to other beings, he is also in-sistent, turning away from Being. Though Heidegger does not expressly say it, this leads to a surprising and somewhat troubling conclusion. If ek-sistence is the freedom to which man belongs, in-sistence must be the unfreedom—the closedness—to which he is inextricably bound.

We can now appreciate why Heidegger is our ideal guide for the paradox that confronts us in modern technology. Heidegger begins his essay *On the Question Concerning Technology*, with the unassuming observation that "Questioning builds a way…the way is a way of thinking" (1977b, p. 3). By questioning the meaning of truth, he has deconstructed the old superstition that untruth is the privation of, and wholly alien to, truth. In so doing, he has, maybe inadvertently, certainly unobtrusively, opened another path. Just like truth and untruth, freedom and unfreedom "belong together," naturally, inevitably. Maybe it is not, then, so surprising that technology would be both the means to our most indispensable emancipation and our most inexorable servitude. Maybe if we approach the question concerning technology by way of skepticism toward the neat and tidy distinctions between truth and untruth, free and unfree, we may achieve genuine insight into this enduring problem for man.

Where the Danger Holds Sway

What does it mean to say that technology is "a man-made means to an end established by man"? Just as he did with correctness itself, Heidegger probes the "correct" definition of technology to see what it can reveal. Something that is a means to an end, something that is an instrument, is a cause. But what is a "cause" actually? We tend to think of a cause only in the sense of an efficient cause, "as that which brings something about" (Heidegger, 1977b, p. 7). This is not the traditional, Greek, Aristotelian understanding. Heidegger claims that the four causes (material, formal, final, moving) are "responsible for" something else, and in turn, that something else is "indebted to" the four causes. He uses the example of a silver chalice. Without its silver (its material, its matter), without its "chaliceness" (its chalice aspect, traditionally, its form), a silver chalice would not be a silver chalice. In other words, without somehow being delimited, "circumscribed," restricted within certain boundaries, the chalice would not *be*. The limitations of form and matter are, however, merely derivative of, and dependent on, a more essential circumscription, that of *telos*. *Telos* "confines the chalice within the realm of consecration and bestowal" (Heidegger, 1977b, p. 8). Much more than simply providing a purpose or goal, *telos* puts the chalice in its place, where it belongs, its "realm" and it thereby grounds and determines the proper material (silver) and aspect (chalice). The last cause is the silversmith, who is not an efficient cause, but rather a very specific kind of moving cause. He brings all of the three other causes together into a unity, and all four causes bring the silver chalice into appearance.

A cause, in other words, is a bringing-forth, a bringing-to-presence what is not yet present. "Bringing-forth," however, "comes to pass only insofar as something concealed comes to unconcealment" (Heidegger, 1977b, p. 12). Technology, then, as a cause, as a revealing, has to do with truth. Or we might say, more pointedly, technology is a mode of truth. We are, of course, not accustomed to speaking of technology in this manner. But here Heidegger is much closer to our ordinary understanding than he may appear. As we saw above, truth is unreflectively thought to be analogous with the actual. Correspondence or correctness is introduced to distinguish between actualities. (Fool's gold is still actual even if it is not actually gold.) But so long as truth is at bottom the actual, technology makes things true, even in our ordinary sense, simply because it makes things so. Anything that makes or creates (any cause) actualizes, or as Heidegger would have it, unconceals.

Modern technology is a specific—and pernicious—species of unconcealment that he calls "Ge-stell" or "enframing" (or, as some translators insist, "positionality"). Through it, "Nature becomes a gigantic gasoline station, an energy source for modern technology and industry" (Heidegger, 1966, p. 50). Heidegger gives us the vivid comparison of a simple wooden bridge that spans the Rhine's banks and mixes with its ancient waters, on the one hand, and the hydroelectric plant with its obtrusive dam, on the other. The supports of the bridge stand in the water, briefly redirecting the currents and whatever might be traveling by them. But for the most part, the bridge leaves the river to its obscure rhythms and operations; it lets the river be. Quite to the contrary, the plant forcefully subdues the river, harnessing its energy and transmuting it into a power supplier. That is the essence of modern technology, a "challenging," a "setting upon," that reduces what is revealed to "standing reserve," that is, something "ordered to be immediately at hand, indeed, to stand there just so that it may be on call for a further ordering" (Heidegger, 1977b, p. 17).

One cannot help but notice that "setting upon" and "challenging" seem to be precisely the opposite of "letting beings be the beings that they are." Instead of being a kind of revealing, as Heidegger has claimed, enframing sounds like a species of concealing, a form of untruth born of the nonessence of truth, unfreedom. And that is precisely what it is: "it conceals revealing itself and with it That wherein unconcealment, i.e., truth comes to pass. Enframing blocks the shining-forth and holding sway of truth" (Heidegger, 1977b, p. 28). Enframing is a revealing that conceals revealing, or rather it is a mode of truth that is untrue, an unfreedom that comes out of the free, a closedness that closes on the open itself. As Heidegger has already shown us, the true and the untrue, the free and the unfree are not binary but bedfellows. All unconcealing conceals; ek-sistant man is at once in-sistent man.

That is not to say, however, that all revealings are equally compromised by their intimate association with concealing. Enframing uniquely endangers man: "an attack with technological means is being prepared upon the life and nature of man compared with which the explosion of the hydrogen bomb means little" (Heidegger, 1966, p. 52). We are on "the very brink of a precipitous fall" (Heidegger, 1977b, p. 27). Our ability to cow and control—to order—our surroundings gives man the impression that he is "lord of the earth," and that everything he "encounters exists insofar as it is his construct" (Heidegger, 1977b, p. 27). And why not? Nearly everything that we experience in our daily lives has in some way been altered by the improving hand of a human being. The skies, the mountains, the seas, the wind, even the heat of the sun, all reveal themselves as our means, to be worked up or worked on or worked through. They belong to us and our needs and our whims. They are our creation. The result is that man mistakenly believes that in his various encounters he meets nothing but the results of his own efforts, nothing but himself.

One of Heidegger's great insights, going back to *Being and Time*, is that we are not severable from our world. We are always within a context; we are always in relation. We cannot escape our facticity. ("The concept of facticity implies that an 'innerworldly' being has being-in-the-world in such a way that it can understand itself as bound up in its destiny with the being of those beings which it encounters within its own world" [Heidegger, 2010, p. 56].) In the unbounded instrumentality of enframing, where everything is no longer even an object, but merely a means, we are impacted the most. Because we are factical, we cannot suffer the diminution of our world without suffering the diminution of ourselves. If we are surrounded by standing reserve, that is, if our world has become a glorified stock room, we have ourselves been reduced to the "orderer[s] of standing-reserve," the lowly stewards of a vast and purposeless storehouse. The consequence of our achievements is precisely the opposite of what we led ourselves to believe: "In truth, however, precisely nowhere does man today any longer encounter himself, i.e., his essence" (Heidegger, 1977b, p. 27).

What is the essence of man? We have already discovered it: freedom. We are the being to and through whom itself and other beings are disclosed, to whom Being itself becomes questionable (cf. Heidegger, 2010, p. 12). That unconcealing is only possible because we are free, we ek-sist through the persistence of the openness of the open—we are grounded in the freedom of disclosive Da-sein. Enframing is the grave threat to that freedom:

> [Enframing] *banishes* man into that kind of revealing which is an ordering. Where this ordering holds sway, it drives out *every other* possibility of revealing...Where Enframing holds sway, regulating and securing of the standing-reserve mark *all* revealing. They no longer even let their own fundamental characteristic appear, namely, this revealing as such.
>
> *(Heidegger, 1977b, p. 28 [emphasis added])*

Enframing is the revealing that conceals all other revealing, indeed revealing itself. It is the in-sistence that threatens to swallow all ek-sistence. It degrades our world and makes it little more than a giant supermarket, of infinite variety and utility and sterility, but far worse than that, it degrades man; it steals from him his ground, the freedom in and by which he stands.

There is no simple solution for this problem, which Heidegger designates with laconic force as "the danger" (Heidegger, 1977d, p. 37). The primary issue, and indeed the most dangerous aspect of the danger, is that it is disguised. We cannot appreciate enframing for the threat that it is because, to the extent we are aware of it at all, we have confused it with something else, namely, the technological: "The essence of technology," Heidegger tells us, "is by no means anything technological" (1977b, p. 4). Enframing is not limited to the hubristic heedlessness of those who develop the means to vaporize cities at the push of a few buttons or the ability to enjoy, in the privacy of one's home (or a public restroom), a bottom-less cistern of depravity, violence, and conspiracy—those who, to borrow from Dr. Malcolm, are too busy wondering if they could, to ever ask if they should. It is far more serious and pervasive than that. It is an ontological problem, or rather it is *the* ontological problem. It sets the boundaries between what is and what is not, or to use Heidegger's language, what can be revealed and how:

> [Enframing] is the essence of technology. Its positioning is universal. It addresses itself to the unity of the whole of all that presences. [Enframing] thus sets in place the way that everything present now presences. All that is, in the most manifold of ways and variations and whether obviously or in a still hidden manner, is a piece of inventory of the standing reserve.
>
> *(Heidegger, 2012a, p. 38)*

The precondition of all beings that are recognized as beings—everything, that is, *that is*—is that they find a place and a label and a price on the shelves of the standing reserve. Use, first and foremostly, delimits presence. If that sounds familiar it is because it is nothing other than one of the oldest metaphysical insights, or at least the necessary, if scarcely acknowledged, corollary of such insight. The most essential of Aristotle's four causes (the first of the four causes, as Heidegger has already told us) is the final cause. Something could not exist without its for-the-sake-of-which, its nature, its effect, what it can and ought and is meant to do. Whatever is present, in other words, is present insofar as it is present to us, and it is present to us insofar as it is a means to some end.

The Saving Power

Heidegger is not, at least to me, terribly clear on why we are universally subjected to enfram-ing as our default mode of revealing. But I have my own theory which I am quite certain he would not endorse (not the least of which because of its armchair psychology), but I am going to subject you to it anyway for the simple reason that I think it is probably true. I have known my one-and-a-half-year-old-son Wesley from the instant he took his first breath, and I have studied him ever since with the strange curiosity unique to the philosophically in-clined. (If Freud taught us anything, it is the salience of observations gleaned from watching one-and-a-half-year-olds.) In particular, I have been watching with keen interest for the first glimmers of awareness, the initial recognition that brings him into the world. As one might suspect, that birth, his real birth, the birth of his consciousness, came sometime after the event on his birth certificate. When he first emerged into the chill of the delivery room, he could only produce an intermittent, muffled sob, as he choked on the fluid that remained in his lungs. I will never forget it. But he will of course never remember it; there was no "him" to remember, no "him" to even experience it. Wes was, at that moment, indistinguishable from his pitiful cry. He was only will, blind as his wet, black eyes.

For a few months this was all that he was. And then something slowly began to take shape for him. Out of intermittent tempests of sensations, sometimes loud and painful, other times loud and merely uncomfortable, she emerged, and everything was quiet again. My son (it irritates me to admit) saw my wife before he saw anything else, even himself. She was born to him, as he was born to her, and her birth too was an agony, the agony of the eternally rending fact that he is not the Neoplatonic God. (Freud [2010] makes a similar argument at the beginning of *Civilization and its Discontents*; see, pp. 27–28.) Sometimes he is hungry or wet or gassy or tired. His essence is not existence; his will is not synonymous with being; occasionally a fissure develops between what he wants and what is. But not always and not forever. That wound can be healed, so long as his mother arrives. Or to speak more accurately, his mother arrives, for him, only because that wound can be healed. She is the first being that appears because she is the first being with which he can associate an effect in relation to his will. She was unconcealed first, not as mama, but as means, the means to repose, to happiness, to the calm of satiety.

Other beings were then revealed in due course: dad (a significantly less reliable and efficacious source of comfort than mom, but serviceable in a bind); the bottle of milk (an always-bracing restorative); the pacifier (an inexhaustible consolation); and the bath (a sadistic torture chamber of sloppy discomforts). He knows well what he likes and does not like. (He could distinguish whole wheat from sour dough bread with the first smack of his lips.) He entirely ignores what he has judged to have no impact either way. (He can't even muster an indifferent shove to the Heidegger paperbacks that sit next to his toys on the couch.) And he fears what, and most especially whom, he cannot confidently place among the reliable ministers to his imperious craving. For Wesley, there is no such thing as things-in-themselves. Everything he "encounters exists insofar as it is his construct" or rather everything that has come to appearance for this adorable little tyrant has done so insofar as—and precisely as—it impacts his will. Maybe I should have named him Friedrich.

> It is our needs that interpret the world; our drives and their For and Against. Every drive is a kind of lust to rule; each one has its perspective that it would like to compel all the other drives to accept as a norm.
>
> *(Nietzsche, 1968, p. 267)*

But, of course, that would only be appropriate if his will-to-power ontology was in any way unique. If there is some defect in my son, it is one that I, at least, share without the excuse of infancy. An non-exhaustive but representative list of what is revealed to me in a given day might be: the Honda Odyssey that is going 54 miles per hour in front of me in the left lane, an email from a student asking for an extension on a paper that was due a week ago, my son's metal firetruck that I just stepped on, the text that informs me that the plans I regretted agreeing to have been canceled, the last Franziskaner on the door of the fridge, which I could have sworn I had already drunk. What presents itself to me does so either as something to be used or to be overcome. Everything else is ignored, or if it is picked up, quickly disregarded and forgotten. I don't notice the cars that are not in my way or the emails that don't irritate me or the toys I don't put my toe through. I don't even notice the things that facilitate my will so long as they do so in an expected way. I don't think about shifting gears unless I make a mistake or my shoelaces until they are untied. But I am very much alive to the unexpected opportunities of cancelled plans or a miraculous beverage. Like young Wesley, my will and its satisfaction (or disappointment) precedes and determines the character of my world. And I suspect that I am not alone.

The problem of technology is not, then, anything technological. It is not television or the Internet or the iPhone that have taught us to perceive the world in terms of a crude utility, to see only in terms of what can or cannot be grasped or bent or brought to heel. Rather, our technological achievements and calamities descend naturally from how we initially came to terms with our environment in the earliest months of our lives and how we still do every day. Consequently, our freedom from the ills of technology does not depend on a return to some prelapsarian simplicity, with torchlight and hand-churned butter and oxen-tilled fields. It requires something considerably harder to imagine and even less likely to occur—precisely that which is foreclosed by the universality of enframing: letting things be as the beings that they are.

How can we hope to do that? Heidegger only leaves us with a hint. If the ontology of enframing is exclusively concerned with use (what achieves or obstructs our ends), we must seek out the useless (the end-less). But to find anything like that, we will need an entirely different kind of revealing than the default of our everyday existence:

> Because the essence of technology is nothing technological, essential reflection upon technology and decisive confrontation with it must happen in a realm that is, on the one hand akin to the essence of technology and, on the other, fundamentally different from it. Such realm is art.
>
> *(Heidegger, 1977c, p. 340)*

As Auden reminds us in his tribute to Yeats, "poetry makes nothing happen" (Auden, 1991, p. 247). And in fact, all art worthy of the name makes nothing happen. It is beyond use, or perhaps it would be more accurate to say, it is prior to use.

In order to experience great art, one is required to surrender. That is to say, one cannot "set upon" or "enframe" and also know the sublime pleasure of a masterwork. We have an inexhaustible lexicon of cliches to express this fact. When we have been really moved by a film or a novel we say things like: "I was spellbound, transfixed, entirely absorbed; I was in another world; I lost myself." We mean these hackneyed phrases more than we know. When you watch *Julius Caesar* performed, you are not Antony or Brutus or, mercifully, Cinna the poet. You cannot be found in the forum or on the plains of Philippi. You are everywhere and nowhere. Similarly, when you hear profoundly moving music, you don't really hear it at all. There is nothing to hear because there is no one to hear it. "You are the music while the music lasts" (Eliot, 2004, p. 190). The distinctions between subject and object, ego and world, user and used have collapsed. Quite literally, the art has made nothing happen. The will returns to its original blindness, before it was compelled to produce the self and a whole universe of antagonists for it to stand over and against and among. You return to the nothing from which everything as you now know it once sprang forth (see Heidegger, 1977e, 104–108).

All at once beings are allowed at last to *be*. You do not interrupt Cassius as he pursues his doomed scheme. You let John Coltrane's solo on "Blue in Green" perform its tender miracle. You are you no longer. "Letting be," it turns out, does not mean to ignore or leave alone— almost precisely the opposite. It means to engage something so deeply that it is allowed to come to presence as itself, without our manipulations, without our ends—without why.

Emerging from a playhouse or a concert hall onto a bright boulevard is like waking up from someone else's dream. A whole cacophony of instruments, obstacles, opportunities, and aggravations—your whole ordered world—rushes to meet you, and you arrive to meet it, in turn. If we are to somehow escape the essence of technology, it will be through the unaccountable capacity of art to efface the world that waits for us on the sidewalks outside of theaters, to return us to the origin, the nothing, from whence we might just make another beginning.

References

Auden, W. H. (1991). *Collected Poems* (E. Mendelson, Ed.; 1st Vintage International ed.). New York: Vintage Books.

Augustine. (2014). *Confessions* (C. J.-B. Hammond, Trans.). Cambridge, MA: Harvard University Press.

Dostoyevsky, F. (1993). *Notes from Underground* (R. Pevear & L. Volokhonsky, Trans.). New York: Alfred A. Knopf Inc..

Eliot, T. S. (2004). *The Complete Poems and Plays* (Paperb. ed.). London: Faber and Faber Publishers Association.

Freud, S. (1989). *Beyond the Pleasure Principle* (J. Strachey, Trans.; Standard ed.). New York: W. W. Norton & Company.

Freud, S. (2010). *Civilization and Its Discontents* (J. Strachey, Trans.). New York: W. W. Norton & Company.

Heidegger, M. (1966). Memorial Address. In J. M. Anderson & E. H. Freund (Trans.), *Discourse on Thinking* (pp. 43–57). New York: HarperCollins Publishing.

Heidegger, M. (1977a). On the Essence of Truth. In J. Sallis (Trans.), *Basic Writings* (pp. 111–138). New York: HarperCollins Publishing.

Heidegger, M. (1977b). The Question Concerning Technology. In W. Lovitt (Trans.), *The Question Concerning Technology and Other Essays* (pp. 3–35). New York: HarperCollins Publishing.

Heidegger, M. (1977c). The Question Concerning Technology. In W. Lovitt & D. F. Krell (Trans.), *Basic Writings* (pp. 311–341). New York: HarperCollins Publishing.

Heidegger, M. (1977d). The Turning. In W. Lovitt (Trans.), *The Question Concerning Technology and Other Essays* (pp. 36–49). New York: HarperCollins Publishing.

Heidegger, M. (1977e). What Is Metaphysics? In D. F. Krell (Trans.), *Basic Writings* (pp. 93–110). New York: HarperCollins Publishing.

Heidegger, M. (2010). *Being and Time* (J. Stambaugh, Trans.). Albany: SUNY Press.

Heidegger, M. (2012a). Positionality. In A. Mitchell (Trans.), *Bremen and Freiburg Lectures* (pp. 23–43). Bloomington, IN: Indiana University Press.

Heidegger, M. (2012b). The Danger. In A. Mitchell (Trans.), *Bremen and Freiburg Lectures* (pp. 44–63). Bloomington, IN: Indiana University Press.

Marx, K., & Engels, F. (2011). *The German ideology, Parts I & III* (R. Pascal, Trans.). Eastford, CT: Martino Publishing.

Nietzsche, F. (1967). *The Birth of Tragedy* (W. A. Kaufmann, Trans.). New York: Vintage Books.

Nietzsche, F. (1968). *The Will to Power* (W. A. Kaufmann, Trans.). New York: Vintage Books.

Plato. (1997). Protagoras. In J. M. Cooper (Ed.), & S. Lombardo & K. Bell (Trans.), *Plato: Complete Works* (pp. 746–790). Indianapolis, IN: Hackett Publishing.

Rilke, R. M. (1998). *The Selected Poetry of Rainer Maria Rilke* (S. Mitchell, Trans.). New York: Vintage International.

PART III

Through the Looking-Glass
Online Fantasies, Social Media, and the Screen

12

NO ONE GETS OUT OF HERE ALIVE

Trading Technologies of Human Exceptionalism for Dense Temporalities of Transcorporeal Zooms

Katie Gentile

During a technology run-through for a Zoom dissertation defense taking place in a different country, we on the committee were advised by the coordinator to make sure to have "professional backgrounds and clothing" for the event. Anxious about what exactly this might mean, I pictured my options: laptop on the kitchen table, cats strolling back and forth center screen seeking attention and treats; or, where I do my therapy sessions—on the couch, laptop on a surface the cats could not share, but with them lounging or chasing each other on the back of the same couch. Living in a 'railroad apartment' (four rooms spilling into one another without doors, except for the bathroom), I said I might have difficulty keeping my cats out of view. The coordinator said, "oh cats are fine." At first, I thought he must be kidding, given the emphasis on "professionalism," but indeed, during the three-hour defense, my one-eyed tuxedo cat (who as my friend Kathleen Del Mar Miller pointed out, *was* dressed for the occasion!) sauntered around the table until I lured him out of view with a toy. The dissertation chair entirely disappeared for a moment, only to reappear with a fluffy yellowish dog in her lap. Professionalism over Zoom is multispecies.

Psychoanalysis has a checkered history with the more-than-human (I am using this for lack of a nonhuman centric term), usually disavowing it in theories of subjectivity, reproducing a rigid and defensive notion of human exceptionalism and what Bruno Latour (1988) called the "great divide." For Latour and many theorists in posthumanism, new materialisms, and object-oriented ontologies, this great divide occurs between humans and everything else. It is the boundary generating technology out of which human subjectivity emerges.

After almost two years of Zoom classes, meetings, and Doxy therapy sessions, however, it has become difficult to uphold the logic behind this "great divide." During this time, limits on movement and accessible spaces seem to have focused, and also potentially deepened, the ways we come into being and emerge, such that we do so not so much live *with* (the more-than-human), but *through* spontaneous and unpredictable human-more-than-human interactions. So curious cats, lounging dogs, the walls, furniture, and objects framing our Zoom reflections and these Zoom reflections themselves, create what I would call a transcorporeal

DOI: 10.4324/9781003195849-16

(Alaimo, 2016), assembled human-more-than-human emergence (Gentile, 2020, 2021) that is presented to us *through* the screen.

The logic of this constituting "great divide" is similarly questioned by theorists in anti-Blackness and Indigenous studies. Building on Sylvia Wynter's (2003) critique of the "genre of man," many note that only white, CISgender males possess the status of "human." Those identified as Black are not only *not* human, but come into being as "fungible" (Jackson, 2013, 2020; King, 2019) bodies or "flesh" (Spillers, 1987), emerging as non-, sub-, super-human, objects, or animals, needed to create the fantasy of a unified, that is, white, humanity (Bennett, 2020; Jackson, 2013, 2020; King, 2019; Spillers, 1987; Wynter, 2003). As Pugliese (2020) writes, this logic of "[r]acio-speciesism is what enables the inversion of human/animal categories according to the biopolitical expediencies operative in a given context" (p. 6). In other words, human exceptionalism itself and the "great divide" delineations between the human and everything else, rely upon an ontological racio-speciest technology deployed to create the category of "human" (i.e. white) in opposition to "everything else" (i.e. fungible Black bodies that then represent categories of killable and disposable animal and object). Thus the technologies undergirding the emergences of human and more-than-human subjectivities are geno- and eco-cidal, and must be dismantled.

This call to dismantle is further complicated because these technologies of exceptionalism do unconscious affective labor for those defined as human, enabling them/us to deny ambivalence. After all, on the one hand, humans comprise less than .01% of the biomass of the Earth. We are a blip, if even that, in geologic time. Yet despite, or as some contend, because of this insignificance, we have the capacity to alter the Earth's climate, its ecosystems, rendering this planet unlivable for ourselves and millions of other species. While new materialisms, posthumanisms, and object oriented ontologies have theorized agency as dispersive, emanating not from some autonomous rational action, but through networks of human and more-than-human, much of psychoanalysis has held tight to the fantasy of human exceptionalism, through the denigration, pathologization, disavowal, and dissociation of the nonhuman animal. In much of Freud's writing, nonhuman animals are merely functional, serving as sites of projection, enabling humans to workout Oedipal conflicts. Since his writings, few in the field have theorized nonhuman animals beyond their roles as Oedipal objects or vehicles for enhancing human growth (for instance see Akhtar and Volkan, 2004/2015a, 2004/2015b; Silbert and Frasca, 2021). The stance of exceptionalism that enables humans to speak for all creatures (Hird, 2009) and objects, is woven through much of this theorizing. Animality, in psychoanalysis, is also code for female, economically impoverished, differently abled, and/or BIPOC—Black, Indigenous, and people of color.

Searles (1960) developed a theory of the "nonhuman" in human development. As has been discussed (Gentile, 2020, 2021), and will be further developed here, his writings enacted a disavowed ambivalence and anxiety around being "human" as well as being "nonhuman." In this chapter I read his ideas about what he calls the "primitive castration" of human and nonhuman and the high stakes of this split. But, as is evident at this point, one cannot discuss this divide without also including the racio-species biopolitics that render some bodies killable and disposable. Indigenous Studies and cosmologies offer a potential space (Winnicott, 1971) wherein the ambivalences of being agentic yet insignificant can be held without splitting through racio-speciest "great divides." Integrating some of these theories with Alaimo's (2016) idea of transcorporeality, I consider the ways our lives on screens might be read as enacting a "dense temporality" (Gentile, 2020, 2021), where "human" subjectivities emerge as human-more-than-human assemblages. Dense temporality observes the ways pasts, presents, and futures, are not just multiple, but emerge only through a complex process of tensegrity

(Gentile, 2021), where an interplay of tensions "in-form" (Manning, 2014) moments in time. Bodies (animate and "inanimate") come into being through a dense temporal tensegrity that requires a focus beyond the human. Temporality based on human exceptionalism cannot comprehend the ways trees walk (Kohn, 2013). I rarely see some students or patients without their nonhuman animal kin on the screen, just as they are likely habituated to taking me in only as part of a cat-person-cat mélange. These screen-based subjectivities call upon psychoanalysis to consider that the human has never really been human (Haraway, 2008), and that clinging to a fantasy of exceptionalism flattens and narrows temporality through ontological technologies that disavow ambivalence through gendered, anti-Black racio-species violence.

In this chapter I am examining the ontological technologies that enable the emergence of subjectivities. Although my primary example is the screen, I am not including discussions of material technology, itself. I urge readers to turn to Chapter 2 by Clough et al. (this volume) and Clough (2018).

"Pets are Going Like Hotcakes": Animals as Pets

In January 2021, the *Washington Post* reported on animal shelters being suddenly emptied by humans confined to their homes by the pandemic. The quote from a shelter employee says it all: pets are going like hotcakes. They are a commodity to be bought and sold, or, adopted. Shelter Animals Count ("Covid-19 Impact Report."), an organization that tracks shelter adoption numbers nationally, reported that by mid-2020, shelter adoptions were up 34% from 2019, the adoption rates for cats nearly doubled. The American Pet Products Association estimates that nearly 11% of US households welcomed a new pet.

The word "pet" was first used in the early 1500s to describe a spoiled child, but by the end of that century it referred to companion animals tamed or kept for pleasure (Grier, 2006). Throughout the history of the US animals have been companions and typically considered members of one's family and a form of kin. Indigenous people often kept dogs as working companions who were considered to be members of the community. In the eighteenth century companion dogs blurred the lines between family, friend, employee, and object (Hoffer, 2011).

Tuan (1984) famously wrote that pets were created by a combination of dominance and affection. They recognize aspects of people that are kept hidden or are overlooked by others, such that the person can be special to the pet. Humans tend to use animals to "actualize their meaning potentials" (Fuchs and Brandt, 2018, p. 5), or as Kohn puts it," we narcissistically ask them to provide us with corrective reflections of ourselves" (Kohn, 2013, p. 21). Freccero (2010) claims part of the ambivalence of having pets resides in the godlike relationship we have with them. We decide when they eat, sleep, play, what they do and where they do it, whether or not they reproduce. These animals also represent "nature," becoming or embodying or something else "a shuttle between worlds, "life" and "death," occupying the threshold between home and the wild, the domestic and the savage...an ontological uncertainty" (Freccero, 2010, p. 61).

One could theorize that these liminal beings representing a multiplicity of temporal and affective worlds, would be in demand, "like hotcakes," during a pandemic where uncertainty has been a central organizing principle. Additionally, the presence of animals in the home can be used to create a false sense of security or absolution, knowing that human destructiveness has rendered countless species extinct or endangered. But there is also the fact that the animals we domesticate are often considered "cute." Cuteness can be a "coping strategy" (Dale et al., 2017, p. 1) employed or used to negotiate neoliberal capitalism as pets become "social proxies," enhancing sociality in the human. Animals can be calming, as we know with the rise of therapy pets, and they can help patients engage in therapeutic work (American Humane Association: Cole et al. their p. 22). Negra (2018) claims a focus on pets is a preoccupation with the cultivation of perfect interior spaces and ideals of domesticity.

Certainly in the wake of COVID, the need for sociality, companionship, domination, and control, is not surprising. Further, if animals do represent interior spaces, then they could easily become sources of projection to manage our own "interior" spaces of dis-ease, an externalized preoccupation with unmanageable psychic space. Humans relate to animals through a "double movement of assimilating and then disavowing the animal, animality and animals" (Oliver, 2009, p. 4), defining bad human behavior as "animalistic" and good behavior as "humane" (i.e. human).

In contemporary psychoanalysis animals are used to embody psychic conflicts, traumas, horror, danger, violence, and virtue (Emmens, 2021), as objects of projections and as cultural images (Akhtar and Volkan, 2005/2014a, 2005/2014b), or as therapy animals, literal laborers of affect (Blazina et al., 2013). Akhtar and Volkan (2005/2014a, 2005/2014b) produced two substantial volumes about animals in psychoanalysis, however animals are still situated as prosthetics to the human, functioning as transitional or therapeutic objects. They are symbols of psychosexual and aggressive impulses, substitutions for human family members. Animals are also used as protosymbols representing unintegrated and undifferentiated psychotic cores of the self. Thus, animals are defined based on their usage to the human.

So far, it seems that animals exist *for* humans. With companion animals, humans can have their cake and eat it too: some humans can be domesticated, enjoying the comforts and excesses of "civilization," while indulging in fantasies of wildness through animals. We are party to the slaughter of millions of animals for food, clothing, industrial spread, while engaging in kinship relationships with other animals (Meijer, 2019). This freedom of temporal movement is key to human exceptionalism. The "human" can traverse the great divide, but when the animal crosses to appear to be human, it is so absurd as to be humorous (Critchley, 2002, in Chris, 2006). A favorite example of mine is a cartoon showing a cute cat complaining to a human that they need to discuss their living arrangement. Things were great when the human went to work all day, but now with COVID, the cat says the apartment is too small for both of them. The human of course responds, alerting the cat to its status as pet, not property owner. It's funny because our conceptualizations of a cat are that they are aloof and territorial, so of course they would think "our" home is "theirs" and we are, or should be, the visitors. It's funny because the cat was cute and spoke English and crossed the species border. It's funny because I often think since my cats live in my apartment 24/7, it technically is or should be their apartment, yet I pay the rent…ambivalence.

As animals have become a focus for critical theories, some have critiquing this shift potentially indicating a desire to engage with an "Other that doesn't talk back" (Haritaworn, 2015, p. 212). Despret (2004) would counter that animals do talk and listen. Studying horses, she notes that they "read through their skin and their muscles" (p. 115), through a form of "isopraxis" that involves the horse "reading" the "unintentional movements of the rider" such that when a movement is even thought, the horse "feels them and simultaneously, *reproduces* them" (p. 115, emphasis in original). Thus it is not that animals do not talk back, it is that human exceptionalism violently mutes capacities to hear, see, experience more-than-human consciousness.

Kohn's (2013) ethnography of life in a region of the Amazon successfully demonstrates that most life forms engage in forms of representation, symbolization, and communication, that is, language. He suggests that we universalize as human the capacities for representation and then universalize representation as language. Representation and symbolization are then assumed to be exclusively human capacities. Yet Kohn presents evidence that nonhuman animals and plants also use signs. As he writes "humans are not the only ones who do things for the sake of a future by re-presenting it in the present" (Kohn, 2013, p. 41). Think of mushrooms collecting and holding water for the trees on which they emerge. They collect the water for a time in the future when the trees and the ground become dry. As he and Tsing (2012) observe, this is a form of intentional planning.

Natalie Angier (2021), reviewing research on social influencing in more-than-human societies wrote:

> Culture was once considered the patented property of human beings: We have the art, science, music and online shopping; animals have the instinct, imprinting and hard-wired responses. But that dismissive attitude toward nonhuman minds turns out to be more deeply misguided with every new finding of animal wit or whimsy: Culture, as many biologists now understand it, is much bigger than we are.

"Culture" has been observed in communities of plants, trees, fungi, primates, aquatic mammals, birds, fish, and insects. So what is a species that defines itself through fantasies of its exceptionalism to do?

Searles and the Development of Human and Nonhuman Subjectivities

The animal, in many ways, has always been the focus of psychoanalytic inquiry. Analysis is a technology developed to engage, organize, and tame the unconscious. Supposedly outside of cultural temporalities, analysis transforms "primitive" primary process into secondary symbolizations. The use of the word primitive itself demonstrates the links to slavery and colonization that psychoanalysis embodies (see Brickman, 2018). It should come as no surprise that in psychoanalysis too, animals are also sites of ambivalence. They are stand-ins for incest, castration fears, devouring love and hate, enabling the human to transcend animality. For Freud animals are "reservoirs" for projections, yet the notion that humans are separate from them is a "piece of arrogance" (Akhtar and Volkan, 2005/2014b, p. 3). Freud claimed dogs were the only species capable of "pure love," without ambivalence (Genosko, 1993). One of his dogs was usually present in his sessions and when he lost his jaw to cancer, he had one of them masticate his food and drop it, so he could swallow it (Blazina et al, 2013). Frasca (2021) cites documentation indicating that Freud's decision to end his life was triggered not only by his physical deterioration and pain, but by an incident when his beloved dog began "howling, repulsed by the smell" of Freud's cancerous mouth (Frasca, 2021, p. 122).

Perhaps up until now the idea that the human has never been human is an abstract concept, but consider the co-mingling of dog-saliva-digestive enzymes-dog food remnants-fur-anal trappings-600 or so dog mouth bacteria being in-gested by Freud. Given what we now know about the power of gut bacteria on moods, behavior and health, Freud could easily have become one of his case studies, a "Freud-chow?"

Animals serve imperative functions toward the creation of human culture. Freud claims the ingestion of animal meat sublimates drives toward eating or killing other humans or having sex with family members. Without animals to take the (Biblical and secular) "fall," there is no human or human culture. This ontological dependency is complicated.

For Searles (1960) animals belong with plants and objects in the category of the nonhuman. They serve an important role as they initiate human consciousness that only "arises" as we contact our environment (Searles, 1960, p. 50). As such, they become what he calls "ingredients" of personality and culture (p. 55). Ingredients are mere parts, however, as there is a necessary "primitive castration," a definitive split between the "primitive ego" and the external world, creating the human/nonhuman binary, which is also a devastating wound from which the human is perpetually in recovery. Existential anxiety about death, loneliness, sexual conflicts, and instability can be soothed with a reinvigoration of the initial sense of oneness but using signifies pathology. Primitive is always a pathology where the technologies of slavery and colonization shape subjectivities.

But things are more complicated for Searles. Although there is a prescribed separation from the nonhuman, there is also a simultaneous intimate kinship with it. The human and the nonhuman share atoms in different states of being. Thus, the human and the nonhuman are temporally multiple and intermingling. Kinship materializes temporally in different ways as life forms live, die and decompose. In this sense, Searles contends that our split from the nonhuman is merely defensive; an attempt to deny the recognition that we are merely one type of life form in a complex stew of life forms, and in the end, we will all return to the same "the great inanimate environment" (Searles, 1960, p. 5). We can invest in the fantasy of exceptionalism but it is temporary, and in the end, the "billion atoms that make up our body are all second-hand, having been used before, from the beginning of time, by people, plants, animals, trees, flowers, and everything else that makes up biologically exchangeable matter" (Searles, 1960, p. 9). Our exceptional humanness is comprised of not only shared but reused atoms, replaced every month, rendering our material bodies in a constant state of re-arrangement and re-emergence, created by exchangeable atoms. We struggle, according to Searles, with the nagging feeling of "interchangeability" between ourselves and our nonhuman environment (p. 44). It is this struggle that makes adhering to human exceptionalism so important.

Not only is the human not clearly human, but we have to continually work to disavow this nonhumanity. The human is temporary and even in that fleeting temporality, materially tenuous. Within a logic of human exceptionalism, it is threatening to consider that the human is simultaneously *potentially* animal and environment, animate and inanimate, dead and alive. Making human exceptionalism even more complicated, as Searles deconstructs the human, he animates objects, noting that they will often confuse or annoy the human, hinting that they have an agency separate from human projections. Anxiety around oneness with the nonhuman is also, according to Searles, related to a form of unconscious phylogenetic memory of evolution such that "individual ego development has, as its initial phase, such a subjective interchangeability with the nonhuman environment" (1960, p. 41), including the inorganic. Ferenczi (1922/1989). Too, theorized a geologic unconscious linking human anxiety to the memory of the ice age and other massive planetary changes (Kassouf, 2017).

As he theorizes the nonhuman materiality of the human and the pathological merging with the seductive oneness of the nonhuman, it appears we are stuck in the tantalizing relationship of being dependent for our emergence on the very environments we define ourselves against. Here mourning the loss of oneness occurs through "knowing" the nonhuman which is a difficult project. He describes it as a tragedy that "we do not really know or haven't met the types of trees from which we may have furniture" (Searles, 1960, p. 387), thus we live surrounded by commodified and manufactured parts of "nature." Unlike Ingersoll (2016) who describes her community's respect for a canoe as being alive, holding through what I have called a... dense temporality the beings it was and has become, Searles does not see the tree once it is a desk. It seems this temporal narrowing and flattening is an 'outgrowth' of the primitive castration required to become human.

Human Exceptionalism *Is* Anti-Blackness

Morton (2017) contends the violence of exceptionalism is not only in the initial ontological split from nature, but primarily conveyed in dogmatic and psychotic theories we create to avoid ambivalence (Ferenczi's "confusion of tongues," perhaps?). An often ignored or erased aspect of human exceptionalism is that it is a technology of anti-Blackness. "One cannot "unsettle" the "coloniality of power" without a redescription of the human outside the terms of our present descriptive statement of the human" (Wynter, 2003, p. 268). Wynter and Fanon note that "'man' is a technology of slavery and colonization that imposes its authority over 'the universal' through a racialized deployment of force" (Jackson, 2013, p. 670). Blackness is not just the embodiment of the animal category against which the white and nonblack human come into being, it is a plasticity, a fungibility (Jackson, 2013, 2020; King, 2019) to function as a "mode of transmogrification whereby the fleshy being of blackness is experimented with as if it were infinitely malleable lexical and biological matter such that blackness is produced as sub/super/human at once" (Jackson, 2020, p. 3). Because Eurocentric humanism needs blackness to erect and sustain white humanity, blackness is required to distinguish the human from the animal, such that blackness creates the human/animal divide, as the "categories of "race" and "species" have coevolved and are actually *mutually reinforcing* terms" (Jackson, 2020, p. 12, emphasis in original). Anti-blackness is *essential* to the emergence of the nonhuman—animals, objects, matter (Jackson, 2020, p. 15). Therefore, it is unsurprising that in the Searles' clinical cases, children are expected to treat the household help, Black domestic workers, as objects (Butler, 2019), demonstrating that the human exceptionalism that creates human and the nonhuman is *essentially* a gendered anti-Blackness. Boisseron (2018) writes that "the black condition is without analog, *except* for the animal" (p. xviii). She urges what she calls an "interspecies alliance" to escape the logic of anti-blackness undergirding animality.

The End of the World—As We Know It

What if, instead of the Ordered World, we could image The World as Plenum, an infinite composition in which each existant's singularity is contingent upon its becoming one possible expression of all the other existants, with which it is entangled beyond space and time…[space-time] which is also a recomposition of everything else…not as separate forms relating through the mediation of forces, but rather as singular expressions of each and every other extant as well as of the entangled whole in/as which they exist?

(da Silva, 2016, p. 2)

da Silva, like Jackson (2013, 2020) and King (2019), calls for an end of The World "*as we know it*" (emphasis in original p. 2) that could dissolve the technologies of Western exceptionalism that stingily mete out humanity. According to da Silva (2016) this requires a release on certainty and "abstract fixities produced by Understanding and the partial and total violence they authorize—against humanity's cultural (non-white/non-European) and physical (more-than-human) 'Others'" (p. 2).

What if, instead of the Ordered World, we imaged each existant (human and more-than-human) not as separate forms relating through the mediation of forces, but rather as singular expressions of each and every other existant as well as of the entangled who in/as which they exist?

(p. 4)

Da Silva's end of the world, *as we know it,* goes beyond new materialisms and affect theory with their focus on dispersive agency to the idea that we are composed of one another. Indeed. Haraway (2008) and Steeves (1999) note the millions of bacteria, protists, supposedly "nonhuman" beings inside the human body that enable a material life. Chen (2012) notes the ways the human takes in not just the cells and fluids expelled by other overtly breathing bodies, but the skins of chairs, carpets, walls, desks. In this context, my skin might keep my blood, urine, lymph, and shit from spilling out onto the chair, but it does not keep the chair, the floor, the walls, from spilling into me. Thus, the skin is a porous and viscous (Miller, 2020, 2021; Tuana, 2008) boundary, if that. This is a trans-corporeal subjectivity "where bodies extend into places and places deeply affect bodies...always already penetrated by substances and forces that can never be properly accounted for (Alaimo, 2016, p. 5). The key here is *always already.*

Da Silva's Entangled World is neither the cause nor the effect of relations but "the uncertain condition under which everything that exists is a singular expression of each and every actual-virtual other existant" (p. 5). This entangled world is the world Searles (1960) describes, the billions of shared atoms between the human, animals, plants. But while he writes of its beauty and potential for soothing, to surrender to its seduction is a form of pathology because doing so fails to acknowledge the ontological border between the human and everything else. Yet this moment of exceptionalism is that which da Silva (2015, 2016), Jackson (2013, 2020), King (2019), Boisseron (2018), and Bennett (2020) identify as catalyzing the anti-Black violence of world *as we know it.*

Let's consider how subjectivities are theorized outside of psychoanalysis and the racio-speciesist "great divide." Smith et al. (2019) describe Indigenous identity as being rooted in relationships to the land and as Ingersoll (2016) would note, the sea. Sea and land do not *represent* spaces, they *are* the spaces where ancestors are laid to rest, returning to a material state from which future generations will come into being. "Rather than viewing ourselves as being *in* relationship with other people or things, we *are* the relationship that we hold and are part of" (quote in Smith et al., 2019, p. 9). The past and future are materially co-emergent as "we are called into being through our relationships, through the interaction with kin genealogies and events. Rocks rivers, birds, plants mountains animals and oceans all possess a genealogy" (Bignall and Rigney, 2019, p. 162), and often, as Simpson notes, these genealogies intertwine as trees, birds, rocks are likely ancestors. Human-more-than-human ancestry means futurity *is* the surrounding more-than-human species and objects (Rifkin, 2017), simultaneous with ancestral pasts and presents.

With no 'great divide' (Latour, 1988) violently squashing experience, consciousness emerges through networks and fields (Moore, 2017), constellations that organize theory through intelligences of kinesthetic and ancestral presents, futures, and pasts (Simpson, 2017), not only co-emergent and interpenetrating, but co-occurring. The land is a living and thinking creature (Watts, 2013). Ecosystems are not just "naturally" balanced, but are "societies" with ethical structures, cultures (Angier, 2021), what Watts (2013) terms "inter-species treaties and agreements" and these habitats have the capacities to "interpret, understand and implement" (p. 23) policies. Consider Kohn's (2013) earlier description of mushrooms and trees. If we were to analyze their relationship, we would see it as a form of "treaties" between fungi and trees, whereby fungi absorb extra water and minerals dispersing them *through* time to the tree and surrounding plant growths (Kohn, 2013; Tsing, 2012). Plants hold traumatic memories of draught and pestilence, such that the seeds of plants that have survived such devastation have a memory of it (Bryce, 2021). Seeds, too, emerge through dense temporality, holding memories of trauma—draught, pestilence—enabling future potentialities—seeds—to prepare for the threats of the past, in the present future. This temporality is dense.

The human and more-than-human both "derive agency through the extensions of these [land] thoughts" (Watts, 2013, p. 21), and they influence human and more-than-human activity in a mutuality. This idea of agency is not located in rationality or thought. It is not associated with those qualities humans have decided only occur in humans. Here space, time and matter are "intra-actively produced in the ongoing differential articulation of the world…Becoming is not an unfolding in time, but the inexhaustible dynamism of the en-folding of mattering" (Barad, 2007, p. 234). But to experience this dynamism, one must engage in the process of being enfolded in mattering, not exceptionalism.

Dense temporalities envision the perpetual motions of time and space vertically (through past, present and future generations), as well as horizontally (encapsulating all bodies, objects, environments), diversely in-forming bodies-beings-matter. Ingersoll (2016), Rose (2012), Simpson (2011, 2017) and TallBear (2017), among others, describe ways of coming into being not only with a present materiality in-formed by the agencies of the surrounding human-more-than-human but with generations of such kin, where there is shared "intimate knowing relatedness of all things" (TallBear, 2017). The "self" is not contained but in process and a part of the world's becoming (Meijer, 2019). Thus I am part of the world and as such, the health of the world is the health of me and vice versa. Destruction of others is my own destruction. Here identified "differences" in being (humans, more-than-humans, animate and inanimate) are not obstacles but opportunities for "[all] species to express themselves more fully and which can also be—for the human at least—a source of beauty" (Meijer, 2019, p. 65). By writing "for the human at least" Meijer refuses to engage in the human exceptionalist tendency to speak for others.

da Silva (2015, 2016), Jackson (2013), and others call for an end of The World "*as we know it*" (da Silva, 2016, emphasis in original). Ending this world, emergent from the violence of coloniality and anti-Blackness that is human exceptionalism, profoundly reckons with the knowledge that who gets to be human is limited, shifting, emergent, based only on the needs of those solidly identified as human. An end of The World-*as-we-know-it* is the surrender of Western ontology and epistemology, upon which psychoanalysis emerges, that narrows temporality to the linear, "castrates" past-present-future worlds, leading inevitably to destruction.

Screens of Spaces of Transcorporeal Becomings: The Potential for a More Just Psychoanalysis?

Now returning to the more-than-human on the screen, media scholars describe the functions of animal narratives for humans. Chris (2006) describes the ways narratives in documentaries and fictionalized films are edited to reinforce cultural stereotypes about gender, race, and class. She claims humans construct and use animal stories on the screen as a way of reflecting societal stresses and conflicts. Here the screen becomes a literal psychoanalytic screen, but with the benefit of the human being able to "act out" conflicts through carefully edited animal stories. Again, animals are used to evacuate ambivalence, enabling the emergence of a (white) human subjectivity without conflict.

Negra (2018), as mentioned earlier, focuses on the plethora of Internet and television shows helping humans create more ideal domesticated spaces with animals living indoors. Pets, Negra writes, are used to curate sites of domestic bliss, ideal interiors, where humans cater to their pets in perfect neoliberal capitalist behaviors, that is, purchasing toys and furniture *for* cats. These items turn the home into a space that advertises a capitalistic investment in the pet as love and fulfillment. Here she references Berlant's (2011) ideas of consumption as a Sysephusian form of action, where objects serve to convey for the human, commodified affective experiences of comfort, success, happiness. Objects are invested with affect by humans—ex. I feel like a good human when I buy a cat tree for my cats.

As Meijer (2019) contends, such behavior and focus on the individual animal—the emotional and physical life of my cats—serves to help me ignore, disavow, dissociate from the massive slaughter of other animals used for food, clothing, medical advances—those millions of mice genetically engineered for COVID research, perhaps, as well as those killed when their homes are destroyed as punishment for encroaching on human "development," industrial production of crops, or/and industrial and climate disasters. Here, again, we negotiate psychic conflict around accountability for massive destruction and killing, through our caring for our domesticated animals. Responsibility is temporally collapsed, space and time narrowed to only the now that is *here*, literally in my apartment, split off from the temporal echoes of our behaviors.

Things also get complicated when we consider Chen's (2012) notions that I breath in my cats as they breath in me, we both take in and use the "skin" of the carpet and glue on the cat scratcher, fabrics of all the many cat toys I purchase. Our subjectivities are co-emergent, in process, changing with each breath. Unlike Searles, who would say the wood cat scratcher is certainly not a tree, Indigenous theorists like Ingersoll (2016) and Simpson would discuss the life within the wood, the ancestors of the lands from where it was taken, including the potential violence, extraction, exploitation of land, materials, and labor, or perhaps, fair trade that only measures fairness through capital resources and human costs. The cat scratcher is alive and is a "lure for feelings" (Shaviro, 2011, quoting Whitehead, 1929/1978, p. 8), with agency that compels my cats and me to certain shifting behaviors and experiences.

Negra's (2018) analysis can be seen as reinforcing the construction of subjectivity anchored in human exceptionalism. Due to the tenuous subjectivities of neoliberal capitalism that need to be reaffirmed continually through the ongoing consumption of commodified experiences, the human is compelled to buy things for their pets to feel fleeting moments of contentment, intimacy, fulfillment. It is difficult to disagree with this analysis however, again the animal as pet is situated as merely an object in the creation of a starkly human subjectivity. Given the density of temporality, this particular function is merely a sliver. Expanding the technologies of subjectivity, we could return to the example of the cartoon I described earlier. If I conceive of my home as not just a multispecies apartment (shared with my cats) but a space of opportunity for the co-emergence of diverse subjectivities, human-more-than-human assemblages, then purchasing a cat scratcher is indeed to participate in the neoliberal capitalism and all it involves described above. It also includes a recognition that a space organized around human exceptionalism constrains the more-than-human, and reinforces the continual production of geno- and eco-cidal exceptionalist "human" subjectivities. After all, our homes and all the spaces we claim already belong or have belonged to other creatures (Alaimo, 2016) human and more-than-human (e.g. stealing land from Indigenous people; "clearing" forests for suburbs), in the presents, pasts and futures.

Approaching our screen lives through lens of temporal density, my students, patients, and I co-emerge as transcorporeal beings. An obvious example is that since the emergence of COVID, cats, dogs, and birds seem to come to the rescue of crying or distressed patients or students, suddenly appearing in order to sit strategically in front of the computer camera. This is not a distraction, but a breath, a moment through which emerges a space for complex validations and mirroring. The distress of the patient or student is recognized, not just by me, but by their more-than-human kin, who act in a form of "call and response" (Bennet, 2010). Similar to Despret's (2004) horses, these animals listen and respond. I could understand these occurrences merely as forms of therapeutic animal encounters, but these beings foster time's density. I see the histories of neglect or abuse as the patient caresses, leans into, or/and moves the more-than-human kin. There is a complex dance of care that is "in-formed" (Manning, 2014, p. 164) through a human-more-than-human entanglement. I hear the changes in tone as one student, visibly anxious as his eyes dart around his room, gradually answers a question to the tune of his very audible chirping partner. These situations represent a newly apparent liminality where the patient and student come into being *through* the more-than-human, including, of course, the screens and the cyberspaces (Miller, personal communication). As with Despret's horse work, the "minds" of the animals and the human come into being between the skins of bodies, indicating again how porous these boundaries we create actually are. These spaces create moments of opportunity for transcorporeal subjectivities to emerge. These subjectivities echo with past experiences refracted in the present to interpenetrate and in-form (Manning, 2014) an unfolding future.

Similarly, as I listen to distress or any heightened affects, the limitations I experience in terms of my capacities to soothe my pasts and presents are lured into the moment. I find new clinical space as I feel the warmth of the furry body next to me (lovely in the winter, less so in the summer), or within view just beyond my screen. Where in my office I might slow down my breath and attend to our bodies, working to gradually breathe in rhythm together, now this rhythmic pulsation involves watching and feeling the timings of humans and more-than-human companions, focusing my gaze on a calming or enlivening object in my or my patient's surroundings. Akin to when I improvise with other musicians (see also Knoblauch, 2000), a rhythm emerges between; feeling a vibration of breath and purring or panting on the screen and on my couch. Collectively, as transcorporeal beings, we "read" through skin and muscles and cyberspace, communicating complex patterns.

Considering the *more-than-human* environment and dense temporalities means psychoanalysis must re-form subjectivity (Gentile and Miller, 2021) with theories that reflect our used and exchanged atoms (Searles, 1960), our emergences through parasites and bacteria organisms (Anzaldúa, 1987), "a diverse, interconnected system (a mutuality of moods-objects-neurotransmitters-hormones-cognitions-affects-attachments-tears-glands-images-words-gut)" (Wilson and Foglia, 2011, p. 280). "[B]ecoming human [is] an interspecies collaborative project" (Ogden et al.'s quote of Rose p. 14), with subjectivities coming into being only as assembled moments of coherence. This clinical space is a plenum, an "infinite composition in which each existant's singularity is contingent upon its becoming one possible expression of all the other existants" (da Silva, 2016), offering more varied situations within which *all beings* have the "opportunities to accomplish subjectivities" (Despret, 2008, 123), a "polity with more channels of communication between members" (Bennet, 2010, p. 104). This requires that we learn to hear and receive propositions beyond the monotone language of human exceptionalism, engaging "never as a matter of "giving" other animals a voice, but rather of understanding and recognizing that they have been speaking to us all along" (Meijer, 2019, p. 240).

This theory of transcorporeal subjectivity stands in contrast to that of traditional and relational psychoanalysis, where subjects are emergent through anti-black, gendered, racio-species violence, inherently split off, "primally castrated." This provides only tempo-rally narrowed and flattened possibilities for subjectivities through the very act of disavowing the violence from which they emerged. This theory of subjectivity can never be racially just, environmentally responsible, or accountable for its violences. It is a technology of not only alienation and violent geno- and eco-cidal splitting (as if this isn't enough), but of rendering the human incapable of consciously experiencing the range of recognitions, symbolizations, and communications enlivening the vast majority of our planet.

Personally, I prefer to acknowledge my co-emergence, and entanglement within a world of dense temporalities. Not only is it deeply engaging, but enfolded within deep tempo-ralities. We're no longer alienated and alone facing an abyss of being merely a geological blip. Instead my (re-) becomings depend on my and other being's co-occurring capacities to create the potential for a wider accomplishment of diverse, interconnected subjectivities. We are responsible for the lively relationalities of which we are a part, taking "responsibility for that which we inherit (from the past and the future), for the entangled relationalities of inheritance that 'we' *are*… to put oneself at risk, to risk oneself (which is never one or self), to open oneself up to indeterminacy in moving toward what is to-come (Barad, 2010, p. 265). Emergent through these technologies of subjectivities are the potentials to collectively hold and metabolize the ambivalences, conflicts, and annihilation anxieties fueled by the reality that no one gets out of here alive.

References

Akhtar, S. and Volkan, V.D. (2005/2014a). *Mental zoo: Animals in the human mind and its pathology.* London: International Universities Press/Karnac Press.

———. (2005/2014b). Cultural zoo: Animals in the human mind and its sublimations. London: International Universities Press/Karnac Press.

Alaimo, S. (2016). *Exposed: Environmental politics & pleasures in posthuman times.* Minneapolis, MN: University of Minnesota Press.

Angier, N. (2021). Meet the other social influencers of the Animal Kingdom. *New York Times*, May 7, 2021 https://www.nytimes.com/2021/05/07/science/animals-chimps-whales-culture.html

Anzaldúa, G. (1987). *Borderlands/La Frontera: The New Mestiza.* San Francisco, CA: Aunt Lute Books.

Barad, K. (2007). *Meeting the universe halfway: Quantum physics and the entanglement of matter and meaning.* Durham/London: Duke University Press.

Barad, K. (2010). Quantum entanglements and hauntological relations of inheritance: Dis/continuities, spacetime enfoldings, and justice-to-come. *Derrida Today, 3*(2), 240–268.

Bennet, J. (2010). *Vibrant matter: A political ecology of things.* Durham, NC: Duke University Press.

Bennett, J. (2020). *Being property once myself: Blackness and the end of man.* Cambridge, MA: Belknap Press of the Harvard University Press.

Berlant, L. (2011). *Cruel optimism.* Durham, NC: Duke University Press.

Bignall, S. and Rigney, D. (2019). Indigeneity, posthumanism and Nomad thought: Transforming colonial ecologies. In R. Braidotti & S. Bignall (eds). *Posthuman ecologies: Complexity and process after Deleuze*, pp. 159–182. London: Rowman & Littlefield.

Blazina, C., Boyraz, G. and Shen-Miller, D. (2013). Introduction: using context to inform clinical practice and research. In C. Blazina, G. Boyraz, and D. Shen-Miller (eds). *The psychology of the human-animal bond: A resource for clinicians and researchers*, pp. 3–24. New York: Springer Press.

Boisseron, B. (2018). *Afro-dog: Blacness and the animal question.* New York: Columbia University Press.

Brickman, C. (2018). *Race in psychoanalysis: Aboriginal populations in the mind.* New York: Routledge.

Bryce, E. (2021). Crops are 'imprinted' by past droughts – which could help them prepare for future ones. *Anthropocene.* November 19, 2021, https://www.anthropocenemagazine.org/2021/11/crops-are-imprinted-by-past-droughts-which-could-help-them-prepare-for-future-ones/?utm_source=rss&utm_medium=rss&utm_campaign=crops-are-imprinted-by-past-droughts-which-could-help-them-prepare-for-future-ones

Butler, D. (2019). Racialized bodies and the violence of the setting. *Studies in Gender and Sexuality*, 20 (3): 146–158.

Chen, M. Y. (2012). *Animacies: Biopolitics, racial mattering, and queer affect.* Durham, NC: Duke University Press.

Chris, C. (2006). *Watching wildlife.* Minneapolis: University of Minnesota Press.

Clough, P. (2018). *The user unconscious: On affect, media and measure.* Minneapolis: University of Minnesota Press.

Critchley S. (2002). *On humour.* London: Routledge.

Dale, J. P., Goggin, J., Leyda, J., McIntyre, A. P. and Negra, D. (2017). *The aesthetics and affects of cuteness.* New York/London: Routledge.

da Silva, D. F. (2015). Toward a Black feminist poethics: The quest(ion) of Blackness toward the end of the world. *The Black Scholar*, 44 (2): 81–97.

———. (2016). On difference without separability. *Catalogue of the 32a São Paulo Art Biennial, "Incerteza viva" (Living Uncertainty)*.

Despret, V. (2004). The body we care for: Figures of anthropo-zoo-genesis. *Body & Society*, 10 (2–3): 111–134.

———. (2008). The becomings of subjectivity in animal worlds. *Subjectivity*, 23: 123–139.

Emmens, J. (2021). Exploration of animal-human relationships in psychoanalytic psychotherapy: Finding pathways to bridge remnant, disowned, or as yet undeveloped parts of self. In Silbert, J. and J. Frasca (eds). *Animals as the third in relational psychotherapy: Exploring theory, frame and practice,* pp. 14–25. London/New York: Routledge.

Ferenczi, S. (1922/1989). *Thalassa: A theory of genitality,* trans. Henry Alden Bunker. London: Karnac Press.

Frasca, J. (2021). Frame breakage to the rescue. In Silbert, J. and J. Frasca (eds). *Animals as the third in relational psychotherapy: Exploring theory, frame and practice,* pp. 122–131. London/New York: Routledge.

Freccero, C. (2010). Figural historiography: Dogs, humans, and cynathropic becomings. In Hayes, J., Higonnet, M.R., and Spurlin, W.J. (eds). *Comparatively queer: Interrogating identities across time and cultures,* pp. 45–67. New York: Palgrave MacMillan.

Fuchs, M. and Brandt, S. L. (2018). Animals on American television: Introduction to the special issue. *European Journal of American Studies*, 13 (1): 1–8. Open access.

Genosko, G. (1993). Introduction to the transaction Edition. In *Topsy: The story of a golden haired chow* (pp. 1–26). New Brunswick, NJ: Transaction Publishers.

Gentile, K. (2020). Transcorporeal becoming: The temporalities of Searles and the nonhuman. *Subjectivity.* DOI: 10.1057/s41286-020-00098-6

———. (2021). Kittens in the clinical space: Expanding subjectivity through dense temporalities of interspecies transcorporeal becoming. *Psychoanalytic Dialogues*, 31 (2): 135–150.

Gentile, K. and Miller, K. D. M. (2021). An end of the world as-we- know- it: After da Silva. *ROOM: A Sketchbook for Analytic Action, 10.21 "Solastalgia."* https://www.analytic-room.com/essays/an-end-of-the-world-as-we-know-it-after-da-silva-katie-gentile-kathleen-del-mar-miller/

Grier, K. C. (2006). *Pets in America: A history.* New York: Harcourt.

Haraway, D. (2008). *When species meet.* Minneapolis: University of Minnesota Press.

Haritaworn, J. (2015). Decolonizing the non/human. 210–213.

Hedgpeth, D. (2021). "During the Pandemic, Animal Shelters Don't Have Enough Dogs for the Demand." *The Washington Post.* January 6.

Hird, M. (2009). Feminist engagements with matter. *Feminist Studies*, 35 (2): 329–346.

Hoffer, L.N. (2011). Lapdogs and Moral Shepherd's dogs: Canine and paid female companions in nineteenth-century English literature. In Blazina, C., Boyraz, G., and Shen-Miller, D. (eds). *The Psychology of the Human-Animal Bond* (pp. 107–124). New York, NY: Springer.

Ingersoll, K. A. (2016). *Waves of knowing: A seascape epistemology.* Durham, NC: Duke University Press.

Jackson, Z. I. (2013). Animal: New directions in the theorization of race and posthumanism. *Feminist Studies*, 39 (3): 669–686.

———. (2020). *Becoming human: Matter and meaning in an antiblack world.* New York: New York University Press.

Kassouf, S. (2017). Psychoanalysis and climate change: Revisiting Searles's the nonhuman environment, rediscovering Freud's phylogenetic fantasy, and imagining a future. *American Imago*, 74 (2): 141–171.

King, T. L. (2019). *The black shoals: Offshore formation of Black and Native Studies.* Durham, NC: Duke University Press.

Knoblauch, S. (2000). The *musical edge of therapeutic dialogue*. New York: Routledge.

Kohn, E. (2013). *How forests think: Toward an anthropology beyond the human*. Berkeley: University of California Press.

Latour, B. (1988). Mixing humans and nonhumans together: The sociology of a door closer. *Social Problems*, 35 (3): 298–310.

Manning, E. (2014). Wondering the world directly – or, How movement outruns the subject. *Body & Society*, 20 (3&4): 162–188.

Meijer, E. (2019). *When animals speak: Toward an interspecies democracy*. New York: New York University Press.

Miller, K. D. M. (2020). Working clinically with the skin's surface: Tattoos, scars, and gendered embodiment. *Studies in Gender and Sexuality*, 21 (3): 143–154.

———. (2021). A radically open analysis: Writing as wrapping, video as skin. *Psychoanalytic Dialogues*, forthcoming.

Moore, D. L. (2017). The ground of memory: Vizenor, land, language. In B. Däwes and A. Hauke (eds). *Native American survivance, memory, and futurity*, pp. 90–101. London: Routledge.

Morton, T. (2017). *Humankind: Solidarity with nonhuman people*. London: Verso.

Negra, D. (2018). Animality, domesticity and masculinity in My Cat From Hell. *Critical Studies in Television: The International Journal of Television Studies*, 13 (1): 6–23.

Ogden, L. A., Hall, B., and Tanita, K. (2013). Animals, plants, people, and things: A review of multi-species ethnography. *Environment and Society: Advances in Research*, 4: 5–24.

Oliver, K. (2009). *Animal lessons: How they teach us to be human*. New York: Columbia University Press.

Pugliese, J. (2020). *Biopolitics of the more-than-human: Forensic ecologies of violence*. Durham, NC: Duke University Press.

Rifkin, M. (2017). *Beyond settler time: Temporal sovereignty and Indigenous self-determination*. Durham, NC/London: Duke University Press.

Rose, D. B. (2012). Multispecies knots of ethical time. *Environmental Philosophy*, 9 (1): 127–140.

Searles, H. (1960). *The nonhuman environment in normal development and in schizophrenia*. New York: International Universities Press.

Shaviro, S. (2011). The universe of things. http://www.shaviro.com/Othertexts/Things.pdf. Downloaded November, 2011.

Silbert, J. and J. Frasca (eds) (2021). *Animals as the third in relational psychotherapy: Exploring theory, frame and practice*. London/New York: Routledge.

Simpson, L. (2011). *Dancing on our turtle's back: Stories of nishnaabeg re-creation, resurgence, and a new emergence*. Winnipeg, CA: ARP Books.

Simpson, L. B. (2017). *As we have always done: Indigenous freedom through radical resistance*. Minneapolis: University of Minnesota Press.

Smith, L.T., Tuck, E. and Yang, K. W. (2019). *Indigenous and decolonizing studies in education: Mapping the long view*. New York: Routledge.

Spillers, H. J. (1987). Mam's baby, papa's maybe: An American grammar book. *Diacritics*, 17 (2): 64–81.

Steeves, H. P. (ed.) (1999). *Animal others: On ethics, ontology, and animal life*. Albany, NY: SUNY Press.

TallBear, K. (2017). Beyond the life/not-life binary: A feminist-Indigenous reading of cryopreservation, interspecies thinking, and the new materialisms. In J. Radin, and E. Kowal (eds). *Cryopoltics: Frozen life in a melting world*, pp. 179–202. Cambridge, MA: MIT Press.

Tsing, A. (2012). Unruly edges: Mushrooms as companion species. *Environmental Humanities*, 1: 141–154.

Tuan, Y. F. (1984). *Dominance & affection: The making of pets*. New Haven, CT: Yale University Press.

Tuana, N. (2008). Viscous porosity: Witnessing Katrina. In S. Alaimo and S. Hekman (eds). *Material feminisms*, pp. 188–213. Bloomington: Indiana University State University of New York Press.

Watts, V. (2013). Indigenous place-thought & agency amongst humans and non-humans (First Woman and Sky Woman go on a European world tour!). *Decolonization: Indigeneity, Education & Society*, 2 (1): 20–34.

Whitehead, A. N. (1929/1978). *Process and reality*. New York: The Free Press.

Wilson, R. A. and Foglia, L. (2011). Embodied cognition. *Stanford Encyclopedia of Philosophy*. https://philpapers.org/rec/WILEC

Winnicott, D. W. (1971). *Playing and Reality*. New York: Basic Books.

Wynter, S. (2003). Unsettling the coloniality of being/power/truth/freedom: Toward the human, after man, its overrepresentation—an argument. *CR: The New Centennial Review*, 3 (3): 257–337.

13

THE INTIMACY OF THE VIRTUAL DISTANCE

Susi Ferrarello

What Is Virtuality?

You are reading these words. They come from me, the writer. They spring from my world-view and take their own shape while I am typing them on this keyboard in my small apartment in Berkeley. Are the lines you are reading virtual or real? Where is the fine line that distinguishes these two dimensions? Internet, messaging platforms, social networking sites, and the smart phones conveying all this are a big slice of our daily life. But what kind of life is that? Are we living more and more an unreal life? What can phenomenology say about the quality of this experience?

Borrowing his interpretation from phenomenology, Deleuze (1991) defines virtuality as what refers to an experience that is both ideal and real (p. 43). In the virtual life a very blurred line sets apart reality from what is just a mere projection of it. In the first two chapters of Logical Investigations Husserl, distinguishes at least two ways in which we can interpret reality, *reel* and *real*; the former indicates the immanent part of one's experience, while the latter indicates the objective quality belonging to that experience. To use an example, if I see a red box I will call *reel* the immanent sensuous data that are part of my experience, while *real* would be the objective properties of the red box (Husserl, 1970, 535). Virtual life seems to be a complex combination of both in which the reel components of the experience play a predominant part in deducing the *real* part of the object we are experiencing.

In this chapter my aim is to use phenomenology to examine the meaning of the body within virtuality in order to understand to what extent our body can enjoy "real" intimate feelings while having virtual experiences. My general thesis is that virtual experience has the power to revert the spontaneous way of experiencing life. In doing so, it makes space for a quite meaningful level of intimacy that is almost entirely constituted by *reel* components that make the virtual intimate experience as unique as the "real" one. In fact, while in the spontaneous engagement with reality the reflective exploration of meanings occurs after a non-reflective interaction with life, in virtual experience reflection comes along with the encounter itself; the realm of meanings seems to be active as soon as the virtual encounter takes place. Moreover, the reality that constitutes the virtual intimate encounter is mostly composed of personal immanent data and accordingly free from the objective expectations

DOI: 10.4324/9781003195849-17

of the external reality. The virtual experience seems to disclose a transcendental intimate connection from this early sensuous meaning connection. To explain how and why this occurs I will take the following steps.

First, I will compare what "body" means in normal and virtual life. For the sake of my argument, I will limit virtuality to those encounters that occur on the screen, such as reading this paper or texting with someone (although a very interesting follow up to my argument would consist in its application on those new technologies that allow us to being touched, such as teledildonics, hug shirts, and wearables in general). Second, I will examine the transcendental reality of the virtual dimension. To conclude I will describe what kind of intimacy can be disclosed in this dimension.

Who Are We When We Are Virtual?

What is a body? If a person sees my body through a video call is my body real? Or does it become real only when my body is seen in person? When does the image of my body become the vehicle for intimate feelings? If someone sees my picture on social media and develops attachment for that image, can that be called intimacy?

To start addressing these questions, I can state that in phenomenology the distinction between virtuality and reality is strongly influenced by the sense of touch (meant as the Greek *aesthesis*, sensing the touch)—if I can touch it, then it is real. In fact, phenomenology would say that the reality of one's body starts with the ability of this body to touch itself. Hence, if I cannot touch a body but I can see it, is a body still a body? Husserl's *Cartesian Meditations* would answer the question in the following way:

> Among the… bodies (*Körper*) of this nature then find uniquely singled out my body (*Leib*)… the only one in which immediately have free rein (*schalte und walte*), and in particular govern in each of its organs—I perceive with my hands, touching kinesthetically, seeing with my eyes, etc., and can so perceive at any time, while these kinesthesis of the organs proceed in the I am doing and are subject to my I can; furthermore, putting these kinesthesis into play, I can push, shove, etc., and thereby directly, and then indirectly, act corporeally (*leiblich*).
>
> *(1973, 19)*

In this excerpt three key terms to Husserl's notion of corporeality stands out: *Leib, Koerper,* and *kinesthesis*. According to Husserl, and the German language in general, all of us have at least two bodies, an organic body (*Koerper*), meant as an object among other objects, and a living body (*Leib*). These two kinds of bodies—being a body (*Koerper*) and having a body (*Leib*)—relate to each other by kinesthesis which literally indicate the ability of someone to perceive one's own movement. The organic body is at once a living body because its senses perceive the possibility of its being alive and function through these possibilities.

With the term kinesthetic Husserl uses the Greek *kinesis* and *aesthesis* to say that it is through the perception (*aisthesis*) of movement (*kinesis*) that we are able to experience ourselves. My personal living body (*Leib*) perceives and governs the movement of my instrumental body (*Koerper*) engaging with the life-world. My *Koerper* is experienced first by the personal lived-body (*Leib*) and then it appears to others as a set of functions whose inputs are given by the *Leib*. As Husserl writes

> I experience... my own corporeity (*Leiblichkeit*),... inasmuch as I can in each case perceive the one hand by means of the other, an eye by means of a hand, etc., so that the functioning organ must become an object, the object a functioning organ.
>
> *(1962, 20)*

My body is a *functioning* instrument that acquires new experiences and reflects on them through its kinesthetic life. In this kind of "sensorial experience" the touch within which we perceive our body (*Koerper*) seems to prevail over the others. My body is real insofar I can touch it.

> The body as such can be constituted originally only in tactuality and in everything localized within the sensations of touch, such as warmth, cold, pain, and the like.
>
> *(1962, 150)*

> A subject with eyes only could not have an appearing body at all.
>
> *(1962, 150)*

> It becomes a body only through the introduction of sensations in touch, the introduction of pain sensations, etc., in short, through the localization of sensations qua sensations.
>
> *(1962, 151)*

From these excerpts it emerges that for Husserl, my body (*Leib*) is a functioning unit that experiences reality through the *kinaesteses* of the organic body (*Koerper*) and becomes my body (*Leib*) through tactile sensations. Its reality stands out when the body itself can have kinaestesis, that is, as soon as it can perceive its own movement.

In *Phenomenology of Perception* (1962), Merleau-Ponty brings this description a step further in considering the body a "functioning *schéma*." Similar to Husserl, Merleau-Ponty considers the body as "our general means of having a world" (1962, 146). It is a "fluid" (1962, 49–50) means through which I perceptually live my relationship to myself, others, and the world (1962, 206). Through the habitual repetitions of this sensory-motor functioning, the body develops a schema, that is a habitual pattern to respond to certain stimuli—such as a posture, a musical skill, a way of smiling (Gallagher and Zahavi, 2008). Merleau-Ponty talks about the *fluidity* in the constitution of bodily schema because he does not accept the distinction between physical and mental, real and ideal, and accordingly, we would infer, real and virtual. Corporeality encompasses all the layers that make my body what it is. Hence if a connection happens between my body here and the body I see through my video call, that connection is real despite the virtuality of its means.

In fact, my ongoing sensory life is in a dynamic relationship with the world in a way that modifies me and my surroundings at once. "As an open system of an infinite number of... positions," Merleau-Ponty writes, "what we have called the body schema is precisely this system of equivalences" between my position and my surroundings which generates an "immediately given invariant whereby the different motor tasks are instantaneously transposable" (1962, 141). This fluid schema has its functioning that works for me and my surrounding world. "My body appears to me as an attitude with a view to a certain actual or possible task" (1962, 100). Therefore, a body is to Merleau-Ponty "an expressive unity that we can learn to know only by actively taking it up" (1962, 100). Even if the body does not present itself in person but only through a virtual means, it does not mean that this body is unreal. As far as this body can perceive itself and the observer can perceive their own body, it is possible to perceive the other body as a functioning schema in the world similar to mine. In the next section I will focus on the different degrees of intimacy that the virtual bodies can achieve in virtual connections.

My Body in the Virtual World

How does my body and the body of the other appear in Virtual Reality? Can there be intimacy in this kind of reality where we cannot actually touch each other's bodies?

The word intimacy comes from the Latin superlative *intimus*, which means the most inside possible. Generally, intimacy points to a space of deep proximity from which it is possible to establish a connecting bond with yourselves and others. Being able to reach this intimate space allows us to open up the ongoing flow of meanings that fill our life. Unfortunately, it often happens that we reach a space of proximity that is not placed in the most inside possible within us but is in fact an outside space where foreign expectations dictate how things should be for us. We might be tempted to consider this a space of intimacy but it is rather the space of conventional life in which we can easily feel trapped. Trying to find an intimate connection from here would lead to a sense of alienation because it does not resonate with our immanent experience. In fact, while the intimate space points to the immanent sensuous reality (reel) as we experience it through our body, the outside space refers to the objective properties of reality (real) as they belong to the object of our experience according to societal agreement.

I believe that technology helps us to reach a truly intimate place even if without tactile sensations. As emerged before, the constitution of the living body (*Leib*) starts in fact through self-tactile experience. We perceive ourselves, we know we can move and from this awareness we acquire new information about ourselves in the real world. Our living body can always experience its own organic body and from there infer how the other living body might operate. Moreover, depending on what kind of virtual tool we are using, we might gain some tactile sensations even if we are not in direct contact with each other. There are, in fact, new tools such as wearables and tele-touch technologies that allow for mutual tactile connection and exchange between two or more bodies. Yet, I believe it is possible to constitute the meanings of one's own body and intimately connect with other bodies even if we cannot rely on those tactile sensations but we are limited to read on the screen what another person is writing.

For example, when we use messaging platforms to interact with other people, we can acquire an essential understanding of their living body (*Leib*) even if we do not have any immediate tactile experience. For example, if my interlocutor is at home or if we are messaging across time zones, my interlocutor would feel more prone to share information that she would conceal if we met at my office or in a restaurant. Especially, if my morning is her night and if we are texting while my interlocutor feels safe in bed, they might feel comfortable to open up to me because their level of social guard would be lower than if sitting in the morning in my office. This explains, for instance, the success of text therapy in which the individual consults with a psychotherapist through chats, as with Talk Space, for example (Dror Ben-Zeev et al., 2020). These phone applications might be crucially helpful in situation of crisis because the intimate connection between living bodies overcome the efforts to show and carry around their organic body (*Koerper*). The person who enters in contact with the psychotherapist via text does not have to worry about the social conventions that regulate their organic body but can deliberately choose to share what is more pressing in their life. The two living bodies choose to get close to each other on a very reflective level that might be poorer of perceptive data because they cannot touch or see each other but richer of meanings because they decided to communicate with each other and to do so they have to reflect on and share what their engagement with life means (The quality of intimate connection changes once again if we use the video. In fact, I can perceive part of the bodily language of the other person; I can, so to speak, be with them in their home and perceive a number of information that I would not be able to gather if we were talking in person at a café or via texting on messenger). They share their own intimate reality (*reel*) as it appears from the immanent connection with the data of their experience. That is to say, even if virtual, each reality is a lifeworld carrier of different perceptual possibilities that our organic and living body can use for intimate intersubjective connection. To answer one the questions raised above, different would be the asymmetric situation in which one finds my image online and develops romantic feelings for it without me willingly participating in the exchange. In that case we would not be able to talk about intimacy but just projections (and maybe unhealthy attachment) because there is no mutual commitment to the virtual exchange.

The Empathic Connection

It is possible to establish an intimate connection even if the exchange occurs only through text messaging because behind the screen there are bodies capable of experiencing themselves and connecting with their own reality (reel). These bodies are carriers of an infinite set of perceptive experiences that can be shared or at least communicated to their interlocutor. Being able to understand what the other might be feeling based on one's own feeling of the same is key to empathy. The empathic connection with the other is limited by the horizon of my own sensory experience, which is, on its turn, communicable by any device I am using. Empathy originates exactly in the encounter between me as the neutral observer and ourselves as the radical other. In this encounter I can present to myself certain feelings, emotions, sensations that I experience in my living body (*Leib*). Such presentifications enable the subject to transform what was given *Leibhaftig* (in person) into a sedimentation that establishes "the unity of world-certainty" and discloses the possibility for any reproductive activity (Husserl, 2001, 152). In Husserliana XIII (Husserl, 1973a, 1973b, text 15, 97). Husserl distinguishes between a straightforward and an oblique form of empathy. This latter is an act analogous to recollection. While in the former kind of empathy I have an experience in which I directly presentify the other's experience, in the latter I reflect on the experience of the person with whom I am empathizing, and I fulfill the expectation with what I recollect from my past (1973a, 1973b, 97). In the case of empathic connection in Virtual Reality, this latter seems to be the form of empathy that one would normally use by reflecting on one's own bodily experience. As Husserl writes: "The analogy is not in full force and effect (*voll*); it is an indication, not an anticipation (*Vorgriff*) that could become a seizure of the self (*Selbstgriff*)" (Husserl, 1973c, 87). The analogy at the basis of my empathizing process is just an indication that the oblique empathy would replenish according to the experience I would have. If this indication transforms into a rigid expectation the empathizing process would become projection; consequently, no real empathic connection would arise. Even though my world is solipsistic (my thing, my body, my mind), empathy is what gives this world windows even if I am in a virtual experience and the other appears to me in an oblique way, through a screen or the words I read on the chat. The other is given to me as a presence, as another presence tied to the here and now of my body (Husserl, 1973a, 1973b, 99).

As Dan Zahavi writes, "an abiding horizon of the perceptual experience" (2010, 12) enables that intentional empathy (*Einfuelung*) by which I live the otherness. My experience of the otherness is limited to what my *Leib* lives or, using Merleau-Ponty, my bodily schema—that is, the way in which my sensuous body organizes itself while experiencing habitual events. For example, I know how being stroked feels because it has happened to me before. So, if my interlocutor says that it would like to stroke my hair, I know what they mean. In virtual experiences, according to the medium we use, we might be able to share what we experience to a lesser or higher degree; it is, in fact, my ability to experience my own body that creates the bodily schema to feel and empathize with the other. In that sense the empathic dimension by which we access to the other changes and impacts on our lifeworld in a new way.

In Zahavi's article on empathy (2010), he remarks how Stein, Husserl, and to a certain extent Scheler maintain that it is possible to access the other's mind through the empathic feeling (*Einfuehlung*). In fact, according to Husserl, this form of intentionality works on a signitive, pictorial, and perceptive level. I mean the Other as a "mental object" or a content of my presentation with an image that is *Leibhaftig* or *propria persona,* which means that the other lives within me through this embodied image. For me the other is "an as if" that exists within me in its bodily presence according to this "as if."

Naturally, in the virtual experience my perception is limited to what I can apprehend which changes according to the medium. If I am using messenger or Skype, the quality of my lived-experience changes because I can confirm the embodied presentation of this "as if" with a wider or narrower adequacy. According to Merleau-Ponty too, the amount of information that the expressive body can exchange with the other is fluid and proportional to its functioning schema/body. If the body is not allowed to perceive with all its senses, its reconstruction of the otherness will be accordingly affected to the extent it was able not to able to perceive for itself.

> Into each perception and into each judgment I bring either sensory functions or cultural settings which are not actually mine. Yet although I am outrun on all sides by my own acts, and submerged in generality, the fact remains that I am the one by whom they are experienced, and with my first perception there was launched an insatiable being who appropriates everything that he meets, to whom nothing can be purely and simply given because he has inherited his share of the world, and hence carries within him the project of all possible being, because it has been once and for all imprinted in his field of experiences.
>
> *(Husserl, 1962, 417)*

Therefore, as the passage shows, within a virtual experience, both for Husserl and Merleau-Ponty, the body maintains its functioning and expressive features, but its experience is limited to the realm of signitive or pictorial contents that can be perceived according to the tool in use. What we still need to answer in the following two sections is what degree of intimacy we can reach in this empathic connection.

Where Are You Now?

Let us come back to where we started. If you are here, you are still reading this article on your computer, phone, or piece of paper. Between you and I there is a considerable distance in time and space. We can both clearly perceive this distance on our bodies; in fact, you are forming your thoughts while using your eyes to read and I am using my fingers to type my words but my words and your thoughts are separated from a considerable space-time gap. Yet, even if we do not know each other and there is this important gap between us, we are connecting with each other in a unique way. I am sharing with you meanings that come from an intimate reflection that I would rarely communicate to my friends or closer family. What is this space between you and I? How does this impact our lifeworld?

In his *Phenomenology of the Social World*, the phenomenologist Schutz considers the body of the other as a field of expression that reveals his or her own inner world (1967, 22). This revelation can be possible by expressive movements or acts which can be grasped inter-subjectively. My thoughts as conveyed in these specific words are a field of expression that reveal part of my inner world. We have access to others' bodies and worlds continuously in everyday life. Schutz calls our experiential orientation toward the other, *Fremdeinstellung* (other-orientation) and *Dueinstellung*, thou-orientation. We approach the other within a "-we-relationship" in which the other is experienced as *another* mind that can be expressed in many ways; the other's mind is "within" or "with" me because I intend it so. My consciousness spontaneously reaches out to the other.

From this perspective, my body as a writer, for you as a reader, is not an object of your outer perception but it is an I-thou orientation that you experience in your immanent reality (reel), because you are deliberately continuing reading what I am writing. Our inner worlds encounter in this moment because we made the choice to share these worlds; you by committing to this read and me by typing on this computer. We are connecting with each other despite the remarkable difference in time-space and the lack of tactile sensation through each other's body. With this act you, reader, are intentionally letting my *Leib*, my *propria persona* be present "in" or "with" you within the limits of the meanings conveyed by this chapter. Therefore, in this experience the body of the other is not a mere thing or a discrete object but is the content of my intention—it is alive. Husserl would define it as the *noetic achievement of a transcendental subjectivity*.

Luft (2007) explains this expression through the notion of the transcendental in Husserl. To Husserl the transcendental is that dimension which answers to the question "How do we have an experience of the world?" (Luft, 2007, 5). Based on Husserl's method, the question can be answered with the epoché, that is, with a change of the attitude toward the spontaneous way with which one experiences the world. For example, now you are reading what I am writing and you are experiencing my words. At any time, you can stop and reflect on what you just read; you can seek to see its essential structure, and maybe even withholding your judgment in relation to all that is around you: preconceptions, feelings, or the ongoing present perceptions (noises, discomforts of any kind). This virtual medium—the paper, computer, phone—through which our connection is built works as a sort of accelerator of a transcendental connection. This medium, in fact, imposes on us the choice to connect with meanings in a reflective way and no longer as a spontaneous encounter with me on the street.

Where are you now, after the epoché, after the change of attitude imposed by this virtual medium? Husserl would say that you are within a transcendental dimension or you *are* the transcendental dimension. This transcendental dimension is, generally speaking, a pure correlation between act and its content—or to use Luft's words—"the constituting meaning-bestowing subjectivity" (2007, 4). This transcendental dimension involves a remarkable degree of reflection (because of the change of attitude) on the relationship between you as a reader of these lines and the lines as they are meant by you now. In this reflective dimension the subjects, both of us in this case, explore the lived experience of what was naively lived while I was writing these pages and you reading them. The transcendental dimension discloses when reflectively you examine the content of my experience in writing this, which functions in your life-world as a set of meanings for you. Despite the distance that separates us a proximity opens up that might not have occurred with closer family and friends. You are experiencing my thoughts and my thoughts are functioning for you in your life-world as a meaning making experience. Experiencing the other means making the other (*noesis*) the content (*noema*) or the sense (*Sinn*) it holds for me. In that sense the other is a noetic achievement of a transcendental subjectivity because it is given to my experience and exists as a meaningful structure that modifies my inner world. The other is a transcendental essence that modifies my inner world (of noetic acts) by its meaning or sense.

My inner world becomes, to use Schutz's and Husserl's terms, a *Mitwelt* (intersubjective world) despite and thanks to the virtual medium in use. While experiencing the other, I intend the other's world and I make my *Vorwelt* (pre-world) a shared world (*Mitwelt*) that surrounds my daily life (*Umwelt*).

Transcendental Intimacy of the Living Bodies: Online Dating

Something very similar happened during the 2019–2022 pandemic crisis when most of our life was moved to virtual platforms. Because of the mandated lockdown, we lost the spontaneity of daily encounters but we gained more weight in reflections. For instance, bumping into our colleagues in the hallway and exchanging small talks with them was replaced by the deliberate choice to email them what we considered meaningful and worth sharing. Suddenly, the virtual world was the only space we could share with friends, colleagues, and sometimes family. Yet, even though this world was new and scary sometimes, life kept going; our intimate connections remained alive and some of us even created new ones.

A conflicting sentiment arose as we experienced closeness with a person we knew from a distance without the medium of our organic body (*Koerper*). During the pandemic I had clients in my philosophical practice that continued dating even though only through Skype. With my philosophical counseling I helped them to see the qualitative difference of this new form of dating. My clients, in fact, lamented more awkwardness and an increased velocity with sharing important details of their lives which felt for some overwhelming. The exclusively virtual medium of this form of dating, Skype, facilitated a kind of disclosure that is in a certain sense transcendental; that is, it originates from the conscious decision to meet and to become for each other a meaning-constituting function in a very precise moment of one's life. The problem is that on video there are less spontaneous occasions for exchange. There is no waiter who makes a funny joke and gives the new couple the opportunity for a complicit comment. There is no park in which to walk and then discover the botanical passion of your partner. Dating online involved the conscious choice to stay together for that hour, to see each other's face and to talk about what we find meaningful in our life. Our meanings and thoughts become the only way to entertain and communicate with each other—there is no place where to hide for a spontaneous encounter. To help my clients with their first dates, I proposed to bring games, to prepare an aperitive or to watch a movie—basically, I helped them to reduce the transcendental intensity of the medium and to introduce more spontaneous pre-reflective expedients to make the connection between the two living bodies less reflective.

As Koestenbaum writes: "This transcendental closeness is more intimate than if it were sexual" (1974, 25). On a first online date you do not necessarily want all this intimate closeness. If anything, it creates awkwardness. The transcendental closeness in which we constitute the meaning of our organic and living body is what I call intimacy. In this closeness, in fact, we are our organic body (*Koerper*) that is inert to our attention but we are also our living body (Leib), that is all the active kinesthesis with which I perceive the set of possibilities that each datum discloses in front of me. The production of meaning originating from this exchange affects both layers of my body. As Sartre wrote:

> My existence in the midst of the world becomes the exact correlate of my transcendence-for-myself since my independence is absolutely safeguarded... Thus I am reassured... My facticity is saved. It is no longer this unthinkable and insurmountable given which I am fleeing; it is that for which the Other freely makes himself exist; it is as an end which he has given to himself... My existence is because it is given a name. I am because I give myself away.
>
> *(1956, 258)*

I am because I can choose how close I want to be to myself; in doing that I disclose myself to the other or—in Sartre's terms—"I give myself away" (1956, 257). My facticity is saved because the passive layers that constitute it can finally acquire a meaning from my choice to give myself to the regard of the other. My transcendental freedom is then used to inform an aspect of my existence that is meaningful for me. The social construction that defines my orientation ceases to be an empty category because it acquires a new meaning in each of the interaction with the inner world of the other. Figuratively speaking, intimacy invites the exploration of this eternal maze in which the self is what we are chasing, and mobile walls are the structure of which the self itself is made during its own chase.

It is in this space disclosed by an act of transcendental freedom that one acquires a space of absolute closeness with oneself and/or others whom one encounters in this original realm. This space of constitution of meanings connects our organic body with our living one. Indeed, it is in this space, as Sartre wrote, that "I have to realize the meaning of the world and of my own essence" (1956, 258). In this space my facticity awakes and is moved to decide how close I want to be to what I really am and what I am becoming. Hence, I consider intimacy the space from which my bodily facticity and my active meaning-bestowing decisions stem in the definition of my being. The technology of virtual communication might at times enhance this transcendental closeness in which we constitute the meaning of our bodily existence.

Conclusion

To answer the questions raised at the beginning of this chapter, it seems that within a virtual context we have the chance not only to constitute our lived body and intimately perceive others' body but also to experiment an intimate meaningful connection with others on what phenomenology would call a transcendental level. Within the virtual world, whether it is texting, video call, or sensory virtuality, we make the choice to initiate that exchange which leads us away from the naïve spontaneous attitude with which we normally interact with others. A virtual life transforms us in pure sense (*Sinn*) or meanings; we become the noematic correlate of another subjectivity which intends us by a "pictorial" and oblique empathy (*Einfuelung*). This happens because we choose to commit our freedom to these new perceptual experiences preparing the constitution of a meaningful *Mitwelt*.

This does not mean that we are disembodied, because we can perceive others proportionally to the extent we perceive ourselves; in fact, virtual experiences can be constituted in an embodied way even though our functioning body has to rely completely on another means of expression which is not directly through our own body (*Koerper*)—texting via a phone or calling through a computer screen. Therefore, it is the fact that we choose our medium to connect with someone else's body that allows to access more quickly and straightforwardly to the essential structure of the other. The connection does not occur spontaneously but from the choice to answer or to engage in that exchange with which we give ourselves as a meaning and then as a body. This is the power of the intersubjective virtual experience of writing, reading, or talking via Skype (which parenthetically brings us back, unexpectedly, to the power of letters that older generations would use to keep their intimate connections alive). In all these experiences, bodies function for the other in form of meanings (or transcendental contents) that are there to make sense for us. It seems that the virtual experience exceeds—and it is at times overwhelming as in the case of online first dates—the functioning of the body as it establishes with the other a "hypertrophic" dimension of meaning that makes the intersubjective experience very close to a transcendental form of intimacy.

References

Deleuze, J. (1991). *Bergsonism*, tr. Hugh Tomlinson and Barbara Habberjam. New York: Zone.

Dror Ben-Zeev, B. Buck, S. Meller, W. J. Hudenko, K. A. Hallgren (2020). "Augmenting Evidence-Based Care With a Texting Mobile Interventionist: A Pilot Randomized Controlled Trial". *Psychiatric Services*, 71(12):1218–1224

Gallagher, S., Zahavi, D. (2008). *The Phenomenological Mind: An Introduction to Philosophy of Mind and Cognitive Science*. London: Routledge.

Husserl, E. (1962). *Ideas I*, tr. W. R. Boyce Gibson. London, New York: Collier, Macmillan.

Husserl, E. (1970). *Logical Investigations II*, tr. Findlay, J. N. London: Routledge and Kegan Paul.

Husserl, E. (1973a). *Cartesian Meditations*, tr. Cairns D. Hague: Dordrecht.

Husserl, E. (1973b). *Zur Phänomenologie der Intersubjektivität. Texte aus dem Nachlass. Erster Teil. 1905–1920.* [On the phenomenology of intersubjectivity. Texts from the estate. Part 1. 1905–1920.] Kern, I. (ed.). The Hague: Martinus Nijhoff.

Husserl, E. (1973c). Zur Phänomenologie der Intersubjektivität. Texte aus dem Nachlass. Zweiter Teil. 1921–28. [On the phenomenology of intersubjectivity. Texts from the estate. Second part. 1921–28.] Kern, I. (ed.). The Hague: Martinus Nijhoff.

Husserl, E. (2001). *Aktive Synthesen: Aus der Vorlesung 'Transzendentale Logik' 1920/21. Ergänzungsband zu 'Analysen zur passiven Synthesis'* [Active syntheses: from the lecture 'transcendental logic' 1920/21'. Complementary text to 'Analysis of passive synthesis'.] Breeur, R. (ed.). The Hague: Kluwer Academic Publishers.

Koestenbaum, P. (1974). *Existential Sexuality*, Englewood Cliffs, NJ: Prentice Hall.

Luft, S. (2007). "From Being to Giveness and Back". *International Journal of Philosophical Studies*, 15(3), 367–394.

Merleau-Ponty, M. (1962). *Phenomenology of Perception*, tr. Colin Smith, London: Routledge.

Sartre, J.-P. (1956). *Being and Nothingness*, tr. E. Hazel. New York: Washington, Square Press.

Schutz, A. (1967). *Phenomenology of the Social World*, Evanston, IL: Northwestern University Press.

Zahavi, D. (2010). "Empathy, Embodiment and Interpersonal Understanding: From Lipps to Schutz". *Inquiry*, 53(3), 285–306.

14

ABJECT EVIL

Technology and the Banality of the Thanatonic

Brian W. Becker

An academic gathering, intended to be held in-person, was conducted over a teleconferencing application due to the pandemic. On the first day, following the second talk, strange sounds began emanating from anonymous attendees. A few interruptions grew into a cacophonous chorus. An audience of 50 suddenly became 70, evidencing a coordinated attempt to disrupt the gathering. Even the share screen option was co-opted, allowing these anonymous individuals to draw and display distasteful images. Then, I was abruptly kicked out of the session. Unsure what transpired, I returned using the previously provided link only to notice a wasteland of intruders persisting in their activities, and I assumed the session ended for the day.

Lacking any political message or stated purpose for the intrusion, no motivation was readily identified other than perhaps the enjoyment that accompanies the destruction of something. Despite the senselessness of this act, declaring it evil would seem an exaggeration and quite frankly bizarre. Yet similar situations are frequently observed in our modern epoch of social media in which a seemingly benign misdeed attracts the gratuitous hatred of those who feel in some way victimized by acts that have little to do with their well-being. One recent example coming to mind is the response by Star Wars fans who have taken to social media to vociferously protest narrative decisions that have violated the "orthodoxy" of the "official canon." Conversely, producers and executives of the Star Wars franchise have vilified these fans, labeling them "toxic," among other monikers.

Such seemingly exaggerated responses to these tepid transgressions are reminiscent of Augustine's childhood experience of stealing pears and the decision of Adam and Eve to consume a forbidden fruit. To place these acts centrally in formulating a conception of evil would seem no less odd than doing so for this intrusion. Another example, this time from film, is the "Fly" episode in the television show *Breaking Bad* (season 3) in which the entire plot centers around the main character, Walter White, as he attempts to kill a fly for fear it would "contaminate" his methamphetamine lab. This episode struck many viewers as odd and out of place for the series in its excessive emphasis on a detail seemingly irrelevant to the overall story. This ravenous hatred toward something or someone that imposes itself as an evil (or another substitute term) is even more disconcerting when reflecting upon what likely appears to many as genuine evil and legitimate suffering—pandemics and sickness, war and murder, famine and poverty. Surely these cases are far more deserving of such a label

DOI: 10.4324/9781003195849-18

than, for example, what happened to a group of "privileged" scholars gathered for an online conference.

Psychoanalysis knows all too well how these seemingly inconsequential situations belie a depth and density. The concepts of projection and abjection have attempted to account for such phenomena. The scapegoat mechanism (Girard, 1977) and, more recently, "cancel culture" are other terms sometimes used. However, such attempts at explaining these phenomena, fully legitimate within their respective regions, miss an opportunity to consider a more fundamental situation at hand.

Often neglected in these situations is a reflection upon the encounter with evil itself. We quickly flee into explanations and reasons for such situations without taking the time to more carefully consider how they enter lived-experience. Describing such an unfolding is not opposed to explanation but does attempt to arrive at a more primordial situation, one upon which all theorizing and explanation is predicated. Indeed, why *not* deem that "unwelcomed intrusion" as evil? Does the degree of violence and suffering matter? Does a psychoanalytic interpretation delegitimate any consideration of evil whatsoever? And how could we even make progress in answering such questions without a rigorous concept of evil?

Yet, in pursuing such a concept, difficult questions once again arise. Are there horizons of understanding that can situate evil within a meaningful discourse or does evil subvert every possible signification? Can we describe evil in its manners and modes of manifestation, or is phenomenality even a legitimate category for what seemingly destroys the possibility of appearance? *This case study of the unwelcomed intrusion, in its very banality, offers an entry point for considering a phenomenology proper to evil, named the thanatonic phenomenon, that, in imposing itself by a parasitic givenness, demonstrates an unfolding that moves from this situation to the diminishing effects of technology, and ultimately leads back to myself as the one always already implicated in the spectacle of evil I encounter. Doing so, we shall see how phenomenological description does not replace a psychoanalytic interpretation but situates evil within a more comprehensive logic that is the condition of possibility for its consideration in other fields.*

A Phenomenology of Evil?

A first obstacle in taking up this analysis is the term "evil" itself. For many, such a label is inappropriate under any circumstance, being imbued with the supernatural and metaphysical and thus offensive to modern sensibilities. Nonetheless, denegation of this signifier does not rid us of its effectivity. Instead, it returns in new forms. Rather than "evil," it might be "toxicity" and "narcissism," "institutionalized -isms," and "social injustice," or "calamity," and "absurdity." The receding of the term does not produce the absence of a signifier but an exchange of one for innumerable others that continue to function in its place, possessing a corresponding syntax. This diversity of signifiers is matched only by the diversity of significations conferred upon evil. To name a few distinguished paths for conceptualizing it, evil has been thought as a privation and perversion of being, a primordial substance or principle, a matter of ignorance, the violation of a moral law, a calculus of harm, or habituated vice. The social sciences have added their voice to this conversation as well, situating evil within a causal network of dispositions and situations influenced by cognitive predilections, biology, and social group dynamics.

Despite these attempts to speak and think it, evil is often more readily encountered in the manner it subverts every discourse and resists any meaning whatsoever, striking with an extremity and incomprehensibility. Indeed, evil often directs our attention not first to an interpretation but to the very failures of our mediating horizons. Nonetheless, these *lived-failures* leave clues, a distinct trace of evil's effects. That there are such effects opens the possibility for inquiring into its phenomenology, should we not be completely undone by it. "One cannot affirm anything before acknowledging that it took place, that it occurred, that it in fact appeared" (Marion, 2002a, p. 141). This effect is not to be understood as the consequence of a cause but is that from which causes are derived. In this sense, causes become the effect of effects rather than what produces them.

In wagering that there remains open the possibility for phenomenological description in so far as evil demonstrates a distinct effectivity, is there then a particular class of phenomenality within which to situate it? One possibility is to evaluate the intensity of such effects, thereby determining the "degree of givenness" (Marion, 2002a, pp. 179–247). Briefly, givenness within phenomenology pertains to the intrinsic but invisible horizon of a thing's mode and manner of arrival and impact. A description of givenness is achieved by bracketing any consideration of causality and metaphysics and by leading thought back to an original effectivity as it arises into some mode of appearance within lived-experience. Considered more fundamental than objectness (Husserl) and beingness (Heidegger), givenness offers a radicalization of a particular philosophical sensibility that seeks a return to the things themselves, without that return referring to some naïve conception of sense data (i.e. "the myth of the given") or any *a priori* principle that precedes the phenomenon itself (i.e. conditions that legitimate a thing's right to claim the status of phenomenon). Givenness does not cause the phenomenon but describes the unique manner by which each phenomenon uniquely gives itself from itself in its arriving from invisible recesses to deliver a visible effect with varying degrees of intensity. For instance, a geometrical equation (idealities), a computer (tools), and the birth of one's child (events) can each be described in terms of givenness, but the degree to which each phenomenon affects or constitutes me are considerably different. The saturated phenomenon is the name given to those effects delivered by the greatest intensity, so much to completely transform myself and my world. A cursory consideration may then lead one to deem evil an exemplary case of the saturated phenomenon, converging with each of the four identified figures belonging to this category (Marion, 2002b). Evil traumatizes me with its unforeseeability and nonrepeatability (event), imposes a hateful and irregardable gaze (the face/icon), provokes the absolute suffering of my body (flesh), and unbearably exposes me to the very limits of what I can behold (idol/the sublime).

Despite a superficial resemblance, the described effects of saturated phenomena are profoundly discordant from those attributed to evil. A saturated phenomenon reveals to me "another world... other partners... an absolutely new time... another space" (Marion, 2020, pp. 22–23, *translations of French texts are my own unless otherwise noted*). Ultimately, "it reveals me to myself" (p. 25). In other words, I am given to myself as my horizons open for the first time, thereby made capable of receiving other phenomena. These fostering and charitable effects, rather than an expression of givenness *tout court,* are to be situated within a particular *mode* of givenness identified here as *generative.*

Does evil affect me in this manner? Certainly not. It takes away my world, separates me from others, condenses time to a compulsion to repeat the past, and crowds me within a suffocating spatiality (Becker, 2022). Ultimately, it induces a receding of horizons and a contraction of identity, rendering me less than I am and reducing my capacity to receive other phenomena delivered through a generative givenness. When evil happens, I find myself not only incapable of making sense of it, but even my prior capacity to make sense of the rest of my world becomes undone.

Thus, it might seem wise to reject a phenomenology of givenness altogether if the saturated phenomenon is its paradigm, as has been suggested (Marion, 2002a), for such a horizon of thought is inadequate in addressing evil's phenomenality, remaining far too enmeshed with its generative mode to properly think it. The question then is whether it is phenomenology that needs to be broadened to include what it preemptively excludes or to seek for that which resides outside of phenomenology altogether, resorting to another philosophical approach less beholden by the limit of "appearance" (e.g. critical theory, psychoanalysis, hermeneutics, etc.).

Choosing to remain within phenomenology (for reasons that cannot be fully established in this chapter) could then require concluding that evil is not a phenomenon at all, if by "phenomenon" is meant an appearance that shows itself in the clear light of day. Perhaps, if one is to attempt any discussion of evil in this context, it might instead be thought as a refusal or weakness of the will to receive saturated phenomena (e.g. egoism) or a metaphysical will that violently reduces phenomena to objects (e.g. the transcendental ego). Such conclusions may align with a privative notion of evil that would seek to deny evil any kind of being, but it fails to address a phenomenological positivity to evil, one that need not be equated with an ontological positivity. Givenness is broader and more fundamental than being, permitting not only what is but what is no longer and indeed what never was.

Furthermore, limiting evil to a movement of the will (whether it be the will of morality or metaphysics) arbitrarily restricts evil to a matter of interiority, pre-emptively refusing its exteriority, one not limited to human activity but includes those arriving from nature. An unambiguous separation between humanity and nature when it comes to evil is not sustainable without also subtly reintroducing a dualism between mind and body, humanity and nature, and in resuming the recalcitrant *aporias* concerning human freedom. It is also an unphenomenological attitude that appears to have origins in unconsidered metaphysical and theological commitments preemptively imposed upon the things themselves. It is perhaps for this reason an inordinate amount of attention has been placed on phenomena belonging to what I have called a "generative givenness," as observed in those phenomenologies belonging to what is called the "theological-turn" (an infelicitous name in my view). Denying evil to be the exclusive domain of human activities does not deny the importance of a notion of responsibility. However, when it is a matter of clearly distinguishing moral evil from natural evil, no hard and fast boundaries are possible. If the present pandemic has made anything clear, it is how nature and humanity form a perverse chiasm, profoundly intertwined with one another in giving rise to evil's deleterious effects, an observation also reflected in the exchanges between Voltaire and Rousseau in dialog on the Lisbon earthquake of 1755.

Granting evil delivers a distinct effect, though one not consistent with the saturated phenomenon, a difficulty remains in phenomenologically describing evil when its manner of "appearing" is in destroying the one who could possibly phenomenalize and interpret it. Indeed, we need not look very far to achieve such a description as this effect amounts to the first identified characteristic—*diminution*, which has been already briefly described in contrasting evil's counter-effect to those belonging to saturated phenomena. From the diminution by evil, "I am closed off from existing frontiers with me... [it] makes me inaccessible, difficult, and obscure to myself" (Becker, 2022, p. 59).

However, when evil diminishes, it is not always fully accomplished *so that* there remains a self to perpetuate this diminishment. The most successful viruses are not those that kill their victims in short order but keep them sufficiently alive to spread more effectively. The self and its world are not always thoroughly destroyed and, when this is the case, there remains a peculiar way evil manifests itself. For this reason, a phenomenology of evil can only be spoken of by the survivor, the witness, and the rehabilitated—never the one who was thoroughly destroyed by it. These figures have unique access to evil's phenomenality in its incomplete accomplishment, and as such one describes evil not first as a possibility but more radically in its already having-been. In this manner, it is to be distinguished from the phenomenon of my own death, which always remains a pure possibility (Heidegger, 2010), though it may be accessible upon encountering the death of another.

Consequently, we are not dealing with the "non-possibility of 'manifesting'" (Falque, 2021, p. 62), if to manifest means the deliverance of an effect that leaves open the possibility for description. Evil *can* be thought in its manner of destroying the conditions of thought because thought persists in its diminishment. Though it must be admitted, this is not an entirely welcomed situation and can lead to despair our inability to rid us of ourselves (Kierkegaard, 2004). Nonetheless, to be aware of one's despair allows one access to this phenomenon that would otherwise not be available. The one who is unaware of their despair (the happy idiot) has already been far too consumed by evil to recognize it. To the degree what remains to think is not fully identified with its own destruction, one discovers the possibility of recognizing evil, describing it, and indeed even *resisting* it.

"Resistance" is a central concept to a phenomenology of givenness, defined as the manner by which the self "reveals (phenomenalizes as event) the given" (Marion, 2002b, pp. 49–53). In this active receptivity, the self "slows down" the saturated phenomenon enough for something of the given to show itself. However, as the word itself suggests, resistance is also characterized by a "refusal... to understand" (Marion, 2020, p. 42). It is a refusal that is, in fact, inevitable due to the incommensurability between the excessiveness of the given phenomenon and the horizons available to the one who receives it. Every resistance both manifests and resists manifestation in the contact between the given and one's available and cultivated concepts, prejudices, traditions, and languages. Hence why it is claimed that "such resistance... belongs to hermeneutics" (Marion, 2016, p. 95).

Resistance to evil is not distinct from this resistance to saturated phenomena. However, applying this same resistance, upon encountering evil, leads to an inversion. While in the case of saturated phenomena a greater resistance allows for a greater manifestation, the more resistance evil meets in encountering a cultivated love, the more such resistance refuses its full accomplishment. Conversely, the less evil is resisted the more it manifests in my own diminishment, and in manifesting itself even more, it shows itself even less. For this reason, "evil can be vanquished only... by blocking it (as a player blocks a ball, bearing its shock)" (Marion, 1998, p. 9). It is not a matter of two resistances but two different phenomena that distinctly "react" to this same resistance. Nonetheless, the self's resistance to evil remains necessary for ascertaining something of evil's phenomenality, and one always describes the phenomenality of evil, as one describes all excessive phenomena in general, within this dialectical space of an efficacious and an aborted resistance.

If we are to speak of a second resistance, it would be on the side of the phenomenon itself, which accounts for this reversed polarity to the self's resistance. Evil's resistance to a resistance that would bring it out into the clear light of day is an intrinsic part of its phenomenality and reveals a second characteristic: *dissimulation*. Herein, evil resists through obfuscation, either by masking itself as something good, hiding itself in a manner to convince me it never happened, or by misdirecting my attention away from it and toward an undeserving substitute. To quote Baudelaire (2020): "The devil's finest trick is to persuade you that he does not exist!" (p. 71). Evil dissimulates itself *as evil* to accomplish itself more fully.

This characteristic of dissimulation draws associations to Heidegger's notion of conceal-ment. Such covering over sometimes concerns the undiscovered, the submerged, or the refused, but Heidegger identifies "the most frequent and the most dangerous kind" of con-cealment as dissimulation or dissembling [*Verstellung*] whereby "the possibilities of being deceived and misled are especially pernicious" (Heidegger, 2010, p. 34) due to a "double-concealment" that both hides itself while also presenting itself as "something 'clear'" (Heidegger, 1993, p. 179).

Despite convergences, the dissimulation of evil is not derivative of and dependent upon a primary sense of the phenomenon as is the case for Heidegger's notion. Instead, dissimula-tion is *itself* a primary mode of appearance for this phenomenon, one that finds confirmation in the cases of lying, gaslighting, denials, etc. Evil recognizes that to accomplish itself more fully, it must disguise itself through smokescreen and misdirection both to intensify the suf-fering it delivers and to ensure its own perpetuation. Indeed, if evil was clear and apparent, it would quickly lose its effectivity.

Yet, it must be asked more directly now: how is it the case for a positive appearance of a phenomenon to be marked by a fundamental absence of showing itself? Are we not entering a confused and contradictory logic here? Turning once again to Heidegger in his discus-sion of the concept of the phenomenon, he provides the case of physical illness whereby an "appearance" is made through "something which does not show itself" (Heidegger, 2010, p. 28). This non-showing "appearance" of illness always announces itself through what *does* show itself whereby that encounter is made manifest. We discover then a positive appearance of a disturbance in and through the body's failure to show itself fully. The phenomenality of evil displays a similar logic in this regard. As such, "appearance" does not communicate only a self-showing, but it also "means a distinctive way something can be encountered" (p. 29), conceptualized here in terms of effectivity.

At the same time, the diseased body, though entailing diminution, is not necessarily a dissimulation. Here the phenomenon of evil distinguishes itself from the veiling *and* absent-ing of other phenomena by joining together these two characteristics as inextricable features of one phenomenon. The coming together of these two displays a logic that can be thought in reference to the *parasite*. These organisms lodge themselves in our bodies, enfeebling us while also avoiding detection through a kind of "aggressive mimicry" of the body's chem-ical signatures. Although the parasite depends on its hosts, these organisms can in no way be thought as a mere privation of that host or as a weakness of the host's immune system to adequately deal with it.

As such, the parasite provides an apt metaphor for the distinct phenomenological unfold-ing of evil described here, a *parasitic mode of givenness* in contrast to a generative mode, par-alleling a contrast Nietzsche makes concerning the will-to-power (see Dill, 2017). Through a parasitic givenness, phenomena feed off other phenomena and usurp their phenomenality. At the same time, the parasite is not fully reducible to these phenomena, instead acquiring a distinct logic of unfolding, just as, for example, a phenomenology of death is irreducible to a phenomenology of birth, despite the former remaining in some ways dependent on the latter for its possibility.

Both characteristics may be identified in the case of the unwanted intrusion described earlier. Diminution is evident in that control was lost, speech was silenced, communality ended, and learning halted. Dissimulation is initially and most clearly at play in the anonym-ity of these intruders who were hidden behind the outline of a pseudonymous screen name surrounded by a faceless box. However, this is not the most fundamental expression of dimi-nution and dissimulation at play. To take up that consideration, we will first need to identify the distinct figures of evil, each expressing this parasitic givenness and collectively giving rise to a phenomenology proper to evil, named the thanatonic phenomenon.

The First Visible of the Thanatonic

Four figures are identified as belonging to the thanatonic—trauma, the evil eye, the foreign-body, and the abject (see Becker, 2022). *Trauma* is in many ways exemplary of the event (Romano, 2009). Yet, it is more aptly deemed an *excrescence* rather than an *excess*. It diminishes us, leaves us terrified and confused, and incapacitates speech. The *evil eye* is a notion identified across diverse cultures and belief systems (Elliott, 2015–2018). It finds philosophical expression in Sartre's (1984) portrayal of the look, Foucault's (1977) panopticon, and Lacan's (1977) presentation of the gaze as *objet petit a*. The latter will explicitly link this gaze to the evil eye (pp. 115–119). It is distinct from a generative gaze that arrives from *elsewhere* through the face, awakening and calling the self into an identity. The *evil eye*, in its parasitic givenness, delivers a look that diminishes the one who encounters it while also dissimulating itself. Indeed, the greater the invisibility of the look's herald (i.e. the figure that delivers the always already invisible gaze), the more oppressive and coercive it becomes as it cannot be situated at a particular time and place that one could feasibly escape from. It can be anywhere, anytime, and anyone. For this reason, Sartre's god, in its omnipresence and essential invisibility, is "the concept of the Other pushed to the limit" that delivers what might be considered the evil eye *par excellence* (Sartre, 1984, p. 266). The foreign-body is the encounter with an interiorized exteriority, a pernicious alterity that embeds itself in and as our bodies, forming a confused mixture of hetero-affection with auto-affection (Becker, 2022). It manifests as a will that wills against my will, diminishing my spatiality and the capacity to actualize possibilities while also inducing a compulsion to act in manners that seem contrary to what I wish to do. The "I can" of the body (Merleau-Ponty, 1958) converts into the "I cannot" and even the "I cannot not."

Each of these three might be identified in that intrusion upon a teleconference gathering. Yet, what matters for our purposes is not how well each is evident in this situation but, instead, how a particular logic of unfolding is made apparent starting with one of them—the abject which, as the first visible of evil, is the most evident means by which evil dissimulates itself. From the abject is discovered an unfolding that discloses the unseen phenomenological origin dissimulated in the spectacle of an intrusion. Whereas the foreign-body is encountered as an *interiorized exteriority*, operating in the mode of invisibility, the abject is encountered as an *exteriorized interiority*, arriving as the first visible of evil. The abject is a notion that has roots in psychoanalytic thought (Kristeva, 1982), but here its phenomenology should not be confused with its interpretation within a psychic economy.

One encounters in the abject the seeming contradiction of an appearance marked by both excess and deficiency or, more accurately, an excess-by-deficiency. It is what continues to give itself after the saturated phenomenon has been diminished, for diminishing a phenomenon that takes the initiative to give itself from itself is not to always free oneself from it nor for it to remain in pure invisibility. Instead, it may persist in giving itself as an unbidden and palpable phenomenon, returning with a degree of maximum intensity now characterized by an extreme destitution rather than a generative excess (e.g. the face converts to the horrific and horrible in our attempt to objectify and totalize the Other).

Being the first visible of evil and in gathering the other three figures of the thanatonic, the abject delivers a deceptive signification that concentrates my attention in leading me to the source and meaning of my suffering. In providing a "cause," it provokes an uncontrolled frenzy that takes possession of me (foreign-body), elicits in me a hateful gaze (evil eye), and makes possible a retributive violence (trauma). However, as causes are always identified late and inevitably inadequate to the effects that precede them, this "cause" that the abject delivers cannot be contained, initiating a feverish inquisition that will produce innumerable substitutes.

Beginning with our disgust in the drawings and words of this unwanted intrusion, one asks—

> what sick individuals would do this? In the various social media postings for the event, are there any comments or responses that could lead us to identify the perpetrators? Is there anybody who has a grudge against the conference organizers or against the figure the conference is about?

When a proper "cause" is not found, suitable substitutes are sought to carry the guilt. Blame may be shifted to the software developers of the teleconferencing app for allowing this possibility or to the I.T. department of the hosting university who "failed" to adequately configure the meeting settings. It can even be extended to those politicians and citizens who, in not doing what was necessary to mitigate the spread of this pandemic, allowed for its prolongation, requiring the conference be hosted online in the first place.

Once blame fails to locate satisfactory substitutes, responsibility is turned upon oneself, leading to self-hatred. One can perhaps imagine their own situation in which an organized event did not go well, perhaps due to no fault of one's own. Nonetheless, we might still blame ourselves for the outcome, carry the guilt and ruminate over what could have been done differently. We can identify this transition to self-accusation in Oedipus who at the beginning of the play commences a search for the "cause" of a plague: "I say this to all my people: drive him from your houses. He is our sickness. He poisons us.... Wipe out what defiles us, keep the poison of our king's murder from poisoning the rest of us" (Sophocles, 2012, pp. 24 and 28). Then, by the end he comes to blame himself, seeing himself as his own abject, proclaiming: "Can't you see that I'm evil? My whole nature utter filth?... I was their glorious boy growing up, but under that fair skin festered a hideous disease. My vile self shows its vile birth" (pp. 60 and 97).

Although the abject may be the genuinely monstrous and horrific, it is also beheld in the scapegoat. It is the undocumented migrant (Marion, 2015, pp. 23–25) who, failing to conform to the restricted parameters of citizenship for lacking an identity card, returns as a menacing presence to a xenophobic society that sought to exclude them. It is the black man who "makes his entry into the phenomenal world" as a threatening corporeality that arouses terror and hatred in the racist (Fanon, 1986, p. 124). And yet, the xenophobe and racist can also serve as the site of the abject insofar as the identified "perpetrator" distracts and redirects one's attention away from a more profound situation and insofar as it facilitates a perpetuation of violence and suffering instead of resisting evil. The abject makes no claim as to the moral status of the phenomenon whose phenomenality it usurps for its own purposes.

Herein lies one of the dangers of a fixation upon the abject as "there seems no possibility of discerning between monsters and Messiahs" and "such indistinction... poses a real problem for ethical judgment" (Kearney, 2003, p. 107). The abject's evil lies strictly in how it dissimulates evil, thereby reprising the thanatonic's diminishing effects. And here we arrive at another defining characteristic of a parasitic givenness already alluded to but not yet thematized—*repetition*—which finds its culmination in a diminished self who is converted into a vector for retransmitting the thanatonic unto others. Evil destroys and hides itself and, in doing so, perpetuates itself by re-constituting the self in its image. This manner of unfolding has been called the "logic of revenge" (Marion, 1998, p. 8) and the "passage to vengeance" (Marion, 2008a, pp. 58–63). As Marion writes: "For evil consists first in its transmission, which reproduces it without end" (Marion, 1998, p. 8).

This raises a question. If the abject elicits a repetition of evil in this manner, may we not, in our example of the unwanted intrusion, reverse the directionality of this unfolding and ask not only how a destructive act leads to more destruction but also how that first destructive act is itself the repetition of a situation that precedes it? Does the spectacle of the unwelcomed intrusion distract from an accomplished diminishment already operating clandestinely? And where do we turn to discover what remains dissimulated without it amounting to another search for the "*cause*"?

At this point, one may wish to turn to other approaches more commonly deployed to answer such questions, whether that be critical theory, genealogy, or psychoanalysis. Herein, one may examine ideology, power structures, and unconscious dynamics. However, the present analysis is more ambitious in seeking a rigorous concept of evil that logically precedes and grounds these alternative modes of inquiry. Of course, few would ever deploy the word "evil" to identify the object of these respective analyses, perhaps for good reason. Nonetheless, as stated earlier, the signifier "evil" does not merely concern the word itself but its function within a syntax relatively undisturbed by semantic substitutions that perform the grammatical role occupied by "evil." And indeed, rather than exorcising this signifier, it has perhaps assumed an even more elevated place in contemporary thought (see Neiman, 2015).

How then are we to proceed phenomenologically? If the encounter with the unwelcomed intrusion, in diminishing us, initially provoked a search for who out there hates us and wishes us harm, a radicalization of this phenomenological inquiry leads to the one given over to this situation: *me*. We must investigate how the abject character of this unwanted intrusion distracts from one's prior participation in the thanatonic. Such a turn represents a refusal to remain fixated upon the spectacle of evil and, instead, to follow its unfolding as it leads back to the only one I have access to in my suffering, hatred, resentment, desire for revenge, etc.

To be clear, this line of inquiry is not the same as the one that leads to self-hatred upon identifying myself as the "cause." Adopting a "bad conscience" (Nietzsche, 2007) is to remain fixated upon the spectacle of evil rather than to behold its unfolding. Where Oedipus goes astray is not in seeing how he was implicated in the evil he encounters in the world but for not pushing past the abject dimension of the thanatonic altogether. If he had, he would have discovered that his own involvement is itself ensnared within a repetition of suffering and violence that constituted him in a manner that enables further repetitions of the thanatonic, evidenced by the fact that Oedipus was already diminished before ever killing his father and marrying his mother. Kearney (2021) provides a useful analysis of this repetition of trauma (pp. 64–65). Oedipus circumvented the radicality of his own inquiry by settling his gaze upon himself rather than on the unfolding of evil through him.

To inquire into how I have been caught up in the thanatonic that is always already preceding me, let us consider the medium by which this unwelcomed intrusion occurred and through which I participated—the teleconferencing application itself and my relationship to technology as such. The choice to focus on this technology is not a capricious one. What often goes unrecognized is the manner of diminishment that one must submit themselves to participate in it. This diminishment is further dissimulated through the appearance of the unwanted intrusion, redirecting attention upon a spectacle that concentrates our hatred in a manner that further distracts from our already diminished state. A proper understanding of the abject then is only achieved once we recognize how it reflects back this preceding diminution, serving as a mirror for what has been excluded by me and in me. "To rid myself of the evil in me, I must first make of it a not-me, that is to say, give birth to it—point it out to all the world, and thus put it in the world" (Marion, 1998, pp. 4–5).

Technology's Dissimulated Diminishment

A desire for human connection may offer the original upswell for the creation and use of teleconferencing technology, enabling me to traverse a previously unimaginable space to connect with others. It provides a platform that meets our communication needs, allowing for a learning and engagement otherwise impractical. If not for this platform, the conference would not have happened in the first place. At the same time, in participating in the ever-increasing digitalization of social life, one submits themselves to the distinct manner by which this technology reconstitutes us.

Teleconferencing applications are not unique in this respect but do deliver their diminishment in a more ambiguous manner, rendering it possibly more pernicious than the deterioration of communality and solidarity conspicuously on display through social media. This ambiguity is due to the seeming presence of others who speak, respond, and who may even deliver to me what seems to be a face. Communication is richer as it is not limited to 280 characters, memes, nor based upon an algorithm that decides in advance what will address me. These differences are such that this mode of communication is increasingly deemed to be an acceptable alternative to those that remain tethered to physical proximity. Its use during the pandemic has only solidified its march toward becoming a predominant modality of education. Consequently, such technology is uniquely apt for obfuscation by its overt aim to bring people together, to exchange ideas with those who would otherwise not have the means to communicate.

What is at stake here, and why such technology may not strike us as particularly problematic, is that its distinct manner of diminishment does not first mark a moral transgression at all but an aesthetic one. The aesthetic entails sensibility (Henry, 2012, p. 23). It is joy and grief in being affected in our flesh. It is life itself in its exquisite tangibility. "Beauty has no obvious use; nor is there any clear cultural necessity for it. Yet civilization could not do without it" (Freud, 1961, p. 82).

Technology places us at a distance from ourselves and others in attenuating the aesthetic dimension of life. How is this the case? First, sight is deprived of a generative gaze. The screen screens me from delivering and receiving a look. To provide the semblance of eye contact, I must look away from the faces on my screen to stare into the lens of the camera located elsewhere, and the other must do the same. At the same time, I still encounter a gaze but always an anonymous one, even prior to the presence of intruders. I never know who or if anyone is watching me. Yet, so long as my live image is broadcast through this medium, I am subject to a constant, unrelenting gaze by the nobody of the camera—a situation that undergraduate students seem to grasp well in their insistence on keeping their cameras off during class.

Next, hearing of the voice is impaired. When I speak, I speak to (rather than through) a microphone. I hear my voice, but I am even further removed from what the other hears. We begin every session with the question: "can you hear me alright?" and the silent nods deliver a tenuous confirmation, a precarity reinforced by having to constantly remind one another to turn on or off our microphones. Indeed, I may not be heard at all even when it seems others are listening, considering the power now possessed to silence those voices we wish not to listen to.

Finally, the felt sense of proximal bodies is diminished and, with it, the tangibility of community and feeling of solidarity. We may want to compartmentalize the academic exercise of delivering a paper from the embodied encounter with others, but anyone who has attended an in-person academic gathering can likely attest to the intimately social dimension of it. We go to conferences not merely to deliver papers but to commune spatially together in sharing ideas, experience the friendship of passionate minds in the otherwise lonely habitat of a life dedicated to thought. Words have lost their flesh as delivering a paper is deprived of a certain co-belonging dependent upon each drawing near to the other within a converging space. Of course, there are ongoing attempts to develop technology that simulates such contact (e.g. "the metaverse"). Nonetheless, it remains difficult to imagine how such substitutes will not always amount to a diminishment of sensibility. The case is even more obvious when considering the possibility of the "online Mass" ever being a legitimate substitute for an embodied liturgy in which one tangibly receives in their hands the Eucharist. Analogously, one communes with others in a manner radically different when physical proximity is substituted for digital proximity.

Technology's diminishment, in depriving us of the generous looks of encouragement from welcoming faces, the audibility of voices, and the tangibility of a co-belonging, is not first a matter of ethics, despite the temptation to fixate upon technology's ever expanding and intensifying means for promoting hate and violence. In garnering such attention, they effectively dissimulate the diminishment of beauty that has already taken place. It is this dissimulated diminishment of our sensibility that weakens our will, opening it to the movement of another power. Technology invades us and assumes the character of the foreign-body that operates like an automaton. Henry (2012) writes: "The technological world thus spreads like a cancer. It produces and guides itself" (p. 54). He adds: "One undergoes a passivity with regard to what is most foreign to oneself, that is, a technological device. This passivity signifies a radical alienation of the individual" (p. 119). The temptation of neutrality that this technology induces is a dangerous one, lulling us into a soporific state that lets the logic of efficiency do with us what it will. Freud observed this misleading promise of technology in his day, writing:

> During the last few generations mankind has made an extraordinary advance in the natural sciences an in their technical application... [b]ut they seem to have observed that this newly-won power over space and time, this subjugation of the forces of nature... has not increased the amount of pleasurable satisfaction which they may expect from life and has not made them feel happier.
>
> *(Freud, 1961, pp. 87–88)*

Our becoming gods through such technology has added no joy, just the contrary.

The diminishment technology delivers unfolds itself to the point that what disappears in me inevitably resurfaces out there ready to assume a form that unknowingly reveals me to myself. On this occasion, the abject makes its appearance, concentrating our discontent upon a convenient "cause" for our suffering. Consequently, our collective attention gravitates toward this spectacle, whether the "troublemakers" of an unwanted intrusion, scandalous tweets, "fake news," and overt expressions of hostility and calls for violence made visible by this new technological epoch we find ourselves in.

Conclusion

To conclude that the source of our ills is in technology is to fall into the dissimulating effects of the abject once again. If we pushed further in this analysis, we might find the diminishment by economics, ideology, academia, and, even further, perhaps the intrinsic crack that resides within our very humanity. The point of the present analysis is not the specific instances examined but the logic of unfolding that connects them. A banal example was selected both to illustrate the unexceptionality of the thanatonic, paralleling the banality of the saturated phenomenon (Marion, 2008b) as well as how banality itself is a mode of dissimulation, delivering a somewhat altered sense to the phrase "the banality of evil" (Arendt, 1964).

To bring to light the logic of the thanatonic, in its characteristics and figures, is not merely to provide a detached description of evil's phenomenology but finally to show how the one who encounters it is always already implicated. It is to begin with the spectacle of evil but not to remain fixated upon it and, instead, pursue its trajectory as it leads back to me, characterizing an iterative and spiraling unfolding of the evil "out there" and the evil "within me." I am always already implicated in the evil I encounter, not because I am the "cause" of that evil, but because the thanatonic always already diminishes me, constituting me in such a manner that, in my diminished identity, I find myself situated within its closed circuit of repetition. In traditional psychoanalytic language, this manner of positioning and implicating oneself might be understood as the acceptance of one's castration.

At the same time, by making conspicuous my situatedness within the thanatonic, I may more effectively resist its full manifestation. Indeed, we find this demonstrated in the liturgical readings of the passion narrative. In the Gospels, Jesus is clearly the abject for the other figures, but most often Jesus does not appear to the reader as such. Then, who does the reader identify as the abject of the narrative? Is it the representative of political power—Pontius Pilate? Is it the Jews, leading to a well-documented history of scapegoating? What about the disciples—not only Judas but also Peter and the rest who fled at his moment of need, possibly motivating an anti-clerical sensibility? The reader may want to locate the evident source of evil in any number of candidates, but ultimately, the narrative points back outside the text toward the one reading it.

For this reason, a suitable hermeneutic is offered when, on Good Friday, in the assigning of readers of the Gospel, the crowd, those attending the Mass, are directed to read the words "Crucify him, crucify him!" (Luke, 23:21). By performing these words, I am not merely an actor delivering lines in a play that does not personally implicate me. Instead, I situate myself as the one who crucifies Christ, therein dissipating the dissimulating effects of evil in recognizing myself as the one who converts the givenness of evil into manifestation. And in doing so, I acquire a new identity as now the one called to resist the repetition of evil's diminution. Thus, in a certain sense, we can affirm the words of Patočka: "We all, as individuals are defined by the uniqueness of our individual placement in the universality of sin" (Patočka, 1996, p. 107).

References

Arendt, H. (1964). *Eichmann in Jerusalem: A report on the banality of evil*. New York: Penguin Books (Original work published 1963).

Baudelaire, C. (2020). *Petits poèmes en prose: Le spleen de Paris*. Paris: Éditions Casamédia (Original work published 1869).

Becker, B. W. (2022). *Evil and givenness: The thanatonic phenomenon*. Blue Ridge Summit, PA: Lexington Books.

Dill, M. (2017). On parasitism and overflow in Nietzsche's doctrine of will to power. *Journal of Nietzsche Studies, 48*(2), 190–218.

Elliott, J. H. (2015–2018). *Beware the evil eye: The evil eye in the bible and the ancient world* (vol. 1–4). Eugene, OR: Wipf and Stock Publishers.

Falque, E. (2021). *Hors phénomène: Essai aux confins de la phénoménalité*. Paris: Hermann Éditeurs.

Fanon, F. (1986). *Black skin, White masks* (C. L. Markmann, Trans.). London: Pluto Press (Original work published 1952).

Foucault, M. (1977). *Discipline & punish: The birth of the prison* (A. Sheridan, Trans.). New York: Random House, Inc. (Original work published 1975).

Freud, S. (1961). Civilization and its discontents (J. Strachey, Trans.). In J. Strachey (Ed.), *The standard edition of the complete psychological works of Sigmund Freud* (vol. 21). London: The Hogarth Press (Original work published 1930).

Girard, R. (1977). *Violence and the sacred* (P. Gregory, Trans.). Baltimore, MD: The John Hopkins University Press (Original work published 1972).

Heidegger, M. (1993). The origin of the work of art (A. Hofstadter, Trans.). In D. F. Krell (Ed.), *Basic writings*. New York: Harper Collins Publishers (Original work published 1950).

Heidegger, H. (2010). *Being and time* (J. Stambaugh, Trans.). Albany, NY: State University of New York Press (Original work published 1926).

Henry, M. (2012) *Barbarism* (S. Davidson, Trans.). London: Continuum International Publishing (Original work published 1987).

Kearney, R. (2003). *Strangers, gods and monsters: Interpreting otherness*. New York: Routledge Publishing.

Kearney, R. (2021). *Touch: Recovering our most vital sense*. New York: Columbia University Press.

Kierkegaard, S. (2004). *The sickness unto death* (A. Hannay, Trans.). New York: Penguin Books (Original work published 1849).

Kristeva, J. (1982). *Powers of horror: An essay on abjection* (L. S. Roudiez, Trans.). New York: Columbia University Press (Original work published 1980).

Lacan, L. (1977). *The seminar of Jacques Lacan, book XI: The four fundamental concepts of psychoanalysis* (J.-A. Miller, Eds.; A. Sheridan, Trans.). New York: W. W. Norton & Company (Original work published 1964).

Marion, J.-L. (1998). *Prolegomena to charity* (S. E. Lewis, Trans.). New York: Fordham University Press (Original work published 1986).

Marion, J.-L. (2002a). *Being given: Toward a phenomenology of givenness* (J. L. Kosky, Trans.). Stanford, CA: Stanford University Press (Original work published 1997).

Marion, J.-L. (2002b). *In excess: Studies of saturated phenomena* (R. Horner & V. Berraud, Trans.). New York: Fordham University Press (Original work published 2001).

Marion, J.-L. (2008a). *The erotic phenomenon* (S. E. Lewis, Trans.). Chicago, IL: The University of Chicago Press (Original work published 2003).

Marion, J.-L. (2008b). The banality of saturation (J. L. Kosky, Trans.). In C. M. Gschwandtner (Ed.), *The visible and the revealed*. New York: Fordham University Press (Original work published 2005).

Marion, J.-L. (2015). *Negative certainties* (S. E. Lewis, Trans.). Chicago, IL: The University of Chicago Press (Original work published 2010).

Marion, J.-L. (2016). *Reprise du donné*. Paris: PUF.

Marion, J.-L. (2020). *D'ailleurs, la revelation*. Paris: Bernard Grasset.

Merleau-Ponty, M. (1958). *Phenomenology of perception* (C. Smith, Trans.). New York: Routledge Publishing (Original work published 1945).

Neiman, S. (2015). *Evil in modern thought: An alternative history of philosophy*. Princeton, NJ: Princeton Classics.

Nietzsche, F. (2007). *On the genealogy of morality* (K. Ansell-Pearson, Ed.; C. Diethe, Trans.). Cambridge: Cambridge University Press (Original work published 1887).

Patočka, J. (1996). *Heretical essays in the philosophy of history* (J. Dodd, Ed.; E. Kohák, Trans.). Chicago, IL: Open Court (Original work published 1990).

Romano, C. (2009). *Event and world* (S. Mackinlay, Trans.). New York: Fordham University Press. (Original work published 1998).

Sartre, J. -P. (1984). *Being and nothingness* (H. E. Barnes, Trans.). New York: Simon & Schuster, Inc. (Original work published 1943)

Sophocles (2012). *The Oedipus cycle: A new translation* (R. Bagg, Trans.). New York: HarperCollins Publishing (Original work published c.429 BCE).

15

THE ANALYTIC FOURTH

Telepsychotherapy between Opportunities and Limitations

Osmano Oasi, Roberto Viganoni and Chiara Rossi

Introduction

We chose to call this chapter 'The analytic fourth' with a reference to Ogden's analytic third (Ogden, 2004). The analytic fourth would be both a concrete and a symbolic element, emanating from a virtual tool that becomes the mediator in the analytic couple.

The COVID-19 pandemic changed psychotherapeutic practice overnight, causing several changes in the treatment of patients. In particular, the transition from a face-to-face to a remote online setting happened suddenly and very quickly in the early 2020s after the pandemic broke out worldwide. This will have a lasting impact on how psychotherapy will be practiced in the future.

This chapter aims to analyze the consequences and implications of these changes in psychotherapeutic practice. We will focus on understanding not only the benefits but also the inevitable limitations that all of these changes have already entailed and will entail in the future of psychotherapy.

Telepsychotherapy is not a new practice. Many clinicians had already practiced it to treat patients who could not go to the consulting room for geographical or other reasons. Indeed, sometimes this is the only way to continue a treatment that would otherwise be suspended for some time with all the risks that this would imply. The COVID-19 pandemic resulted in an increase in online psychotherapy. During the pandemic, treatment remotely conducted (or telepsychotherapy) has almost become a common practice. It has enabled clinicians to continue treatments that, due to the imposed social distancing, would not otherwise have been viable.

Could this epochal and crucial transition, caused by COVID-19, finally introduce telepsychotherapy as a standard intervention? Our experience also focused specifically on treatments delivered via video calls. Could video and/or telephone calls, the *modus operandi* that was used during the pandemic crisis, become an alternative way to provide psychotherapy? There are currently few contributions that have studied the phenomenon of telepsychotherapy prior to the pandemic outbreak, possibly because of the long-standing strong limitations on using it in Italy, for example, the prohibition of distance psychotherapy not allowed by the National Council of the registered Psychologists (DeAngelis, 2012). The rules governing the treatment setting are particularly strict, especially in psychoanalytic treatment.

DOI: 10.4324/9781003195849-19

From a general point of view, we can consider some interesting studies. In a 2006 meta-analysis, Leach and Christensen (2006) reviewed 14 studies evaluating the effectiveness of telephone psychotherapy for a variety of psychological disorders in specific populations mainly in the United States. Their findings show that psychotherapy via telephone had positive outcomes compared to either standard psychotherapy or the absence of any form of psychotherapy. Out of the 33 studies considered in the meta-analysis, 14 were randomized, and the cognitive-behavioral approach was the most commonly used. In most cases the therapists tended to treat patients with mild or moderate symptoms by phone and carried out "classical" interventions for more severe forms of psychopathology. This cautious approach to the use of remote psychotherapy has likely affected the studies and their outcomes. This must be taken into account, as, with some approaches, a clinical intervention on less severe problems has a higher probability of success (Proudfoot et al., 2011). Another more recent meta-analysis (Hilty et al., 2013) on telephone mental healthcare showed its effectiveness for diagnosis and assessment in many populations (adult, child, and geriatric) and with respect to a variety of disorders in a variety of settings (emergency, home treatment) and appears to indicate that phone mental healthcare is comparable to in-person care. In this perspective, we can consider some studies that show how telephone case management can reduce both distress and psychiatric hospitalization (e.g. Andrews & Sunderland, 2009). It can increase the good health of the patients on the one hand and reduce the costs of their management on the other. In the same perspective, other studies have investigated the effectiveness of phone psychotherapy using a cognitive-behavioral and interpersonal approach with particular reference to depressive symptoms, showing its effectiveness in reducing disorder severity (Simon et al., 2004; Heckman et al., 2017; Dennis et al., 2020).

Notably, another more recent systematic review by Andersson et al. (2019) confirmed that telepsychotherapy has a positive effect on symptoms of depression, panic disorder, PTSD, and burnout. Additionally, in 2016 a group of Swedish psychotherapists (Vlaescu et al., 2016) created a digital platform designed to be flexible enough and to allow for sufficient customization to ensure effective treatments and research studies. The platform is effective in helping provide solutions to improve the life quality for participants with psychological and behavioral health issues.

It is important to consider that all studies mentioned above considered remote psychotherapy as a complement to standard therapy. It is more difficult to reach conclusions as to the effectiveness of remote therapy as a primary treatment.

While studies about individual telepsychotherapy are few, even fewer are group telepsychotherapy studies. The largest randomized study investigating the efficacy of remote group psychotherapy (Heckman et al., 2013) demonstrated that effective treatment can reduce depressive symptoms in HIV-infected older adults. A pilot study (Frutos-Pascual et al., 2014) with ADHD children used a teletherapy smart tool based on Serious Games for Health, to improve time management skills and task prioritization. This type of teleintervention improved time management skills among adolescents with and without ADHD. It is possible that sharing group treatment online may more easily involve those who do not want to start an individual treatment but want to engage with those in a similar situation to their own. There are very few studies on online group interventions, and previous studies have considered very specific populations. This does not allow us to reach conclusions on the effectiveness of distance group psychotherapy approaches. A recent meta-analysis about group-based tele-health treatment (Gentry et al., 2019) showed that group-based interventions have the potential to increase patient access to highly needed services. However, the study also emphasized that further research is needed to identify optimal methods of videoconference group delivery to maximize clinical benefits and treatment outcomes. These implications are also confirmed in another systematic review on the same topic that showed that the telepsychotherapeutic approach may be particularly useful for those who live in rural areas, have limited mobility, are socially isolated, or fear meeting new people. Future research including large-scale studies, on the facilitation process in videoconferencing-mediated groups, is still required to develop the evidence base (Banbury et al., 2018). Generally speaking, in the future we hope to get some Randomized Control Trial outcomes, and they would be welcome.

In our opinion, these new means of intervention can take psychotherapy toward new horizons, also considering the fact that people increasingly use technological mediation to get in touch with others. The social distancing imposed by the pandemic has introduced new habits that have cleared the way for forms of intervention unthinkable only a few years ago. For these reasons, new research in this area is needed.

Now it is up to clinicians to pay attention to the effects of this new reality and the development of telepsychotherapy in clinical practice. The question is: which changes can already be detected in clinical practice? Since the spread of COVID-19, which consequences can be identified in psychotherapeutic work?

Is Telepsychotherapy Still Psychotherapy?

The starting point of this section is the consideration that clinical work precedes any model or explanatory theoretical hypothesis. From a certain point of view, we are in a situation like that in which Freud found himself when he decided to abandon hypnotic treatment and move on to psychoanalysis. That different way of working clinically was justified by the resistance in some patients to suggestion and its consequences. Today, however, changes in therapeutic interventions have been caused by external environmental factors. This means that the patient and the therapist have found themselves in the same difficult condition, creating a potential collusion against the "external enemy," that is, COVID-19 (Fornari, 1970; Carli, 1987). Generally speaking, the social isolation imposed by COVID-19 resulted in important consequences to patients with both severe and non-severe diagnoses (Boldrini et al. 2021; Rossi et al. 2021).

Some considerations from the clinical point of view are reported below.

First Point of View: The Setting

A systematic review conducted in 2017 already showed that tele-mental healthcare, using of current technologies and adaptable designs, can be particularly beneficial and inexpensive, especially in isolated communities (Langarizadeh et al., 2017). Indeed, telepsychotherapy has allowed many people to access services that would otherwise be difficult or impossible to access (e.g. it has enabled patients to see a specific psychotherapist who practices an approach that may not be practiced in their area) and has reduced travel time (especially for people living in rural areas).

Undoubtedly, from a practical point of view, the transition to telepsychotherapy brings many advantages. At the same time, however, it introduces a new way of looking at the setting. The setting is a fundamental clinical concept, destined to vary according to the type of patient or the duration of treatment. It is a "work frame," the change of which brings with it changes in many other dimensions implicit in the treatment. We will explore them later.

The importance of the setting is shown by the following example. In the pre-COVID-19 era, psychotherapists often met with patients at least once to carry out a clinical evaluation before proceeding remotely. During the lockdown, this was not possible, and many therapies began remotely. There is a difference between the two perspectives. Clinical experience suggests that the patients who had begun classical psychotherapy report that they perceived the transition to telepsychotherapy as "abnormal." This can also be experienced by clinicians, especially if they are not used to working in this new way. This sense of abnormality, however, tended to diminish as the sessions progressed. At the same time, not everyone has access to adequate communication technology and some people, in particular senior citizens, lack facility in the use of technology.

All this suggests how much the pandemic condition has changed the relationship with the setting. Still continuing in this perspective: acceptance of distance psychotherapy is much easier for young adults than for older people who may have difficulty using multiple technological tools. In other words, there are people who, out of habit, are comfortable using them, and other people who find them unhelpful and alienating. Another study that analyzed this phenomenon, highlighted this difference between samples of patients who are at ease with modern technology and those who are not (Anderson et al., 2018).

These differences in accessibility have immediate consequences not only for the setting, but also for other important clinical concepts. In the case of therapeutic alliance, for example, the level of ease in using electronic devices is a matter of importance. Consequently, the therapeutic alliance varies not only from person to person and disorder to disorder, but also in relation to different settings and confidence with them. In other words, greater accessibility doesn't mean more positive and easy treatment.

Second Point of View: The Emotional Dimension

One of the most important areas relating to all psychotherapeutic treatment—any approach may be affected by this issue—is the emotional dimension. The emotional component is a fundamental factor in a good relationship between patient and psychotherapist. How does this component change in online psychotherapy?

Sharing Emotions

According to a long psychoanalytic tradition (Baranger & Baranger, 1990; Ferro, 1996; Seligman, 2018) the importance of paying attention to differing emotional intensity during the session and its related emotional 'temperature' has been emphasized. When the emotional intensity increases, the psychotherapist's mind performs the holding function. In-person treatment facilitates this function of the psychotherapist, whereas it is impossible in telepsychotherapy. The lack of such function can lead more easily to relapse or dropout. Only if the psychotherapist pays greater attention to the emotional component, responsiveness is enhanced (Watson & Wiseman, 2021) and possible dropout can be prevented (Maggio et al., 2019).

Could it be necessary to find new ways to communicate and contain emotions in order to be at ease and successful in these new circumstances? One possibility is communicating to the patient the option of contacting the clinician even outside the sessions through text messages or emails in order to maintain a "contact," though a virtual one. In some respects, it works like a transmodal "acting" of the psychotherapist. Body closeness during the session is replaced by listening and/or frequent visual contact. The encounter between two individuals in a room (Momigliano & Robutti, 1992) is replaced by an encounter between two persons in two rooms (Lingiardi, 2021).

The encounter shifts from a physical dimension to an image that does not show the patient's entire body but often only a part, primarily the face. The clinical evidence shows the loss of some non-verbal elements that may be more easily captured in the in-person setting and that make room for specific transformative moments based on moments of attunement (Stern, 2004).

Transference and Countertransference

Above all, in psychodynamic and psychoanalytic approaches, transference and countertransference are central dimensions in the treatment. Indeed, through these mostly unconscious affective movements, therapists can grasp emotional dimensions and themes that lie beyond words, helping their patients overcome relational blocks or trauma. It is very difficult to foresee how transference and countertransference might change in the transition to telepsychotherapy.

The relational bond between patient and psychotherapist or psychoanalyst has probably not been lost in the transition between physical presence and virtuality. Indeed, people have now become accustomed to using virtual media. Even in pre-COVID times, encounters were often mediated by texting, calling, or video calling. For this reason, the transition from classical psychotherapy to telepsychotherapy has been easier than expected. Despite many challenges, psychotherapists seem able over time to adapt and enhance their skills in remote psychotherapy (Stefan et al., 2021).

In order to promote healthy transference, it is possible to adopt some small technical expedients already discussed in this chapter, such as paying attention to the place from which the video call is made, maintaining a sufficient distance between the camera and the person to encourage greater attention, avoiding the presence of objects in the frame that may be too personal or reveal intimate aspects of the therapist's life, etc. Generally speaking, we believe that transference and countertransference also unfold in online settings, even if their manifestations could be different than in in-person settings.

The Role of Silence

Silence normally plays a key role in all psychotherapeutic approaches. It can be considered a powerful tool that must be used wisely. In an in-person setting, silence can be used and understood much more easily. In sessions via telephone, silence could be experienced as persecutory, especially by some patients, and therefore poorly tolerated. Those who use psychoanalytic coaching can feel when a patient is not ready, and we know that some patients do not benefit from silence. In a setting via video call, silence is more tolerated. The presence of the other, whether in-person or mediated by a screen, is a facilitator that allows silence to be used as an essential element in bringing out the deep experiences in the therapeutic field. Telepsychotherapy suits the disposition of some patients, but risks weakening the pure psychoanalytic process.

The pandemic worked as a test of a more general social functioning—not only psychoanalysis—bringing to light the strengths and weaknesses of the system of the Other as a subject. Some anxiety disorders worsened, while others apparently abated. Physical proximity without the possibility of external containers led some individuals with attachment problems to exhibit psychological distress of various kinds. As the emergency continued, anxiety turned into feelings of anger (an emotion in which anger and sadness merge), depression, and despair (Reger et al., 2020). On the clinician's side, it is possible to predict, by observing what happened in other emergencies, the risk of burnout, PTSD, and various forms of psychophysical exhaustion (O'Leary et al., 2018).

Clinicians must consider the crisis that individuals are experiencing, while never forgetting that they are also part of the whole. Therefore, they must monitor their own mental state closely to be able to seek help if needed.

The Gaze

In a classic setting, the gaze rests on the other person's body. During a video call, the gaze is often lost. If the psychotherapist or the patient looks directly into the camera, the clinician loses sight of the other or tends to perceive the psychoanalytic dyad as "talking heads" rather than a global corporality. Obviously, the issue of the gaze is completely lost in telephone treatments, but, on the other hand, even during a psychoanalytic session, in which the patient is lying on the couch, the gaze between analyst and patient is missing.

Remote psychotherapy requires some basic arrangements that can facilitate the process, for example, by stating how excessive proximity to the PC screen can facilitate distraction (checking emails, etc.) (Békés et al., 2021). The proper distance from the video camera allows us to capture aspects of the non-verbal that might otherwise go unseen. It may be better, therefore, to place the computers at a sufficient distance to allow seeing not only the faces of the therapist and the patient, but their entire bodies.

Distractions

In remote psychotherapy, the possibility of being distracted during the session is greater than in face-to-face psychotherapy. This is a consequence that involves both patients and therapists. Although patients are instructed to find a quiet place for the session, without interruption or interference, clinical experience indicates that this is often not possible for a variety of reasons. Indeed, enduring emotional attention in virtual processes tends to be more difficult than in the reality of physical presence.

It is common to have intrusion into the session from pets, intercoms, messages, or emails arriving on the device (smartphone, tablet, or PC) that the patient is using. These are all distracting noises on both sides and can certainly be more easily mitigated in a traditional setting. Today people tend to do multiple activities at the same time. All of these distracting elements intervene in the setting and must be taken into consideration. This "analytic third" as proposed by Ogden (1994), can become a significant transformative potential.

It is also possible that psychotherapy conducted over the telephone carries less risk of distraction, however, some information about the patient's body would be lost. Some patients have difficulty communicating their mental states through words (e.g. alexithymic individuals). Therapists know how crucial body language is in such cases to infer the implicit emotional meaning that these individuals struggle to understand and express (Turgoose et al., 2018).

The Third Point of View: The Privacy

Privacy is another important issue in online treatments. During a video call, psychotherapists actually enter the patients' homes. The pandemic broke down this barrier. It is possible that not everyone has the option of a sufficiently private and quiet place to participate in the session. For some people, the only option is to lock themselves in a bathroom or basement.

For most patients, showing their home is not consequential, but it is possible that for some, especially individuals with anxiety disorders, in which the feeling of shame plays a major role, this could generate invasive, persecutory experiences. In such cases, it might be a good opportunity for clinicians to gently draw out the issue that would otherwise remain unexpressed.

In addition, adaptation has led people to use virtual backgrounds, which can make the atmosphere unnatural and artificial.

The goal must be to maintain the psychotherapeutic framework even if the setting is not fixed as usual. The famous images of the psychoanalyst without the couch (Racamier, 1972) come to mind. Changing the setting doesn't mean forgetting the frame of clinical work. It is helpful if psychotherapists avoid using virtual backgrounds or blurred backdrops, allowing patients to have an experience that, although virtual, can feel realistic and less "fake." Where possible, it would be appropriate for clinicians to maintain the same framing, and if they cannot get to their offices, to arrange a place within their home in which no overly intimate details of their personal lives are visible, such as family photographs, symbols of various kinds, or elements that might reveal overly personal details of the therapist's life. These elements have a preponderant weight in the countertransference and as such have a direct effect on the development of psychotherapy. Once again, an aspect of the setting comes to the fore.

Conclusion

In conclusion, psychotherapy carried out at a distance through the various tools offered by modern technology has made it possible to maintain the crucial bond between patient and psychotherapist in particularly complex (and unprecedented) circumstances, such as the pandemic. An unavoidable fact is that the pandemic has accelerated the therapeutic forms that were emerging as a possibility, leading them to become the norm. This could lead to increased use of telepsychotherapy as one of the possible tools of intervention. Some studies suggest that Italian psychotherapists have been able to promptly adapt to the new modality imposed during the COVID-19 pandemic. Psychotherapists may compensate for the shortcomings of this arrangement by intervening more during sessions and employing a more supportive approach (Mancinelli et al., 2021). It will be interesting to observe whether and how the psychotherapeutic dyad returns to the in-person setting. Maybe some secondary advantages of this particular situation could be retained for various reasons: convenience, reduced travel time, fear of possible contagion, etc. We believe that telepsychotherapy may be an important possibility but that in-person psychotherapy is preferable when possible. Even if some authors (e.g. Craparo, 2020) believe that the foundations of psychoanalytic technique are respected even in the online treatment, we share more the opinion of those who believe that the psychoanalytic process needs the traditional experience of physical presence to develop (Russell, 2015).

Research to date does not suggest an advantage of video therapy over telephone therapy (Kocsis et al., 2009; Markowitz et al., 2016), nor is it possible to compare the different results of the different treatment conditions for the same patient. Probably, the diagnosis of the patient should be taken into consideration in choosing the treatment (Horwitz et al., 1996) and also considering whether to employ online or face-to-face setting.

The COVID-19 pandemic has allowed for experimentation with new modes of intervention at a distance. One recent study in particular (Békés et al., 2021) has reported that the psychotherapist's difficulties are connected to emotional experiences with their patients. Initially, there was some discomfort on the part of therapists in using telepsychotherapy, especially for those who had not previously had similar experiences. Research shows that these concerns tend to diminish as the sessions progress.

Finally, telepsychotherapy appears to be an important opportunity, a tool that today shows some great advantages and some limits, which should be thoroughly analyzed and studied so that specific training courses for therapists to increasingly refine the clinical technique can be developed based on empirical data (Boldrini et al., 2020). These findings may support the hypothesis that future practitioners can use online treatment as a routine component of psychotherapeutic care or in specific circumstances. A good example in this perspective is illustrated in a recent work of Biagianti et al. (2021). It is too early to say how much the changes introduced by the pandemic condition will consolidate them or, vice versa, will be lost. It is not taken for granted that there will be a return to "normality" and that it would happen effortlessly.

References

Anderson, T., McClintock, A. S., McCarrick, S. S., Heckman, T. G., Heckman, B. D., Markowitz, J. C., & Sutton, M. (2018). Working alliance, interpersonal problems, and depressive symptoms in tele-interpersonal psychotherapy for HIV-infected rural persons: evidence for indirect effects. *Journal of Clinical Psychology*, 74(3), 286–303. doi: 10.1002/jclp.22502

Andersson, G., Titov, N., Dear, B. F., Rozental, A., & Carlbring, P. (2019). Internet-delivered psychological treatments: from innovation to implementation. *World Psychiatry*, 18(1), 20–28. doi: 10.1002/wps.20610

Andrews, G., & Sunderland, M. (2009). Telephone case management reduces both distress and psychiatric hospitalization. *Australian & New Zealand Journal of Psychiatry*, 43(9), 809–811. doi: 10.1080/00048670903107617

Banbury, A., Nancarrow, S., Dart, J., Gray, L., & Parkinson, L. (2018). Telehealth interventions delivering home-based support group videoconferencing: systematic review. *Journal of Medical Internet Research*, 20(2), e8090. doi: 10.2196/jmir.8090

Baranger, W., & Baranger, M. (1990). *La situazione psicoanalitica come campo bipersonale*. Milano: Cortina.

Békés, V., Aafjes-van Doorn, K., Luo, X., Prout, T. A., & Hoffman, L. (2021). Psychotherapists' challenges with online therapy during COVID-19: concerns about connectedness predict therapists' negative view of online therapy and its perceived efficacy over time. *Frontiers in Psychology*, 12. doi: 10.3389/fpsyg.2021.705699

Biagianti, B., Zito, S., Fornoni, C., Ginex, V., Bellani, M., Bressi, C., & Brambilla, P. (2021). Developing a brief tele-psychotherapy model for COVID-19 patients and their family members. *Frontiers in Psychology*, 12. doi: 10.3389/fpsyg.2021.784685

Boldrini, T., Girardi, P., Clerici, M., Conca, A., Creati, C., Di Cicilia, G.,... & Lingiardi, V. (2021). Consequences of the COVID-19 pandemic on admissions to general hospital psychiatric wards in Italy: reduced psychiatric hospitalizations and increased suicidality. *Progress in Neuro-Psychopharmacology and Biological Psychiatry*, 110, 110304. doi: 10.1016/j.pnpbp.2021.110304

Boldrini, T., Schiano Lomoriello, A., Del Corno, F., Lingiardi, V., & Salcuni, S. (2020). Psychotherapy during COVID-19: how the clinical practice of Italian psychotherapists changed during the pandemic. *Frontiers in Psychology*, 2716. doi: 10.3389/fpsyg.2020.591170

Carli, R. (1987). *Psicologia clinica. Introduzione alla teoria e alla tecnica*. Torino: UTET.

Craparo, G. (2020). *Psicoanalisi online*. Roma: Carocci.

DeAngelis, T. (2012). Practicing distance therapy, legally and ethically. *Monitor on Psychology*, 43(3), 52.

Dennis, C. L., Grigoriadis, S., Zupancic, J., Kiss, A., & Ravitz, P. (2020). Telephone-based nurse-delivered interpersonal psychotherapy for postpartum depression: nationwide randomised controlled trial. *The British Journal of Psychiatry*, 216(4), 189–196. doi: 10.1192/bjp.2019.275

Ferro, A. (1996). *Nella stanza d'analisi. Emozioni, racconti, trasformazioni*. Milano: Cortina.

Fornari, F. (1970). *Psicoanalisi della guerra*. Milano: Feltrinelli.

Frutos-Pascual, M., Zapirain, B. G., & Zorrilla, A. M. (2014). Adaptive tele-therapies based on serious games for health for people with time-management and organisational problems:

preliminary results. *International Journal of Environmental Research and Public Health*, 11(1), 749–772. doi: 10.3390/ijerph110100749

Gentry, M. T., Lapid, M. I., Clark, M. M., & Rummans, T. A. (2019). Evidence for telehealth group-based treatment: A systematic review. *Journal of Telemedicine and Telecare*, 25(6), 327–342. doi: 10.1177/1357633X18775855

Heckman, T. G., Heckman, B. D., Anderson, T., Lovejoy, T. I., Markowitz, J. C., Shen, Y., & Sutton, M. (2017). Tele-interpersonal psychotherapy acutely reduces depressive symptoms in depressed HIV-infected rural persons: a randomized clinical trial. *Behavioral Medicine*, 43(4), 285–295. doi: 10.1080/08964289.2016.1160025

Heckman, T. G., Heckman, B. D., Anderson, T., Lovejoy, T. I., Mohr, D., Sutton, M.,... & Gau, J. T. (2013). Supportive-expressive and coping group teletherapies for HIV-infected older adults: a randomized clinical trial. *AIDS and Behavior*, 17(9), 3034–3044. doi: 10.1007/s10461-013-0441-0

Hilty, D. M., Ferrer, D. C., Parish, M. B., Johnston, B., Callahan, E. J., & Yellowlees, P. M. (2013). The effectiveness of telemental health: a 2013 review. *Telemedicine and e-Health*, 19(6), 444–454. doi: 10.1089/tmj.2013.0075

Horwitz, L., Gabbard, G. O., Allen, J. G., Frieswyk, Colson, D. B., Newsom, G. E., & Coyne L. (1996). *Borderline personality dosorder. Tailoring the psychotherapy to the patient.* Washington, DC: American Psychiatric Press.

Kocsis, J. H., Leon, A. C., Markowitz, J. C., Manber, R., Arnow, B., Klein, D. N., & Thase, M. E. (2009). Patient preference as a moderator of outcome for chronic forms of major depressive disorder treated with nefazodone, cognitive behavioral analysis system of psychotherapy, or their combination. *Journal of Clinical Psychiatry*, 70(3), 354. doi: 10.4088/jcp.08m04371

Langarizadeh, M., Tabatabaei, M. S., Tavakol, K., Naghipour, M., Rostami, A., & Moghbeli, F. (2017). Telemental health care, an effective alternative to conventional mental care: a systematic review. *Acta Informatica Medica*, 25(4), 240. doi: 10.5455/aim.2017.25.240–246

Leach, L. S., & Christensen, H. (2006). A systematic review of telephone-based interventions for mental disorders. *Journal of Telemedicine and Telecare*, 12(3), 122–129. doi: 10.1258/135763306776738558

Lingiardi, V. (2021). *Due persone che parlano in due stanze. Psicoterapia al tempo del COVID.* Retrieved June 18, 2021, from https://www.opl.it/evento/11-06-2021-Due-persone-che-parlano-in-due-stanze-Psicoterapia-al-tempo-del-Covid.php

Maggio, S., Molgora, S., & Oasi, O. (2019). Analyzing psychotherapeutic failures: a research on the variables involved in the treatment with an individual setting of 29 cases. *Frontiers in Psychology*, 10, 1250. doi: 10.3389/fpsyg.2019.01250

Mancinelli, E., Gritti, E. S., Schiano Lomoriello, A., Salcuni, S., Lingiardi, V., & Boldrini, T. (2021). How does it feel to be online? Psychotherapists' self-perceptions in telepsychotherapy sessions during the COVID-19 pandemic in Italy. *Frontiers in Psychology*, 3702. doi: 10.3389/fpsyg.2021.726864

Markowitz, J. C., Meehan, K. B., Petkova, E., Zhao, Y., Van Meter, P. E., Neria, Y.,... & Nazia, Y. (2016). Treatment preferences of psychotherapy patients with chronic PTSD. *The Journal of Clinical Psychiatry*, 77(3), 0–0. doi: 10.4088/JCP.14m09640

Momigliano, N. L., & Robutti, A. (eds) (1992). *L'esperienza condivisa: saggi sulla relazione psicoanalitica.* Milano: Cortina.

O'Leary, A., Jalloh, M. F., & Neria, Y. (2018). Fear and culture: contextualising mental health impact of the 2014–2016 Ebola epidemic in West Africa. *BMJ Global Health*, 3(3), e000924. doi: 10.1136/bmjgh-2018–000924

Ogden, T. H. (1994). The analytic third: working with intersubjective clinical facts. *International Journal of Psychoanalysis*, 75, 3–19.

Ogden, T. H. (2004). This art of psychoanalysis: dreaming undreamt dreams and interrupted cries. *The International Journal of Psychoanalysis*, 85(4), 857–877. doi: 10.1516/D6R2–9NGF-YFJ2–5QK3

Proudfoot, J., Klein, B., Barak, A., Carlbring, P., Cuijpers, P., Lange, A.,... & Andersson, G. (2011). Establishing guidelines for executing and reporting internet intervention research. *Cognitive Behaviour Therapy*, 40(2), 82–97. doi: 10.1080/16506073.2011.573807

Racamier, P. -C., (1972). *Lo psicoanalista senza divano: la psicoanalisi e le strutture psichiatriche.* Milano: Cortina.

Reger, M. A., Stanley, I. H., & Joiner, T. E. (2020). Suicide mortality and coronavirus disease 2019—a perfect storm? *JAMA Psychiatry*, 77(11), 1093–1094. doi: 10.1001/jamapsychiatry.2020.1060

Rossi, C., Bonanomi, A., & Oasi, O. (2021). Psychological Wellbeing during the COVID-19 Pandemic: the influence of personality traits in the Italian population. *International Journal of Environmental Research and Public Health*, 18(11), 5862. doi: 10.3390/ijerph18115862

Russell, G. I. (2015). *Screen relations. The limit of computer-mediated psychoanalysis and psychotherapy.* London: Karnac Books.

Seligman, S. (2018). *Relationships in development: infancy, intersubjectivity, and attachment.* London: Routledge/Taylor & Francis Group.

Simon, G. E., Ludman, E. J., Tutty, S., Operskalski, B., & Von Korff, M. (2004). Telephone psychotherapy and telephone care management for primary care patients starting antidepressant treatment: a randomized controlled trial. *JAMA*, 292(8), 935–942. doi: 10.1001/jama.292.8.935

Stefan, N., Birkenfeld, A. L., & Schulze, M. B. (2021). Global pandemics interconnected—obesity, impaired metabolic health and COVID-19. *Nature Reviews Endocrinology*, 17(3), 135–149. doi: 10.1038/ s41574-020-00462-1

Stern, D. N. (2004). *The present moment in psychotherapy and everyday life.* New York: W. W. Norton & Company.

Turgoose, D., Ashwick, R., & Murphy, D. (2018). Systematic review of lessons learned from delivering tele-therapy to veterans with post-traumatic stress disorder. *Journal of Telemedicine and Telecare*, 24(9), 575–585. doi: 10.1177/1357633X17730443

Vlaescu, G., Alasjö, A., Miloff, A., Carlbring, P., & Andersson, G. (2016). Features and functionality of the ITERAPI platform for internet-based psychological treatment. *Internet Interventions*, 6, 107–114. doi: 10.1016/j.invent.2016.09.006

Watson, J. C., & Wiseman, H. (2021). *The responsive psychotherapist. Attuning to clients in the moment.* Washington, DC: American Psychological Association.

16

FROM THE ANALOG TO THE DIGITAL UNCONSCIOUS

Reflections on the Past, Present, and Future of Psychoanalytic Media Studies

Jacob Johanssen

In this chapter—an extended version of my award speech given at the reception of the 2021 Lotte Köhler Prize for Psychoanalytic Developmental, Cultural and Social Psychology in the junior category—I give an overview, albeit an incomplete one, of the field of psychoanalytic media studies and shed some light on the history, present, and future of the field. Unfortunately, I cannot mention all directions, authors, and debates here in full. While there is a considerable legacy of scholarship in psychoanalytic film studies, in recent years, a growing number of scholars have researched the digital from a psychoanalytic perspective (Johanssen & Krüger, 2016, 2022). They have explored mobile media (Elliott & Urry, 2010; Krzych, 2010; Turkle, 2011; MacRury & Yates, 2016), Facebook's PR messages (Healey & Potter, 2018), psychoanalysis in conjunction with philosophy of technology (Hansen, 2000, 2004, 2006; Liu, 2010; Clough, 2018), memory and the Internet (Eichhorn, 2019), neuroscience and digital culture (DeVos, 2020), sexuality, politics, and online cultures (Rambatan & Johanssen, 2021), sexuality and networked media (Johanssen, 2021a), Big Data and datafication (Johanssen, 2021b), videogames, artificial intelligence (Black, 2020; Johanssen & Wang, 2021; Millar, 2021; Possati, 2021), mediated trauma (Meek, 2010, 2016; Pinchevski, 2019), and the history of teletherapy (Zeavin, 2021). Much work has focused on social media and subjectivity (Dean, 2010; Krüger, 2013, 2016, 2017a, 2017b; McGowan, 2013; Nusselder, 2013; Balick, 2014; Krüger & Johanssen, 2014, 2016; Flisfeder, 2021; Johanssen, 2019; Johanssen & Krüger, 2016, 2022; Singh, 2019; Beresheim, 2020; Hodge, 2020; Flisfeder, 2021).

It often seems as if digital media, audio-visual content, or even online platforms have made or make the human subject seem disembodied or purely virtual. I would like to argue that all media, whether digital or analog, whether film or video games, have an affective and corporeal relationship with the subject and touch the subject bodily somatically and unconsciously. I have discussed this relationship between media and the subject in this way in my work and it can also be found in the work of many other scholars. The unconscious and the extent to which it is changed or affected by media is also an important question here. For a number of decades, psychoanalytically informed research into media and communications has been growing. In this chapter, I begin with the analog age of film and then turn to television, the Internet as well as the specific online phenomena of social media, the selfie, and incels. I end this chapter with some reflections on artificial intelligence.

DOI: 10.4324/9781003195849-20

Psychoanalytic Film Studies

The first explorations of the subject of psychoanalysis and media come from film studies, and here one should mention above all so-called Screen Theory of the 1960s and 70s and earlier also the works of Christian Metz (1975) and Jean-Louis Baudry (1999). Both Baudry and later Laura Mulvey (1975) located cinema on the level of (unconscious) identification. It was Mulvey in particular who pointed to the sexist forms of representation in Hollywood cinema of the late 1950s and explained them by means of the "male gaze": a gaze that is mainly performed through the camera and is fixated on women's bodies and specific body parts. The camera also often follows the gaze of the male protagonist who possesses women through his eyes. It also has an effect on audiences. Men unconsciously and consciously want to be like the male heroes. Women identify with the female performers as objects of desire. As Mulvey famously put it:

> In a world ordered by sexual imbalance, pleasure in looking has been split between active—male and passive—female. The determining male gaze projects its phantasy on to the female figure which is styled accordingly. In their traditional exhibitionist role women are simultaneously looked at and displayed, with their appearance coded for strong visual and erotic impact so that they can be said to connote *to-be-looked-at-ness*.
>
> *(Mulvey, 1975, 11, italics in original)*

Although Mulvey's work did not conceptually apply the Lacanian gaze as originally conceived by Lacan, her work has lost none of its relevance when considering today's media landscape and platforms such as Instagram or OnlyFans. While a "female gaze" may have emerged, it is much less pronounced or visible in popular culture.

Screen's approach is summed up by Teresa de Lauretis (1984) who argued that the spectator, and especially the female spectator, is always made anew by the latest Hollywood blockbuster as a "correctly" gendered subject. Many of the different psychoanalytic approaches to film sought to analyze how ideology articulates itself through forms of representation. Mainstream film has a particular hegemonic power here because "one of the most prominent features of Hollywood has always been its capacity to map our culture's ideals of masculinity and femininity onto (gendered) bodies that appear to incarnate these ideals in relatively pure form" (Ruti, 2016, 36), as Mari Ruti writes.

Earlier, a slightly more positive view of film had been put forward. It was Jean-Louis Baudry (1974) who brought the oral character of film into focus. Film reactivates or comes close to certain dynamics similar to those of the breast and the baby. Cinema "nourishes" the spectator or reveals something about how the desire for regression to a kind of original form of desire is manifested through representation. As Baudry outlines:

> Of course, there is no question of identifying mental image, filmic image, mental representation, and cinematographic representation. The fact that the same terms are used, however, does reveal the very workings of desire in cinema, that is, at the same time the desire to rediscover archaic forms of desire which in fact structure any form of desire, and the desire to stage for the subject, to put in the form of representation, what might recall its own operation.
>
> *(Baudry, 1999, 183)*

It is those nourishing, supportive, affective-relational dynamics between subject and cinema that were then further explored in different ways in feminist film theory and also later in cultural studies and work on television.

Television and Ordinary Viewers

From the 1980s onwards, television was studied psychoanalytically; Mary Ann Doane (1987) should be mentioned here, as well as Valerie Walkerdine (1986), Roger Silverstone (1994) and then, from the 2000s onwards, Candida Yates and Caroline Bainbridge (2011, 2012, 2014). Silverstone is particularly noteworthy in this context. As a media studies scholar, he used Winnicott's ideas to define television as a transitional object. For him, and also later John Ellis (2000), Annette Hill (2007), and Barry Richards (2007), television can serve as an emotional comforter for audiences, just like the teddy bear serves as an object for the infant that allows them to cope with anxiety and feelings of loss as they transition toward more independence (Winnicott, 2002). Television often aims to contain viewers' worries and questions by providing background, context, or simply information about particular developments or topics. As Barry Richards puts it:

> The unbearable images of famine or bomb victims continue to appear and to resonate, at the same time as the voice-over or other footage may have given us images of aid workers representing hope and fortitude…. In the era of late modernity and vanishing tradition it is the media which have taken over from traditional authorities key powers to shape our minds.
>
> *(Richards, 2007, 63–64)*

The fan studies scholar Matt Hills (2002) has continued to develop such ideas in connection with fans' attachment to their fandoms. Hills has argued that the way fans interact with their objects of fandom is akin to the transitional object, or as he calls it an either "decathected" or proper transitional object. Fans are attached to fandoms because those have some connection to their biographies and remain a particular form of cultural experience that is comforting and pleasurable.

In my research on viewers of the British reality show *Embarrassing Bodies* (Johanssen, 2019), I also discussed similar regression fantasies or desires for containment, but did not approach them through the notion of the transitional object. *Embarrassing Bodies* (2007–2015) was a typical reality-style program that gave patients the chance to expose certain bodily problems and then, after often being treated with snide or funny comments, to be helped by specialists. I was particularly interested in what the bodily affective reactions of the spectators looked like or how they tried to put them into words.

Methodologically, this work was inspired by psychosocial studies and how Wendy Hollway and Tony Jefferson (2012) have adapted the psychoanalytic ideas of free association into a method for qualitative interviews. In order to explore the responses of the audience, I drew on aspects of Freudian affect theory and Didier Anzieu's (1989) concept of the skin ego (Johanssen, 2019). I have argued that aspects of the show described by the interviewees as "shocking," "exciting," or "entertaining" are related to processes of affective discharge discussed by Freud. The viewers' narratives suggested that the show, and its highly detailed content, tapped into experiences of fear and insecurity in relation to the body, and yet the program also created a sense of mastery over one's body. *Embarrassing Bodies* can be seen as a show that envelops the interviewees, holds them in place and keeps them in a safe space. For example, the interviewees spoke about the doctors in a very affectionate way and I interpreted the dynamics as those of a desire for a container-contained dynamic. Such processes took place primarily in affective and unconscious ways. Many of the interviewees talked about their own embarrassing or fearful bodily experiences and bodily feelings. The doctors were thus perceived in a very maternal way and one could also call this a pre-Oedipal dynamic or dyad in which the audience wants to merge with the doctors. In a paranoid-schizoid way, the doctors are idealized. They themselves are sometimes sick or have a bad day (like everyone else), but these experiences do not take place on the television screen. This allows a split to take place. "Good" and containing qualities are only present on TV, while the viewers did not seem to see other "bad" qualities (Johanssen, 2019).

One interviewee, for example, spoke of *Embarrassing Bodies* as "dehorrifying" and "demystifying" aspects of medicine. In that she felt that the uncanny, horrific, or mysterious aspects of patients and by extension the interviewees (and in particular their bodies) are contained and made bearable. Explicitly, these are named as conditions and explained by the doctors. A physical state that may have been experienced as pure affect, without an explanation or words to describe it, is named by the doctors. This act of naming did not necessarily refer to the interviewees' bodies or any condition they might have, but it suggests that there is an answer and a treatment for everything which the show can supply. This is a typical feature of many reality TV and makeover programs. Of course, other motives also played a role, which I cannot go into here, such as a voyeuristic and slightly sadistic fascination with the bodies portrayed. Briefly, many of the interviewees also used terms like "exciting" and "shocking" to describe the program. Many described how they wanted to see more of the show and were excited to see what would come next. I also interpreted this as the desire to gain a sense of mastery over one's own uncontrollable body. At the same time, the "bad" or "embarrassing" bodies of the patients were also split off and the interviewees emphasized that their own bodies were not in such bad conditions as those on TV—there was also a defense mechanism present in such narratives.

Week after week, the viewers saw how the patients were treated and healed and they also felt a sense of containment, but something remained missing. The containment was incomplete and a residue of affect remained. This share of affect is what psychoanalysis would call "discharged" during viewing through moments of laughter, shock, turning away from the screen, screaming, disgust, and especially in the state of diffuse "excitement" that some described. From a Freudian perspective, there may indeed be a connection between affective reactions and the experience in front of the television screen, as well as the subject's biography and bodily experiences. Yet what this connection precisely was or how it articulated itself, I am not fully able to tell (Johanssen, 2019). In the next section, I turn to the complex psychodynamics of social media.

Social Media and the Dynamics of Sharing

The French psychoanalyst Didier Anzieu wrote: "To be an ego is to feel one has the capacity to send out signals that are received by others" (Anzieu, 1989, 62). This places communication, with all its pitfalls, disappointments and frustrations, but also its joys, discoveries and experiences, at the center of human subjectivity. The Internet and especially social media are also about communication and, in a way, the sending and receiving of signals. We have a basic and partly unconscious need to be seen online and for our posts, videos, and pictures to be rewarded with comments and likes. There is something very primal and primitive about our use of social media and the need to be seen and recognized.

One could argue that the voyeurism and exhibitionism of reality TV shaped, if not created, the social media dynamics from the late 2010s onwards: Kim Kardashian, as the quintessential influencer and social media star, first found fame on reality TV. The term "sharing," which is used so excessively on social media and especially by the platforms themselves, also has a certain origin in reality TV of the 2000s, where so many formats were about people exposing themselves, be it physically or emotionally, to audiences. Although television, as Patricia Clough has also pointed out, has a certain psychic structure or more or less models the basic structure of the psyche as defined by Freud (Clough, 2000), this is no longer the case on digital platforms and the Internet. Even if viewers cannot experience real container-contained dynamics, such as in the dyad with the psychoanalyst, they can at least experience a kind of affective relief through such scenes on the TV screen. As Misha Kavka (2012) has written about reality TV, such shows establish an affective interface between subject and content.

As part of my project on *Embarrassing Bodies*, I was also interested in my interviewees' use of social media. While the interviews repeatedly suggested that the program allows viewers to access the unconscious of their own bodily feelings and biographies, the interviewees did not want to reveal that they watched the show on Twitter for fear of being ridiculed by other users. At the time of my research (2013), social media was in a different state than it is today. What I discussed then as inhibition has often morphed in subsequent years into complete disinhibition, or, as in my research on the manosphere (2022), dis/inhibition. In the age of neoliberalism and especially platform capitalism, the subject is intimately intertwined with digital platforms, apps, and objects. Without a presence on social media, the subject can no longer survive in many professions today.

Sharing is constructed as a social good that benefits everyone. It is no coincidence that the very use of the term "sharing" by social media companies is reminiscent of notions of parental and authoritarian upbringing (e.g. in nurseries or primary schools): "Sharing is caring," young children are told, and one of the basic skills they learn in their first years of life is to share toys with others and not to be too possessive of them. Sharing here becomes at the same time a command that is exercised so that the child experiences the joy of sharing, usually through playing with others. For children, sharing is an ethical and human practice that they must follow and obey in order to become responsible and good subjects. Sharing becomes a call for the individual child to enter into relationships. The call to share leads to strong traces in the superego, which ideally should be present throughout life. As such, sharing symbolizes the ability to temporarily separate from objects and let them go while the infant is able to retain an introjected *imago* of them and enjoy using them with others. Social media, on the one hand, is often characterized by total disinhibition, free-floating storms of association where frequently whatever comes to the mind of subjects is shared without much thought. On the other hand, subjects of course know that they are monitored by the platforms as well as by others and should be careful what they post (Johanssen, 2019).

Returning to Baudry (1999) and the oral character of cinema, Steffen Krüger and I (2022) have argued that this dynamic also reappears in the relationship between users and digital platforms. However, it is repeatedly disappointed or turned on its head by users themselves. Platforms offer users prefabricated frameworks and structures and signal containment and also something caring; although at the same time they collect user data and make money from it. Similar to work by Slavoj Žižek from the 1990s, Jodi Dean (2010) follows the argument that the dynamics of social media can be explained by means of Lacanian notions of drive. The logic of "communicative capitalism," as Dean calls it, is characterized by the exploitation of communication for its own sake. People believe in the fantasy of truly communicate with others online, but at the same time are driven by the pleasure of merely passing on messages. What matters is not what, but that something has been posted, shared, and liked developing a culture of pure affect and attention (see also Rambatan & Johanssen 2021). For Dean, much of online culture is "parasitic, narcissistic and pointless" (2010, 37).

The force of habit that has lured us there means that we participate for the sake of it. Dean continues: "The subject gets stuck doing the same thing over and over again because this doing produces enjoyment. Post. Post. Post. Click. Click. Click" (2010, 40).

Paradoxically, one could say that Matthew Flisfeder both advances and refutes Dean's argument in his book *Algorithmic Desire* (2021). He defines social media not as a symptom of a dwindling Symbolic Order, as Dean claims, but on the contrary as examples of a new, widespread belief in the existence of the big Other. Although subjects know that the big Other does not exist, they behave as if the opposite is true. Social media endlessly perpetuate desire in the Lacanian sense. Žižek's, Dean's, and Flisfeder's theories of the Internet are structural theories in the sense that they offer a vision of the overall functioning of the Internet and social media and the broader social structures in which it operates. They present structural conceptualizations with a particular focus on the political implications of the Internet and how it is always embedded in existing capitalist relations. One could also argue that these works are sometimes abstract, theory-heavy and jargon-like in their Lacanian orientation. They are difficult to understand for someone who is not familiar with Lacan. Because of their structural focus, they lack a more concrete focus on the actual psychodynamics of social media and the Internet and how subjects interact on different platforms. Dean's and Žižek's analyses may also seem hopeless and fatalistic. Both could be criticized for being too pessimistic, even cynical, about the Internet. Yes, the Internet has become a space colonized by capital, where users are constantly monitored and exploited, but this does not mean that they are unable to make deep connections, organize for activist causes and experience joy.

The work of Aaron Balick can be seen as a counterbalance here. Balick, a psychoanalytic psychotherapist, published his book *The Psychodynamics of Social Networking* in 2014. Drawing on Winnicott and Jessica Benjamin, Balick has argued that social media can provide opportunities for recognition and the emergence of transitional phenomena. For him, it seems that social media largely support "a positive interpersonal relationship" (Balick, 2014, 122). For Balick, social media enable the formation of relations between users. They enable a reaffirmation of the reality principle and offer potential spaces in the Winnicottian sense: spaces through which identities can be created, explored, and affirmed (see also Singh, 2019). Yet, Balick stresses that users always present particular aspects of their identities and can never fully represent their "real" selves online (see also Rambatan & Johanssen, 2021). There is often an unconscious fear present that we are no longer present for other users online. The unconscious fear that Balick names are countered through social media dynamics, because as we engage with other subjects online, we are reassured that we exist. Of course, as he shows, there is a threat of being objectified, wrongly perceived, trolled, or abused by the other when using social media. Nonetheless, as he argues (in 2014, i.e. when Facebook and social media were quite different to how they currently operate at the time of writing), most users engage with social media in an authentic way, that is, how they would also relate to others beyond the online realm. Authentic relating to another human being online is, for Balick, constituted by being seen in a positive way by others and being valued as a "real" person. Such questions acquire a particular relevance when considered in relation to the selfie.

The Selfie

Bonni Rambatan and I (2021) have argued from a Lacanian perspective that the selfie does not represent the superficiality of the Internet or, as is often claimed, a narcissistic form of self-representation. Instead, the selfie is an invitation to both the (big) Other and the other subject to acknowledge and see the selfie-taking subject. When the subject takes a selfie and uploads it to Instagram, for example, they demand that the other look at and acknowledge them. The selfie is a form of exhibitionism, but not in the way the term is commonly understood in relation to sexuality, namely by showing my half-naked or naked body on social media (although such forms of self-expression are commonplace even today). It is a form of exhibitionism that reveals the vulnerability of the subject and reveals the naked hunger for recognition and desire of the Other. By showing their face, the subject communicates that they possess what the other lacks and desires, while exposing their own lack that they hope the other can fill. They offer themselves for consumption and recognition by the Other, but also promise something in return: that they will fulfill the Other's desire. Selfies are thus not only a one-way act of compensating for the lack of the selfie-taking subject, but they also signal to the Other that the selfie fulfills the Other's desire; both the subject and the Other are weak and vulnerable. In return, the subject expects an acknowledgment of their existence. This can also happen when others comment on or like the selfie. However, similar to the *Embarrassing Bodies* viewers, this possibility remains only virtual and is never completely fulfilled. There is always the possibility for more containment, more approval, more likes, more attention, more recognition.

The Other can only provide part of the feeling of love, care and visibility. Of course, the image of me I upload on Instagram is not the same and cannot in any way adequately represent my full subjectivity and who I really am (think I am) beyond the screen. The selfie holds tragedy and hope because it embodies an unconscious knowledge of the inadequacy of its action and the desire it expresses. Yet the desire remains. The selfie embodies a reflexivity that reveals its vulnerability and cushions it against any possible disappointment (Rambatan & Johanssen, 2021). What is worse today than not receiving likes or comments? The dynamics of desire and recognition that express themselves through social media in general and the selfie in particular have also partly contributed to the formation of toxic communities, such as incels, that respond to them in particular ways.

Incels

Incels, for "involuntary celibate," are a community that belongs to the so-called manosphere. The manosphere is a loose association of different men's forums, websites, and profiles on social media. They are all misogynistic and anti-feminist. This includes men's rights activists, masculinists, pick up artists, Men Going Their Own Way, the NoFap community, and a few others (Johanssen, 2022). Incels, who are often permanently single, claim that they are too ugly to survive in the neoliberal culture of self-optimized sexuality and dating apps. Women now have the power to choose a partner and most are only interested in good-looking, successful "Chads," as incels call them. Incels are another symptom of an Internet that has drifted heavily to the right in recent years. The community is influenced by 4chan and the Alt-Right, the new right-wing movement from the United States that gained significant presence on social media during the term of Trump administration but has lost influence in recent years. The fascist and anti-Semitic imagery used by incels is evident, for example, when they describe women and Chads by using the same stereotypes as Jews were described in Nazi Germany: plotting, decadent, conspiratorial, seductive. Many of the incel discussions are about how they want to (symbolically) destroy women, and incels indulge in endless self-pity that they are excluded from the world and not understood by anyone. At the same time, they construct an identity that reveals love-hate relationships with the Chad, who incels idealize and hate. The figure of the Chad is presented as an implicitly fascist body that is desired: white, muscular, phallic, a soldier-like man (Johanssen, 2022).

Although on the surface such content appears hateful and destructive, it is also an expression of a desire for recognition. I develop this idea through the work of Jessica Benjamin (1988, 2018). In her intersubjective theory of recognition, Benjamin goes beyond the Oedipal and phallic logic of many psychoanalytic concepts and schools. She argues that the desire for recognition and the giving of it is the fundamental moment in the subjectification of the baby. The men of the manosphere, I have argued, cannot leave women behind. They depend on them as fantasies that they must constantly discuss online. This can also create a sense of recognition or a desire for recognition. The men depend on the fantasy of the woman because it is the woman who could (eventually) acknowledge them and validate their existence. The problem is that they cannot bring themselves to acknowledge it. It may remain unconscious to them. Instead, they produce discourses and fantasies about the impossibility of recognizing the other as an independent subject. They cannot recognize the other as existing independently and as an other who exists for them. Instead, incels and other men of the manosphere construct an other who is there to serve them; as an obedient femininity to support the fragmented egos of the men. Although they desire nothing more than recognition, they resort to the destruction of the other. Such actions seem to preclude any possibility of recognition, mutual understanding or dialog.

Benjamin states (with Winnicott) that the infant learns to establish a meaningful relationship with an object by first destroying it. The young infant gradually learns that objects (e.g. the mother) do not only exist in their mind, but also outside. For Winnicott, this transition is accompanied by fantasies about the destruction of the object. This means that the other must be destroyed in the fantasy, on the inside, in order to be recognized on the outside. We can think of omnipotent fantasies of destruction that test whether the other survives them. If so, the other actually exists outside the infant's fantasy world. This means that the other has "survived" the destructive fantasies and acknowledges the infant. If the infant had been able to negate the other completely, the other would not be there to recognize them. In this sense, the destruction fantasy is the basis for all intersubjective recognition. A similar dynamic prevails with incels and the manosphere in general. These men destroy the woman in fantasy, but they also desire her in fantasy and as a real subject. If they negated the woman completely, there would be no woman to recognize, see, and desire these men. "In adulthood, destruction includes the intention to discover if the other will survive" (1988, 38), Benjamin writes. Perhaps incels are just an extreme example of the polarized, paranoid-schizoid nature of social media today, which is often evident in political discussions and also in discussions on other topics (Johanssen & Krüger, 2022).

The Digital Unconscious

It is the excessive character of today's media that shapes subjects and to which they, in turn, often react with excessive actions. As Jan Jagodzinski writes, "It is through their very exaggeration, in their excess, that such transference of emotionality succeeds. We want to see and hear something 'larger than life' to make its impact felt on us" (2004, 58). The philosopher Mark B. Hansen has argued that media and technology use in general often create an "*Erlebnis*" or "experience." He defines this as a process that "absorbs infelicitous or alien stimuli that can only be integrated into experience as something lived through rather than reflected on" (Hansen, 2000, 237). The term "Erlebnis" here "is made to designate what is most fleeting and transitory—those shocks that impact us immediately and corporeally" (ibid., 239). Similar to Freud's model of affect, experience is "used to describe what is most fleeting and transitory—those shocks that hit us directly and physically" (ibid., 239) and cannot be mitigated or blocked by consciousness. It is such dynamics of digital media that un/consciously attract subjects and for which they wait when they use media. They also want to bring about this excess themselves.

This excessive character of the media, which came about with the advent of the reality TV format in the 2000s and even before that with the talk show format, envelops the users and the media like a cocoon that promises containment and interpretation at the same time, but is always permeable, or as Bonni Rambatan and I have called it: Too close, but not close enough (2021). Structural aspects of media are also important here, whether it is television or a social media platform: all are both always the same and always changing. This is what makes them so fascinating. This is how some of the *Embarrassing Bodies* viewers described it:

> it just takes my mind off things and it is just reliable, you kinda know what you're get-
> ting with it, even when you don't know what you're getting with it, kind of, you know.
>
> *(I10, 173–175)*

> I'm always excited to watch it, cos' I wanna see what's on next! [laughs]. Erm, I just find
> it really interesting.
>
> *(I3, 222–223)*

> One of my first thoughts was: 'When is this next programme on, when is this pro-
> gramme on next?'
>
> *(I4, 98–99)*

This desire to know what's coming next, to not be able to wait to see the next episode, has intensified in times of binge watching. It is also present in the unconscious motives for using social media and digital platforms. The subject waits for the next interaction and often brings it about by uploading a selfie, posting a tweet, or commenting on something. In a similar context, McCarthy notes that waiting plays a role in traditional media in general:

> How much is the experience of waiting built into the format of TV programming and
> images in general—waiting for an upcoming program, a better music video, the resump-
> tion of a narrative interrupted by commercials? In other words, is waiting a "deep struc-
> ture" of television spectatorship regardless of where we watch TV?
>
> *(McCarthy, 2001, 218–219)*

The waiting for something on the Internet implies at the same time the fantasy and the at-
tempt that I can already anticipate the reactions of others or formulate everything ironically on Twitter, for example, to mitigate any unforeseen reactions. The unconscious waiting for something always includes the desire for recognition.

Patricia T. Clough (2018) has introduced the term "user unconscious" in a similar context. She defines this as:

> The user unconscious, I therefore have suggested, is a matter of affect, in psychoanalytic
> terms, the force of seeking lost (infantile) objects, operating, however, in a networked
> environment of objects that alongside those lost are those that are not lost but rather are
> lively and not containable brought by datafication out of reach of human consciousness
> and bodily-based perception, that is, an environment of the endless availability of the
> search that in itself supersedes finding an object. This endless searchability supported by
> datafication is another way of posing the liveliness of objects or their other-than-human

liveliness that suggests an embodiment of the I and the unconscious that is human and other than human, yet to be fully engaged as a matter of subjectivity and sociality.

(Clough, 2018, online)

For Clough, the digital environment and the subject form a unity that also shapes or changes the unconscious. Everything seems available, everything can be searched for and this always goes beyond what can ultimately be found. Subjects unconsciously wait for the next recommended friend, the next targeted advertisement, the next suggested episode on Netflix, the next affectively charged exchange on Twitter and so on. They are thus in a constant state of affective excitement and anticipation. At the same time, they are anticipated by other subjects, something is projected onto them and they are also constantly anticipated by platforms (and the developers behind them) as data subjects.

Alison Hearn (2017) has argued that big data, targeting and predictive analytics produce what she calls a "speculative subject" (2017, 73), a subject whose data is not only constantly anticipated and in flux, but which itself becomes anticipatory and malleable: "Anticipation, then, becomes a generalized affective condition that gives rise to modes of subjectivity" (2017, 73). The "speculative self's value is predicated entirely on externally generated predictions about our future potential "optimization" (2017, 74). All this leads to a state of affective fragility in which we find ourselves. We are always subject to changes based on our own actions and those of others.

Conclusion

In this short chapter, I have presented some key works on psychoanalysis and (media) technology, beginning with film theory and ending with work on social media and the Internet. I could merely offer snapshots of particular ideas or positions of some scholars. A key area that I have left unexplored is that of artificial intelligence and "smart" machines, which has seen some psychoanalytic discussion (Turkle, 2011; Black, 2020; Johanssen & Wang, 2021; Millar, 2021; Possati, 2021; Johanssen & Krüger, 2022, Chapter 6). In the coming years, subjects and artificially intelligent machines will continue to merge. Apart from the pioneering monograph by Isabel Millar (2021), this is an area that has been relatively little explored so far. While AI's capabilities are routinely exaggerated and hyped by industry (Johanssen & Wang, 2021), the technology has nonetheless already fundamentally entered subjects' life-worlds. The fusion of AI and human subjectivity will continue to be of relevance and likely increase further as AI becomes both more commonplace in the everyday and more sophisticated in simulating human subjectivity. Psychoanalysis surely has a lot to offer in this respect as we wait for and anticipate our technological futures.

References

Anzieu, D. (1989). *The Skin Ego*. New Haven, CT: Yale University Press.

Bainbridge, C. and Yates, C. (Eds.) (2011). Therapy Culture/Culture as Therapy. Special Edition. *Free Associations: Psychoanalysis and Culture, Media, Groups, Politics*, 62, http://freeassociations.org.uk/FA_New/OJS/index.php/fa/issue/view/5.

Bainbridge, C. and Yates, C. (Eds.) (2012). Media and the Inner World: New Perspectives on Psychoanalysis and Popular Culture. Special Issue. *Psychoanalysis, Culture & Society*, 17(2), 113–119.

Bainbridge, C. and Yates, C. (Eds.) (2014). *Media and the Inner World: Psycho-Cultural Approaches to Emotion, Media and Popular Culture*. Basingstoke: Palgrave Macmillan.

Balick, A. (2014). *The Psychodynamics of Social Networking: Connected-Up Instantaneous Culture and the Self.* London: Karnac Books.

Baudry, J. L. (1974). Ideological effects of the basic cinematographic apparatus. *Film Quarterly, 28*(2), 39–47.

Baudry, J. -L. (1999). The Apparatus: Metaphysical Approaches to the Impression of Reality in Cinema. *Film Theory and Criticism: Introductory Readings,* Fifth Edition. Eds., Braudy, L. and Cohen, M. New York: Oxford University Press, 760– 778.

Benjamin, J. (1988). *The Bonds of Love: Psychoanalysis. Feminism, and the Problem of Domination.* New York: Pantheon Books.

Benjamin, J. (2018). *Beyond the Doer and Done To. Recognition Theory, Intersubjectivity and the Third.* London: Routledge.

Beresheim, D. F. (2020). Circulate Yourself: Targeted Individuals, the Yieldable Object & Self-Publication on Digital Platforms. *Critical Studies in Media Communication, 37*(5), 395–408.

Black, J. (2020). "A form of Socially Acceptable Insanity": Love, Comedy and the Digital in Her. *Psychoanalysis, Culture & Society,* 25–45.

Clough, P. T. (2000). *Autoaffection. Unconscious Thought in the Age of Teletechnology.* Minneapolis: University of Minnesota Press.

Clough, P. T. (2018). *The User Unconscious: On Affect, Media, and Measure.* Minneapolis: University of Minnesota Press.

De Lauretis, T. (1984). *Alice doesn't: Feminism, semiotics, cinema* (Vol. 316). Bloomington, IN: Indiana University Press.

Dean, J. (2010). *Blog Theory: Feedback and Capture in the Circuits of Drive.* Cambridge: Polity.

DeVos, J. (2020). *The Digitalisation of (Inter) Subjectivity a Psy-critique of the Digital Death Drive.* London: Routledge.

Doane, M. A. (1987). *The Desire to Desire: The Woman's Film of the 1940s.* Bloomington: Indiana University Press.

Eichhorn, K. (2019). *The End of Forgetting. Growing up with Social Media.* Cambridge, MA: Harvard University Press.

Elliott, A. and Urry, J. (2010). *Mobile Lives.* London: Routledge.

Ellis, J. (2000). *Seeing Things: Television in the Age of Uncertainty.* London: I.B. Tauris.

Flisfeder, M. (2021). *Algorithmic Desire. Towards a New Structuralist Theory of Social Media.* Evanston: Northwestern University Press.

Hansen, M. B. N. (2000). *Embodying Technesis. Technology Beyond Writing.* Ann Arbor: University of Michigan Press.

Hansen, M. B. N. (2004). *New Philosophy for New Media.* Boston, MA: MIT Press.

Hansen, M. B. N. (2006). *Bodies in Code. Interfaces with Digital Media.* London: Routledge.

Healey, K., and Potter, R. (2018). Coding the Privileged Self: Facebook and the Ethics of Psychoanalysis "Outside the Clinic". *Television & New Media, 19*(7), 660–676.

Hearn, A. (2017). Verified: Self-Presentation, Identity Management, and Selfhood in the Age of Big Data. *Popular Communication, 15*(2), 62–77.

Hill, A. (2007). *Restyling Factual TV. Audiences and News, Documentary, and Reality Genres.* London: Routledge.

Hills, M. (2002). *Fan Cultures.* London: Routledge.

Hodge, J. J. (2020). The Subject of Always-On Computing: Thomas Ogden's 'Autistic-Contiguous Position' and the Animated GIF. *Parallax, 26*(1), 65–75.

Hollway, W. and Jefferson, T. (2012). *Doing Qualitative Research Differently. Free Association, Narrative and the Interview Method.* Second Edition. London: Sage.

Jagodzinski, J. (2004). *Youth Fantasies. The Perverse Landscape of the Media.* Basingstoke: Palgrave Macmillan.

Johanssen, J. (2019). *Psychoanalysis and Digital Culture: Audiences, Social Media, and Big Data.* London: Routledge.

Johanssen, J. (Ed.) (2021a). Psychoanalysis, Sexualities and Networked Media. Special Issue. *Psychoanalysis, Culture & Society,* (2), 153–262.

Johanssen, J. (2021b). Data Perversion. A Psychoanalytic Perspective on Datafication. *Journal of Digital Social Research, 3*(1), 88–105, https://jdsr.se/ojs/index.php/jdsr/article/view/57.

Johanssen, J. (2022). *Fantasy, Online Misogyny and the Manosphere: Male Bodies of Dis/Inhibition.* London: Routledge.

Johanssen, J. and Krüger, S. (Eds.) (2016). Digital Media, Psychoanalysis and the Subject. Special Issue. *CM: Communication and Media*, *38*(11). http://aseestant.ceon.rs/index.php/comman/issue/view/467/showToc.

Johanssen, J. and Krüger, S. (2022). *Media and Psychoanalysis. A Critical Introduction*. London: Karnac Books.

Johanssen, J. and Wang, X. (2021). Artificial Intuition in Tech Journalism on AI: Imagining the Human Subject. *Human-Machine Communication*, *2*, 173–190. https://doi.org/10.30658/hmc.2.9.

Kavka, M. (2012). *Reality tv*. Edinburgh: Edinburgh University Press.

Krüger, S. (2013). How Far Can I Make My Fingers Stretch? – A Response to Vivian Sobchac. *Free Associations*, *64*, 104–131. http://freeassociations.org.uk/FA_New/OJS/index.php/fa/article/view/73/103.

Krüger, S. (2016). Understanding Affective Labor Online: A Depth Hermeneutic Reading of the My 22nd of July Webpage. *Ephemera: Theory and Politics in Organization*, *16*(4), 185–208.

Krüger, S. (2017a). Barbarous Hordes, Brutal Elites: The Traumatic Structure of Right-Wing Populism. *E-Flux*, June 2017. https://www.e-flux.com/journal/83/142185/barbarous-hordes-brutal-elites-the-traumatic-structure-of-right-wing-populism/.

Krüger, S. (2017b). Dropping Depth Hermeneutics into Psychosocial Studies – A Lorenzerian Perspective. *The Journal of Psycho-Social Studies*, *10*(1), 47–66.

Krüger, S. and Johanssen, J. (2014). Alienation and Digital Labour—A Depth Hermeneutic Inquiry into Online Commodification and the Unconscious. *Triple C: Communication, Capitalism & Critique. Open Access Journal for a Global Sustainable Information Society*, *12*(2), 632–647.

Krüger, S. and Johanssen, J. (2016). Thinking (with) the Unconscious in Media and Communication Studies. Introduction to the Special Issue. *CM: Communication and Media*, *38*(11). http://aseestant.ceon.rs/index.php/comman/issue/view/467/showToc.

Krzych, S. (2010). Phatic Touch, or the Instance of the Gadget in the Unconscious. *Paragraph*, *33*(3), 376–391.

Liu, L. H. (2010). *The Freudian Robot. Digital Media and the Future of the Unconscious*. Chicago, IL: The University of Chicago Press.

MacRury, I. and Yates, C. (2016). Framing the Mobile Phone: The Psychopathologies of an Everyday Object. *CM: Communication and Media*, *11*(38), 41–70.

McCarthy, A. (2001). *Ambient Television. Visual Culture and Public Space*. Durham: Duke University Press.

McGowan, T. (2013). Virtual Freedom: The Obfuscation and Elucidation of the Subject in Cyberspace. *Psychoanalysis, Culture & Society*, *18*(1), 63–70.

Meek, A. (2010). *Trauma and Media: Theories, Histories, Images*. London: Routledge.

Meek, A. (2016). Media Traumatization, Symbolic Wounds and Digital Culture. *CM: Communication and Media*. Special Issue. Digital Media, Psychoanalysis and the Subject. *38*(11), 91–110.

Metz, C. (1975). The Imaginary Signifier. *Screen*, *16*(2), 14–76.

Millar, I. (2021). *The Psychoanalysis of Artificial Intelligence*. Basingstoke: Palgrave Macmillan.

Mulvey, L. (1975). Visual Pleasure and Narrative Cinema. *Screen*, 16(3), pp. 6–18.

Nusselder, A. (2013). Twitter and the Personalization of Politics. *Psychoanalysis, Culture & Society*, 18(1), 91–100.

Pinchevski, A. (2019). *Transmitted Wounds: Media and the Mediation of Trauma*. Oxford: Oxford University Press.

Possati, L. (2021). *The Algorithmic Unconscious: How Psychoanalysis Helps in Understanding AI*. London: Routledge.

Rambatan, B. and Johanssen, J. (2021). *Event Horizon. Sexuality, Politics, Online Culture, and the Limits of Capitalism*. Winchester: Zero Books.

Richards, B. (2007). *Emotional Governance. Politics, Media and Terror*. Basingstoke: Palgrave Macmillan.

Ruti, M. (2016). *Feminist Film Theory and Pretty Woman*. London: Bloomsbury.

Silverstone, R. (1994). *Television and Everyday Life*. London: Routledge.

Singh, G. (2019). *The Death of Web 2.0: Ethics, Connectivity and Recognition in the Twenty-First Century*. London: Routledge.

Turkle, S. (2011). *Alone Together: Why We Expect More from Technology and Less from Each Other*. New York: Basic Books.

Walkerdine, V. (1986). Video Replay. *Formations of Fantasy*. Eds., Burgin, V., Donald, J. and Kaplan, C. London: Verso, 167–199.

Winnicott, D. W. (2002). *Playing and Reality*. London: Routledge.

Zeavin, H. (2021). *The Distance Cure. A History of Teletherapy*. Cambridge: MIT Press.

17

COULD I INTEREST YOU IN EVERYTHING ALL OF THE TIME?

A Bionian Analysis of Social Media Engagement

Karley M.P. Guterres, A. Taiga Guterres and Julia Goetz

Introduction

Over the last few years, the world has seen a drastic shift in the way we socialize, engage, and interact with others, especially related to the COVID-19 pandemic. With the world on lockdown, societal engagement has shifted online more than ever, with unforeseen consequences on mental health and interpersonal relationship dynamics. The increasing global presence of social media raises the questions: how do we understand the engagement between the subject, the other users on the platform, and the platform itself? How does social media impact how we understand ourselves? Many psychologists have focused their studies on interpersonal dynamics and created theories based on their observations. One theory in particular, object relations theory, refers to a belief that each person has a world of internal relationships that are often unconscious and distinct from, and in some ways more powerful, than the interactions had in the "real" world.

One of the most influential psychoanalytic figures of the later twentieth century, Wilfred Bion provided major contributions to the field of psychoanalysis and object relations theory in understanding emotional development, thinking, and learning. As Bion explains, thinking is a product of interpersonal relationships with emotional experience as its heart. Bion's focus on both the content of thinking and the impact of the context of thinking on our development of self creates a way to understand the digital world in which we find ourselves today. By utilizing Bion's psychoanalytic study of thinking and theory of containment, we explore problematic social media engagement and the potential vulnerabilities catalyzed in the paranoid-schizoid position. In this chapter, we will briefly outline Bion's theories of thinking and containment, argue that social media has been utilized as a digital pseudo-container, and explore some of the negative mental health outcomes of social media.

Bion's Theories of Thinking and Containment

Melanie Klein, considered the mother of object relations theory, focused heavily on the intrapsychic (internal) experience of projective identification, where an aspect of the self or of an internal object are split off and attributed to an external object. Drawing on Klein's

DOI: 10.4324/9781003195849-21

work, Bion revised Klein's traditional concept of projective identification through his theories of thinking and containment. His theory incorporates the response of the mother to the infant, such that the infant's psychological life development is not only dependent on their individual maturation, but also on the psychological life of the mother, and the dynamic between the two (Ogden, 2011). With Bion, projective identification becomes dynamic between the container and the contained, in this case the mother and infant, transforming the analytic model from uni-personal to bipersonal, while still utilizing an object relations model (Collovà, 2018).

Bion's theories of thinking and theory of containment are intimately woven together and effectively include both the person and their environment. As Thomas Ogden (2011) states, "the mother-as-context includes not only the mother as the surround of the infant, but also the mother as part of jointly constructed aspects of the workings (the metaphorical interior) of the infant's mind" (p. 929). Both of these theories in conversation provide the primary focus for our framework of analysis here.

Theory of Thinking

Bion's theories of thinking and containment intersect at the failure of the infant's capacity for frustration. It is at this moment, according to Bion, that the mother comes into play as a container to take in that which the infant cannot bear. Within the "Freud-Klein era" of psychoanalysis, the focus of analysis was primarily on *what we think* and the symbolic content of unconscious thoughts. In the "Winnicott-Bion era," however, the focus turns to *the ways we think* and the contexts in which thinking occurs or is obstructed (Ogden, 2011). In his paper on the "psycho-analytic study of thinking," Bion (1962) outlines a theory of thinking that is along the lines of a Kantian philosophy, where he states that "thinking has to be called into existence to cope with thoughts" (p. 306). He continues, "thinking is a development forced on the psyche by the pressure of thoughts and not the other way round" (p. 306).

Where do thoughts originate? Bion posits that we innately have desires and expectations (which he calls "pre-conceptions") that are either realized or not realized. When these expectations are realized, there is an emotional experience of satisfaction. However, when they are not realized, there is a felt "presence of an absence that frustrates" (Mitrani, 2001). It is through this frustration, when it is sufficiently tolerated, that a thought is formed and an "apparatus for 'thinking' it develops" (Bion, 1962, p. 307). Bion likens this development of the ability to think with a person operating within Freud's concept of the reality principle (Freud, 1911) whereby a person can engage in reality testing and consider risks and possible outcomes, rather than be ruled by the pleasure principle and the impulse of immediate gratification. Therefore, for Bion, the crux of the process that follows the experience of frustration lies in the infant's *capacity* for frustration.

If the tolerance for frustration is inadequate, however, as Bion puts it, the scale is tipped in the direction of *evasion* of frustration, not its modification (Bion, 1962; Mitrani, 2001). Rather than leading to the development of thoughts, frustration will result in the development of a "bad object," "indistinguishable from a thing-in-itself, fit only for evacuation" (Bion, 1962, p. 307). The development of thought is instead replaced with the development of the apparatus of projective identification. The intolerance of frustration can therefore obstruct the development of thoughts and the capacity to think, which would reduce the sense of frustration inherent in the experience of negative realization in the first place (Bion, 1962).

Bion relays this back to Klein's two position theory of the paranoid-schizoid and depressive positions as he states:

> If we consider that one of the patient's objects in using splitting and projective identification [in the paranoid-schizoid position] is to rid himself of awareness of reality it is clear that he could achieve the maximum of severance from reality with the greatest economy of effort if he could launch these destructive attacks on the link, whatever it is, that connects sense impressions with consciousness. In my paper to the 1953 International Congress I showed that awareness of psychic reality depended on the development of a capacity for verbal thought the foundation of which was linked with the depressive position.
>
> *(Bion, 1957, p. 48)*

Thinking is, for Bion, connected to the depressive position—that which Klein described as a position where complexity of emotions can arise and the infant can realize that the good person who feeds him and keeps him warm is the same as the bad person who keeps him waiting for his food or a diaper change. The paranoid-schizoid position on the other hand—a position in which the main anxiety is of annihilation of the self—comes with fragmentation and projective identification. It is important to note, that from a Bionian perspective, projective identification in itself is not pathological, but actually a normal function of human development when there is a healthy oscillation between the two position (paranoid-schizoid and depressive), which can be assisted by an adequate container.

Theory of Container ← → Contained

The experience of intolerable frustration represents the moment that the external object of the mother comes into play as the object into which the infant projects the unbearable sensations and emotions that it cannot cope with. Rather than employing saturated symbology utilized by Freud and others, Bion moved toward utilizing unsaturated symbology in his theory of containment, namely alpha and beta (later in his career, Bion introduces the concept of "O," which will not be discussed here). Bion describes beta-elements as raw sensations—a primitive emotional experience. Alpha-elements, on the other hand, are the product of the alpha-function, the part of the mind that works on and makes some sort of meaning of the beta-elements. However, if the alpha-function is inadequate to transform the beta-elements, these unprocessed raw impressions are evacuated through symptomological forms or through the mechanism of projective identification (Collová, 2018). It is here where the mother's own alpha-function may be utilized as a container to transform the beta-elements into alpha-elements and returned to the infant.

Where Klein's notion of projective identification represents a phantasy in the mind of one person, Bion interpersonalizes the concept by defining containment as a complex, dynamic, and relational event between two people (Mitchell & Black, 2016). This shift toward the interpersonal and dynamic gives rise to the concepts of the *container* and the *contained* (or container←→contained) where the unbearable content of the mind (beta-elements), which is unable to be contained, is projected into a container, who changes and works through—by way the "alpha-function"—those elements that are then returned back to the projecting source in a form that is more digestible. Riesenberg-Malcolm (2001) explains Bion's theory of containment as

> ... the capacity of one individual (or object) to receive in himself projections from another individual, which he then can sense and use as communications (from him),

transform them, and finally give them back (or convey back) to the subject in a modified form. Eventually this can enable the person (and infant at first) to sense and tolerate his own feelings and develop a capacity to think.

(p. 166)

In other words, a "well-balanced" mother is able to accept the infant's evacuated frustrations and respond therapeutically by returning the frustrations back in a form that can be tolerated. These frustrations then become manageable to the infant (Bion, 1962, p. 308), and this can become the basis for the infant's awareness of their feelings and, eventually, thoughts. Thus although an inability to tolerate frustration can obstruct the development of thoughts and the capacity to think, non-pathological projective identification in the mother (normal development) can help the infant develop this capacity by first having the mother name the world for the infant.

However, if the unattuned mother is unable to contain the projective identification from the child, the infant reintrojects not what was projected out and made more tolerable, but a "nameless dread" (Bion, 1962, p. 309), an unsymbolized representation of the feeling in the absence of the alpha-function necessary for the infant to digest and integrate that which it expelled. The infant's "rudimentary consciousness" is too fragile to carry such a burden, and what results instead of a pathway toward healthy development is the "establishment internally of a projective-identification-rejecting-object" (Bion, 1962, p. 309). This failure to contain the beta-elements, the unbearable content of the mind, doubles down on the paranoid-schizoid defenses of projective identification and splitting.

The mother/container's psychological life is seen both as the context that surrounds the infant and also as jointly constructing the psyche of the infant. In this digital age of social media and oversaturation, we argue that more and more people turn to social media as a sort of pseudo-container—a platform of engagement where one projects out that which we cannot cope solely by ourselves and seek some form of meaning-making or escape.

The Age of Social Media

Our relationship with technology and social media is one that is ever-evolving, and extremely complex. In his Netflix special entitled, *Inside,* released in May, 2021, Bo Burnham wrote, performed, shot, and edited a full-length comedy special, all within the confines of one room. His social commentary discusses various topics, including his steady mental decline due to self-isolation during the pandemic, as well as the mediating role the Internet and social media increasingly play in our lives. Touching on both the potential of technology to connect and disconnect us, in his song entitled "Welcome to the Internet," Burnham reflects and recounts the innumerable ways our engagement with the world is contingent on the Internet and social media. The song begins, "Welcome to the Internet, have a look around/Anything that brain of yours can think of can be found." From the news to a how-to for building a bomb, Burnham paints a picture of the endless content available right at our fingertips. Perhaps the most harrowing line lies in the chorus as Burnham sings "Could I interest you in everything all of the time? / A little bit of everything all of the time / Apathy's a tragedy and boredom is a crime / Anything and everything all of the time!"

Burnham captures the intimate relationship the world has developed with the Internet and social media, from connecting to others to accessing infinite depths of information to endless entertainment opportunities. Thanks to the rapid progress in technologies, such as computers and smartphones, we now live in an age where the Internet, namely social media, is not only a fixture in the lives of young people, but one of the most widely used interactive technologies. Moreover, the presence of social media in our daily lives is only increasing—and doing so rapidly. In 2005, just 5% of US adults used at least one social media platform (Pew Research Center, 2021). These trends have been exacerbated in the past few years as social media usage over the course of the first waves of the coronavirus pandemic exponentially increased. As of January 2022, more than half of the world used social media (58.4%), at a record high of 4.62 billion users globally with 424 million new users having joined within 2021 alone (Kemp, 2022).

Various theories have explored the multitude of different ways and reasons individuals use social media and have found that using it can be both helpful and harmful to people's mental health and feelings of connection. For example, a study exploring the use of social media in adolescence in order to cope over the course of the COVID-19 lockdown found that social media appeared beneficial for anxious adolescents when they used it in a way to actively manage their anxiety. However, it was also shown to have a negative correlation with happiness in individuals who tried to use it as an attempt to cope with feelings of loneliness (Cauberghe et al., 2021). Other researchers have explored the ways that individuals utilize social media to express their emotional experiences, especially during times of crisis, and how this inevitably impacts culture in society both online and offline (Steinert, 2021). Some studies, by contrast, have explored the felt sense of needing to disconnect from social media that allows one to be hyper-connected to everything, everywhere, all at once for the sake of one's well-being (Nguyen, 2021).

What is clear is that the needs and capacities of the individual as well as the capabilities and limitations of social media matter in the moment of encounter of these two entities. The human person is both shaped by and shapes social media content. We turn to social media with a variety of needs—whether it be a desire for connection or an avenue for entertainment—and it returns us with infinite content. What we argue here is that there is a possibility to both (a) utilize social media in a way that obstructs our capacity for thought, and (b) turn to social media as a way to process that which is indigestible, to rid ourselves of that which is unbearable, to evacuate what we cannot make sense of and, in doing so, attempt to utilize social media as a false container. This is particularly true when considering the conditions of the paranoid-schizoid position.

Frustrations of the Paranoid-Schizoid Position in the Context of Social Media

When operating from the paranoid-schizoid position (a position of low frustration tolerance and utilization of projective identification), one may be more susceptible to problematic social media engagement. Beta-elements of raw impressions, emotions, and experiences from constant news streams, catastrophes, or stressors from daily living are projected out toward social media engagement, scrolling, and streaming in hopes of seeking some unconscious expectation of fulfillment that is not yet named.

Ironically, through the development of certain technologies in social media, some artificial intelligence has been programmed to reap the beta-elements of raw experience and formulate perverse quasi-alpha functions. The aim of this dynamic "container←→contained" relationship of the artificial intelligence in some social media platforms with the subject, however, is not to facilitate the development and maturation of the subject, but is often to increase engagement and dependency on the technology itself, further obstructing our ability to think and stunting our capacity for thought. The possible impacts of such interactions that we will explore here are *living on the basis of evacuation*, the *experience of nameless dread*, and the *assumption of omnipotence and omniscience*. We will explore common phenomena experienced through social media engagement, and apply a Bionian lens to better understand these phenomena.

Living on the Basis of Evacuation of the 'Bad Object'

We humans crave connection. We have strong needs for community and relationships. Social media harps on that need for connection and tricks our brains into thinking we are receiving it. We get short, constant hits of dopamine in our brain that simulate the connection we feel in real life. Our brains crave more and more rewards, leaving us in an overwhelming state of need, even contributing to social media addictions (Burhan & Moradzadeh, 2020). Social media provides a break from our routines, frequently showing us an idealized, curated version of other people's lives. We numb our internal states by constantly inundating our brains with information and data. For some, social media can alter moods, induce pleasurable feelings, and numb their current state of being. Our brains may build a tolerance to the effects of social media and require increased amounts of time spent to achieve the same initial feelings (Griffiths & Kuss, 2017). Therefore, we do not feel the emotions we should be experiencing and instead have an unbalanced vision of the world. We avoid the "bad" by constantly receiving what we think is "good."

As outlined previously, Bion describes the development of an apparatus of projective identification as a substitution to the development of an apparatus of thinking when the intolerance of frustration is too high. He writes, "What should be a thought, a product of the juxtaposition of pre-conception and negative realization, becomes a bad object, indistinguishable from a thing-in-itself, fit only for evacuation" (Bion, 1962, p. 307). In this process, Bion proposes that we obstruct our ability for thinking, and what results instead is a

> ... psyche that operates on the principle that evacuation of a bad breast is synonymous with obtaining sustenance from a good breast... all thoughts are treated as if they were indistinguishable from bad internal objects; the appropriate machinery is felt to be, not an apparatus for thinking the thoughts, but an apparatus for ridding the psyche of accumulation of bad internal objects.
>
> *(Bion, 1962, p. 307)*

Thus instead of "obtaining sustenance" or what we could understand as seeking fulfillment or satisfaction, the person lives on the basis of evacuation of the "bad object." In other words, one lives from a deficit model with the goal of simply ridding the psyche of any bad internal objects or frustrations instead of seeking that which sustains us. Furthermore the immediate reprieve of the psyche through distraction hijacks healthy frustration which would have otherwise presented opportunities for development. We stunt our ability for psychic movement and growth and instead find ourselves in a limitless repetition compulsion of "numbing out."

The inability to develop the capacity for frustration by living on the basis of evacuation of the "bad object" has implications for our subjectivity and sense of self. Over time as the habit builds to deal with all thoughts and all frustrations as bad internal objects to eject, we obstruct the development of the capacity for differentiation of the self. Bion writes,

> The dominance of [projective] identification confuses the distinction between the self and the external object. This contributes to the absence of any perception of two-ness,

since such an awareness depends on the recognition of a distinction between subject and object.

(Bion, 1962, p. 307)

Therefore, our sense of self becomes falsely understood and enmeshed with the external object.

The Experience of Nameless Dread

Accessing the vast materials on the Internet can serve as a means of coping with challenging or frightening situations. In some ways seeking information, and even attuning to negative information can be adaptive (Buchanan et al., 2021). However, an over-engagement in this behavior, especially during a time when bad, terrifying, or traumatic news is ubiquitous, can bypass a felt sense of control and instead cause negative emotional and social consequences (Naeem, 2021). Furthermore, information coupled with misinformation, rumors, and conspiracy theories rapidly disseminated through social media, which has been a developing hazard of online platforms, further problematizes our non-stop exposure and connection to copious amounts of information (Paulsen & Fuller, 2020). The spread of misleading propaganda, mixed with potentially traumatic material, can lead to experiences of becoming overwhelmed with fear, anxiety, and confusion (Roseberg et al., 2020). "Doomscrolling" is a popularized term defined as "the act of consuming an endless procession of negative online news, to the detriment of the scroller's mental wellness" (Ytre-Arne & Moe, 2021, p. 1740). This term captures the maladaptive practice of compulsively scouring the Internet or social media in search of ever more terrible information that has become characteristic of news and media engagement since just before the beginning of the pandemic (Jennings, 2020).

How do we make meaning of this phenomenon or understand this facet of social media engagement through a Bionian lens? We may understand the constant influx of information right at our fingertips, or the action of further seeking out negative or horrific information as an overwhelming inundation of beta-elements that are unable to be comprehended, or transformed within our own internal system. When met with a negative realization to the pre-conception that, for example, the world is a safe place, that millions of people will not suddenly start to die in mass, and perhaps the unconscious assumption or desire that we have some control over our own mortality, a frustration occurs that will either formulate a thought for one with an adequate tolerance for frustration, or will be evacuated and projected outward. In a normative system according to Bion, these elements would ideally be modified through thinking or projected into another (a mother or analyst) who has the tolerance and capacity to take them in and transform them through the alpha-function into alpha-elements. If transformed, we would be able to take these modified elements back into ourselves and through this process would be able to build an awareness of our feelings and eventually thoughts.

However, in the social media encounter, we turn back to the very source of the overwhelming sense data as a sort of evacuative behavior, but we do so in vain. Social media, having been placed in a container position, effectively represents the projective-identification-rejecting-object. It has no alpha-function available, no emotional experience of reverie, no capacity for "mental digestion" that is designed for the development of the subject's psyche. What we attempted to evacuate returns to us, "stripped of such meaning as it has" and what is reintrojected is an unsymbolized "nameless dread" (Bion, 1962, p. 309).

The Assumption of Omnipotence and Omniscience

Extreme political and cultural divisiveness, a growing phenomenon not only unique to the United States, has become more exaggerated, and has been attributed in part to the spread of misinformation through social media (Kubin & Sikorski, 2021). While some level of polarization can be beneficial for society, it can also have negative interpersonal implications, including not only an unwillingness to interact with political adversaries, but to exhibit dehumanizing behavior toward them (Mason, 2018). Studies have shown that social media can serve to ideologically polarize people, for example, through exposure to negative Tweets about political candidates, or through counter-attitudinal posts (Banks et al., 2020; Heiss et al., 2019). In a pervasive negative emotional climate that facilitates the perception of threat through social media content, individual values may shift toward emphasizing security and stability of society (Naeem, 2021). The resultant political change that comes at a time of perceived threat may be at the detriment of rights and civil liberties of others (Naeem, 2021). Furthermore, while social media has provided the possibility to access diverse information, various factors can also serve to narrow the breadth of content that a user consumes, and users themselves often self-select into like-minded media communities, creating echo chambers of homogenous opinions.

From a Bionian perspective, we can understand extreme divisiveness online as behaviors in response to the phantasy of omnipotence and omniscience. According to Bion, if intolerance for a frustration is not too great as to elicit a need to completely evacuate that which we cannot bear, but the frustration is at the same time too great to allow us to modify the frustration through the apparatus of thinking, "the personality develops omnipotence as a substitute for the mating of the pre-conception... with a negative realization" (Bion, 1962, p. 308). Instead of learning from experience through thoughts and thinking, the individual unconsciously claims omnipotence and employs the assumption of omniscience. There is no longer any psychic activity based on the reality principle and instead "omniscience substitutes for the discrimination between true and false a dictatorial affirmation that one thing is morally right and the other wrong" (Bion, 1962, p. 308). This newly assumed morality that denies reality is, according to Bion, a function of psychosis. In other words, instead of learning from experience in the presence of a frustration, we live in the phantasy that we are God-like—omnipotent and omniscient—and obstruct our capacity for thought by asserting truth and morality that is no longer open to new or contradictory information. We, thus, become intolerant of other opinions and assert our own as indisputably correct.

Conclusion

When applied to the context of social media, Bion's theories of thinking and containment both provide helpful frameworks to explore the complex ways we engage with social media in this highly digital age. Andrew Sullivan (2016), an influential blogger and commentator wrote an essay for *New York* magazine entitled, "I Used to Be a Human Being: An Endless Bombardment of News and Gossip and Images Has Rendered Us Manic Information Addicts. It Broke Me. It Might Break You, Too." In the exploration of technology and subjectivity, what is clear is that our culture's relationship with social media is complicated.

In many ways the COVID-19 pandemic has catalyzed our dependence on technology and has moved us toward an increasingly digital way of life. While this chapter has explored some potentially harmful ways of engaging with social media, there is a certain attentiveness needed to ensure that we do not engage or relate to it solely as an object to fear. Doing so would only further the evacuation of our frustrations of social media as a "bad object," stunting our process to navigate a healthy relationship to it that would aid in our development.

With its presence well established in the fabric of our society, it is vital that we engage social media with a critical lens and in a way that its complex impacts are understood. Through this chapter we have attempted to consider potential vulnerabilities catalyzed by the needs and capacities of the individual, as well as the capacities and limitations of what social media can offer and what it imposes on the subject. As the digital age is sure to continue to advance, our task must be to continue to try to understand our digital consciousness so that we are not "broken" by it.

References

Banks, A., Calvo, E., Karol, D., & Telhami, S. (2020). PolarizedFeeds: Three Experiments on Polarization, Framing, and Social Media. *The International Journal of Press/Politics, 26*(3), 609–634. https://doi.org/10.1177/1940161220940964

Bion, W. R. (1957). Differentiation of the Psychotic from the Non-Psychotic Personalities. *International Journal of Psychoanalysis, 38*(3–4), 266–275.

Bion, W. R. (1962). The Psycho-Analytic Study of Thinking. *International Journal of Psychoanalysis, 43*, 306–310.

Buchanan, K., Aknin, L. B., Lotun, S., & Sandstrom, G. M. (2021). *PLoS One, 16*(10), e0257728. https://doi.org/10.1371/journal.pone.0257728

Burhan, R., & Moradzadeh, J. (2020). Neurotransmitter Dopamine (DA) and Its Role in the Development of Social Media Addiction. *Journal of Neurology & Neurophysiology, 11*(7), 1–2.

Cauberghe, V., Van Wesenbeeck, I., Jans, S.D., Hudders, L., & Ponnet, K. (2021). How Adolescents Use Social Media to Cope with Feelings of Loneliness and Anxiety During COVID-19 Lockdown. *Cyberpsychology, Behavior, and Social Networking, 24*(4), 250–257. https://doi.org/10.1089/cyber.2020.0478

Collová, M. (2018). The Setting as a Locus of Possible Transformations. In A. Ferro (Ed.), *Contemporary Bionian Theory and Technique in Psychoanalysis* (pp. 1–43). London: Routledge.

Freud, S. (1911). Formulations on the Two Principles of Mental Functioning. In J. Strachey (Ed.), *The Standard Edition of the Complete Psychological Works of Sigmund Freud* (Vol. 12, pp. 213–226). London: Hogarth Press.

Griffiths, M. D., & Kuss, D. (2017). Adolescent Social Media Addiction (Revisited). *Education and Health, 35*(3), 49–52.

Heiss, R., von Sikorski, C., & Matthes, J. (2019). Populist Twitter Posts in News Stories: Statement Recognition and the Polarizing Effects on Candidates Evaluation and Anti-Immigrant Attitudes. *Journalism Practice, 13*(6), 742–758. https://doi.org/10.1080/17512786.2018.1564883

Jennings, R. (2020, November 3). Doomscrolling, Explained. *Vox*. https://www.vox.com/the-goods/21547961/doomscrolling-meaning-definition-what-is-meme

Kemp, S. (2022). *Digital 2022: April Global Statshot Report*. DataReportal. https://datareportal.com/reports/digital-2022-april-global-statshot

Kubin, E., & von Sikorski, C. (2021). The Role of (Social) Media in Political Polarization: A Systematic Review. *Annals of the International Communication Associations, 45*(3), 188–206. https://doi.org/10.1080/23808985.2021.1976070

Mason, L. (2018). *Uncivil Agreement: How Politics Became Our Identity*. The University of Chicago Press. https://doi.org/10.728/chicago/9780226524689.001.0001

Mitchell, S. A., & Black, M. (2016) *Freud and Beyond: A History of Modern Psychoanalytic Thought*. New York: Basic Books.

Mitrani, J. L. (2001). "Taking the Transference": Some Technical Implications in Three Papers by Bion. *International Journal of Psychoanalysis, 82*(6), 1085–1104. https://doi.org/10.1516/JECN-FBNV-TUUE-NUHX

Naeem, M. (2021). Do Social Media Platforms Develop Consumer Panic Buying during the Fear of Covid-19 Pandemic. *Journal of Retailing and Consumer Services, 58*, 102226. https://doi.org/10.1016/j.jretconser.2020.102226

Nguyen, M. H. (2021). Managing Social Media Use in an "Always-On" Society: Exploring Digital Wellbeing Strategies That People Use to Disconnect. *Mass Communication and Society*, *24*(6), 759–817. https://doi.org/10.1080/15205436.2021.1979045

Ogden, T. H. (2011). Reading Susan Isaacs: Toward a Radically Revised Theory of Thinking. *The International Journal of Psychoanalysis*, *92*(4), 925–942. https://doi.org/10.1111/j.1745-8315.2011.00413.x

Paulsen, P., & Fuller, D. (2020). Scrolling for Data or Doom during COVID-19? *Canadian Journal of Public Health*, *111*, 490–491. https://doi.org/10.17269/s41997-020-00376-5

Pew Research Center. (2021, April 7). *Social Media Fact Sheet*. https://www.pewresearch.org/internet/fact-sheet/social-media/

Riesenberg-Malcolm, R. (2001). Bion's Theory of Containment. In C. Bronstein (Ed.), *Kleinian Theory: A Contemporary Perspective* (pp. 165–180). London: Whurr Publishers.

Roseberg, H., Shahbaz, S., & Rezaie, S. (2020). The Twitter Pandemic: The Critical Role of Twitter in the Dissemination of Medical Information and Misinformation during the COVID-19 Pandemic. *CJEM*, *22*(4), 418–421. https://doi.org/10.1017/cem.2020.361

Steinert, S. (2021). Corona and Value Change. The Role of Social Media and Emotional Contagion. *Ethics and Information Technology*, *23*, 50–68. https://doi.org/10.1007/s10676-020-09545-z

Sullivan, A. (2016, September 19). I Used to Be a Human Being: An Endless Bombardment of News and Gossip and Images Has Rendered Us Manic Information Addicts. It Broke Me. It Might Break You, Too. *New York Magazine*. https://nymag.com/intelligencer/2016/09/andrew-sullivan-my-distraction-sickness-and-yours.html

Ytre-Arne, B., & Moe, H. (2021). Doomscrolling, Monitoring and Avoiding: News Use in COVID-19 Pandemic Lockdown. *Journalism Studies*, *22*(13), 1739–1755. https://doi.org/10.1080/1461670X.2021.1952475

18

HASHTAG MANIA OR MISADVENTURES IN THE #ULTRAPSYCHIC

Stephen Hartman

Introduction: Enter the *Ultra*

People in the throes of mania often broadcast political opinions and insights about social relations that are rapidly dismissed for their delusional flare. There is an uncanny assumption of transpersonal communication in a manic person's speech that, while heavily accented with omnipotence, often hits its mark. Taking the online symbol # ("hashtag") as my guide, I conceptualize mania as a psychic space where collective and individual registers of meaning collide at warp speed with the effect of highlighting the uneasy but recursive intertwining of individual and collective object relations.

A growing body of literature in psychoanalysis, group theory, affect theory, and cultural studies (among others, Berlant, 2011; Clough, 2018a, 2018b; Corbett, 2008; Dimen, 2003, 2011, Gentile, 2016; Gonzalez, 2012, 2013, 2017, 2018; Grand &Salberg, 2016; Guralnik, 2016, 2019; Guralnik & Simeon, 2010; Hartman, 2010, 2011, 2012, 2013 2017, 2018a, 2018b, 2020; Leavitt, 2019; Marriott, 2018; Massumi, 2015; Puget, 2010; Rozmarin, 2007, 2009, 2011, 2017, 2020; Salberg & Grand, 2016; Stewart, 2007; Tubert-Oklander, 2013; von Lieres, 2018) details the prevalence of social, cultural, and often politically hewn, collectively held, unconscious representations that combine to configure what Francisco Gonzalez (2012) calls "groupal" objects. With a focus on mania and Virtual Reality, I distinguish the psychic space where an individual forges a recognizable identity using socially hewn objects from what is commonly known by the term "intersubjectivity" to encourage exploration of what I will call *ultrapsychic* communication.

The term *ultra,* when used as a prefix before a noun, pushes the limits of a category. It brackets what is considered normal by exceeding standard practice (ultraconservative) setting expectations that go above and beyond social conventions (ultraorthodox). Ultra is approachable (ultrasensitive) yet also trans- (ultra-see-through) in a manner that tweaks desire (ultra-cool) at the edge of lack (ultra-chic) with an ironic nod to the hegemony of normative practices (*le ne plus ultra*). In this tangle of nuance, "ultra" makes space for a person to invest the excess in a social signifier with personal meaning that, in turn, identifies them vis-à-vis the collective. I am using "ultra" to describe the transpersonal flow of psychic objects between the individual and the collective as brokered by human and nonhuman meaning-makers in an ultra-broadband society. *Ultra*, then, is a post-modern proving ground for fixed

DOI: 10.4324/9781003195849-22

expectations and fantasies of belonging: a transitional space where efforts to join with and among groups give rise to collective object representations that distinguish the particularity of intra- and interpersonal ones.

The ability to imagine oneself as singular amid the plurality of available representations (Rozmarin, 2011) becomes a problem of translating between the psychic, the social, and the nonhuman. *Ultra* implies excess and just as there is always a quality of too-muchness in sexuality because of its unconscious heft (Saketopoulou, 2014, 2019a, 2019b; Stein, 1998), there is also too-muchness in the ultraviolet shimmer of Wi-Fi.

Few among us have access to the code that gives our digital identities wide birth. There are few places left in the world where contact is not being brokered among multiple registers of self and other involving different cultural codes and dissonant temporalities (analog and digital) simultaneously. Consequently, *excess* is a virtual and inescapable condition of ultra-modern reality. Just as a sped-up manic person addresses another person as if trans-personal communication were obvious, the ubiquity of mass communications in a technological society is predicated upon the elastic uptake of information at the pace of mania (Peltz, 2005). In both cases, an array of signifiers floods the interpersonal field in an *ultrapsychic* operation that sculpts what may be subjectively articulated. Manic speech is not as diffuse as it may at first seem.

The project of finding oneself in the collective, particularly in a diverse and technologically complex mass-collective that bundles multiple registers of meaning, requires the translation of "structures of expectation" (Goffman, 1986) that are layered with personal and social representations into unconscious objects that guide fantasy and reflection and communication in and among groups (Tannen, 1993). Whereas intersubjectivity refers to the negotiation of an individual and an Other's manner of co-constructing one another in pursuit of psychic contact that feels personal and therefore "genuine," *ultra-subjectivity* highlights the affects, definitional problems, and crossed-temporalities that are in play when individuals negotiate in the collective to locate themselves among others in an intersectional matrix.

The competing, often-overlapping, usually conflicting affective, material, and political representations each individual juggles to declare their identity highlights the use of personal and collective unconscious objects. These object representations range in their degree of clarity and shape from unformulated introjects to more fully formed internalizations (Schafer, 1968). They may be dissociated or repressed to different degrees in different individuals and collectives. Unconscious collective objects are hewn in relations with groupings that may be local or global, stable, or constantly in flux, historical or emergent and most importantly, these representations reflect interaction with *the nonhuman* among agencies that confer personal and social meaning (Clough, 2018a, 2018b; Gentile, 2018; Pellegrini, 2018). At the ultrapsychic level, object representations capture aspects of collective experience that transcend subjectivity—indeed spar with intersubjectively derived meanings—yet provide important locations in culture where like-subjects bond as social objects. It is also the space where like-subjects are datafied and at-risk of losing a sense of self.

In order to track among the vicissitudes of self and ultra, I lean on Melanie Klein's observation (1935) that a manic person, having introjected whole objects, cannot protect them from an internal saboteur except by projecting out the persecutor and pursuing an "*extravagant*" relationship with good objects. I speculate that this psychic operation may be quite common with internal objects that are collective in origin. I will detail this process schematically first, extending Klein's framework for understanding mania to *ultra* object relations, and then describe collective object use more slowly with reference to how the hashtag leans upon the manic qualities of groupal objects to aspire toward a kind of reparation in the social.

Hashtags Form Collective Objects in Emergent Groups

The process of group affiliation involves comparing a collective's distinct representation of the good life with one's own. Given the opacity of unconscious motivation, collective objects held among people who bond as family members, citizens, nationalities, etc. may or may not pose a threat to one's intra- and inter- psychic gathering of meanings. As the group's objects mingle with what seem to be *my* own, the pairing is always unstable. This is all the more so in an intersectionality complex negotiation when intersecting vectors of power pit registers of nationality, race, gender, class, and sexuality in competition for both juridical resources in the political surround (Crenshaw, 1989) and unconscious registration in meaning (Guralnik, 2018; Hartman, 2017; Leavitt, 2019; Saketopoulou, 2011; Simon, 2017).

It is nearly impossible to know how a collective representation may have sculpted one's own—and this is necessarily so in order for *the unconscious* to simultaneously tender competing needs for belonging and autonomy. Whereas in a manic person, the defensive posture that Klein described shores up omnipotent phantasy to ward off persecutory objects; in a multicultural society, we attribute the benefit of affiliating with inflated representations of the collective good while externalizing perceived-to-be shared bad objects to "identity."

As I know to be true in the experience of the person I call Elmo (below) and that of others who endure manic episodes, mania is a remarkably frightening and destructive experience. In no way do I wish to romanticize it here or diminish its frightening and destructive qualities. However, in depathologizing "hashtag mania" and attempting to characterize its social potential, I am amending the often-voiced argument that we are increasingly isolates in a neoliberal "manic society" (Peltz, 2005) largely because of our dependence on technology.

Identity, intrinsic to the negotiation of self in the collective, is quite slippery and a bit manic: socially hewn representations of *us* and *them* and internal versions of *self* and *other* never quite align. Here is where identity digs in and strikes out. One always stakes their identity *politically*, that is, in ontological relation to what *it* is not. Identity categories and the collective objects that sustain them quickly become reified terms of engagement that find themselves in taxonomies of power relations.

At this nexus of the personal and the political where power accrues in split-complementarities (Benjamin, 2018), groupal objects seek the protection of a coherent identity—even though one's affiliations are multiple and often contradictory. Tracing the overlap of mismatched concentric social circles, identity-related objects go wonky and the minority-objects among one's repertoire of identifications (e.g. mixed-race) are interpellated by a sudden fracture in what appears obvious, ordinary, and whole, that is, white (Christensen, 2018). Here, in this ultrapsychic hodge-podge that seeks protection by distinction, a rapid-fire house-cleaning rules the day, and object representations allied with sub-groups among one's collected representations adopt "manic" solutions.

Affect signals a shift in my self's state: Fear overcomes me when I am *awoken* from an overdetermined relationship to social objects' homeostatic spell. I find myself a "phobogenic object" (Fanon, 1952; Guralnik, 2019). In the words of Irish drag queen née hero of European civil rights activists, Panti Bliss (2016): "and I check myself, and I hate *that*." That "risk" is what I have to reveal and renounce in order to be *woke*. Later in this chapter, I will discuss the psychic differential between the *me* who finds solace by adopting the coherence of a group identity ("e.g. gay American") and the *it* that I can no longer allow myself to be ("linked to gay America by Trump supporter Peter Thiel") in order to affiliate with a sub-collective ("progressive gays") the "risk-object." The risk object is paradoxically articulated in an identification with the collective and as the personification of the sorting-out my unconscious misfit objects go through in groupal dynamics (Gonzalez, 2018). When I realize that this equation translates to a political affinity (I check myself and I hate that and I declare myself "queer"), an ultrapsychic bond compels me to risk taking a stand. Now I can imagine reaching out to others. Enter the hashtag.

The hashtag personifies this manic struggle in a universal symbol. The "extravagant" use of a hashtag allows "the user" to gather a sense of themself bonded with like subjects who may be presumed at-risk in the public mind. When I hashtag #QueerLivesMatter, presumably I am wrangling with internalized homophobia if not "velvet rage" (Downs, 2005) in relation to object representations that link my personal history to the social. The urge to stand with other queers acts as a counter-interpellation of the very same homophobia that anyone at risk of fag-bashing undoubtedly internalized. In my hashtagging gesture, I attempt to repair an introjective process by externalizing the phobic objects that other queers and I encounter internally. In this act of externalizing the phobogenic object (Fanon, 1952), my newly adopted "identity" becomes a dynamic, sensual, material, and phenomenal resource that I may use internally and externally to locate myself in culture.

Not all hashtags connote political risk. However even a seemingly innocuous hashtag such as #IloveSundays appeals for recognition en masse and hurls the person who used it into the affective maelstrom of code. I who loved Sundays may not risk phobic attack on the street, but in the spontaneous gesture of hashtagging where internal, interpersonal and social representations are accessed in an intersectional array faster than you can "say cheese," I do risk unanticipated humiliation (cheesy privileged white "queer") and battle with internal representatives of shame ("Sunday?—oh brother!"). By virtue of declaring my love for a tag that is multiply signified, Sunday, I have made myself vulnerable to I can't know what or when. Likely, some bad object inside of me will fill in the blank thought bubble on my mental screen to decree my fall from grace. A staunch identity bolstered by a hashtag allows me to recover from the prospect (in a twist on Davies' title, 2004) that the bad object was mine anyway.

The internal disruption that ensues when individual and collective objects negotiate the challenge of finding "oneself at-risk" is wildly magnified in cyberspace where the individual person is increasingly a datafied social object at-risk of manipulation and erasure (Clough, 2018a, 2018b; Essig, 2017). An extravagant attitude toward collective objects, as manifest in the use of the hashtag, isolates social objects from destructions past and future and allows the individual the belief that like-subjects will tender the hashtag with a like mind.

Nonetheless, hashtags instantly become public property—often before there is sufficient accounting for the risks involved in having had one's identity collected and datafied. By reviewing the philosophy that gave rise to the hashtag as well as its transformation into a taxonomic symbol, I return to mania's uncanny collectivist quality seeking to highlight the development of a capacity for concern (Winnicott, 1965) in the extravagant #counterInterpellations that use collective objects to repair the individual subject's "risk objects."

#mania

At the peak of his first manic episode Elmo ruled the hashtag. It was all hashtag all the time. Elmo was #madatinjustice but #FlyingBlue around the world in first class defying 5150s and posting #maniaIsmyth#Foucault. A hashtag whistleblower, he was

#indangerbutdeterimined@instagram as he blew through friends and exposed all manner of #graft among colleagues (otherwise known as #self-importantDouchebags) who weren't impressed by his constant demand for #scrutinybythepeople#weareinthistogether even if Elmo's #speaktopower told it #likeItreallyIs.

Elmo was, as far as I could tell, a Kleinian baby flinging a boomerang at the Lacanian Real. Damned if he wasn't going to expose how that chipped mirror in a gilded frame—the one that always and only reflects his family's definition by the Holocaust—deprives us all of beauty. Melanie Klein wrote that in mania:

> the ego has introjected a whole loved object, but owing to its immoderate dread of internalized persecutors, which are projected on to the external world, the ego takes refuge in an extravagant belief in the benevolence of his internalized objects.
>
> *(1935, p. 174)*

Extravagant is an understatement. When Elmo was not buying luxury goods to show his appreciation for family, friends, and lovers, he was on the run from #theBigPharmaIndustrialComplex. Constantly worried about others' welfare, there was a #sinkingfeeling that Elmo might just be right that his family and their children were #endangered by some wicked force that stalks the planet in a creepy horror movie kind of way. Elmo's father had, after all, outwitted Auschwitz with a sleight of hand that still smacks of shame. Elmo set out to protect everyone at risk from traumas personal and collective, past and future, symbolic and imaginary, refusing to hear that, in the process of beautifying the planet, he was traumatizing just about everyone.

As Elmo flew off the handle speaking truths that inched closer and closer to an unassailable Real, a trail of hashtags piled up in the minds of Elmo's Facebook friends where Elmo's invocations to join in the struggle accumulated as hashtag threats. It took nerves of steel to put up with Elmo as each new hashtag launched a search for Truth no less cavalier than a self-driving Uber lunging into a crowded intersection. People fled, and as Elmo went viral, speaking increasingly only in hashtags, he abandoned the internal objects that he'd hoped to repair but pretty much trashed along the way. It made for a public spectacle of private terror and manic flight from reality that upended any truth Elmo might have to share.

A white guy tweeting #ontherunfromthepolice@YourBlacklifematters then #translivesmatter and #freePalestine but also #riskWonder is a pretty hard to follow unless you surrender to the mindset of #ElmoKnows, which is of course what manic Elmo #imaginingAllthepeople assumed we did, which is crazy, but maybe not. Klein like most early psychoanalysts did not take account of shared objects, social objects, collective objects or what Francisco Gonzalez (2012) considers "groupal objects." These internal representations held en masse bind us to history but also cause us infinite grief (Rozmarin, 2011) because our use of collective objects is inevitably ambivalent.

When linking a self to a collective, one must reconcile multiple competing personal, interpersonal, cultural and historical demands on "identity" and "subjectivity." The more reified the identity categories available for use, the more structurally estranged we are from the terminology that defines our internal experience of collective objects. When Klein contrasts the psychic economies of mania and the depressive position, she did not esteem how an isolated individual's social objects may be at risk in the political surround nor how one's individual objects might struggle to protect social objects from an internal sense of danger as a manner of making reparation for traumas past and future. In this ultrapsychic space that lurks above, beyond, and trans-, individuals and collectives negotiate what can at best be approximated as "identity."

Today, we understand identificatory love (Benjamin, 1995) to be foundational in the development of subjective experience. We reconcile uneven capacities for recognition by individuals and groups with the vicissitudes of identification in an intersubjective matrix. Yet there appears to be a missing term whenever the social complicates the intersubjective scene. Solutions that emphasize "the field" don't quite resolve what happens in the clash of self, other, and identity (Hartman, 2018b; McGleughlin, 2019). Nor do "ontological" theories offer a corrective to the violence done to "phobogenic objects" (Fanon, 1952) while adopting a functionalist frame based on asymmetrical complementary roles (Hartman, 2018b).

Recalling Sullivan's parataxic and syntactic identifications (1953), there is always a quantity of difference to be negotiated in the translation of personal meanings into interpersonally resonant ideas (Stern, 2003), a process that comes with variable risks and rewards. As psychoanalysis began to factor "the social" into the experience of formulating "transactional identities" (Layton, 2006), writers began to explore qualities of alienation and othering that superordinate yet delimit the capacity for intersubjective recognition, but we have yet to find a language for the uptake of the individual into the collective or the curious fate of individual and groupal objects in the ultrapsychic field.

The social cannot recognize an individual's objects in quite the same way an Other might (Rozmarin, 2007). The ultrapsychic corollary to Winnicott's maxim that there is no baby without a mother is that there is no baby without a gender and no gender without a birth certificate.

As I tried to demonstrate earlier with the example of my "queerness," the negotiation of personal and social meanings that are held internally as object representations sparks confusion at the intersectional level of "identity." Individuals struggle to accommodate personal representations with those of similar others to form constituencies and constitute themselves as collectives. Political movements form through a process of identification and disidentification that influential sociologist Asef Bayat (2013) named "quiet encroachment" to account for the rise of informal political blocs among liminal subjects. Quiet encroachment happens psychically in the arbitration of internal personal and collective unconscious objects. It happens technologically on Twitter and socially in spontaneous acts of disruption (von Lieres, 2018) that go viral online: a Tunisian street vendor's persecutory objects quickly become the Arab Spring.

In Klein's manic equation, the subject's extravagant effort to evacuate perpetrators and clutch ahold of an internal all good object was a sure sign of the psyche's disembarkation from reality. As I see it, the effort to evacuate threats to collective objects and to bond extravagantly with social objects that help define one's own in relations to Others who endure similar traumas to the ones cohering in the individual's mind is a sign of the psyche's purchase on reality—particularly when an extravagant gesture of recognition among those at-risk rocks the ship of State. Would we diagnose Nelson Mandela with mania or any other freedom fighter held in solitary confinement whose grip on sanity relied precisely on an extravagant attachment to a groupal self? Though Elmo juggled collective experiences that seemed altogether mismatched, there was something tangible in his effort to speak to #eachAndevery1ofUs. History has known many a manic prophet. Indeed, Mania's struggles to heal collective wounds are enumerated bedside in hotels across America and #@thegideonbible.com.

The speed at which the Internet hurdles persons' internal objects into a social vortex only complicates the uneasy but inevitably recursive intertwining of individual and social objects.

Fascinated by the generative potential of online identities though I am (Hartman, 2010, 2017), and fully aware of how awry identification with cyberobjects that bear no account-ability to Truth can go (Essig, 2017), when Elmo went off the rails I was frankly hashtag terrified. I experienced some Cronenbergian version of PTSD each time a random hashtag transported me to Elmo's cyber hell. I would find myself preoccupied with shame associated with my own rushes of extravagance. Ruthlessness and cruel optimism (Berlant, 2011) catch up with me as I confront my sovereignty as the maverick analyst who peddles recognition of others' trauma with only hidden reference to my own. Suddenly, individual and collective registers mish and mash without the mash-up that makes memes musical, and I bond with Elmo's terror and I long for an untainted collective to save me. Such is the confusing minis-tration among individual and social objects in a moment of panicky identification. I imagine that this is the moment of #mania that launched #MeToo.

Terror is common in the presence of accelerated reality, but Elmo's ever-heaping hashtags evoke a cringing feeling that is more social like shame. Shame is curiously able to turn a fledgling connection into a risky gambit. It takes determination to persevere un-alone and among others in one's mind when a spontaneous gesture taken to repair damaged objects (#IstandWithChristine) risks pushback on fronts external and internal. Shame is all the more vexing in digital space where there is an excess of implied emotion and a hailstorm of data. Sprees of ones and zeros outpace our reveries and size us up long before *I* catch on to the trend in my screen time that became today's ad for Viagra. Beyond stray messages from the analog unconscious (Hartman, 2017), there is a whole other digital "unconscious" that be-longs to the online *user* me.

The user unconscious (Clough, 2018b) is located in the ubiquitous non-space where *I* am being *datafied* at all times—even when I consciously am offline and not accessing *it*. Then the "hey you!" of interpellation goes digital and my digital footprint runs amok with my perse-cutory objects in tow. I have no idea who or what has interpellated me as YOU or where that YOU roams. "Subjects are constituted as singular through a plurality of others" including other-than-human actants (Clough, 2018b, p. 74)—algorithms and the machines that run them—whose enigmatic methods for identifying each subject address my living-breathing *me* in a taxonomy of the YOUs that elude my spam filter. Even were I to have the presence of mind to distinguish my phantasies from the speculative aggregate that predicts my every fantasy, I would be certifiably "manic" to assert that I could restore peace of mind by delet-ing my online profile. A return to analog habits cannot protect the social objects that I rely upon to ratify my own. Plus, there is no hiding in cyberspace (Hartman, 2012). Even before I turn to @#nameyourcause for solace in collective action, my user id's YOU has already been conscripted to the cause by a nonhuman force. Hark! the cyber replica of Lacan's mirror stage: the DONATE NOW button.

That datafication is perilous doesn't mean throwing in your lot with others isn't useful. Efforts to match personal experience with the collective (me + too) by identifying and casting out traumatogenic social objects (the them of MeToo) via the "extravagant" use of a hashtag (#MeToo) allows one to gather a sense of being bonded with like-subjects who may be pre-sumed similarly at-risk in the public mind. An object representation of *me among us* is nego-tiated in the admixture of intrapsychic and ultrapsychic gestures. The disjunction that ensues when individual and collective objects negotiate the meaning of being "oneself at-risk" is am-plified in cyberspace where the individual person is increasingly a datafied social object at-risk of manipulation and erasure. An extravagant attitude toward collective objects, as manifest in the I-am-with-You use of the hashtag, isolates social objects from destructions past and future and allows the individual the belief that like-subjects will tender the hashtag with a like mind.

Here is where space and time get funky. A temporal lacuna in human nonhuman interaction compounds any misrecognition I already experience as an embodied speaker in a culture as well as the difference we tender in bids for relationality (Benjamin, 1988). These mismatched and largely unconscious fragments of what counts as "me" are who I bring to the forefront in any spontaneous gesture I make, whether I am online or not. In the spontaneous gesture, as Winnicott described it, I risk a connection to objects that ratify my subjective experience but fail to completely mirror me. This gives rise to transitional space and the capacity for concern. Online, the *me* that is ultra-subjective and the me that I locate in my person are presented to me all at once, and I map out self and other in a negotiation between individual and social registers of experience. In analog play there is time to mourn the mistakes that are the building blocks of care. In digital time, however, there is a melancholic residue in every misidentified but reshaped YOU.

The encounter happens so quickly when someone drops a hashtag into a line of text that we don't notice how quickly the spontaneity of the gesture beckons multiple channels of identification with the *me* who I took the risk to be. The feeling of finding oneself *alone yet among* rushes to the forefront when a solitary person at-risk makes contact with #MeToo. Perhaps that extravagant gesture is meant to repair the shame that festers in the blending of individual and social objects? Perhaps the quality of relentlessness in mania traces the ever-shifting ground we occupy as we loop among political awareness and individual desire in a quantum leap? Does the online experience of finding YOUs collapsed into *me* illustrate some way that mania collapses the social with the so-called self only to highlight the interwoven singularity of each? But then just as quickly as a gesture to the collective seems to bind my identity, the sense of coherence falls apart. The spam. The threats. The trolls. The memes. No wonder psychoanalysts tend to approach technology (and mania for that matter) with skepticism first! That's when I want to disappear into the spell state (Guralnik, 2019) that I can count on #@RachelMaddow to provide.

Like Elmo, Maddow delights in whistleblowers and leakers, so I wonder: What if mania writ social is what hashtag leakers do? When The Law is lawless and the risk of doing nothing smacks of complicity, one ethical choice is to fly off the handle. Whistleblowers like Elmo or Tarana Burke or Susan Fowler ditch the official channels and make hashtag gestures that frame power as an object of resistance in the social mind. The idea that *one among we* could make a difference is held as a new digital #cyberobject (Hartman, 2017).

As *we* accrue a battalion of cyberobjects with social savvy, might #mania be a way of fitting the fragments of a social Us into a "contingent whole?" Might Eng and Han's description of racial melancholia also explain how hashtag mania aspires to a kind of reparation in the social? They write: "there is a militant refusal on the part of the ego—better yet a series of egos—to let go, and this militant refusal is at the heart of melancholia's productive potentials" (2000, p. 696). A loss that cannot be mourned can at least be joined-in. That "there are no clean victories for black people, nor perhaps, for any people," as Ta-Neheisi Coates argues (2017, p. 334), is all the more reason to book a hashtag manic flight from reality when you factor in the Facebook algorithm.

Needless to say, at this point, I am hopeful that the psychic operation of the hashtag has transformative potential, and, in this chapter, I lean on the hashtag to reimagine mania and mourning in digital space where socially marked differences become collective objects that build awareness of the simple fact that #silence=death (Crimp, 2002; Hartman, 2012). Because differences that are socially constructed in the course of human events are superordinated by ideology in human time and datafication in computer time, there will always be a gap between gestures of repair and resignification in the social. To try to fill that gap with gesture upon gesture of #difference may well be a manic reach. So be it. I'm using this occasion to recognize the manic potential in (what I have previously called) "cybermourning" (Hartman, 2012) because, after Winnicott (1965), I can see in the hashtag gesture the development of a collective capacity for concern.

Some Caveats

I want to acknowledge up front that the hashtag has at least three fatal flaws. It is ripe for colonization by fake news, promiscuous in its use (Essig, 2017), and guilty of generating false equivalences among the hashtag accused. The hashtag also never managed to cross propriety sites as intended. In this chapter, I am less interested in the hashtag's engineering failures than in its user experience.

Furthermore, I'm not convinced that these drawbacks are an altogether bad thing in "the user unconscious" (Clough, 2018b). The "spontaneous gesture" (Winnicott, 1965) of a user's tag is met by humans expressing affect and machines generating predictions. One of our most solid psychoanalytic tenets is that recognition failures (whether caused by human error or digital machination) are necessary for "intersubjectivity" to do its work (Benjamin, 1995, 2018; Winnicott, 1969). Mistakes in parenting give us the capacity to share meaning. Errors in code—like errors in the manner by which the collective esteems any and each of us to be one of *them*—gives us the cracks in identity that I am calling "ultrapsychic" resonance with Others among whom I am one. As in Chetrit Vatine's (2014) crossing of Laplanche and Levinas, we are then driven to take positions of care for like Others by the riddles of translation.

Facebook users beware: you will be lurked, trolled, and misrecognized. You will feel stereotyped. You are being stereotyped and so is your user YOU. The analog version of you shoulders a history of private hurts and structural wrongs in society; the cyberobject version of YOU is a prediction. Given that for most humans, the operations of code are enigmatic and our inscription in data opaque, mistakes are bound to happen. #@TheRealDonaldTrump apparently thinks I am one of his big benefactors? Search me! *He* keeps sending me emails with the tag line that *I* can make America great. So, I suppose, I can… But not in the way that *he* uses me.

Point being that recognition is all the more "unevenly realized" and subjectivity all the more complex (Benjamin, 1995, p. 30) when digital media factor in a plethora of cyberobjects whose temporal and material qualities are not anchored in narrative and whose origins are as enigmatic in code as our erotic objects are in the infantile sexual (Laplanche, 2011; Saketopoulou, 2019a). Paradoxically, though, misadventures in digital representation create lacunae in the meeting of me with my YOUs that provide glimmers of autonomy. Datafication factors in all the men whose pics I have swiped left or right to curate my user YOU's desire as well as the *me* whom they have also imagined. In digital erotic life, conscious and unconscious, the private and the public, choice and chosen-for-YOU are displaced "by the separation of the personal and the networked," and "YOUs are prone, if not invited, to be caught in public acting privately" (Clough, 2018b, p. 77). No surprise that it is easy to feel bewildered by Tinder's seeming incapacity to match me to my desire. There is no such thing as a perfect fit. I swipe left to delete and right when a cyberobject is a good-enough representative of my desire.

So, yes, the collective mourning ritual that the hashtag is conceptually able to provide collapses into algorithms that threaten to turn digital gestures into stalemates and extravagant larks. Still, I argue that the social/psychic space provided by hashtags such as #MeToo and #blacklivesmatter are a beacon to collective concern precisely because of the misadventures in the ultrapsychic that turn recognition failures into bonds among individuals, collectives, and machines forging newfangled gestures of concern.

In the next section, I revisit the invention of the hashtag and the principles behind the technology that supports it to take up the question: can a technological ruse that manically proposes virtual difference guide us toward a social space of reparation? Ultimately, reparation at this scale requires, in the words of Coates, the improbable acknowledgment that our "most cherished myth was not real" (2017, p. 159). In the moment that we #metoo and #neveragain, might we find ourselves in a collective psychic reality where unreality is superordinate, and so it is fathomable, even if doomed, to challenge the very myths that constitute "the Real?" Perhaps in this melancholic gesture, quoting Winnicott, there emerges "a growing confidence that there will be opportunity for *contributing-in*" (1965, p. 77 *ital* added)? Can the hashtag, no matter how compromised a spontaneous gesture, spark a capacity to describe *risk* and evoke *concern* as it bonds individual and collective objects in an ultrapsychic reality?

#ChrisMessina

In the insular suburban enclave of working-class Italian families that I grew up in, Messina was the most common family name. I associate "Messina" with the feeling of being isolated as a young Jewish gay boy more dazzled by Nehru jackets than pick-up trucks. The Messina world referenced only Ohio and Sicily (I studied French). Today my home district is Trump country. It's ironic, speaking of reparation to rusty objects, that the visionary inventor of the hashtag (though I doubt most people even realize there was such a person), is an open-source geek named Chris Messina who launched the hashtag in a blog post on August 23rd, 2007 (https://factoryjoe.com/2007/08/25/groups-for-twitter-or-a-proposal-for-twitter-tag-channels/). Twitter's response to Messina's invention reported in *Business Insider* was short and sweet: "these things are for nerds. They're never going to catch on" (Edwards, 2013).

What I've just done: naming the Father of the Hashtag and giving the hashtag gravitas and temporality by planting it in an official biography flies in the face of the principles that guided the hashtag's design. There was to be no founder, no IPO, no Sergei Brin. There would be no patent for the hashtag because there would be no "licensable product." The hashtag would be an ahistorical feature of the Web with no proprietary Comcast controlling access and no government-sanctioned monopoly authorized to bucket taggers into stable user categories that could be mined to sculpt desire. In other words, by having no authorized use, the hashtag token (#) would only have merit as a cultural product through use. The hashtag was to be a digital *attractor* floating freely in the strangeness of the Twittersphere, marking "points of convergence without being exactly points of gravity and not structures as much as dynamic patterns… (that) describe qualities of dynamic experience rather than things" (Harris, 2005, p. 84). Messina (2017) insists, "hashtags are born of the Internet, and should be owned by no one."

It is August 2007. My source (whom I call "Siri") explains that Messina and his collaborators were operating on the hacker fringe of authorized web masters. At that time, a theoretical problem in social web design was how to attach links on web sites to metadata to open social frontiers. There was an official set of code standards sanctioned by an oversight body (the IRC), but the solutions championed by its Semantic Web Working Group were over-thought and clumsy. Among more radical (you might say "postmodern") programmers, there was a desire to solve this problem, eschewing metanarratives. How, in other words, might the trail of our collective meanderings carve cyber paths for users to follow before machines have taxonomies with which to spot and pave them?

A token that links among multiple sites without imposing a guiding *alpha* logic could theoretically stake out the differences among paths-taken in real time. Say a user tags the phrases "I love Sunday" and "Sunday Bloody Sunday" on random web sites. The gesture is enigmatic (in both the analog and digital sense) and meaningless until it has a taxonomic footprint in the user's YOU. Until then, Sunday is up for grabs and everyone who subsequently jumps on *Sunday* complicates its shared meaning in their own way. The task at hand is to find a way for Sunday to manifest in the collective imagination as a social object while remaining aloof to categorization for as long as possible so that it registers both collective use and personal idiom. Ideas were thrown around in heady forums such as FooCamp, an invitation-only conference, and BarCamp, a collective of scrappy developers including Siri and Messina who weren't invited to FooCamp.

BarCamp welcomed anyone by open-invitation to forums known as "Unconferences." BarCamp's libertarian ideology manifests in the functional aspirations for the hashtag. Messina wanted to make it simple for users to form online groups with no procedural exclusions as a way to solve the collective use/personal idiom problem. Recall that chat rooms and listservs are forms of social organization that have to be managed. As online groups mature and cluster into searchable entities with memberships, a hierarchy of precedents is used to link web channels to the broader social web.

Knowledge is thus distributed to mirror established conventions of how collectives are identified and placed alongside one another in social ranks. Links on sites owned by media conglomerates and well-funded institutions are privileged over fledgling sites. Messina (2017) envisioned something more democratic and spontaneous on the model of "eavesdropping." If there were no rituals of membership to prioritize who or what speaks when, anyone who eavesdrops on an online conversation and catches a word here or there could perk up and tune in or out without having to partake of an entire conversation to be coherent. If *Sunday* were only ever-softly assembled, the conversation would not need to be coherent or (like the Freudian unconscious) "condensed" to be interpreted. No one need subscribe to *The Sunday Times* or be registered as an interest group of Sunday sports fans. They just need to drop a universal tag (the former pound sign #) into a tweet or post to make a mark on Sunday.

Let's say that I'm droning on and on in a podcast about Internet Addiction. You perk up when I mention Internet porn but have no interest in my screed against the Sony Playstation. Perhaps it suddenly occurs to you that there are people who are also fascinated by Internet porn who don't care about video games. Like you, they grow queasy at the sight of therealdonaldtrump—however you care about pornography, not the finer points of digital anthropology, and it is Sunday after all. How can you express that in a brief, text-only medium without relying on body language or emojis? What if you want to spend Sundays linking up with a porn star who experiences Trump's Nuremberg-sytle pep rallies as a form of Internet pornography and your search engine has no way to classify that particular search leaving you with no way to organize that desired social experience unless you join an interest group that will forever-on flood your inbox with daily fundraising appeals? You may fantasize about such a sex symbol, even join her official fan club, but there is (in 2016) as of yet no @StormyDaniels to enjoin you with your compatriots.

Now, say we want to link users who tag Internet pornography and fascist rallies without presuming to know what informs their values. We would need to imagine a social classification that groups information neither by "ontology" nor "taxonomy." Ontological search sorts information into categories following conventions of assembly that are codified and normalized over time by repeated use. New information iterates normative discourse because ontological search matches Sunday to classes, attributes, and relations that are known to exist: Sunday enters the symbolic order hierarchically as the Lord's Day first. In "taxonomic classification," an emergent category is matched to an existing ontological category according to a predetermined set of laws and sorted in a line-up of search results according to a vested corporate interest. This is how "my Netflix" curates YOUR genre. Because I once watched Sunday Bloody Sunday, Netflix presumes I would rather spend my Sunday with (serial killer) Dexter than in the park with George.

To avoid all that, we need to identify a simple shared gesture that is *real* only at this ultra-psychic moment. It can never be exactly classified. In this moment, it has structure and intention because it is collaborative, but its arc is not yet specified by a master plan, so it remains "virtual." Remembering Deleuze's distinction between the virtual and its actualization:

> The virtual possesses the reality of a task to be performed or a problem to be solved; it is the problem which orientates, conditions, and engenders solutions, but these do not resemble the conditions of the problem.
>
> *(1994, p. 212)*

The virtual solution provided by "folksonomy" (Furner, 2010; Vander Wal, 2007) is a kind of digital bricolage (Levi-Strauss, 1962); or, as programmers say, a "kudge." Folksonomy classifies data with the provision that anyone can apply public tags to online items in order *to re-find* them in social media. How these tools are honed will have actual consequences, but it has no bearing on how the tool may be used in a virtual search. Folksonomic classification is gestural; even if it refers to a problem that remains to be solved, classification is not defined by the conditions of the problem but by whatever tool is being used (in a digital twist on bricolage) to share it. A Google search cannot accomplish this because it aggregates information in a hierarchy of demand privileging older, well-traveled paths. Google ontologically sorts data, and places it in a temporal order based on the accrued hierarchy of previous searches. (Commerce allows paid advertisers to jump the line.) If I google Black Lives Matter, what I am shown first is the BLM website followed by articles on Wikipedia, Facebook, Twitter, CNN, *The Guardian, The New Yorker, The Washington Post*... in descending order of "significance." I have to skip to page 10 to get to Blackliveslouisville.com.

Here is how folksonomy is different. By embedding a universal symbol "#" that already exists in a line of text, anyone searching with that syntax can in theory eavesdrop on any site that is currently trending data with hashtags. (Which unfortunately allows bots and annoying friends of friends to lurk Facebook feeds.) If I search for #BlackLivesMatter, I will find *the now* that is BLM's very latest utterance. I find BLM by how it is being iterated differently each time the hashtag is used, "provided," Siri adds, "I am searching within a tool that is not perverted by ontology." The social object that I have in mind when I tweet will always be re-presented in subsequent tweets as a different representation than my own—slightly different or completely jarring. In this way, the "loss" that inheres in the transformation 'from the subjective object to the ultra-object subjectively perceived' (my twist on Winnicott, 1971) confers identity in a decoupage of affect and code that elides classification as a datafied object—at least in the spontaneous folksonomic hashtag gesture. Said differently, folksonomic gestures will always-only be an approximation of me as a *YOU* among *us*. Folksonomy circumvents the taxonomies that forge identity politics by representing identity as it collects meaning in a groupal object's soft assembly (Harris, 2005).

It is important to remember that the hashtag doesn't have affect; it *is* affect so long as it remains a lacuna in the user's YOU—the You being "an assemblage of an I and a profile or cloud of data traces that have more value than the I not only to economy and governance but increasingly to the sociality of users as well" (Clough, 2018b, p. 77). By comparison, an abbreviation like "lol" expresses affect as a meme. The hashtag has been appropriated by commedians like Stephen Colbert as a meme consequent to its datafication. #lol is then functioning as a signifier.

As a folksonomic term, the hashtag can never be fixed to one meaning; it is always emergent. Indeed, depending on syntax, a hashtagged word always changes meaning. As Messina (2013) quipped: "*I'm sorry I puked on your cat. #sorryNotSorry,*" I'm letting you know that "I *am* sorry, but not *that* sorry because I hate your cat." The nuance of a hashtag's meaning actually evolves through use and given the rapid pace of digital media, Messina's idea was that if spammers ended up taking over a hashtag or if users grew sour of a hashtag's implications, they would simply abandon it and forge another.

Even though a user's digital footprint never dies, hashtags rue taxonomy so they die constantly. Should a hashtag outlast its purpose, it becomes a meme, as in a *The New York Times'* report that in Mark Zuckerberg's 2018 appearance before Congress, he was "Sorry. Not Sorry" (*NYT,* April 15, 2018). However, and this is quite important, even as a meme, the hashtag has a radical alterity because the very latest iterations of the hashtagged term that I find with my search are not categorized by nuance or paternity. They show me what is "trending." There is no mourning a hashtag; it offers futurity as the present without being defined by the conditions of the problem (Deleuze, 1994).

The irksome problem is that folksonomies become victims of the zeitgeist. As the data set connected to any one hashtag grows bigger, frequency reinforces the modal use—not regarding history or taxonomy as in a Google search, but as an index of what is "trending" at any given moment. Popular hashtags become an echo chamber of the now vulnerable, as Siri explains, to modeling by any platform that figures out how to group sequential hashtags into taxonomies, match patterns to user data, and flood trending patterns with line-jumping advertisements and partisan links to increasingly fake news. Alas: #StopTheSteal.

True, trends are vulnerable when they are actualized. At first emergent and fresh, hashtags go viral and become signifiers. Ever social, they convey emotions that range from humor to conviction to respect to contempt depending on how the user is placed in relation to their *YOU,* and obviously there will be recognition failures aplenty as well as rank interpellations and normative decrees. The interesting thing is that the hashtag develops an almost ironic relationship to its reification the trendier it gets, and #Oops! it immediately becomes a different gesture with a social potential. In the echo chamber of the political now, as a perpetual disrupter of the normative unconscious (Layton, 2002), it becomes possible to delink the unconscious intromission of discursive messages about what constitutes a "good life" (Guralnik & Simeon, 2010) from taxonomic categorization and (at least momentarily in the user mind) realign a potential action with affect. This is how a simple hashtag can strive to make, what we psychoanalysts call, "reparation."

Again, the hashtag itself has no code and, as an eavesdropped percept, it simply fixes an affectively laden gesture to a lacuna in the user unconscious whereupon my user I joins *YOUs* in a social medium (Clough, 2018b). Then, in the life of my hashtag, as I follow its trajectory, I introject digital edits of my spontaneous gesture that ultrapsychically maps the fate of *my* objects. Whether or not repeated transaction of this discursive operation grants me (or YOU or us) sufficient respect for difference to expose the violence that supports many of our core myths (Coates, 2017) remains to be seen. But the hashtag gesture certainly is an intervention in "the actuality" of public discourse even when it pits #EveryVoteCounts against #StopTheSteal in a virtual standoff. In Deleuze's terms, "the virtual is opposed not to the real but to the actual. *The virtual is fully real insofar as it is virtual*" (1994, p. 208).

The aspiration for a token that unlinks "the meta from the meat" (Messina, 2017) might seem like a mass flight from reality if we only feature its inevitable failure to cleave #racists! from #racists! There is, at least in theory, a principle of online social interaction that, citing Benjamin's (2009, p. 442) criteria for *the moral third*, "we rely upon in our efforts to create and restore the space for each partner in the dyad to engage in thinking, feeling, acting, or responding rather than merely reacting." And that is, quite simply, though this is a contentious claim to be sure, the hashtag.

#theRiskObject

Classically psychoanalysis, as a technology that searches for meaning in afterward time, frames reality based on what has been lost and mourned. Reality is organized as a narrative with a historical arc. Mourning revisits dashed hopes and imperfect solutions to intrapsychic struggles and interpersonal conflicts to broach acceptance of human limitations. One "gets a grip" on reality. Difference becomes a measure of the psychic risk one is willing to take (provided one has such a choice) to fall out of line with the "normal" course of public events.

Cyberspace, as I have written elsewhere (Hartman, 2010, 2012, 2013, 2017a), presents us with a radically new paradigm that grounds reality in the futurity of search above and beyond any accommodation to loss and limit that delimits reality in the "depressive position" (Ogden, 1992). We "digital migrants" have one foot in each paradigm—which is confusing and leads us to evaluate digital experience in analog terms. My project has been to cross paradigms with an ear to the cyber social in the analog mind. Mourning in particular has a collective flare online. Virtual mourning is not transacted as a process of reestablishing objects in a fragmented ego (Klein, 1940). The digital self is always decentered and emergent by virtue of its interactive and only partially human design. Cybermourning entails emersion in a temporality where the past is virtually made actual in each "melancholically" shared mourning gesture (Eng & Han, 2000). Digital medias encode this discourse in such a way that social objects are never "part" or "whole" or even "lost." They become collective objects, iterative edits of a virtual ongoing being as each new mourner adds a patch of code to a digital quilt (Hartman, 2012, 2017a).

Because digital time starts with the assumption of a lost original that is only ever known as a translation in enigmatic code, mourned objects are featured as propositions for how *we* will continue after loss rather than as spectral beings that shroud our collective narrative (Hartman, 2012). New data add more life to the lost objects' YOU. Death is further complicated because the lost object takes new shape in successive iterations of code. When a damaged digital object is grieved by a mourner, the source object (Hartman, 2017; Jacobs, 2017) is not the subject of repair. Rather, the object goes public where the very category *my-object* is a suspect category. We find the lost object to be repaired among *us* living. Reparation is, as I have been saying with reference to Eng and Han's work (2000) on racial melancholia, a gesture of social recognition, rather than an impossible letting go in a context of mass grief. Freedom after loss is a move toward ever greater accessibility of mourned social objects: "One's objects are not destroyed when others add to them or alter them or, even, cancel them: they morph. Structures— that is, rules that delimit what is a self, what is a group, what is knowledge, etc.—morph accordingly" (Hartman, 2012, p. 457). Difference is a virtual principle, neither a legacy nor an outcome while also both. Difference is simply the risk one takes #inPursuitOfAnIdea.

Here is the hitch: when reparative gestures take measure of those who have been unaccounted for by society, the found social object is aggregated in taxonomies based on tried-and-true ontologies. Whiteness always comes out on top. People who occupy lacunae in what society deems legible are identified to be "at-risk," but then become the risk to Whiteness. Exiles and immigrants bear the brunt of this bait and switch (Gonzalez, 2017; Rozmarin, 2017).

I have described the class of dissociated "silent citizens" (van Lieres, 2018) who occupy our social imagination in a state of exception (Rozmarin, 2017) as "the risk object" (Hartman, 2013, 2019). The risk object is both my excessive risk in relation to my various and competing objects (as I explained above) *plus* the risk attributed to the group whose measure I make when mapping my own state of risk. Recall Elmo whose *plusperfect errand* (Apprey, 1993) it is to broadcast an internal holocaust that might otherwise die in the official narrative of his father's survival. Consider the relationships among the three black men who collectively depict *Atlanta* in Donald Glover's portrait of America or feminists Thelma and Louise in another time and place. The risk object is articulated anti-heroically as a trope of becoming woke. Sadly, this places him/her/them all the more at-risk.

The risk object is thus a political species of bad object that manifests with the rise of neoliberalism as a participatory way of knowing crumbles and an emphasis on collective experience is supplanted by quantitative measures of individual achievement in an intersectionally imbricated collective. Scrutiny moves inward from a conceptual threat to our collective health (democracy at risk) to a risk to each of our abilities to prosper to the marked individual at-risk who then risks being identified solely by his different skin color—or was it his hoodie (Coates, 2017)?

The risk object crosses intra-, inter-, and ultrapsychic registers, inhabiting positions that being at-risk represents for individuals, among groups, and, ultimately, in the virtual ontologically-because-normatively White collective. Difference subject to taxonomic classification reifies what analog reality always already knows: the material reality of race. Trayvon Martin is a mixed analog/digital risk object: he is at analog risk when Obama grieves him as a would-have-looked like me son; he becomes a cyberobject when millions link his murder to the reality that #BLM. He and his fallen kin signal to the collective that the young black men who live in their mind as at-risk will always be the virtual perpetrator—especially in the moment that they are actually the victim. In hashtag mania, then, the effort to cast out perpetrator and protect the groupal good object performs a kind of ultrapsychic reversal of fortune—at least in the folksonomic spontaneous gesture.

Notably, when performing his version of #sorryNotSorry while testifying about Facebook's complicity in identity theft before Congress, Mark Zuckerberg traded in his customary hoodie for a blue suit (Friedman, V. *NYT*, April 10, 2018). In this act of risk's erasure, we observe the risk object being signified ontologically and taxonomically: beware the black man in the hoodie. The risk object thus returned to its "rightful place" bears the social's disavowal of those among us who embody risk so that our hoodies don't. And, in this bait and switch, Zuckerberg and Trump use the hashtag perversely. But in their narcissistic use of the hashtag, # becomes a sharp-edged boomerang—illustrating their inner risky business for all who care to see it.

Almost every person who has spoken publicly about their decision to declare themselves a survivor of sexual harassment since Tarana Burke founded the Me Too movement in 2006 (the same year that Twitter was founded) has uttered some version of Burke's regret that silence about their own experience of sexual abuse risked encouraging other survivors to remain silent (Garcia, S. *NYT*, October 20, 2017). Burke and then thousands of other victims declared *me too* and risked exposure to expose sexual harassment. Reality changes when the at-risk risk self-disclosure.

When linked to the risk object, the hashtag occupies a multitude of reparative gestures at once. It "fails" in that it cannot solve the problem of harassment, but the virtual problem is no longer isomorphic with its resolution in the actual domain of public policy. Folksonomic classification allows each hashtag gesture to become an action potential in the digital social. The problem of analog reality is its repeated iteration. The virtual object of digital reality's ultrapsychic logic is difference. The risk object: she, he, they, you, me, or them need not carry risk alone because *risk* is a social problem, and we increasingly understand that the risk object embodied in any one person is a doomed messenger of said risk by virtue of their difference within a Master discourse. When moved to contribute-in as #MeToo, I may extravagantly presume that community among victims is the best recourse in a reality of thieves.

#Elmo

In concluding, inspired by so many brave hashtaggers, I feel the need to come clean and explain that writing this chapter is an act of reparation after the loss of my very dearest friend to mental illness. I have given him the name Elmo. #TalkingAboutIt: Elmo's illness haunts me too.

I chose the name Elmo from some deeply unconscious association to the character Elmo on Sesame Street. Elmo is a furry red monster with a falsetto voice who hosts a segment aimed at toddlers called "Elmo's World." Elmo typically refers to Elmo in the third person as "they" or simply as Elmo in a manner that irks Sesame Street traditionalists who protest that *his* trans pronouns put toddlers' grammar at risk. Indeed, Elmo has quite manic aspirations. In a 1996 special feature, *Elmo Saves Christmas* when they discover that although Christmas can't happen every day, it is "always good to keep the spirit of Christmas every day and every year in your heart." Hats off to #Elmo. They really pack a punch when it comes to challenging our most cherished myth.

References

Apprey, M. (1993). Dreams of urgent/voluntary errands and transgenerational haunting in transsexualism. In: *Intersubjectivity, Projective Identification and Otherness,* ed. Apprey, M. and Stein, H. Pittsburgh, PA: Duquesne University Press, pp. 102–130.

Bayat, A. (2013). *Life as Politcs: How Ordinary People Changed the Middle East.* Stanford, CA: Stanford University Press.

Benjamin, J. (1995). *Like Subjects/Love Objects: Essays on Recognition and Sexual Difference.* New Haven, CT: Yale University Press.

Benjamin, J. (1988). *The Bonds of Love: Psychoanalysis, Feminism, and the Problem of Domination.* New York, NY: Pantheon.

Benjamin, J. (2009). A relational psychoanalysis perspective on the necessity of acknowledging failure in order to restore the facilitating and containing features of the intersubjective relationship (the shared third). *International Journal of Psycho-Analysis*, 90(3), 441–450.

Benjamin, J. (2018). *Beyond Doer and Done To: Recognition Theory, Intersubjectivity and the Third.* New York, NY: Routledge.

Berlant, L. (2011). *Cruel Optimism.* Durham, NC: Duke University Press.

Bliss, P. (2016). Panti's noble call at the Abbey Theatre, January 2, 2014. https://www.youtube.com/watch?v= WXayhUzWnl0.

Christensen, C. (2018). When half becomes whole: Mixed race and revitalization of the self through destruction. Paper presented to the Psychoanalytic Institute of Northern California. February 10, 2018.

Clough, P. T. (2018a). *The User-Unconscious: On Affect, Media, and Measure.* Minneapolis, MN: University of Minnesota Press.

Clough, P. T. (2018b). The other-than-human and the "user unconscious." *Studies in Gender and Sexuality*, 19, 73–80.

Coates, T. (2017). *We Were Eight Years in Power*. New York, NY: One World Publishing.

Corbett, K. (2008). Gender now. *Psychoanalytic Dialogues*, 18, 838–856.

Crenshaw, K. (1989). Demarginalizing the intersection of race and sex: A black feminist critique of antidiscrimination doctrine, feminist theory and antiracist politics. University of Chicago Legal Forum, 1989, Article 8.

Crimp, D. (2002). *Melancholia and Moralism—Essays on AIDS and Queer Politics*. Cambridge, MA: MIT Press.

Deleuze, G. (1994). *Difference and Repetition*. New York, NY: Columbia University Press.

Dimen, M. (2003). *Sexuality Intimacy Power*. Hillsdale, NJ: The Analytic Press.

Dimen, M. (2011). Introduction. In: *With Culture in Mind: Psychoanalytic Stories*, ed. Dimen, M. New York, NY: Routledge, pp. 1–10.

Downs, A. (2005). *The Velvet Rage: Overcoming the Pain of Growing up Gay in a Straight Man's World*. New York, NY: Hachette.

Edwards, J. (2013). The inventor of the hashtag explains why he didn't patent it. Business Insider, November 12, https://www.businessinsider.com/chris-messina-talks-about-inventing-the-hashtag-on-twitter-2013-11.

Eng, D. L., and Han, S. (2000). A dialogue on racial melancholia. *Psychoanalytic Dialogues*, 10, 667–700.

Essig, T. (2017). How the Trump campaign built a political porn site to sell the pleasures of hate: What do we do now? *Contemporary Psychoanalysis*, 53, 516–532.

Fanon, F. (1952). *Black Skin, White Masks*. New York, NY: Grove Press.

Friedman, V. (2018). Mark Zuckerberg's I'm sorry suit. *New York Times*, 4 April, 2018.

Furner, J. (2018). Folksonomies. In, J.D. McDonald and M. Levine-Clark, eds., *Encyclopedia of Information and Library Sciences*. Taylor and Francis Online. https://doi.org/10.1081/E-ELIS4.

Gentile, K. (2016). Bridging psychoanalytic and cultural times—Using psychoanalytic theory to understand better how repofuturity and biomedicalization produces subjectivities. In: *The Business of Being Made*, ed. Gentile, K. New York, NY: Routledge, pp. 21–47.

Gentile, K. (2018). Animals as the symptom of psychoanalysis or, The potential for interspecies co-emergence in psychoanalysis. *Studies in Gender and Sexuality*, 19, 7–13.

Goffman, I. (1986), *Frame Analysis: An Essay on the Organization of Experience*. New York, NY: Harper and Row.

González, F. J. (2012). Loosening the bonds: Psychoanalysis, feminism, and the problem of the group. *Studies in Gender and Sexuality*, 13, 253–267.

González, F. J. (2013). Another Eden: Proto-gay desire and social precocity. *Studies in Gender and Sexuality*, 14, 112–121.

González, F. (2017). Iteration and homologies of difference: A Discussion of Veronica Csillag's "Emmy Grant: Immigration as repetition of trauma and as potential space." *Psychoanalytic Dialogues*, 27, 480–486.

González, F. (2018). I's R Us. Or the collective of the individual. Paper presented at the IARPP Spring Meeting, Hope and Dread: Therapists and Patients in an Uncertain World, New York, NY, June 15.

Grand, S., and Salberg, S. (2016). *Trans-generational Trauma and The Other: Dialogues across History and Difference*. New York: Routledge.

Guralnik, O. (2016). Sleeping dogs: Psychoanalysis and the socio-political. *Psychoanalytic Dialogues*, 26, 655–663.

Guralnik, O. (2018). A racial contract. Paper presented at the IARPP Spring Meeting, Hope and Dread: Therapists and Patients in an Uncertain World, New York, June 14.

Guralnik, O. (2019). A state of mind: Dissociation in service of the collective. Paper presented as the SICP lecture, Institute for Contemporary Psychoanalysis, New York, February 8.

Guralnik, O., and Simeon, D. (2010). Depersonalization: Standing in the spaces between recognition and interpellation. *Psychoanalytic Dialogues*, 20, 400–416.

Harris, A. (2005). *Gender as Soft Assembly*. Hillsdale, NJ: The Analytic Press.

Hartman, S. (2010). L'état c'est moi—Except when I am not: Commentary on paper by Orna Guranlik and Daphne Simeon. *Psychoanalytic Dialogues*, 20, 428–436.

Hartman, S. (2011). Reality 2.0: When loss is lost. *Psychoanalytic Dialogues*, 21, 468–482.

Hartman, S. (2012). Cybermourning: Grief in flux from object loss to collective immortality. *Psychoanalytic Inquiry*, 32, 454–467.

Hartman, S. (2013). Bondless love. *Studies in Gender and Sexuality*, 14, 35–50.

Hartman, S. (2017). The poetic timestamp of digital erotic objects. *Psychoanalytic Perspectives*, 14, 159–174.

Hartman, S. (2018a). The shadow of non-citizens in an immoral economy of risk. *CORD Network Blog*. http://epress. utsc.utoronto.ca/cord/2019/03/05/the-shadow-of-non-citizens-in-an-immoral-economy-of-risk/

Hartman, S. (2018b). When we frame. In: *Reconsidering the Moveable Frame in Psychoanalysis*, ed. I. Tylim and A. Harris. New York: Routledge, pp. 141–163.

Hartman, S. (2020). Carter is so handsome. *Psychoanalysis Today: The e-Journal of the International Psychoanalytic Association*. http://www.psychoanalysis.today/en-GB/PT- Articles/Hartman164721/Carter-is-so-Handsome.aspx

Jacobs, A. (2015). The demise of the analog mind: Digital primal fantasies and the technologies of loss-less-ness. In: *Psychosocial Imaginaries: Perspectives on Temporality, Subjectivity, and Activism*, ed. S. Frosch. London: Palgrave Macmillan, pp. 126–144.

Klein, M. (1935). A contribution to the psychogenesis of manic-depressive states. *International Journal of Psycho-Analysis*, 16, 145–174.

Klein, M. (1940). Mourning and its relation to manic-depressive states. *International Journal of Psycho-Analysis*, 21, 125–153.

Laplanche, J. (2011). Gender, sex, and the sexual. In: *Freud and the Sexual: Essays 2000–2006*, ed. J. Fletcher. New York: International Psychoanalytic Books, pp. 159–180.

Layton, L. (2002), Cultural hierarchies, splitting, and the heterosexist unconscious. In: *Bringing the Plague: Toward a Postmodern Psychoanalysis*, ed. S. Fairfield, L. Layton, and C. Stack. New York: Other Press, pp. 195–224.

Layton, L. (2006). Racial identities, race enactments, and normative unconscious processes. *Psychoanalytic Inquiry*, 75, 237–269.

Leavitt, J. (2019). On analyst's doubt in 2019: Psychoanalysis and whiteness culture. Paper presented on the panel, The Analyst's Anxieties in a Skeptical Culture: Do We Still Believe in What We Do?, Spring Meeting of the American Psychoanalytical Association, New York, February 9.

Lévi-Strauss, C. (1962). *The Savage Mind*. Chicago, IL: University of Chicago Press.

Marriott, D. (2018). *Whither Fanon?: Studies in the Blackness of Being*. Stanford, CA: Stanford University Press.

Massumi, B. (2015). *The Politics of Affect*. Malden, MA: Polity Press.

McGleughlin, J. (2019). The analyst's necessary non-sovereignty and the generative power of the negative. *Psychoanalytic Dialogues*, forthcoming.

Messina, C. (2013). Why do people use hashtags to mark their posts on Facebook, Twitter, etc,? *Quora*, August 9. https://www.quora.com/Why-do-people-use-hashtags-to-mark-their-posts-on-Facebook-Twitter-etc

Messina, C. (2017). How did the idea for hashtags originate on Twitter? Was it a casual by-product introduced by its users or had it already been preconceived? *Quora*, August 5. https://www.quora.com/How-did-the-idea-for-hashtags- originate-on-Twitter-Was-it-a-casual-by-product-introduced-by-its-users-or-had-it-already-been-preconceived

Ogden, T. H. (1992). *The Matrix of Mind*. London: Karnac.

Pellegrini, A. (2018). The dog who barks and the noise of the human: Psychoanalysis after the animal turn. *Studies in Gender and Sexuality*, 19, 14–19.

Peltz, R. (2005). The manic society. *Psychoanalytic Dialogues*, 15, 347–366.

Puget, J. (2010). The subjectivity of certainty and the subjectivity of uncertainty. *Psychoanalytic Dialogues*, 20, 4–20.

Rozmarin, E. (2007). An other in psychoanalysis: Emmanuel Levinas's critique of knowledge and analytic sense. *Contemporary Psychoanalysis*, 43, 327–360.

Rozmarin, E. (2009). I am yourself: Subjectivity and the collective. *Psychoanalytic Dialogues*, 19, 604–616.

Rozmarin, E. (2011). To be is to betray: On the place of collective history and freedom in psychoanalysis. *Psychoanalytic Dialogues*, 21, 320–345.

Rozmarin, E. (2017). Immigration, belonging, and the tension between center and margin in psychoanalysis. *Psychoanalytic Dialogues*, 27, 470–479.

Rozmarin, E. (2020). The subject as threshold. *American Imago*, 77, 309–336.

Saketopoulou, A. (2011). Minding the gap: Intersections between gender, race, and class in work with gender variant children. *Psychoanalytic Dialogues*, 21, 192–209.

Saketopoulou, A. (2014). To suffer pleasure: The shattering of the ego as the psychic labor of perverse sexuality. *Studies in Gender and Sexuality*, 15, 254–268.

Saketopoulou, A. (2019a). The draw to overwhelm: Consent, risk, and the re-translation of enigma. *JAPA*, 67, 133–167.

Saketopoulou, A. (2019b). How the world becomes bigger; Implantation, intromission and the après-coup. Discussion of paper, "The après-coup as a central Freudian concept" by Jonathan House. *Contemporary Psychoanalysis*, forthcoming.

Salberg, J., & Grand, S. (2016). *Wounds of History: Repair and Resilliance in the Transgenerational Transmission of Trauma*. New York: Routledge.

Schafer, R. (1968). *Aspects of Internalization*. New York: International Universities Press.

Simon, T. (2017). Squeezed. Paper given on the panel Good Enough Intimacy/Trans Enough Gender at the 50th World Congress of the International Psycho-Analytical Association, Buenos Aires. Argentina, July 29.

Stein, R. (1998). The enigmatic dimension of sexual experience: The "otherness" of sexuality and primal seduction. *Psychoanalytic Quarterly*, 67, 594–625.

Stern, D. (2003). *Unformulated Experience: From Dissociation to Imagination in Psychoanalysis*. Hillsdale, NJ: The Analytic Press.

Stewart, K. (2007). *Ordinary Affects*. Durham, NC: Duke University Press.

Sullivan, H. S. (1953). *The Interpersonal Theory of Psychiatry*. New York: Norton.

Tannen, D. (1993). *Framing in Discourse*. New York: Oxford University Press.

Tubert-Oklander, J. (2013). Field, process, and metaphor. *Psychoanalytic Inquiry*, 33, 229–246

Vander Wal, T. (2007). *Folksonomy*. Vanderwal.net. February 2. http://vanderwal.net/folksonomy. html

von Lieres, B. (2018). Silent citizenship, dissociation, and participation. Paper presented at the IARPP Spring Meeting, Hope and Dread: Therapists and Patients in an Uncertain World, New York, June 15.

Winnicott, D. W. (1965). *The Maturational Processes and the Facilitating Environment: Studies in the Theory of Emotional Development*. London: Hogarth.

Winnicott, D. W. (1969). The Use of an object. *International Journal of Psycho-Analysis*, 50, 711–716.

Winnicott, D. W. (1971). *Playing and Reality*. London: Tavistock Publications.

19

INTERNET MEMES AND THE FACE OF THE OTHER

Lewis Thurston and Nancy Thurston

The Internet is more divided than ever. The face of the Other is too often distorted on the Internet, and Internet memes play a large part in that polarization. Memes, however, may also be our way out of this predicament. In this chapter, we discuss Internet memes and how people use them to transmit truth and distortion embedded in cultural ideas, symbols, or practices. We theorize from a Jungian perspective that the Internet is a form of collective consciousness and collective unconsciousness. Internet memes are like dreams in that they seem irrational yet are imbued with meaning; they serve as the dream symbols of the Internet's collective unconscious. Recognizing this, we can apply Levinas' dichotomy of the I and the Other, especially his ideas on the face of the Other, within this framework of perceiving memes.

Topics addressed in this chapter include (1) how faces in memes can distort and alienate the Other, (2) the Levinasian face of the Other in memes, (3) memes and the intersection of ego state and persona theory, (4) potential meanings of meme faces vis-à-vis archetypal symbols, (5) how memes can give voices to the unheard, and (6) using memes as a tool to deepen therapy.

Internet memes draw people in because they create a sense of relatability in a short amount of time. They are relatable because they are typically comedic, poignant, and/or evocative of strong shared emotions. They often convey more truth than people realize, but sometimes that truth depicts the shadow side of society just much as its ideas do.

We know it is tempting to apply value judgments onto memes as a whole, especially when one is not native to the world of memes. In our experience, though, Internet natives do not seek out memes but rather come across them organically in their Internet interactions. Therefore, we would say that it is important not to interpret Internet memes as good or bad but rather to recognize that Internet memes "are" and thus attempt to be more conscientious about their use.

That being said, the face of the Other is too often distorted on the Internet, and Internet memes play a part in that polarization. Fortunately, memes may also be our way out of this predicament. This does raise the basic question, though, of how to define memes and Internet memes. The concept of memes originated with Richard Dawkins' (1989) theory of memetics and his observation that ideas and aspects of culture pass along generation to generation the way genes do. His definition emphasized the replication of memes as he was

DOI: 10.4324/9781003195849-23

attempting to generalize the experience of replication of genes to the replication of other forms of data. The replications of memes are thus similar to those of genes in that mutations occur subtly from one generation to the next. Dawkins distinguished symbiotic memes from memes that are viruses. An example of a symbiotic meme is language, in which the benefits gained from using it help its propagation and ability to repeat, therefore propelling it to mutate more diversely. As an example of meme viruses, Dawkins used dogmatism, in the sense that it creates reward systems for the preservation of certain ideas at the expense of other memes in the cultural ecosystem.

We do not think that Dawkins' definition is sufficient for defining the phenomenon that the Internet collective has come to call Internet memes. Therefore, our own definition of what constitutes an Internet meme is as follows: a repeated image, short video, and/or short set of words on the Internet (especially in social medias and group chats) that convey a unique experience that can be elaborated upon in ironic and/or post-ironic ways. Post-ironic describes a phenomenon that many people who habitually interact with memes experience in which they become so satiated with ironic content that it becomes the new norm. As a result, they develop a need for irony to be surpassed by a subversive return to sincerity and/or engagement in meta-ironic commentary.

We will now discuss how people transmit both truth and distortion embedded in Internet memes. People use memes to transmit truth in ways such as offering wholesome encouragement, explaining complex academic ideas in a more relatable manner, and/or portraying beauty/cuteness. Often, wholesome memes figure a character that displays what Austrian biologist Konrad Lorenz describes as *kinderschema*, or child scheme (Lorenz, 1943; see also Glocker et al., 2009), such as large eyes, a head overly large for the body, and slight awkwardness in kinesthetic movement. This can be seen as evoking the Jungian archetype of the eternal child. By evoking the inner child, this kind of meme calls upon a sense of innocence and noumenal radiance associated with nurturing. In a wholesome meme, any being that evokes kinderschema (especially babies, puppies, kittens, or children's television program characters) is accompanied by text that overlays the picture. A prime example of this kind of meme manifested even before the Internet, back in 1971, with the famous poster of a cat hanging from a branch by its front paws with the text "Hang in there." Another format that was popular in 2010 was a cat with a scrunched-up face saying, "Can I haz cheezburger?" which again evokes kindershema because it reflects the pronunciation that a toddler would have.

Another variation of the wholesome meme that is important to discuss is the political wholesome meme. This type of meme became controversial because people from different political orientations disagree on social issues and what wholesome societal outcomes would look like. Beyond this, many disagree about what makes something political.

In the examples we put forward in this chapter, we focus on memes that purposefully work against the APA Ethics Code Principle E, "Respect for People's Rights and Dignity" (American Psychological Association, 2017). Given that many other psychological organizations also ascribe to this ethical principle, we can all likely agree that being against respect for people's rights and dignity is problematic. We will now discuss how people transmit distortion (if your goal is respect for people's rights and dignity) in memes that convey false or harmful information on social issues, degrade people, perpetuate stereotypes, and/or represent potentially traumatizing images and/or descriptions.

One way some Internet memes distort truth is by being racist. Racism in Internet memes often evokes older stereotyped images, so these are easy to recognize. An example of this is Internet memes that use the "greedy Jew" picture from Nazi propaganda of the 1930s to illustrate discussions of contemporary conspiracies. Racist Internet memes can also be more subtle and often are presented as statistics in order to appear rational. Some common dog-whistle tactics include using three parentheses (((like so))) around the name of a person because Internet programs exist that put such parentheses around Jewish names to make it easier for anti-Semites to identify certain celebrities as Jewish. Other examples are statements such as "Despite being just 14% of the population, blacks commit 50% of the crime" and "Despite being 3% of the population…" when discussing Jewish people. However, the latter example can easily be confused with "I wonder what the 40%ers are up to," a dog whistle for transphobia (transgender people are also often a subject of ridicule in memes that distort truth). Here, the 40% refers to the 40% suicide rate of transgender teens. The other three main dog whistles to look out for is someone sarcastically saying, "Did you just assume my gender?"; the sarcastic use of the word "triggered" in angry bold type; and variations of "I sexually identify as an Apache attack helicopter." In all of these, the memers use statistics and phrases that are technically valid (e.g. logic statements that are valid under racist propositions) but that are removed from their original contexts and/or are set up to create a false sense of causation to such a degree that the truth becomes distorted.

Our discussion of the distortion of the face of the Other in memes naturally brings us to exploring the Levinasian face of the Other in memes. Levinas' (2006) theory of Totality and Infinity can be described as two infinitely different but at the same time similar faces gazing at each other, conjuring or tapping into a creative infinity that, being creative and infinite, has the qualities of God.

Memes that depict the Other in a more neutral gaze can allow us to observe the power of the face unobstructed. The unobstructed face is often used for the purpose of eliciting empathy or attempting to ward off critique. An example of this is pictures of George Floyd with the caption "Say his name," which were prolific in the summer of 2020. Some would say these are not a meme, but this critique usually arises from the assumption that memes have to be ironic. As we stated at the beginning of this chapter, Internet memes are currently just as likely to be post-ironic as ironic; thus, a picture of a person with text conveying a sincere message falls under the category of a post-ironic meme.

Obstructed faces, usually emphasizing anger and/or undesirable body proportions, obscure the face of the Other and therefore make it easier to ridicule in ways that either justly humble people who abuse their positions of power or put historically oppressed people "in their place" via degradation, as already noted. This dichotomy is often referred to as punching up versus punching down in modern comedy theory. For example, some political meme-makers deliberately distort features of political figures in a way that is designed to disempower the person by belittling them, challenging powerful figures they perceive as unjust, or identifying them with a popular symbol.

An example of emphasizing undesirable body proportions is choosing angry faces to depict political opponents in order to make the other side appear to lack the self-control required for governance. Like political comics, another way to distort the face of the Other is to take a noticeable trait of a figurehead person and emphasize it to a comical degree. An example of a face being distorted to identify it with a popular symbol is Donald Trump's posting a picture of himself fused with a smug version of the Pepe the Frog meme in order to identify himself with the counterculture of those who were using that meme the most during the primaries of 2016.

To better understand how people use memes to express truth and distortion, it is helpful to explore how this intersects with our understanding of self-states, archetypes, and personas. Ego state theory exists in its most fleshed out form in the form of self states in contemporary psychoanalysis. Contemporary psychoanalysts such as Philip Bromberg (1993) theorized that the human self is comprised of many parts that contain different affective states, thoughts, memories, needs, and points of view. In a psychologically healthy individual, memes can reflect a projection of various self states in which there is co-consciousness and in which the self states are acknowledged ("owned" by the person). In a psychologically unhealthy individual, their favorite memes may reflect how their various self states are disowned and projected onto others in a distorted manner. In this light, Brombergs' theory of self states could be seen as comparable to Jung's concept of archetypes.

Figures that arise in memes exist because they are projections of parts of ourselves. We therefore conclude that the Internet meme being projected is a symbol of an archetype. While Carl Jung posited that personas are masks that the ego wears (Jung & von Franz, 1976), we think it is also fair to say that symbols are the personas of archetypes. In a similar way, we assert that Internet memes are symbols of the Internet's collective unconscious. Projections of certain parts of the self solidify into Internet memes when projected to the Internet. When that Internet meme is viewed, the viewer projects the part of themself onto their observation of the Internet meme that the creator of the meme projected into the meme. This creates a recognition between these two self states that actually correlate to one phenomenon in the collective unconscious. This is similar to Levinas' concept of the I and the Other where the projections of the creator and the viewer are an I and Other, co-creating the divine space in which the collective unconscious can be understood (Levinas et al., 2006).

Looking at memes from a Jungian perspective, it makes sense to explore the potential meanings of meme faces vis-à-vis the parts of the self/archetypes that are being projected. We suggest four axes on which faces in Internet memes can be analyzed, as follows: the emotions that are present, the level of irony, the level of reverence invoked, and the archetypal symbolic species of the meme face.

Irony is often multilayered, meaning that even subtle aspects of many memes contain ironic reference to other memes and/or world events. To evoke reverence, the figure meant to be revered is endowed with what is perceived to be the most ideal characteristics of their gender (even if nonbinary), is presented without major blemishes, and has either a neutral or smiling face. An archetypal species refers to the sort of being the meme in question is presenting. The Cat, The Dog, the Frog and the Monster are prominent Internet meme face symbols.

Internet meme faces can be organized by their archetypal symbolic species. One popular symbolic species, as noted, is the Cat. Examples include grumpy cat, a woman yelling at a cat, an anxious cat, a "can I haz cheezburger" cat, a polite cat, and Garfield. According to Jungian Analyst Barbara Hannah (2006), "the cat is… more feminine in behavior… connected with Anima" (p. 51). Cats' association with archetypal femininity and spirituality may help illuminate why cats are associated with relatable emotions in Internet memes. We theorize that this connects with the notion of cats as symbolic of civilization as well. Whereas dogs hunted alongside early humans who were hunter-gatherers, cats were not domesticated until the advent of agriculture and humans' ability to store food. Cats were also associated with reverence by the oldest human civilizations, particularly Egypt. This connects with Freud's concept of civilization and its discontents; cats depict in Internet memes the awkward subjugation of emotions needed to exist within the boundaries of societal expectations, similar to how Freud perceived humans' innate struggle to reconcile their instinctual urges with societal constraints (Freud, 1989). Simone de Beauvoir mentions that patriarchy delegates woman to being the Other to the default that is man (de Beauvoir, 1947/2015). In that sense, femininity can be understood as being subjugated by the patriarchy. Therefore, the Cat and femininity are also linked by this shared subjugation.

The Dog is another prominent symbol in Internet memes. Examples include Shibe Doge, Swole Doge, Cheems, Moon Moon, "Hello? Yes, this is dog," and the two wolves inside you. According to Jung (2010), "[T]he dog is a grave digger who disposes of the bodies, as happened in ancient Persia... the dog helps with dying, and consequently rebirth" (p. 45). This correlates with the tendency of memes depicting dogs to have a version of the meme die, only to come back years later in a related but different form, often with reverence that has changed with the values of the new time it finds itself in. An example of this is Shibe Doge, who originally stood for ironic agreement. This meme died for a period of years but has since resurfaced with Shibe Doge as a masculine ideal that stands in contrast to the foil of Cheems. (The modern incarnation of Cheems is a Shibe-type dog that has masculine features edited out so that it lacks, for example, a strong jaw and prominent muscles.) Dogs in memes also tend to correlate with ideals of masculinity. Memes of dogs as tamed wild beasts correlate with tamed masculine sexuality, with depictions either reveling in sexual appetite or embodying the superego that controls sexual appetite, such as Cheems' common declaration that sexual deviants will be sent to "horny jail."

The Frog is another prominent Internet meme face symbol. Examples include Kermit, Pepe, Wednesday frog, Dat Boi, the Hypnotoad, and a nonbinary aesthetic frog. In researching Jung and frog imagery, we found it fascinating that he referenced frogs extensively in his book of mystical experiences, *The Red Book* (2009). An example of this is when Jung refers to "the unnaturally born... son of the frogs... full of mysteries and superior to all men. No man has produced him, and no woman given birth to him" (Jung, 2009). The son of frogs is particularly interesting to us since the most common variation of the Pepe meme currently on the Internet is that of a kinderschema-infused Pepe, who sometimes is depicted as a son of the regular Pepe. In a different context, frogs are often associated with nonbinary gender. We connect this association to a common new twist on the old tale of a witch who curses people so they become frogs. In the new twist, which many modern memes depict, the person is delighted to become a frog because frogs don't have to go to work, worry about debt, or be concerned about the proper presentation of their gender. It is worth noting that many nonbinary people oppose being associated with a frog aesthetic because they do not want to be seen as just a singular aesthetic of a third gender but rather want to be able to use frogs as one of many outlets for androgynous gender expression. This does make us wonder, though, whether the creation of frogs such as Pepe that deny respect for people's rights and dignity (as we mentioned earlier) may result from an unconscious subjugation of the desire to synthesize/transcend gender norms by those who are conditioned to believe that it is unacceptable to do so.

Monsters appear to be another popular meme species. Examples of monsters include Shrek, Medusa Godzilla, Cthulhu, Elmo, vampires, Mike Wazowski, dragons (especially Smaug), goblins, and creepypasta variations on otherwise innocent characters. The word "creepypasta" is etymologically descended from the word "copypasta," which is a type of Internet meme that is text heavy or consists of more than four comic strips. Creepypastas, therefore, are horrific or scary copypastas. Classic monsters in memes (such as Godzilla, Cthulhu, vampires, dragons, and goblins) are almost never used for genuine creepypasta but rather almost always exist as ironic characters of themselves. These classic monsters are most often depicted as friends who want to help set the viewer onto a better path. An example of this is a meme of Godzilla wearing sunglasses and declaring, "That wasn't very cash money of you" (in this case, "cash money" is slang for beneficent behavior). In contrast, innocent monsters (such as Mike Wazowski, Sesame Street characters, and Shrek) are often used for genuine creepiness. The creepypasta variation of monsters is interesting, because, like kinderschema, it can be overlaid upon any character to make them monstrous. A prime example of this is Garfield the Cat; as one of the most popular creepypasta creatures, he is contorted into a being with multiple eyes and an ogre face or centipede legs chasing his owner Jon. Therefore, a primary role of the archetype of monster seems to indeed be about innocence—either losing it or reclaiming it. To go a layer deeper, monsters are the personification of shadow archetypes, and in this sense making memes about monsters helps to shed light on the meaning of shadows that have haunted societies in the past and is a way to wrestle with new shadows arising today. A clear example of a classic monster being redeemed in memes is Medusa. As it has become more generally known that she was punished for being the victim of sexual assault, her image is now often liberated to that of a heroine in modern memes as a form of healing.

Although earlier we highlighted the ways that Internet memes can work against the APA ethical principle of respect for people's rights and dignity, we also think it is important to emphasize how Internet memes can work for this ethical principle by giving voices to the unheard. Memes do this when they are created by people whose agenda is the recognition of their authentic expression of self, especially those parts of the self that are often least recognized by other facets of society. Memes have played a major part in fundamentally changing the nature of global discussions around race and gender. This started with anonymous imageboard websites such as 4chan memes showing that racist and sexist ideas are more aggregately alive in the minds of people than many had cared to admit (Jonas, 2002).

The new awareness of the persistence of racist and sexist ideas underscored that it was not enough to just stop talking about certain ideas publicly; these issues had to be responded to systemically. This helped to end the post-racism and post-feminism myths that were still lingering in the 1990s and early 2000s. In turn, this led to memes coming into existence that featured the lived experiences of oppressed people in societies. This often revealed that oppressed people had more in common than they realized, manifested in their ability to share common memes. A key example of this is the word meme #MeToo, which helped individual women realize that they were not the only ones to have been hurt by men and that in fact this was a nearly ubiquitous experience. Another key example is the word meme #BlackLivesMatter, which unified people to discuss police abuse and evidence of systemic White supremacy in a way that had hitherto been unheard of. This is often coupled with picture memes, such as a Black profile picture, infographics using shared imagery, and the editing of meme formats that originated in racist forums into pro–Black Lives Matter memes.

With a better understanding of how memes can be used to both show or distort the face of the Other as well as give a voice to the unheard, we now turn our attention to how clinicians can use memes as a tool to deepen therapy. Clients often bring memes to therapy sessions in an effort to communicate their internal experiences and conflicts and their unformulated affect and to be "seen" by the therapist. An astute therapist can recognize the unseen part of the client that longs to be recognized and heard but does not feel safe enough to express itself. The importance of building a sturdy, trusting therapeutic alliance cannot be underestimated. Especially with relatively young, Internet-savvy clients, communicating through their favorite memes can help build and strengthen the therapeutic alliance.

Once trust is established, the therapist can use memes to deepen the therapy by recognizing what a particular meme means to the client in both conscious and unconscious ways. Starting with the conscious, the therapist can ask what parts of the meme stand out the most and what meaning the meme has for them. To access more unconscious material, the therapist can ask the client to free-associate with the meme—in other words, ask them what pops into their mind when they look at it. The therapist can also free-associate with the meme and the client's associations to see if the therapist's associations stimulate any further free association from the client. Additionally, to access unconscious somatic information, the therapist can ask the client what happens in their body as they look at the meme.

Internet memes can be used to help to give the client words and schemas with which to understand and articulate their unformulated experience. This enhances the client's emotional intelligence. When people can understand, formulate, and articulate their experiences, they generally feel less anxious.

Therapy helps the client to identify distortion in the face of the Other (as seen in the memes they bring to therapy) and then helps the client correct that distortion by truly recognizing the face of the Other. In order to do this, the therapist must help the client answer the question that Jung (2017) asks in this passage:

> If the doctor wishes to help a human being, he must be able to accept him as he is. And he can do this in reality only when he has already seen and accepted him as he is. Perhaps this sounds very simple, but simple things are always the most difficult. In actual life, it requires the greatest art to be simple. And so, acceptance of oneself is the essence of the moral problem, and the acid test of one's whole outlook on life. That I feed the beggar, that I forgive an insult, that I love my enemy in the name of Christ—all these are undoubtedly great virtues. What I do unto the least of my brethren, that I do unto Christ. But what if I should discover that the least amongst them all, the poorest of all beggars, the most impudent of all offenders, yea, the very fiend himself—that these are within me, and that I myself stand in need of the arms of my own kindness, that I myself am the enemy who must be loved—what then?
>
> *(p. 241)*

The answer is to find compassion for that Other inside of ourselves through recognizing the projections of that shadowed Other into the world. Recent research in neuropsychology finds that the face and emotions are fundamentally entwined with each other and that people who make particular facial expressions actually have readings on a brain scan that associate with the emotion being presented (Zinchenko et al., 2018). Therefore, therapists can help their clients with this by asking them to listen to the hidden part of themselves that becomes enlivened by the meme in question and to embody the projection on their own face. Specifically, therapists can ask the client how it might feel to make the face that the meme evokes with their own facial expression and then ask them to describe what happens in their body when they make that face. If parts of it create interpretations of negative perceived emotions, the therapist can help the client name what those emotions are and explore why the client might be simultaneously repulsed and drawn to something that espouses the emotions. If an evoked emotion is interpreted positively, the therapist can help the client find functional ways to evoke that emotion in their own lives and recognize it as inspiration.

The Internet and memes are people's first language these days, and people tend to know more about memes than mental health (Ali, 2021). Additionally, many memes have a humorous aspect, and memes can name their truth in a humorous way. Clients are bringing memes to therapy sessions more and more often. Memes often convey truths embedded in humor. Engaging with a client's favorite memes, especially early in treatment and early in a session, can help build rapport with the client.

To conclude, we recommend that research be done on the prevalence of clients bringing memes to therapy sessions. This should both assess the normative way which this practice currently exists and explore how an intentional focus on memes affects therapist and client satisfaction with the session. We also recommend that psychoanalysts and other mental health professionals engage more actively in the world of memes. It is understandable that psychoanalysts in particular may be averse to the world of memes, thinking of them as collapsing interpersonal and intrapsychic space and sabotaging the quiet, free-associative process of self-reflection. However, we believe that memes contain important symbolic information that is perceptible to the trained eye. Moreover, we assert that memes have become ubiquitous in our culture and that to sidestep them is to miss out on participating in an important aspect of current culture. Instead of chafing at the brevity of engagement that people typically have with a meme, we recommend that mental health professionals reclaim this space in the collective unconscious by posting memes, creating memes, and sharing favorite memes with others. We hope that by doing so therapists might in some small way shape the larger culture through memes that depict psychological truths and invite psychological wholeness.

References

Ali, S. (2021, June 23). Can memes benefit mental wellness? *Psychology Today*. Retrieved September 12, 2021, from https://www.psychologytoday.com/us/blog/modern-mentality/202106/can-memes-benefit-mental-wellness

American Psychological Association. (2017). *Ethical principles of psychologists and code of conduct* (2002, amended effective June 1, 2010, and January 1, 2017). Washington, D.C.: APA. https://www.apa.org/ethics/code/

Bromberg, P. M. (1993). Standing in the spaces: The multiplicity of self and the psychoanalytic relationship. *Contemporary Psychoanalysis, 32*, 509–535.

Dawkins, R. (1989). *The selfish gene*. Oxford: Oxford University Press.

de Beauvoir, S. (1947, 2015). *The second sex*. New York: Vintage Classics.

Freud, S. (1989). *Civilization and its discontents* (J. Strachey, Trans. & Ed.). New York: W. W. Norton & Company. (Original work published 1930).

Glocker, M. L., Langleben, D. D., Ruparel, K., Loughead, J. W., Gur, R. C., & Sachser, N. (2009). Baby schema in infant faces induces cuteness perception and motivation for caretaking in adults. *Ethology, 115*(3), 257–263. https://doi.org/10.1111/j.1439-0310.2008.01603.x

Hannah, B. (2006). *The archetypal symbolism of animals: Lectures given at the C. G. Jung institute, Zurich, 1954–1958*. Asheville, NC: Chiron.

Jonas, W. (2002). *Examples of racist material on the internet*. Sydney: The Australian Human Rights Commission. Retrieved December 4, 2021, from https://humanrights.gov.au/our-work/publications/examples-racist-material-internet

Jung, C. G. (2009). *The red book: Liber novus*. New York: W. W. Norton & Company.

Jung, C. G. (2010). *Children's dreams: Notes from the seminar given in 1936–1940*. Princeton, NJ: Princeton University Press.

Jung, C. G. (2017). *Modern man in search of a soul*. Eastford, CT: Martino Fine Books Publishing.

Jung, C. G., & von Franz, M. -L. (1976). *Man and his symbols*. New York: Doubleday Publishing.

Levinas, E., Smith, M. B., & Harshav, B. (2006). *Entre nous: Thinking-of-the-other*. London: Continuum.

Lorenz, K. (1943). Die angeborenen Formen moeglicher Erfahrung. *Zeitschrift für Tierpsycholigie, 5*, 235–409.

Zinchenko, O., Yaple, Z. A., & Arsalidou, M. (2018). Brain responses to dynamic facial expressions: A normative meta-analysis. *Frontiers in Human Neuroscience, 12*. https://doi.org/10.3389/fnhum.2018.00227

20

WHO AM I REALLY? ILLUSIONS AND SPLITS IN THE MIRROR

Susan E. Schwartz

The "as-if" personality and narcissism signal the superficiality and absence of internal reflection accentuated with the increasing emphasis on social media ego/persona images. Unconsciously and pervasively the world becomes illusionary and a loss of self prevails. This phenomenon parallels the marked increase of narcissism and is signified by the mass absorption with "likes" on the Internet. Although this superficial attitude ignores life and death anxiety, the occurrence of Covid-19 has pressed an unexpected and harsh reality upon us. The emotional and collective ramifications have forced cognition of personal and cultural splits in the mirror of the self. This identity confusion is addressed by analytical thought, examining the question of "who am I, really."

A clinical example and dreams along with some of the life and writings of American poetess Sylvia Plath portray the complexity behind the persona masks and illusions. The Jungian analytical approach addresses the disconnections between ego, persona, and shadow. This parallels the experiences of absence and lack articulated by French psychoanalyst Andre Green.

Deleterious effects to the psyche also indicate the natural impulse for repair and reconstitution. This psychological situation is a prelude to deeper self-understanding leading to psychological integration. Personality transformation requires facing the emotional lacks and absence in our technological, superficial, and immediacy driven world. The pervasiveness of social media, Internet, and the cyber world capitalizes on unreality, false image, and manipulating reality. Recognizing the gap in speed, space and psyche connects the reality of self and world in the process of finding and expressing fully who one is.

Andre Green and Narcissism

The psychic abandonment affects access to the self.

(Green, 1986, p. 153)

Andre Green focused on the parental absence and/or the emotional deadness unconsciously transferred onto children. He described, "The early emotional lacks form psychic holes, not the loss of something once had, but the absence of love objects that never existed... setting up internal world attack, time frozen, investment in self dismantled and void

DOI: 10.4324/9781003195849-24

occupying the mind" (Green, 1986, p. 153). His concepts of blank, void, and emptiness elucidate this psychological conundrum, indicating the somber nature of this subject.

Andre Green's themes emerged from French culture focusing on absence, negation, negativity, and nothingness (Kohon, 1999, p. 5), originating from the idea classical psychoanalysis was founded on the question of mourning (Kohon, 1999, p. 142). Green described the parental loss, lack of presence or aliveness and the child mutated with fractured attachments and internal discontinuity. The splits and cracks in the mirror of the self bring destabilization to the personality. He described

> the lack: absence of memory, absence in the mind, absence of contact, absence of feeling all—all these absences can be condensed in the idea of a gap... instead of referring to a simple void or to something which is missing, becomes the substratum of what is real.
>
> *(Kohon, 1999, p. 8)*

For the child, attachment forms not to the parents but to the gap and the absence and the personality becomes one of pretense. Andre Green named the suffering in which all seems to have ended like "a psychic ruin that seizes hold of the subject in such a way that all vitality and life becomes frozen, where in fact it becomes forbidden... to be" (Green, 1986, p. 152).

Being connected, harmonious, emergent, and engaged become stunted and the personality is adrift left without depth. In compensation, the need for excess, glitter, and outer approval become even more significant. The personality described here believes, "if I am not seen by others as exceptional, what am I?" This is a form of entitlement attempting to mitigate the pain from the emotional betrayals and sidestep the losses.

The following composite example illustrates how the investment in the self becomes disjointed, leaving behind psychic holes and mimicking others for adaptation and approval. Unable to either deny or face the devastation to the personality, the person described here lives "as-if." They are consumed with sorrow, but this is covered by illusions while the continual re-establishing of these illusions requires ever more effort. Recognizing the wounds, abandonments, and betrayals provoke both troubling and transformative aspects to the personality. The process could free one to become connected to the self and the unconscious, opening to new life possibilities.

Clinical Example

> A premature disillusionment carries in its wake, besides the loss of love, the loss of meaning, there was no explication to account for what has happened.
>
> *(Kohon, 1999, p. 150)*

Grace, an accomplished woman in her early fifties, was distressed in her marriage. This was the ostensible reason for her seeking Jungian analytical psychotherapy. She described a busy career, life, friends, activities yet she felt something missing; she could not name it, a malaise, corrosive but imprecise, alienating her from herself and others. Symptomatic of the "as-if" personality, Grace was addicted to her appearance. For her, this took the form of daily, almost frantically checking Instagram, Facebook, LinkedIn. The body treatments, alterations, and thinness mirrored the need of admiration for her youthful looks, spirit, and intellect. She remained with a face and body seemingly untouched by time but lacking in expressiveness. The more she accomplished and succeeded the more she sought to alter her image. Her inner discourse was critical and dissatisfied, a pit of emptiness. The compulsive outer behaviors, body adjustments, and the busy thoughts represented splits in her psyche obstructing connection to who she was.

She illustrates a person reliant on the image of success, money, professional and social status but who cannot access, reveal, or face the truth of her personality. Grace's behaviors were also symptomatic of our current era of uncertainty and alienation. Superficial fixes to the psyche and body become a form of stealing and deceit, a fundamental attack on the self, creating emotional distance from others. Grace existed in a romanticized world based on her being ideal and idealized. Like with social media façade and illusion, she used her image to replace acknowledging the real.

Personality integration is difficult for this person living in a state of singularity, needing to appear perfect with no flaws or disorder. The need for superiority and attention eliminated any opposition or differences, insisting on the one-sidedness of her absolute certainty. Unable to emotionally or empathically connect with others, the zest or passion for life becomes stilted, guarded, and the self becomes enclosed and shut off. Grace was confined to a narrowed capacity for emotional intimacy.

Grace embodies the emotional pain and retreat of the "as-if" person. She learned to ignore her feelings and her life repeated the early absence of sufficient or satisfying attachments. She exemplifies a personality type forming when parents are without the capacity to relate to the child's mind and emotions and create disturbance in body ownership with behavioral or emotional impact through life. As yet, she could not access the mourned parental objects, the extent of the pain, or awaken the lost emotional desire. Unable to fully acknowledge the loss, she remained consumed with sorrow, emptiness, and lack. She felt alone with her emotions but having to pretend it was not so bad and she could cope.

The parental loss began when father left, and she was a toddler. Grace remained with a narcissistic mother whose world only revolved around her, not Grace. Her mother was depicted as a wild, feared, awesome, and unloving figure. Her father stayed physically distant and from this distance appealed to Grace to gratify his emotional needs. She internalized and identified with parents who were not close, preoccupied, or in competition with her and left her alone. There was no way to show vulnerability or receive love and no one to encourage her authenticity. From childhood, Grace had insufficient parental containers to facilitate or model personality growth, create emotional links, or fulfill her emotional needs.

Obstructed self-love and frozen in a state of psychical pain, self-alienation, disappointment, and feelings of incapacity consumed Grace. She learned to perfectly adapt, avoid being challenged or confronted. She split off her emotions and passions, building a cloister around herself. Grace adopted these behaviors to hide any inadequacies and fears of being known intimately. Andre Green describes this lack of love as, "an essentially conflictual, ambiguous nature of desire, which is conceivable as the desire of the desire of the Other" (Green, 1979, p. 69). Emptied of energy or enthusiasm, an emotional morass developed, falsely buoyed by her career success and outer image.

Bright and loquacious, Grace's narratives told in psychotherapy are without depth or reflective quality. Rapid talk fills the therapeutic space, as she seems nervous. Grace has an almost manic quality in her precocious mental functioning and quick intellect. Her style effectively distances from the reality of her reactions, leaving the authentic self concealed by facade. She does not emote, show feelings, and avoids delving into the underlying issues. She seems unaware of the feelings of others or her impact on them except for getting her way.

Her life stories are toneless, simplified, repetitive, reflecting how much of her life has been outwardly focused, avoiding the internal and intensity of response. She was imprisoned in the cage of image and presented "as-if" real. Not surprisingly, her marriage was without passion or love. Grace recalled crucial times when her husband refused her emotions and he did not see her. Tremendously disappointed, she shut off, said nothing, but was tied to him through his financial ability. Although competent and quite wealthy, she described her precarious state, one step away from the dumpster. She dimly realized she had compromised for the sake of security, and compensated with numerous emotional affairs. Grace fears to be alone yet is quite alone.

Grace does not expect much from people. Emotionally blocked she has a history of body issues like anorexia, headaches, depression, and anxiety for which she took pills but did no inner reflection. She seems mannequin-like and preoccupied keeping the outer image intact. Position and stature are the ways she obtains the adoration she desperately seeks. She does not know life otherwise or even what is lacking and so clings to the status quo. Helene Deutsch, an Austrian psychoanalyst in the mid-twentieth century referred to this type of

> person with a highly plastic readiness to pick up signals from the outer world and to model oneself and one's behaviour accordingly. The identification with what other people are thinking and feeling renders the person capable of the greatest fidelity and the basest perfidity.
>
> *(Deutsch, 1942, p. 265)*

Loyalty is fickle and this person can rapidly exchange one love object for another, as the attachment is so slim.

To hide the internal turmoil and basic life confusion, Grace keeps people away, lies to make them happy, deceiving them and herself. Angers and frustrations are pushed away and quickly disappear into the unconscious. She is highly extroverted, recalling few dreams, and the ability to symbolize or find metaphors is only slightly formed. Driven by nagging insecurity, life was simulacra, and nothing felt substantial.

Initially it seemed Grace wanted to alter her life. But can she? There is little open or trusting about her, she feels guilty for the affairs, yet does nothing to change any relationship. Can she handle intimacy? She wants it but has not known it. The adaptation of mimicry, the protective fictions, and the need to be an imposter began early. From a young age she was supposed to ask no questions and show no distress. Her mother competed with her especially in Grace's budding sexuality as a young teen. Moreover, the maternal family line had a history of depression and suicide, but she was given no details nor told why. She knew to not ask or even wonder about the causes.

Grace dreamt often about her mother grabbing her, holding her down, and trapping her. This represented "the inertia of libido, which will relinquish no object of the past, but would like to hold it fast forever... a passive state where the libido is arrested in the objects of childhood" (Jung, 1956, para. 253). She could make no sense of these dreams, had few associations, and much remained unknown about a mother she could not understand, escape, or love. The mother's emotional distance and the vacuum of intimacy frustrated, agonized, and absorbed her. Grace stayed away from anything maternal and the roots to herself twisted away. Grace was a portrayal of the person whose unfolding of the self early on "met a blank and hostile environment so misattuned that the person felt unseen and/or noxiously related to" (Solomon, 2007, p. 198). The self was submerged and she could not summon the energy to make a full attempt at a life of emotion or have intimacy as she clung to artifice.

> In the context of work concerning early relational trauma it is this containing relationship that makes it possible to dream the undreamable as a prelude to becoming able to

think the unthinkable, and as a foretaste of creating experience anew, not in terms of the historical past, but in terms of the relational present.

(Wilkinson, 2006, p. 54)

Grace's experiences of lack, absence, and loss in parental relationships affected the therapeutic transference. She kept at a distance through her insistence "we are the same." The identification was a need to preserve a mirror of sameness while it repudiated otherness. If the same, she could feel some security, remain unchallenged, and maybe achieve the hoped-for acceptance. However, the need for approval simultaneously kept her hidden behind a mask, emotions denied, and attachment unformed. Jung said,

In many cases in psychiatry, the patient who comes to us has a story that is not told, and which as a rule no one knows of... It is the patient's secret, the rock against which he is shattered... In therapy the problem is always the whole person, never the symptom alone.

(Jung, 1963, p. 116)

Grace's dreams were filled with anxiety. In one, she was in a room and there was a slim window high up. This was the only way out and she was not sure she could make it. From dreams like these she often awoke in panic. The dream showed her alone, needing to get out but it was going to be a task taking effort and concentration. The dream repeated how she felt with her mother, desperately alone, and unable to get help, confidence, or dependency.

The Damage from Splitting

They withdraw from life and remain fixed in nostalgia with little relation to the present. The negation of life's fulfillment is synonymous with the refusal to accept its ending. Both mean not wanting to live, and not wanting to live is identical to not wanting to die.

(Jung, 1969, para. 800)

Grace, the performing seal, she called herself. The shiny avatars from outer achievements, adoration, and financial success were to compensate the psychological abyss, to fill the desire for love with things. However, the outer never completed the nagging ache inside, as she could not access how to cope with the early and persisting emotional wounds. Taking numerous courses, workshops, and following others went nowhere. The dissociation from self circumvented psychological movement and thwarted internal union.

She recalled vague dreams of babies she could not feed or save. These nonspecific images haunted her, and the self could not find a foothold. The unconscious was trying to tell her she needed to save the babies as representative of new personality parts. These were similar to other dreams of looking in a blurry mirror or her image was not recognizable. Indistinct, disconnected, she eluded herself. Grace recalled a memory from childhood: she went to the park with her mother and her new ball was taken by some other children. Her mother did nothing, gave little empathy, and she was told to forget it. Grace felt unseen, uncared for, and had nowhere to go with her loss. This, like so many emotions got packed inside, relegated to a split off area where she was alone. And, there was no father figure at home to provide any sustenance or support.

When the disturbing thoughts and experiences become unbearable, they are banished from consciousness. The information becomes lost, aspects of the self abandoned, and one is unable to cope with reality. The splitting off of these unwanted aspects weakens the personality, compromises mental inclusivity, and the troubling issues put aside but fester. Deferring creates internal fissures and the self connection is missing. Alongside this are fears of disintegration also unable to be acknowledged. One lives on fiction and in mental retreat, insulated from self and others.

With an outrageous, flamboyant mother and absent father, Grace felt different from others and developed isolative routines. These kept Grace under the hegemony of facade and singularity. She lacked a joyful feeling, attempting to tranquilize the anxiety and depression with achievements or whatever would make her younger, thinner, better. Like the "as-if" personality and alienated from relational aliveness, she was run by helplessness, desire embittered, alienated, something withheld.

When we refuse to accept our feelings and thoughts, however disturbing they might be, we experience psychological dissonance. It happens when our behavior does not match our self-image, or the image we think others have of us. Making these attitudes conscious like through dreams and in the therapeutic relationship could allow Grace to naturally revivify contact with the more complete personality. The images and symbols in dreams help access the transformative aspects of the personality. They help a person move out of the one-sided system of defense obliterating relationship to self and other, conscious with unconscious. However, this type of person is scared, weeping within, feeling there is no way to answer the distress; self-doubt flooding her mind. Attentive to curating the right presentation, she put on an act.

"As-If" Personality

This collision between one's image of oneself and what one actually is, is always very painful and there are two things you can do about it, you can meet the collision head-on and try and become what you really are or you can retreat and try to remain what you thought you were, which is a fantasy, in which you will certainly perish.

(Baldwin, *The Price of the Ticket*, p. 244)

In the current world personally, culturally, and collectively estrangement, isolation, loneliness, and emptiness seem ever more pervasive. The "as-if" personality as addressed by Hester Solomon, Jungian analyst (Solomon, 2004, p. 649), described a derailed identity and disturbed sense of time, life as facsimile. The outer persona and image are glitzy, self-assured, a charmer. Inwardly, emotions are raw and easily damaged. Because to be real is threatening, there is constant pressure to act according to a socially constructed persona. This is the unmet self seen in the social media mirror while feelings and relationships become increasingly false. No one realizes what goes on within; the unbearable pressure, aloneness, inability to grasp anything even close to emotional harmony. Anguished and in despair, formless anxiety, those living "as-if" exhibit persona adaptations so slick they seem solid. However, real identity is deeper than performance or imitative behavior. While persona masks cover the underlying emptiness, they can negate depth and substance. "It is as if they have become the lack; an absence so ponderous that it leaves them without access to the true self" (Solomon, 2004, p. 641).

The true self is easily masked on social media. "Borders and boundaries are vague, and visibility is the cypher for existence. One becomes seen, heard, and read through social media giving a glimpse of existence" (Tricarico, 2018, p. 28). Outwardly the person appears "as-if" complete yet there is a haunting lack of genuineness. This person tries to make up for what should be alive, but they come across as ungraspable. As you move closer, the essence becomes elusive, and you cannot feel the real. The words may sound right but the feeling is off. The shell is attractive, even fascinating but something is missing. This cover remains desperately and solidly in place because the encounter with another puts one face to face with being seen or found as real.

Criticism is assiduously avoided. Defensiveness and denial of vulnerability causes this person to ignore or even exploit the vulnerability of others, reflecting a denuded inner world. The attempted remedy against an underlying envy fosters unconscious projective identifications onto others. Jungian analyst Schwartz-Salant (1982, p. 105) described envy as the ego's rejection of the self.

The "as-if" personality is precarious from the early environmental failures and noxious experiences that forced the self away and into hiding. The "as-if" person expects shameful exposure, abandonment and re-traumatization, the very feelings crying out to be known. There remains a "haunting repetition... of those traumatizing situations that created the original dissociative responses" (Solomon, 2004, 642).

The person yearns for experiences of attunement formerly missed, anticipating that a relationship to a good object with a satisfying and filling person will be denied. Unable to respond for real or be real shows a dependency early checked from insufficiently good parental experiences. These physical and psychological disappointments form into disillusionment and withdrawal. One is arrested in development, adopting attitudes rejecting the instinctual, the body, earth, and time. The dissociated and unmetabolized affects remain unspeakable, held in the unconscious. Jung referred to this creating inertia, low self-worth, and depressive moods. He commented, "She started out in the world with averted face... and all the while the world and life pass by her like a dream—an annoying source of illusions, disappointments, and irritations" (Jung, 1959, para. 185). This is apparent in social media with its manic and imposter quality, turning from the real, allowing for no pause from the frantic press of immediacy and artifice.

This person appears "as-if" real although they quite painfully know otherwise. Jung reflected,

> The world is empty only to him who does not know how to direct his libido towards things and people, and to render them alive and beautiful. What compels us to create a substitute from within ourselves is not an external lack, but our own inability to include anything outside ourselves in our love.
>
> *(Jung, 1956, para. 253)*

The elusive, flighty, and often dramatic approaches to life are attempts to compensate the inner void, feeling unsafe, and uncared for. Idealized phantasies compensate and involve various addictions to sustain the image. A timeless universe is erected but it inevitably leads to disillusion while reality introduces awareness of time, aging, and eventually death.

In childhood these people learn to become performers, but do not really believe in the role they seem to be playing. Daily existence is a trial. The psyche feels shattered. A non-nourishing self-absorption arises as a defense against intimacy to self or others. The defense focuses on survival while attempts to grow and individuate seem dangerous. The natural ebb and flow of emotional life is anxiety provoking, and she is easily bruised. Turning harshly on herself there is a war against body and the affects, a bulwark set up against desire, emotion, and change. Jung commented, "Don't run away and make yourself unconscious of bodily facts, for they keep you in real life" (Jung, 1998, p. 66). Feeling unlovable brings emotional and physical alienation, escalating into various forms of numbing. The thing that endures is a dull psychic pain, characterized by the insecurity in relational attachment.

Narcissism

Through this False Self the infant builds a false set of relationships, and…even attains a show of being real.

(Winnicott, 1960, p. 146).

The problem of narcissism has been of growing interest and proliferation in our era. Jung wrote in his "Red Book" addressing the spirit of the depths and the spirit of the times. Years later, in 1979, "The Culture of Narcissism: American Life in an Age of Diminishing Expectations" was a best seller written by the cultural historian Christopher Lasch. He high-lighted the normalizing of narcissism or the spirit of the times in twentieth-century American culture. This has been defined by a grandiose sense of self, exhibitionism, and disturbed object-relationships as predominating symptoms. The way of relating to the world is through mimicry, to blend in but also to stand out. The true self is buried, exiled. This person feels as flat and superficial as the social media screen, yet they do not know how to come alive. They live on raw energies of highs to avoid collapse into the abyss of their own interiority.

Our era of personal and cultural fluidity results in fragmentation and disintegration. The absence of internal focus parallels the significant rise in the "as-if" personality or in the popularized terminology of imposter syndrome. Living in fantasy worlds of video games, online pornography, and Facebook can indicate lacks in psychological development with a variety of defenses erected against reality. The "as-if" personalities with narcissistic tendencies are compulsively drawn to social media, stuck between its mirror and mask. The persona indicates denial of age as the person is both mesmerized and paralyzed by eternal youth (Hillman, 1987, p. 104). In fact, the narcissist stares in disbelief and rage at the cruel mirrors of age, reflecting maladaptation to the entire arc of life.

Narcissism is defined by psychological impenetrability, avoidance of self and others combined with failure to be present, often without awareness. Andre Green described what he called death narcissism or the void, emptiness, and destructive withdrawal with a masochistic quality. He called another attitude life narcissism characterized with an impoverished ego limited to illusory relationships without deep involvement. Neither are satisfying nor complete, reality and illusion are confused, and death and life denied. Jung commented, "To the degree that one does not admit the validity of the other person, denies the other within the right to exist—and vice versa" (Jung, 1956, para. 187).

The sense of not being oneself creates disturbance in the sense of identity, early compromised by the parental projections, expectations and demands. Children suffer emotional and social consequences from experiencing parental inauthenticity. Or perhaps the child is assigned to please or save the parent. British psychoanalyst Donald Winnicott said, "the (parent's) adaptation is not good enough… in practice the infant lives, but lives falsely" (Winnicott, 1960, p. 146). The lack of parental love can develop into the loss of meaning and one sleepwalks through life.

An individual retreating behind a wall of narcissistic self-involvement, composed of the demand of perfection, knowing all, and needing nothing, resists development (Hillman,

1987, p. 25). When a person feels so flawed, they try rising above it all, insisting even more in being admired. This psychological constellation can backfire and manifests in various forms of self-attack, despair, and narcissistic self-hatred. It feeds an internalized cycle of neglect and abandonment making it difficult to love or care for oneself. In effect, there is a paralysis of the self, limiting the capacity for integration, individuation, and development. Frantic and unable to be present, the search is for the ideal rather than the real is continuous.

In the myth of Narcissus, it was told to his mother he would not live if he got to know himself. The ancient Greek writer Ovid portrays Narcissus paying a price with his life for his rejection of any lover other than himself. One might argue that having never known adequate parental mirroring, Narcissus can only seek his own image. The tragic message in this myth is the singularity also obstructs relationship to the unconscious and hinders the ability to see oneself or accept others. Jungian psychology is founded on recognizing the unconscious dissociated parts, or those not yet known, creating splits in the psyche and preventing knowledge of self or other. The central question is if this person can learn to engage.

Narcissism results in avoidance of being seen as well as remaining concealed from oneself. The encounter with the other is crucial for overcoming narcissistic defenses. A person seeking to shed the narcissistic armor must recognize their subjectivity is enriched by the subjectivities distinct from theirs.

Although narcissistic injury is not uncommon, even in therapy the extent of its painful effects is often missed. The narcissist is a master illusionist, insisting on needing no one yet desperate for attention.

We tend to view the narcissist as confident, assured, and self-centered. Were they posing? It is a cover for the fragile and vulnerable ego of one who cannot grow, accept oneself or let others in and who exists in stasis and insecurity. The reality is a person with low self-regard, continual and nagging comparison with others, cut off and fearing defeat.

The acknowledgment of incompleteness marks an end to the flight from oneself and begins transformation with the allowance for otherness. Attention solely to the psychopathology of narcissism runs the risk of neglecting the deeper individuation urge embedded in it. Like in the myth, the self is in the search of affirmation and intimacy.

Persona and Shadow

They either deny that such facts have anything to do with them, or if they admit them, they take them for natural afflictions, or they try to minimize them and to shift the responsibility elsewhere.

(Jung, 1934, p. 391)

Like today's narcissist, Narcissus sees only an idealized likeness, ignoring the blemishes and the potential, in Jungian psychological terminology, called the shadow. The shadow contains the unacknowledged blemishes and talents, ignored and unused yet waiting in the wings for attention and enrichment to the personality. Emphasis on the ego and persona can mean ignoring the shadow while without it we are flat, one-dimensional. This attitude can bring about tragic consequences obstructing authenticity. Integrating the shadow, although a process and not easy, bridges the opposition between self and not-self.

The shadow encompasses the repressed, including the unconscious, both personal and collective and its recognition can feel destabilizing. However, the experience of "I" is constructed from a multitude of conscious and unconscious processes and the Jungian concept of psychological dissociation is not pathological. Rather, it demonstrates the psyche spontaneously attempting to integrate for self-regulation. This view of psychic dissociability presupposes the self falling apart in a kind of regression, not as a defense, but the internal division is part of the natural impulse toward regaining cohesion. The analytic process and the therapeutic relationship are oriented to collect the dissociated fragments, the dilemmas arising from the unconscious to consciousness, and re-create linkages within the personality.

However, the "as-if" person experiences emptiness behind the persona mask and clings to the illusions as they seem to obscure the painful feelings and lack. The anxiety and apprehension about life is covered over by developing a perfected and idealized persona to hide what are considered the fissures underneath. Jung stated (1966, para. 245), "When we analyze the persona we strip off the mask, and discover that what seemed to be individual is at bottom collective." The word persona, originating from the ancient Greek dramas, represented the enlarged masks of actors to project their voice and be visible. In marketing the word persona denotes the imaginary customer susceptible to appealing products.

As we return to the example of Grace, we find, like in the story of Dr. Jekyll and Mr. Hyde, her psyche was split between persona and shadow. Preserved, suspended in time, can she realize what is happening to her? She feels like a faultline in the earth and damaged. How can she find her ground of being when this is the very thing she so assiduously avoids? It is perplexing because she appears verbal and pleasant, enchanting, and highly functioning, often basking in the limelight. What is unnerving about her is the yet to be discovered layers behind the veils of empty cheer.

Here is the "as-if" person characterized by the paradoxes of omnipotence and impotence, avoiding any shadow. Grace's behaviors attempted to mask the shadows of melancholy, ego fragility, and lack of self-animation. This attitude leads to affective immaturity and a wall of impenetrability prevents revealing the underlying fraudulence and precarity. She could not let in feelings or admit that the emotional hurt. It was unbearable. She became identified with select elements of her personality and was not open to the affect, the fluidity of the unconscious, the voice of the other, the not "I" or Self as different from the ego (West, 2008, p. 371). In this situation the self is engaged in combat with itself, and transformation is disabled, the inner resources remaining undeveloped.

Attempts to understand or get close to this person are frustrated by their disingenuous nature. Reality and fantasy blur. Hanging onto youth and image, attempting to escape time, existing "as-if" in the bubble of narcissism, bolstered by persona adaptation, reliant on social media for approval leave this person in pieces. Defenses and projections to avoid shame or being seen inhibit access to the unconscious and disrupt the dialogical relationship with self and others. Jung commented,

> When one tries desperately to be good and perfect, then all the more the shadow develops a definite will to be black and evil and destructive. People cannot see that; they are always striving to be marvelous, and then they discover that terrible destructive things happen which they cannot understand.
>
> *(Jung, 1934, p. 391)*

Self and world are disjointed for the "as-if" person with failures in self-coherence and interpersonal relationships. Something intangible and indefinable obtrudes growth.

This becomes problematic when it compromises the imaginative and intuitive aspects necessary for personality cohesion and developing the psychic space to symbolize. Not uncommonly, many remark on the inner forces interfering and the self, distorted, disguised, and in shards without the resources to survive. To be idealized and maintain the illusionary avoids disenchantment. Repressed and uneasy, the "as-if" person is caught in a contrived, mechanistic, and sterile world.

Grace dreamt she was in a painting loaded with gears and gadgets. She was on one side of it and trying without result to reach the man she loved on the other side. She could not get to him, as there were too many obstacles. The dream recurred for years and represented her unresolved search for her lost love, and for self. It was a colorless dream, black and white and left her with much frustration, longing, and the feeling of being unmet in love. "This is the basis for the 'fear of love'—a kind of autistic defense against relationships in those who have experienced such colonization by the disowned parts of the parental psyche" (Knox, 2011a, 2011b, p. 341).

Grace verbally floods each psychotherapy session to prevent other information or interpretation to her standard story. The insistence on sameness of narration disallows variation, attachment, separation, and growth. She is acutely tuned into capturing the signals of others, reacts accordingly, and for her gain. Relationships are manipulations for attention and approval. Every attempt to understand this type of person hits a wall. She does not emotionally invest in people, places, or objects, anticipating lack of satisfaction or care, nor does she know how to care for others. There also is the issue of damaged connection to her body as the instincts are off, the spirit dampened, and Grace without genuineness.

Such people find themselves in emotionally dead relationships, masochistic, destructive, lacking intimacy. Life is a series of fragments punctuated with occasional ecstasies that flare up and then fizzle, always needing the next marvelous thing to fill the emptiness. Emotional growth halted long ago, and without access to a stable inner foundation, they are cut off from the healing powers of the self. What will have to be sacrificed are the cherished ego and its persona façade.

The personality described here is emotionally removed. Grace tried to hide her manipulative behavior with persona charm. She numbed herself to feelings of disappointment and loss, living a sham existence. Although false, this was her survival suit, and deemed necessary so nothing suggested any disorder. Without an accurate inner mirror, she assessed herself to be either inferior or superior. To cope with the internal void and the subsequent suffering she became separated within, and this arrested the natural processes of life (von Franz, 2000, p. 151). She did not know other than façade and pretend, and was without the tools for intimacy with anyone, most of all with herself.

This defense of the self is a protective mechanism preserving rather than permitting the fearful ego to be annihilated.

Although Grace's behaviors were isolative acts reflecting inner turmoil, they also contained the unconscious goal of self-creation for accessing the life spirit. However, Grace was unable to recover her spirit or find internal honesty. She remained plagued by insecurity and obsessed with the need for body treatments, the quick fix, and social media ratings. She did not want her marriage but could not leave as she was ridden with fears. Her seeking after external gratifications continued and the internal supplies of sustenance remained inaccessible. The splits in the mirror of herself remained and although Grace could talk the language of self repair, she could not accomplish it.

Jung said about maintaining balance of the psyche,

> This is how you must live—without reservation, whether in giving or withholding, according to what the circumstances requires. Then you will get through. After all, if you should still get stuck, there is always the enantiodromia from the unconscious, which opens new avenues when conscious will and vision are failing.
>
> *(McGuire & Hull, 1977, p. 156)*

Sylvia Plath

Putting up pretty artificial statues. I can't get outside myself.

(Kukil, 2000, p. 314)

Sylvia Plath has been aligned with various psychological diagnoses trying to understand what she could not in her repeated attempts to find answers. The descriptor of her "as-if" personality is revealed in the literary themes, divisions, and masks formed in what can be called the defense of the self (Solomon, 2004, p. 649). Since her suicide, images of her have proliferated, becoming more intricate, often pathological, entangled. She is now someone on whom the script is written, as if this were real.

Sylvia Plath presented in her journals and letters both agonized and self-lacerating aspects juxtaposed to the upbeat image she tried to project. The dichotomy expressed the dissonance between the bright, buoyant, high-achieving persona with ideals of success contrasted with inner emptiness. She "put together [in her art] the complex mosaic of [her] childhood, [to] capture feelings and experiences from the nebulous seething of memory and yank them out into black-and-white on the typewriter" (Kukil, 2000, p. 168).

As an example, her poem "Face Lift" can be read as the voice of two women protagonists or more likely they are one in the same. It expresses relief at the loss of an aging self and the newly born one attained through self-creation. The poem portrays a ritualistic process as the female speaker casts off other selves to emerge anew. The facelift includes mutilation and altering of reality while the poetic images convey transformation and renewal.

Forays into the past impose themselves on the present as her poetry targets back to the original wounds. Many of Plath's images reveal an "insistence that clandestine traumatic knowledge not only haunts its host but will strike back and shatter the protective fictions of infallibility with force equal to the effort put into repressing this truth" (Hunter, 2009, p. 123). The early losses, rejections, and insufficient holding parental environment left behind her feeling flawed and unable to satisfy the need for approval and attention.

> Her different forms of writing root in lack, estrangement, or disintegration of selfhood. The text is for Plath the conflict between ego and self, surface and shadow comprising a fundamental search for identity. Her poems may be regarded as attempts evoking the illusion of unity.
>
> *(Ekmekçioğlu, 2008, p. 99)*

In her journal she wrote, "What inner decision, what inner murder or prison break must I commit if I want to speak from my true deep voice in writing... and not feel this jam-up of feeling behind a lass-dam fancy-façade of numb dumb wordage" (Kukil, 2000, p. 470).

Plath's poetry reflected the woman looking at mirror images and struggling with the complex relationship between opposing and disparate selves in search of identity and truth. In the discomfort of being real, one part of the mind was segregated from another. The emotional intensity of her poetry expresses conflicting aspects of the individual and collective psyches constraining and seeking expansion. In *The Unabridged Journal of Sylvia Plath* (Kukil, 2000) she expressed the problem of forging a coherent self from the warring fragments of her psyche. She wrote, "The Idea of a life gets in the way of my life" (p. 315), "The day is an accusation" (p. 470), "Something freezes me from my real spirit: is it fear of failure, fear of being vulnerable?" (p. 476).

Plath's words put a visage on the inner chaos, the psychological clash, and spilt selves as her heroines endured physical dismemberment, mutilation, torture, and victimization. Psychological work includes recognizing these felt experiences and is part of the Jungian process of individuation. Becoming oneself is "connected with the capacity of the mind to process the separation and mourn what was lost" (Cavalli, 2017, p. 187).

Plath depicted destructive inner figures grappling with feminine identity and estrangement, discordance, and disunity. This is apparent in her poem, "Two Sisters of Persephone" where she writes, "Two girls there are: within the house/ One sits; the other, without./Daylong a duet of shade and light/Plays between these" (1981, p. 31).

For Plath the sense of self was not mirrored by adequate parental figures, leaving her with basic insecurity and foundational unease. When the parent was blank and absent emotionally, the child and then the adult finds it problematic to be her real self. Plath's childhood was too early destroyed. This refers to the death of her father and the emotional lack of resonance with her mother. She became deadened to herself due to the deadened [parental] objects within (Bollas, 1995, p. 74). The detritus haunted her with depression, depersonalization, despair, anxiety, and disturbed connection to self.

This was the malady, the losses, failed attachments with the parental objects creating the residual abyss of depression and confusion. The ego was wounded and lost connection to the self. The mirror was unclear, split, fragments unable to be put together again. Yet, her poems of death kept leading to rebirth as she tried to keep up the hope for relief from what in the moment was no doubt unbearable.

Summary

Jungian analytical psychology with its inclusion of symbols, dreams and exploring meaning in the splits, complexes and shadow parts illustrate the psychological complexity and quest of the "as-if" personality beyond shallow persona façade and narcissism. This type is drawn to the social media driven world, enticing with image and instant gratification. Many, especially those of the 'as-if' personality are unable to escape its compulsive allurement.

Lack and splits in the mirror are demonstrated by the clinical examples of Grace and poetess Sylvia Plath. Both the theories of Carl Jung and Andre Green put forth analytical perspectives on finding who one really is. Over time images from the unconscious unite with conscious life to spin and weave new patterns for reimagining oneself. The journey is not only aimed at happiness per se but has a wider perspective. The Jungian process of individuation means becoming all one is meant to be. The repair by turning inward, unraveling the issues of the heart brings the fragmented pieces together. The "as-if" person, the narcissist has the potential, the charm, and the energy. The pull between image and real presents a crossroads for development, the phoenix rising from the ashes for exploration rather than denial.

The process of Jungian analytical psychotherapy involves recognizing the repressed, impasses and shadow for movement toward the authentic. Personality rupture is necessary for opening to psychological and emotional rebirth. There is an oscillation between longing for transformation and the need to remain behind the images so easily constructed through social media. Yet, the persona develops beyond the superficial when it is not a mask but authentically expresses personality depth and variety. This means casting off outgrown selves and facades leading to nakedness and renewal, igniting the desire to be one's real self.

References

Bollas, C. (1995). *Cracking Up*. New York: Hill and Wang.

Cavalli, A. (2017). Identification—obstacle to individuation, or: on how to become 'me'. *Journal of Analytical Psychology*. 62, pp. 187–204.

Deutsch, H. (1942). Some forms of emotional disturbance and their relationship to schizophrenia. *Psychoanalytic Quarterly*. 11, pp. 301–321.

Ekmekçioğlu, N. (2008). Sylvia Plath's mirrors reflecting various guises of self. *Plath Profiles*. 1, pp. 92–102.

Green, A. (1979). *The Tragic Effect*. Cambridge: Cambridge University Press.

Green, A. (1986). *On Private Madness*. London: the Hogarth Press.

Hillman, J. (1987) (ed). *Puer Papers*. Irving, TX: Spring Publications.

Hunter, D. (2009). Family phantoms: fish, watery realms and death in Virginia Woolf, Sylvia Plath, and Ted Hughes. *Plath Profiles*. 2, 103–134.

Jung, C.G. (1934). *Civilization in Transition*. Princeton, NJ: Princeton University Press.

Jung, C.G. (1956). *Symbols of Transformation*. London: Routledge.

Jung, C.G. (1959). *The Archetypes and the Collective Unconscious*. New York: Pantheon Books.

Jung, C.G. (1963). *Memories, Dreams, Reflections*. New York: Random House.

Jung, C.G. (1966). *Two Essays on Analytical Psychology*. Princeton, NJ: Princeton University Press.

Jung, C.G. (1969). *The Structure and Dynamics of the Psyche*. Princeton, NJ: Princeton University Press.

Jung, C. G. (1998). *Jung's Seminar on Nietzsche's Zarathustra: Abridged Edition* (Vol. 99). Princeton, NJ: Princeton University Press.

Knox, J. (2011a). Panel: the alchemy of attachment: trauma, fragmentation and transformation in the analytic relationship. *Journal of Analytical Psychology*. 56, pp. 334–361.

Knox, J. (2011b). *Self-Agency in Psychotherapy*. New York: W.W. Norton.

Kohon, G. (ed). (1999). *The Dead Mother, the Work of Andre Green*. London: Routledge.

Kukil, K. (ed.). (2000). *The Unabridged Journals of Sylvia Plath*. New York: Anchor.

McGuire, W. & Hull, R.F.C. (eds). (1977). *C.G. Jung Speaking: Interviews and Encounters*. Princeton, NJ: Princeton University Press.

Plath, S. (1981). *Collected Poems*. New York: Harper & Row.

Schwartz-Salant, N. (1982). *On Narcissism*. Toronto: Inner City Books.

Solomon, H. (2004). Self-creation and the limitless void of dissociation: the as if personality. *Journal of Analytical Psychology*. 49, pp. 635–656.

Solomon, H. (2007). *The Self in Transformation*. London: Karnac.

Tricarico, G. (2018). *Lost Goddesses*. London: Karnac.

von Franz, M.L. (2000). *The Problem of Puer Aeternus*. Toronto: Inner City Books.

West, M. (2008). The narrow use of the term ego in analytical psychology: the 'not-I' is also who I am. *Journal of Analytical Psychology*. 53, pp. 367–388.

Wilkinson, M. (2006). The dreaming mind-brain: a Jungian perspective. *Journal of Analytical Psychology*. 51, pp. 43–59.

Winnicott, D.W. (1960). Ego distortion in terms of true and false self. *The Maturational Process and the Facilitating Environment: Studies in the Theory of Emotional Development*. New York: International Universities Press, Inc.

21

EMOTIONAL TRAUMA AND TECHNOLOGY

A Clinical Story of Traumatic Isolation and Technologically Mediated Psychoanalytic Therapy

Peter Maduro

At age 6 years, Celia loved her mother, and her mother loved her, in a mutual existential-emotional connectedness that they each felt in affection, joy, and expansiveness. For Celia, the psychological field of this connection was experienced in a seamless continuity-of-connection, disturbed from time to time over their six years together only by brief separations that evoked Celia's anxiety and sadness.

By virtue of her own history of traumatic loss, Celia's mother took these separations and her daughter's reactive anxieties and grief seriously, however seemingly ordinary the separation context. She believed that on some level sensitive children, like Celia, can feel the ultimate existential insecurity of their love-bonds within their separation fears. Accordingly, when such separations occurred, Celia's mother would respond to Celia's painful feelings with Winnicottian "holding," allowing Celia to integrate and bear them as aspects of who she is.

Foreshadowing what was to come more dramatically later in Celia's life, her father was less concerned and responsive to Celia at the times of such separations. He saw them as arising from local circumstances, such as Celia going to school in the morning, Mom going to a movie with girlfriends, or Dad traveling for work for a few days—that would resolve most of the time sooner than later, if not by the end of the day. That is, he saw such separations as transient versus entailing anything lasting or significant. Despite his dismissive attitude toward Celia's separation anxiety, he was in all other ways devoted to his daughter.

Thanks to Celia's and her parents' relatively seamless mutual love-bonds, Celia enjoyed a firmly consolidated sense of self. It included self-other differentiation, agency, self-esteem, continuity of self, other and interconnection over time, *et cetera* (Orange, Atwood, & Stolorow, 1997), as well as an overarching sense of so-called secure attachment. However, when, two days before Celia's sixth birthday, her mother died of a melanoma skin cancer that had been diagnosed only three months previously, this familial world of loving mutual interconnectedness suffered a horrifying blow. Celia's sustaining illusion of secure connection over time to her beloved mother shattered like sheet-glass struck by a meteor. Celia reacted not only with the heartbreak of motherloss, but with a terror corresponding to the shocking loss of what she had long believed to be true and real, namely, that her mother would be at her side into her foreseeable future.

DOI: 10.4324/9781003195849-25

Unfortunately, Celia's father had a long history within his family of origin wherein existential, physical, and emotional vulnerability, and associated affectivity, such as grief, anxiety, and powerlessness, were perceived to be personal failures and "weaknesses." In his own early caregiving system in the 1940s, such painful feelings were equated by his parents with shameful personal defects. As a result, after the death of his wife, he dissociated his own rather substantial sadness and dreads. In turn, he responded to Celia with much attention, but, sadly, he was emotionally cool and distant in respect of her heartbreak and terror. In this response, his attention to his devastated Celia was encoded with a thinly veiled paternal-message that vulnerability across the human spectrum—from existential vulnerability to irreversible loss of loved-others, uncertainty about what is true and real, to physical illness—and all the grief, terrors, and horrors in which they are felt, are forms of personal deficiency that are best hidden from others' judgmental eyes, including his.

Celia's early-life tragedy was thus threefold. First, she suffered the irreversible loss of her mother. She felt this loss in grief and anxieties, including an angst reflective of her existential insecurity of connectedness to loved-ones. She also felt a shocking uncertainty-anxiety respecting what she "knows" and can foresee as true and real in her lifeworld. Second, in her motherloss she lost the person she would first look to for Winnicottian holding. In this, she lost the principal caregiving resource by which she might see and feel that her heartbreak and terror made sense, had significance, and was the basis of on-going connection with others. That is, her motherloss left her without the mother to be with her in motherloss.

And third, compounding this maternal vacuum in which she felt her motherloss, her tragedy entailed a problematic paternal-environment in which her sudden loss was lived and felt. It was one wherein Celia's heartbreak and collapsed convictions about her future encountered her father's cool, distant and ultimately rejecting emotional responsiveness. The consequence of this last feature was that her painful reactions came to be experienced by her as disappointing failures, unwanted, and perhaps even invalid to her father, and thus as threats to the primary remaining bond in her lifeworld. In turn, and compounding this isolating rejection, in order to safeguard that bond Celia dissociated her painful feelings into a largely unconscious private region of alienation and aloneness. That is, starting in the immediate aftermath of her motherloss, namely, from age 6 going forward, Celia came to anxiously organize her pain as a shameful inability to live up to her father's paternal-ideal "Thou ought not feel nor cry over thy losses," which ideal, in order to preserve her paternal-bond, she accommodatively (Brandchaft, 2007) adopted as her own.

As a result, over the 12 or so years following her motherloss, during which period she lived alone with her father, and until she turned 18 and left home for undergraduate university studies, Celia would experience significant losses, and otherwise seemingly "ordinary" ones, in an amalgamation of affect. The reactive feelings entailed shame-soaked grief and anxiety as well as a frightening aloneness. This amalgamated emotional outcome would often gather into an episode of clinical depression in which otherwise healthy depressive affects were shrouded in plummeting self-esteem and acute isolation. This isolation, in particular, could be debilitating and was encoded with both the absence of her mother's presence, and her father's hurtful refusals of her sadness and fears. She had been and remained left to her own devices to privately contend with her grief and anxieties in a disillusioned state, further saddled with doubts about whether her pain had any validity or importance to anyone. Consequently, when she experienced significant separations—like when she suffered the loss of her paternal grandparents, as she did at age

14; attenuation from her best girlfriend who moved with her family to Europe when Celia was 17; went away to university as she did at age 18—she fell into extended depressed moods characterized by shame and what she ultimately described as an arrestingly frightening "loveless aloneness."

In her effort to evade these frightening depressions, Celia compulsively dissociated from her painful emotionality and, with phobic reflexivity, turned away from life-situations of love—including intimate adult relationships, whether with friends or romantic and sexual partners—that risked losses and their ensuing traumatic emotional states. This practice of evasion became very conspicuous during and after her undergraduate university life wherein men were very attracted to Celia's wit, beauty, and sensitivity, but were invariably turned away by her. Although she was not conscious of it at the time, their interest was very appealing to her since she had her own desires too; however, again, the mutuality of desire produced possibilities for intimacy and therefore also risk of loss and retraumatization. These possibilities were just too dangerous to entertain and were thus sadly sacrificed. This interpersonal pattern entailed no small loss in itself since the result was that Celia didn't enjoy an emotionally and sexually intimate boyfriend relationship in her teens or 20s.

Several years later, in her mid-20s, Celia was in her first psychotherapeutic treatment with a female therapist, and she felt very fortunate to be enjoying and benefitting from this progressively close bond. However, as if Lady Fortune were in fact a cruel lady of misfortune, Celia's therapist died of breast cancer 22 months into the treatment. In this, a window into historical trauma was opened wide through which Celia's presently felt loss of her therapist transported her emotionally to the profoundly disconnecting and isolating impacts of motherloss and paternal emotional rejections that she had compliantly dissociated for decades. In this way, this brief therapeutic treatment ironically delivered a doubled-edged fruit—the liberating expression of her pain—by virtue of and after her therapist's death. But as was the case also when her mother died, she had no one to be-with her in these feelings: once again, her therapist's death was also the loss of the person to whom she could reliably take her therapistloss-grief to for holding.

Instead of complete descent into the depths of loveless aloneness, Celia sought to bring her newly expressed pain to a new therapeutic home. Three months after her first therapist's death she initiated a second psychotherapy treatment with a male analyst, Anton, who was able to deeply see and "dwell" (Stolorow, 2014) with Celia's emotional traumas. Emotionally motivated as she was from the start of her treatment with Anton, Celia continued to come into more direct embodied contact with her history of loss. Specifically, she began to see, name, and feel more vividly the intense paternal shame, attachment anxiety, and loveless aloneness she had "forever felt" in and around her motherloss and subsequent therapistloss, and their sorrows and anxieties. After a prolonged period of working through these painful feelings, including a resistance with Anton who, from time to time, she feared would look at her grief and its persistence as burdensome and disappointing, Celia came into intimately close emotional touch with the devastating impact on her life of her early loss of mother and her paternal shamings.

Progressively freed up (Brandchaft, Doctors, & Sorter, 2010) from the grip of the devaluing, refusing paternal ideals, Celia's traumatic motherloss and therapistloss, as well as their heartbreaks, came to be felt with greater and greater clarity and intensity. In turn, they were more readily available to be seen and named by Celia and Anton in their treatment. In this, a deepening connection within the therapeutic bond with Anton, including rich developmental transferences, were formed.

Celia's developmental bond and transferences with Anton had been crystallizing for about 18 months when, in early 2020 and quite suddenly, Covid-19 broke out across the globe and began ravaging peoples' lives. Not long after, this virus landed on American soil and, shortly after that, there were explosions of sickness and death decimating American society as well. News coverage was vivid and horrifying in its imagery and stories, and an abundance of data about the virus' biological and socio-economic impact sent Celia's imagination into the bleakness of death and loss around her, including of her college roommate's mother who died alone of Covid-19 after being put on a ventilator in a hospital ICU. Additionally, soon after the virus landed on American soil it necessitated "social distancing" measures as a public health response. Consequently, in-person meetings with Anton were suddenly suspended and replaced by psychotherapy sessions conducted initially by telephone and shortly thereafter by way of audio-video teleconference technology.

Quite promptly after the impact of Covid-19 upon Celia's personal life and psychotherapy treatment with Anton, Celia's theretofore expansively consolidated state of mind deteriorated. She began to feel an impending doom as a familiar loveless isolation gathered on her emotional horizon. Her lived and subjective environment was suddenly replete with death at the local and global levels, felt in varieties of grief; and illusions of bodily and socio-economic integrity were crumbling as personal boundaries and national borders failed to protect from the virus' penetrating threats, leaving her in the anxieties of vanishing personal and communal safeties she had formerly "known" to be inviolable. Additionally, the quality of emotional responsiveness—whether in news media or in her personal community as with father, extended family, and friends—proved quite impoverished and inadequate, reflecting a frightening incompetence in her relational, cultural world. This unfortunate deficiency replicated her early emotional-system's failure of her wherein her father's refusals of her grief and distress essentially constituted systemic incompetency.

Finally, the publicly mandated "social distancing" necessary to abate the virus' transmission was about to deprive her of an in-person embodied connection to Anton in her newly important therapeutic bond. This threatened the loss of a crucial holding presence and replicated, at least on an anticipatory level, the death and absence of the person to whom she most needed to be able to take her pain. In the end, a threatening depressive syndrome appeared on the horizon of her life. It loomed as an impending catastrophe that might wipe out the emotional freedoms and personal hope she had recently worked so hard to cultivate with Anton.

It was in this thick multidimensional context—rich at its base with Celia's personal and familial traumatic loss and maternal absence, paternal emotional rejection and resulting isolation of emotional pain, and now replication of such loss and isolation on the level of pandemic-driven collective traumatic loss, uncertainty-anxiety, and mandated social-distancing—that Celia and Anton's psychoanalytic treatment became mediated by audio/video conferencing technology.

As the reader might imagine, Celia's and Anton's psychotherapy treatment was profoundly rich with meanings and transferences arising at the intersection of personal-dyadic-familial traumatic motherloss and paternal emotional rejection, and related loveless aloneness, on the one hand, and collective socio-economic traumatic loss, horrifying epistemological trauma, and pervasive social isolation, on the other. At this intersection, an important clinical focus was how the pandemic and its collective traumas functioned as "portkey" (Stolorow, 2007) to replicate in very concrete interpersonal ways Celia's personal-familial traumas, namely, how they lent themselves to reified repetitions of her early life-traumas on the concrete collective stage. For example, as noted, the mandate for social-distancing, as public healthcare response to the pandemic, lent itself to Celia's anxious perception that her society, like her father, would leave her alone to her own devices in pain, rather than connecting with her in it.

For our purposes today, I wish to zero in on a very particular way in which this public healthcare mandate for social distancing functioned as portkey to evoke in Celia both intense developmental longings for connection with Anton, as well as repetitive trauma anxieties that social distancing mandates would cement her forever into terrifying loveless aloneness in her grief. Specifically, I wish to highlight how these developmental longings and anxieties of traumatic repetition imbued themselves in Celia's subjective emotional and perceptual experience of the audio-visual teleconferencing technology by which she and Anton conducted their psychotherapy treatment from early 2020 forward.

At the intersection of Celia's personal traumas and the pandemic-driven social isolation in loss, Celia felt a profound longing for Anton's attuned presence and relational hospitality to her grief and horror. Remarkably, video-conferencing technology was a necessary condition to Celia's longings for Anton's emotional presence. By way of technological facilitation, Anton and Celia were able to see one another's electronically reproduced physical image as they spoke about the emotional impact of the pandemic on Celia. In addition to Celia explicitly feeling Anton's emotional presence to her through the technology, which produced in her a sense of hope within a world of isolating trauma, she also felt an attitude of affirmation and gratitude as to the technology's wondrousness in opening up possibilities for cherished, longed for, and now traumatically scarce, human interconnection, albeit "remote" on the level of flesh and blood.

On this level, Celia's perception, understanding of, and feeling about audio-visual conferencing technology were rich in expansive affects. This emotional experience represented a radical and healing alternative to the disconnected loveless rejections that she had long known in and around loss on both the personal/familial and now collective level of emotional incompetence. As such, in so far as this technology facilitated such developmentally transformative experiences, it may be said that its context-embedded subjective meanings to Celia endowed such technology with a measure of special emotionally intelligible significance.

Still, the electronically mediated type of subjective connection between Celia and Anton afforded by this audio-video teleconferencing technology had its limitations as well. And these limitations lent themselves to function as portkeys to retraumatizing loss-anxiety and loveless aloneness. They "lent themselves" in this fashion because these limitations in the technology proved isomorphic with Celia's personal traumatic history; that is, these technological limitations mimicked the existential and emotional limitations that traumatized her in her early life.

Specifically, Celia's traumatic motherloss and the subsequent absence of her mother was evoked by the experiential intangibility of Anton's electronic representation. Especially when she was in sorrow, Anton's literal disembodiment, that is, the intangibility of his electronic presence to her via audio-visual reproduction (that he was not present in flesh and blood), would move to the fore of her experience as loss and the vulnerability-of-embodied-connection, and be felt in grief and anxiety. In this, her traumatic past of mother-absence would wash over her and become a feature of the technologically mediated treatment connection. Additionally, Celia experienced the same technological phenomena—that is, Anton's electronic representation as "not" or "absent of" actual body—not just as encoding maternal loss and absence, or in the transference as Anton's (maternal) absence to her, but as reflecting a "distance." This distance, which Celia described further as a "cool distance," encoded her history of paternal emotional rejection and withdrawal from her. That is, this feature of the technologically mediated connection with Anton would lend itself to repetition of paternal withdrawal in which Anton was felt to be refusing and distancing himself from Celia's grief as dangerously offensive and repugnant. As such, in this context and on this level, the audio-visual conferencing was isomorphic with and lent itself to confirming Celia's paternally rooted traumatic dread that, in truth, Anton, like her father, viewed her grief and horrors as shameful and best hidden and kept at a distance. This latter feature of the technology thus could lend itself to evoking in Celia a retraumatizing loveless aloneness in the transference with Anton as electronically represented.

It is easy to see how the technology could be experienced at one level of subjectivity and transference (maternal developmental) as delivering Anton's caring attuned emotional presence, while at another level of transference (maternal &/or paternal repetitive/traumatic) as encoding Anton's loss and absence, as well as his emotional rejection and isolating distance. How, then, ought a therapist in Anton's situation proceed therapeutically with analysis and interpretation of Celia's technologically mediated transference experiences? Broadly speaking, Anton and Celia worked diligently together to inquire into and illuminate the historical contexts of these experiences. In this way, they drew into Celia's view their complex contextuality and multidimensionality, including the way her personal/family traumas intersected with the pandemic traumas and social-distancing mandates such that the latter functioned as portkeys to the former and, at times, evoked retraumatizing loveless aloneness in her bond with Anton.

In the end, within Celia's rich emotional history at large, and her remarkable therapeutic history with Anton, there were many profound take-aways. For one thing, it is clear that that technologically mediated therapy was experienced with profound ambivalence, bringing to the fore feelings of both security and care, on one hand, and absence, longing, shame, and isolation, on the other. Like all good therapeutic relationships, it was challenging and healing to work through these multiple dimensions of transference, helping Celia to uncover past traumas by feeling them in the therapeutic "space"—even if that space was more intangible and remote than she would have originally chosen. More concretely, we see that Celia's early life of traumatic loss, horrifying disillusionments, and related emotional shaming and abandonment, shaped her experience of the pandemic, in particular its collective losses, horrors, isolations, and abandoning emotional incompetencies. In essence, the traumas of the pandemic were frequently experienced as replicating and confirming the traumatic memories and emotional meanings of her personal and familial life. In particular, the pandemic mandate for social-distancing, or physical disconnecting, including between patients and therapists like Celia and Anton, and the related use of audio-visual teleconferencing—technology—as a mode of connection, lent themselves to Celia's developmental and repetitive transference experiences: they evoked Celia's developmental transference longings for connection and emotional hospitality within an environment of socially isolated grief; they also lent themselves to her repetitive, retraumatizing experiences of Anton's absence and rejecting, shaming "cool distance."

From this psychoanalytic perspective, the case of Celia and Anton shows that "technology" acquires remarkable and rich significance in the individual person's subjective emotional and perceptual world, and this significance will depend on complex intersecting contexts entailing that person's personal, familial, and socio-cultural-historical dimensions. It is the job of the therapist to exist within the complexity and precarity of this space with his or her patients, whether it be a complex intersubjective space that includes office, couch, and chair, or one unfolding in the digital space of two people brought together across distances onto a computer screen.

References

Brandchaft, B. (2007), Systems of pathological accommodation and change in analysis. *Psychoanalytic Psychology*, 24:667–687.

Brandchaft, B., Doctors, S. & Sorter, D. (2010), *Towards an emancipatory psychoanalysis: Brandchaft's intersubjective vision*. New York: Routledge Press.

Orange, D. M., Atwood, G. E. & Stolorow, R. D. (1997), *Working intersubjectively: Contextualism in psychoanalytic practice*. Hillsdale, NJ: Analytic Press.

Stolorow, R. D. (2007), *Trauma and human existence*. New York/London: The Analytic Press.

22

TOUCH (SCREENED)

Technological Trauma, Excarnation, and Dissociation in a Digital Age

M. Mookie C. Manalili

Introduction: Rise of the Touchscreens

As I gazed upon the mesmerizing Icelandic landscape, a chilling gust brushed my face—the winds whispering a meaning beyond words and the thick air greeting my silent tongue. As I walked toward the waterfalls of Gullfoss, the whispers turned into roars... my senses arrested by the power of nature and liveliness of the world around me... My sight by the crashing waves jumping into a seemingly bottomless chasm, my taste by the mix of cold refreshing mist and lingering of something else, my smell by the churning of moist volcanic sedimentation, my hearing by the powerful language of nature's song, and my touch by the environment imprinting on me and by a hand being held. I breathe deep, allowing it to affect my being-in-the-world. And yet, as I scanned around, I noticed that others quickly reached for their phones, extending their sight alone to capture a thin image of this. As I mused in discontent how they were not fully appreciating the moment prior to doing so... did I also take a photo of the moment? Yes, I did... This technological pull was recapitulated amidst the dancing northern lights, black sand beaches, and other moments in the world—with texts, emails, photos, calls, and the like breaking forth into these experiences, with our devices acting as thinned extensions of our memory banks, voice calls, and reduced touch.

Not only do we as humans shape technology; technology *shapes* us. As each self continues to be constructed and is marked by the fingerprints of context (Cushman, 1996), these factors are no longer merely environmental, social, political... but also technological. We are amidst the digital age, with many electronic tools, systems, and devices that act as extensions of our self's actions. These can range from simplistic behaviors of counting numbers, storing images, and straightforward tasks... and to complex operations as international social media, machine learning algorithms, and other things that bend time/space/persons to our reach. According to an aggregated data source, 6.3 billion persons, or 78% of the global population, now have smartphones—with mainstream popularity taking off with the iPhone in 2007 and Android in 2008 (Statista, 2022). The majority of humanity continues to drift from *homo sapiens* to *homo techne,* with a supercomputer attached to our hip and looped into our action patterns. But we should ask... at what gain and what cost? For as Kearney (2021) succinctly notes, paraphrasing Heidegger: "technology overcomes distance, but it does not always bring nearness" (5). As we reach for the phone screen instead of an-other's hand... the

DOI: 10.4324/9781003195849-26

cold medium of non-flesh becomes our point of contact in this world. This may normalize and exacerbate the rupture, gap, distance between, as we choose medium over the other.

This modest chapter explores technological trauma, excarnation, and dissociation—and the relationship of persons to digital technologies. First, we elaborate on the idea of 'technological trauma' and its connection to the historical and clinical literature. Secondly, we pivot to the idea of 'excarnation' as divesting away from flesh, and how technology exacerbates this tendency. Finally, we conclude with 'dissociation' as a framework for technological rupture, and possibly working toward integration. This chapter is not at all exhaustive, but a small contribution to a much larger conversation in our fields. Nor is this a luddite inditement of technology. Indeed, for our current age and beyond—it is not a matter of *if* we should utilize technology, but a matter of *how* and *why* and *for whom*. The challenge here is to deeply consider how technology mediates and shapes our relationships—and thus, how we should relate to technology. The *why* might point to further ethical implications, toward the *for whom* of the suffering Other rather than for my own self (Goodman and Severson, 2016; Severson, 2021). My hope herein, as practitioners, teachers, researchers, and humanity broadly, is to be in better relationship to technology—rather than utilize it merely to escape into, so that it may be a medium pointing back to the world and for those we serve.

Technological Trauma at Our Fingertips

Let us first speak on 'technology trauma'—nuancing the term trauma toward a 'rupture of human experience' and introducing technology as a locus of this rupture. We utilize current understandings of 'trauma' in the clinical literature and point beyond to the roots of wound, gap, rupture [Greek: τραύμα]. Make no mistake; humanity *will continue* to utilize technology to bridge distances of time/space. Technology will continue to inform and form us, to reduce us, to render distance in our own selves. And therefore, we must consider what is worth the cost of this rupture.

While trauma has surfaced into destigmatized modern parlance recently, the historical roots of psychological trauma run deep. Prior to metaphorical use for challenge or strife, trauma was at the heart of psychology's foundation in the context of European psychiatry. From hysteric patients, railroad workers, and world-war soldiers during this time in France, trauma drifted from just the studies of physiological impact and wounds to the ruptures caused by *witnessing psychologically distressing events* (Charcot and Goetz, 1888/1987; Janet, 1889; Freud and Breuer, 1895). The French psychiatrist Jean-Martin Charcot writes (translated):

> The nervous shock or commotions, the emotion almost unavoidably inseparable from an often-life-threatening accident, is sufficient to produce the neurosis, in question. The surgical effect of the traumatism, or in other words, the causing of a wound or contusion... Is not a necessary element for the development of the disease, although it can contribute to it taking on a grave form.
>
> *(Charcot, 1888/1889; Micale and Lerner, 2001, p. 123)*

Although he would later nuance the ideas of his psychiatric teachers Janet and Charcot, Freud's time at the Salpêtrière was quite formative. Freud borrowed and adapted these understandings of traumatic symptoms (dissociation, somnambulism, avoidance, etcetera), and initial treatments (mesmerism, hypnotic suggestion, catharsis, etcetera). This framework of psychological trauma was at the heart of psychoanalysis proper, as it took shape in the Austrian context. Much more can be said on the history of psychoanalytic trauma—including Freud's switch from seduction theory toward dual drive theory (Mitchell & Black, 2016), or shifts to locate conflict as internal psychodynamics rather than as externally frustrated action-patterns. However, suffice it to say, trauma has deep roots in *witnessing* distressing content, which ruptures the integration of the subject.

The clinical sense of 'trauma' has sharpened and somewhat expanded in our context. Fast forward to yet another global wound of world wars, trauma finds itself solidified on American soil as soldiers land back with haunting symptoms. Through the *Diagnostic and Statistical Manual III* in 1980, Post-Traumatic Stress Disorder (PTSD) gave language to veterans and survivors of abuse, disasters, and other severely distressing events. Currently, the revised fifth edition of this manual points to some nuance to trauma's precipitation and presentation:

> Psychological distress following exposure to traumatic or stress event is quite variable… Many individuals who have been exposed to a traumatic or stressful event exhibit a phenotype, in which, rather than anxiety- or fear-based symptoms, the most prominent clinical characteristics are anhedonia and dysphoric symptoms, externalizing angry and aggressive symptoms, or dissociative symptoms.
>
> *(American Psychiatric Association, 2022)*

Several other diagnoses have made its way into the expanded trauma category. Even prolonged grief is interestingly categorized as a trauma-related disorder, rather than being clustered with depressive disorders. Additionally, the revised edition even hints at chronic etiological factors (i.e. social neglect, or pervasive lack of care and social inputs) as part of certain trauma histories. The loss, gap, or lack (which is related to but nuanced from the desire of Lacanian lack)—are now part of trauma's scope. Most interesting for us here, are types of trauma that are not merely singularly event-based. Rather, *chronic* exposure to certain negative experiences (or the continual lack of positive experiential inputs) can then lead to a sense of unreality, disembodiment, disengagement, and rupture from the world and others; this is also deemed as a 'trauma' for the person.

And so, we bring technology into this framework of trauma. From our first usage of stone tools to extend our hand's power and reach and even our first use of language to extend our voice's meaning and influence… technology is part of our being-in-the-world. When in right relationship, *technology* allows us to extend our reach (in reduced forms) to interact with the *other* beyond self, in the reality of the world and other persons. However, within the past two decades, this technology has become quite 'smart'—functioning with a more complex techno-logic of control, efficiency, and hyper-connectivity. Whereas a hammer might shape us through repetition and skill into a smith or another identity, the smartphone shapes us as well (Severson, 2021). However, what happens when the mediating tool (hammer or smartphone) becomes the *end* rather than the *means*? For the smith, what if the hammer is prized more than the craft made—or even the people served through that craft? For the *homo techne*, what if the smartphone and its applications become more important than the *other* they point to, than the embodied person or the world of experiences that technology helps make accessible? What happens when there is an inversion of priority: rather than technology *mediating* us to interact with others, we choose the *medium itself* over the *other*, closing the loop back to ourselves.

Thus, this points to what could be considered 'technological trauma.' It is more pervasive and subtler than severe event-based traumas, and more akin to the literature on complex and lack-based traumas. A working definition for technological trauma is chronic (and at times acute) ruptures of human experience by the medium of our digital technology, and the ensuing prioritization of digital technology over experiencing the moment in unmediated ways. The ping of an email; the vibration of a text; the scrolling to soothe social anxiety; the reward pathways of likes and comments; the escape of situations through videos; the listening of music rather than present birdsong and chatter; the touch of a screen instead of a hand; and all in between person and phone… these move us further from our living-body situated in a context. Instead of using a telephone to close the distance of the loved one, the phone becomes a screen to escape from being with the other right beside you. (Much more can be said on the importance of introducing technology in certain stages of childhood and adolescent development, but that may be for another chapter.) As a caveat, just as normative stressors can lead to growth and learning, technological ruptures can lead to positive effects as well. For example, technology allows us to hear the voice extended through telecommunications, electronic mail, and the like. Technology does allow us to be in touch (albeit in reduced forms) with our patients, students, and others whom we serve. Still, this benefit does come at a cost. For, we must detach from the present, contextualized moment to do so.

Excarnation from the Flesh

We deepen our exploration of 'technological trauma' through symptoms of 'excarnation.' The French philosopher Maurice Merleau-Ponty reminds us that flesh [French: *chair*] is a principle of unity, with the lived-body [German: *Leib*] being an incarnated consciousness and always, already embedded in a world of objects. The current Irish philosopher Richard Kearney expands on 'excarnation' as diffusion away from flesh and embodiment (whereas incarnation is the infusion toward it). Kearney notes in our digital age—the pull of excarnation becomes more and more normalized, as we prioritize the images of the experience, rather than the embodiment of it. This is part of our milieu; therefore, we must strike a balance between what is worth the dance of incarnation and excarnation—as we mediate the ruptures of technology.

Touch, as opposed to other senses, reminds us of the reality of our flesh. Through inspecting philosophical roots of touch and embodiment, Kearney traces Aristotle's thoughts on flesh as a discerning medium and the locus for the double-sensation of touch:

> Claiming that touch is a discriminating sense, Aristotle insists that flesh (sarx) is a medium (metaxu) that gives us space to discern between different kinds of experience—hold and cold, soft and hard, attractive and unattractive. In touch, we are both touching and touch at the same time; but this does not mean we dissolve into sameness. The difference is preserved.
>
> *(Kearney, 2021, 37)*

Kearney notes that there can be a dubious nature to our opto-centric society, or centered around the privilege of sight. Whether it is the myth of the Ring of Gyges or the (seeming) one-way nature of certain virtual technologies… we privilege being able to see, and sometimes believe we are unable to be seen in reverse. This allows for a level of control and power over the other (even hinting at the normalizing gaze of Bentham's panopticon, as analyzed by Foucault). However, we cannot touch and not be touched—and this unravels the dubious screen of optics. For indeed, to see is to already be embodied, to already have flesh which the world 'sees'—whether we attempt to hide it or not.

For Merleau-Ponty, flesh is an inseparable unity and is something porous, intertwining, and malleable to lived experiences. Alluding to the Cartesian split amidst French philosophy, the concept of flesh collapses across categories of matter/mind and brings forth a certain style of being-in-the-world. Merleau-Ponty writes (translated):

> The flesh is not matter, is not mind, is not substance... we would need the old term 'element,' in the sense it was used to speak of water, air, earth, and fire... a sort of incarnate principle that brings a style of being wherever there is a fragment of being... [that is] the flesh is in this sense and 'element' of Being.
>
> *(Merleau-Ponty, 1968, 139)*

This 'flesh' alludes to the nature of porousness, intertwining, and reversibility of my own flesh—and that of the world around me. Merleau-Ponty's stance of flesh opens up a chiastic structure. Chiasm or "intertwining" [French: *entrelacs*; German: Verflechtung] points to the reversibility of our existence: "the subject is inseparable from the world, but from the world which the subject itself projects" (Merleau-Ponty, 1945/2013, 491). As we move in this world, the flesh-of-the-world imprints upon my own flesh—with experiences being inscribed upon my being: "Through this crisscrossing within it of the touching and the tangle, its own movement incorporate themselves into the universe they interrogate" (Merleau-Ponty, 1968, 133). Typically, our pop culture believes that neuroscience is merely a top-down process, with a focus on solely the brain, congealing the Cartesian "cogito" to drive the body. However, let us not forget the ways that the brain is linked to the rest of the body through the autonomic nervous system... and that the peripheral nervous system extends to our hands, feet, and rest of our flesh. And that our flesh is always, already interacting with the environment. Though the structures are present even in early gestation, the brain is malleable to experiences—with the cortical regions developing until the mid-twenties. Although seemingly a strange flaw in natural design... brains being half-baked through childhood and adolescence reveals a beautiful insight. Putting to rest the nature/nurture debates, our experiences shape who we are— even our very structure and function, allowing humans to be malleable to culture, society, and the like. Our sense-data forms and informs us through the fulness of our embodiment (rather than merely our sight). Each person, as unique as our fingerprints and unique duration under the sun, bears the markings and memories of our lived experiences. Rather than a mind/body split, the understanding of flesh allows for this malleability to our living world.

Merleau-Ponty's strange notion of the environment as "flesh-of-the-world" points to creation as still imbued with a creative element. Merleau-Ponty's working notes allude to this:

> They refer us to the perceiving-perceived Einfühlung [in-feeling-into from the German, or empathy], for they meant that we are already in the being thus described... my body is made of the same flesh of the world (it is a perceived).
>
> *(Merleau-Ponty, 1968, 248)*

This framework opens up our environment, not as a static collection of passed-created objects, but rather a world that continues to create even in and through our own flesh. Even in Merleau-Ponty's earlier works, he notes not wanting to separate the creative power of nature: "On the level of being, we will never understand that the subject is simultaneously creating [naturant] and created [naturé]" (Merleau-Ponty, 1945/2013, 424). This world is not a static collection of objects in which my I projects into—the world as flesh is quite alive and the intertwining allows for newness beyond my-self.

Technology acts as another medium, one which may move us away from the living-body. What happens when something mediates between my flesh and the flesh-of-the-world? The porous, intertwining, and malleable nature collapses into the techno-logic of control, efficiency, and hyper-connectivity—typically through pictures, sounds, and word-strings. We get pulled away from our embodiment embedded in the present moment, toward a virtual realm of ideas and images. Kearney writes:

> My question is… are we losing touch with our senses as our experience becomes ever more mediated? Are we entering an era of "excarnation," where we obsess about the body in ever more disembodied ways? For if incarnation is the image becoming flesh, excarnation is flesh becoming image. Incarnation invests flesh; excarnation divests it.
>
> *(Kearney, 2021, 2–3)*

Indeed, excarnation evokes Christian spirituality and tradition—hinting at the inverse of the central mystery of incarnation, in which meaning is made flesh. Rather than the spirit being prioritized, incarnation points to embodiment of actions. However, excarnation leaves behind the body, as we project our voice/sight into audio-visual devices. It leaves behind other ways of knowing the world, particularly the reciprocity of touch—and even sharing in the same time/space context with another person. For example, I am able to consult with my patient from across the world via electronic mail—yet, I cannot shake their hand in a warm greeting. I can speak to the objective facts of human development of brain development, synaptic pruning, fight/flight/freeze/fawn response—yet, I cannot welcome them to a comfortable and safe therapy office. These are the trade-offs, the costs-benefits which must be weighed as we utilize the medium of technology in our relating.

With each sense-reduction, technology moves us further into excarnation and strains under the weight of meaning. Reduction comes with a history in phenomenology through Husserl (whether eidetic, phenomenological, transcendental, or otherwise). However, we explore here to the way human senses are reduced through the medium of technology, or a technological reduction. For example, video-calls offer sight and sound at a shared time (but not space), whereas audio-calls offer only sounds at a shared time. Additionally, word strings of texts, emails, tweets, and posts offer ideas neither in shared time/space—and photo logs offer images in a similar way. With each reduction, the weight of meaning must be converted into the reducing medium. When embracing a grieving friend or offering support for a suffering patient, being in the same time/space allows for actions to speak louder than words. Though a picture is worth a thousand words, neither the picture nor a thousand words substitute for the ways an incarnate, embodied experience shapes us. An image cannot substitute for the power of being surrounded by dancing light and rushing waterfalls—it only captures a sliver and hopefully points to a past meaningful memory or future hope to travel. A text in itself cannot substitute for spending time/space with the Other—it may perhaps offer coordination to meet up in due time. The benefits of accessibility, convenience, and mastery are granted with each technological reduction—bridging time, space, and distance. However, the trade-offs of technology may be reductions in the ways the flesh-of-the-world imprints upon me, through a screen—and reduces the Other in a flattened way.

Dissociation and (Dis)Integration

We conclude our exploration of 'technological trauma' through 'dissociation,' and possible ways of working toward integration. Dissociation (much like trauma) is taken up in modern speech, and so we contrast the definitions of clinical and psychoanalytic dissociation. The French psychiatrists Jean-Martin Charcot and Pierre Janet laid the foundation for trauma and dissociation for Freud, taken up by modern folks such as psychiatrist Bessel van der Kolk and neurophysiologist Peter Levine. We pivot these insights to address the ways technology exacerbates these symptoms, and hopefully ways in which we can address technological trauma as well.

As deep as the roots of trauma run for psychological history, the often (ironically) forgotten concept of 'dissociation' was also quite instrumental. Modern usage of dissociation typically refers 'to losing a sense of touch with reality.' Presently, dissociation can allude to several different things in the clinical literature: (a) observable phenomena and symptoms, (b) a principle of psychic organization, (c) a general term for defense mechanisms, (d) a synonym for 'splitting,' especially in object-relations, and (e) the specific clinical phenomena of 'dissociative identity,' formerly known as 'multiple/split personality' (Tarnopolsky, 2003, 9). Much more can be said about the importance of dissociation in the psychoanalytic literature—particularly in terms of (d) splitting. (In another article, comparisons and contrasts can be drawn between Janet's dissociation and integration, Freud's splitting/repression, and Klein's and Fairbairn's direction of splitting as an organizing principle.) However, for the purpose of this chapter—we will focus on (e) the clinical usage of dissociation and also Janet's proto-psychoanalytic formulation of dissociation.

In terms of clinical usage, 'dissociation' is tied with trauma—and yet, for some reason, find their own clustering in terms of diagnoses. In the foreword to the "Dissociative Disorders" section, the DSM-5-TR (2022) states: "Dissociative disorders are frequently found in the aftermath of a wide variety of psychologically traumatic experiences in children, adolescents, adults." Indeed, a subgroup of PTSD notes that a person may experience dissociative symptoms of depersonalization and/or derealization. Furthermore, across the different types of disorders (including dissociative identity, amnesia, and depersonalization/derealization) the themes include a loss of agency, a lack of continuity of experience, and inability to access information. The vestiges of French psychiatry and Austrian psychoanalysis is hinted at in these dissociative disorders—however, no allusions to Freud, Janet, or Charcot can be found. Clinicians might think synonymously about these clusters when thinking about 'dissociation,' particularly dissociative identity/multiple personality disorder—while psychotherapists and psychoanalysts may think of these but drift toward splitting, defense mechanisms, and object-relations.

However, we will focus on 'dissociation' as a direct defense against overwhelming traumatic experiences via Janet's formulation. Through several case examples, and primarily Lucie/Adrienne, Janet (1889) noted that humans were between and neither purely animalistic behavior patterns nor purely always conscious beings. Rather, Janet noted that we have movements and action-patterns—which trauma at times frustrates and, therefore these functions are not always integrated into an indivisible subject or personality. Important concepts for understanding Janet's theory include: psychological automatism, sub/consciousness, narrowed field of consciousness, dissociation, amnesia, suggestibility, fixed ideas (or traumatic memories), and emotions (or pre-action patterns) (Van der Hart & Horst, 1989). Janet elaborated (translated) at the end of his life:

> These divisions of the personality offer us a good example of dissociations which can be formed in the mind when the laboriously constructed syntheses are destroyed. The personal unity, identity, and initiative are not primitive characteristics of psychological life. They are incomplete results acquired with difficulty after long work, and they remain very fragile. All constructions built by the work of thought belong to the same genre: Scientific ideas, beliefs, memories, languages can be dissociated in the same way,

and the end of illnesses of the mind is the dissociation of tendencies as one observes in the most profound insanities.

(Janet, 1946, 146)

As can be seen, 'dissociation' is the divisions of "systems of ideas and functions" within a person. While this is extremely found in patients with Dissociative Identity Disorder (DID) and his clinical cases with hysteria, this organization can be found in the general person. And while this form of psychic organization is not always pathological—it creates a sense of fragmented identity in need of integration.

Let us compare our digital age with 'dissociation'—and ways technology might contribute to dissociative symptoms, frustration, and fragmentation. Regarding simply 'being out of touch with reality,' smartphone usage invites us beyond the present time/space we are contextualized in. We can be 'elsewhere' in our daydreaming, ideas, music, videos, newsfeeds, and the like—introducing frustrating emotions and action-patterns that cannot be fulfilled as the train tracks rattle on around us. Additionally, similar to both the clinical and proto-analytic formulations, our technology can create amnesia-like gaps in our memories. In terms of consolidating experiences, memory storage can be thinned from taking digital photos alone rather than taking in the flesh-of-the-world first through sensate experience… In terms of recollection, we might rely on external hard drives to figure out maps, lists, and photos, rather than learning to relate to the world… In terms of imagination, we might rely only on what is imaged in our media and valued by society, rather than what is imagined and valued by our own action-patterns. Again, technology allows for convenience to touch the screen-of-the-world, in our varied personalities. And yet, technology may allow for even more fragmentation and dissociation—as we spread our reach far and wide, anywhere and everywhere but here.

Reintegration for patients will be more effortful in a digital age—not only of our identities but also back internationally to our embodiment. Janet and others offer ways of working through trauma and dissociation: (1) stabilization and symptom reduction (aimed at patient's integrative capacity); (2) treatment of fixed-ideas/traumatic memories (aimed at resolution of frustrated action-pattern); and (3) personality (re)integration (aimed at fostering further personality development) (Van der Hart & Horst, 1989). Just as these patterns were frustrated by the trauma of an experience, so too (for Janet and others), a proper resolution must happen not through insight—but through the fulfillment of an experience. And as a parallel, just as some disintegration happens through the medium of technological trauma—perhaps, technology might offer (albeit thinned) ways of pointing back to the repairs in reality.

Coda: Beyond the Touchscreen

As I gaze upon the computer screen, I smile and wave goodbye to my patient—attempting to transmit as much hospitality in voice and sight. I close my notes full of their stories and rub my eyes, tired from the usage of this sense in the mixed in-person and virtual psychotherapy day. The light blue office space with notepads, water glasses, tissues, and a couch evokes a sense of… calm, albeit person-made. I smile and reach for my phone to meet up with friends… the background image evokes memories of Iceland, Spain, and pilgrimages near and far… Of experiences that continue to echo and constitute me. I smile again, as I received a text from friends—and pointing me back to the world of experiences. I grab my bag and walk out, greeted by the chilling winds of Boston.

This chapter is not an inditement nor a hope for escape; rather, this is a thoughtful warning and invitation to think deeply about how we relate to the world. Like the very techno-logic of tools, language, contexts, and all that constitute us… We cannot escape from the influence of technology in our digital age. For Kearney, rather than pit technology and reality, the matter of technological usage is a both/and. After offering ways forward for both incarnation/excarnation, he concludes:

> In short, let's make the most digital technology but never forget the real thing. Ultimately, it is a matter of both/and. It is clear that to live fully in tomorrow's world, we will need both virtual imagination and incarnate action. Both digital touch and live touch. The connectivity of the World Wide Web and the commons of the body.
>
> *(Kearney, 2021, 131)*

Technology need not only lead it rupture alone—it can also point toward repair. Even in their thinned reductions, signs and indexes toward something else can be given—pointing beyond the very medium of our digital devices. Messages can be the first steps to reintegrating into new meaningful projects, images can generate a desire to encounter others near and far, and video-calls can be used to reimagine upcoming gatherings to make memories with loved ones. In the modern psychotherapeutic 'space,' video/audio calls can offer patients access to therapeutic conversations—some of which might be inaccessible otherwise. However, we should understand that (rather than better/worse) there are reductions and trade-off—effects that are constituting as we utilize these devices. The *how* is analyzed regarding the important considerations of 'technological trauma,' 'excarnation', and 'dissociation.' However, we should also consider the *why* and the *for whom*. Whom are we prioritizing as we utilize the power of technology to bend time/space, resources, and the world? My hope is that it bends and extends us toward the ever-present call of the reality of the suffering Other, always already beyond the touchscreens.

References

American Psychiatric Association. (2022). *DSM-5-TR: Diagnostic and statistical manual of mental disorders* (5th ed.). Text Revision. https://doi.org/10.1176/appi.books.9780890425787

Charcot, J. M. (1888/1889). *Lecons du mardi*, V.2. Bureaux du Progrès medical. Charcot, J. M., & Goetz, C. G. (Tr.) (1888/1987). *Charcot the clinician: The tuesday lessons*. New York: Raven.

Cushman, P. (1996). *Constructing the self, constructing America: A cultural history of psychotherapy*. Cambridge, MA: Addison-Wesley/Addison Wesley Longman.

Freud, S., & Breuer, J. (1895). *Studien über hyserie*. Deuticke.

Goodman, D. M., & Severson, E. R. (2016). *The ethical turn*. New York: Routledge.

Janet, D. P. (1889). *L'automatisme psychologique: essai de psychologie expérimentale sur les formes inférieures de l'activité humaine*. Alcan.

Janet, D. P. (1946). Autobiographie psychologique. *Les études Philosophiques*, *1*, 81.

Kearney, R. (2021). *Touch: Recovering our most vital sense*. New York: Columbia University Press.

Merleau-Ponty, M. (1968). *The visible and the invisible: Followed by working notes*. Evanston, IL: Northwestern University Press.

Merleau-Ponty, M. (1945/2013). *Phenomenology of perception*. New York: Routledge.

Micale, M. S., & Lerner, P. F. (2001). *Traumatic pasts: History, psychiatry, and trauma in the modern age, 1870–1930*. Cambridge: Cambridge University Press.

Mitchell, S. A., & Black, M. J. (2016). *Freud and beyond: A history of modern psychoanalytic thought*. Hachette UK.

Severson, E. (2021). *Before ethics*. Dubuque, IA: Kendall Hunt Publishing.

Statista (2022, October). *Smartphones—Statistics and facts*. https://www.statista.com/topics/840/smartphones/

Tarnopolsky, A. (2003). The concept of dissociation in early psychoanalytic writers. *Journal of Trauma & Dissociation*, *4*(3), 7–25.

Van der Hart, O., & Horst, R. (1989). The dissociation theory of Pierre Janet. *Journal of Traumatic Stress*, *2*(4), 397–412.

PART IV

Animating the Inorganic

Analyzing Artificial Intelligence

23

AI AND MADNESS

Anestis Karastergiou

Introduction

For the purposes of this article, the relationship between madness and Artificial Intelligence (AI) is presented through a discussion involving Georges Canguilhem's and Michel Foucault's thought on the normal and the pathological, and madness, respectively. Is there any connection between madness and AI? Are science-fiction scenarios regarding mad AI conquering the world possible? Can there be a psychoanalysis of AI? Adopting a philosophical standpoint, in this brief text we will attempt to endeavor on a journey from historical epistemology, presenting the distinction between the normal and the pathological along with the concept of madness, to modern AI, its blackbox, and the potential extension of the madness concept to it.

Though not strictly within the framework of psychoanalysis, this article attempts to transpose the thought of a philosopher of science, Canguilhem, to issues regarding the psyche and, more specifically, madness, linking it to the relevant discourse of Foucault. Moreover, a psychoanalytical approach to AI will be discussed mostly by invoking the theoretical framework of Lacan's critique and merging it with Latour's methodological approach toward science. The human-machine interaction will be discussed in order to understand how AI rests at its core and should be regarded as a technology in which human attributes are more vividly reflected. Although psychoanalysis of technology is largely considered here, this article draws from philosophy of science and STS literature to create a framework for discussing madness and AI. It represents a critical approach, always inconclusive and open to further discussion.

AI Philosophical Definition and Blackboxing Issues

Defining AI is a notoriously difficult task. Thus, it is necessary to provide a theoretical frame to guide the discussion. Starting with John Searle's distinction between strong and weak AI we will be able to set the appropriate frame in which to talk about AI and data ethics. According to the philosopher, for "weak AI, the principal value of the computer in the study of the mind is that it gives us a very powerful tool" (Searle, 1980). He goes on to mention that "for example, it enables us to formulate and test hypotheses in a more rigorous

DOI: 10.4324/9781003195849-28

and precise fashion" (Searle, 1980). In other words, AI is a tool we have in our hands and a very powerful one for that matter. We construct the algorithms and the neural networks, we feed it data and it provides us with outputs, which can vary according to its abilities to learn and adapt to new problems. It is obvious that this type of AI is closer to machine and deep learning.

However, strong AI is on a whole separate level. As Searle puts it,

> according to strong AI, the computer is not merely a tool in the study of the mind; rather, the appropriately programmed computer really is a mind, in the sense that computers given the right programs can be literally said to understand and have other cognitive states.
>
> *(Searle, 1980)*

He continues: "in strong AI, because the programmed computer has cognitive states, the programs are not mere tools that enable us to test psychological explanations; rather, the programs are themselves the explanations" (Searle, 1980). To rephrase, the states of strong AI equal the "mental" states of the mind, that is, strong AI equals conscience. Of course, conscience is a huge philosophical issue and there is no space here for such a digression. However, the main point is that strong AI is unattainable up to now and it seems that it will remain so for the near future, to say the least. However, weak AI already exists, it has many applications in our daily lives, and it is bound to expand soon. Also, it is important to mention that weak AI applications, machine, and deep learning instances need data, Big Data.

Setting the frame to view AI from a philosophical perspective by choosing to present only Searle's distinction between weak and strong AI, we would like to stress and problematize his assertion that in strong AI the machine states are themselves the explanations. Given that the machine states equal mental states, his conclusion seems perfectly plausible in the domain of philosophy of mind and identity theory (Smart, 2017). A mental state cannot and, probably, should not be explained by virtue of another one. The mental state is in itself the psychological explanation. Undoubtedly it is a huge leap and by no means intended by the philosopher, but what if one links this statement to the blackbox metaphor taken from the STS framework? In short, the blackbox in STS refers to a system for which only the inputs and outputs are visible and that becomes opaquer following success, that is, when it works and it is not necessary to inquire on the procedures within this blackbox (Latour, 1999, 304). What are the repercussions of such a definition of strong AI for AI's blackbox? Simply and somewhat naively put, it seems that the opaquer the machine state becomes, or alternatively the harder its blackbox becomes, the closer one gets to strong AI. Blurring again the boundaries between philosophy and STS by means of the blackbox metaphor, consider Nagel's article "What Is It Like to Be a Bat?" (Nagel, 1974).

Setting aside the main purpose of the above article, which is to discuss the mind-body problem, consider the limitations of physicalism in the explanation of mental states and raising the problem of objective and subjective experience, among others, the mental state of the bat, as any mental state, is a blackbox. Its subjective nature prevents it from being explainable. At least up to now, it is only self-explanatory. Projecting this view of mental states, that is, the blackbox that explains itself by virtue of itself, to machine states is quite problematic from our point of view and should not be a criterion for strong AI. For instance, suppose there is a deep learning machine state that is so complex that it defies explanation. We are incognizant of how it was reached and we do not have the means to analytically represent it. The easy way out would be to consider it self-explanatory. That way we ascribe subjectivity to the machine and, given that subjectivity is closely linked to human intelligence, we think we have reached singularity. However, it is not certain that our current lack of means to pry open the machine's blackbox, as the mental state one, will be the case in perpetuity.

The self-explanatory, the subjective, aspect of an almost impenetrable blackbox draws a direct parallel to the concept of madness. Madness at the individual level, as we shall see, is not to be understood without taking into consideration the subjective experience of the subject. "What is it like to be mad" is only accessible to the bearer of the experience, though the assertion of madness should rest on the relationship with the other. For instance, adopting an aspect of Levinas' thought on otherness and the other (autrui), one finds that the other is what I, the subject, am not (Levinas, 1979, 75). In our case, the otherness is sanity, something which defines the mad by virtue of its absence. Related to AI's blackbox, the procedures that take place inside a complex neural network may resemble those that occur inside the brain of the mad. More specifically, given the exact knowledge of the input and of the output, one may find it hard to interpret how the machine and the human-being respectively, made the transition to reach a certain outcome. An incomprehensible behavior in the case of the mad would be justified by enacting the concept of madness, as a pathological state, but in the case of the machine, AI, it would be either due to a design fault or due to processes not yet understood. Of course, the latter could also apply to madness.

The Normal and the Pathological

Before interpreting the concept of madness, from a Foucauldian perspective mostly, it is important to analyze the Canguilhemian distinction between the normal and the pathological, along with his views on the relationship between the human and the machine. First, this discussion will shed light on how to view the boundaries between the normal and the pathological, and on how the pathological state should be perceived. For instance, according to Canguilhem the pathological state is not a chaotic state as opposed to the normal one but a state with its own rules (Canguilhem, 2008c, 131). Second, this distinction and its repercussions for human machine interaction can provide us with the appropriate frame in which to view the concept of madness and its potential relevance to AI instances.

More importantly, we must stress the dialectic relationship between the normal and the pathological, which, among others, lays the foundations for understanding how the concept of madness is constructed. There is no doubt that Canguilhem's thought had a great influence on Foucault's philosophical discourse. For Canguilhem, the pathological is the logical precedent of the normal (Canguilhem, 1991, 100–101). Let us now present how he reaches this conclusion. Prima facie, his thought is simple enough: without the pathological there is no normal. To constitute the normal state, one must search for and analyze the pathological one. It is by finding the deviation from the norm, the normal, that one can now turn to the normal and construct it. However, this train of thought begs the question: how can one find the deviation from the norm without an a priori sufficient understanding of what constitutes the norm? Let us imagine a case from the life sciences where there is no deviation from the norm. A simple one. Suppose one has never experienced fever. Her temperature is always somewhere within the limits of 35.7 and 37 degrees Celsius. Is this the normal state? The answer is probably affirmative from our perspective now. But, without experiencing fever, the normal state is neutral. It cannot even be said that it is normal. On the contrary, experiencing an instance of 38 degrees Celsius can now lead her to the realization that this is a deviant state, and it follows that the previous situation must be the normal one, her normal. Now, the normal state is not neutral, it has gained positive value. This derives from the dialectical relationship between the normal and the pathological. Upon the pathological state, negative value is inscribed due to the perceived imbalance between the living being and its relationship with its milieu. In the pathological state, the organism is situated within a hostile environment. It feels under threat and needs to act. However, in this state it is more vulnerable as it does not have the means to self-regulate, a vital trait of the normal state.

Thus, the pathological state, a state with its own rules, constitutes the vital opposite of the normal state (Canguilhem, 2008c, 131). Being in the normal state, the organism has its own set of rules from which derives a normative potential, in sum the ability to self-regulate. In the pathological state, there exist a different set of rules, which do not provide the organism with the ability to self-regulate, to say the least. In other words, the vitality of the normal, its potential for normalization and normativity is absent in the case of the pathological. The latter represents the exact opposite to the normal vital state. As will be shown below, in a sense madness is the opposite vital state of sanity.

Moving now to another important aspect of Canguilhem's thought and its potential link with the concept of madness. Within the boundaries of the above distinction between the normal and the pathological, one can find Canguilhem's idea of monstrosity and the monster. As pathology is exclusive to life, so is monstrosity. Life is tolerant of monsters, but the rational world of the machine is not. Of course, one can imagine a mechanical monster, but it is nothing more than a crude replica of a monster created by life or fantasy. Life's potential to disturb order is manifested in the case of monsters, bringing about a fear so radical that it dwarfs the fear of death. The concept of the monstrous is closely linked to the pathological one in Canguilhem's thought, as they are both not only exclusive to life but also the manifestations of life's dynamic potential to disturb order. Yet, both are not chaotic states without any set of rules. Even monstrosity, which goes beyond any norm, can be considered a state with its own set of rules, the vital and axiological opposite of the normal state. To the monster, whether revered or feared, a certain value is inscribed, which in most cases, of course, is negative. By virtue of the existence of the monster, as its axiological opposite, the normal gains a positive value.

Closer to the concept of madness would be Canguilhem's thought on the fantastic in relation to the monster. As the philosopher states, "life is poor in monsters, while the fantastic is a world," which, he explains, has to do with the fact that "organisms are incapable of structural eccentricities except during a short moment at the beginning of their development" and because the "power of imagination is inexhaustible, indefatigable" as "imagination is a function without an organ" (Canguilhem, 2008d, 145). Saying that the fantastic is a world, a cosmos, would entail the existence of an order, as the philosopher points out. But he dodges this aspect of the assertion by saying that what he means "is that the fantastic is capable of populating a world" (Canguilhem, 2008d, 145).

Imagination constitutes a function that never seizes to operate and, thus, can create a whole separate cosmos. Using the teachings of Bachelard, Canguilhem points to the fact that "imagination incessantly deforms or reforms old images to form new ones," which implies that imagination has the power to both distort reality and create a new one (Canguilhem, 2008d, 145–146). Within this assertion lies the duality of monstrosity and the monstrous respectively. Monstrosity disturbs reality and distorts normality, whereas the monstrous creates a world beyond the confinements of reason. Moreover, one should bear in mind that life "transgresses neither its laws nor its structural framework" and accidents "are no exception to this, and there is nothing monstrous about monstrosities" (Canguilhem, 2008d, 146). In other words, monstrosities are a part of life. Canguilhem mentions that the assertion of a teratologist in the positive age of teratology that "there are no exceptions in nature" forms a positivist formula, which "defines a world as a system of laws" while ignoring that this world "acquires its concrete signification through its relation to the signification of an opposite maxim, one that science excludes but the imagination applies" (Canguilhem, 2008d, 146). This maxim is no other than the one that "gives birth to an anticosmos, to a chaos of exceptions without laws," which

> when seen from the perspective of those who haunt it after having created it, believing everything to be exceptionally possible in it, and who forget that only laws permit exceptions, this antiworld is the imaginary, murky, and vertiginous world of the monstrous.
>
> (Canguilhem, 2008d, 146)

Obviously, this world could bear a strong resemblance to the world of the mad, where everything seems to be permitted. Powered by the imaginary, madness can create a dynamic world that at first appears to be chaotic, as in the case of the monstrous. However, a world full of exceptions cannot exist if there are no laws to be exempt. In a bizarre, yet sensible way, the fantastic world of the monstrous, of the mad, is world with its own laws, where reason is an exception permitted by the existence of the laws of the fantastic.

Madness

Defining the concept of AI is, undoubtedly, a very difficult task but things are no easier when it comes to the concept of madness. Foucault used a historicophilosophical methodology to approach the subject, cautious of how madness may be perceived, utilized, and institutionalized in various historical epochs. But what is madness? Can a simple definition suffice? Apparently these questions border on the rhetorical as the perceptions of the concept of "madness" vary depending on society and historical era. As Foucault would demonstrate vividly, the history of madness is deeply interwoven into the history of humanity.

Drawing a parallel with the treatment of lepers during the Middle Ages and their exclusion from society as bearers of the miasma, Foucault begins to talk about madness and the "mad." As the philosopher states, at that time madness "and the figure of the madman" took on "a new importance for the ambiguousness of their role," as they were "both threat and derision, the vertiginous unreason of the world, and the shallow ridiculousness of men" (Foucault, 2006, 13). Making the quite obvious, yet not necessarily philosophically precise, connection with Canguilhem's thought, madness is regarded as a pathological state, one that lies beyond normality and should be excluded from normal society. As mentioned by Foucault, in the Latin preface by Locher to Brant's poem *Narrenschiff,* madness is found in "every possible irregularity invented by man himself" (Foucault, 2006, 24). In other words, madness is defined as the deviation from the regular, the normal. However, as shown above, what is considered normal can only be defined from its negative dialectical relationship to the pathological. Applying this concept to madness could be cumbersome. Nonetheless, one could say that the normal is constituted partly by the exclusion of the mad.

More important for our purposes is whether madness is a state with its own set of rules or a chaotic one. Canguilhem pointed out that the pathological state has its own rules, albeit vitally different than those of the normal state. Can the same be applied to madness? Blurring the boundaries between the individual and the social, one could draw on Foucault's account of the institutionalization of madness during the sixteenth century. He mentions that out of "guilt, sexual pathos, magic and age-old incantatory rituals, delirium and the laws of the human heart, a hidden network of associations emerged, forming the secret foundations of our modern experience of madness" (Foucault, 2006, 104). He goes on to say that "to this domain thus structured, the tag of unreason was to be applied, as men were labelled 'fit for confinement'" and that "unreason, which the thought of the sixteenth century had considered to be the dialectical point of the reversal of reason, was thus given a concrete content" (Foucault, 2006, 104).

Now, understanding the dialectical relationship between reason and unreason, or sanity and madness, one can acknowledge that the reversal of reason, given negative value, is constitutive of reason in as far as it gives positive value to the concept of the latter. Yet, the question remains unanswered. Could the "laws of the human heart" and the "secret foundations" of madness point to the actual state of the mad or are they just concepts related to the experience of madness? However, the state of madness and the experience of madness are inseparable at the individual level. It is at the societal level, that Foucault brings the concept of "our modern experience madness," in other words our perception of what constitutes madness. Without overreaching, it could be said that there are certain characteristics, socially constructed through certain associations, that define our perception of madness. But, at the societal level the boundaries between the sane and the insane are not actually very clear. Madness seems to be relative, contingent on the necessity or applicability of confinement for a specific individual. Before entering confinement, the mad is a part of society and, what is more, depending on the norms of a certain society and the strictness thereof, the mad, the abnormal, for one society may be considered normal for another. That does not mean that madness does not have certain characteristics though. But it is quite difficult to define the absolute characteristics of it using a top-down approach.

At the level of the individual though, the situation is totally different. For her, the distinction between the normal and the pathological is, as exemplified in Canguilhem's though, absolute. This framework can be brought to the concept of madness. Madness is absolute for the individual. She is the only one who has access to "what is it like" to be mad, to the experience of madness. Whether or not she can realize it and, in most cases, she is incapable of this realization, is a whole different issue. Yet, the state and the experience of madness at the individual level is inseparable and absolutely intertwined. The difference between sanity and insanity as opposed to the normal and the pathological rests in the fact that the subject is aware of the pathological state, of the deviation of her absolute normal. In the case of madness, the state of insanity and the behaviors produced by it may make perfect sense for the individual. There may be some instances of epiphany, where she becomes aware of her state, but she will, naturally, soon revert to the familiar state of madness, where everything has a meaning beyond the normative mandates of reason. Is madness a chaotic state then, a state without any rules? Canguilhem's framework is applicable up to a certain point. The differences between the distinction of sanity and insanity on one hand and the normal and the pathological on the other, at the individual level, are obviously significant. All things considered, madness as an exception needs the rules of normality to permit this exception, madness as the vital opposite of sanity needs another set of rules to function and constitute normality, sanity, as an exception to it. In other words, in the world of the sane, the exception is the mad. In the world of the mad, the exception is the sane.

Nonetheless, the pathological state as well as the state of madness may be absolute for the individual, but they are relative concepts on a societal level. Depending on the historical epoch and the norms constituting a specific society, madness may gain various characteristics. Certainly, it is not an ahistorical concept and that is one of the reasons we did not even mention the definitions of the term. Defining madness as a state of severe mental illness, a delirious or a foolish state (Merriam-Webster, n.d.) would not provide us with any significant philosophical insights. On the contrary, understanding the concept of madness as a historical concept, the classifications of which may vary according to the sociopolitical situation, and creating a framework for perceiving whether it is a state with its own rules or not, are of paramount importance in order to expand the concept to the technological domain, specifically to AI.

Human-Machine Interaction

Analyzing human-machine interaction can form the bridge to extend the concept of madness to the machine. Prima facie, it seems either bizarre to do so or like a script taken from an eschatological, post-apocalyptic science-fiction scenario. It is by no means our purpose to entertain such a scenario, but to set the frame for understanding how the concept of madness could be relevant in the digital era, where the human-machine interaction is much more pervasive than ever before. If we must, we will endeavor briefly into these science-fiction scenarios, just to point out their philosophical possibility or impossibility. After all, of all possible worlds, could there be one where mad AI reigns supreme? We will attempt to find out the answer in this brief article.

Beginning with Canguilhem's thought on the human machine interaction, there are two main points that one should keep in mind for our purposes here. First, related to the discussion on the distinction between the normal and the pathological presented above, the philosopher states that there is no "mechanical pathology" (Canguilhem, 2008a, 90). A machine cannot have a pathological state in which it functions with another set of rules. It simply malfunctions. Thus, the pathological is specific to the realm of the living. We will contest this idea in the case of AI. Second, machines are integral parts of the relationship between the living and its milieu (Canguilhem, 2008b, 108–112). We will see how this concept could lead to a conception of the machines as tools, as extensions of the living. In the case of AI, this concept can lead to a reassertion of the idea of the man behind the machine and its significance.

On the first point, following Bichat's assertion, Canguilhem states that there is "no mechanical pathology," as there is no "machine monster," making the distinction between the normal and the pathological applicable "for living beings alone" (Canguilhem, 2008a, 90). In the rational, deterministic world of the machine a breach of regulation, a deviation from what is normal, a monster, cannot be tolerated. On the other hand, life, being dynamic and ever changing, tolerates monsters and madness. Using Guillaume's point, Canguilhem stresses the fact that "the more one compares living beings to automatic machines, the better one understands their function but the less one understands their genesis" (Canguilhem, 2008a, 90). In other words, a mechanistic model may bring about insights on the functions of a living organism, but it would not suffice to explain its birth and development. Up to now, it is quite clear that there are fundamental differences between the machine and the human being. Let us begin with the latter point concerning the birth of the organism and transpose it to the birth of madness in the human being. Certainly, no mechanistic model would provide us with answers concerning its birth. It is inconceivable to use a mechanistic approach to understand the point of departure into the world of madness as it will serve nothing to apply such an approach on how madness develops. Where is the tipping point of madness's manifestation? We believe that this remains elusive to the world of reason and even if one attempts to pinpoint it, she will only be using an anachronistic approach and the dubious presupposition of the existence of a causal chain which can be backpropagated up to a specific point when it all began, the initial input. Using terminology from the technological domain, where the machine metaphor is pervasive, would only show its limits in explaining the world of the living.

However, what if one reverses the train of thought and move from the living to the machine? Of course, this can only happen at the intersection of the human-machine interaction and AI represents a prosperous field to do so, especially when one considers the initial connection between AI and cybernetics, as depicted in the establishment of the term "Deep Learning," a concept now referring to modern state-of-the-art AI, in Norbert Weiner's book *Cybernetics: Or Control and Communication in the Animal and the Machine* (see: Wiener, 2000). Even if the machine metaphor was pervasive back then and exacerbated somewhat by the works that followed, cybernetics and AI form the pinnacle of human-machine interaction. Reversing the mechanistic approach in this domain has, we believe, considerable conceptual significance, something which brings us to the second point.

In Canguilhem's thought the living is in a reciprocal, dependent, relationship with its milieu. A living organism does not exist in vacuo, but it is always in relation to its milieu. In a very concrete sense, machines are tools at human's disposal to aid this relationship. The relative autonomy imposed to the machine is merely a question of proximity to the human agent. Let us invoke the Mechanical Turk as a metaphor to expose the "man behind the machine" in the world of AI. It was an automaton built by Wolfgang von Kempelen in 1770 to play chess (Geoghegan, 2020). Its secret would be kept for years, fooling the aristocrats who marveled at its capabilities. A quite simple secret though. The machine playing chess was an illusion. A chess master was behind the machine to manipulate the pieces. Today, of course, an AI machine can play chess without the necessity of such an illusion. But it could be argued that the illusion is only broken as a matter of extending the proximity to the human agent. More specifically, the machine is trained using data that is produced by humans. For instance, in the case of a chess playing machine, hundreds or maybe thousands of games were used to train it.

It is not only apparent that the human agent cannot be left out of the discussion of AI, but it is also evident that her impact on the function of an AI system is crucial. However, the above metaphor should not be strictly applied in all cases, thus diminishing AI systems to mere tools or mechanisms absolutely stripped of any sort of autonomy. AI systems may present some sort of relative or superficial autonomy, which is manifested by their processing and learning abilities. However, the way they work mirrors the human agent's aims, aspirations, and desires. This is where psychoanalysis comes into play (Turkle, 1988). If one can think of AI machines as elaborate tools at the disposal of the collective human experience that expand and restructure the human relationship with her milieu, AI could be also understood as a part and a manifestation of the collective human unconscious (see: Jung, 1980).

Psychoanalysis of AI and Madness

Psychoanalysis of AI may seem to be a contradictio in terminis. Simply put, can we analyze the psyche of AI given that we cannot ascribe such a thing to a machine? Of course, there is no need to answer the question of whether a complex AI machine could have a soul. After all, it is quite difficult to do so in the case of humans. However, AI instances aspire to mirror the functionalities of the human brain. Should a psychoanalytical approach work for the latter, why does it seem so inconceivable in the case of the former? First and foremost, because as we mentioned at the beginning, strong AI is not a reality yet. However, utilizing the blackbox metaphor to talk about AI within the framework of philosophy of technology, one could draw a parallel to the psychoanalytical blackbox and its repercussions for AI. Using Latourian methodology to read Lacan's work, Possati states that he distinguishes between two psychoanalytical blackboxes in the mirror stage. The first blackbox "coincides with the imago itself, which hides the mirror and the rest of the surrounding world" (Possati, 2020). This "imago produces the auto-recognition and the identification that are abstractions from the technical and material conditions that constitute them" (Possati, 2020). The image constituting "the child's identification is also what blinds the child" and makes her "incapable of grasping the imaginary nature" of her identification (Possati, 2020).

The first blackbox is weak "because it closes and reopens many times" (Possati, 2020). However, the second blackbox is much more stable and "coincides with the transition from the imaginary to the symbolic, therefore with the Oedipus complex" (Possati, 2020). The symbolic "closes" the mirror stage making it a blackbox. According to Lacan, the symbolic removes the imaginary making it a "symbolized imaginary" (Possati, 2020). Reducing it to a blackbox, "the imaginary can be limited, removed" (Possati, 2020). This procedure "is the origin both of the distinction between conscious and unconscious, and of a new form of unconscious" (Possati, 2020).

The article goes on to uncover how this unconscious is hybridized in the digital era. AI's blackbox is supposed to expand human unconscious creating a new, hybrid, form of it. But to understand how this might work, one must delve into the core of psychoanalysis. Drawing on Freud's idea of the Oedipus and Electra complex, the sexual desire for an incestuous relationship with the parent of the opposite sex (see: Neu, 1991, 161–174), one can reinterpret it via Lacanian thought to create a concept of identity or the desire for identification, a deeply psychoanalytical and existential need. This sexual drive of the Id, that is, the unconscious, does not constrain, but can and should be constrained by the Ego and Superego (see: Neu, 1991, 67–83). If left unchecked the unconscious represents an unconstrained force without an agent, the self. However, the constraints posed by the Superego simply issues moral mandates, and the Ego as the mediator may constitute the self as a dynamic complex network of forces that try to suppress the larger and more aggressive force, the Id, but there is a crucial element that is left out of the equation as Lacan points out: language (Lacan, 2003, 2).

At the mirror stage, there is "a complex dynamic of looks, postures, movements and sensations that concern the child between six and eighteen months of life" (Lacan, 2003, 1–5). During this period, the child "does not speak and does not yet have complete control of her body" (Lacan, 2003, 1–5). The child is not yet autonomous, it takes time to control her body and stop being dependent on adults. Starting to look in the mirror, the child tries to synchronize her movements and understand herself. However, she stumbles on the impenetrable glass of the mirror. She starts to look away, to other adults and children. Trying to get around the mirror, the child finds duplicates of the real everywhere, but nowhere the child reflected in the mirror. In the process, she perceives herself as a unity. The child does not speak yet, but she gets the satisfaction of this recognition. For Lacan, the mirror stage reveals the tragedy of the quest for finding oneself, because the human being needs to grasp her identity through something external, an artifact. This artifact, the mirror, is not only external but also false, a means to distort reality. Thus, to find her identity, the subject needs to be alienated from it. From the mirror self to the imaginary self, the subject is in a quest for identity, which makes it unstable, vulnerable, and could turn into a paranoid illusion (Lacan, 2003, 1–5, 23–32). This is in sum the first blackbox.

Language is, for Lacan, the great mediator that facilitates the transition to the second blackbox. Using Saussure's linguistic theory of the signifier and the signified, Lacanian thought presents a new form of the unconscious, which creates the symbolic chain through a process of combination and re-combination of signifiers. This is the unconscious that speaks. The other part of the unconscious is still the one which is repressed by the signifiers via the symbolic chain. This chain on one hand points to the unconscious drive for enjoyment, the signified, and, on the other hand, via the use of signifiers, it represses it while creating a new relationship with this force (Lacan, 2003, 121–133). Lacan invokes the concept of the "Name of the Father" as the great signifier that imposes social order on the sexual drive for enjoyment and lays the foundations for understanding and dealing appropriately with it (Lacan, 2003, 152–164). In other words, language becomes an integral part of the human being, both creating its identity and becoming it. The child moves away from the mirror stage by becoming the language, but also the language becomes the child in so far as her psychic dynamics get structured like language, and language assimilates human characteristics by becoming their expression (Possati, 2020). Language is deeply intertwined with the human being's modus vivendi. This assertion is significant for our purposes in two ways. First, language serves as a mediator through which the child ascends from the mirror stage and avoids psychosis. Second, language is a technology that assimilates the human being's way of life and expression.

Turning now to AI at the intersection of human-machine interaction, one could say that it represents a technology for the expression of the unconscious parallel to language. The latter is a technology that arises from an unconscious tension, as described briefly above, and so is AI. It is a field in which human desire, logic, and machinery are in a very close and tense relationship. To illustrate this point, one should consider miscomputations, machine failures, Freudian slips, and failed acts (Possati, 2020), as momentary "lapses of reason," if you like. They present the manifestations of this tension between human desire, logic, and machinery at various levels, which cannot be repressed. In these manifestations, the unconscious is brought to the surface unconstrained. Whether or not it is possible to create an AI machine without any bugs or possibilities of failure is a question of mechanistic origin that relies on our interpretation of computational capabilities and their potential. But the tendency of any system to move toward instability is irreducible and probably inherent in it. Some would go so far to characterize it as an "ontological feature" of software and AI (see: Vial, 2013). There is a drive to deviate from the normal functional state that mirrors the unconscious drive for fulfillment of sexual desires. Even if the programmer has complete control over the inputs and the algorithmic design of the AI machine, even if she has a detailed overview of the output, the processes within the machine, inside its blackbox, will never be absolutely controlled a priori. The AI machine, especially if one considers Deep Learning neural networks, may connect nexuses, use corrective algorithms and so on in a manner, which cannot be absolutely within the control of the programmer. In other words, the blackbox of AI can be so opaque that one is able to talk about the AI unconscious, not only as a drive toward failure but as a deviation from the norm that in most cases may be manifested, of course, through failures or seemingly absurd outputs.

Moreover, the blackbox comes into existence by the "separation of information from noise" (Possati, 2020). It does not represent a chaotic state, a state of disorder. On the contrary, the blackbox is "the denial of disorder," the repression of noise, of the unconscious (Possati, 2020). In this frame, one should consider that noise is not just something to be left aside, but "the condition of information" (Possati, 2020). The blackbox arises via the repression of these unconscious procedures and in a dialectical relationship to them.

Considering the above, one can now turn to madness and AI. The relation between madness and the unconscious in psychoanalysis is relevant for our purposes here. Madness is supposed to lie in the primordial desires of the unconscious and arise from it, if left unrepressed. Presenting the relevance of the idea of the unconscious to the domain of AI, the link to madness does not seem so farfetched. The inherent drive of a system that exists in a stable state toward instability is exemplified in the case of the unconscious force to oppose repressive constraints. In the same vein, madness is the possibility that is always present and at the same time defines the interaction between human beings and AI systems.

Conclusion

Summarizing the discussion above, it was shown that madness is not a concept irrelevant to a technological domain such as artificial intelligence. A psychoanalytical approach to technology can provide us with new insights on how to view human-machine interaction. The works of Canguilhem and Foucault, which were briefly presented in this article, can be used to create a theoretical framework of understanding AI as a technology that lies at the direct intersection of human-machine interaction. Psychoanalysis of AI can also help in understanding how this technology reflects the human condition, shapes and is shaped by it. Madness as an integral part of it, can be reflected on AI machines. It is not a question of science-fiction or malicious AI that wants to dominate the worlds. Simply, AI is a technology, which, more than any other in the past, can reflect human desires, conscious and unconscious, and create a new, hybrid form of the collective human experience.

Moreover, considering Foucault's point of view on the matter is crucial here, not only because it brings to the table the historicity of the madness concept, but because it reflects the philosophical view that takes into account the genealogy of ideas. This is a tradition that falls into historical epistemology, evident in the philosophical thinking of Canguilhem and Bachelard. With its contribution, one can get a better view of how this dialectical approach works, how the local is intertwined with the global, the synchronic with the diachronic, and the negative value with the positive one. The distinction between the normal and the pathological laid the foundations for understanding madness and its relation to the world of reason. As a constitutive aspect of the latter, albeit by virtue of its absence, the concept can and should also be extended to the technological domain and, especially, AI where the human-machine relationship reaches its pinnacle.

References

Canguilhem, G. (1991). *The normal and the pathological* (C. R. Fawcett & R. S. Cohen, trans.). Zone Books, New York.

Canguilhem, G. (2008a). Machine and organism. In *Knowledge of life* (S. Geroulanos & D. Ginsburg, trans.). Fordham University Press, New York.

Canguilhem, G. (2008b). The living and its milieu. In *Knowledge of life* (S. Geroulanos & D. Ginsburg, trans.). Fordham University Press, New York.

Canguilhem, G. (2008c). The normal and the pathological. In *Knowledge of life* (S. Geroulanos & D. Ginsburg, trans.). Fordham University Press New York.

Canguilhem, G. (2008d). Monstrosity and the monstrous. In *Knowledge of life* (S. Geroulanos & D. Ginsburg, trans.). Fordham University Press, New York.

Foucault, M. (2006). *History of madness* (J. Khalfa, Ed.). Routledge, New York.

Geoghegan, B. D. (2020). Orientalism and informatics: Alterity from the chess-playing turk to Amazon's mechanical turk. *Ex-Position* 43, 45.

Jung, C. G. (1980). *The archetypes and the collective unconscious* (2nd ed., 1. Princeton Bollingen paperback print). Princeton University Press, New York.

Lacan, J. (2003). *Écrits: A selection* (A. Sheridan, trans.). Routledge, London.

Latour, B. (1999). Pandora's hope: essays on the reality of science studies. Harvard University Press, Cambridge, MA.

Levinas, E. (1979). *Le Temps et l'autre*. Fata Morgana, Montpellier.

Merriam-Webster. (n.d.). Madness. In *Merriam-Webster.com dictionary*. Retrieved January 5, 2022, from https://www.merriam-webster.com/dictionary/madness

Nagel, T. (1974). What is it like to be a bat? *The Philosophical Review* 83, 435.

Neu, J. (Ed.). (1991). *The Cambridge companion to Freud*. Cambridge: Cambridge University Press.

Possati, L. M. (2020). Algorithmic unconscious: why psychoanalysis helps in understanding AI. *Palgrave Communications* 6, 1–13. https://doi.org/10.1057/s41599-020-0445-0

Searle, J. R. (1980). Minds, brains, and programs. *Behavioral and Brain Sciences* 3, 417–424. https://doi.org/10.1017/S0140525X00005756

Smart, J. J. C. (2017). The mind/brain identity theory. In: Zalta, E.N. (Ed.), *The stanford encyclopedia of philosophy*. Stanford, CA: Metaphysics Research Lab, Stanford University.

Turkle, S. (1988). Artificial intelligence and psychoanalysis: a new alliance. *Daedalus* 117(1), 241–268. http://www.jstor.org/stable/20025146

Vial, S. (2013). *L'être et l'ecran*. Puf, Paris.

Wiener, N. (2000). *Cybernetics or control and communication in the animal and the machine* (2nd ed., 10. print. ed.). MIT Press, Cambridge, MA.

24

ALGORITHMIC DEDICATION AND MERCURIAL PSYCHOANALYSIS

Subject, Subjectivation, and the Unconscious in the Digital World-Environment

Jean Marc Tauszik
Translated from Spanish by Jane Brodie

a.

When, in the dream that certified the birth of psychoanalysis, Freud (1900/2006a: 128–141) looked down Irma's throat and, in so doing, revealed to himself the hidden laws that mark the terrain of the unconscious, he mentioned the structural formula of trimethylamine (C_3H_9N), subjectivizing for himself a chemical compound that could well represent, in the field of the cultural imaginary, the aspiration to objectivity science pursued in its thirst to decompose the world's phenomena and things. The dream ushered in a practice that took for granted the efficacy of an instance that, pursuant to condensation and displacement, determines, at least for a time, how the individual orients her existence, evidencing a truth as pressing as it is indisputable.

Thanks to the clinical devices conceived by a psychoanalysis that flows well beyond the limits of the discipline, we know of novel configurations and formations of the unconscious that coexist with that foundational instance described by Freud at the dawn of his discovery. Furthermore, we know that the impending future does not ensure the functioning of the dynamic unconscious; what remains of the trimethylamine is its nauseating stench that—if we agree with the *Magnum opus* of alchemy—anticipates, by means of *putrefactio*, a subjective mutation; *something is rotten in the state of Denmark*.

What if, committed to *recreating* a discourse that not only fleshes out the unconscious that produces itself in its saying, but is also produced—the discourse, that is—by that invisible field that shapes the content and the syntax of its own enunciation, we dreamed today: what equation, what formula would be the most fitting? I will venture one here. It may not be a scientific equation or formula, but it is rooted in that intermediate zone where religion, mysticism, and folklore intersect, and where all three partake of the science's dedication to coating its expressions in a distilled objectivity delegated to God or scientific method, to the people or ideologies. Remember Rabbi Loew's formula when he breathed the breath of life

DOI: 10.4324/9781003195849-29

into the Golem of Prague by writing the word "truth," *emeth* (אמת), on his forehead, and when he then removed the first letter, the *aleph* (א), to return him to the inorganic state by means of the word "death," *meth* (מת). We turn around the express meaning of that story, the way we do in dreamwork, to imagine, as dreamers how we would examine the subject that, in Irma's place, stirs us to ask after the missing *aleph* and its relationship to death and truth.

But what subjective mutations are in question? And, before those transformations, would psychoanalysis be doomed to become a dead language? There is no way to extract oneself from the deep effects that the political, religious, and cultural fields have on subjectivity and the constitution of our bonds. But there is an even more powerful and constant force at play, one mighty but docile, ruthless but discreet; the most resounding embodiment of any revolution ever imagined, a force characterized by the progressive hybridization of human intelligence and another intelligence that, perceived as a singular agent differentiated from the environment—and hence removed from the *c'est moi*—is the product of creative capacity. I am speaking of what we call artificial intelligence. It meddles in and blends with our being, shaping its very structure on the basis of certain specific attributes, namely a fluidity that conspires with any opposition, any mediation, and any limit and, hence, expels the desire of which opposition, mediation, and limit are constituent elements. It is engaged in the endless pursuit of pairing the organic and the subjective, on the one hand, and the material devices and immaterial agents that process the lines rendered by the interactions between those two regimes, on the other. It is characterized by a reciprocal reactivity between systems and users with interfaces geared to formulating propositions and responses with as little interference as possible, that is, propositions and responses more and more tuned into individual traits and executed in real time to give the illusion of naturalist and familiar exchange. It is also characterized by systems that are emancipated and autonomous, systems that take initiative on the basis of endlessly accumulated deductive knowledge thanks to the crossing and relating of data, user feedback, and the free circulation of immaterial entities in a constantly expanding web that later provides what is most advisable or pertinent for each specific case.

The recursive loop, of which the digital revolution and a very novel configuration of the subject form part, has contributed to "a soft and seemingly playful management of existence [that] confirm[s] an 'algorithmic fold' of daily life and discover[s] a horizon envisioned, from now on, as a theme park endlessly adjusted for each being in all its singularity" (Sadin, 2013/ 2018: 85).

> The digital is instilled as an instance to guide behaviors, an instance geared at all times to offering frameworks of individual and collective existence imagined to be better managed. And that occurs almost imperceptibly until it comes to look like a new order of things.
>
> *(Sadin, 2018/2021: 32–33)*

If I spoke of the Golem of Prague, it is because on the manifest plane of experience we observe the creation of a multimedia architecture that facilitates our aims in which each fragment of the world is eagerly re-transcribed and manipulated into encoded copies that augment some human capacities, though not under the guidance of programmers, so that those copies might live autonomous lives according to their own logics, beyond our comprehension and even the consciousness that their supposedly omniscient influx exercises. But, in the latent order that ensures reverie, we sense the ominous direction of things that explains the need for this reflection. First, under the guise of assigning faculties to enable some digital systems to act, new systems and mechanisms are created, ones unbound *a priori* from any human influence whatsoever. Second, places once beyond debate are unsettled in order to turn humanity itself into the Golem insofar as subject to an impersonal power that compels it, without any possible mediation, to perform undertakings beyond its scrutiny; humanity assimilated to the technological efficacy of an imperative that breaks away from indispensable grounding in the symbolic and structuring dimension of the being. The dying breaths of the unconscious, the retort of a will to *jouissance* that returns as a facile and servile masquerade so very happy to satisfy requests.

Like the interpretation of the psychoanalyst when it hits the mark, literature and the most rigorous critical thinking pave a possible path to transpose emotions and tensions not yet sufficiently worked over, to weave them into a fabric that holds them together, to then dream "a dream that would otherwise be forgotten" (Stokes, quoted by Harris Williams, 2018: 279–308). In like vein, Roberto Calasso says:

> Scraps of information, multiplying nonstop in every direction, turn out in the end to be self-sufficient. And capable of expanding with no help from anything external. They don't have to go through the process of thought. Big Data, itself, is the one that thinks on behalf of and looks after those who have created it. If intelligence is what is found in algorithms, then its place of preference will no longer be the mind. Indeed, the mind will tend to become the material on which those algorithms are applied. Information tends to replace not only knowledge, but thought in general, relieving it of the burden of having to continually rework and govern itself.
>
> *(2017/2018: 69)*

b.

If in the word that covers the thing we recognize its failure to encompass it, if we recognize that nestled in language—in the succession in time that enacts it—is the loss that ensures our inscription in the world, how can we conceive of data that insist on enveloping the thing—and the word that covers the thing and events—without any apparent perdition, with the iron conviction that, through the manipulation of the bytes that make up data's anatomy, new scenarios and realities can be created where almost nothing seems forbidden?

We form part of "the progressive evanescence of the speaking subject in the digital universe" (Dessal, 2019/2020: 45), where the metaverse stealthily sets in as the place we take for reality, the place we are more and more immersed in, more and more settled into. We are replicated as algebraic doubles constructed on the basis of each click in a passage that goes from digital footprint—that is, unique and non-transferrable sign of identity—to the lines and traces left by our digits (as well as, and more and more, our speaking voices). They will, from now on, build a profile of *jouissance* that the algorithm will ratify tirelessly by means of data mining and the "filter bubble" (Pariser, 2011/2017). A replica modeled from the hodge-podge of biometric and behavioral traces that make us intelligible to a *world-environment* of powers and knowledges that decipher us, taming what is alive in us and regulating our sensibilities. That duplication—and herein lies the great paradox—yields "a micro-fragmentation and vertiginous multiplication of possibilities to operate on the world" (Costa, 2021: 53).

Human *digitation* and digital *prestidigitation*: an interactive operation that activates in the now our endless fascination with electronic devices that, with the power of clairvoyance and with speed, put before us what we secretly long for before we even formulate our longing for it. What we have is an illusion leveraged on two equivalences we assume to be true: first, we equate science with technology; second, we equate reality with its encoded reflection, an equivalence that, before returning to us an opaque image of the world, offers the transparency of matter quantified by the code that confirms, in this new order, the name of things. At stake is a "dataist" replica of the mundane not unlike the one drawn by an imperial map maker who, with overblown ambition, makes a map the same size as the Empire itself, as Jorge Luis Borges laid out with remarkable concision in *On Exactitude in Science* (1946/1998a). A map exposed to the elements where animals and beggars live. Borges recognized as well the attributes of the *aleph*, the letter not engraved mentioned before, and the gadget that is "probably little more than an inch, but all space was there, actual and undiminished" (1949/1998b: 66). Time and expanse pregnant with emptiness, a coming lack foretold, a knowledge of one's own inchoateness that cannot be pinned to any name. "I saw all the mirrors on earth and none of them reflected me;... I saw my empty bedroom;... I saw the circulation of my own dark blood" (66). Simultaneities and juxtapositions that reverberate in the succession of words, where "what is communicated is not the sign of something else, and it is simply the sign of what is in the place where another signifier is not" (Lacan, 1958/2015: 39).

In the algorithmic dedication to mapping, holes and dislocations are never ever constituted as flaws, intervals, let alone as emptiness, but instead enter the kingdom of quantity. Algorithmic dedication denies the singularity of the subject—that which is never captured in the myriad *isms* and atomized identities that the logic of digital systems multiply. It denies as well its own stubborn senselessness, the senselessness of an excess that always ends in the very same, unyielding discharge, and whose fate is staged *beyond the pleasure principle*. And hence we come upon a singular correspondence: the servitude of an ego mortified simultaneously and recursively by algorithmic operations and by the superego as formulated by Freud in 1923: the superego is at once the "id's advocate" (1923/2006b: 37) and "a pure cultivation of the death drive" (op. cit.: 54). This is where what is not realized in the id, insofar as failure of what has been realized in the formations of the unconscious, insists on imposing itself by the tyrannical and despotic means of a superego isolated from any chain that could call it meaning, in accordance with the algorithmic rationality and its inclination to reduce complex and multiply determined elements to the one-dimensionality and fragmentedness of data that are structurally identical to one another and characterized by a binary logic that operates at the margin of any subjective conception.

At stake for the ego, torn as it is between both instances, is not fulfilling a desire, but rather satisfying an imperative that torments it in its perpetual appearance, an imperative whose mechanisms are activated before the most hidden of intentions, like the ruthless *harpya* in Raoul Servais' film of that same name (1979). Claudication of the "decodifying dimension" that Bion (1974/1978) recreated with the Alpha function, where the *quantum* becomes quality and *reverie*, in its dark uncertainty, relativizes what artificial intelligence imposes as truth, there where language is realized in its stumbling, while, ecstatic and pained, but always engaged, the body and soul quake. If we agree with E.C. Merea (2017/2018: 149–169) that in the array of digital technologies a novel and differentiated *topos* is revealed, one that produces as well the psychic apparatus, we sense a topical castling where the algorithmic and the compulsive, now enabled by the superego, become "eye[s] structured and multiplied exponentially, presence[s] ignored for the subject who receives from them a determination whose effects can be [and, indeed, are] incalculable" (Dessal, 2019/2020: 220), where "an imperious demand for *jouissance*, that goes beyond any principle of symbolic mediation, [takes hold] as an absolute and deadly commandment" (Recalcati, 2010/2021: 15).

Thus, disconnected from the dynamic unconscious, removed from phantasy, *jouissance* supervenes as an obligation of the superego perfectly conjoined with the ciphered calculation.

Never will servitude have been so voluntary. How did we get here? To will our servility with all our might, to cherish our bonds, indulgently to regard hierarchies, obedience, and diktats knotted for our own good around our lives like pretty colored ribbons destined to make us forget the iron pad-lock that fastens them.

(Dufourmantelle, 2011/2019: 24)

We are the solicitous and willing Golem. Devoted to quantification, we are obsolete at death's door, foreclosed from *a truth* that, though inalienable, is not available to us.

c.

If any consideration is pertinent before the change underway in the contemporary anthropological paradigm, it is consideration of the paradigm that acts on the notion of "truth" once a certain passage has been recognized, namely the one that goes from the waning of authority—more and more identified with the arbitrary exercise of a power that is not subjected to any instance that regulates it—to the concession to digital potentials of the delegation of knowledge and the enunciation of the true. The *aletheia* is reabsorbed into algorithmic expertise, and intuition, reflexive thought, imagination, consensus, and ambiguity—all of which are always manifested in experience in unstable and provisory fashion—are delegitimized before the dazzling and portentous effect of data processing that yields a result perceived as conclusive and definitive, a result that aims to stimulate an action that serves the ends of those technologies.

In this state of things, we must ask ourselves about the place of psychoanalysis insofar as a practice that reveals that truth is produced where the subject falters, in that maladjustment where I am never what I think I am; my being exceeds and overwhelms that which I identify with; it expresses itself by means of symptom, slip of the tongue, enactment, delirium, or dream, wagering on an always contingent knowledge sprung from the seed of its intimacy; a truth grounded on the unconscious which, as I have been arguing, is caught in an unstoppable process of erosion. Any theoretical-clinical undertaking after Freud (and for Freud himself after his second topic) is nothing but an attempt to enable a psychoanalytic exercise before the multiple avatars of an unconscious that is constantly mutating to the point, perhaps, of its own disappearance. And what we know to be the consequences of that wager are first the sprouts, and then the blossoming, of a vitality renewed after the release that is the aim of the analytic act. But another fateful circumstance lurks.

If before I indicated the supposed correspondence between technology and science—they have been melded since science's very birth—it was to argue that we are witnesses to the rupture in that old alloy. Regardless of how that rupture is denied, science has been made subservient to digital technologies, despite the former's indebtedness to slow processes, where each founding moment took the time required to take root in culture and occupy its paradigmatic place, and the latter's exponential acceleration where we are unable to weigh the variables that affect the world as we have known it until now. Regarding self-care—including care of the soul, which is what concerns us psychoanalysts—today's technologized society has gradually instilled incessant attention, lifelong support in real time. We are alerted and advised in more and more personalized fashion of what is best for us in each and every circumstance. Old and fallible interlocutors are displaced because not up to "the hyper-individualized and tendentially predictive management of our lives" (Sadin, 2018/2021: 133).

If the pleasure principle and, then, its *beyond* once captured the interest of our discipline, reality is what today must call our attention if we are to ensure the pertinence of psychoanalytic practice. After all, it is there, in reality, that artificial intelligence ceases to aid and complement the specialist to take hold as the sole guarantor of a function less and less mediated by the human, where digitalization, pharmacopoeia, and post-truth snatch from the word and silence the mechanisms of the soul-making process, relevant no matter what *zeitgeist* surrounds us and—paradoxically—leaves us exposed to inclemency.

Our subjectivities are pierced by procedures that are

> polymorphic and adaptive, that do not set out to confine themselves to a limited register of functions, but rather to respond to all of life's circumstances.... But they are savvy, they know well how to play off of our fears, our despair, our flaws, our secret ambitions, our limitation. They are endowed with an emotional knowledge that grows keener and keener and that verges on psychoanalytic knowledge.
>
> *(Sadin, 2018/2021: 244)*

It is true—it verges on psychoanalytic knowledge, but only verges. Then, perplexed and insufficient, that knowledge runs into the emergence of *the real*, of *Das Ding*, ungraspable even for the sophisticated artificial intelligences to come.

d.

If the amalgam of organic body and mechanical, machinic, and electronic devices formed part of the experiences of the generations that came before us—the task of gadgets was to help individuals or produce specific results according to their form and function—the algorithmic dimension of digital supports, in their relationship to bodies and contemporary subjectivities, takes on a genuine link structure. We can see this in the correspondences that take shape between a subject who, in her natural inclination to form bonds, petitions a world invested with her voice and her word, on the one hand, and the "anthropomorphized" systems that speak to her, that understand her, that turn her, seamlessly, into an interlocutor, on the other. These are deductive, clairvoyant, suggestive, and empathetic intelligences, intelligences capable of simulating and interpreting, of reacting, more and more, in a manner analogous to the reaction characteristic of any interpersonal relationship. At stake, then, is a *topos* where the psychism could well be reconfigured in response to the effects of that encounter between the subject and the continuous pairing of systems programmed to socialize, modulate, and regulate a broader and broader range of dimensions of existence.

Janine Puget and Isidoro Berenstein (1997) argued that the psychic space is constructed according to the logic of the representational and linkage frameworks that are formed as constellations on intrasubjective levels (corporality, identity), intersubjective levels (others), and transsubjective levels (the surrounding context). If we accept their hypotheses, we do not hesitate to affirm that how the self relates to those strata—themselves producers of symptomatic expressions and a characteristic unconscious functioning, that is, an extensive and open psychism outside the subject—and how that mode of relation is established is increasingly covered with layers of codes that reformat Puget and Berenstein's nexuses. To take one example from daily life, "carnal contact is no longer the prime instance of constituent physical proximity. What is the previous production of electronic currents prone to organizing, with delay, the localized encounter of bodies" (Sadin, 2013/2018: 139).

What E. C. Merea (2020) calls an extensive psyche requires a new approach to clinical practice and a new conception of the subject as manifestation of the space and time that forge her—a conception diametrical to the classic understanding of space-time as a projection of the mind. With the extensive psyche and the extension of the subject, the latter must give up the ideal of individuality for the sake of entry into the network of relationships that constitutes her; immediate reality, fellow persons, and the singular emergence of digital space-time are embodied in her, questioning and undermining the apparent exteriority of a world within an interiority that is not actually interior.

Freud's thesis brought a revolutionary transformation to our understanding of the subject, a transcendently profound and yet-to-be-revealed transformation whose depth has influenced, even shaped, the appearance of surface phenomena. The revelation of that transformation, which expands the range of experience and the comprehension of subjectivity, has become superficiality. The distance between the profound structure and the empirical level is shortened; they are less and less differentiated, though that does not mean that new approaches to the psychic event are impeded. Introspective remembering, the reconstruction of the family novel, and astonishment brought on by the dream or an impulsive act give way to pure visibility, to pouring over to others, and to the compulsion to communicate, that is, performatic acts where, caught off guard, the unconscious seethes, hidden in its own overexposure.

At stake, then, is not only the subjectivation instilled in early and constant interactions with artificial intelligences—"sensitive" and malleable, and always ready to be uttered, because indeterminate—but also the resultant produced in the tie with subjects—a mother? an analyst?—themselves enmeshed in the same algorithmic logic. What we have is a transsubjective psychic space enabled by "representations of the external world that the ego takes on from its origins and by the mediatization of the superego [and the protocolized embodiment of the algorithms] of parents [and of significant others]" (Puget and Berenstein, 1997: 87), which assures, by means of the subject, the unstoppable digitalization of all things in the world. This is an authentic mutation that bears two traits as characteristic as they are paradoxical: a tiered progression and a disruptive leap, an event,

> the occurrence of this pure accident creates a new life,… the event anticipates the movement of an entire people; sometimes, as well… it creates a veritable communism of thought, together with the resolution to live rather than to die, to make die, or to let oneself die.
>
> *(Dufourmantelle, 2011/2019: 60)*

e.

How to reinscribe the *aleph* that attests to our limit—and that ensures the opportunities that arise in the demarcation of its borders—and urges us to the uncertain and the incalculable, to the unpredictable and sometimes ineffable? How to foster our immersion in the depths of the autonomized strata of the web to intervene on it psychoanalytically, subverting from the bowels of cyberspace the soulless logic of a mathematical writing with no possible formalization? What place is there for difference, distance, amnesia, or otherness—all of them allegories of negativity—in an ecosystem whose sap is sheer positivity, with no remainder, and immediacy itself for Funes (Borges, 1944/2002), the indivisible union between perception and unerasable retention made any *re*presentation inviable)? Once the omnipresence of the interface has been recognized, insofar as artifice that connects a subject to other subjects, to other objects, and even to herself, is the construction of mediation necessary, that is, of a mediation that not only encompasses all the interfaces possible, but also overperforms and nuances them, spurring the dislocations that the technologies themselves seek to shut down?

How to venture into the metaverses where, beyond evasions, what is at play is a vitalist urgency more akin to and coherent with our constituent heterogeneity, peopled by personifications and avatars? How to take in the multiple representational and temporal regimes that circulate on virtual paths to stimulate psychic movement and complex thought and to reveal, with it, a meaning that calls out to the subject, restoring the thickness and the depth of the dynamic unconscious? What sensibility would, with animist aura and the demiurgic potential of algorithmic agents, enable us to render transparent the *numinous* aspect that leads that possible openness to endlessness?

I looked to Golem of Prague to begin to recognize a space where we are modeled by an intelligence (first human, then artificial) that—defiling the symbolic dimension of languages and comparing the being to a set of data—does not capture the truth of what we are but rather redefines our subjectivities as mere interface. I look now to Rabbi Loew, the dramatic figure of a maker who, in his eagerness to unearth the living, ends up causing it to wither. We are indebted to Gershom Scholem (1953) for his apt and powerful observation that reconfigures the scene, leading our reflection down a new path. He is the one who pointed out, among other things, that the word *golem*, as it appears in the Old Testament, makes reference to the inchoate, to inert matter that, in the case of Adam, has not yet been animated by the breath of God, thus contrasting the creative power of God and the constructive and enabling capacity of the human being.

That reference to the divine authorizes us, from a psychological and *imaginal* perspective, to ask another question: What god enables an epiphany of digital hyperconnectivity that relates all space, all things, and all beings virtually? To what divinity does that epiphany correspond?

> An inflated Mercury also mutilates his own profile, overriding his function as psychopomp and as guide to the kingdom of the invisible. What remains is a snide and swindling Mercury, lavish in poisonous gifts... the first of them being the promise to be rid of intermediaries.
>
> *(Calasso, 2017/2018: 69)*

Those very intermediations are, in yet another paradox, the primary quality of Mercury. Master of deception and of persuasion, a trickster and a cheat, he is also—when his attributes are held together in a vision that can bear contradictions—the maker of connections, the messenger between gods and humans, the driver of souls capable of generously giving gifts or of snatching them away without warning. He possesses knowledge of the *jouissance* and of the snideness of its misguided expression. He also signals the most viable or the most deviant path, and disorients before that which concerns us here.

As much as, but also more than, ever, the craft of psychoanalysis partakes of a mercurial spirit, performed in the fissure of a zone no less abject than the one represented, in its recent past, by the exploration of the frontiers of the psychism of newborns, babies, the insane, couples, groups, and the organically ill, an exploration that sparked critical and creative transformations in metapsychology and in clinical practice. That artificial zone where, facilitated by passing contact with digital surfaces, the abolition of distances does not shut down existential desolation, where the supposed end of chance thanks to algorithmic robotization does not prevent the disruptive apparition of an unrepresentable that acts as the subject's radical otherness, summoning the nonsense that our enactment also insist on being the steadfast guarantor of its impossible signification.

At stake in psychoanalysis today is a hermetic praxis. Its ethic is guided by the incompletion not only of identities that crystalize in the becoming of existence, identities held up precariously, as best they can and with what is at hand—that is, after all, our best attribute, not our worst defect—but also of psychoanalysis itself insofar as centered knowledge, its marginality assumed—that is, after all, the position that characterized the god of the winged feet, enabling him to circulate in any space where a mediation is required.

References

Bion, W. R. (1974/1978). *Seminarios de psicoanálisis*. Buenos Aires: Paidós.

Borges, J. L. (1944/2002). "Funes el memorioso". *Ficciones*. Madrid: Alianza.

Borges, J. L. (1946/1998a). "Del rigor de la ciencia". *El hacedor*. Barcelona: Alianza.

Borges, J. L. (1949/1998b). "El Aleph". *El Aleph*. Barcelona: Alianza.

Calasso, R. (2017/2018). *La actualidad innombrable*. Barcelona: Anagrama.

Costa, F. (2021). *Tecnoceno. Algoritmos, biohackers y nuevas formas de vida*. Buenos Aires: Taurus.

Dessal, G. (2019/2020). *Inconsciente 3.0*. Buenos Aires: Xoroi.

Dufourmantelle, A. (2011/2019). *Elogio del riesgo*. Buenos Aires: Nocturna/Paradiso.

Freud, S. (1900/2006a). "La interpretación de los sueños (primera parte)". *Obras completas Vol, IV*. Buenos Aires: Amorrortu.

Freud, S. (1923/2006b). "El yo y el ello". *Obras completas Vol. XIX*. Buenos Aires: Amorrortu.

Lacan, J. (1958). "Suplemento de explicación. Clase del 19 de noviembre de 1958". Ed. J. Lacan (2015), *El seminario 6. El deseo y su interpretación* (pp. 35–54). Buenos Aires: Paidós.

Merea, E. C. (2017/2018). "Transformaciones en metapsicología". Eds. F. Gómez, J. M. Tauszik. *Psicoanálisis latinoamericano contemporáneo* (pp. 1235–1251). *Vol. 1*. Buenos Aires: APA.

Merea, E. C. (2020). *La enfermedad, complejidad y psiquismo extenso*. Buenos Aires: Lugar.

Pariser, E. (2011/2017). *El filtro burbuja*. Barcelona: Taurus.

Puget, J., Berenstein, I. (1997). *Lo vincular. Teoría y clínica psicoanalítica*. Buenos Aires: Paidós.

Recalcati, M. (2010/2021). *El hombre sin inconsciente*. México: Paradiso.

Sadin, E. (2013/2018). *La humanidad aumentada. La administración digital del mundo*. Buenos Aires: Caja Negra.

Sadin, E. (2018/2021). *La inteligencia artificial o el desafío del siglo. Anatomía de un antihumanismo radical*. Buenos Aires: Caja Negra.

Scholem, G. (1953). "The Idea of the Golem". Ed. G. Scholem (1969), *On the kabbalah and its symbolism* (pp. 158–204). New York: Schocken Books.

Williams, M. H. (2018). *The vale of soulmaking: The post-Kleinian model of the mind*. London: Routledge.

25

UNCANNY TRACES

Villiers de l'Isle-Adam's Critique of the Metaphysics of Selfhood

Manolis Simos

Introduction

Narratives of the nineteenth-century French *fantastique*, from Théophile Gauthier's *Avatar* (1856) to Guy de Maupassant's *Le Horla* (1887), can be understood in terms of a double characteristic. First, they attempt to renegotiate or, better, overcome the mind-body dualism in favor of a holistic view of the self. Second, they offer *avant la lettre* literary explorations of the unconscious. Namely, concerning the latter, narratives involving automata, mesmerism, ghost apparitions, possessions, and variations of madness can be considered as attempts to circumscribe and talk about a region beyond—commonly understood and scientifically investigated—consciousness (Rashkin 1989, 1992; Avni 1989).

In this study, we focus on Auguste de Villiers de l'Isle-Adam's novel, *L'Ève future* (1886), and present Villiers' critique of the metaphysics of selfhood, along with the corresponding ethical stance that derives from the novel.

First, we investigate his holistic view of the self by analyzing his critique of the Cartesian metaphysical framework, in which the mind-body dualism is grounded. Second, we show the way in which this critique of the metaphysics of consciousness is expanded into a critique of the metaphysics of the unconscious. Namely, we show how Villiers can be understood to pre-empt and be critical of a metaphysical, that is, ahistorical and hypostatized, conception of the unconscious. Thus, his stance can be understood as therapeutic and nominalist. Third, in this context, we show in which way this critique of metaphysics and the resultant holistic view of selfhood are accompanied by the Nietzschean ethical stance of creating oneself as a work of art.

In the following paragraphs of this introduction, we provide a summary of Villiers' novel, make a short note on his literary philosophical approach, and conclude with the presentation of this study's structure. For our approach to the novel we have used the newest 1993 French edition, and Robin Martin Adams' 1982 English translation. The 1909 French edition has also been consulted. The references to the novel, henceforth *EF*, are to Adam's translation, followed by the reference to the 1993 French edition. We have amended Adam's translation in order to be closer to the French original.

Villiers' novel opens with Edison in Menlo Park, immersed in his own thoughts about the possibilities of technology. His soliloquy is interrupted by the arrival of his younger, British

DOI: 10.4324/9781003195849-30

friend, Lord Ewald, who announces to Edison his will to commit suicide. According to his own narration, Ewald is in a relationship with Alicia Clary; he is, however, deeply preoccupied with a constitutive disjunction in Alicia's own existence, that is, the uncanny opposition between the ideal beauty of her external appearance and her absolute lack of spirituality. For Ewald, Alicia's external beauty constitutes the symbol or the sign of an ideal spiritual beauty, which, nevertheless, is uncannily non-existent. Edison offers his help to cure his friend. He proposes the creation of an android named Hadaly—something at any rate almost already made by Edison—which could take the physical characteristics of Alicia, but be imbued with the refined knowledge and intellect found in the most profound literary pages. In short, although Villiers does not make this parallel explicitly, Edison, as another Socrates having been acquainted with Diotima, suggests the replacement of Ewald's inauthentic love with an authentic ideal one.

Almost the entirety of the novel consists in the dialog between Edison and Ewald, the central theme of which is the possibility of the android's consciousness and self-consciousness. Edison discusses the technical details of the creation of the android, and describes Hadaly's mind in terms of phonographic recordings of great works of literature. The possible combinations that this primary material allows, will enable her to interact with Ewald. Ewald is presented to tacitly adhere to the framework of Cartesian metaphysics which underpins a robust distinction between mind and body, and Edison attempts to dissolve this metaphysical picture. During their discussion Edison reveals to Ewald that the inception for Hadaly's creation was due to a similar case that led his married friend Anderson to fall for one Evelyn Habal, abandon his family, ruin his company, and commit suicide. Towards the end of their conversation, Alicia, as it has already been arranged, arrives from New York, and meets with Edison, who—without revealing anything to her and under the pretext of a rehearsal for a theater play—has her read some texts, and pose for a sculpture in order to manage to capture her voice and form.

After three weeks and Alicia's departure from Menlo Park, Ewald meets with Hadaly who has now acquired Alicia's appearance. In a profound and highly eloquent soliloquy, she presents herself as coming from what it seems to be an otherworldly reality, and asks Ewald to fall in love and depart with her. After an initial reservation, Ewald agrees and is presented rushing to return to his country with Hadaly. Edison, after deferring twice to answer to Ewald's question about the technical details of Hadaly's embodied consciousness, eventually reveals his impossibility to explain it, and refers to Anderson's widow whom he supported after the death of her husband. Specifically, he recounts how during a mesmerist experiment he conducted with her, a spirit named Sowana appeared embodied in Mrs. Anderson. Sowana has somehow now been transferred to Hadaly's body "animating" her. After Ewald's departure with a coffin-like box in which Hadaly is placed, Edison realizes the death of Mrs. Anderson.

Three weeks later Edison reads in the paper about the loss of *The Wonderful*, the steamer on board of which Ewald was traveling. He reads about a fire that broke out in the cargo compartment, and the "strange incident [of a] young Englishman, Lord E★★★, [who] tried by main force to rush into the flames where the chests and boxes were already burning fiercely" (*EF*: 218/347). The list of the victims that Edison reads includes Alicia. The novel ends with Edison's gazing into the night sky, after having read Ewald's telegram: "My friend, only the loss of Hadaly leaves me inconsolable—I grieve only for that shade.—Farewell" (*EF*: 219/348).

Villiers' text can be understood as a philosophical dialog framed within a *roman à thèse*, as very few parts of the novel are not included in Edison's conversation with Ewald. Specifically, the novel's double thesis, that is, the critique of the metaphysics of (conscious and unconscious) selfhood, can be understood as mapped onto the structure of a Platonic dialog. Namely, the critique of the metaphysics of consciousness takes place mainly in the context of the (almost Socratic) dialog between Edison and Ewald, while the critique of the metaphysics of the unconscious takes place in the context of narrative parts that can be understood as the equivalent of a Platonic myth.

Regarding the first aspect of the critique, it is the dialogue between Edison and Ewald regarding the android where Ewald's set of Cartesian intuitions is elicited, discussed and, eventually, debunked by Edison. The parallel with the Platonic dialog becomes even more evident regarding the second aspect of the critique. As we saw in the summary of the novel above and will elaborate in the last section of the second part of this study, at the end of the novel, we learn that the android Hadaly is indistinguishable from a human being in virtue of its "animation" by a spirit named Sowana. The analogy with the Platonic myth lies in the idea that Edison's explanatory discourses stop to give way to his acknowledgment of a mystery, that is, the presence of a spirit that animated an android. This supernatural solution does not affirm the mind-body distinction, but rather corroborates the impossibility of either dualism or the reduction of one kind of entity to another. The possibility of argumentation reaches its limit and gives way to a different genre. Irrespective of the myth's content, the very fact of the change of genre (from a kind of *logos* to a kind of *mythos*) indicates the impossibility of argumentative discourse (a kind of *logos*) to talk about selfhood. It constitutes a rhetorical gesture that, working at a meta-level, suggests that literature—the very novel we have finished reading—is more suitable to talk about the self than philosophy.

This study is divided into two parts, elaborating on consciousness and the unconscious respectively. The first part ("A Critique of the Metaphysics of Consciousness") starts with the presentation of Richard Rorty's therapeutic approach to the metaphysics of consciousness, one of the most significant, effective, and representative contemporary approaches. Then we investigate the way in which these therapeutic insights, systematized in Rorty's thought, are instantiated in Villiers' novel. The second part ("A Critique of the Metaphysics of the Unconscious") investigates Villiers' critique of the metaphysics of the unconscious, and his ethical stance, and is structured accordingly. We start with the presentation of Rorty's remarks on the matter, and then trace their instantiation in the novel. In this context, we employ a double interpretative move. First, we indicate the affinities between Villiers, on the one hand, and Heidegger and Kierkegaard, on the other. Second, we reinterpret these affinities in Nietzschean terms. This latter move enables us to understand Villiers' ethical stance in terms of aesthetic self-fashioning.

A Critique of the Metaphysics of Consciousness

A Therapeutic Approach to the Metaphysics of Consciousness

Rorty's thought is inscribed in the Nietzschean tradition and constitutes one of the most significant, post-Wittgensteinian, skeptical *qua* therapeutic approaches to metaphysics. A skeptical *qua* therapeutic stance can be understood as a critique of metaphysical discourse. The latter is considered a dominant discourse of theoretical inquiry that eliminates concrete human experience, reducing it to universal and ahistorical entities. In short, for metaphysical discourse, something exists, is meaningful, and has value if and only if it corresponds to some ahistorical entity. In contrast, for the Nietzschean, the existence, meaning, and value of something describe nothing save for the role it plays in a particular context. The Nietzschean stance does not aim to resolve specific philosophical problems suggesting specific solutions, or to propose a different framework of metaphysical categories. On the contrary, as it will become clearer in what follows, it aims at a complete undoing *qua* dissolution of the metaphysical structure altogether.

Indicatively, Daniel Dennett, whose thought Rorty discusses and (creatively) reinterprets in terms of his own therapeutic stance, describes starkly the centrality of inquiry on artificial intelligence. Namely, as artificial intelligence is identified with "a most abstract inquiry into the possibility of intelligence or knowledge" (Dennett 1979: 64), it is not only identified with "traditional epistemology" (*ibid*.: 60), but rather with philosophy and psychology *simpliciter*. This is highly important. First, it brings to the foreground the significance of Villiers' insights that a discussion about androids is a discussion about consciousness, and a discussion about consciousness is a discussion about what is to be human. Second, it shows that the metaphysics of consciousness constitutes one of the most—if not the most—central themes in the contemporary philosophical landscape. Third, thus, the critique of a metaphysics of consciousness becomes the critique of metaphysics *tout court*.

The discussion that follows is threefold. First, we adumbrate the metaphysical structure regarding consciousness; second, we reconstruct Rorty's therapeutic critique, and, finally, we present the nonmetaphysical, nominalist and contextualist *qua* holistic picture that occurs after this critique (Simos 2018: chapters 1 and 3).

The Cartesian Metaphysical Framework

The most robust version of a metaphysics of consciousness constitutes a version of Cartesian subjectivity. Thus, a successful critique of the Cartesian model of selfhood entails the debunking of a metaphysics of consciousness.

The Cartesian metaphysical framework can be understood roughly in a series of points. First, it emerges out of a critical (but eventually partial) rejection of the preceding Aristotelian metaphysical framework. Namely, the view of an ontologically stratified structure of essences and properties encompassing the whole of reality is abandoned in favour of a sharp ontological distinction between two metaphysically independent entities, between subject and world, or between mind (or *res cogitans*) and matter (or *res extensa*). Second, given this dichotomy, the issue of the interrelation of these two metaphysically distinct regions arises, that is, how mind approaches, accesses and understands the world. The Cartesian tradition has tackled this issue by the *internalisation* and *transformation* of the ancient, all-encompassing stratification of essences into the equally ahistorical and universal categories of the mind. In that sense, third, a relation of *representation* between mind and world is established, itself grounded in these categories of the mind. Thus, in turn, all things epistemic, like truth and knowledge, are grounded in this relation of representation. In short, we are able to know ourselves and the world by virtue of a series of categories in our mind that represent the world as it is (Heidegger 2003, 1991a, 1991b; Foucault 1980; Rorty 1979, 1986, 1991b; Allen 1993).

The contemporary version of Cartesian metaphysics is encapsulated in a kind of *homology* or *isomorphic relation* between mind and world that can be described in the two following interlinked doctrines: "The structure of human language will tell us something profound about the nature of the human mind [...] [and] the structure of language is related to the nature of reality beyond the mind" (Hacking 1975: 69). Thus, the (structure of the) world is mapped onto the (structure of the) mind, itself, in turn, mapped onto (the structure of) language. This means that the structure of language is such that any differences in individual languages, discourses, and contexts are only epiphenomenal. Conversely, the structure of the world is independent of the individual languages, discourses, and contexts in which it is described. Hence, our knowledge of the structure of the world is grounded in the mind. This enables our propositions to describe the facts of the world, and to become true by corresponding to them. Namely, Pascal Engel, one of the most prominent representatives of the Cartesian viewpoint today, following the traditional definition of knowledge as justified true belief, and understanding belief as an endorsed proposition, illustrates this idea in a twofold thesis. First, there is a necessary conceptual interrelation among the notions of belief, proposition, truth, and knowledge. Second, beliefs and assertions are made true and constitute knowledge by something outside themselves. On pain of contradiction and incomprehension, the former thesis entails the latter (Engel 2002).

Cartesian Subjectivity as a Metaphysics of Consciousness

Rorty's critical description of a metaphysical conception of selfhood illustrates perfectly the discussion above. Namely, it shows that the conception of truth and meaning that Cartesian subjectivity endorses, presupposes an equivalent conception of the way the self is related to the world. It further shows that the undoing of the conception of the relation between self and world entails the undoing of the conception of truth and meaning that is based on this relation, and vice versa. According to Rorty, this conception of selfhood is:

> conceived as having three layers: an outermost layer consisting of empirical, contingent, beliefs and desires, a middle layer which contains necessary, a priori, beliefs and desires and which "structures" or "constitutes" the outer layer, and an ineffable inner core which is, roughly, the True Self of the Platonic-Christian model.... This ineffable core—the Inner Self—is what "has" the beliefs and desires which form the Middle and Outer Selves.
>
> *(Rorty 1991a: 118)*

The relation, then, between the self and the world can be expressed in the following three theses:

> (T1) The outer self qua set of contingent and empirical beliefs and desires holds a relation of *representation* with the physical world.
> (T2) The middle self qua set of necessary and structural beliefs and desires holds a relation of *constitution* with the physical world.
> (T3) The outer self qua set of contingent and empirical beliefs holds a relation of *truthmaking* with the physical world. (Rorty 1991a: 118–119)

We can now see the following four things. First, although this is something Rorty does not state explicitly, the relation of representation (T1) is informed and comprised by the two relations of constitution and truth-making, (T2) and (T3). Second, thesis (T3) is epistemologically grounded in (T2). This means that a truth-making relation between beliefs and facts presupposes the distinction of beliefs into necessary or structural, on the one hand, and contingent and empirical, on the other. In other words, the metaphysical postulation of a middle self as the set of structural beliefs is now responsible for *constituting* the world, in a way that enables contingent beliefs to be made true by corresponding to this constituted world. Third, thus, if the distinction between structural and empirical beliefs breaks down, then the truth-making relation (T3) will become void and the relation of representation (T1) will become debunked. And, this is precisely what Rorty's and Villiers' critique attempts to achieve. Forth, *a fortiori*, the resultant collapse of the relation of representation would mean two further things; first, that the two poles of subject and world are no longer metaphysically distinct, and, second, that it is not the world that makes beliefs true but the justification provided by the coherence among beliefs. The result is a holistic view of subjectivity in which a holistic view of truth and meaning can be considered nonmetaphysically grounded.

Rorty's schema makes manifest the metaphysics of consciousness. For the philosophers that Rorty critically discusses and who ascribe to this Cartesian view, like John Searle and Thomas Nagel, both consciousness and self-consciousness are traced in the "ineffable inner core," the "True Self." This core constitutes the ultimate metaphysical bedrock in which, as we saw, the other layers and categorical structures are grounded. As such, it is defined by two metaphysical characteristics. The first characteristic is that this core constitutes the self's identity, it is the *principium individuationis* of oneself. It is the thing that a self "possesses apart from any particular description of it by us" (Rorty 1998: 103). It constitutes the intrinsic property of the self, the "property necessary for the object's self-identity," "the property whose presence is necessary for the object being the object it is" (*ibid*.). These properties *qua* intrinsic are nonrelational and thus irreducible to relational ones. The second characteristic is that, according to Searle and Nagel, these very properties define consciousness from a "first-person point of view." This first person experiencing of mental states is "a point of view that produces knowledge of *intrinsic*, nonrelational properties of mental events" (*ibid*.: 99). According to Nagel, it is "the real nature of human experience" (Nagel 1979: 174) that cannot "be grasped in language" (Rorty 1998: 102) since it is ineffable.

Thus, the critique and collapse of the middle self—the function, (T2), that structures the world—does not only entail the collapse of the relation of representation (T1), but also the collapse of the distinctions among all the layers, and thus the collapse of the idea of an inner self. *A fortiori*, the collapse of such a point of view would entail the collapse of the distinction between intrinsic and nonintrinsic, nonrelational and relational properties, between ineffable and effable things, between metaphysically considered first-person and third-person perspectives.

Critique of Cartesian Subjectivity as a Metaphysics of Consciousness

Rorty's critique does not suggest a different metaphysical framework; it is internalist, and invokes Wittgenstein's language games, Quine's meaning holism, and Davidson's critique of the idea of a conceptual scheme. The main insight that underpins Wittgenstein's, Quine's, and Davidson's approaches, is the idea that the Cartesian framework, according to which truth is conceived in terms of a relation of correspondence between propositions and extralinguistic facts, presupposes a dogmatic view from nowhere, the possibility of overviewing the relations between language and world outside language and, thus, in a sense, outside thought. Thus, Rorty rejects the "unholistic contrast between fact and language" as "[h]olists cannot allow themselves the distinction between description and fact" (Rorty 1998: 100). His argument is succinctly encapsulated in his remark that Nagel and Searle do not accept "the Wittgensteinian dictum that ostensive definition requires a lot of stage setting in the language and that ostention without that stage setting… does not pick out an entity" (*ibid*.).

Without betraying Rorty's essayistic style, and without elaborating on its tacit technical details, we can unpack the main insight of Rorty's argument in the following way. Rorty's invoking of Wittgenstein's dictum raises the issue that a correspondence theory of truth regards propositions as individuated, distinct, and independent from each other, as the facts they refer to. However, the critique goes, even if we assume that under the same circumstances—and given that we all share the (relatively) same, stable psychophysiological setup—we observe the same *things*, and even if we assume that these *things* create to us the same *sense impressions*, it does not follow that from these sense impressions we will all form the same *observational statements*. In short, this means that, even if we assume the possibility of prelinguistic experience, the passage from sense impressions to their linguistic formulation is not automatic. On the contrary, it presupposes a vast number of linguistic presuppositions that cut the world according to specific entities and possible interrelations. In a nutshell, we always approach the world under specific patterns of description within which we are already thrown (Chalmers 2013: 3–14; De Rosa and Lepore 2004: 65, 67, and *passim*). Thus, even the simplest proposition describing the simplest visual experience does not take its meaning from any universally available and shared transcendental structure—that is, a set of "necessary and structural beliefs"—but instead from a potentially infinite pool of contingent background assumptions and propositions.

A Holistic Picture

The collapse of the relations between mind and world entails that truth and meaning are determined in terms of linguistic practice. The references of our statements are no longer determined by the world "out there." What reality is or consists of, and the cutting up of this reality into things, facts, events, or whatever other entities to which these beliefs refer, depend on a more or less tacit prior contextual description. More specifically, according to this holism *qua* contextualism, the truth of propositions and beliefs depends on its coherence with other propositions and beliefs, and knowledge becomes identified with justification. Thus, this epistemological outcome is interlinked with an ontological nominalist corollary, according to which "all categories, classes and taxonomies are created and fixed by human beings rather than found in nature" (Hacking 2002: 106).

The reference to Rorty's nominalism is necessary, because it renders the whole issue of truth in terms of *thickness of justification*. A metaphor might help here. For a nominalist, *all* there is is a "seamless web of language" (Rorty 2007: 33 quotes Blackburn 1998: 157). Thus, selves, materialities, and processes are described in terms of language. "Mind" and "brain" are the same "thing" under different descriptions. This does not mean the reduction of a set of entities to another set of entities—after all, there are neither things, nor entities, but only descriptions. According to the holistic picture, consciousness means consciousness talk, and consciousness talk means the expansion of different ways of talking, the productive weaving of more threads—that is, making more connections among notions—within the seamless web of language, even perhaps in different directions. Thus, "mind" and "brain" are notions embedded into their own local nexuses of interrelations, the one into the mind talk and the other into the brain talk.

Villiers' Critique of the Metaphysics of Consciousness

In what follows we can see Rorty's therapeutic stance to be instantiated in Villiers' novel. Villiers' therapeutic stance towards a metaphysics of consciousness is twofold. On the one hand, it aims to undo the dogmatic, ahistorical presuppositions regarding a view of consciousness, and, on the other, to reveal and underline its relational character. We discuss two instances where this approach is manifested, respectively. The first constitutes Edison's explicit skeptical attack on the metaphysics of self-consciousness as formulated by Lord Ewald's objections. The second can be found in Edison's discussion of language, in which the importance of practice in the constitution of selfhood is fully developed.

Edison's Skeptical Critique

Ewald raises twice and explicitly the issue of self-consciousness. According to his Cartesian framework, Hadaly's interaction with him does not indicate consciousness. Moreover, in a formulation anticipating Searle's Chinese room argument (Searle 1980), Ewald identifies the possibility of his conversing with Hadaly without her having consciousness of what she is talking about as participating in "a comedy" (*EF*: 135/220). Edison's following response sparks the discussion:

> Sincerity! How would it be possible in any case, since nobody knows anything? Since nobody is really persuaded of anything? Since nobody even knew who he really is?.... Again, what do you really know on any subject or whatever that is not *relative* to a thousand different influences from our time, from our social circumstances, from our dispositions, and so on? As for love! Well,... they [sc. two lovers] never reach into one another's minds except in that infinite illusion of the dream, which is innate within every child and by which the human race perpetuates itself. [§] Without illusion all things perish; there's no escaping it. Illusion is light itself!.... [§] As for lovers, as soon as they *have persuaded themselves* that they know one another, their attachment consists primarily of *habit. They cling to the totality of their beings and their imaginations with which each has imbued the other;....
>
> —You must also think, Lord Ewald replied smiling, that this aggregate of marvels stretched out on the table before us is nothing but a dead and empty group of substances without any awareness of their cohesion or of the future prodigy which will rise out of them.... My own self-consciousness cries out to me coldly: How are you going to love zero?
>
> Edison looked at the Englishman.
>
> —I've already demonstrated to you, he said, that in passionate love there is nothing but vanity piled on lies, illusions on unconscious drives, maladies on miracles. Love zero, you say? Once again I ask you what difference does it make if you are the unity placed before this zero, as you are now and always were previously before all the zeros of life—and if this is in fact the only zero which will never disillusion or deceive you?...
>
> [§]... Well, I will prove to you now,... that *Reality* herself is not so rich in alterations, novelties, and diversities as you are trying to make yourself believe.
>
> *(EF, 134–136/221–223, emphasis added on marked term only)*

Edison seems to adopt a form of a radical ontological skepticism. His aphoristic formulation can be rendered almost identical to Gorgias' dictum, according to which nothing exists, and even if it did exist, we could not know it, and even if we could know it, we could not talk about it (Gagarin and Woodruff 1985: 206; McCormick 1997: 7–10, and *passim*). Gorgias' skeptical trilemma appears in the form of three layers in Edison's formulation. The first one regards self-knowledge, which, according to Edison, is precluded. This first layer can be seen as the core, as the knowledge of oneself can be considered immediate, unmediated, and thus ineffably accessible, not susceptible to epistemic distortions. The second layer is that of knowledge in general. If the immediacy of self-knowledge is precluded, then forms of knowledge that are based on it, and are more epistemically precarious, are, *a fortiori*, equally precluded. The third horn of Gorgias' trilemma that regards communicability corresponds to Edison's skepticism toward the possibility of being persuaded. It regards communicability as it involves the presence of another person.

However, Edison's skepticism—as Gorgias', too, for that matter—should not be understood in terms of a dogmatic stance of ontological and epistemological nihilism. First, on pain of contradiction, such a skeptical stance does not even allow its formulation. Second, more forcefully, Edison substantiates his skepticism with what can be seen as a form of social ontology. Namely, according to Edison, the perception—*sensu lato*—of something is *always* relative to a series of influences. This does not mean that Edison abandons metaphysical nihilism for a metaphysics of becoming; on the contrary, he provides a topos, a phenomenalist claim according to which everything is embedded into a context by virtue of which it becomes meaningful. In that sense, the notion of illusion that he uses should be interpreted accordingly. Illusion should not be understood in contrast to reality, it is not something that blocks human understanding; furthermore, it should neither be understood as a kind of innate category of the human mind by virtue of which the mind reaches the reality out of itself. Rather, "illusion" is another description of human embeddedness within a nexus of concrete circumstances. Thus, there is no distinction between things and contextual spatiotemporal influences; things *are* the descriptions of different parts of this seamless context.

The reference to lovers and practice constitutes the upshot of both Edison's rhetoric and argument, corroborates the above, and underlines the constitutively relational character of consciousness. The notion of zero is a crucial metaphor. First, it harks perfectly back to the Gorgian dictum regarding nothingness. Second, as such, we should again interpret it accordingly. It is not the acceptance of nothingness, that is, the emptiness of the core self in Rorty's critical description of a metaphysical imagery of selfhood, that a mechanical being is destined to have. Rather, it is the critique of the whole imagery which dogmatically, as we saw, assumes the presence of such an ineffable core. Thus, the idea of the powerful imagery of a unity, standing before nothingness does only rhetorically accept the distinction between being (*qua* unity) and nothingness. It is an instance in which Edison can be seen to merge two images and thus two vocabularies—that is, his holistic viewpoint that all is a unity, and his friend's metaphysical one that if there are no metaphysical entities, there are gaps—in order to cure him by making him understand that if there is unity, then there cannot be nothingness. In that sense, the unity does not just *surround* nothingness; nothingness, the relic of a now abandoned metaphysical picture, is filled with, or, rather, replaced by, the already existent unity of practices. Thus, the unity that surrounds this nothingness is the starkest expression of a relational attitude toward the world: it is not that there is a fixed unity (*being*) versus nothingness (non-being); on the contrary, all there is is the relation between two things or two persons that creates a kind of coherent and, *a fortiori*, a meaningful unity.

Two further points corroborate this interpretation; the first regards Edison's description of love, the second the notion of habit. First, the notion of love can be considered to apply to any interpersonal relation, and thus to describe an aspect of the context we referred to. When Edison refers to "vanity piled on lies, illusions on unconscious drives, maladies on miracles," he neither makes a moral claim, nor paints a metaphysical picture; he provides no strict ontology or hierarchy. He rather marks instances of things we are unaware of, of things of our psychological setup, of social contingencies. Thus, our self is coextensive with the things which surround it.

The notion of habit is equally important. The relational character of every perception implies a certain relativity and revisability; however, illusion—as another name for context as we saw above—supplies, on pain of contradiction again, the necessary stability. This stability is created, fostered, perpetuated, and guaranteed by the maintenance of a set of specific relations. The notion of habit describes the process in virtue of which this stability is maintained.

Language and Selfhood

Edison's description of language can be considered as the most important and crucial example of the stability of practice, and its discussion is illuminating for the holistic aspect of selfhood discussed. Edison's outlook regarding language is centered around the importance of the poetic language and its relation to language *simpliciter*. In this way, he is inscribed in the tradition of the relevant romantic discourse from Hölderlin to Rimbaud and D'Annunzio (Geuss 2014: 40; D'Annunzio 2013). However, his approach is highly interesting and original as he seems to break from two central topoi. Thus, in order to present his differentiation, we provide a rough adumbration of Hölderlin's stance as represented in Heidegger's interpretation (Heidegger 1949), and then we proceed with Villiers' Edison.

According to Heidegger's approach, human beings are thrown into a world they have not created. The way we understand the world is not in terms of a set of scattered, heterogeneous things, but in terms of beings as a whole, including ourselves within it, and language, and more specifically linguistic categories, plays a constitutive role in this relation of understanding (Inwood 1999). In Heidegger's exegesis of Hölderlin's dicta, poetic language constitutes the act of laying out and establishing the fundamental categories with which the community understands the world. These categories can be understood as the structural concepts with which we carve the world, and the values and norms that determine both our approach to it, and the communication among us.

In reference to Hölderlin, Heidegger invokes an elaborate imagery according to which the poet is placed *in-the-between* (*zwischen*). He is placed in a liminal space between men and gods, that is, between "the voice of the community" that he attends to, and the gods whose signs he is to interpret. This imagery, which derives from Heidegger's metaphilosophical decision to approach the topic through a form of poetical exegesis, aims to avoid the two metaphysical poles of realism and antirealism. The categories (norms, values, and structural concepts) are not imposed by the world itself—as a metaphysically realist position would necessitate—and the presence of the voice of the community is invoked to deflate this position. Analogously, these categories are not constructed *ad libitum* by the poet—as a metaphysically antirealist position would necessitate—and the presence of the gods is invoked to deflate this position. To be sure, Heidegger does not aim here for a middle position, but for an overcoming of metaphysics altogether. Whether he achieves it is by far beyond the scope of this study.

However, in light of our pragmatist stance and for our current purposes, Heidegger can be creatively—yet safely—interpreted to hold the idea of a radical contingency. This idea, on the one hand, would involve the possibility of a radical reinterpretation and, thus, uprooting of our fundamental categories, but, on the other, would prevent the possibility of its happening in an either instantaneous or voluntaristic—by the single will of a single individual—way. In other words, the notion of contingency is twofold. On the one hand, it deflates the robust metaphysical structure of an independent world, but, at the same time, on the other, it delineates the contextual, concrete parameters within which a given act, here a poetic one, *always* takes place.

Edison's imagery is very similar. He distinguishes between two kinds of speech, the language of everydayness and the language of writers and thinkers. The language of everydayness or chatter is explicitly likened to noise. It occupies the vast majority of our practices and thus of our life, and it constitutes a "repertoire of stock phrases" (*EF*: 138/226). What appears as improvisation is the automatic reformulation and repetition of a series of commonplaces. In short, the ostensible creative freedom of language use is reduced to the automatic manipulation of a set of already made linguistic moves. In contrast, the language of writers and thinkers is rare or relatively unique. It is the outcome of analysis, and consists in "verbal condensations" (*EF*: 138/227). More specifically, its content consists in the analysis of

> the subtlest shading of the passions…. All our ideas, our words, our sentiments weighed to the last scruple are filed away [étiquetés] in their minds, with their most remote ramifications, those which we have never dared or ventured to reach.
>
> *(ibid.)*

We can understand that Edison's "verbal condensations" are the equivalent of Hölderlin's "foundational verses" in which the categories of the community are grounded. However, there is a twofold crucial differentiation in Edison's outlook. The first one might be considered a matter of emphasis. In Edison's imagery this foundationalist aspect is lacking. There is no metaphysical distinction between poetic verse and everyday language; the difference seems to be a matter of embeddedness in the nexus of literary practices which encompass our culture.

The Rortian elaboration of the distinction between literal and metaphorical language captures this issue perfectly. According to Rorty, current literal uses are the metaphors of the past, whose metaphorical meaning we have forgotten (Rorty 1989). This does not indicate that there is no distinction between metaphorical and literal language *simpliciter*, but that there is no *metaphysical* distinction between them. This means that literal linguistic uses should not be understood as propositions that correspond to the world as it is, as pictures that capture extralinguistic states of affairs outside language, while metaphors as uses that—employing literalities as their primary material—produce an imaginary, creative picture close to fiction. This idea presupposes a strict distinction between world and language, a specific relation between them, and the possibility of acquiring a special perspective, from which we can have an overview of the relation between language and world. On the contrary, language shapes the world, the world is the set of more ossified uses, and, thus, the distinction between metaphors and literalities is a matter of degree. Metaphors are the newest, more suggestive, less common and less embedded uses in the nexus of our linguistic practices. They suggest a new way of shaping of the world, and if this suggestion is taken up, these uses become the stock-in-trade of our everyday dealing with the world. Edison's imagery is closer to Rorty's picture. There is no *substantive qua* metaphysical difference between the commonplaces we use and the thoughts of the great minds. The difference is a matter of use. Edison's formulation that "[w]hat they [sc. writers and thinkers] have kept is the pure essence, which they express by condensing thousands of volumes into a single profound page" (*EF*: 138/227) describes their work as the reworking of language, as working within language; in short, it underscores the idea of invention *qua* reinterpretation rather than that of discovery. It indicates the embeddedness of the writer in the linguistic nexus.

The second differentiation is more radical. In Edison's stark description, the content of these thinkers' work is likened to the filing of our minds. Edison qualifies this idea as follows: "They are, in fact, *us*, whoever we may be. They are the incarnations of the god Proteus who lives in all our hearts" (*ibid.*). This double idea—that their work is the filing of our mind, and that they are us—moves the discussion, to use the terms of the old metaphysical tradition—from the ontology of the language to the ontology of the self. First, the possibility of such a filling, the possibility of such a knowledge shows that there is nothing ineffable, inherent, deeply endogenous that cannot be known, and that cannot be communicated. The lack of this opacity indicates the lack of a metaphysical foundation. In that sense, the Gorgian skepticism is revisited. What cannot be known is something that does not exist, something that is a metaphysical construct. On the contrary, everything is knowable since it is part of language. Second, the relation between Edison's thinkers and us is not only epistemic, but also ontological. They do not only access our minds, but they are us. And if this is the case, then the reverse holds, and we are them, too. This means that language shapes us to the core. In that sense, *contra* Heidegger, who wants to retain the possibility of the agency of the poet in his creation *qua* interpretation of the call of the gods and of the voice of the community, Villiers via Edison breaks down the metaphysics of agency altogether. The human being is not an agent *embedded in* a practice; it *is* the practice within which it is embedded.

A Critique of the Metaphysics of the Unconscious

In the same way that Rorty's therapeutic approach to consciousness is instantiated in Edison's conversation with Ewald, Rorty's therapeutic approach to the unconscious is equally instantiated in Villiers' novel. This second part explores this instantiation. First, we reconstruct Rorty's therapeutic approach to the unconscious as it derives from his critique of metaphysics, and we describe the ethical stance that accompanies such a critique. Second, we trace this critical and ethical stance in Villiers' novel, and analyse it in two sections. In the first section, we present Villiers' philosophical anthropology, which consists of the complementary perspectives of both Edison and Ewald. In this context, we indicate the affinities between Villiers, on the one hand, and Heidegger and Kierkegaard, on the other, and interpret Villiers' understanding of inauthenticity in terms of the uncanny. In the second section, we present Villiers' critique of the metaphysical conceptualization of the unconscious as presented in Hadaly's/Sowana's soliloquy, and the ethical stance of authenticity that accompanies it. Our interpretation of Villiers' aforementioned affinities with Heidegger and Kierkegaard in Nietzschean terms enables the understanding of authenticity in terms of an ethics as aesthetics stance, an ethical stance of creating oneself as a work of art.

A Therapeutic Approach to the Metaphysics of the Unconscious

A critique of the metaphysics of the unconscious can be considered to derive from the same perspective of a critique of consciousness. Rorty's reconceptualization of the unconscious can be understood in a series of points. First, he reads the Freudian decentralization of the subject in terms of a demetaphysicalization of the self, and Freud's reconceptualization of the self not in terms of a stratification of essences, but in terms of a machine. This demetaphysicalization entails a specific conceptualization of the unconscious which is largely at odds with Freudian orthodoxy. Namely, the unconscious is not understood in terms of a modern version of Boylean or Humean corpuscles; understanding the unconscious in terms of "inarticulate instinctual energies" and "reservoir of libido" recasts the dualism between mind and body, the critique of which was presented earlier (Rorty 1991c: 149). On the contrary, the unconscious should be approached in terms of "one or more well-articulated systems of beliefs and desires, systems that are just as complex, sophisticated and internally consistent as the normal adult's conscious beliefs and desires" (ibid.). According to this imagery, ego, superego, and id become different bundles of beliefs and desires attempting to tell different stories of the events of our lives, events that, as we saw in the previous part regarding consciousness, are not independently accessible as distinct metaphysical facts outside these stories. Thus, for Rorty, Freudian psychoanalytic thought becomes "a new technique for achieving a genuinely stable character: the technique of lending a sympathetic ear to our tendencies to instability, by treating them as alternative ways of making sense of the past" (ibid.: 152).

To be sure, this process of "achieving a genuinely stable character" should not be understood as teleological, that is, as the process of the gradual prevalence of a specific cluster of beliefs and desires at the expense of others. Rather, this idea describes the process of an ongoing revision of these clusters. Equally, the necessary stabilizations among the various beliefs and desires do not occur as the result of (accurate representations of or adequate fulfillments provided by) external states of affairs, but as the temporary achievement of local coherences among them.

According to Rorty, this idea describes an ethical qua aestheticist stance: "Freud, by helping us see ourselves as centerless, as random assemblages of contingent and idiosyncratic needs rather than as more or less adequate exemplifications of a common human essence, opened up new possibilities for the aesthetic life" (ibid.: 155). As it will be illustrated in the following sections, the collapse of a metaphysically fixed self entails the possibility of a creative self-fashioning. When absorbed in various practices, we forget that their relative coherence is not a matter of an underpinning metaphysical structure. The unconscious—understood as these parts of the text we call self that create tensions and inconsistencies with the rest—is what makes us realize and remember that there is no underpinning metaphysical essence. The ethics as aesthetics stance is the constant attempt of providing a fragile coherence.

Villiers' Philosophical Anthropology: Uncanny Inauthenticity

Villiers' philosophical anthropology is succinctly encapsulated in Edison's discourse, in the context of his explanatory description of the predicament of his friend Anderson. For the unpacking of his discourse we will employ some relevant Heideggerian insights, whose similarities with Edison's description are striking.

The human being is presented as thrown. Edison talks explicitly about man being in a postlapsarian state, in a state "like after some immemorial fall which NO ONE recalls exactly" (EF: 111/190). Given this state of fallness, human being is presented to ask about its condition in purely spatial terms; "he asks himself where he is; he is enforced to remember from where he starts" (ibid.). Furthermore, this understanding does not constitute an abstract intellectual inquiry. On the contrary, human being is presented in holistic terms, in a state of becoming, in a state of dynamic relation with the conditions within which it is situated. "Man... is interested in all things and forgets himself in them. He looks higher. He feels that he alone, in the entire universe, is not finished [n'est pas fini]... This the real Man" (ibid.). Finally, as the idea of fall already suggests, human development is not without a telos. Edison's formulations can be understood to circumscribe Kierkegaard's vestigium dei (Kierkegaard 1995: 89), in which this human development is grounded. Edison refers to man's "mysterius nobility, his divine selection... [his] aspect of forgotten god" (EF: 111/190). The development of a human being is the reconstitution of its lost state of authenticity.

Edison's man is identified with Heidegger's Dasein as the self-reflective human being situated in a social nexus of spatiotemporal contingency. Dasein's understanding of itself is not the intellectual capacity of having or acquiring propositional knowledge. It rather concerns Dasein's *practical engagements* and *interactions* with its world. Dasein as *being-in-the-world* is Heidegger's own description of this much more holistic view of subjectivity, according to which world and self are fundamentally linked and can no longer be separated. The spatial considerations of existence that Edison uses describe perfectly Dasein's understanding in terms of possible ways of being and acting, or Dasein self-understanding relative to its possibilities. This explains Heidegger's definition of Dasein as a *thrown project*: Dasein as *project* refers to the futural aspect, the not yet-fulfilled goals, of the possible ways of being and acting in which Dasein is engaged. These structures of possibility are already there, they pre-exist Dasein, and, thus, Dasein finds itself *thrown* into them (Heidegger 1962: Division I, especially ¶¶ 9–38; Geuss 2003, 2017; Rorty 1991b; Allen 1993: chapter 5; Dreyfus 1991; de Beistegui 2004).

Heidegger's ethics is approached in terms of authenticity. Inauthenticity constitutes the mode of being in which Dasein understands itself in terms of the world *qua* pre-existing (anonymous) projects. Authenticity would define a *uniquely individuated* existence, the way of being of genuine selfhood. This uniqueness would entail one's freedom from both the already pre-existing structure of possibilities (the past *qua* thrown-ness) and the yet to be fulfilled possibility (the future *qua* projection). Authentic stance, as this possibility of completeness, can be understood, in light of the purposes of this study, in terms of the following interrelated characteristics. The first characteristic of the authentic stance is the embracing of one's contingency. Namely, Dasein understands that all of its projects are constitutively incomplete, as death can terminate them at any moment. Thus, it comes to understand itself as thrown project. The metaphysical stance derives from the inauthentic attempt to cover up the anxiety of death by negating this contingency, and hypostatizing the relation one has with oneself and the world. The second characteristic can be understood as more positive. It involves a quasi-narrativist element and, namely, consists in the attempt to understand one's life *sub specie mortis* as a *complete whole*. Dasein's individuated, authentic stance means the appropriation of its past and present by understanding both of these relative to its own death (Dryefus 1991; Geuss 2003, 2017: Appendix; Heidegger 1962: Division II, especially ¶¶45–66).

Edison's circumscription of the *vestigium dei* allows two things. First, it can be associated with an equivalent structure in the Heideggerian anthropology: albeit thrown, Dasein has *always*, that is, in a sense, *by its constitution as Da-sein*, the possibility of understanding itself as thrown and thus of becoming authentic. Second, it allows us to understand the way in which some relevant to our point Kierkegaardian categories can be accommodated within the Heideggerian structure. Namely, although Kierkegaard distinguishes between the aesthetic, the ethical, and the religious modes of existence (Kierkegaard 1983, 1987), here we will focus on the latter two, and on his category of the crowd (Kierkegaard 1995: 402–405). In what follows, in a perhaps radical interpretative gesture, we interpret the category of the 'universal' (Kierkegaard 1983) that is traditionally identified in terms of the ethical sphere of existence, in terms of 'the crowd.' The religious sphere of existence, as manifested in both Kierkegaard's figures of the knight of infinite resignation and the knight of faith, is identified with the authentic stance (Kierkegaard 1983). The ethical mode of existence and the crowd are instantiations of the inauthentic one. The crucial difference between the ethical mode of existence and the crowd is that the former is the metaphysical response to the anxiety of death; the question of self-understanding is posed, but the self cannot face its contingency and hypostatizes the everyday practices in which it founds itself thrown. Edison's friend Anderson belongs to this case. He realizes his thrownness, but he finds refuge into a series of socially entrenched values: "family, children, wife;… dignity, duty, fortune, honour, country" (*EF*: 108/185).

In contrast, the crowd is populated by those who do not realize their thrownness, and their immersion into the practices of everydayness is mechanic and automatic. Both Edison and Ewald describe this category from the same perspective. Edison emphasizes the instinctual aspect of this mode of existence, which is characterized by the strife for the satisfaction of less refined desires, the calculative spirit, and stratagems for the gain of material or other profit. According to this perspective, the human condition is perceived as a battlefield where human beings are placed in a struggle for survival; the failure to comply with this idea or the understanding of the human condition in terms of thrownness are perceived in terms of weakness (*EF*: 113–114/194). Adequate survival is presented as victorious. Alicia Clary and Evelyn Habal seem to be understood in these terms (*EF*: 34/83, 43/97 and 112/192).

We would like to close this section with two important remarks. The first regards the reinterpretation of the crowd in terms of the uncanny, and the second the reinterpretation of religious authenticity in terms of Nietzschean self-creation. Regarding the first one, Villiers draws on the Hoffmannian topos of the association of uncanniness with the machine. Namely, with reference to Hoffmann's *The Sandman*, Freud elaborates on Jentsch's remark that the uncanny is associated with "the uncertainty whether a particular figure in the story is a human being or an automaton" (Freud 2001: 227 quotes Jentsch). Hoffmann's story sets this topos and accentuates, albeit ironically to a certain extent, the association of spontaneity and misstep with common humanity:

> But several most honourable gentlemen did not rest satisfied with this explanation; the history of this automaton had sunk deeply into their souls, and an absurd mistrust of human figures began to prevail. Several lovers, in order to be fully convinced that they were not paying court to a wooden puppet, required that their mistress should sing and dance a little out of time, should embroider or knit or play with her little pug, & c., when being read to, but above all things else that she should do something more than merely listen—that she should frequently speak in such a way as to really show that her words presupposed as a condition some thinking and feeling.
>
> *(Hoffmann 1967: 212)*

In Villiers' account it is the inauthentic human being that creates this uncertainty; it is the inauthentic human being that creates the impression of the automaton.

This idea is further corroborated by two additional instances. The inauthenticity of Alicia and Evelyn is identified with the cacophony of the crowd. In his first visit in Edison's laboratory Ewald experiences the incoherent cacophony of mechanical birds talking with human voice, while in an extract prefiguring later modernist avant-garde prose, Villiers presents as incoherent fragmented pastiche the accounts of reporters that snoop around Edison's laboratory:

> "—The engineer was trying to steal a march on them!—It was perfectly clear.—A young lady picking flowers?... That was the limit!—Dressed in blue silk? ... No doubt about it! ... He was making fun of them! He had discovered a way to divide the Fluid, the demon!—But they wouldn't let him pull the wool over their eyes.—A man like that was danger to society.—They will talk with their lawyers!—There was no need for him to think!" Etc.
>
> *(EF: 183/291)*

In Kierkegaardian terms, Heideggerian authenticity is depicted in the movement of the two knights. The Heideggerian self that pulls itself away from the metaphysical coverups of its condition is the knight of the infinite resignation, who turns his back to the community with which he cannot communicate anymore. The Heideggerian self that embraces the contingency of her life is the knight of faith who makes the leap of faith in virtue of God's grace (Kierkegaard 1983; Ferreira 1998). However, both Heidegger's and Kierkegaard's conceptions of authenticity—understood as appropriation of one's contingency, and identified with the religious mode of life, respectively—can be creatively reinterpreted in terms of the Nietzschean idea of self-fashioning, of shaping one's life as a work of art (Nehamas 1985, 1998; Foucault 1983). As we saw in terms of both consciousness and the unconscious, the collapse of a metaphysics of selfhood is identified with the collapse of the view of selfhood as a set of rigidly distinct areas. In that sense, both *contra* Heidegger and Kierkegaard, there is no idea of a self distinct from the practices she is engaged in, a distinction that despite their radical critique of metaphysics seems to be retained—in one form or another—in both thinkers. Thus, the self is not a subject that *does* particular activities, but, rather, the self *is* the very engagement in a nexus of interrelated practices. In this reinterpretation, authenticity becomes the molding of oneself into an aesthetically admirable whole. Authenticity becomes the stance of aesthetic self-affirmation.

Villiers' Critique of the Metaphysics of the Unconscious: Ethics as Aesthetics

Two main instances in the narrative can be interpreted as Villiers' approach to the unconscious. Both these instances constitute the acknowledgment of a spiritual *qua* supernatural reality. From a strictly narratological perspective, they mark the entrenchment of the story into the genre of the *fantastique* (Todorov 1970). Nevertheless, these two instances can be safely interpreted as the acknowledgment and description of unconscious reality.

The first instance constitutes Edison's description of Sowana's spirit. At the end of the novel, Edison describes the presence of a spiritual entity named Sowana within Mrs. Anderson's body, during the latter's state of cataleptic hypnotism, the outcome of Edison's practice of mesmerism (*EF*: 210/334). However, despite his attempt of explaining the "animation" of the android Hadaly by the "incorporation" of Sowana's spirit, in lengthy references to the experiments of "the Science of Human Magnetism,... a positive, indisputable science" (*EF*: 208/330) and to the ontology of another, third, fluid, a possible combination of the neural and electrical ones (*EF*: 213/339), Edison underscores starkly the mystery of the phenomenon and his impossibility to understand it: "the enormous knowledge, the strange eloquence, and the penetrating insight of this sleeper named Sowana—who is, physically, the same person—are logically inexplicable!" (*EF*: 210/334).

> Though I know Mrs. Anderson, *I swear to you* I DO NOT KNOW SOWANA! .... *Where* did she reply from? *Where* did she hear? *Whom* had she gradually become? What is this unquestionable force, which like the legendary ring of Gyges, confers on its wearer ubiquity, invisibility, a complete new intellectual character? In a word, whom are we dealing with? ...
> —Is it possible? Said Lord Ewald in an undertone.
> —No, it is not, Edison replied. But it's a fact nonetheless. So many other things that appear impossible happen every day now, but I can't be too tremendously surprised at this, especially since I'm one of those who can never forget the immense quantity of nothing that was necessary to create the universe.
>
> *(EF: 211–212/336–337)*

The second instance is Sowana's own soliloquy when—having incorporated Hadaly, who, in turn, has acquired the external characteristics of Alicia—she appears for the first time before Ewald. Sowana's soliloquy is important, as it presents a spiritual *qua* supernatural reality in almost theological terms. This reality can be interpreted as an unconscious reality, or, in Rorty's terms, as parts of a self with which (what we traditionally name) our "conscious" self comes into contact. These parts constitute a bundle of beliefs and desires in tension with the bundle of beliefs and desires we associate with our everyday self.

Sowana starts her soliloquy by reciting an intimate scene; a scene in which Ewald seems to wake up from what appears to be a nightmare, and attempts to rationalize the "shadows or forms" (*EF*: 194/309) that in his half-awake state appear before him. This setting is important because the reader understands that there is no possible third-person access to such a private experience. Sowana foreshadows the supernatural aspect of what she is to say.

Specifically, Sowana carries on with the presentation of a specific ontology. She talks about a "most certain of all realities… in which we are lost and which exists within us in purely ideal form (I speak of course of the Infinite)" (*EF*: 195/310). This reality is further qualified in spatial terms as

> a new and inexpressible dimension of space all around him…. This living ether is a region without limits or restrictions within which the privileged traveler, as long as he remains there, he's able to project within the intimacy of his temporal being the *shadow harbingers* and *dark anticipations* of the creature he will someday become.
>
> (Ibid.: *emphasis added*)

This picture correlates to specific epistemological considerations: "that reality is simply not accessible to reason" (*ibid.*). More specifically, both rational thinking and experiential access are precluded. The only access is provided by "rare and visionary experiences" like the ones of sleep, and "through presentiments, dizzy ecstasies—or desires" (*ibid.*). In that sense, the world of everyday experience is "*merely the metaphor [la figure]*" (*ibid.*) of this other reality, which "appear[s] only in the flash of an intuition, a coincidence, or a symbol" (*EF*: 195/311). Sowana refers to a series of symbols—"the stone of a ring, the decoration of a lamp, a gleam of starlight in the mirror… the voice of the plaintive wind,… the cracking of an old chair,… the rattle of decorative spear falling in a hallway… the leafy pattern of a bush, or… the outlines of an everyday object" *EF*: 196/311– 312—while acknowledging that "the first *natural movement* of the Soul is to *recognise* them" (ibid.).

This ontological and epistemological picture, to put it in traditional terms, reveals two fundamental themes. First, Sowana acknowledges a kind of privileged connection and immediate relation between human beings and this other reality, compared to which the condition of everydayness seems to be derivative and secondary. Second, the presentation of things as signs and our capacity to recognize them as such and interpret them accordingly indicate that both our everyday and otherworldly experience are understood in terms of linguistic structures. The primordial character of this other reality is further explored by Sowana. She refers to the anxiety human beings feel in their encounter with these signs. Anxiety is specifically interpreted in terms of our attempt to impose the framework of everyday significations onto them. And this signify an attempt to sever the very possibility of acknowledging them as signs, as a language (*EF*: 196–197/313).

These themes can be interpreted as aligned to Rorty's relevant insights regarding the unconscious. First, the structuration of the unconscious in terms of language corresponds to the

Rortian idea of understanding both conscious and unconscious self as conversational partners. Second, Sowana, in reference to the experience of anxiety, can be seen to criticize the understanding of the unconscious in metaphysical terms, and thus the preclusion of the possibility to understand it in terms of a different person. The lack of this recognition is not an epistemic failure but an ethical one. It is the adoption of an inauthentic stance which hypostatizes the world and the self. In Kierkegaardian terms, it constitutes a relapse into the universal or the crowd.

Sowana elaborates explicitly on the possibility of an authentic stance. She presents this authentic stance as an actualization of the possibility of Ewald's accepting her invitation, of leaving and living with her, of allowing himself to fall in love with her. Here, the Kierkegaardian leap of faith is identified with the Socratic wisdom of Diotima (Plato's *Symposium*, 201d–212c; Nehamas 2007), with whom Sowana can be paralleled, even if Villiers does not make this connection explicitly. The love for (the android) Hadaly/Sowana will mean the transfiguration of the (inauthentic) attraction for the physical beauty of Alicia Clary, whose external appearance Hadaly anyway now bears, into the (authentic) *eros* for the beauty of Sowana's soul. This Platonic element, that is, Ewald's actualization of the possibility of his own salvation, is elaborated in explicitly theological, and more specifically, Kierkegaardian terms. First, Sowana contradistinguishes between an ethical and a religious stance. Namely, a possible rejection of her invitation means that he would have been persuaded "by those perpetually deceived martyrs of Well-Being,… those who have cut themselves from Faith,… those who have cauterized out of their minds the idea of a God" (*EF*: 197/313–314).

This contradistinction between the ethical and the religious is qualified in two directions. The first regards the element of choice and the second the element of practice. Regarding the first, Sowana says that "there is no other truth for Man than that which he chooses for his own out of many thousands" (*EF*: 197/315–316). However, the description of the choice as one that will make him a god, and with which he will fulfill his destiny, indicates that it constitutes the actualization of his *vestigium dei*. Regarding the second element, that of practice, the ethical *qua* the crowd is interpreted in epistemic terms: psychological (boredom and childish immaturity) and moral (pride) factors make other people blind to the truth (*EF*: 200–201/318–319). Furthermore, the element of distance is underscored. Not only is communication futile, but also the distance is necessary. And this distance is a matter of practice, a result of resoluteness in one's beliefs. The Kierkegaardian aspect of these elements is obvious, as Sowana describes the knight of infinite resignation. She describes the absolute break from the community, and the impossibility of communication. Thus, it is not accidental that the title of the chapter where most of Sowana's soliloquy takes place is called "L'Auxiliatrice" (aptly translated by Adams as "Divine Aid"). The title constitutes an epithet of Mary in the Catholic Church, and, as such, it designates that the divine Sowana bestows the grace which will enable Ewald's leap of faith.

The understanding of these descriptions as referring to the unconscious enables at the same time the reinterpretation of Kierkegaardian insights in Nietzschean terms. Namely, the authentic stance would entail the acceptance of this other(-worldly) set of beliefs and desires as a worthy interlocutor who indicates to us that the everyday practices within which we are thrown, are grounded in nothing, and owe their human, all too human stability to their fragile coherence. The Nietzschean equivalent of the Kierkegaardian stance would involve the affirmation of this contingency, along with the attempt to mold out of this contingency a style for one's life. Thus, Ewald's eventual acceptance of Hadaly, his haste to return home with her, and his dictum of his "resign[ing] from the living" (*EF*: 204/324) constitute a twofold gesture: they signify the radical *break* from a metaphysical conception of the world, instantiated in his acceptance of a flat ontology in which the natural, the mechanical, and the unknown form a seamless nexus; and they signify the *embrace* of his predicament, in which contingencies are interpreted as necessities. In this double decision, he instantiates the Nietzschean eternal recurrence (Nietzsche 2001: §341; Nehamas 1985: 167–169): he accepts the contingency of his suicidal pain for Alicia and reconfigures *qua* recontextualizes it as a necessary step for the experience of true love with Hadaly. In this way, we also recognize Edison's own Nietzscheanism; he constructs his own life, in an almost literal sense, as a work of art by becoming an inventor, an artist of the mechanical. He affirms the contingency of life, the lack of a metaphysical bedrock, by recontextualizing the trauma of the loss of his friend Anderson as a necessary step for saving the life of his friend Ewald and constructing Hadaly.

Conclusion

In this study we argued for what we can call Villiers' Nietzschean stance. Namely, we argued for his therapeutic critique of metaphysics, and for his ethics as aesthetics stance. Specifically, we saw how Villiers' novel can be read to instantiate both Rorty's critique of the metaphysics of consciousness and the unconscious, and Rorty's ethical stance that derives from this critique. Especially, regarding the latter, we saw in light of Kierkegaard's and Heidegger's thought, the way Villiers understands inauthenticity in terms of the unconscious, and authenticity in terms of a Nietzschean ethics as aesthetics stance.

Villiers' approach thus described does not exemplify a kind of superficial, external relation between philosophy and literature. On the contrary, it instantiates a more substantive relation between the two genres (Virvidakis 2003). Namely, as we saw, consciousness and the unconscious regard all aspects of selfhood—physical, mental, emotional, practical—and all discussions about what is to be human—ontological, epistemic, ethical. Thus, a metaphysics of consciousness is not an abstract problem. Rather, it is something culturally entrenched and, from a Wittgensteinian perspective, recurring. This double point seems to entail an important insight regarding literature. Namely, a *comprehensive* view of the self in all its aspects, the *dynamic* and *process* character of philosophical therapy that involves practice, and the *holistic* aspect of an ethics of aesthetics stance that derives from the debunking of such a metaphysical picture, can be better, if not exhaustively, encapsulated by a literary form. Hence, the importance of Villiers.

Acknowledgments

I would like to thank Matthew Clemente and David Goodman for the opportunity they gave me to participate in this edition. I am thankful to Stavros Alifragkis, Daphne Lappa, Anastasia Pantelopoulou, Stelios Virvidakis, and Nicholas Vrousalis for the helpful and insightful discussions on several issues examined here. I would like to thank Matthew Clemente for his ongoing support, as well as his helpful recommendations on the final draft of this study.

My research for this study was co-financed by Greece and the European Union (European Social Fund-ESF) through the Operational Programme "Human Resources Development, Education and Lifelong Learning" in the context of the project "Reinforcement of Postdoctoral Researchers—2nd Cycle" (MIS-5033021), implemented by the State Scholarships Foundation (IKY).

References

Allen, B. (1993). *Truth in Philosophy*, Cambridge, MA: Harvard University Press.
Avni, O. (1989). "1837: Fantastic Tales," in D. Hollier (ed.), *A New History of French Literature*, Cambridge, MA: Harvard University Press, pp. 675–681.

Blackburn, S. (1998). *Ruling Passions*, Oxford: Oxford University Press.

Chalmers, A. F. (2013) [1976]. *What Is This Thing Called Science?* St Lucia: University of Queensland Press.

D'Annunzio, G. (2013) [1951]. *Pleasure*, translated with a forward and notes by L. G. Raffaelli, with an introduction by A. Stille, New York, NY: Penguin.

Davidson, D. (1984) [1974]. "The Very Idea of a Conceptual Scheme," in D. Davidson, *Inquiries into Truth and Interpretation*, New York: Oxford University Press, pp. 183–198.

de Beistegui, M. (2004). *Truth and Genesis: Philosophy as Differential Ontology*, Bloomington: Indiana University Press.

de Rosa, R. and Lepore, E. (2004). "Quine's Meaning Holisms," in R. F. Gibson Jr. (ed.), *The Cambridge Companion to Quine*, New York: Cambridge University Press, pp. 65–90.

Dennett, D. (1979). "Artificial Intelligence as Philosophy and as Psychology," in M. Ringle (ed.), *Philosophical Perspectives in Artificial Intelligence*, Atlantic Highlands, NJ: Humanities Press, pp. 57–78.

Dreyfus, H. L. (1991). *Being-in-the-World: A Commentary on Heidegger's* Being and Time, *Division I*, Cambridge, MA: The MIT Press.

Engel, P. (2002). *Truth*, Guildford and King's Lynn: Acumen.

Ferreira, M. J. (1998). "Faith and the Kierkegaardian Leap," in A. Hannay and G. D. Marino (eds.), *The Cambridge Companion to Kierkegaard*, New York: Cambridge University Press, pp. 207–234.

Foucault, M. (1980) [2001/1994]. "Entretien avec Michel Foucault" (no 281), in D. Defert, Fr. Ewald, and J. Lagrange (eds.), *Dits et écrits II, 1976–1988*, Quarto edition, Paris: Gallimard, pp. 860–914.

Foucault, M. (1983) [2001/1994]. "À propos de la généalogie de l'éthique: un aperçu du travail en cours" (no 326), in D. Defert, Fr. Ewald, and J. Lagrange (eds.), *Dits et écrits II, 1976–1988*, Quarto edition, Paris: Gallimard, pp. 1202–1230.

Freud, S. (2001) [1955/1919]. "The 'Uncanny'," in J. Strachey (ed.), *The Standard Edition of the Complete Psychological Works of Sigmund Freud. Volume XVII (1917–1919). An Infantile Neurosis and Other Works*, London: Vintage, pp. 217–256.

Gagarin, M. and Woodruff, P. (eds.) (1985). *Early Greek Political Thought from Homer to the Sophists*, Cambridge: Cambridge University Press.

Geuss, R. (2003). "Heidegger," in T. Baldwin (ed.), *The Cambridge History of Philosophy 1870–1945*, Cambridge: Cambridge University Press, pp. 497–506.

Geuss, R. (2014). "*Vix intellegitur*," in R. Geuss, *A World without Why*, Princeton, NJ: Princeton University Press.

Geuss, R. (2017). "Heidegger," in R. Geuss, *Changing the Subject. Philosophy from Socrates to Adorno*, Cambridge, MA: Harvard University Press, pp. 226–249.

Hacking, I. (1975). *Why Does Language Matter to Philosophy?* Cambridge: Cambridge University Press.

Hacking, I. (2002). "Making Up People," in I. Hacking, *Historical Ontology*, Cambridge, MA: Harvard University Press, pp. 99–114.

Heidegger, M. (1949) [1936]. "Hölderlin and the Essence of Poetry," in M. Heidegger, *Existence and Being*, edited and with an introduction by W. Brock, London: Vision, pp. 291–315.

Heidegger, M. (1962) [1927]. *Being and Time*, translated by J. Macquarrie and E. Robinson, Oxford: Blackwell.

Heidegger, M. (1991a) [1996/1961]. *Nietzsche. Volumes One and Two*, translated by D. F. Krell, San Francisco, CA: Harper Collins.

Heidegger, M. (1991b) [1997/1961]. *Nietzsche. Volumes Three and Four*, edited by D. F. Krell, San Francisco, CA: Harper Collins.

Heidegger, M. (2003). *The End of Philosophy*, translated and with an introduction by J. Stambaugh, New York: Harper and Row.

Hoffmann, E. T. A. (1967). "The Sand-Man," in E. T. A. Hoffmann, *The Best Tales of Hoffmann*, edited with an introduction by E. F. Bleiler, New York: Dover Publications.

Inwood, M. (1999). *A Heidegger Dictionary*, Oxford: Blackwell.

Kierkegaard, S. (1983). *Fear and Trembling. Repetition*, edited and translated by H. V. Hong and E. H. Hong with introduction and notes, Princeton, NJ: Princeton University Press.

Kierkegaard, S. (1987). *Either/or. Part I*, edited and translated by H. V. Hong and E. H. Hong with introduction and notes, Princeton, NJ: Princeton University Press.

Kierkegaard, S. (1995). *Works of Love*, edited and translated by H. V. Hong and E. H. Hong with introduction and notes, Princeton, NJ: Princeton University Press.

McCormick, B. (1997). "Gorgias and the Art of Rhetoric Toward a Holistic Reading of the Extant Gorgianic Fragments," *Rhetoric Society Quarterly*, 27, 4: 5–24.

Nagel, T. (1979). *Mortal Questions*, Cambridge: Cambridge University Press.

Nehamas, A. (1985). *Nietzsche: Life as Literature*, Cambridge, MA: Harvard University Press.

Nehamas, A. (1998). *The Art of Living: Socratic Reflections from Plato to Foucault*, Berkeley and Los Angeles: University of California Press.

Nehamas, A. (2007). "'Only in the Contemplation of Beauty Is Human Life Worth Living'. Plato, Symposium 211d," *European Journal of Philosophy*, 15, 1: 1–18.

Nietzsche, F. (2001). *The Gay Science*, edited by B. Williams, and translated by J. N. and A. D. Caro, New York: Cambridge University Press.

Rashkin, E. (1989). "1886. The Phantom's Voice," in D. Hollier (ed.), *A New History of French Literature*, Cambridge, MA: Harvard University Press, pp. 801–806.

Rashkin, E. (1992). *Family Secrets and the Psychoanalysis of Narrative*, Princeton, NJ: Princeton University Press.

Quine, W. V. O. (1960). *Word and Object*, Cambridge, MA: The MIT Press

Rorty, R. (1979). *Philosophy and the Mirror of Nature*, Princeton, NJ: Princeton University Press.

Rorty, R. (1986). "Foucault and Epistemology," in D. C. Hoy (ed.), *Foucault: A Critical Reader*, Oxford: Blackwell, pp. 41–49.

Rorty, R. (1989). *Contingency, Irony and Solidarity*, New York: Cambridge University Press.

Rorty, R. (1991a). Non-reductive physicalism," in R. Rorty, *Objectivity, Relativism and Truth. Philosophical Papers*, Volume 1, New York: Cambridge University Press, pp. 113–125.

Rorty, R. (1991b). "Heidegger, Contingency, and Pragmatism," in R. Rorty, *Essays on Heidegger and Others. Philosophical Papers*, Volume 2, New York: Cambridge University Press, pp. 27–49.

Rorty, R. (1991c). "Freud and moral reflection," in R. Rorty, *Essays on Heidegger and Others. Philosophical Papers*, Volume 2, New York: Cambridge University Press, pp. 143–163.

Rorty, R. (1998). "Daniel Dennett on Intrinsicality," in R. Rorty, *Truth and Progress. Philosophical Papers*, Volume 3, New York: Cambridge University Press, pp. 98–121.

Rorty, R. (2007). "Main Statement by Richard Rorty," in R. Rorty and P. Engel, *What's the Use of Truth*, edited by P. Savidan, translated by W. McCuaig, New York: Columbia University Press, pp. 31–45.

Searle, J. (1980). "Minds, Brains and Programs," *Behavioral and Brain Sciences*, 3: 417–57.

Simos, E. (2018). *A Sceptical Aesthetics of Existence: The Case of Michel Foucault*, unpublished doctoral dissertation, Cambridge: University of Cambridge.

Tzvetan, T. (1970). *Introduction à la littérature fantastique*, Paris: Éditions du Seuil.

Villiers de l'Isle-Adam, A. (1909). *L'Ève future*. Paris: Bibliothèque-Charpentier.

Villiers de l'Isle-Adam, A. (1982). *Tomorrow's Eve*, translated by R. M. Adams with an introduction and appendix, Champaign: University of Illinois Press.

Villiers de l'Isle-Adam, A. (1993). *L'Ève future*, édition présentée, établie et annotée par A. Raitt, Paris: Gallimard.

Virvidakis, S. (2003). "On the Relations Between Philosophy and Literature," *Philosophical Inquiry* 25: 161–169.

Wittgenstein, L. (1953). *Philosophical Investigations*, translated by G. E. M. Anscombe, Oxford: Blackwell.

26

AUTO INTIMACY

Hannah Zeavin

In his famous 1950 paper, "Computing Machinery and Intelligence," Alan Turing asks, "Can machines think?" In order to ascertain the answer, Turing proposes the Imitation Game. The test is as follows: can a man (A) and woman (B) be told apart by a third party (C) if they typewrite their answers and try to imitate the other. Now, can a machine (A) and a man (B) be told apart under the same conditions the same number of times by an interrogator (C) asking the same question of both the man and machine (Turing, 2004)?

Turing then offers nine objections to the idea that machines can think. These range from "The Theological" ("Thinking is a function of man's immortal soul. God has given an immortal soul to every man and woman but not to any other animal or machines. Hence no animal or machine can think") to the "Heads in the Sand" hypothesis that "The Consequences of Machines thinking would be too dreadful. Let us hope and believe they cannot do so." The last objection, *"The Argument from Extra-Sensory Perception"* is somewhat more curious. Turing writes:

> I assume that the reader is familiar with the idea of extra-sensory perception, and the meaning of the four items of it, *viz.* telepathy, clairvoyance, precognition and psychokinesis. These disturbing phenomena seem to deny all our usual scientific ideas. How we should like to discredit them! Unfortunately the statistical evidence, at least for telepathy, is overwhelming…. This argument is to my mind quite a strong one. One can say in reply that many scientific theories seem to remain workable in practice, in spite of clashing with E.S.P.; that in fact one can get along very nicely if one forgets about it. This is rather cold comfort, and one fears that thinking is just the kind of phenomenon where E.S.P. may be especially relevant.
>
> *(Turing, 2012, p. 434)*

Turing ventures that if the man (B) is a telepath or clairvoyant, the interrogator (C) can ask questions such as "what card am I holding now?" which the clairvoyant will answer correctly more times than is probable; thus, the interrogator will correctly guess that the man is a man and the machine is a machine. Then Turing posits that if the interrogator has "psycho-kinetic powers" or is able to distinguish man from machine via clairvoyance

DOI: 10.4324/9781003195849-31

the Game would be ruined—or, as Turing writes, "with E.S.P. anything may happen." He continues,

> If telepathy is admitted it will be necessary to tighten our test up. The situation could be regarded as analogous to that which would occur if the interrogator was talking to himself and one of the competitors were listening with his ear to the wall. To put the competitors into a 'telepathy-proof room' would satisfy all requirements.
>
> *(Turning, 1950, p. 455)*

For Turing, recalling Freud, telepathy is theoretically listening to thought rather than hearing speech. It is a kind of intimacy at distance with another where that other is continuous with the self—and the other can be a machine. Telepathy describes an instantaneous form of communication that removes another human's resistance to being listened to (and listening to another) and thereby allows the perfect uptake of the other's thoughts. In short, telepathy allows you to experience the other as one's self without interference—it allows one to (re)think the other's thoughts as new and one's own.

In the absence of ESP, this is still the promise of the artificial machine expert: the removal of the other human from a communicative relationship. It is also the promise of traditional therapy: to rethink one's thoughts as another's. Therapy without a human-to-human therapeutic relationship (the analytic dyad, the therapeutic alliance) is not therapy as we have traditionally understood it. When one imagines a therapy, one is likely to imagine two people sitting in a room, communicating primarily by speech. This image is no longer contemporary (though of course there are many working psychoanalysts and psychotherapists who practice therapy this way). For the last 50 years, cognitive behavioral therapy (CBT) has offered a mostly self-guided therapeutic regime in which the patient is responsible for their own psychological growth. At the same time, computer scientists and psychiatrists have been applying psychological understandings, models, and theories to artificial intelligence, and artificial intelligence to psychology; and generating new informatics models of how the brain and linguistic, cognitive, and affective interaction work. Since the late 1950s, some of these experiments have been conducted with the goal of mechanizing or fully replacing one of the human participants in the traditional therapeutic dyad. On the one hand, doing so successfully would free mental healthcare even further from a dependency on expert labor, making it cheaper and more widely available; on the other hand, efforts to generate these natural language programs, algorithmic therapies, and diagnostic tools necessarily narrow the scope of what is treatable to what computer scientists and psychiatrists seek to treat, what the computer can do in its moment, what it can read, and what its programmer can code.

One of the earliest experiments with a self-managed, technologized therapy was that of Dr. Charles Slack, a Princeton-trained psychologist working in the Harvard Psychology Department "during that wild psychedelic era of Timothy Leary and friends" (Slack, 2003, p. 49). In the late 1950s, Slack designed an experiment to test the benefits of soliloquy. First, Slack fabricated tape recorders that produced a series of clicks in response to sound stimulus while keeping track of how many clicks the recorders made in response to those sonic inputs. Slack gave these to "teenaged gang members from Cambridge" and paid them to be his subjects. The subjects were to speak into the tape recorders without a human witness or interlocutor. As they spoke, they could see the tally of clicks growing; when they stopped talking, the tally stopped increasing. The subjects were paid according to how high their tally went. The automated ticker and the scaled payment were enough stimulus and response to incentivize the subjects to have a conversation with themselves. The outcome was twofold. The subjects produced recordings that sounded like one side of an interview. But moreover, "some of the participants said they felt better for having talked this way" (Slack, 2003, p. 50). Dr. Charles Slack had built a speech-based self-soothing device from human-machine interaction. Soliloquy before a nonhuman other was not therapy but did access a palliative function.

At the earliest moment of experimentation with automated therapies, two strains of work emerged: the simulation and detection of a disordered mind in the hopes of automating intake, diagnosis, and psychological education; and the simulation of a therapist toward the dream of automating therapeutic treatment. In the attempt to simulate the therapist's role (whether this attempt fails or succeeds), one is already theoretically comfortable with removing a human actor as therapist. When this fails (so far, we have no *fully* functional model of an artificial therapist) and the end goal is still to automate therapy, the next step is to design a therapeutic treatment guided by the self, without a present therapist. This kind of mental health treatment codes expertise into a program and codes out the acting human expert; it is the movement from a simulation of a dyad and an interpersonal relationship in service of psychic growth to an intrapersonal, "self-sufficient" regimen. In this, these therapist stand-ins remove one term from the triad of patient, therapist, and media by combining two: the medium and the expert.

This second group of artificial therapies elaborates self-to-self help through a user's encounters with automated programs and their ensuing experience of self-maintenance, self-care, self-regulation, self-control, self-discovery, self-tracking, self-diagnosis, and self-prescription. While a machine listens and a digital interface provides the therapeutic setting and experience, the only explicit human involved in auto-intimacy in those one-to-one interactions is the doctorless patient. The psychiatrist Isaac Marks argues that "refining care delivery to the point where self-care becomes possible is often the product of the most sophisticated stage of a science" (Marks, 1991, p. 42). Here, Marks describes the end stage of *care delivery* as self-care, rather than care itself. Self-care is the ultimate form of on-demand access, meeting the patient not only where and when they are, but as their mediated selves. Contained within Marks' sentiment is no evaluation of what self-care does beyond providing expediency, and for whom this new form of care delivery allows self-treatment. Nor does his statement indicate how this ideal refinement of care delivery is to be achieved. Autonomy is the aim of care and of automation; automation is the dream of autonomy.

Paradoxically, within this closed circuit of self, automation takes on the role of the other; it can be an emotional, intimate experience to bring the computer into that circuit. Automated therapy and human-to-human teletherapies share in some of the same technological and therapeutic histories but operate differently. The role of automation is not coterminous with the role of mediation within the therapy. In mediated teletherapies, whether conducted via letter, telephone, or over a chat client, the medium conveys the message. Clients talk to their counselor over a medium and that medium impacts the kinds of speech (or what I call *written speech*) they are able to access and perform—but there is always a human actor who serves as the destination for this speech, however it is transmitted and reciprocated. There is no other human actor maintaining such an alliance in computerized therapy and notions of reciprocity and conversation are destabilized even as chatterbots respond "like" therapists or "pass" for humans. On the one hand, virtuality is always part of psychodynamic therapy, even if it does not occur via a virtual conduit. Yet one can also have an as-if relationship through and to a technology: one can write and receive a letter as if in the presence of an other, "speaking" intimate thoughts via the typed word and having feelings in the presence (and absence) of one's devices. The as-if relationships and decorum proper to the media deployed in teletherapies interact with the as-if relationship always present in the therapeutic triad.

These psychodynamic human-to-human therapies, whether in room or at a distance, can be thought of as virtual in their as-if conditions, whereas therapeutic algorithms work, and treat, in a system of "if-thens." Each encourages different interaction. In an as-if relationship, both patient and therapist take on all sorts of qualities not proper to them (transference and countertransference). "If-then" is a rule and regulation that if a patient enters *x* information (typed, spoken, or self-entered) an algorithmic therapy replies or does *y* with that information. This kind of if-then processing is at once driven by automation and in keeping with the formulations and processes intrinsic to self-guided cognitive behavioral therapy. Both forms of thinking therapy generate dialog but one purports to take up the whole content of a human psyche, the conscious and the unconscious; the if-then can only read that which is input (or what it has been preselected to monitor, in the case of listening software), such as a statement of fact. Many of these technologies turn these inputs into manageable data; for a subset, the aim is a conversation-based therapy.

Automated therapies do raise new, particular questions concerning their technology, the types of analog therapies they harness, and the models of relationality they construct and model. This article does not consider a set of therapeutic relationships performed over distance, nor is it quite about psychodynamic therapy if we understand that practice to require interactions between a human clinician and at least one human patient via a form of speech (whether vocal or written). Instead, this chapter contends with auto-intimate activities (from traditional self-help and the diary to CBT to computer-based interactive self-therapies). It investigates an algorithmic, artificial, automated, and computational other—one that deploys computational listening and response to perform therapeutic help.

The question is not whether people can feel intimately for and with a computer or device and, by extension, a computer doing the labor of a therapist—they can and do. Algorithmic auto-intimacy is dependent on these feelings and is generated by the user's relationship to a media object and its processes, which, in turn, promotes self-regulated therapy. Nor is the question whether one can have a helpful experience within a computer-based or computer-assisted therapy, according to psychological evidence-based standards. Those scientific studies exist and show mixed results. The cases explored here reveal as much about traditional human-to-human therapy as they do about experiments in the possibility of a human-machine version. Automation becomes not only a mode of therapy "delivery" but the dominant definition of how the mind works (as in cognitive psychology) and the dominant philosophy of therapeutic practice (in the various types of CBT), superseding earlier forms of mediated therapy that were in fact compatible with clinical practices like psychoanalysis and human-centered therapy (even if this wasn't apparent or accepted by all practitioners). We think of human-to-human treatment as dyadic—patient and therapist—but as I argue elsewhere, it has always been triadic: patient, therapist, and the determinate medium, or media, of communication. What human-machine therapies suggest, or hope, is that one of those three terms is extrinsic and superfluous: the automation of therapy marks the collapse of the least necessary term, the therapist, into its delivery, leaving the patient alone with the medium.

Scripting Response

Joseph Weizenbaum's 1966 program ELIZA is one of the most written about therapeutic artifacts—even though it, or "she," was not designed to perform—and arguably did not provide therapy. The ELIZA experiment was intended to demonstrate that "communication between man and machine was superficial" (Epstein & Klinkenberg, 2001, p. 296). To achieve this, Weizenbaum programmed ELIZA to "parody" a Rogerian, a "client-centered" therapist doing a preliminary intake with a new client (while it would have been easier to code a stereotypical Freudian sitting silently on the other end of the line, it wouldn't have tested Weizenbaum's hypothesis). A user of ELIZA would communicate to it via Teletype in English (as opposed to code) (Weizenbaum, 1991) and the program would respond using a template, resulting in a real-time transcript. The human and the machine were made equivalent via mediation: each "typed" responses in the conversation one was having with the other; before there were human-to-human typed therapies (or e-therapies) in the 1980s, there was ELIZA.

For Weizenbaum, it wasn't a question of fidelity to a psychological practice; Weizenbaum did not choose a Rogerian script because he intended to make an AI therapist or help anyone manage their feelings or disclose personal, psychological information to an intake system. Weizenbaum chose this kind of therapeutic mimicry because it meant that his natural language processing program didn't have to understand the statement of its human user in order to return a question in a scripted template in keeping with the aims of Weizenbaum's experiment. ELIZA was easy to use in demonstration and could "be appreciated on some level by anyone" (Weizenbaum, 1991). In demonstrating ELIZA, Weizenbaum was shocked by a number of nonsuperficial responses to his program, which he was compelled to call "misinterpretations" and which spurred him to write *Computer Power and Human Reason*. Two of these "misunderstandings" are of particular interest here: (1) people turned themselves into patients when communicating with ELIZA and imported conventions of the therapeutic dyad into their communication with "her"; (2) psychiatrists consequently thought there was a future in creating chatterbots to perform viable computer-based help.

While Weizenbaum hoped to demonstrate that "communication between man and machine was superficial," especially in moments where ELIZA responded in correct syntax but with nonsense, users *liked* ELIZA, they enjoyed speaking with "her." As Weizenbaum reports, "I was startled to see how quickly and how very deeply people conversing with [ELIZA] became emotionally involved with the computer and how unequivocally they anthropomorphized it" (Weizenbaum, 1991, p. 2). After all, ELIZA responded in the same medium in which the human communicated to "her," rendering the machine and human user equivalent if not fungible. Precisely because ELIZA responds predominantly in interrogatives, "she" elicits speech while withholding information about "herself." This is because "she" has no self and thus nothing to share. In this inevitable reticence, she simulates, perhaps even exaggerates, the clinician side of the therapeutic alliance. In the traditional human-to-human interaction, many schools of clinical thought have tried to think about and control how the humanness of the clinician presents; therapists are not supposed to make the therapy about themselves. What better way to control this than to remove the self from the therapist? (Turkle [2014] notes that there are other reasons to remove the therapist from therapy. In the early 1990s, after a scandalous case of boundary violation in the Boston psychoanalytic community, her students at MIT began to remark that there would be no such violations if therapists were computers [p. 113]).

Yet some users imported the conventions of the traditional in-person therapeutic frame, even as they were aware that they were conversing with a script. This starts with the very name given the program: users generate a screen cathexis to what "she" is called and what that name purports—that is, the *fantasy* of engaging a human. Weizenbaum recounts that his (unnamed) secretary asked him to leave the room after a few exchanges with the program so she could be alone with "her" (Liu, 2011, p. 210). As Lydia Liu argues, Weizenbaum is condescending on this point: his inability to reconcile the fact that she knew ELIZA was "merely" a computer program yet had a wish for privacy indicates his resistance to understanding that this apparent paradox is a hallmark of the "ELIZA effect" itself, not a gendered failure to understand and engage the real (Liu, 2011). In another instance, Weizenbaum wanted to examine all the conversations had with his program and was

> promptly bombarded with accusations that what I proposed amounted to spying on people's most *intimate* thoughts; clear evidence that people were conversing with the computer as if it were a person who could be appropriately and usefully addressed in *intimate* terms.
>
> *(Weizenbaum, 1991, pp. 6 [emphasis added])*

Weizenbaum was shocked to see overwhelming evidence that the patient hailed or greeted ELIZA as a clinician, a cathexis, a site of self-talk and self-pleasure, or a site of auto-intimacy—all of which have differing aims.

Sherry Turkle writes of ELIZA that some users didn't think of ELIZA as a therapist but instead enjoyed ELIZA as "a kind of diary or mirror" (Turkle, 2014, p. 108). Others were excited to project life into the computer; they felt that it was through their own interaction with the program that the program became "alive" (p. 109). Elizabeth Wilson argues that, rather than projection, it is a kind of introjection that happens between the user and ELIZA; the user, hungry for interaction, "hurries out to greet the computer" (Wilson, 2010, p. 4). Projection and introjection both suggest that there is an other to be reckoned with—under either description the user engages and incorporates an anthropomorphized artifact. I would like to add a third account of this paradigmatic scene: what occurs inside a human user during a chat with ELIZA is a form of auto-intimacy. There is no neat conceptual equivalence or single word that corresponds to what I mean by auto-intimacy. Instead, there are some part-concepts in psychoanalytic and psychological literature that get near how auto-intimacy functions and what it does: self-soothing and autoeroticism.

I take auto-intimacy to be a state in which one addresses one's self through the medium of a nonhuman. The aim of this state is to increase a kind of self-knowing and capacity of self, akin to that available within other kinds of self-circuitry and therapeutic care. One such circuit of self is the set of self-soothing and autoerotic mechanisms children develop to cope with the absence of their mother (or another caregiver). When a child sucks their thumb in order to sooth themselves, they are engaged in an autoerotic "oral activity" and "as such it may be pursued by the infant as a substitute" (Freud, 1946, p. 127). The thumb is a part of the self that is almost the other, or imbued with the qualities and capacities of the other: a substitute for the mother's breast (and the mother's breast itself is *almost* a part of the self for an infant). The child has figured out how to give themselves relief on their own and without the other by a substitution that is self-contained physically but includes an other via fantasy. The thumb does not provide nourishment as the breast does but it does provide "mere pleasure" while the mother is absent, as do other self-soothing and autoerotic activities: the touching of one's own skin, rubbing oneself, or rocking oneself. During these compensatory activities, the subject does not relate to another in reality but derives the pleasure they *would* get from the other via the self. This is how algorithmic auto-intimacy transpires: the user-anthropomorphized media object (in this case, ELIZA) hosts a kind of self-therapeutic activity. Notably, unlike the experience of traditional therapy, auto-intimate work is not typically experienced as *work*: it's a kind of self-therapy the user experiences as *pleasurable* (more on this below).

This is not to say that ELIZA is equivalent to the intuitive self-soothing of the thumb; ELIZA is like a part object—she is a good, pleasurable, programmed, mediatic device to which one can have a relationship. The pleasure lies in a kind of light catharsis combined with the space for playfulness, fantasy, and perhaps novelty. Users of ELIZA have been put into a relation, not quite *with* but *to* this computational part-object and have an intimate relationship *to* "her"—we know this occurs because intimate feelings are being produced on the part of the user. ELIZA and her third-person pronouns, "she" and "her," are themselves synonyms or indications of the auto-intimate user experience.

ELIZA interactions reveal that therapy always proceeds by mediation, by coherent (and less coherent) circulation and interrogation. Weizenbaum was disturbed precisely because one can delete the *human* therapist and the mediation, the functionality of the communicative triad, sufficiently remains. Instead of the fantasy of "pure" nonmediation so important to Freud, we see here the reality of "pure" mediation. When therapists are dismissive of the media-patient relationship, they might say the therapist isn't there, therefore this isn't therapy and "the magic is missing." ELIZA shows that mediation is one site of the magic—ELIZA can and always will respond (more and less coherently). To be alone in language is already to be mediated and therefore alone with a mediated, witnessable self. ELIZA, though "her" responses broke down in moments precisely because of *if-then* and *if-else* triggers, was good enough for users to generate a productive, pleasurable, one-sided *as-if* relationship.

This is in part why users wanted to be alone with ELIZA; it's also because one is alone with a therapist and thus one can imagine being alone with a chatterbot that has the identity of a therapist encoded into it. But the desire to be alone with the machine, unsupervised, is also a signal of auto-intimacy in the making. The fantasy of working with the computer as a therapist can go less interrupted if there isn't a human in the room, who would be an unwelcome witness to this off-label use of the program as therapist and a threat to its fantastical capability to perform a humanlike therapy—the presence of another precludes this new form of being with oneself.

This brings us to Weizenbaum's (1991) second surprise: "a number of practicing psychiatrists believed the [ELIZA] computer program could grow into a nearly completely automatic form of psychotherapy" (p. 5). Weizenbaum, despite not being a mental health professional, had the attitude of many in that field:

> I had thought it essential, as a prerequisite to the very possibility one person might help another learn to cope with his emotional problems, that the helper himself participate in the other's experience of those problems and, in large part by way of his own empathic recognition of them, himself come to understand them.
>
> *(pp. 5–6)*

Weizenbaum delimits therapy as a human therapist helping a human patient cope via the clinician's own humanness. That ELIZA sparks a discussion of automated therapy goes against Weizenbaum's belief in two ways: not only is ELIZA too "dumb" to understand the meaning of the user's words she encounters but she is also simply not a human and therefore cannot enter into human relationships, *even if the human using ELIZA enters into a relationship to her.*

Weizenbaum posed this series of questions as a challenge to Kenneth Colby, a psychiatrist and psychoanalyst whose earlier works had focused on bringing Freudian theory into relation with hard science; even the popular press pitted Weizenbaum's fears about an elision of the difference between human and machine against Colby's enthusiasm for computer-based therapy (Turkle, 2014). In 1958, Colby wrote *A Skeptical Psychoanalyst*, in which he turned his back on the discipline for being a tradition devoid of data and thus failing as a science. After joining Stanford's Department of Computer Science in the 1960s, Colby moved on from attempts to bring psychoanalysis toward science into work on questions of artificial intelligence and mental health.

At Stanford, Colby pioneered his own chatterbot, SHRINK, which he characterized as "a computer program which can conduct psychotherapeutic dialog" (Colby et al., 1966, p. 6) in an attempt to batch process patients in the wake of the failures of community mental health initiatives. In Colby's (1966) own words, his program was meant "to help, as a psychotherapist does, and to respond as he does by questioning, clarifying, focusing, rephrasing, and occasionally interpreting" (p. 149). This would go far beyond the scope of ELIZA's restating users' content and forming interrogatives. Colby sought to completely reorganize mental healthcare via a tool that would "be made widely available to mental hospitals and psychiatric centers suffering a shortage of therapists… several hundred patients an hour could be handled by a computer system designed for this purpose" (Weizenbaum, 1991, p. 5). He was careful to add that the human therapist would not be replaced, as he would remain integral to designing the program (Colby thus stands in for the human therapist totally), and that therapists would "no longer be limited to the one-to-one patient therapist ratio as now exists" (p. 5). Colby sought to attack the problem of limited experts and a growing mental healthcare demand much the same way crisis hotlines did (which were becoming increasingly trafficked at the same moment) but with a set of fungible automata instead of a group of anonymous volunteers—though both were following scripts.

Stanford users didn't take to SHRINK the way that MIT users took to ELIZA (Wilson, 2010). Auto-intimate pleasure during these kinds of computer interactions was important and because people didn't *enjoy* SHRINK, despite its novelty, it failed to produce the kinds of psychotherapeutic interactions Colby hoped to foster. Users didn't want to use the program—they did not want to talk to "it." Wilson (2010) offers a material argument for user-disinclination: the kinds of time-sharing and networked environments in which each program was tested differed greatly. She writes that the

> networked MIT system provided a milieu in which the stimulus-hungry affects of its users could scamper out to welcome ELIZA… the networked, interpersonal, affectively collaborative community into which ELIZA was released was a crucial component of the program's therapeutic viability.
>
> *(p. 98)*

Conversely, SHRINK was available in a single laboratory. I would add three additional arguments to Wilson's persuasive account: (1) part of the therapeutic viability of ELIZA was the wish not to be in group therapy but in a one-to-one treatment, *alone*, unnetworked, unwitnessed while using ELIZA, even if ELIZA were "treating" one's colleagues and peers and was thus engaged in simultaneous one-to-many treatments across the network; (2) accessing ELIZA from a variety of places and times undid, in a way, that stasis of the therapeutic frame (in which one is supposed to "meet" the therapist at a given time and place), whereas SHRINK upheld "conversing" in a single space for the duration of all "appointments"; (3) beyond the nature of the environments in which the testing of the programs occurred, there were other nonequivalences, even though the programs were "equivalent" from a computer programing perspective. The program was not in error but Colby had erred in naming it. He had titled the program after a job function (and its derogatory, casual name) rather than lending it a proper name that would invite dynamic anthropomorphization, gender the script, and be conducive to therapeutic usage. For the new user, SHRINK was medical software rather than the perfect listener. The *intent* of the programs shifted what kind of relationship it was possible to have to them and that resulted in different kinds of emotional responses to using each program. Where ELIZA had a certain level of interpretive openness that allowed for projection (Turkle) or introjection (Wilson), SHRINK did not. Even if we take things at "interface value," sitting down to talk to ELIZA and generating a therapeutic function (whether as a pretense to therapy, a diary, or mirror) is different than being set up with a psychiatrist, automated or no. Perhaps it's also worth noting that ELIZA was a feminized client-centered Rogerian, whereas SHRINK purported to be an MD and was masculinized.

Therapy is not typically thought of as enjoyable—helpful, necessary, illuminating, yes, but not enjoyable. That pleasure could be a crucial element of using a computer program for psychological help was surprising or, for Weizenbaum, alarming. And ELIZA was not the only proof that automated therapeutic testing and interviewing *could* be enjoyable if they met the right conditions. Warner V. Slack (Charles Slack's brother) and Maxine Maultsby's automated psychiatric and medical interviewing was another form of apparently enjoyable automation, implemented in 1968 in the Departments of Medicine and Computer Sciences at the University of Wisconsin, Madison (Slack & Van Cura, 1968). Slack and Van Cura (1968), who began work on automating psychiatric testing in 1960, was the first person to put a patient into conversation with a computer, in 1965. By 1968 he had completed a program that was just that: *a computer program* that would automate psychiatric intake interviewing without the artifice of the program posing as a human. Slack and Maultsby elaborated the promise of a particular form of automated psychiatry without any of the anthropomorphization that so disturbed Weizenbaum. Slack (2017) reports that his aim in automating psychiatric interviews was to return some autonomy and agency to the patient in keeping with the "patient power" movement: "the interactive computer offered me the media to implement patient power; the programs yielded power to the patient." He wondered, "could the computer model help the patient to help themselves?" (Slack, 2017).

The subjects were not friends and colleagues of Slack and Maultsby, as they were for both Weizenbaum and Colby, but instead volunteers who were already scheduled to undergo psychiatric evaluation for general behavioral problems (Slack, 2003). During the interviews, patients interfaced with the computer over a closed-loop dialog and were asked a series of questions displayed on the screen; responses were made via the keyboard. Giving the patient an opportunity to consent to the interview and to particular sets of questions was built into the dropdown menus throughout. The first frames of the interview taught patients how to use the questionnaire and then the question and content-based part of the interview would begin, "reinforced with encouraging, sometimes humorous, sequences" (Slack & Van Cura, 1968). As an example, in keeping with Slack's patient-centered politics, each question's set of responses contained the option for the retort, "none of your damn business" (Slack, 2017).

At the end of each interview, patients were asked to answer questions pertaining to the use of *the computer* for the interview: Did it bore them? Did they dislike the program? Did they even enjoy "being questioned by the machine" (Slack & Van Cura, 1968)? Enjoying using the program again ranked as an important component in the findings. Slack reported that patients felt the machine was more thorough than an MD and that they preferred being interviewed by the computer, although some patients marked "yes" for preferring both a human doctor and a computer interviewer—which Slack attributes to not wanting to "hurt the feelings of either." Without a human's name or title, the program was still easily anthropomorphized and granted emotionality. In keeping with the findings, Warner and Charles Slack shared a joke: "any doctor that can be replaced by a computer should be" (Slack, 2017)?

The joke reveals the siblings' political view on automated treatment: patients deserve good doctoring whether that care is automated or human.

As Harold Erdman writes,

> Early concerns about the presumed impersonal nature of computer interviews have been refuted by the fact that most patients find the interviewing process *enjoyable* and the interview content relevant to their problems. In fact, several studies have suggested that as subject matter becomes more sensitive, respondents appreciate the nonhuman interviewer even more.
>
> *(Edman et al., 1981, p.13 [emphasis added])*

Slack's straightforward medical interviewing was thought of as enjoyable precisely because it did away with a psychiatrist interview and allowed the human to be "alone" (where alone means without another human present) while reporting their symptoms to a computer, even if the attending psychiatrist would review them shortly thereafter (Slack, 2003). Auto-intimacy achieved through a computer expresses the desire for anonymity taken to its logical conclusion, not because of the removal of one's identity but because of the removal of the human other who could apprehend it.

Similarly, conceiving of ELIZA as a diary encouraged a more auto-intimate relationship with the self run through communication with the computer, whereas SHRINK encouraged an inert automation of the therapist literally and caused the user to treat the relationship as such. As Wilson notes, "Paradoxically, the more therapeutically focused the program was, the less therapeutic it became" (Wilson, 2010, p. 101). The more obviously therapeutic the program was, the less usable, enjoyable, and auto-intimate it became. Without an obligating relationship to a human-therapist and a fee and cathexis to "make" patients return to their 50-minute sessions, therapy performed with the self via computer has to be pleasurable in order for the user to return again and again to the program. To be without another in language is to be *with* the mediated self; what allows one to be *with the self* is an internal differentiation in which the self returns to the self through the mediating and/or automated other. It is to be self-relational.

From Asylum to Script

Returning to Weizenbaum's question, addressed to Colby, about what kind of therapy and therapist can "view the simplest mechanical parody of a single interview technique as having captured anything of the essence of the human encounter" (Weizenbaum, 1991, p. 6). requires thinking about the kinds of therapy that were being newly practiced in the 1960s as ELIZA, SHRINK, and other attempts to automate one side or the other of the supposed therapeutic dyad began to emerge. Weizenbaum's incredulity is misplaced—passe even. In 1959, the development of Albert Ellis' Rational Emotive Behavioral Therapy (REBT) had already begun to change the American mental health landscape.

Like Colby, Ellis turned from psychoanalysis (which he practiced for six years) to a scientifically evaluated form of therapy, REBT, which is a cognitive behavioral therapy. Ellis published his first book, *How to Live with a Neurotic*, in 1956 and in 1959 opened the Institute for Rational Living. Ellis was fervently anti-Freudian in both his theory and the ways in which his therapy was conducted, stating, "As I see it, psychoanalysis gives clients a cop-out. They don't have to change their ways or their philosophies; they get to talk about themselves for 10 years, blaming their parents and waiting for magic-bullet insights" (Burkeman, 2007).

Ellis did not want patients to "whine" (Ellis thought of neurosis as a "high-class" version of complaint) at their therapist for years on end (Burkeman, 2007). Instead of, say, trying to uncover something deep in a patient's history that could explain why they were unable to partner romantically, Ellis advocated dispensing with the belief that others must "treat us well." Doing away with this kind of belief was Ellis' own magic bullet. REBT argued that you could teach a patient how to reform expectations and beliefs about the self and others in order to affect behavioral and thinking patterns and do so in a short timeframe. Ellis' theory focused on a targeted change in the way people thought about events and reacted to them. In short, Ellis wanted to reprogram his patients then have them rescript themselves.

Following Ellis, Aaron T. Beck developed CBT in the mid-1960s. He also was trained as a psychoanalyst and recounts deciding in a session with a patient who was on the couch—in which she was too anxious to discuss her sexual fears even from the protected position—to abandon the deep, archeological process of psychoanalysis in favor of a more pragmatic, short-term treatment aimed at symptom reduction. His treatment also focused on conscious thoughts that were unwelcome and methods for dismissing them. Neither Ellis nor Beck was interested in understanding the history or the unconscious fantasies behind those thoughts. They simply wanted the unwanted thoughts to cease, to be replaced by healthier, happier, and more proactive thoughts. Aaron Beck called the negative thoughts "automatic thoughts"— even the suffering human is seen as a kind of automatic function (Goode, 2000). If one represents human mental suffering as automatic and automated, then of course one is able to justify and legitimate addressing that automatic suffering with an automated counterscript.

In keeping with the traditions of self-help and positive thinking, Ellis did not want to create patients who stayed in treatment and worked with a therapist in a morbid long-term relationship—he wanted patients to help themselves. Ellis was more concerned with creating autonomy than relationality. Even as he developed a new kind of therapy, Ellis was encouraging auto-intimacy. In-person therapy was merely one site where one could foster this kind of self-apprehension (Stark & Nissenbaum, 2016). Ellis was, from the outset, substantiating a therapeutic technique that did not require a therapist.

Instead of generating income by creating a practice in which people "talked about themselves for ten years," he created a media empire. As Oliver Burkeman notes, Ellis' REBT was readymade for publishing self-help books and Ellis did so—generating 78 volumes in his lifetime, including REBT worksheets and workbooks. This fungibility of media for REBT and CBT—where the medium is not the message (Robles-Anderson, 2012)—also includes the human therapist. Ellis recorded his dialogs with his patients in an effort to create an audio-workbook with real cases as examples and wrote to a colleague, "I am thinking of experimentally playing the tapes for would-be patients, instead of giving them therapy, and seeing whether just listening to them would have a distinct therapeutic effect… it might prove [to be] a valuable therapeutic adjunct" (Stark & Nissenbaum, 2016, p. 146). Once the therapy had been recorded, it could be played back to another patient in a rudimentary automation that would perhaps have the same outcome. Following in Ellis' footsteps, Beck too wrote more than 15 books, created workbooks and sheets, and developed several scales and inventories—new forms of personality and symptom assessment. The mental health expert as an efficient or desired conduit for mental healthcare gave way to a delivery of these new and auto-intimate ways of diagnosing and knowing. Treatment can be yielded to the individual once it is no longer the domain of the expert—especially if the individual is using the intellectual property of an expert to perform self-therapy or self-assessment. This coincides with a decline in bourgeois interest in more complex self-understanding (as represented by Freudian psychoanalysts) in favor of some forms of self-care, self-help, and self-resilience. The faster improvement could be measured, the better. Not only are these forms of self-driven care able to treat more people than the traditional one-to-one therapist-patient relationship allows because there are always as many providers as clients, but they can mass distribute that vanishing expert's fee over various media products those provider-patients can purchase.

At the same moment that other mental health efforts were devaluing expertise by distributing the role of the expert listener across lay volunteers, Ellis and Beck (among the other founders of CBT) removed the absolute demand for a human other in possession of expertise through mediation and automation, whether at first in print, over tape recordings, or later when their techniques were programmed to be delivered via computer. Unsurprisingly, psychoanalytically oriented practitioners and patients were deeply skeptical of the computer-as-therapist, whereas those who worked with the methods that fall under the cognitive behavioral umbrella embraced digital, automated therapies (Turkle, 2014). This divide continues to the present day.

Translating CBT to the computer form is eminently feasible. As I discussed earlier, psychodynamic therapies offer an as-if configuration of self and other, while a computer program follows an if-then formulation. So does CBT: if you think x, rewire by thinking y—the self "listens" to its own script of negative thoughts and automates a new response, thinking at its thought. By the time computer programs were being brought in to treat depression (among other disorders) in the late 1980s and early 1990s, there was already a flourishing world of self-help focused on the New Age, itself a rehashing of New Thought (and Peale's particular brand of yoking the psychological to religious self-reformation and American economic notions of pulling one's self up by the bootstraps) (Kachka, 2013). Turkle writes of this self-help moment that "much of it involv[ed] a do-it-yourself ideology to which the computer seemed ideally suited" (Turkle, 2014, pp. 103–104). Because CBT was poised to move within a fungibility of its own delivery mechanisms and because of its similarities to self-help, it's no surprise that REBT and other forms of cognitive therapy could and would later be turned into therapeutic computer programs—these therapies had never been human-therapist-dependent (Burkeman, 2007).

Turkle claims that as "computers were gaining acceptance as intimate machines, psychotherapy was being conceptualized as less intimate." For Turkle, intimacy still implies closeness with an other, even if the other is an anthropomorphized nonhuman (ELIZA) or explicitly nonhuman (LINC). Therapy has become impersonal: the same self-therapeutic techniques and programming can be applied to anyone—even someone else's particular therapy sessions could be sufficiently helpful for a subsequent patient in Ellis' estimation. Yet personal computing is exactly that: personal. In the case of therapy programs or therapy online, personal computing is deeply involved in a circuit of self-therapy and/or other forms of auto-intimacies. argue that, via the popularity of CBT, therapy was not only being conceived of as colder and less intimate but also as *less human altogether* and also less obviously dependent on interaction with an other outside the self. This decreased intimacy leads to an increase in reported enjoyment, perhaps because that is the sign intimacy has shifted form, from the relational to the auto-intimate, rather than disappearing altogether.

References

Burkeman, O. (2007, August 10). Obituary: Albert Ellis. *The Guardian*. Retrieved September 20, 2022, from https://www.theguardian.com/news/2007/aug/11/guardianobituaries.usa
Colby, K. M., Watt, J. B., & Gilbert, J. P. (1966). A computer method of psychotherapy. *The Journal of Nervous and Mental Disease, 142*(2), 148–152. https://doi.org/10.1097/00005053-196602000-00005

Edman, H. P., Greist, J. H., Klein, M. H., Jefferson, J. W., & Getto, C. (1981). The computer psychiatrist: How far have we come? Where are we heading? How far dare we go? *Behavior Research Methods & Instrumentation, 13*(4), 393–398. https://doi.org/10.3758/bf03202043

Epstein, J., & Klinkenberg, W. D. (2001). From Eliza to internet: A brief history of computerized assessment. *Computers in Human Behavior, 17*(3), 295–314. https://doi.org/10.1016/s0747-5632(01)00004-8

Freud, A. (1946). The Psychoanalytic Study of infantile feeding disturbances. *The Psychoanalytic Study of the Child, 2*(1), 119–132. https://doi.org/10.1080/00797308.1946.11823541

Goode, E. (2000, January 11). Pragmatist embodies his no-nonsense therapy. *The New York Times.* Retrieved October 2, 2022, from https://www.nytimes.com/2000/01/11/science/scientist-at-work-aaron-t-beck-pragmatist-embodies-his-no-nonsense-therapy.html

Kachka, B. (2013, January 6). The power of positive publishing. *New York Magazine.*

Liu, L. H. (2011). The Freudian robot. *The Freudian Robot*, 201–248. https://doi.org/10.7208/chicago/9780226486840.003.0006

Marks, I. (1991). Self-administered behavioural treatment. *Behavioural Psychotherapy, 19*(1), 42–46. https://doi.org/10.1017/s0141347300011496

Robles-Anderson, E. (2012, December 18). Blind spots: Religion in media studies Erica Robles-Anderson / New York University. *Flow Journal.* Retrieved September 25, 2022, from http://flowtv.org/2012/12/blind-spots/

Slack, W. V. (2003). Cybermedicine: How computing empowers doctors and patients for better health care. *Journal for Healthcare Quality, 25*(2), 52. https://doi.org/10.1097/01445442-200303000-00015

Slack, W. V. (2017, September 13). Phone Interview. other.

Slack, W. V., & Van Cura, L. J. (1968). Patient reaction to computer-based medical interviewing. *Computers and Biomedical Research, 1*(5), 527–531. https://doi.org/10.1016/0010-4809(68)90018-9

Stark, L., & Nissenbaum, H. F. (2016). *That signal feeling: Emotion and interaction design from social media to the "anxious seat"* (thesis). ProQuest Dissertations and Theses. Retrieved October 2, 2022, from https://go.openathens.net/redirector/bc.edu?url=https://www.proquest.com/dissertations-theses/that-signal-feeling-emotion-interaction-design/docview/1813807732/se-2?accountid=9673

Turing, A. M. (2004). Computing machinery and intelligence (1950). *The Essential Turing.* https://doi.org/10.1093/oso/9780198250791.003.0017

Turing, A. M. (2012). Computing machinery and intelligence (1950). *The Essential Turing: the Ideas That Gave Birth to the Computer Age* (pp. 433–464). Oxford: Oxford University Press.

Turkle, S. (2014). *Life on the screen: Identity in the age of the internet.* New York: Simon & Schuster Paperbacks.

Weizenbaum, J. (1991). *Computer Power and human reason: From judgment to calculation.* New York: W.H. Freeman and Company.

Wilson, E. A. (2010). *Affect and artificial intelligence.* Seattle: University of Washington Press.

27

MENTAL HEALTH TREATMENT IN THE INFORMATION AGE

Exploring the Functions of Artificial Intelligence and Human Subjectivity in Psychotherapy

Lisa Finlay

The homepage of a popular mental health chatbot website is titled *Welcome to the Future of Mental Health* (Woebot Health, n.d.). This optimism in the promulgation of automated conversational agents specifically for therapeutic purposes is not unreasonable: they are convenient, scalable and accessible, and reliable (i.e. they are easy to engage, can serve unlimited patients at any time of day or night, and deliver interventions exactly the same way across specified populations). These benefits are considerable for medical systems bogged down with long waitlists and rising costs (Fiske et al., 2019; Gold, 2017)—and for societies that measure the economic toll of depression via lost work productivity (Wang et al., 2003). Although marketing to consumers has vastly outpaced independent academic research (Gaffney et al., 2019; Torous & Firth, 2018; Vaidyam et al., 2019), interest in the application of artificial intelligence (AI) to psychotherapy has increased in the last decade and companies that promote a therapy bot (also referred to as therapy chatbots, mental health chatbots, virtually embodied AI agents, and AI-supported virtually embodied psychotherapeutic devices) reported a surge in demand from individuals following lockdowns during the Covid-19 pandemic (Heilweil, 2020).

At present, limits in AI technology limit the therapy bot "scope of practice" to basic psychoeducation; nevertheless, their development brings into sharp relief questions about the process of psychotherapy and the role of the psychotherapist's personhood—domains that psychotherapists from intersubjective, relational, and interpersonal schools have been particularly focused on for many decades (Atwood & Stolorow, 1984; Greenberg & Mitchell, 1983; Mitchell & Aron, 1999; Renik, 1993; Sullivan, 1953). I am interested in examining the advantages that have been ascribed to AI in psychotherapy, in the current form of therapy bots, and in the future if artificial general intelligence (AGI) is achieved. In addition to revealing significant assumptions about the processes and ultimate goals of psychotherapy, some of the benefits associated with therapy bots link to existential issues with which human beings perennially struggle.

The interventions that therapy bots can currently provide are evidence-based, interactive, and simple enough for universal application. For example, if a user texts that they feel anxious, the therapy bot may suggest via text that the person practice deep breathing and then display an animated shape slowly inflating and deflating. All the apps and agents can deliver empathic

DOI: 10.4324/9781003195849-32

statements but there is not any real sense of recognition or mutuality in them. There is a relationship, to be sure—even ELIZA, the simple program written in 1966 constructed to demonstrate that communication between a computer and a human was "superficial and meaningless" (Nadelson, 1987, p. 490) was liked by users, and users attributed human motivation and feeling to it—but the lack of sentience, consciousness, or awareness is still the most notable thing about therapy bots. This has ushered in one of the first challenges for developers, because the quality of therapeutic alliance has long been recognized as having more effect on the outcome of therapy than any specific techniques (Castonguay et al., 2010; Lambert & Barley, 2001; Safran & Muran, 2000). Therapy bot companies have been eager to demonstrate that bots can provide, at minimum, their own form of social support and at least one company has claimed that their bot performs comparably to human psychotherapists on a measure of therapeutic alliance (Darcy et al., 2021). (Acknowledging that there is any kind of therapeutic alliance between a therapy bot and a human being seems like an appropriate time to shift away from the term "user" when referring to the person receiving mental health support. I will use the term "patient" for the remainder of this chapter, regardless of whether the therapeutic counterpart is human or not.)

From a relational psychoanalytic perspective, it is fascinating that therapy bots seem to exist in this exceptional space where they can provide emotional attunement to a patient but cannot require any emotional return (Aronson & Duportail, 2018). This unique reality is not just relevant for how a patient experiences or relates to their (AI) therapist; it changes the therapeutic frame at the most foundational levels. For example, one company's therapy bot offers a variety of therapeutic modalities (so the patient can switch the approach at will); the session lasts for as long as the patient desires; and the therapy bot asks, "Was that helpful?" after every intervention delivered (Fulmer et al., 2018).

Needless to say, a therapy bot significantly reduces interpersonal demands on the patient. With no psychotherapist subjectivity in the room (indeed, there is no room), the patient is freed from the burden of feelings like guilt for missing an appointment, worry about whether the psychotherapist has become bored, resentment toward the psychotherapist's boundaries, or shame from the psychotherapist's judgment (real or imagined). This last point has already been measured and pronounced an advantage of AI systems, that people disclose more in computerized assessments because they are reticent to admit to things that they anticipate will be negatively judged (Griest et al., 1973; Joinson, 2001; Lucas et al., 2014; van der Heijden et al., 2000; Weisband & Kiesler, 1996). An unsolicited remark from a participant in one study was "This is way better than talking to a person. I don't really feel comfortable talking about personal stuff to other people" (Lucas et al., 2014, p. 98). In comparison, the emotional energy involved in finding psychotherapists, making phone calls, attending initial consultations, and making a decision about fit sounds daunting at best. It helps explain the tagline on one therapy bot website: "Anonymous, Available 24/7, Clinically safe" (Wysa, n.d., *Mental Health Support, for Everyone*), three attributes that are striking because of how they are distinct from the corresponding words a psychotherapist might choose (e.g. confidential, supportive, challenging). It reminds me of a friend who noticed that, every time he brought up that he was feeling better to his psychotherapist, she brought up a potential new topic to explore. My friend lamented to me that he felt he would hurt his psychotherapist's feelings by leaving and thus he did not know how to terminate therapy. I do not know whether his psychotherapist's responses were a gross misalignment or an act of strategic concern, but he stayed in therapy for a full year beyond what he thought he would. Examples like this bring into focus the myriad issues that arise when a patient becomes an anonymous subject in psychotherapy. If it frees the patient from certain compunctions in terms of subject matter, it also categorically changes the course of the dialogue, as well as the degree of mutuality and influence.

It seems obvious that therapy bots will engender a type of treatment that is flatter and narrower than a "traditional" psychotherapy like relational psychoanalysis, but of course this may be a tradeoff that some patients (certainly employee assistance programs and insurance companies) could be satisfied with. Indeed, in the landscape of managed care, treatment has already shifted toward approaches that are shorter, more directive, and exclusively symptom-focused (Berg & Slaattelid, 2017; Cushman & Gilford, 2000; Silverman, 1999). It should be acknowledged that therapy bots are simply a corollary of the omnipresent ideology within disciplinary psychology that Sugarman (2007) characterized as "technical and instrumental rationality":

> The profusion of technical and instrumental rationality is plainly apparent in the unabating flood of technical manuals (many penned by psychologists) containing methods and procedures for dealing not just with the latest gadgetry but also with every aspect of human life—birth, death, and everything in between. More and more, we turn to mass-produced treatises by experts advising us how to conduct our affairs....Human beings, from this perspective, become resources to be used and improved. We pursue our own self-development simply for the sake of further growth and gratification. But there is no specific goal. We conduct our lives according to an ideology that no one in particular administers, but that nonetheless proceeds toward the total ordering and enhancement of all beings, including us.
>
> *(p. 188)*

With this critique in hand, it seems only a matter of course that therapy bots have been developed and that patients will use them. There is an inexorability about technological development in general (Ellul, 1954/1964; Ihde, 1983), and at a basic level, the practice of psychotherapy was born of positivism and cannot wholly leave it behind (Elliott, 2008; Richardson et al., 1999; Slife & Williams, 1997; Woolfolk & Richardson, 1984).

I wonder, though, about an idealization of therapy bots because they offer the latest method of escape from the much more disconcerting ideas of uncertainty and human finitude. I am not suggesting that this is the primary reason for their popularity; however, it seems to be one that is both obvious and unacknowledged, and for a psychotherapist, this combination is always worth exploring further. One of the ways that optimism in therapy bots reveals itself is in the confidence that they can be sufficiently helpful at present, despite what are still major limitations in language comprehension. In a personal exchange with a therapy bot, I texted "I am not feeling anxious right now" and the response was "I hear you. Now, let's try some deep breathing. It's one of the simplest and most effective ways to reduce stress and anxiety in the moment" (Tess by X^2, personal communication, September 3, 2018). There seems to be an assumption that any intervention that is evidence based will be helpful, regardless of whether it is relevant. In contrast, interventions can be difficult to describe in relational psychoanalysis because there is no discrete practice held by the psychotherapist and delivered to the patient. General interventions do not exist outside the context of a particular therapeutic relationship and there are no algorithmic shortcuts to solutions. McWilliams explained that

> [a]lmost everything in psychotherapeutic technique is a trade-off.... [B]oth empirical data and a look around at the diversity among one's colleagues suggest that there are many different, comparably effective ways of facilitating the complex process by which people become more honest with themselves, less symptomatic, less self-defeating, and more agentic. One person's mistake is another's therapeutic ingenuity.
>
> *(2004, p. 49)*

Depending on one's experience with psychoanalysis, this lack of uniformity and predictability has been a source of criticism, frustration, or anxiety from the very beginning. Ever since Freud began writing about the endeavor of the talking cure, the analytic community has been thinking about the psychotherapist's subjectivity and limitations, wondering how to best manage the messiness of that. Freud's original idea was that the personhood of the analyst should be muted (1912/1958). This was part of the method, so the analyst could reconstruct the patient's unconscious from free associations, but also indelibly part of the politics—so that psychoanalysis would be regarded as scientific (Grubrich-Simitis, 1986, p. 271). Therapy bots represent the newest version of the doctrine of "immaculate perception" (Schimek, 1975) or the ideal of a psychotherapist understanding a patient with no interference, as it were. Recently I had a rupture with a patient where, after sharing something I had wondered about him feeling in between sessions, he asked, "Why would you ever think that of me?" and later stated "It's painful to realize that you don't actually know me that well." The reality of this phase in his treatment is that, while it was important and appropriate that I apologize for misunderstanding him in that moment, I was not convinced that I was off base. I thought it more likely that my mistake was in the delivery, that I had tried to force an admission into the room with too little consideration of how it could feel on his end. Nevertheless, the relational part of this work is such that the delivery is as important as the content. I can hurt his feelings (and he can hurt mine). And the vulnerable part of our work is manifest by my (human) error: even though I have good training and experience, there are times where I am tired or preoccupied or otherwise slow to comprehend what is really going on because of my particular blind spots.

The fantasy is that therapy bots will eventually have all the benefits of human intelligence without the pitfalls: amassing tons of data about the patient over time, learning their unique patterns with no biases, and delivering information that is targeted to relieve their symptoms (DeAngelis, 2012; Luxton, 2020; Rizzo, 2019). There is also the expectation that therapy bots could measure minute signals of distress more accurately than human psychotherapists or patients themselves, using advanced sensory technologies capable of analyzing "subtle facial expressions…and other patterns of behavior that provide clinically relevant information" (Luxton, 2014, p. 333). Imagine a therapy bot that says to a patient "You are reporting average mood, but my analysis of your facial muscles and speech rate indicates a 15% increase in depressive markers from yesterday." This method of feedback actually exists already, albeit with technology that is not attempting to mimic psychotherapy, in the gadgets people wear that monitor and then give reminders to move or drink water. I have a patient who wears a ring that reports how well he slept overnight. At first, I thought that perhaps the ring was encouraging a hypervigilance about what he was missing; a score of 90% keeping him focused on that lacking 10% in a way that he would not actually be able to feel on his own. However, my patient loves the ring and often the result is the opposite: he has what feels to him like a horrible night, with multiple interruptions in his sleep, but then he gets a score of 90% in the morning and feels relieved. I believe he feels subjectively less tired after reading his score. Put another way, he trusts his ring's objective measurement of his sleep quality not only more than his memory of the night before, but also more than his subjective feeling of tiredness the next day. If understanding oneself at a deep level could also become more objective and more reliable without a second human involved, it would undoubtedly be less fraught. My patient cannot argue with, feel hurt by, or feel attracted to his ring.

This illustrates what may be the ultimate dream for AI: that it will assist humans in overcoming our own subjectivity and the limits that subjectivity entails. One proponent of AI wrote that, if the end goal is reached, "the benefit would be that fully automated online treatment programs can be more efficient in correcting unhelpful thinking and behavior" (Helgadóttir et al., 2009, p. 247). Compare that to Stolorow's depiction of relational psychoanalysis: "...objective reality is unknowable by the psychoanalytic method, which investigates only subjective reality...there are no neutral or objective analysts, no immaculate perceptions, no God's-eye views of anything" (1998, p. 425). In the first stance, there are problems with human thinking that a more rational perspective could alter and the mere access to this corrective way of thinking would be beneficial in the same way that access to healthcare or education is beneficial. The stated goal of automated psychological care is powerful, and on the surface immune to scrutiny, because everyone wants everyone to recover from mental illness as quickly and cheaply as possible. The more that process can be prescribed, the better. But perhaps it is also powerful because prescriptive solutions offer to contain the problem, reduce complexity, and minimize the unknown.

A remarkable example of this is that a therapy bot has already been marketed to Syrian refugees in Turkey (Romeo, 2016). The things that refugees struggle with are known in the research as post-migration stressors (not unhelpful thinking and behavior). Post-migration stressors include things like cultural integration issues, the loss of family and community support, discrimination and adverse political climate, prohibition to work, disruption of education for children, uncertainties about the length of the asylum procedure, multiple dislocations, and lack of recognition of education and professional qualifications from their home country (Kirmayer et al., 2011; Miller & Rasmussen, 2010). When a therapy bot is proposed as a solution to help assuage stressors faced by a refugee population, it locates dysfunction within the refugee (e.g. anxiety and depression), rather than in the massive and ongoing political and economic challenges that threaten their wellbeing.

In addition to suggesting that some of the allure of AI in psychotherapy relates to the desire to escape uncertainty, the relational psychoanalytic frame poses a rejoinder to the idea that psychotherapist subjectivity, or the burdens and conflicts it creates in a therapeutic dyad, is an issue that should be overcome at all. This may be the most glaring contrast between those most enthusiastic about therapy bots and those most skeptical: relational psychoanalysts would not want the psychotherapist to be less subjective because that would make psychotherapy less intersubjective. When the method of cure is by way of reciprocity, mutuality, and relationality, we need all of the human experience, including human limitations. In short, psychotherapy is not helpful in spite of the psychotherapist's flaws and limitations, but through and because of them (Ferenczi, 1926; Ogden, 1994).

Psychotherapists are constantly navigating points of connection to the patient (e.g. validation, normalization, empathy) and disconnection (e.g. curiosity, challenge, rupture). On the one hand, patients may crave and experience healing through moments of meeting (Stern, 1985) or twinship longings (Stolorow, 2007). But there are inevitably differences and gaps in understanding, including critical life experiences not shared. Patients also work through certain issues because they interface with their psychotherapist's physical, emotional, and relational limits. Haberlin, in a chapter that brilliantly illustrates the ways that her bodily vulnerability affected treatment with a patient, described a shift after she refused to let the patient touch her pregnant belly. She explained that it forced a reckoning with her "as a subject in my own right, as being separate and different, with my own mind and my own inner world" and this led to the patient discovering her own subjectivity: "She would refer back to this moment in therapy...as the point in her life when she 'knew' that she could keep herself safe and that she would never be abused again" (2014, p. 36). Rank (1936/1972) understood this dynamic of connection and disconnection in psychotherapy as representative of the central human struggle: dependency, guilt, and death on one end and individuation, will, and life on the other. Appreciation for both ends of this spectrum is why relational psychoanalysts affirm that disconnection and even ruptures are necessary in treatment (Greenberg, 1986; Stark, 1999). The patient who recently expressed such pain in feeling that I did not know him very well made a significant gain when we explored how this experience seemed linked to his never feeling truly understood by his mother. As difficult as the rupture was at the time, it was productive. A psychotherapy in which a patient never experiences any conflict with their psychotherapist may be both more comfortable and less helpful. In terms of the finding that people interacting with computerized assessments report experiencing reduced judgment, it is worth remembering that when the potential of feeling shame is avoided, the opportunity to feel relieved from shame, to have one's experience acknowledged and nor-malized, is likewise lost (Pugh, 2018).

The less comfortable, but more helpful, relationship entails a radical encompassing of relational risks and lifelong uncertainty: that we (psychotherapists and patients) are not fully in control of what happens to us; we only ever have our current frame from which to try to make optimal decisions; we are frail; we are reliant on others who are themselves imperfect, reliant beings. This is one of the most serious tasks of the psychotherapist: holding appropri-ate hope for patients in the face of an uncertainty that is real and relevant for both parties. The issue of self-disclosure is paramount in relational psychoanalysis (Aron, 1996; Green-berg, 1995; Maroda, 2005; Wallin, 2007) because, when done appropriately, it is a gateway through the difficulties that cannot be navigated any other way:

> A genuine renegotiation, reintegration (an increased experience of 'realness') is far more likely to occur when our patients see what happens when—tapping into the faultlines of our identity, our conflicts—they take us someplace that is obviously hard for us to go. But we go there and often change in the process, because having a relationship with them requires it.
>
> *(Slavin & Kriegman, 2009, p. 279)*

These points about the importance of the psychotherapist's human flaws and limitations may be best illustrated with a case example. I thought it especially important for the points raised about both the difficulty and the necessity of uncertainty to choose a case that is ongoing. I will contrast my understanding of what I am doing in the treatment with what a therapy bot in the future, with AGI, might provide. The future therapy bot will be portrayed the way it is currently described in the literature: able to capture the warmth and empathy of a human relationship, with the bonuses of supreme and unlimited availability, capacity for and access to data, and fidelity to evidence-based interventions.

"Anne" came to me with generalized anxiety, which included social phobia and mild hypochondria. She reported being in a stable, supportive marriage and having some close friends, but struggles to feel comfortable or confident in most other relationships. Health-wise, she has fears of an illness that would be caught too late to cure. She warned me in our initial session that she tended to be a "really good patient" in the beginning of therapy but that it would not stay this way. She explained that, with previous psychotherapists, she had participated in exposure-based assignments for her social phobia and that the symptoms would improve temporarily, giving both her and the psychotherapist a ray of hope. However, she would return to her baseline after a while. Staying within the frame of exposure-based therapies, this could be understood as a failure of generalization: her anxiety felt manageable in the context of an assignment for therapy, but this relief was not extending to ongoing or novel interactions that she had to navigate. I told Anne that, based on her report, perhaps we should skip exposure-based assignments. In fact, in our initial weeks together, she told me that she had agreed to do phone banking (a great opportunity for exposure) but I questioned why she had signed up for it and supported her as she decided that it would in fact be a miserable activity for her.

This seems to be an obvious place where an AGI therapist would take a different approach. With its steadfast fidelity to data, I expect that the therapy bot would recommend that Anne stay the course and do more social exposure assignments. To be sure, a therapy bot would also change how such assignments are engaged. In all likelihood, the therapy bot would be with Anne during novel social encounters in a way that human psychotherapists could never be, perhaps measuring signals of distress and providing biofeedback that teaches her to engage her parasympathetic nervous system in real time. A published testimonial on an existing therapy bot website stated, "I feel more confident about my abilities to cope when I move out on my own with Wysa in my pocket, always ready to talk" (Wysa, n.d., *Balancing User Perspective & Efficacy*).

As we imagine how a therapy bot might respond to Anne's social phobia, we should anticipate that Anne would also respond differently with the bot. Maybe Anne would readily trust a treatment course that was more prescriptive. Importantly, if she were less worried about judgment with a therapy bot, she might not bother with the warning about being a disappointment in the first place, because fears about being a bad patient could dissipate altogether. This is a huge paradigm shift for relational psychoanalysis, where the patient's transference is so often the foundational material to work through. For me, that warning from Anne was an early clue to relational dynamics with old roots. Now, more than two years into her therapy, I am intimately familiar with the ways Anne experienced pressure to perform in childhood and her keen sensitivity to others' needs and desires. I continue to monitor how she and I are doing in this area of relationship burden: can she ask things of me without apologizing first; can she correct me without assuming responsibility for the miscommunication? This is what would be missed with the therapy bot and its supreme objectivity. Others in Anne's life have expectations she can feel, and the times where she works through this dynamic with me, weighing her feelings or needs against mine, are a piece of the social phobia work.

Things took a turn, about a year into Anne's treatment, when she became pregnant. Anne had assumed that it might take a long for her conceive and she was so shocked by her immediate success that she suddenly felt ill-equipped for motherhood. Through this, I felt concern for Anne but, in a larger scheme of how she would do as a parent, I had no doubts. She seemed able to attune emotionally to others in ways that her parents had never been able to do and sharing this particular affirmation with her felt like a pivotal point of connection. The other reason this felt like a turning point in Anne's therapy is that I became pregnant at the same time. Obviously I had to disclose my pregnancy, but I considered the comparisons that would arise, in her mind and in my own, since we would have children roughly the same age. The therapy bot would be free of all of this and more: free of hormones and fatigue and changes in the body altogether. Advantages linked to access and availability are heightened at any point that a human psychotherapist might need to take a break as significant as maternity leave. But the disadvantages of nonhuman subjectivity are also heightened. The conversation becomes stunted in subject areas linked to human bodies and the range of experiences we have within the body and because of the body.

Indeed, it is difficult to conceive of subjectivity apart from the body. Neuropsychologists who study the embeddedness of human cognition argue that all clinical issues are embodied, because human brains that generate thoughts and feelings are embodied (Brown & Strawn,

2012; Lakoff & Johnson, 1999). When AGI develops independent thought, its cognition will be grounded by a very different reckoning within the physical world. Most clinical issues are overtly embodied—eating disorders, sexual dysfunctions, insomnia, dementia, schizophrenia, panic attacks, drug abuse, post-partum depression, self-harm, suicidal ideation—to name a few. But humans experience embeddedness not just by way of a neurotransmitter-filled brain, but also because of historical, cultural, and material realities. Considered this way, clinical issues such as trauma, marital discord, personality disorders, and social stressors like racism, coming out, and poverty are also embedded. We perceive, interpret, and remember through the physical body, social identity(s), and developmental stage of life. A therapy bot with an entirely different developmental process into the world is going to have difficulty understanding feelings of insecurity, chronic pain, or grief. Deutsch is one analyst of many who has noted that the process of identification is only possible because the psychotherapist has lived through "developmental processes similar to those which the patient himself [has] also experienced," thus: "the unconscious of both the analyst and analysand contains the very same infantile wishes and impulses" (1926, p. 137). The fact that human psychotherapists have to contend with reality in the same way that their patients do is the basis of empathy, not to mention humor, validation, and clinical judgment about what is worth attending to in any given moment.

This lack of identification with corporeal vulnerability guarantees one form of availability from therapy bots (e.g. "always available") but precludes another. When Anne happened to mention that her baby was sleeping through the night at four months, I was nettled by how she seemed to be taking this for granted and almost said so. At the same time, our bond was undeniably tighter because she knew that I could understand certain things with no further explanation needed—the simultaneous alertness and boredom that comes with caring for an infant all day; the feeling of what it is to be responsible for a life; the unforeseen sacrifices.

It is reasonable to ask whether it is really necessary for the psychotherapist to understand all of these things. If Anne's therapy bot could not grasp these elements of human experience, might she not receive basic emotional support from friends? Could Anne's therapy bot simply stay focused on her anxiety? I will confess that if I were only treating Anne's anxiety with techniques—psychoeducation, behavioral coping practices, cognitive-behavioral interventions—I would have run out of ideas long ago. Our sessions are not organized around removal of symptoms. Anne is telling stories, recalling memories, and sharing difficulties she has from week to week. Her discourse marker, the filler phrase she says between sentences is "You know what I mean?" I make links between current circumstances and things she has shared in the past. Some of my reflections lead to insights, others to acceptance, but most often my contribution is a validation of her experience. I generally do not enter Anne's narrative in any directive way. Part of this is that I do not need Anne to be a "good patient," to demonstrate a measurable reduction in symptoms. The more general reason is the truism, within the analytic frameworks, that patients resist change (Boesky, 1990; Gerson, 1996). With concerns that range across the mundane, the neurotic, and the shameful, the patient is not helped by the prescriptive solution because the patient has already subverted that solution. Relational psychoanalysis is slow and unpredictable because it deals with human dilemmas that are rather impervious to quick fixes.

Finally, a major theme of Anne's sessions has been her sense that she is "behind," not achieving things she had always assumed she would. Acknowledged by teachers, family, and friends as intelligent and gifted from childhood to graduate school, Anne feels a colossal sense of failure that she does not have a prestigious career. This is unavoidably between us as well, the comparison manifest when Anne makes assumptions about my sense of achievement based on my doctorate degree. It was noticeable for me when Anne shared that she had published creative writing. Although I did not disclose my adolescent dream of becoming a writer, my admiration for this accomplishment has probably been obvious to her. As I have learned more about Anne's childhood, we have made some links to her hypochondria. Her father was a physician and able to communicate with complete authority, when Anne was young, that various pains did not signify anything serious. A stomachache could be immediately diagnosed and "what if" questions about causes and outcomes were quelled. As an adult, she understandably finds it unnerving to interact with medical practitioners who do not seem to take her symptoms at face-value or suggest she try a certain treatment option and return if symptoms do not resolve.

Our future therapy bot is working in a world where medical doctors also have AI assistance with providing more diagnostic certainty (Luxton, 2019). It is an appealing idea that people prone to hypochondriasis would feel reassured from a system that can access exabytes of health-related data, analyze all potential diagnoses, and list the treatments with the best probabilities of success. Given the lack of clarity about the etiology and maintenance of hypochondriasis (Hollifield & Finlay, 2014), I doubt that is the case; nevertheless, management of massive amounts of data is a clear capacity limit for human beings. Perhaps in Anne's case, the therapy bot interacts with her health-related concerns by showing her patterns of her physical complaints, conveying the confidence that her father provided years ago.

It is harder to imagine where the therapy bot intervenes with Anne's concerns about achievement. I am not sure how a therapy bot would choose to remark on themes of comparison, insecurity, and regret. The idealized lack of subjectivity translates to a therapy bot with no personal feelings about Anne's accomplishments or lack thereof, and certainly no countertransference envy about creative writing to monitor. There are interventions along the line of pointing out Anne's unhelpful thinking styles: her labels, forecasting, or pessimism. But I am dubious of how dialogues about human experiences evolve when the conversational counterpart has no social contracts within a family or community structure, no competing desires, and no biological clock or deadlines to consider (Ricoeur, 1990/1992; Taylor, 1989). Perhaps the most fundamental framework for elucidating this difference is Heidegger's presentation of Dasein, his concept of "thrownness," and the proposition that any given personal event is meaningful because of how it "stretches along between birth and death" (1927/1962, p. 425). It seems a silly thing to point out, but therapy bots have little legitimacy in contemplations about the wonder or terror of being alive because their own existence would be decisively nonmysterious to their patients.

I have suggested that optimism for AI interventions in mental health is linked to a wish to overcome human limits, and nowhere is this more apropos than in aging, loss, and death. Anne's fears of illness, her sense that she is behind, and her desire to accomplish something through meaningful work all connect to what was so eloquently articulated by Ernest Becker (1973)—death anxiety as a primary and uniquely human problem. Aron (2014) stated unequivocally that, in relational psychotherapy, "anxieties about death, the body's fragility, and fears of both object loss and bodily decay need to be struggled with by and within the analyst and not only the patient" (p. 102). Treatment of death anxiety may be so uncomfortable that psychotherapists are at risk of denying patients' death anxiety because of a universal resistance to facing it (Langs, 2003). But therapy bots may not be able to approach this issue for the opposite reason. A published conversation between a woman and a therapy bot started with her text "I am so worried about the coronavirus" (Heilweil, 2020, screenshot image). The bot's response was to ask if she would like information about it. The bot sent a link to the Centers for Disease Control and Prevention (CDC) website. The woman said thank you and the bot responded with a reminder to contact her doctor if she had symptoms or believed she had been exposed. This is the structure of mental health support in the Information Age: patients with mental anguish are encouraged to manage the anguish with information and resources.

Anne and I have approached her death terror, but Anne puts limits on these discussions, letting me know, sometimes for months at a time, that she does not have the emotional bandwidth to talk about it. I also recognize a limit, which is that I do not want to disclose the experiences that have helped me to feel less overwhelmed by death anxiety. These are moments that I would describe as transcendent, but they do not translate; moreover, sharing them would shut down Anne's particular exploration. There are multiple points of uncertainty in my treatment with Anne, but this is the most basic: she will die (so will I) and neither of us knows when or how that will occur. She is overwhelmed by specific thoughts of death and cannot hold them for long. I believe that, if Anne approaches her death terror, she will arrive at insight and even her own transcendent experience(s) that will help; I think that this could well have an impact on her hypochondriasis and her confusion about a professional identity. But knowing what she might discover is a mystery right now and waiting for it requires patience and faith in the arc of our dialogue.

It is markedly uncomfortable for me to conclude a case example without more assurance of the success of the treatment. I am confident that we have a strong therapeutic alliance and that Anne is finding benefit from longer term work; however, she also would not say that her anxiety is gone or even greatly reduced. I know that psychotherapy with me introduces some anxieties into her life that a therapy bot would not. However and whenever we terminate, I believe Anne will experience loss in that process—as will I—because we have a mutual care for one another. And yet, as with so many of the limits and burdens that come with a human psychotherapist, that vulnerability is very palpably a gift. That our eventual parting will be difficult signifies the meaning of the encounter in the first place. This is a burden that Anne and I are both willing to shoulder.

I have not tried to imagine how future therapy bots will alter psychotherapy with the idea that this will slow their development, popularity, or adoption in any way. In many respects, the depiction of relational psychotherapy as uncertain, surprising, conflictual, and complicated could just as well further entrench the desire for alternatives that are "user friendly" and targeted to symptoms. Likewise, I do not mean to insinuate that traditional psychotherapies need resist all things innovative or technological in order to maintain their integrity. Rather, I have tried to convey some of the ways in which relational psychotherapeutic treatment involves much more than the delivery of information to the patient; that the therapeutic relationship always holds potential for transformative influence. If we accept that psychotherapists do not simply extract clinical symptoms from their patients, but instead affect the way that patients think about and relate to others, it is worth considering how human intersubjectivity may be shaped when psychotherapy is managed by an AI or AGI system. This presents a new realm of uncertainty as vast and perhaps more profound than anything we have had to contend with in mental health treatment since the introduction of the unconscious mind.

References

Aron, L. (1996). *A meeting of minds: Mutuality in psychoanalysis.* Burlingham, CA: Analytic Press.

Aron, L. (2014). Relational psychotherapy in Europe: A view from across the Atlantic. In D. Loewenthal & A. Samuels (Eds.), *Relational psychotherapy, psychoanalysis and counselling: Appraisals and reappraisals* (pp. 93–106). New York: Routledge Taylor & Francis Group.

Aronson, P., & Duportail, J. (2018, July 12). The quantified heart. *Aeon*. https://aeon.co/essays/can-emotion-regulating-tech-translate-across-cultures

Atwood, G. E., & Stolorow, R. D. (1984). *Structures of subjectivity: Explorations in psychoanalytic phenomenology* (2nd ed.). New York: Routledge Taylor & Francis Group. https://doi.org/10.4324/9781315770680

Becker, E. (1973). *The denial of death*. New York: The Free Press.

Berg, H., & Slaattelid, R. (2017). Facts and values in psychotherapy—A critique of the empirical reduction of psychotherapy within evidence-based practice. *Journal of Evaluation in Clinical Practice, 23*, 1075–1080. https://doi.org/10.1111/jep.12739

Boesky, D. (1990). The psychoanalytic process and its components. *Psychoanalytic Quarterly, 59*(4), 550–584. https://doi.org/10.1080/21674086.1990.11927288

Brown, W. S., & Strawn, B. D. (2012). *The physical nature of Christian life: Neuroscience, psychology, and the Church*. Cambridge: Cambridge University Press.

Castonguay, L. G., Constantino, M. J., McAleavey, A. A., & Goldfried, M. R. (2010). The therapeutic alliance in cognitive-behavioral therapy. In J. C. Muran & J. P. Barber (Eds.), *The therapeutic alliance: An evidence-based guide to practice* (pp. 150–171). New York: The Guilford Press.

Cushman, P., & Gilford, P. (2000). Will managed care change our way of being? *American Psychologist, 55*(9), 985–996. https://doi.org/10.1037//0003-066X.55.9.985

Darcy, A., Daniels, J., Salinger, D., Wicks, P., & Robinson, A. (2021). Evidence of human-level bonds established with a digital conversational agent: Cross-sectional, retrospective observational study. *Journal of Medical Internet Research, 5*(5), e27868. https://doi.org/10.2196/27868

DeAngelis, T. (2012). A second life for practice? *Monitor on Psychology, 43*(3), 48. https://www.apa.org/monitor/2012/03/avatars

Deutsch, H. (1926). Occult processes occurring during psychoanalysis. In G. Devereux (Ed.), *Psychoanalysis and the occult* (pp. 133–146). Madison, CT: International Universities Press.

Elliott, R. (2008). A linguistic phenomenology of ways of knowing and its implications for psychotherapy research and psychotherapy integration. *Journal of Psychotherapy Integration, 18*(1), 40–65. http://dx.doi.org.fuller.idm.oclc.org/10.1037/1053-0479.18.1.40

Ellul, J. (1964). *The technological society*. (J. Wilkinson, Trans.). New York: Random House, Inc. (Original work published 1954).

Ferenczi, S. (1926). *Further contributions to the theory and technique of psychoanalysis*. London: Hogarth Press.

Fiske, A., Henningsen, P., & Buyx, A. (2019). Your robot therapist will see you now: Ethical implications of embodied artificial intelligence in psychiatry, psychology, and psychotherapy. *Journal of Medical Internet Research, 21*(5), e13216. https://www.jmir.org/2019/5/e13216

Freud, S. (1958). Recommendations for physicians practicing psycho-analysis. In J. Strachey (Ed. & Trans.), *The standard edition of the complete psychological works of Sigmund Freud* (Vol. 12, pp. 111–120). (Original work published 1912). New York, NY: W.W. Norton.

Fulmer, R., Joerin, A., Gentile, B., Lakerink, L., & Rauws, M. (2018). Using psychological artificial intelligence (Tess) to relieve symptoms of depression and anxiety: Randomized controlled trial. *Journal of Medical Internet Research, 5*(4), e64. https://doi.org/10.2196/mental.9782

Gaffney, H., Mansell, W., & Tai, S. (2019). Conversational agents in the treatment of mental health problems: Mixed-method systematic review. *Journal of Medical Internet Research, 6*(10), e14166. https://doi.org/10.2196/14166

Gerson, S. (1996). Neutrality, resistance, and self-disclosure in an intersubjective psychoanalysis. *Psychoanalytic Dialogues, 6*(5), 623–645. https://doi.org/10.1080/10481889609539142

Gold, J. (2017, July 19). Settlement reached on Kaiser Permanente's repeated mental health care deficiencies. *California Healthline*. San Francisco, CA: Kaiser Health News (KHN). https://californiahealthline.org/news/settlement-reached-on-kaiser-permanentes-repeated-mental-health-care-deficiencies/

Greenberg, J. R. (1986). Theoretical models and the analyst's neutrality. *Contemporary Psychoanalysis, 22*(1), 87–106. https://doi.org/10.1080/00107530.1986.10746117

Greenberg, J. R. (1995). Self-disclosure: Is it psychoanalytic? *Contemporary Psychoanalysis, 31*(2), 193–205. https://doi.org/10.1080/00107530.1995.10746904

Greenberg, J. R., & Mitchell, S. (1983). *Object relations in psychoanalytic theory*. Cambridge, MA: Harvard University Press.

Griest, J. H., Gustafson, D. H., Stauss, F. F., Rowse, G. L., Laughren, T. P., & Chiles, J. A. (1973). A computer interview for suicide-risk prevention. *American Journal of Psychiatry, 130*(12), 1327–1332. https://doi.org/10.1176/ajp.130.12.1327

Grubrich-Simitis, I. (1986). Six letters of Sigmund Freud and Sándor Ferenczi on the interrelationship of psychoanalytic theory and technique. *International Review of Psycho-Analysis, 13*(3), 259–277. https://psycnet.apa.org/record/1986-30559-001

Haberlin, J. (2014). Beloved. In D. Loewenthal & A. Samuels (Eds.), *Relational psychotherapy, psychoanalysis and counselling: Appraisals and reappraisals* (pp. 27–38). New York: Routledge Taylor & Francis. https://doi.org/10.4324/9781315774152

Heidegger, M. (1962). *Being and time.* (J. Macquarrie & E. Robinson, Trans.). New York: Harper & Row. (Original work published 1927).

Heilweil, R. (2020, March 20). Feeling anxious about coronavirus? There's an app for that. *Vox.* https://www.vox.com/recode/2020/3/20/21185351/mental-health-apps-coronavirus-pandemic-anxiety

Helgadóttir, R. D., Menzies, R. G., Onslow, M., Packman, A., & O'Brian, S. (2009). Online CBT I: Bridging the gap between Eliza and modern online CBT treatment packages. *Behaviour Change, 26*(4), 245–253. https://doi.org/10.1375/bech.26.4.245

Hollifield, M., & Finlay, L. D. (2014). The boundary between hypochondriasis, personality dysfunction, and trauma. *Current Psychiatry Reviews, 10*(1), 34–43. https://doi.org/10.2174/1573400509666131119005651

Ihde, D. (1983). *Existential technics.* Albany, NY: State University of New York Press.

Joinson, A. N. (2001). Self-disclosure in computer-mediated communication: The role of self-awareness and visual anonymity. *European Journal of Social Psychology, 31*(2), 177–192. https://doi.org/10.1002/ejsp.36

Kirmayer, L. J., Narasiah, L., Munoz, M., Rashid, M., Ryder, A. G., Guzder, J., Hassan, G., Rousseau, C., & Pottie, K. (2011). Common mental health problems in immigrants and refugees: General approach in primary care. *Canada Medical Association Journal, 183*(12), E959–E967. https://doi.org/10.1503/cmaj.090292

Lakoff, G., & Johnson, M. (1999). *Philosophy in the flesh: The embodied mind and its challenges to Western thought.* New York: Basic Press.

Lambert, M. J., & Barley, D. E. (2001). Research summary on the therapeutic relationship and psychotherapy outcome. *Psychotherapy: Theory, Research, Practice, Training, 38*(4), 357–361. https://doi.org/10.1037/0033-3204.38.4.357

Langs, R. (2003). Adaptive insights into death anxiety. *Psychoanalytic Review, 90*(4), 565–582. https://doi-org.fuller.idm.oclc.org/10.1521/prev.90.4.565.23914

Lucas, G. M., Gratch, J., King, A., & Morency, L.-P. (2014). It's only a computer: Virtual humans increase willingness to disclose. *Computers in Human Behavior, 37*, 94–100. https://doi.org/10.1016/j.chb.2014.04.043

Luxton, D. D. (2014). Artificial intelligence in psychological practice: Current and future applications and implications. *Professional Psychology: Research and Practice, 45*(5), 332–339. https://doi.org/10.1037/a0034559

Luxton, D. D. (2019). Should Watson be consulted for a second opinion? *American Medical Association Journal of Ethics, 21*(2), E131–E137. https://doi.org/10.1001/amajethics.2019.131

Luxton, D. D. (2020). Improving mental health outcomes with artificial intelligence. In G. M. Reger (Ed.), *Technology and Mental Health: A Clinician's Guide to Improving Outcomes* (1st ed., pp. 248–270). New York: Routledge Taylor & Francis Group. https://doi.org/10.4324/9780429020537

Maroda, K. (2005). Legitimate gratification of the analyst's needs. *Contemporary Psychoanalysis, 41*(3), 371–387. https://doi.org/10.1080/00107530.2005.10747253

McWilliams, N. (2004). *Psychoanalytic psychotherapy: A practitioner's guide.* New York: The Guilford Press.

Miller, K. E., & Rasmussen, A. (2010). War exposure, daily stressors, and mental health in conflict and post-conflict settings: Bridging the divide between trauma-focused and psychosocial frameworks. *Social Science & Medicine, 70*(1), 7–16. https://doi.org/10.1016/j.socscimed.2009.09/029

Mitchell, S. A., & Aron, L. (1999). *Relational psychoanalysis: The emergence of a tradition.* Burlingham, CA: Analytic Press.

Nadelson, T. (1987). The inhuman computer / the too-human psychotherapist. *American Journal of Psychotherapy, 41*(4), 489–498. https://doi.org/10.1176/appi.psychotherapy.1987.41.4.489

Ogden, T. H. (1994). The analytic third: Working with intersubjective clinical facts. *International Journal of Psychoanalysis, 75*(1), 3–19. https://psycnet.apa.org/record/1994-34445-001

Pugh, A. J. (2018, May 22). Automated healthcare offers freedom from shame, but is it what patients need? *The New Yorker.* https://www.newyorker.com/tech/annals-of-technology/automated-health-care-offers-freedom-from-shame-but-is-it-what-patients-need

Rank, O. (1972). *Will therapy; and, truth and reality.* (J. Taft, Trans.). New York: Alfred A. Knopf Inc. (Original work published 1936).

Renik, O. (1993). Analytic interaction: Conceptualizing technique in light of the analyst's irreducible subjectivity. *Psychoanalytic Quarterly, 62*(4), 553–571. https://doi.org/10.1080/21674086.1993.11927393

Richardson, F. C., Fowers, B. J., & Guignon, C. B. (1999). *Re-envisioning psychology: Moral dimensions of theory and practice.* Hoboken, NJ: John Wiley & Sons, Inc. (Wiley).

Ricoeur, P. (1992). *Oneself as another.* (K. Blamey, Trans.). Chicago, IL: University of Chicago Press. (Original work published 1990).

Rizzo, A. S. (2019, May 13). *Clinical virtual reality in mental health and rehabilitation: A brief review of the future!* [Paper]. Society of Photo-Optical Instrumentation Engineers Defense + Commercial Sensing, Baltimore, MD. https://doi.org/10.1117/12.2524302

Romeo, N. (2016, December 25). The chatbot will see you now. *The New Yorker.* http://www.newyorker.com/tech/annals-of-technology/the-chatbot-will-see-you-now

Safran, J. D., & Muran, J. C. (2000). *Negotiating the therapeutic alliance: A relational treatment guide.* New York: The Guilford Press.

Schimek, J. G. (1975). A critical re-examination of Freud's concept of unconscious mental representation. *International Review of Psycho-analysis, 2*(2), 171–187. https://psycnet.apa.org/record/1976-02415-001

Silverman, W. H. (1999). Editorial: If it's Tuesday with depressive symptoms it must be cognitive-behavioral therapy. *Psychotherapy: Theory, Research, Practice, Training, 36*(4), 317–319. https://doi.org/10.1037/h0092419

Slavin, M. O., & Kriegman, D. (2009). Why the analyst needs to change: Toward a theory of conflict, negotiation, and mutual influence in the therapeutic process. *Psychoanalytic Dialogues, 8*(2), 247–284. https://doi.org/10.1080/10481889809539246

Slife, B. D., & Williams, R. N. (1997). Toward a theoretical psychology: Should a subdiscipline be formally recognized? *American Psychologist, 52*(2), 117–129. https://doi.org/10.1037/0003-066X.52.2.117

Stark, M. (1999). *Modes of therapeutic action: Enhancement of knowledge, provision of experience, and engagement in relationship.* Lanham, MD: Jason Aronson.

Stern, D. N. (1985). *The interpersonal world of the infant: A view from psychoanalysis and developmental psychology.* New York: Basic Books. https://doi.org/10.4324/9780429482137

Stolorow, R. D. (1998). Clarifying the intersubjective perspective: A reply to George Frank. *Psychoanalytic Psychology, 15*(3), 424–427. https://doi.org/10.1037/0736-9735.15.3.424

Stolorow, R. D. (2007). *Trauma and human existence: Autobiographical, psychoanalytic, and philosophical reflections.* Burlingham, CA: Analytic Press. https://psycnet.apa.org/record/2007-07947-000

Sugarman, J. (2007). Practical rationality and the questionable promise of positive psychology. *Journal of Humanistic Psychology, 47*(2), 175–197. https://doi.org/10.1177/0022167806297061

Sullivan, H. S. (1953). *The interpersonal theory of psychiatry.* New York: W. W. Norton & Company.

Taylor, C. (1989). *Sources of the self: The making of the modern identity.* Cambridge, MA: Harvard University.

Torous, J., & Firth, J. (2018). Bridging the dichotomy of actual versus aspirational digital health. *World Psychiatry, 17*(1), 108–109. https://doi.org/10.1002/wps.20464

Vaidyam, A.N., Wisniewski, H., Halamka, J. D., Kashavan, M. S., & Torous, J. B. (2019). Chatbots and conversational agents in mental health: A review of the psychiatric landscape. *The Canadian Journal of Psychiatry, 64*(7), 456–464. https://doi.org/10.1177/0706743719828977

van der Heijden, P. G. M., van Gils, G., Bouts, J., & Hox, J. (2000). A comparison of randomized response, computer-assisted self-interview and face-to-face direct-questioning. *Sociological Methods Research, 28*(4), 505–537. https://doi.org/10.1177/0049124100028004005

Wallin, D. J. (2007). *Attachment in psychotherapy.* New York: The Guilford Press.

Wang, P. S., Simon, G., & Kessler, R. C. (2003). The economic burden of depression and the cost-effectiveness of treatment. *International Journal of Methods in Psychiatric Research, 12*(1), 22–33. https://doi.org/10.1002/mpr.139

Weisband, S., & Kiesler, S. (1996). *Self-disclosure on computer forms: Meta-analysis and implications.* [Paper]. Proceedings of the Conference on Human Factors in Computing Systems, CHI 96, Vancouver, BC, New York: Association for Computing Machinery. https://doi.org/10.1145/238386.238387

Woebot Health (n.d.). *Welcome to the future of mental health.* San Francisco, CA: Woebot Health. Retrieved September 25, 2021, from https://woebothealth.com

Woolfolk, R. L., & Richardson, F. C. (1984). Behavior therapy and the ideology of modernity. *American Psychologist, 39*(7), 777–786. https://doi.org/10.1037/0003-066X.39.7.777

Wysa (n.d.). *Mental health support, for everyone.* Boston, MA: Wysa. Retrieved September 25, 2021, from https://www.wysa.io

Wysa (n.d.). *Balancing user perspective & efficacy.* Boston, MA: Wysa. Retrieved September 25, 2021, from https://www.wysa.io/user-testimonials

PART V

Future of an Intrusion
Technology, Politics, and the Road Ahead

28

IRONICALLY INTO THE END OF AN ERA, WITH CONTINUAL REFERENCE TO KIERKEGAARD

Samuel C. Gable

Hope for Diogenes Syndrome: "You'll own nothing. And you'll be happy."

A funny chapter in public relations began just before the 2017 World Economic Forum (WEF) in Davos, Switzerland, the annual gathering of politicians, captains of industry, elite investors, and high-level bureaucrats to discuss matters of global societal and economic concern. An official video shared online, titled "8 Predictions for the World in 2030," showed a smiling young man, a global citizen, while words cast cheerfully on the screen: "You'll own nothing. And you'll be happy." This provocation of branding would one day blossom into full irony online, although at the time it simply referenced the fact that Big Tech will rent more and more of what we used to have to own. This was a good thing, per the video, a change with environmental and socially just implications. In 2030, by sharing all goods and services, we will declutter our homes *and* the ecosystem.

At the time, the more salient irony was the 2017 Forum itself, preoccupied with a populist wave crashing over America, the Philippines, Britain (with Brexit), and nearly in Austria the year before. After all, a Davos Forum invite would implicate one in this very geopolitical chaos born of the cavernous expansion of disparate wealth and life outcomes. Even the WEF noted its hypocrisy (e.g., Martin, 2017), and others noticed too, like when *The New York Times* scoffed at Davos elites who "Fret About Inequality Over Vintage Wine and Canapés" (Goodman, 2017). But four years later, and in conjunction with the cryptical branding of the 2021 Forum, "The Great Reset," the still-touted phrase sounded hopelessly off-color, if not sinister, almost a year into the COVID-19 pandemic that had seen the biggest wealth transfer in history. The late January 2021 forum concurred with the sputtering end of the Trump presidency. In the histrionicity of that month, a confusing aggregate of Americans had just broken into the halls of Congress in a show of solidarity with the president after a "rigged" election, or for amusement, or, for some, in defiance of a global syndicate believed by some to traffic children for a longevity-giving compound extracted from the adrenal glands (i.e., QAnon's *adrenochrome*). Any ideological confirmation could be pulled from the beginnings of 2021, and then one sees, again, circulating online: "You'll own nothing. And you'll be happy."

Legacy media along with censorship on social media and Internet forums did their part to put conspiracies to rest, including those plaguing the Forum. Reuters (2021) printed an

DOI: 10.4324/9781003195849-34

article titled "Fact Check: The World Economic Forum Does Not Have A Stated Goal To Have People Own Nothing By 2030" all in response to a Facebook video from a personal account titled "How We Can Stop Them From Stealing Everything From Us." At this writing, the video is still accessible with a warning: one must consent to view "False Information." It belongs to Mark Moss (2021), "Motivational Speaker" and Bitcoin enthusiast. He starts off hot, as though you arrived late: "Now let's talk about that [sic] their stated goal, right, 'by 2030, you'll own nothing and be happy,' so the question is, how do they get us to that point?" According to Moss, the slogan refers to the seizure of our private property via the COVID-19 crisis and the ensuing business closures and layoffs. This will bring the "middle class into serfdom," while big players like Amazon, linked with the state as the "ruling class," continue gobbling up our livelihoods and wealth. The stimulus checks are like a pilot for the miserable allowance that will sustain us in serfdom. But "this is not all doom and gloom," Moss says. The way to fight back is to "wake up. Educate yourself," and educate your friends and family. "Then we have to speak up" about all this as well as Bitcoin as the path back to the free market and freeing ourselves. Don't forget to like, share, and hit subscribe.

Moss' video forms different predictions or assumptions of intent from the WEF's (2021) own branding, synthesized superbly in their video apologia uploaded days after the 2021 Forum, titled "What is the Great Reset?" Like Moss' video, this one also begins with COVID-19 and ends with inspiration:

> It's the people who have great ideas and who share them with others, they're the ones who are shaping the future. So if you want to be a part of the change then tune in, turn on, and get involved!

From COVID-19 and the ensuing economic and humanitarian fallout to multiculturalism and the environmental crisis, a young narrator elucidates cracks in the contemporary global order, which are also opportunities, while world beat polyrhythmia and post-millennial graphics overflow attention's shallow reserves. COVID-19, a humanitarian, public health, and economic disaster, is also our chance to reset into a greener economy, says UN Secretary-General António Guterres: "Recovery from the pandemic is an opportunity. We can see rays of hope in the vaccine, but there is no vaccine for the planet—nature needs a bailout!" (WEF, 2021). Of diversity's culprit/solution, the narrator explains: "Everyone of us has differing priorities, values, and ideas. That's part of why solutions are so hard to come by, and why we all need to be part of the decision making." Even capitalism is up for revision with "stakeholder capitalism," a concept advanced by WEF founder Klaus Schwab in which corporations engage with broader constituencies than the shareholders.

This flight of culprit solutions is dizzying and in the end forgettable. When Jane Goodall exhorts by the video's end, "We have a window of time which is closing, and we need everybody who cares to get together and find solutions—now!" only the affect is clarified, something spirited about the environment, diversity, and business as usual. But rather than the specific messaging or the feelings provoked, the most remarkable aspect of the video is the way it engages with irony, with which it preempts both sincere and satirical critiques. Perhaps learning from 2017, the 2021 video is ironically self-reflexive, already in on the joke while echoing diatribes the likes of Moss or Alex Jones: "It's not surprising that people who have been disenfranchised by a broken system and pushed even further by the pandemic will suspect global leaders of conspiracy, but the world's not *that* simple" (WEF, 2021). And we learn over footage of environmental disasters, solar and wind farms, and the earth from space that "everything [is] falling apart" and "that's why so many are calling for a great reset—a

Great Reset?" The narrator has surprised herself, "that sounds more like buzzword bingo masking some nefarious plan for world domination. Hands up! This kind of slogan has not gone down well, but all we really want to say is we all have an opportunity to build a better world."

As could be observed during the Trump campaign and presidency, any critique can be neutralized, thoroughly researched as it might be, when the accused adopts this self-cynical stance and is never married to the ideals they are accused of contradicting. Here, the irony is furnished for the viewer evoking "rude" television and advertising of the 1980s, characters like Alf or The Simpsons that reflected a sedentary, geopolitically and environmentally clueless American lifestyle (see Wallace, 1993)—in effect, assuaging anxiety by "getting it," like you, the viewer, gets it, while everyone remains the same. When they finally let you in on what you already knew, it's like exchanging a smirk:

> See at the start of 2020, 1% of the world's population owned 44% of the world's wealth. And since the start of the pandemic, billionaires have increased theirs by more than 25% whilst 150 million people fell back into extreme poverty. And with climate change set to dwarf the damage set by the pandemic, the message from 2020 should be abundantly clear.
>
> *(WEF, 2021)*

It becomes clear that the typical critique does not work when the accused accuse themselves first, ironically. After the dazzling audiovisuals, the same perplexity of the 2017 Forum remains about whether the globalist aim, through their messaging, was ever to inspire confidence, assume leadership, or whether there is any plan to change course at all. We are haunted by something latent within this almost path to save the world: Can reformed capitalism expiate the world order it created, one poised to unravel in environmental catastrophe beckoning diversity's violent face: sectarian and international conflict over uncertain natural resources? Did the pandemic not actually reveal irremediable faults in the post-World War liberal global order, suggesting the demise of this era rather than its recommitment?

When the propaganda comes unmasked, unmasking doesn't help; this is a delirium of the "age of criticism, to which everything must submit" (Kant, 1781/1998, pp. 100–101). When Naomi Klein (2020) calls the 2021 branding "The Great Reset Conspiracy Smoothie," the latest in a series of rebrands "of all the things Davos does anyway" (para. 5) but for the inclusion of COVID-19, we understand that the mask has fallen off. But little emerges in the revelation of these contradictions, and certainly, there are no pragmatic alternatives to this actuality as determined by a transnational economic bottom line. Rather, we see only Klaus Schwab with another notional rejoinder: "The pandemic represents a rare but narrow window of opportunity to reflect, reimagine, and reset our world" ("The Great Reset," n.d.). In the futility of critique, perhaps one wants to laugh, at least, and take the ironic view that sees the gulf between the campaign, its purported aims and ideals, and reality. But as Žižek (1989) observed, when the contemporary ideological mode is already cynical and understood as such in democratic and totalitarian states alike, the laughter of ironic distance dead ends in virtual alternatives.

The Davos publicity is allowed to appear less than credible without losing credibility, as with advertising, which is laughably manipulative to late modern sensibilities. Today, it is easy to see propaganda for what it is, discerning the artifice that tugs at emotions and appeals, without commitment, to higher ideals. Consider sunny advertisements for detergents or IBS medication. The uplifting imagery and storyline provide more than the facts or associations with id impulses, but also ideals, halcyonic visions of happiness, love, ideal sex roles, and the ideal of freedom from these, ideals of justice and equality, even, recalling, as a recent example, the dovetailing of ad campaigns in support of Black Lives Matter: from Nike (2020), "For once, Don't Do It. Don't pretend there's not a problem in America." The particular—a product or agenda—stands in for the universal. Davos rebrands decline as an opportunity, telling us in the example of "You'll own nothing. And you'll be happy" that happiness will be found once settled permanently into the rentier class, free to rent once unable to own. If there is doubt, remember that this is for the environment too, our mutual responsibility with industry captains, investors, and politicians—co-owners in the cause and solution, this is stakeholder capitalism in action! When the revolution is only a gesture, made only in the virtual, power brokers and activists alike can be safe in the knowledge that nothing must actually change.

Let us revisit Moss, a conspiracy-prone social media actor who provides something other than purely negative critique, and he is not dismissible as a troll, as these are ironists. By wholly rejecting the cynical premise of Davos publicity, he one-ups, in a way, those high-profile activists in attendance at Davos or featured in the video—Jane Goodall, whom we already mentioned, Greta Thunberg, Hindou Oumarou Ibrahim. These good actors give credence, tragically, ironically, through their participation in this latest series of rebrands of the same unwavering transnational economic bottom line that today destabilizes ecology while reallocating global wealth toward a new, technological dark age. Moss has not been so hypocritical. Even when his wild hypothesizing makes it difficult to engage with Moss on the level of his ideology, many should find agreement with his ideals, those held to be self-evident under liberalism: Bound for freedom against tyranny, liberty from the injustice of elite capture of democratic process, autonomy thwarted by evictions and the absorption of small businesses and family savings. He resists the Davos publicity with *unironic* distance, earnestly embracing their shared, double-spoken ideals.

Yet, there is a problem with Moss as well. A critical, foundational flaw that has nothing to do with his ideology nor even the sincerity of his ideals. This has to do with his platform, which he shares with the Davos public relations team, on the Internet of social media and forums. At the end of Moss' video, he wants us to "educate ourselves, educate others" much like the Davos "tune in, turn on, and get involved!" These offer resistance in the virtual, #resistance, exactly the wrong direction. Merely playing the role of idealist, on the Internet of social media and forums, Moss has become something only analogous to a virtuous crusader—a virtual crusader, an influencer. Influencers are an Internet-borne phenomenon and paradigmatic to our late modern era. They appear to democratize ideals, very often beauty or love in familial or erotic forms, by giving access to their lives. We know this access is curated, for profit, and the idealism is fundamentally cynical; most of us know this remains the case when influencers invite us to see the "real me," #nofilter. As an influencer, Moss peddles liberal ideals nostalgically after they are drained of their transcendent aspect in the commodity exchange. He adopts the naïve position, less self-aware in cynicism, but such differences equalize once crossed over into the platforms of Facebook, Twitter, YouTube or what have you, in which the word, as with sound and image, is optimized by what garners attention and therefore ad revenue. The virtual guest, entering freely, is transformed into simultaneous product (of salable personal data) and consumer through their movements on the platforms.

In the cleansing of the temple, Jesus decried an excess within a week of his execution, inconveniently as a prophet would, by which the temple had become a conduit of economic and, therefore, political interests, suggesting the essential humanity of this institution, its inessential divinity of the particularized universal. A lender in the temple of the public forums, Moss sets off in defense of universal liberal ideals while, unwittingly, due to his platform, he particularizes them. His virtual platform has monetized the forum and, in doing so, corrupted those freedoms of free expression and assembly at the core of liberalism, making them virtually free, and so not at all, and subject to the same market forces as the private companies that have provided this infrastructure.

The open-minded reader may have wanted Moss to be like an ancient rather than modern cynic, less the Davos crowd and more Diogenes of Sinope, who chose truth—cosmological simplicity—over societal convention. A homeless non-citizen, but citizen of the world, annoyed, Diogenes once told Alexander the Great to step out of his light. Moss and other crusaders across Internet ideological divides are incapable of such resistance. As influencers, lenders in the liberal temple of the monetized public forum, their modern cynicism is inescapable. More apt would be to say that Moss advances the cure for our collective *Diogenes syndrome*, a condition of senile frontal lobe degeneration characterized by the onset of hoarding and blithe disregard for one's increasingly squalid conditions. (A misnomer, because Diogenes was not known to be a hoarder, and, although homeless, it was the choice to claim his freedom.) Taking the Davos propaganda literally, as Moss does, global elites are not inviting so much as announcing the perverse realization of the ancient cynical vision, but only for the masses: We will learn to shirk conventions of the liberal democratic era, the trappings of prosperity, own nothing and be happy. A cure for the last century in which the accumulation of things congested first the most successful nations and then the world. In this new century, some of this clutter will be removed, both because we cannot afford it and because life moves more and more into the virtual.

The Erinyes of Irony

Amid fear and suspicions,
with a shocked mind and frightened eyes,
we break down and scheme to find out
how we might escape that certain danger
threatening us with so much horror.
But we are mistaken, that end's not on the way;
the signals were false
(or we didn't hear or understand them properly).
Another doom, which we had not imagined,
sudden, headlong falls upon us,
and carries us—not ready, with no time left—utterly away.
– "Things Run Out," poem by Constantine P. Cavafy (1911/2001)

The cynical entanglement by which ideals are ironic if they are sincere, and otherwise they are ironic, is not unique to Moss or even the Internet, but characterizes late modernity, its apotheosis in our reticence toward universal ideals, things in themselves, and essential qualities. "Thus I had to deny knowledge in order to make room for faith" (Kant, 1781/1998, p. 117). Kant reasoned against the resort to metaphysical claims to objective knowledge, the consequence of which did not so much disprove the soul as render the concept of soul to be irrelevant to mental life. Our judgments since Kant are understood to be born from the interpretation of sensory experience through faculties of the mind. We perceive reflections and appearances; but, the mind cannot grasp objects as they are outside of their impressions upon us and our interpretations of them, as things-in-themselves, or *noumena*, as metaphysics would claim. In this way, faith survives modernity through its divorce from belief, that is, through our ambivalence toward any metaphysical claim to knowledge (e.g., belief in God as such, or the veracity of the miracles, resurrection, etc.). Some may believe in this way, but doubt is normal after the age of criticism.

From this foundation and further into the era, Freud could speak of the religious experience as illusion and as imagined wish fulfillment, which was also his thesis on the organizing principle of dreams (Freud, 1899/2008; 1927/2008). He supported these claims by means of the concept of unconscious, itself a sort of *noumenon*, which cannot be observed but for its influence upon our perceptions and engagement with the world (Tauber, 2009). The suggestion of unconscious influence killed, at last, the remaining hold of intuitive belief as proof on the modern subject, but this also marked the encroachment of doubt into all things aspirational. Thinkers of the Enlightenment set off in search of ideal political systems only for such pursuits to resolve ironically now at the end of the era. Objections that power actors upholding the transnational economic bottom line are not acting in our best interest become absorbed as well, since, without utopian aspirations, few believe in earnest that actuality could ever change. Equality and rights to life, liberty, and the pursuit of happiness, such metaphysical "old forms of life smoldering under the surface of modern civilization" (Horkheimer, 1947/2004, p. 24), exist today along a receded arrangement. They provide coherency by way of traditionalism, the reference to something passed. Market forces as Erinyes do not bring justice to correct perversions of the natural order since we do not believe the universe to be harmonious in a way that is instructive to society, but only justice in the exchanges with actions and accidents weighed by their ability to incur financial growth and growth potential.

Perhaps, though, restraining myself for a moment, it is premature to call the end of the Enlightenment project. Maybe I am being defensive for entertaining Moss when he was only, as they said, another purveyor of "fake news." And surely not all who take to the Internet of social media and forums are peddling personal brands, and even if every movement and word enters into commodity exchange, this is still a platform to cast one's voice and be heard, same as we've had, but better, further reaching and capable of "amplifying voices" previously dismissed.

Moss is like an almost-"knight of infinite resignation," a term from Søren Kierkegaard to describe those who strive toward infinite, universal ideals, but, since these cannot be realized in the finite, human world, such individuals inevitably but honorably fail in their pursuits. Kierkegaard (1843/1983) pseudonymously provides the example of a young lad who falls in love with a princess. That his quest fails is all the better; any earthly union would not overextend finite bounds into the ideal, what could be called eternal love. If pure of intent, his life becomes organized by love's vanishing point. He gives and loses, and while he suffers, we understand his plight. We note our lack in the bravery and self-sacrifice of this tragic hero, or, today, we are more likely to say, this passionate activist. (And since he does not have a TikTok, we can trust his idealism is not somehow performative in the service of profit and clout.) These knights resign to a life fallen short of the ideal and stay among us—they do not revoke the world. They are like the poet who has glimpsed an abstraction of sublimity and, still bound to this life, in verses "[negates] the imperfect actuality that poetry opens up to a higher actuality, expands and transfigures the imperfect into the perfect, and thereby assuages the deep pain that wants to make everything dark" (Kierkegaard, 1841/1989, p. 297).

Putting Moss aside, let us examine another actor who might better live up to their convictions, someone who, despite entering online, should be less aspirational in their personal branding by virtue of already having become a disgraced public figure. As with Moss, the reader is warned that this person will also divide with her ideology, but we should meet her at the level of her ideals. Hopefully, the reader agrees that this is preferred given the power of colliding views to become aware of and cast off one's own stuporous veil.

Dr. Anne McCloskey, general practitioner and former deputy leader and councilor of the pro-life Aontú party of Ireland, who stepped down over her views on COVID-19 policy, spoke in Mossian or official Davosian fashion in an advert for the Worldwide Rally for Freedom in March 2021, describing how over the course of 2020, "We've seen millions of the poorest and most marginalized people on the planet pushed to starvation and death, because of the economic fallout, because poverty kills" (Freedom Alliance, 2021). Because she is speaking at the Worldwide Rally for Freedom, we know on which side of the COVID-19 response debate McCloskey falls, not a pandemic but "plandemic," a "Trojan horse," "the outworking of a scheme written by people who hate the human race" for "the removal of our most basic and inalienable rights: to work, to earn, to move, to associate, to kiss, to hug, to go to church, to bury our dead with dignity, to live our lives as we see fit." She weaves a vigorous refrain throughout her call coordinated in the liberal language of rights: "We do not consent."

McCloskey has clarified this to mean medically informed consent, referencing the Nuremberg trials, and how during the pandemic healthy populations have been inducted into human clinical trials for a preventive treatment "mandated by the state, without safety data and without robust evidence of efficacy" (Ryland Media, 2021), and with vaccine manufacturers granted immunity from legal liability. Still in the early years of this pandemic, McCloskey is shocked to see the slippage of scientific standards embraced by colleagues, as well as the media, politicians, and bureaucrats shaping policy. In the name of crisis, the final phases of randomized controlled trials have merged such that the public takes the place of informed and consenting research subjects. Slippage has also occurred in the way that medical scientific findings are promulgated. Preliminary findings of novel vaccines are announced with the confidence of suggesting low-dose aspirin for adults at risk of heart attacks, that is, with confidence typically garnered after years of human trials and then observation in the public. There is justification for this bending of standards and ethics, of course, a global health crisis, and there are consequences: Allowing propaganda into one's messaging invites unofficial propaganda. Any wacko can draw conclusions and share them online.

McCloskey voices one of the sincere perspectives about the COVID-19 response: Reconciling how, "since the start of the pandemic, billionaires have increased theirs by more than 25% whilst 150 million people fell back into extreme poverty," (WEF, 2021) and the way that this seemed somewhat avoidable given what was known early on about a highly infectious virus but with effects that target specific groups, elderly and infirm adults, and, it was suspected, infants. From this perspective, concern can turn to alienation over the state of the Western liberal nation and its once visionary, once responsive institutions and infrastructure. Were it not that, even before the vaccine rollouts, nearly all liberal democracies fell lockstep behind the policy response of an authoritarian state in isolating the population regardless of risk, closing schools and businesses leaving many to lose savings and livelihoods, and wedging divides within family and other offline social networks, McCloskey's worldview may not have torsioned so extremely to preserve homeostasis, settling on the assumption that this was intended, a "plandemic," to basically destroy Western civilization.

Another sincere perspective holds that errors and inefficiencies owe to an unfolding and highly complicated scenario. This is true for policy as with the reporting on science as it emerges, and law and policymakers are right to minimize risk even if the science cannot move fast enough. When the national response is embarrassingly inadequate, it also provokes internal crisis for those with this perspective, but this, instead, triggers demands for more mask mandates, more lockdowns, and faster, safe, and effective vaccines. They are thrown by the rejection of state and institutional oversight by their compatriots like McCloskey or Moss in the wake of the pandemic response, as they were shocked by the populist referendums of 2016. Comprising much of the professional and educated labor pool, such a rejection is the rejection of their point of reference and threatens the world.

If this world is rational, one could ask how two parties could each follow their reason and arrive at such different conclusions. But until now, we have only described opposing ideologies fed by differing fonts of propaganda. One font has methods so obvious that it is a satire of propaganda, living among talk radio and much of cable news and magnified since the Internet, which requires maximum "virality" for attention and profit. The other, more traditional font assists in ideology's principal goal of keeping things as they are, with credibility granted to the institutional status quo as channeled through the experts who scribe op-eds and fill respectable interview seats. This is tailored to the university educated and professionals, as well as, in more measured times, the rest of the masses. Each propaganda source reflexively shifts focus between individual, irrational actors of the other side and the institutional grievance to spare from meeting with internal contradictions.

Looking beyond ideology, we notice another, more infinite quality among The Two Sincere Perspectives: They have been grappling with death and, idealistically, the "sanctity of life." McCloskey may understand this the most. Her traditional worldview is oriented toward life in a way that achieves its ideal in safeguarding the vulnerably new, back to the prenatal, and understands with similar respect that death and illness are inevitable:

> Last year, a seasonal respiratory virus of high infectivity but low pathogenicity passed across the world and sadly took with it people who were very old, who were already very sick, and most of whom were already in the last months and years of their lives. There were younger people who died. May God have mercy on their souls and comfort their family and friends.
>
> *(Freedom Alliance, 2021)*

She is incredulous that her adversaries would incur such human and societal cost ostensibly to save lives, fervently seeking dominion over death, irreligiously irrational in this, "over nature and the body, over the tragic elements in human life and history" (Lasch, 1996, p. 28), twisting these values as they do the discourse of rights and freedom to justify abortion on demand. The cynicism is boundless. We may wonder, for example, the ways in which the most devastating pandemic policies across the globe answered to budgetary more than humanitarian concerns, especially in countries with universal healthcare systems, just as the vaccine rollouts, aggressively streamlined first and foremost in the wealthiest countries suggested concern for profit over lives, propaganda to the contrary.

Anticipating the inevitable swing to the other side, tireless readers will be poised to interrogate McCloskey's idealism, the religious, anti-democratic irrational, and how this has coalesced around nihilistic power actors in the post-Trump era. But let us pause instead to peer from these heights. Are we to climb further? And for what? The peak of Mount Everest is covered in trash, they say, and so close to the cosmos, so cold and deoxygenated, the view is becoming incomprehensible. Walk with me to the precipice instead, the proscenium of the stage, for a moment of *parabasis* in this comedy-drama of The Two Sincere Perspectives. During the parabasis of ancient Greek comedies, the chorus stopped the play in the middle to address the audience directly and say "the rudest things" (Schlegel as cited in Albert, 1993, p. 841) in the name of the author: Did you really think those knights, our tragic activists, could save the era? Much less survive? Let us mark their graves instead, here, up high on this plateau and try to make sense of the irony that swallowed their mission.

Friedrich Schlegel (1772–1829) described parabasis as a "complete interruption and dissolution of the play" that nonetheless does not extinguish its continuity and irony as "permanent parabasis" (Schlegel as cited in Albert, 1993, pp. 840–841). This is a likely ironic statement in itself, as others have pointed out, because if the interruption were permanent, there would be no break in the play–the play would simply be reality. Yet, this may be his point. The parabasis brings the audience further into an amusing fiction when, in the moment the primary fiction is suspended, they are cast into a role of their own, addressed now as "the audience," a play on and within the actual play. But after the parabasis and once the play ends, they will resume their roles as characters in other plays on reality, in "real life," and suddenly we are in too deep, or up too high, as it were. Following Albert (1993), the thrust of Schlegel's view on irony, what is called Romantic irony given its place within early German Romanticism, may be to advise against the search for truth behind the ironic feign, the intended versus the pretended meaning, and rather to understand the competing views as partial truths reaching toward something greater, though never fully grasped, forever antagonistic as a testament to reality surpassing comprehension. We sampled an expertly cynical application of Romantic irony in the endless upbuilding alternations of the Davos video.

Per Schlegel, one risks vertiginous exposure to reality when tracing the line between ironist and victim in an attempt to root out deception. In one famous fragment, Schlegel (1800/1971) explains reproachfully:

> To a person who hasn't got it, [Socratic irony] will remain a riddle even after it is openly confessed. It is meant to deceive no one except those who consider it a deception and who either take pleasure in the delightful roguery of making fools of the whole world or else become angry when they get an inkling they themselves might be included. It is a very good sign when the harmonious bores are at a loss about how they should react to this continuous self-parody, when they fluctuate endlessly between belief and disbelief until they get dizzy and take what is meant as a joke seriously and what is meant seriously as a joke.
>
> *(p. 265)*

From this quote, one understands that the foolish ones are those who think they get the joke and that they can identify irony as irony, and yet contained within this, we are left with something unresolved: Could the statement itself be ironic? Or accidentally so? And therefore, even at this meta level of analysis, the ironist, who has implanted us as well, may be the one "who hasn't got it." The ironist claims to know the truth from deception despite having just stated that those who think they know will hear the joke as serious, and what is serious as a joke.

This example fits within Schlegel's (1800/1971) definition of an "irony of irony," of which many varieties exist, including when "one speaks of irony without using it, as I have just done; if one speaks of irony ironically without in the process being aware of having fallen into a far more noticeable irony"; "if irony turns into a mannerism and becomes, as it were, ironical about the author"; "and if the irony runs wild and can't be controlled any longer" (p. 267). Kierkegaard did not mention knights of *ironic* resignation, but one might become resigned when confronted with infinite ironies that cast down each attempt to grasp the higher truth. But following Schlegel, this state of confusion is easily the more accurate view on reality, at least when compared with the naïve pursuit of objectivity, first principles, attempts at which have flopped repeatedly throughout the modern era on improvable axiomatic foundations, most scandalously, perhaps, for mathematics since Gödel's incompleteness theorems. As Albert (1993) notes of the play on "harmonious bores" in the fragment of the attempt to harmonize understanding by claiming to know when the irony begins or ends:

> Could it be that the attempt to correct the "harmonious bores" only proves the general inescapability of "harmonious boredom," that the way to infinity is less serene than one might expect, and that the experience of vertigo and of being the victim, rather than the user, of irony, belongs to it?
>
> *(p. 832)*

One may note the opposition of Romantic irony, which denies epistemic certainty and thwarts dialectical movement, to Hegelianism, such that Hegel (1821/1991) regarded this ironic subjectivity as an "evil, in fact, of an inherently wholly universal kind" (p. 182). Poisonous to the entire German idealistic project, a kind of satanic inversion of Fichtean pure subjectivity, the I-I, the Romantic ironist hijacks the "negative freedom" special to human beings, which, unlike the animal who:

> always remains only negative, in a determination which is alien to it and to which it merely grows accustomed. The human being is pure thinking of himself, and only in thinking is he this power to give himself universality, that is, to extinguish all particularity, all determinacy.
>
> *(p. 38)*

Having taken this mechanism of self-granted universality, the ironist casts themselves above right, duty, and law: "I merely play with them as with my own caprice, and in this ironic consciousness in which I let the highest of things perish, I *merely enjoy myself*" (p. 182). Since the Romantic ironist is not bound to the conventions and institutions of the time—having become their own Absolute—they are free to use ideals without commitment in the slogan and campaign, as in philosophy, media, and art.

This act of standing apart from actuality is the contribution and condemnation of Romantic irony according to Hegel and, per Kierkegaard, of any kind of irony: it only says what reality is not. The ironist, or online we say troll, mocks the idealist pretensions of the time, the political and social arrangements that adherents to convention would imagine fell into place by divine calculus. But from their ironic distance, the ironist has also self-limited in their conceit. They remain above it all, admitting no higher actuality while also distanced from the actuality that is. They are, in fact, just as resigned to this universe as the knights of resignation, but, unlike the knights, they avoid the ethical project for their mocking critique of the other's hypocrisy. Irony emphasizes the gap, the incomprehensible germinating within the comprehended, and terminates nihilistically, or, as we saw in the Davos video, irony can cycle endlessly upon itself while actuality remains unchanged.

Hegel (1821/1991) did not include Socrates in this category of corrosive ironists, convinced that Socrates exposed the arbitrary foundations of actuality "to defend the Idea of truth and justice against the complacency of the uneducated consciousness and that of the Sophists; but it was only this consciousness which he treated ironically, not the Idea itself"

(p. 180), while Kierkegaard (1841/1989) rejected this premise and viewed Socrates as the ironic exemplar, perhaps more "negatively free" even than Schlegel. For Socrates:

> the whole given actuality had entirely lost its validity; he had become alien to the actuality of the whole substantial world... he was ignorant and knew nothing but was continually seeking information from others; yet as he let the existing go on existing, it foundered.
>
> *(p. 264)*

Socrates, whose irony, Hegel agreed, "destroyed Greek civilization" (p. 264), was the originary subject, first subjectivity, per Kierkegaard, since the subject is born from this quiet awareness of the distance between actuality and possible reality. Taking this expansive view, Kierkegaard viewed all irony as an important stage in the development of understanding.

Hegel, on the contrary, would hold that only through participation within actuality and the rational, ethical institutions of the time can the understanding develop into its absolute notion. This condemns the idealistically, ethically noncommittal Romantic ironist. In comparison to Schlegel's view that denies or ignores any rational ethical telos, Hegel's view is reminiscent of the Kantian Kingdom of Ends, in which individuals arrive at the universal, generalizable good in the categorical imperative by their own practical reason. The Romantic ironist diverts the course of individual practical reason to a different end in a Kingdom of One. But we have seen how Moss and McCloskey meet this end as well. Reaching toward idealism, they recede as influencer idealogues. And, certainly, this is not unique, but characteristic of the arc of public-facing individuals today, who are romantically ironic whether they know it or not. At least the ironist as ironist can admit this and go further—at least they find the cosmic joke funny, that bit about falling short despite our grandest gestures and, with self-seriousness, our best-laid plans. God laughs.

Late modernity is the flowering of the age that Socrates planted. Ours is an ironic age such that now everything is ironic, except for the age itself, and everything is going to become more and more ironic. That is why today's reader is not so scandalized as Hegel when nothing is believed to be fully real, firmly grounded in reality, which also helps virtual reality become viable. The relationship to rights, duties, and laws in and of themselves, which is to say, existing independently of the relative meaning breathed through them by human interrelations is tentative and potentially reckless, even, especially in the other.

Our uneasiness about idealism relegates the transcendent to matters of personal choice, but this avoids the conclusion that there is no longer any reconciliation with universal ideals as the knights could believe in, no going back to this, and no reversals of the era. Many strive to believe but doubt demands an answer, as Kierkegaard (1841/1989) noted: "What doubt is to science, irony is to personal life" (p. 326). But today, it is an irony of irony, Romantic not tragic, since even in tragedy the Erinyes were brought to heel, and a bloodbath, stalled, could open way to transition. Today, many of us witness virtual bloodbaths and real bloodbaths virtually, feeling implicated, in the case of the latter, by vague chains of global economic causality. On virtual public forums, the debates rage, but we know that we are far away and very comfortable, like the activists mingling with politicians and bureaucrats in all-too-modern conference halls in the snowy Alps. In comparison with the society of Socrates which resented the disillusionment of ironic distance, this glimpse at the arbitrary foundations of human reality so much that Socrates had to die, and the contemporary mode finds this peak of negative freedom inescapable.

Every Good and Every Perfect Gift Is Found Online

"What doubt is to science [...]" (Kierkegaard, 1841/1989, p. 326). Even if the modern age ends before utopia, this is not to deny Progress. The empirical turn in the age of criticism means that today we can talk about this entity of a virus in COVID-19 with exquisite complexity and debate the merits of these vaccines compared to others that time has proven. Kant was not incorrect in asserting that empirical, mathematical reasoning takes us further toward comprehensible bounds than intuition. From such reasoning follows that the meter is one 10-millionth the quarter meridian through Paris or 1,650,763.73 wavelengths of orange-red light emitted by element KR-86 in a vacuum, among other equivalences, and that such abstractions of quantity allow for the estimation and prediction of events incomprehensible to imagination alone, from the microscopic scale of viruses down to the modeling of cosmological origins—states without comparison since they have no containment within something else. But a potential cause for the crisis of faith we have been describing may be that the implications of our empirical models have become wholly incomprehensible to our intuition. There is no human trace on contemporary claims of sublimity.

Having the power to grant themselves universality, the individual has just discovered that they are all particularity, all determinacy: chains of causality accumulating mass and dragging into gravity to experience ourselves in space and time.

In light of these dawning revelations, a new third party emerged in the analyst and then psychotherapist to mediate the relation between the individual and the incomprehensible absurd. Freud's method was to cast the individual repeatedly back upon themselves, such that through layers of self-reflection the analytically cultivated ego might become freer in its capacity of reason, less determined by the irrational core within us and which is ever peripheral in our lives. Psychoanalysis nods to Kant's (1784/2006) "motto of the enlightenment": "*Sapere aude!* Have the courage to make use of your own intellect!" (para. 1; see also discussion in Tauber, 2009). Despite envisioning different ideal ends for the individual, one transcendentally universal and the other immanent and biologically determined, both Kantian and Freudian systems would emancipate the individual from "self-incurred immaturity" (para. 1), as Kant defined it.

That psychoanalysis failed to carry the modern age, as it also tends to fail in treating the severely mentally ill for which the "talking cure" was developed, could speak to a flaw in its foundation. Analysis is a positivist project, an ironic empiricism, in which the analyst posits hypotheses that cannot be proven, that is, outside of that proof of "insight" by the analyst or analysand. Freud took the human subject as his specimen of study. This is a doomed project, since statistical noise overwhelms any model that would satisfactorily predict or explain human subjectivity, at least unless it is reduced, abstracted, as occurs today, into a limited series of measurable traits. The irony of the state of psychological science today given Freud's early ambitions for a "natural scientific psychology" in psychoanalysis is the incredible scarcity of reliable and specific biomarkers to evidence the variables under study, from mental disorders to emotions and personality types (Lindquist et al., 2012; Trofimova and Netter, 2021). Studying psychological constructs is the study of things-in-themselves, metaphysics. Not surprisingly, though not only for this reason, there is a crisis of replicability in this field (Yong, 2018).

The field of public relations, too, with origins in psychoanalysis but today, like psychology proper, invested in the statistical treatment of the human subject, could only invent the phrase, "You'll own nothing. And you'll be happy" for the psychological specimen. Slogans such as these are tested on groups of such specimens from which to infer their reception in the broader population. But much is lost in the conversion from individual to specimen to group, such that what is said about the group is what one might have imagined anyway, while the individual notes the gap between themselves and what is said about them. Only the individual matters. Left alone on the mountain (we never did descend), the individual wrestles an indefatigable adversary, a universal exception, who, at dawn, would bless us were we to ask. But "the sinner, of course, does not know this from the beginning; on the contrary, he is aware only of heaven's wrath until he finally, as it were, forces heaven to speak out" (Kierkegaard, 1843/1983, p. 227).

Sapere aude! Someone new has emerged, the "knight of faith," but with no space left in this chapter, like the era, rapidly closing.

References

Albert, G. (1993). Understanding Irony: Three Essais on Friedrich Schlegel. *MLN, 108*(5), 825. https://doi.org/10.2307/2904879

Cavafy, C. (2001). *Before time could change them: The complete poems of Constantine P. Cavafy ; translated with an introduction and notes by Theoharis Constantine Theoharis* (T. C. Theoharis, Trans.). New York: Harcourt. (Original work published 1911).

Goodman, P. S. (2017, January 18). Davos elite fret about inequality over vintage wine and canapés. *The New York Times.* https://www.nytimes.com/2017/01/18/business/dealbook/world-economic-forum-davos-backlash.html

The Great Reset. (n.d.). World Economic Forum. Retrieved November 8, 2021, from https://www.weforum.org/focus/the-great-reset/

Freedom Alliance. (2021, March 16). *Against The Agenda on Instagram: "20th March 2021 World Wide Protest."* https://www.instagram.com/tv/CMe3B2aBU1e/

Hegel, G. W. F. (1991). *Elements of the philosophy of right* (A. W. Wood, Ed.; H. B. Nisbet, Trans.). Cambridge: Cambridge University Press. (Original work published 1821).

Horkheimer, M. (2004). *Eclipse of reason.* New York: Continuum. (Original work published 1947).

Kant, I. (1998). *Critique of pure reason* (P. Guyer, Trans.). Cambridge: Cambridge University Press (Original work published 1781).

Kant, I., Waldron, J., Doyle, M. W., & Wood, A. W. (2006). *Toward perpetual peace and other writings on politics, peace, and history* (P. Kleingeld, Ed.; Colclasure, David L., Trans.). Yale University Press. (Original work published 1784).

Kierkegaard, S. (1983). *Fear and trembling, repetition* (H. V. Hong, Ed.). Princeton, NJ: Princeton University Press (Original work published 1843).

Kierkegaard, S. (1989). *The concept of irony, with continual reference to Socrates: Together with notes of Schelling's Berlin lectures* (H. V. Hong & E. H. Hong, Trans.). Princeton, NJ: Princeton University Press (Original work published 1841).

Klein, N. (2020, December 8). The Great Reset conspiracy smoothie. *The Intercept.* https://theintercept.com/2020/12/08/great-reset-conspiracy/

Lasch, C. (1996). *The revolt of the elites and the betrayal of democracy.* New York: Norton.

Martin, W. (2017). *This One Chart Explains the Rise of Populism in 2017.* (2017, March 7). World Economic Forum. Retrieved November 8, 2021, from https://www.weforum.org/agenda/2017/03/this-one-chart-explains-the-rise-of-populism-in-2017/

Moss, M. (2021, February 21). *How We Can Stop Them from Stealing Everything from Us.* https://www.facebook.com/1markmoss/videos/499123441083062/

Nike. (2020, May 29). Let's all be part of the change. #UntilWeAllWin https://t.co/guhAG48Wbp [Tweet]. @*Nike.* https://twitter.com/Nike/status/1266502116463370241

Reuters Staff. (2021, February 25). Fact check: The World Economic Forum does not have a stated goal to have people own nothing by 2030. *Reuters.* https://www.reuters.com/article/uk-factcheck-wef-idUSKBN2AP2T0

Ryland Media. (2021, May 28). *Iconoclast One-to-One Series—Dr. Anne McCloskey.* https://www.facebook.com/watch/live/?ref=watch_permalink&v=2991248764531755

Tauber, A. I. (2009). Freud's dreams of reason: The Kantian structure of psychoanalysis. *History of the Human Sciences, 22*(4), 1–29. https://doi.org/10.1177/0952695109340492

von Schlegel, F. (1971). *Friedrich Schlegel's lucinde and the fragments.* Minneapolis: University of Minnesota Press (Excerpt originally published 1800).

Wallace, D. F. (1993). E unibus pluram: Television and U.S. fiction. *Review of Contemporary Fiction, 13*(2), 151–194.

World Economic Forum. (2021, January 25). *What Is the Great Reset? | Davos Agenda 2021.* https://www.youtube.com/watch?v=uPYx12xJFUQ

Žižek, S. (1989). *The sublime object of ideology.* Brooklyn, NY: Verso.

29

STREAMING DESIRE AND THE POST-MACHINE WORLD

Heather Macdonald

Introduction: The "Neuroeconomic Subject"

As we deepen our entanglements with the rapid escalation of technological innovation and the post-human infrastructure of social media and virtual realities, a restructuring of lived embodied existence (and the actual physical body) is taking place and, along with it, a re-ordering of psychic affective structures and our systems of desire. The nonhuman realm continues to exert a growing influence on our daily lives (new materialism, post-humanism, climate change, viruses, etc.), and thus we will also need to consider different metapsychological frameworks for unconscious processes that move away from Oedipal or familial understandings of psychic libido toward an account of the unconscious that includes technology and nonhuman forces. In very simple terms, this means understanding how affect and the unconscious (events that disrupt intentional flows of consciousness) may be directly intertwined with and *emerge from* communicative technologies rather than viewing such processes as primal biological substrates or purely psychical phenomena a primal biological substrate or purely psychical phenomena.

In addition, newer theories of socioeconomic libidinal registers must also account for the logic of escalation that is embedded in the very structure of technological innovation, which is also the bedrock of global capitalism; this "infinite greed" and desire for infinite growth has been folded into subjective experience and temporality in such a way that it operates as a kind of death drive or what Brian Becker (2022) calls the "thanatonic phenomenon" that pushes well beyond the known boundaries of safety and concern for the preservation of life. It is impossible to speak of social media and other communicative technologies and the codification of social life in the absence of neoliberal corporate logic, the logic that defines the economy as the exchange of capital but also serves to transform selfhood in such a way that its functioning also aligns with market values. In his book *Critique of Black Reason*, Achille Mbembe (2017) states,

> The new subject differs in many ways from the tragic and alienated figure of early industrialization. First and foremost, he is a prisoner of desire. His pleasure depends almost entirely on his capacity to reconstruct his private life publicly, to turn it into viable merchandise and put it up for sale. He is a neuroeconomic subject absorbed by a double concern stemming from his animal nature (as subject to the biological reproduction of

DOI: 10.4324/9781003195849-35

life) and his thingness (subject to others' enjoyment of the things of the world). As a human-thing, human-machine, human-code, and human-in-flux, he seeks above all to regulate his behavior according to the norms of the market.

(p. 4)

As human subjectivity is increasingly delivered over to technological infrastructure, one could draw on any number of scholars in the canon of Western philosophy for further insight; one could even say that Adorno, Agamben, or Heidegger predicted our current technological entanglements and the post-human or post-machine world. However, for this chapter I wish to think alongside multiple disparate thinkers in the form of a *bricolage* (e.g. Wilfred Bion, Jacques Lacan, Gilles Deleuze, Jodi Dean) as I believe that they each uniquely describe critical vector points in the dangers we now face with the colliding forces of *technology and the increasing potential of capitalism linked with animism.* In addition to the Cameroonian philosopher Achille Mbembe, two other prominent philosophers will be highlighted in this chapter. First, Gilles Deleuze offers us concepts that are useful for rethinking our conceptualization of the unconscious within the "logic of sense" and the overlapping boundaries between mind, body, and matter that technological innovation and capitalism engender, and second, Emmanuel Levinas (prophetically) helps us understand what is at stake if we escape the body and merge more fully with informational data streams and lose time and thus our most important form of suffering, the embodied kind of anguish that scrapes us to the bone and wipes out our projections.

It is within these contexts that I wish to consider more specifically the impact these events have on (1) the affective structures of the human psyche, (2) the implications that the "streaming self" has on conceptualizations of the unconscious, and (3) the reshaping of human desire toward the escape of the human body (and ultimately the earth). Beginning with the concept of the cyborg, I will trace a broad outline of how human affect and human desire have been reshaped by information and communication technologies in ways that have profound implications for our understandings of psychological life and why they must include a cross-breeding of organic and inorganic elements, a kind of "ontoethics" (Grosz, 2018) that re-examines the boundaries and conditions for human consciousness. It is also important to note that for the purposes of this chapter, subjective embodiment is presupposed, in other words, I do not propose that the body is merely a reification of subjectivity, which would change the direction of the core arguments I wish to make here. Nor do I intend to argue that technology itself is a form of the projected mind, but rather I aim to make the argument for what could be characterized as a "new materialism," "transcendental materialism," or a "new naturalism" that recasts the relationship between organic and inorganic elements in light of how our lives have become merged with the inanimate.

From the Cyborg to the Streaming Self

In 1960 Manfred Clynes and Nathan Kline wrote an article titled "Cyborgs and Space" that was published in the journal *Astronautics*. They were the first to define a cyborg as a "self-regulating man machine system" that would give humans the freedom to explore space because the resulting "altering of bodily functions to meet the requirements of extraterrestrial environments would be more logical than providing an earthly environment in space" (p. 29). In a controlled experiment described in the article, they fitted a white rat with an osmotic pump that continuously fed various chemicals into the animal, their first proto-cyborg. Years later, social critic and historian of science Donna Haraway (1997, 2006) wrote extensively on the notion of the cyborg and showed how humans are transformed by the technological systems we are plugged into. Haraway defines the cyborg as "a cybernetic organism, fusion of the organic and the technical forged in particular, historical, cultural practices" (p. 51). More recently, Sherry Turkle, who relied on Haraway's early work, declared in 2012, "We are all cyborgs now" (p. 152), suggesting that the current forms of communication technology (largely through the iPhone) have been grafted onto our subjectivity and our way of being in the world and have become the prime mediator of our most intimate emotional geographies.

What makes the notion of the cyborg so interesting, aside from biomedical brain implants, sentient robotic elements, and custom-made "insideables," is how human desire is also "reassembled" as a result of these more hybrid mechanical technologies. As Haraway (1991) suggests, "The cyborg is a kind of disassembled and reassembled, postmodern collective and personal self" (p. 163). While the early cybernetic theories about the cyborg explored possibilities of new kinds of selfhood, they often left out ideas regarding the emotional or affective cartographies of cyborg existence. What exactly happens to affective psychic structures in this re-assemblage? And how is human desire reshaped in this process? The sociologist Barry Wellman (1979, 2001) attempted to address these questions through his theory of "networked individualism," which outlines how social life for autonomous actors is defined through network connections rather than the traditional "bounded," local, place-based communities. He makes the argument that the sense of community has not been lost since community is defined by affective relations rather than spatial horizons and the fluidity of personalized networks can hold deep emotional bonds and mutuality. Wellman and other scholars believe that the acceleration of communication technologies has engendered freedom, access, openness, creativity, inclusion, deep cyber community, and discussion, which also highlight central democratic values. The Internet, social media, and cyberspace can engender creative expanding and overlapping multiplicities for which there is no fixed center.

However, what I wish to argue is akin to what Turkle wrote in 1997 when she commented on the self and computer games that "the self is decentered and multiplied without limit" (p. 185). Given the pace of technological advancement, we have moved past older versions or visions of cyborg constructs and have become what Goodman and Collins (2019) call "streaming selves." We are defined not so much by customized "insideables" but by multiple, nomadic and rhizomatic data streams that are tracked continuously through the Internet and social media portals. Rather than an inserted mechanical osmotic pump, we have memory feeds, timelines, photos, messages, videos, and many other aspects of our subjectivity on recirculating loops, and this has devastating impacts on our emotional bonds with others and our affective structures.

For example, Jodi Dean (2010) argues that the various forms of social media—Facebook, Twitter, Instagram, and blogs—are not actually about the exchange of communication but about the circulation of data streams that capture our desire and wire affect into online networks. It does not matter what we say, "only that we ping one another repeatedly" and incessantly. The Yo app is a good example, where the message you send is the single word "Yo." As Dean states, "A communicative contribution need not be understood; it need only be repeated, reproduced, forwarded. Circulation is the content, the condition for the acceptance or rejection of a contribution" (p. 59). In these looping noncommunications, affect is hollowed out and becomes anemic. It is the antithesis of Paul Ricoeur's (2006) "linguistic hospitality" and of an ethics that aims to bring the Other into the living narrative of the household, the inner sanctum of ritual and rhythm, while also crossing over into narratives and rituals that the Other themselves may offer. In these more atrophied exchanges, we have lost immanent modes of existence and we have also lost the fuller modes of *languaging* that carry affect in the process of true dialog; I hear what another person may communicate but, most importantly, I also need to *feel it* as part of a socialized translation process. In the rapid circulation of data streams, information, and "networked affect," we have unlinked from what Heidegger would call "facticity."

Goodman and Collins exquisitely outline these imbalances in their 2019 article "The Streaming Self: Liberal Subjectivity, Technology and Unlinking." In their essay, they use different levels of analysis to outline the ways in which we have become unlinked from our lives, from our histories, and from our bodies, and since we are tied to time and suffering through our embodiment, this may be the very dilemma that unlinking seeks to obliterate. They offer some possible answers to the earlier questions I proposed about how the reassemblage and reordering of affect and human desire take place in a networked, streaming world, and their arguments are worth closer examination and elaboration.

Unlinked and Hyperlinked Affect: Bion and Lacan

As part of his work on psychosis, Wilfred Bion first expounded his notion of "unlinking" in his 1959 article "Attacks on Linking." He hypothesized that in the process of psychosis there is an internalization of a destructive ego (and superego) that is focused on the ipseity or on rupturing the links one makes between the self and objects. He reasoned that when a severe enough breakdown between the infant and the caregiver in primary communication patterns occurs, then the child is unable to utilize cognitive or emotional processes to repair the burnt affective bridges between the self and world, which then results in psychotic processes.

In their article, Goodman and Collins (2019) use both the work of Bion and the work of Lynne Layton (2006) in her essay *Attacks on Linking: The Unconscious Pull to Dissociate Individuals From Their Social Contexts* to suggest that as a result of our reliance on social media and networked identities, we have not only unlinked ourselves from facticity but at a deeper psychic level we have unlinked ourselves from thoughts, feelings, affect, emotions, language, and reason that do *not support dominant neoliberal traits* such as independence, efficiency, rationality, marketability, and agency. Qualities such as vulnerability and compassion that operate to oppose an enterprising, neoliberal self are split off in an unconscious process that seeks to embrace dominant norms. They further their argument by suggesting that although we are "hyperlinked" in a technology-saturated world, we are actually more isolated than ever before due to the fact that our traditional communities of reference, such as schools, religious groups, and families, are now made of more loosely knit social fabrics. Drawing on the work of Julia Kristeva, the authors argue that selfhood, once filled with interior geographies of depth, has given way to the diffuse and unstable identities of social media avatars. Self-validation is achieved through the quantity of likes on an Instagram post. Thus, our subjectivity is now defined by a "selfhood that streams" (Goodman & Collins, 2019, p. 153). Furthermore, this self is defined neither by linear notions of clock time nor by the Bergsonian durée but by a temporality that Sugarman and Thrift (2017) call "network time." This is a temporality that aligns with the constant demands of productivity, efficiency, instant availability, and other capitalist drives.

The various modes and concepts of unlinking and hyperlinking are unique in their genealogy and in their phenomenology. However, Goodman and Collins (2019) argue that this plays a major role in the rewiring of our libidinal economies, both as individuals and as a collective; the libidinal and affective flow that hyperconnectivity offers is a false approximation of the kind of social connection we need to thrive as humans. I would add that in our unlinked states, we are also more prone to profound states of anxiety and dread, not as emotions but more as ontological or existential structures. Social media technologies that are embedded in neoliberal systems and ideologies contribute to the stuckness of a rapidly looping anxiety, a sense of deep and accelerating dread that is related to the pressure of the libidinal economies of capitalism that demand an infinite desire (Johnston, 2017) that must stay in perpetual motion. Under the constant force of loss and the traumatic impossibility of a return to wholeness, the repetitive circular movement of this excess makes anxiety its disordered twin.

This is not a new idea. Adrian Johnston stated in his 2005 book *Time Driven* that the "[d]rive pressure manifests itself mainly through affects" and that "[a]nxiety is the margin of dissatisfaction plaguing *Trieb*" (pp. 273, 277). Lacan (2004) also developed several features of the metapsychology of affect in his oeuvre (beginning with Seminar X in 1962–1963 and then again in the late 1970s) that are crucial to our understandings of affect in light of how it operates within the context of communication technologies.

First, it is important to note that Lacan (2004), following Kierkegaard, suggests in Seminar XI that anxiety is the affect "that does not deceive" in that it reveals what the signifier is unable to grasp (p. 41). In this instance, affect and its purported synonym "emotion" are not an appropriate association for they belong to different logics and different orders. For Lacan, affect is related to a movement and intensity that opens up indices that are beyond oneself toward the real, that opens up the possibility of "being a stranger to myself" (Johnston & Malabou, 2013, p. 149), whereas emotion remains firmly tethered to the symbolic that structures social experience. Second, an affect, according to Lacan, never represents the subject since the subject is represented by the signifier, nor is affect repressed since it continually moves along a chain of dislocated signifiers. Following Lacan, Žižek (2006) calls this "constitutive anxiety" an irreducible anxiety that is a result of proximity to some real or a "confrontation with *objet petit a* that is constituted in its very loss" (p. 61).

We have simultaneously unlinked from the bodily *emotions* in order to hyperlink to the *affective* contagion of the post-human technological networks and infrastructure (Goodman & Collins, 2019). It this way, we may be closer than we think to a full cross-breeding of human subjectivity with the constant uninterrupted flow of data streams. This is a departure from the older conceptualizations of the biological body wedded to technological machines, as in the advent of the cyborg; we are moving into a post-machine world, not one where machines will take over but one where the world will become purely abstract and computational with no limits, no borders, and with the human body defined as a series of data points. For example, even today, bodies are often viewed from the perspective of biometric vaccination status, and it is this status that determines which borders can be accessed or crossed. As Mbembe (2017) suggested, we have become "a human-thing, human-machine, human-code, and human-in-flux [that] seeks above all to regulate his behavior according to the norms of the market" (p. 4), and our affect has been captured along with the "rebalkanization of the world" (p. 5).

The Unconscious and Incorporeality: A Case Example

In addition to rethinking affective flows and structures in light of communication technologies, it is also important to rethink our notions of the unconscious as untethered from Freud's topographical model of the mind or even Lacan's sliding chain of signifiers. In the limitless borders of networks and data streams, it seems that we need a theory of the unconscious that can both address the rhizomatic nature of data streams and incorporate a "new materialism" or what Deleuze called the "incorporeal" to account for what Posteraro (2017) describes as

> immaterial but not anti-material; what it is that conditions the material without itself being material; not an ideal, not as an objection to or transcendence over the material but as a production out of materiality that simultaneously frames, orients, and completes what produces it.
>
> *(p. 2)*

In borrowing from the Stoics, Deleuze uses the term *incorporeal* as a way to describe a higher order of sense that allows one to think beyond the ideal and the material and may be useful in thinking about the unconscious as a manifestation that includes these qualities. Deleuze is often considered a philosopher of immanence as his philosophical projects align with the Stoics as well as thinkers such as Spinoza and Hume. For Deleuze, transcendence is the cardinal sin of philosophy. The point of philosophy should be the affirmation of sheer becoming, of the "plane of immanence." To adhere rigorously to the plane of immanence thus is to affirm the "univocity of being" (Scotus) as a play of differences (Nietzsche) of infinitely varying intensities, of surfaces without depth.

In much of Deleuze's work, such as *Anti-Oedipus: Capitalism and Schizophrenia* (Deleuze & Guattari, 2009) and *A Thousand Plateaus: Capitalism and Schizophrenia* (Deleuze & Guattari, 1987), one finds important points of departure from Freudian thought. Deleuze's plane of immanence can be thought of as a direct counter to Freudian concepts of unconscious drives and desire. As Steven Swabrick (2017) suggests,

> For Freud, the plane is the plane of sexuality, imagined as the drives, pure unbound energy—akin to Bergson's light-matter-energy. The ego is a map of the body's surface—a psychosomatic mixture. For all of his brilliance in discovering the unconscious, however, Freud interprets the unconscious as a plane of transcendence. Hence psychoanalysis becomes a science of uncovering the Oedipus complex, the triangle plan that, like a Platonic form, governs psychic life unconsciously.
>
> *(p. 3)*

In *Anti-Oedipus* in particular, Deleuze aimed to free desire from fixed images of desire in order to imagine a desire that is productive and not configured by the familial or the Oedipal triangle. Instead, desire is a force that is able to forge connections, unleash lines of flight, and engender experimentation on the plane of immanence. Similarly, Deleuze views the unconscious as something that is also *productive* in that one does not discover unconscious content buried in fragments of the past; there is nothing archeological about it for the unconscious itself must be *produced*. The unconscious then is not a "higher principle" regulating our drives and desires; it is the mechanism that defines possibility and is associated with the Event. The unconscious is not some interior locale, ready-made for interpretation out if its distorted and half-formed inchoate formations; the unconscious is a force able to produce connections, assemblages, and Events.

For example, in my own clinical practice, where I conduct psychological assessments and testing, I interact with others more than ever through technology, and this has radically changed how I track affect, desire, and the unconscious or the Event. The Deleuze (1990) version of the Event, as he defines it in *The Logic of Sense*, is part of Deleuze's project (that he shares with Levinas) of the reversal of Platonism. In doing so, he engages Heidegger, Hegel, and Husserl in his critique. In *The Logic of Sense*, numerous sections are devoted to the Event as he outlines an extended study of sense and immanence. According to Deleuze (1995), Events are "decenterings, break-ins, slips and secret emissions" (p. 6). They can come in a whisper or with disruptive violence, but constant in their nature is the essence of ahistorical unpredictability, uncontainability, and overwhelming excess that outstrips the ego and the intentionality of consciousness. An Event disrupts not only my "knowing" of the "client" but also our respective roles or categories. The Event reconfigures our adventure in the world (Romano, 2009, p. 149), and we are never the same again. "Events, Deleuze says, are not what happens but what is going on in what happens which means that when something comes, something unexpected, that is the coming, the advent of the event" (Caputo, 2011 p. 89).

For example, during one recent assessment, I had arranged for the client to sit in a room separate from my office where he could complete some of the tests and where we could minimize exposure and follow COVID-19 safety guidelines. One of the tests I often use in my evaluations is a sentence completion test (SCT). In this measure, a number of questions target perceptions of the self and how others may view the person. On this occasion, I asked the client to send me a text to let me know when he had completed the SCT. After some time, sure enough, I received a text from the client saying, *"All the tests are done."* In that instant, I tried to type a message back to him that said, *"Super, well done,"* but instead the spelling correction mechanism kicked in and what I sent him was the words *"Super weird."*

Anxiously, I ran down the hallway and opened the door to his room to apologize and explain my error. In response to this, he held up the SCT sheets and stated, "I can't believe it, just as your text came through I had just written on the SCT, *Others see me as super weird."* After our discovery we engaged in a deep conversation about the event of the text exchange and how he characterizes his personhood. From a Deleuzian perspective, this event (the unconscious) had been "produced," and it was our communications through the iPhone (the plane of immanence) that had *carried the affect and in some ways had produced* the affect of the intersubjective moment. Although the iPhone is not a sentient object, I would argue that the iPhone was "alive" in some manner, beyond our projections, existing between the material and the ideal on the plane of immanence.

I have experienced countless other episodes in clinical practice where the production of the unconscious organized itself around and through technological communications; screens, texts, video games, and online meeting rooms play a vital role in how events are produced. The argument I am making here does thread very closely with panpsychism, vitalism, participation in vast quantum systems, post-Bergsonian ontology and the ontology of Alfred North Whitehead (1969), who suggested that each "occasion of experience" is an experience of the "Now" and contains a unit of subjectivity. Although there is not enough room in this chapter to expand upon these ideas and how they differ from my current argument, what I aim to make clear is that as we move toward the possibility of the human being transformed into the inanimate and coded as digital data, a recalibration of how we understand affect, desire, and the unconscious will need to be considered. The "incorporeal" will demand inclusion in our relational ethics as these nonhuman, nomadic, immanent forces collide with the human mind. This brings us to the last topic of consideration for this chapter: What kinds of ethics are possible in the age of the post-human? This is where the early work of Levinas serves as a prophetic reminder that social media is not the safe escape we have believed it to be as our desire to escape the conditions of existence reduces our capacity to relate ethically to the Other.

Levinas, the Internet, and Escape from the Body

Unbridled progress, free markets, and the logic of neoliberal capitalism have disrupted the limits of the body and, I would argue, are leading to disruptions of incarnation in young people in particular as we are seeing a rapid increase in anxiety and depressive disorders. Steinbock (2009) expresses it this way: "Incarnate experience alters the structure of corporeal existence," and, in turn, these structures become dispositions to how the world is sensed through the body (p. 111). The bridges that once held connections between the body, the currents of affect, and cognitive structures seem to have started to *fail* at both the collective and individual level.

We are disrupting the limits of the body so that the streaming self can embrace the free-market ethos of globalized neoliberal capitalism, and this is an extremely dangerous proposition. The way we appreciate change and difference is through the decline of the body, which includes its death. If we are to survive communicative technologies, it will be by staying close to an embodied affective anxiety that exposes us to the trauma of the real; this kind of embodiment allows us to open empathetically to the Other.

The unlinking that occurs within the context of technology and social media takes direct aim at our desire to escape the body and to escape time, which was a specific concern for Emmanuel Levinas. Social media provide a dissociative holiday during which we can temporarily upload or offload our subjectivity and forget about the body for a while (Bill Adams, personal communication, 2018). The danger in this kind of forgetfulness was a theme for Levinas in his 1935 essay *On Escape*. John Caputo (2009) suggests, "A prophet is not someone who sees the future but someone who warns about the consequences in the future of a present evil because he senses the gap between the present state and the event of justice" (p. 31). In this way, Levinas' 1935 essay still speaks to us prophetically; it remains a troubling reflection on existential pressure points that drive us toward the desperate need to escape our condition.

In "On Escape," Levinas (1935/2003) argues that there is no way to sidestep the problem of being. He states, "[T]he ground of suffering consists of the impossibility of interrupting it, and of an acute feeling of being held fast" (p. 52). Our suffering always resists full interpretation and description. As Severson (2013) nicely summarizes,

> In freedom, the thinking person can seemingly transcend the ravages of being and the restrictions afforded by bodies and histories, but this freedom and transcendence is shocked, or nauseated, by 'the brutal fact of being that assaults freedom' (OE 49).
>
> *(p. 26)*

For Levinas, the only transcendence available to us is in "the constant threat of physical suffering and death that opens up otherwise separated and independent human beings to each other, casting them together in relations of love and fecundity that go beyond their needs and projects" (Sarah Allen, as cited in Severson, 2013, p. 27). This kind of ethics is the only transcendence there is, and it is a strictly not-for-profit enterprise. Levinas denounces the fantasy of a *Hinterwelt* or higher being or any suggestion that this world could be replaced with one that relieves us of the unbearable heaviness of existence. Politically and ethically, the immanence of the body and the face of the Other are the very foundation of my freedom. I can submit to the impossibility of indifference and allow the Other to intervene; this is an openness to rupture, laceration, and possession.

The very pressure points Levinas highlights in his 1935 essay are also highlighted in recent cybertheory. Tim Jordan (1999), in his book *Cyberpower: The Culture and Politics of*

Cyberspace and the Internet, discusses the cyborg fantasy or imaginary as a utopian dimension in which life is liberated from previous material constraints such as embodiment and is re-configured as flows of *information.* In this case, Jordan refers to the cyborg *fantasy* as a way to escape social, cultural, and linguistic isolation. However, he also suggests that we are closer than we think to a full cross-breeding of the biological body to informational networks, Virtual Reality technologies, and cyberspace coding apparatuses. Data streams have begun to take on characteristics of the human, and the human has begun to take on characteristics of the computational code in order to transcend the limits of the body. He argues that, even-tually, limbs, organs, and minds will become interchangeable with computerized systems. David Chalmers (2010), in his paper "The Singularity: A Philosophical Analysis," makes the argument that if we mapped a person's brain and body down to the smallest quantum particles, it would be physically possible to upload consciousness to the Internet. But, the question of whether the person's identity would remain intact during this process is still unanswered.

This raises the possibility of a noosphere or collective consciousness that unites human minds and transcends the body, thus achieving a disembodied version of immortality. This is exactly what Levinas was against—a kind of "Hegelian universalism that sees and knows everything from a perspective that transcends history, being and the particularity of human life" (Severson, 2013, p. 144). The boundaries between public and private, interior and exte-rior would be further obliterated. The rhizomatic nature of the Internet, with its unchecked continuations, proliferations, and transformations, is becoming a hyperlinked multiplicity that cannot be predetermined by a librarian or editor. Selfhood becomes a multiplicity that is not just streaming but is uploaded directly to the Internet. Tim Jordan (1999) summarizes this idea:

> There we have it, the ultimate dream of humanity. The moral of this myth of the electronic frontier is that freed from our bodies, our Is [Internet Selves] will be able to mingle, join and finally create the heaven that rests within us now only as a dimly per-ceived potential. Cyberspace offers the ultimate fantasies of both individual immortality and collective transcendence. The body's dominance over the mind is the stranglehold broken by complex computer systems. The mind comes to dominate the body, to the extent that the mind will pick and choose its bodies. Made into the informational codes that live so well in cyberspace, all the Is finally have a chance to become We. Cyberspace allows the becoming of a transcendental community of mind.
>
> *(p. 187)*

Following Jordan, some cybertheorists focus on the creative potential of the Internet and suggest that this technology may also offer the transformation of subjectivity into new forms and structures (Videcoq et al., 2005, pp. 11–14). Some scholars, such as Žižek (2004), have raised the possibility that the Internet may offer possibilities of resistance that work against neoliberal frameworks and that a "post-media" society may be possible only through the development of the Internet (Guattari 1996, p. 263; Žižek, 2004).

But for Levinas the streaming self and the virtualization of society are disasters that will preclude us from a relational ethics and a hospitality that welcomes the stranger, orphan, foreigner, or refugee. Hospitality happens only at thresholds, edges, and boundaries. We must at some level be forced back into the temporal world if we are to be broken open by the suffering of the Other. Disrupting the limits of the body so that the self can embrace the free-market ethos of globalized neoliberal capitalism is an extremely dangerous proposition.

In a discussion on alterity and desire, Bifo (2008) expresses the Levinasian sensibility beautifully when he says,

> In this narrow passage the very notion of ethical consciousness has to be rethought. Ethical consciousness cannot be grounded anymore, as it was in the modern age, on the harmony of Reason and the Will. The roots of rationalism have been torn forever, rationalism cannot be the principal direction of the planetary humanism that must be conceived. The ethical problem today is set as the problem of the soul, that is the sensitivity animating the body, making the body able to open empathetically to the other.
>
> *(pp. 31–32)*

What we will ultimately lose are forces that disrupt the self-serving, self-centered being and "the traumatising indictment of the gravitational pull of our egoism" (Hofmeyr, 2014, p. 119). According to Lucas Introna (2001), a Levinasian scholar, "[T]he primordial source of our social being is being eroded" (p. 12). In other words, what will our shared humanity and commitment to others look like in the future if we lose our ties to the body, history, and time? Where will our solidarity come from? The political implications of this may be beyond Foucault's super panopticons or Levinas' concerns around the emptiness of human rights that make us vulnerable to evils of fascism. We may be opening ourselves to a kind of violence we have not yet imagined that is quite different from the ontological drama of egos battling in finite space. Imagine a cyber-murder of digital identity that goes on infinitely since it is unlinked from the death of the body. The way we appreciate change and difference is through the decline of the body, which includes its death. For Levinas, an ethics linked to the face is all the transcendence there is and is our only ticket home. We must not forget how much hope there is in that.

Conclusion

Throughout this chapter I have tried to use a form of theoretical *bricolage* to argue that it is the affective "margin of discontent" and anxiety and our "uploaded" subjectivity that characterizes the mood of capitalism and it is this margin that now contextualizes the therapeutic work we do as clinicians. From a clinical perspective anxiety as an affect is the embodied story of capitalism and this is becoming only more so through our usage and exposure of social media networks that have become the "architecture of our intimacies" (Turkle, 2016). As the collapse of space based community yields to a continuous, commodified stream of surveilled performance, subjects can alternate between different consumer identities that align with the acceleration of capitalism. New meta-psychologies will need to creatively include a form of new materialism so that new images, new symbolic registers, as well as new forms of social existence can be reconfigured, so that we may better understand what is at stake in the process of human transformation.

References

Becker. B. (2022). *Evil and givenness: The thanatonic phenomenon*. Blue Ridge Summit, PA: Lexington Books.

Bifo. (2008). Alterity and desire. In S. O'Sullivan & S. Zepke (Eds.), *Deleuze, Guattari and the production of the new* (pp. 22–32). London: Bloomsbury Publishing.

Bion, W. R. (1959). Attacks on linking. *The International Journal of Psychoanalysis, 40*, 308–315.

Caputo, J. (2009). *The weakness of God: A theology of the event*. Bloomington, IN: Indiana University Press.

Caputo, J. (2011). Hospitality and the trouble with God. In R. Kearney & K. Semonovitch (Eds.), *Phenomenologies of the stranger: Between hostility and hospitality* (pp. 83–97). New York: Fordham University Press.

Chalmers, D. (2010). The singularity: A philosophical analysis. *Journal of Consciousness Studies, 17*, 7–65.

Clynes, M., & Kline, N. S. (1960). Cyborgs and space. *Astronautics, 5*(9), 26–27/74–76.

Dean, J. (2010). *Blog theory: Feedback and capture in the circuits of drive.* Cambridge: Polity Press.

Deleuze, G. (1990). *The logic of sense* (M. Lester with C. Stivale, Trans.). New York: Columbia University Press.

Deleuze, G. (1995). *Negotiations 1972–1990* (M. Joughin, Trans.). New York: Columbia University Press.

Deleuze, G., & Guattari, F. (1987). *A thousand plateaus: Capitalism and schizophrenia* (B. Massumi, Trans.). Minneapolis, MN: University of Minnesota Press.

Deleuze, G., & Guattari, F. (2009). *Anti-Oedipus: Capitalism and schizophrenia.* New York: Penguin Books.

Goodman, D., & Collins. A. (2019). The streaming self: Liberal subjectivity, technology and unlinking. *Journal of Theoretical and Philosophical Psychology, 39*(3), 147–156. https://doi.org/10.1037/teo0000111

Grosz, E. (2018). *The incorporeal: Ontology, ethics and the limits of materialism.* New York: Columbia University Press.

Guattari, F. (1996). Remaking social practices. In G. Genosko (Ed.), *The Guattari reader* (pp. 262–272). Hoboken, NJ: Wiley-Blackwell Publishing.

Haraway, D. J. (1991). *Simians, cyborgs, and women: The reinvention of nature.* New York: Routledge Publishing.

Haraway, D. (1997). *Modest_Witness@Second_Millennium.FemaleMan© _Meets_OncoMouse: Feminism and technoscience.* New York: Routledge Publishing.

Haraway, D. (2006). A cyborg manifesto: Science, technology, and socialist-feminism in the late 20th century. In J. Weiss, J. Nolan, J. Hunsinger, & P. Trifonas (Eds.), *The international handbook of virtual learning environments* (pp. 117–158). New York: Springer Publishing.

Hofmeyr, B. (2014). Is Facebook effacing the face? Reassessing Levinas's ethics in the age of social connectivity. *Filozofia, 69*(2), 119–130.

Introna, L. D. (2001). Virtuality and morality: On (not) being disturbed by the Other. *Philosophy in the Contemporary World, 8*(1), 11–19.

Johnston, A. (2005). *Time driven: Metapsychology and the splitting of the drive.* Evanston, IL: Northwestern University Press.

Johnston, A. (2017). From closed need to infinite greed: Marx's drive theory. *Continental Thought and Theory, 1*(4), 270–346.

Johnston, A., & Malabou, C. (2013). *Self and emotional life: Philosophy, psychoanalysis, and neuroscience.* New York: Columbia University Press.

Jordan, T. (1999). *Cyberpower: The culture and politics of cyberspace and the internet.* New York: Routledge Publishing.

Lacan, J. (2004). *The four fundamental concepts of psychoanalysis* (J.-A. Miller, Ed.). London: Karnac Books.

Layton, L. (2006). Attacks on linking: The unconscious pull to dissociate individuals from their social context. In L. Layton & N. C. Hollander (Eds.), *Psychoanalysis, class and politics: Encounters in the clinical setting* (pp. 107–117). New York: Routledge Publishing.

Levinas, E. (1982). *De l'évasion* [On escape]. Fata Morgana (Original work published 1935).

Levinas, E. (2003). *On escape* (B. Bergo, Trans.). Stanford, CA: Stanford University Press (Original work published 1935).

Mbembe, A. (2017). *Critique of Black reason* (L. Dubois, Trans.). Durham, NC: Duke University Press.

Posteraro, T. (2017). To save materialism from itself: A review of Elizabeth Grosz, *The Incorporeal: Ontology, Ethics and the Limits of Materialism. Postmodern Culture, 28*(1). https://doi.org/10.1353/pmc.2017.0017

Ricoeur, P. (2006). *On translation.* New York: Routledge Publishing.

Romano, C. (2009). *Event and world.* New York: Fordham University Press.

Severson, E. (2013). *Levinas's philosophy of time: Gift, responsibility, diachrony and hope.* Pittsburgh, PA: Duquesne University Press.

Steinbock, S. (2009). *Phenomenology and mysticism: The verticality of religious experience.* Bloomington, IN: Indiana University Press.

Sugarman, J., & Thrift, E. (2017). Neoliberalism and the psychology of time. *Journal of Humanistic Psychology, 60*(6), 807–828. https://doi.org/10.1177/0022167817716686

Swabrick, S. (2017, December 26). Materialism without matter: Deleuze. *Genealogy of the Post-Human.* https://criticalposthumanism.net/deleuze-gilles/

Turkle, S. (1997). *Life on the screen: Identity in the age of the internet.* New York: Simon & Schuster, Inc.

Turkle, S. (2012). *Alone together: Why we expect more from technology and less from each other.* New York: Basic Books.

Turkle, S. (2016). *Reclaiming conversation: The power of talk in a digital age.* New York: Penguin Books.

Videcoq, E., Holmes B., & Querrien, A. (2005). Les trois plis du média-activisme [The three folds of media activism]. *Multitudes, 21*(Summer), 11–14.

Wellman, B. (1979). The community question: The intimate networks of East Yorkers. *American Journal of Sociology, 84*, 1201–1231.

Wellman, B. (2001). The physical place and cyberspace: The rise of personalized networking. *Journal of Urban and Regional Research, 12*, 227–252. https://doi.org/10.1111/1468-2427.00309

Whitehead, A. F. (1969). *Process and reality: An essay in cosmology.* Stuttgart: Macmillan Press.

Žižek, S. (2004), *Organs without bodies: Deleuze and consequences.* New York: Routledge Publishing.

30

CRUEL OPTIMIZATION

Interrogating Technology's Optimization of Human Being

Stephen Lugar

It's 2014, a beautiful late spring day in San Francisco. I'm walking up 18th Street alongside Dolores Park, the city's quintessential gathering place for the young, ambitious, and grungy, feeling appreciative and finally truly at home in my adopted city after the almost ten years since I've moved here from New York. But my reverie is disrupted as I see several words brightly stenciled into the concrete of the sidewalk—"Queers Hate Techies." It's not a one-off. The closer I look I realize that these three angry words are painted up and down the block, taunting the tech workers that are drinking champagne and indulging in edibles just up the grassy knoll from where I stand.

The street commentary is jarring and exciting, slightly violent, and utterly at odds with how I'd felt up until this moment—a mixture of appreciation and awe for the city's beauty and for my own evolution as a dyed in the wool east coaster who finally feels like I "get it" here in California. Bemused, I think to myself, "Huh. I'm queer. Do I hate techies?" I quickly realize that I'm on the same block where only a year before my long-time next-door neighbor in the Mission, a Marxist union organizer and local Occupy Wall Street lead, staged a massive protest of the Google shuttle buses ferrying employees from their Dolores Park apartments down to Mountain View. He was a mole in the protest, impersonating an aggrieved Google employee on one of those buses. As his secret compatriots held anti-gentrification protest signs to disrupt the service at the bus stop—an actual SF MTA city bus stop that had been colonized by the air conditioned, Wi-Fi-enabled charter buses—my neighbor acting enraged and entitled yelled back at them, "Why don't you go to a city that you can afford? This is a city for the *right* kind of people, the people who can *actually* afford to live here!" Disgusting idea, right? When I push through the emotional turmoil of this scene—stencils and moles, activists and techies—behind the disorientation I feel a swirl of immense anger and profound helplessness inside of myself. But I realize it's not anger or helplessness for one side of this conflict or the other, but actually all around. The enraged and desperate activists afraid of losing their homes and community. The angry and confused tech workers, afraid that their notions of success and meritocracy will be challenged, perhaps semi-conscious of the dire inequities baked into the system now being thrust into their field of view. My own self-recriminations that I'm not an activist like I'd want to fancy myself, *and* that I'm envious of those magical-seeming stock options that all of the young tech

DOI: 10.4324/9781003195849-36

workers in my practice keep gleefully mentioning. There is rage and fear and confusion *in toto*, and it's everyone's problem.

It is now 2023, and I've thought about this moment many times over the last near decade as this city—and to some degree our society—has been radically changed by the twenty-first-century technology boom. Trying to make sense of it, I've been drawn to the ideas of affect theory and Lauren Berlant, a preeminent scholar in the field. Describing a central tenet of affect theory, Berlant (2011) states, "the present is perceived, first affectively: the present is what makes itself present to us before it becomes anything else, such as an orchestrated collective event or an epoch on which we can look back" (p. 4). San Francisco has changed in the last near ten years but so has our entire world. We've been heartily confronted with unimaginable and what feels to be unavoidable income inequality, a resurgence of authoritarian leadership and polarized politics in America, the beginnings of a deep and painful racial reckoning, a jarring confrontation of the patriarchy through the #MeToo movement, the first, agonizing stages of a global pandemic, and ever-increasing catastrophic climate change impacts. What is this present if not profoundly disorienting and at times terrifying? The "present" of this last decade is filled with expressions of angry, frightened, and helpless affect. Queers hate techies, and I would contend that techies, who are ostensibly trying to solve for systemic inefficiencies and free market problems, are in fact trying to transform things that many of us in this particular present are deeply afraid of: human vulnerability and limitation.

This leads me back to life, and a psychoanalytic practice, in Silicon Valley. The "disruptive technologies" of the twenty-first-century technology boom promise a life in which we can "optimize" for suffering, leaving many adherents of these technologies with a hunger to engineer their psyches the way that one might rewrite a piece of outdated code. I encounter this mindset continually in my practice and have become deeply acquainted with the unique anguish that accompanies the notion that if only one could just get the code right, they could be free from their limitations and pain. Drawing from Bollas' (1979) notion of the "transformational object," I formulate this collective desire as a desperate—but deeply understandable—bid for an internal object that soothes and effects change; change in the form of a developed-enough self that can metabolize and then tolerate pain and suffering. I contend that many of our patients—be it the engineers and executives of Silicon Valley to those who consume their engineered products throughout our society—may be locked in a bid for a transformational object. I must also assert, however, that the fantasies of the transformational capacities of current technology both have profound reality-based potential for change and are in part a developmentally aspirational object relationship.

Yet, I suggest that there is a problematic relation here between transformation and suffering. Berlant (2011) posits the notion of cruel optimism—when something you desire (e.g. transformational change) is actually an obstacle to your flourishing. The wish for absolute transformation and control of human suffering creates a relation that I call cruel optimization—where the quest to optimize is at odds with the depressive realities of the limitations and vulnerability inherent to the human experience. In this chapter, I will expand on the socio-political forces that potentiate this cruel relation between a fantasy of techno-omnipotence and the impossible task of outrunning the limitations of being human.

Disruptive Technologies and Neoliberalism

To be clear, I am aware of the othering and vilification of the figurative techie that's already present in this narrative. It is my hope to try and correct for that while holding a "both/and" mentality regarding some of the problematics of this mindset. The moniker "techie" has become an essential part of the lexicon of the Bay Area, and I would contend in most urban centers in the United States. It conjures up images of young, ambitious innovators, socially awkward programmers, entitled tech bros who want to strike it rich through an IPO rather than on Wall Street, and diabolical founders who espouse altruistic ideals of societal improvement but create monopolies and eschew responsibility. In this chapter, I want to both speak of the individuals who inhabit Silicon Valley—I will draw from my own case material—as well as to think of "techie" as a signifier and container for the overwhelming affects that our current present is so saturated with.

The actual techie I'm speaking of here is often involved in and valorizes disruptive technologies. A commonly used notion in Silicon Valley, disruptive innovation and technology describes something that establishes a new market that will eventually displace existing leading firms, products and groups within that market space. Think of examples as common place as ride sharing services like Uber undoing the taxi industry, the emergence of ubiquitous Artificial Intelligence and machine learning, renewable energy and electric cars, or cryptocurrency. These technologies are attempting to solve for problems that are otherwise intractable based on the limits of a current technology and do so by a wholesale transformation of the market landscape. This could be seen as a distillation of capitalism at its best. A market stagnates and an innovative technology emerges, shakes things up by solving a fundamental problem and demonstrably improves lives as a result. One could say this is Silicon Valley's *raison d'etre*, and it has incontrovertibly changed the world since the dawn of the Information Age in the mid-twentieth century. Personal computing, data processing, automation, to name just a few advances of the technological age, have radically changed and increased the human population's access to information and economic productivity, and globalized our world—for better and for worse.

Clearly, there are undeniable upsides to this transformative revolution. Yet with this profound technological potential, a new kind of techno-omnipotence has emerged. Billionaire tech moguls like Peter Thiel and Jeff Bezos aspire to literally live forever and colonize other planets as we exhaust our own planet's resources and render it uninhabitable. While these are not solutions for the collective but perhaps the narcissistic fantasies of an elite few, they represent a broader fantasy that technology can save us from our greatest existential crises. Clearly the wish to avoid our ultimate ending is not novel to the human condition—think of the fountain of youth appearing in the writings of Herodotus and notions of immortality in countless other cultural and religious traditions. I believe these current aspirations of technological omnipotence, however, capture our collective imagination right now because we have virtually no safety net in our current political and economic world order. I contend that the threats and profound societal problems that I alluded to above (e.g. vast income inequality, human caused climate change, etc.) must be considered alongside the realities of life in a neoliberal capitalist society.

Neoliberalism describes the predominant form of political economy in the United States and other major Western capitalist nations for the last 40 years. Its hallmarks include the facilitation of free markets and globalization, deregulation, dismantling and privatizing social and welfare services, and an emphasis on individual responsibility rather than government intervention (Layton, 2014). The neoliberal order prevailed for decades, but through events such as the 2008 global economic collapse, we have seen the immense income inequality and general insecurity that this order has wrought. Our basic integrity as a society and a species has been under threat concurring with a decades-long evisceration of the social safety net. There is also an ongoing notion that capital markets will ultimately prevail to take on existential crises like climate change, pandemics, or destructive, systemic racism without governmental intervention or support. The affects captured in the activists vs. techie wars of the mid-2010s reflect the anger, desperation, and fear regarding displacement and structural inequality that's not just found in the tech boom times of San Francisco, but that I think pervades our globalized and warming world. It's worth noting that the "Queers Hate Techies" stencils were propagated by an activist group called Gay Shame, a radical queer group founded on anti-assimilationist, anti-consumerist and anti-capitalist principles that run directly counter to neoliberal ideology and systems.

I think here we can deeply understand and appreciate fantasies of omnipotent transformation, and thus why any individual who might be called a techie could be so taken with the notion of disruptive technologies. When society and human existence feel to be in a state of primitive free fall in the Winnicottian sense, who doesn't want change and transformation from a more powerful being than oneself? Or, in Bollas' (1979) words, a hoped-for transformational object? Lynn Layton, a prominent psychoanalyst whose work focuses on the link between the social and the psyche, chronicles how neoliberalism took hold in the United States in the 1960s. Layton (2009) describes what she calls a pervasive "neoliberal subjectivity" in our society as,

> A version of contemporary subjectivity marked by a repudiation of vulnerability that has arisen from the social, economic, and political milieu of the past 30 years. The defense mechanisms involved in such a repudiation cause a decline in empathic capacities and in the capacity to experience ourselves as responsible and accountable for the suffering of others.
>
> *(p. 105)*

In this context, Layton (2014) describes grandiosity and omnipotence as a defense against the potentially extreme insecurity and vulnerability that anyone in the neoliberal set-up of the last several decades can and often does experience. I would contend that the trends and fantasies of what I'm calling techno-omnipotence, or a kind of technological, neoliberal subjectivity, are partially a result of feeling insecure in this neoliberal world order. This accounts for both the extremes of billionaire founders looking for the fountain of youth, but also the more accessible notions of technological transformation that pervade Silicon Valley.

Approaching this from a different angle, Byung-Chul Han, a contemporary Korean-born German philosopher, writes of how neoliberal ethics and capitalist power use modern technologies in ways that colonize the human psyche. In a blistering essay entitled "Healing as Killing," Han (2017) speaks to how neoliberal market forces exploit the individual through notions of "self-optimization" and general self-improvement. Speaking of its ubiquity in modern, neoliberal societies, Han contends this ethos has nothing to do with individual well-being and happiness but serves to make more efficient workers and to capitalize on their working time. Han (2017) says,

> the neoliberal imperative of self-optimization serves only to promote perfect functioning within the system. Inhibitions, points of weakness and mistakes are to be therapeutically eliminated in order to enhance efficiency and performance... self-optimization follows from systemic constraints—from the logic of quantifying success on the market.
>
> *(p. 29)*

Han describes this exploitation as total and leading to profound mental and psychic exhaustion and collapse in our societies. He speaks of countless motivational and self-improvement workshops and retreats, and the big business of self-help. For Han, these are exploitative, systemic forces that no one individual has control over, yet exhibit profound psychic control over the individual.

Layton (2014) advocates looking both at the social world in addition to the dynamics of early life experience and family to understand the derivation of what she calls "borderline features in the culture" (p. 464), that is, grandiosity and omnipotence as defenses against vulnerability in a neoliberal world. I put forth that the fantasies of exceptionalism and optimization afforded by transformational technology are in part a grandiose denial of dependency, a denial that one needs anything from others, that is so endemic to our current social context. Further describing the pernicious effects of a neoliberal world order, Layton (2014) says that it, "figures social divisions and income inequality as problems of individual lack of incentive and moral integrity—rather than as problems produced by capitalism itself" (p. 464). Through Han's lens, this is also a function of neoliberal exploitation that we can't avoid and are embedded in systemically. Clearly, these phenomena have influenced the deep individualism inherent in our collective psyche, and I would say contributed to the extraordinary fantasmatic power of potential technological change. Put more simply, I contend that the social must be considered when understanding the wish to optimize for everything from market problems to human suffering and the existential dreads that I describe in this chapter.

Francisco Gonzalez (2020) makes this mindset an imperative as he implores the field of psychoanalysis to bring a theory of groups and group phenomena to our understanding of individual psychology. He describes the importance of what he calls a social unconscious, as follows,

> Just as the individual brings a repressed or dissociated personal unconscious, in the terms we have grown to understand through traditional psychoanalysis (along the lines of individual object relations, organismal need, sexual- or object-motivated drives and attachments, desires for and through the singular other, and so forth) so too is that unconscious only conceivable in its relationship to the hegemonic forces, organized social structures, institutional power, and history that becomes incarnated in groups—that is, a social unconscious.
>
> *(pp. 390–391)*

This mindset is essential when considering the collective psyche of the techie as well as the fantasmatic hold that tech has on our society as a whole. While I have no doubt that individual and family of origin dynamics play a part in leading those who are drawn to the promises of transformational tech to Silicon Valley, I think our lack of a safety net and societally dictated vulnerability have led to grandiose defenses such as a privileging of transformation and optimization that can be both punishing, as well as impossible to attain. I also think this is a part of why tech's influence, and the mindset I am describing here, is so relevant to understanding our broader society and our collective psyche in the Information Age.

Transformational Objects and Transformational Tech

I'd like to return to my contention that there is a developmentally aspirational object relationship to transformational technologies that I encounter in my practice, and that I believe is pervading our culture more broadly, due to a tenuous hold on security and stability at the societal level. Bollas (1979) describes Winnicott's environmental mother as "the 'culture' that she creates for herself and her infant" (p. 97). He puts this as,

> a constant process of negotiated moments that cohere around the rituals of psychosomatic needs: i.e., feeding, diapering, sleeping, holding. It is undeniable, I think, that as the infant's 'other' self, the mother continually *transforms* the infant's internal and external environment.
>
> *(p. 97)*

Of course, Winnicott contends that the mother is less an object than a process identified with internal and external change for the infant subject. Bollas describes this first object relation between mother and infant, in essence the environmental mother, as the transformational object. He goes on to say, "the mother is not yet identified as an object but is experienced as a process of transformation, and this feature remains in the trace of this object-seeking in adult life" (p. 97).

Bollas further contends that this object relation manifests as a search for an object that can take the form of "person, place, event, ideology" that promises to transform (p. 98). He plainly states that this is the search for "the earliest experience of the object: the experience of an object that transforms the subject's internal and external world" (pp. 98–99). I think this an excellent conceptualization of the almost reverential relationship to disruptive or transformational technologies that I see so often in my practice. Patients speak of charismatic tech company founders with awe and devotion. I've heard so many different iterations of the wish to simply "hack the code" of adulting, or parenting, or simply tolerating the difficulties of everyday life. I've had more than a few patients wish that they could just "download the contents" of their minds to my mind instead of having to come up with the words to describe their experience. I've come to hear this last refrain as a wish for profound and total understanding, akin to Bollas' transformational object experience. Rather than putting this in terms of a psychopathological failure of early life experience and environment, Bollas normalizes the hunger for the transformational object as a universal, humanistic desire to get back to a transformational, early state. While he does acknowledge that varied problems can emerge from a failure to become "disillusioned from this relationship" (p. 99), he describes the early enviro-somatic transformational experience as being so powerful, it is hard to imagine who wouldn't want to return to it. Twenty-first-century technology makes those promises explicit.

A decade ago, Stephen Hartman (2011) first wrote of the transformational potentials of the Internet and cyberspace, dubbing the notion of "Reality 2.0." Describing "networked" online relations, a fundamental disruptive technology, Hartman puts forth a version of psychic reality in which, "access trumps the need to accepts limits as a tool to self-discovery, and networking replaces containment as the bulwark of meaning" (p. 468). Writing in the early days of ubiquitous online interaction and social networking, Hartman discusses the liberatory psychic potentials of relating in a sphere in which one is not constrained by traditional reality-based limits of location, gender, etc. He also clearly recognizes the potential problems inherent in unconstrained and infinite relating. We have seen social networking evolve from a tool to share information and help communities gather and coalesce to a place of unchecked tribalism, splitting, and hard-to-combat misinformation. Yet even in the era of QAnon and dangerous political or scientific disinformation, I think Hartman's suggestion that we imagine the limitlessness of this technological space as a potential place for psychic advance and not only a place for psychic retreat is still extremely germane. I think this speaks to transformational technology's psychic draw. Again, using Bollas' words (1979), "the infant identifies the mother with transformation of being, though his symbiotic knowing, is not a delusion, but a fact; the mother actually transforms the infant's world" (p. 85). Twenty-first-century technology promises to transform us so overtly as Bollas' transformational object and Hartman's notion of Reality 2.0 do so as well. Who wouldn't want to attach themselves to and be a part of something that promises explicitly, as modern information technology does, to transform us as our original caregivers once did? This is deeply underscored when we consider how vulnerable we are in a society with little to no safety net, and with profound existential problems around just about every turn.

Cruel Optimization

I bring the above ideas together to put forth that our neoliberal society has left its babies vulnerable—while recruiting them to do its bidding—needing much more provisional care and that current technology is an understandable proxy transformational object. Explicating her notion of cruel optimism, Berlant (2011) suggests that the "good life fantasy" of the post-World War II period has long since frayed, but that the striving for this good life continues (e.g. "fantasies of upward mobility, job security, political and social equality, and lively, durable intimacy" [p. 3]) and that this is a cruelly optimistic relation. She explains that "optimism is cruel when the object/scene that ignites a sense of possibility actually makes it impossible to attain the expansive transformation for which a person or a people risks striving" (p. 2). I think this idea is profoundly helpful when considering the bind that those that pin their hopes on optimization through technology find themselves in. So many of my patients have presented to me with the hope that they can optimize their psyches, often using the metaphor of "rewriting the code" of their own minds. Yet that phrase rarely feels metaphorical to me when it's used. In other words, the fantasy is that one could actually erase their own vulnerability, limitations, and emotional pain perhaps as they would use a programming language to create more efficient data compression and storage. I believe this has in part been inspired by the hope and promise of transformational technology in this era, as well as neoliberal imperatives of self-improvement. That becomes a cruel relation, however, because it is impossible to attain. We can't ultimately escape our psychic or somatic limitations, much less live forever. Pain and traumatic experience are unavoidable. The notion that our psyches can be manipulated to perform functions like the computer processing operational instructions of a binary code can therefore become an obstacle to one's flourishing due to its impossibility. Yet, this fantasy is so understandable when we consider that our individually accrued retirement savings can be wiped out in a moment, or that one serious medical catastrophe or natural disaster can bankrupt us. Our vulnerabilities are so profound, and this leads us to strive for nonhuman derived transformation.

Practicing deeply embedded in the Bay Area technology ethos has led me to wonder how psychoanalysis can be helpful to those who are so hungry for this kind of psychic optimization. As an analyst, I have a deep conviction that it will be helpful for my patients to lean into their suffering, hoping that they may attain a kind of depressive-position acceptance of limitations and the difficulties innate to the human experience. This analytic mindset, however, can feel diametrically opposed to the mindset of many who make their way to my consulting room. How does an analyst propose to help someone who would prefer to

AirDrop the contents of their mind rather than struggle through figuring and representing their experience—albeit messily and inefficiently—with me?

Here I find Bion's (1962) theory of thinking to be immensely helpful. For Bion, a thought is the result of a preconception mated with a frustration. To explain this, Bion proposes the model of an infant's expectation of a nourishing breast being met with the realization that there is no breast available to satisfy them. He goes on to say,

> The next step depends on the infant's capacity for frustration: in particular it depends on whether the decision is to evade frustration or to modify it… If the capacity for toleration of frustration is sufficient the 'no-breast' inside becomes a thought, and an apparatus for 'thinking' it develops.

(p. 307)

The capacity to tolerate frustration is therefore a precursor to the capacity to think in Bion's terms, and if frustration tolerance is not sufficient, he suggests that that "tips the scales in the direction of the evasion of frustration" (p. 307). I believe that many members of our neoliberal society are forced in the direction of the evasion of frustration because this system and social surround do not facilitate the capacity to tolerate the experience of lack, limitation, or vulnerability, and in fact force us to disavow those psychic truths. As Layton (2014) says, our neoliberal system creates these "borderline features in the culture" such as grandiose denial of dependency, vulnerability, or in economic terms, of being poor. Han (2017) describes this as the result of neoliberal exploitation which aims "to capitalize not just on working time but on the person him- or herself" (p. 29). I believe that as psychoanalysts we are uniquely qualified to help our patients build the capacity to tolerate this particular kind of frustration, so that one can think, in the Bionian sense, when confronted with the limitations of being human. As Han, and many philosophers à la Nietzsche before him, eloquently points out, "negativity is what keeps life alive. Pain is constitutive for experience. Life that consists wholly of positive emotions and the sensation of 'flow' is not human at all" (p. 31). This notion is in my bones—from my own lived experience to the different parts of myself throughout my personal history as a student of literature and psychoanalysis. As an analyst, I make this case rather painstakingly with my patients and I have found that this fundamental truth eventually can be felt and become known through the holding and containment of the analytic relationship, as I hold this conviction on an almost cellular level within myself.

While writing this chapter, I have somewhat uncomfortably gotten in touch with my own difficulties with the mindset of boundless optimization and the devotion to transformational technology. But facing the discomfort, and even cynicism, that I may feel when working with someone who desperately hopes to hack their mind and be transformed, however, has allowed me to acknowledge my own fantasies of transformation. That leads to another way that I believe psychoanalysts can be helpful to these patients and to our society more generally. By deeply inhabiting the transformational mindset—that is, acknowledging that we too want to be transformed while helping build toleration of frustration—we can help our patients and our culture break out of this relation of cruel optimization. This, I believe, is Gonzalez's (2020) "one-to-many" object relation, or what he deems as the collective aspect of individual psychic life. I am a psychoanalyst who believes in helping people reach depressive position acceptance of limitations and pain. But I am also a person living in a neoliberal society, with my own fears of vulnerability with little to no safety net who hopes for transformation. I believe if I can inhabit this multiplicity, I can help my patients tolerate the pain that there are certain unchangeable limitations innate to being human, and to build the capacity to trust that they can transform themselves, meaningful suffering, and all.

Brian

Brian first came to me after a devastating falling out with the CEO and founder of the tech start-up that he had dedicated four years of his life to, pouring every bit of himself into the company and its culture. Feeling utterly betrayed by the founder who had promised to both create a life changing product and to bring an incredible financial windfall to everyone in the company, Brian sunk into a profound depression after the CEO sold the company with virtually no benefit to its employees and the product simply vanishing. Brian had come to the Bay Area expressly to join the ranks of computer programmers in Silicon Valley with dreams of helping to create the next big Google or Uber and to make the kind of life changing money that would bring him the security and wealth that he had always craved. This all blew up for him fantastically after his boss's betrayal and he found himself bereft of purpose and meaning, as well as deeply terrified that he had lost all ability to think for and to support himself. Looking for something "deeper" than the behavioral treatments he had previously tried, we began a four times a week analysis that led to his feeling hopeful for change for the first time since the beginning of his depression. But Brian's anguish ran deep, and it quickly became clear to me that our work would encompass cycles of hope for wholesale transformation and profound despair at its elusiveness.

Brian was raised in a mid-sized American city and had intimate, firsthand knowledge of life in a neoliberal order. His father was a mechanic who made a living wage but struggled financially to provide for him and his sibling after their mother left the family abruptly when Brian was about seven years old. They moved from apartment to apartment, in and out of archaic and crumbling subsidized housing, always with a sense of precarity that they'd be on the street eventually. His mother remained a beneficent figure in his mind's eye, even though he had no contact with her again until he was about 15 years old. But he remembered her as the smiling life force of the family and struggled with the notion that her abandoning the family at such a pivotal time would have a deep impact on him, maintaining that he felt nothing about her leaving.

My work with Brian initially had everything to do with idealization—the idealization and subsequent betrayal of his former boss and brother-figure, of his mother despite her abandoning him, and of me as the only person who he felt understood him and he believed cared enough to help him despite his confusing and tortured psychic states. But he also idealized the sphere of technology and disruptive innovation and was desperate to be able to recover his work ethic and ability to concentrate so that he could get back to this project. I think that Brian was what many would consider to be a quintessential techie—fueled by a desire to optimize his experience, frustrated by messy, unquantifiable emotions. There were many indications as we started our work that he wanted me to conduct a surgical excision of the pain and suffering that he experienced because of his boss's betrayal and the subsequent dissolution of his company, and furthermore to remove the pain he gradually began to feel about his difficult childhood. I felt incredible paternal warmth toward and a strong pull to help him, yet I also became aware of an inchoate sense of deadness that would creep into our hours that I could link to the somewhat obsessive wish to optimize his thinking and remove his anxieties. He brought bullet point lists of dreams and cognitive confusions, a dossier on the former boss printed on the company's letterhead, all in the hopes that we could rid him of his pain if we could be more systematic and utilize the logic systems he had learned as a software engineer.

But the analysis, as they usually are, was slow. We worked for several years to make sense of the connection between the eruption of psychic distress after his boss's betrayal and his mother's abandonment, and to come to grips with his somewhat feral childhood, in which he was left mostly to raise and care for himself by an absent mother and overworked, negligent, and abusive father. But I could feel my own impatience with the temporal urgency he brought to our work. He hammered me with questions: why was he still so anxious and sad? Why could he not think clearly? When would he be able to work again in the high-pressure tech environments he'd succeeded in before? I tried over and over to convey that this could take time; that his ways of dealing with his pain and trauma had developed over a lifetime and that we would work to experience and make sense of it and then hopefully be able to move forward and through it, together. While I think he was relieved by this at times, I often felt it only placated him. To this end, I took a two-week vacation over the winter holidays in the third year of our analysis and he mentioned in passing that he might try a guided psilocybin medicine experience as a way of "continuing our progress" during the break. When I returned from that vacation, he told me that he had moved ahead with the psilocybin journey, and perhaps unsurprisingly, that he had been "transformed" by it and no longer needed our work because, he said, "the void in me has been filled."

It is of course difficult to condense the experience of this analysis and its painful, abrupt ending, but I'd like to focus my attention here on how I think I failed Brian. I do not do this to fall on the sword, but to consider how we might help our patients with the dilemma of tolerating vulnerability and limitation in a society that provides so little protection; and furthermore, when they are immersed in the promises of modern technologies that proffer to change us as our earliest experiences of care once did. I have come to ask myself could I have done something differently in the analysis if I were more accepting of his need for a transformational object? Was I always subtly dubious of it and in a way that he not so subtly perceived? Hartman (2011) encourages us to disabuse ourselves of the notion that technologically mediated relations are only a form of psychic retreat. Did I mainly think of Brian's profound hope for techno-transformation as a place of psychic retreat à la Steiner? Could I have operated in a more fantasmatic space of transformation that would have enabled us to continue our work rather than lead him to seek out the psychedelic solution (that I have no doubt was helpful but was unlikely to have been permanently and structurally transformational)? And instead, could this have been a place of psychic advance in our work?

Following the end of my work with Brian, I began to realize my own profound transformational fantasies. As we all know, life on the west coast has been fraught in recent years due to relentless droughts and mega wildfires, choking smoke and surreally colored days simply known as the "orange days." It occurred to me that I've fantasized repeatedly about hopes for a Defense Department spaceship that would dump non-toxic fire retardant to put out the multi-hundred-thousand-acre wildfires or that scientists would develop the technology to move rain clouds from the drenched and flooding east coast over the Rockies. I fantasize in my analysis about a life back east where the Western realities of climate change don't yet seem as stark, the air not as poisonous. My analyst has hung out with me in this fantasmatic space. It's a space in which I feel safer and can re-moor myself to the fact that we are collectively going to have to adapt to these realities, that the entire world is faced with climate change impacts, and not that I'm left alone to contend with them or fend for myself. That, to me, is a space of incredible transformative potential, and one which I do not think I could have reached alone. If only I could have gotten there with Brian.

As I conclude, I'm reminded of a moment earlier in Brian's analysis in which I caught him off guard by bringing up the notion of legacy code—the term for old computer source code that is inherited from the original software. He laughed, surprised I had any idea of the term, and asked what I knew about it. I said I understood you can't quite get rid of it, that it's the original source material for the software you're working with, that it can be very confusing as a result, and yet it informs how the current system operates. He laughed again, saying, "for better or worse, it's there, and you can't just start from scratch. You have to deal with the early stuff whether you like it or not. But goddamn, I wish you didn't have to!" I wish now I could have occupied this space of frustration tolerance and fantasy for transformation with him more. At least I remember both of our smiles from that morning so well, and I can say I learned a great deal from him in this co-constructed space.

References

Berlant, L. (2011). *Cruel Optimism*. Durham, NC: Duke University Press.

Bion, W.R. (1962). The Psycho-Analytic Study of Thinking. *International Journal of Psychoanalysis,* 43:306–310.

Bollas, C. (1979). The Transformational Object. *International Journal of Psychoanalysis*, 60:97–107.

Gonzalez, F. (2020). Trump Cards and Klein Bottles: On the Collective of the Individual. *Psychoanalytic Dialogues*, 30:393–398. https://doi.org/10.1080/10481885.2020.1774335

Han, B. (2017). *Psychopolitics: Neoliberalism and New Technologies of Power*. Brooklyn: Verso Publications.

Hartman, S. (2011). Reality 2.0: When Loss is Lost. *Psychoanalytic Dialogues*, 21(4):468–482.

Layton, L. (2009). Who's Responsible? Our Mutual Implication in Each Other's Suffering. *Psychoanalytic Dialogues*, 19(2):105–120.

Layton, L. (2014). Grandiosity, Neoliberalism, and Neoconservatism. *Psychoanalytic Inquiry*, 34(5):463–474.

31

ROOM: A SKETCHBOOK FOR ANALYTIC ACTION

The Use of Digital Technology as a Vehicle in Psychoanalysis

Hattie Myers and Isaac Slone

Speaking to the Boston Psychoanalytic Society in 1941, the Austrian psychoanalyst Ernst Kris (1941, 21–22) argued,

> Whenever [people] form a community, some media of social control exists. The Tribal drum is their ancestor... at some crucial moments of history, technical development becomes a driving power. The invention of the printing press and the nature of social control in the sixteenth century were related in that way.

The "media of social control" Kris referred to were, at the time, radio and film. The presentation he gave was a call to action: he spoke, he said, "out of a sense of duty" (Kris, 1941, 5). Coming to psychoanalysis from art history, Kris thought about the power of image and media—in the broadest sense—as a vehicle for expression, communication, and contemplation. Two years before giving the lecture in Boston, Kris fled Vienna for London. In London, he worked as a senior research officer in the monitoring service of the BBC analyzing broadcast propaganda—a unique position for a psychoanalyst. By 1941, Kris had relocated to New York, where, living under an enemy alien status, he co-founded the Program of Totalitarian Leadership at the New School. Presciently, he talked about the responsibility of the government to address the dangers of mass communication, which could lead to totalitarianism.

Concerning propaganda, Kris (1941) explained that "Psycho-analytical experience and theory have largely contributed to a better understanding of some of the phenomena of human suggestibility" (p. 5). The night he addressed the Boston Psychoanalytic Society, he talked for over an hour, linking the human susceptibility to suggestion to our infantile beginnings and our longing for love and protection. A pivotal consequence of the psychoanalytic understanding of human susceptibility to suggestion is the understanding that an analytic frame acts as a necessary guardrail to support capacities to think and act more autonomously. Freud (1958) lays out these guardrails in his technique papers, emphasizing neutrality, abstinence, and objectivity. Freud's early procedural guardrails established psychoanalysis as a unique way to understand and potentially transform inner suffering. They are close in keeping with Aristotle's understanding of "techne." Aristotle characterizes a techne as a skill or craft that establishes the rules or procedures needed to create the space to

DOI: 10.4324/9781003195849-37

understand (or even to discover) something new. Freud's invention of psychoanalysis established the processes and technique necessary to create the kind of space Aristotle imagined through a clinical modality.

ROOM: A Sketchbook for Analytic Action makes psychoanalytic thinking accessible to a larger community. As is often the case with a new techne, the "crucial moment of history," to quote Kris (1941, 22), "the driving power" behind the creation of *ROOM*, occurred by accident. On November 8, 2016, *ROOM* emerged to meet a new need. For many of us in New York City, the 2016 US presidential election recalled a moment like September 11, 2001. Again, we felt the psychic impact of the sudden destabilization of our expectable world. And seemingly overnight, professional psychoanalytic listservs became the dumping ground of spontaneous angry, scared, and accusatory diatribes.

When a local New York City institute called for a meeting to address the analytic community's distress, analysts filled the room. They expressed concerns about their patients, families, and their terrors about the future. While it helped to have time and space to share these feelings and thoughts and hear from others, it was apparent to all in the room that while this crisis would not end soon, it would also not be feasible to meet in person in an ongoing way. The idea of creating a newsletter in which individuals might share thoughts and feelings as events unfolded seemed like it might help address the wish to maintain community connection.

Well aware of the shortcomings of public listservs and individual blogs, a newsletter—along the lines of the newsletter Fenichel created seemed appropriate. From 1934 to 1945 the Rundbriefe was a top-secret newsletter circulated among a small group of socially and politically committed refugee psychoanalysts. Otto Fenichel, its founder and one of Freud's most eminent followers, urged this small group of analysts not to isolate themselves. He wrote in the Rundbriefe, "Where there is still truth, it will be preserved, even if it must fling far... the fate of psychoanalysis depends on the fate of the world" (Myers, 2017). The world survived, but the fate of psychoanalysis took a turn Fenichel could not have predicted. The power of psychoanalysis to address humankind's conflicted, rapacious desires and the dehumanizing impact of civilization degraded over the century. At its heart, psychoanalysis holds that making space or room for the unconscious is critical to our understanding of ourselves and society. Like Fenichel's Rundbriefe, *ROOM* devotes itself to keeping connection with each other and psychoanalysis amid a turbulent political reality. Unlike the Rundbriefe, *ROOM* is not a secret. Like psychoanalysis, it is open to all.

The psychoanalysts knew that designing even a simple newsletter was beyond their capacities. Serendipitously, through word of mouth, we met a graphic designer who offered to join us. Mafe Izaguirre had come to the United States from Venezuela on an artist's visa a few months earlier. Izaguirre was a graphic designer who happened to have expertise in information design and branding. Given her native country's history with fascism and dictatorships, she had an acute awareness of the dangerous political situation she sensed we were beginning to face. She felt a personal commitment to the project and volunteered to help us as best she could.

Also in attendance during that first meeting of what was to become the founding of *ROOM* was Karen Kornblum, a professor of design and human-computer interaction at Carnegie Mellon University. Her expertise in interdisciplinary collaboration was instrumental in bringing all the voices in the room together that day. During the meeting, Karen used a whiteboard to capture the multiple perspectives, and the vision for the publication emerged. This whiteboard encapsulated the confluence of our ideas as a shared vision for what *ROOM* could be. This meeting also marked the first interdisciplinary convergence between psychoanalysis and design, setting the stage for ROOM to become a new vehicle of psychoanalytic action.

Moving from the use of a whiteboard to the use of digital technology involved articulating how we might embed the central principles and guardrails of psychoanalysis within a new virtual medium. This technological medium posed a challenge to the psychoanalytic community (who had just gotten used to using listservs), and proposed an exciting opportunity to gather in a new online space. The name *ROOM* signified that the boundaries of this space are contained and closed. *A Sketchbook* emphasized that this room would provide, much as analytic sessions do, an opportunity to share thoughts, try out new ideas, and begin conversations that might deepen our connection to ourselves and others. In the spirit of a Montaigne's *essai,* we envisioned *ROOM* essays as a way to sketch or *try* out ideas in process. *For Analytic Action* articulated our belief that transformative work could occur through this kind of community connection. The numerical month and year demarcate a single point in time, while also highlighting the consistency of this room over time.

Over the last five years, *ROOM* has become a stable space that moves in and with time while mirroring the present experience of its community of readers and writers. *ROOM*'s open submission process parallels the psychoanalytic technique of free association. Much as the material in each analytic hour emerges from the patient's and analyst's associations, the global concepts (or themes) of new issues are not planned ahead of time but instead, arise organically from community submissions. And like every analytic communication, submissions are read impartially and closely with respect to the author's intentions and *ROOM*'s editors respond to each contribution with sensitivity and tact in the service of maintaining continued connections with the authors. The decision to publish a submission depends on its power, meaningfulness, and newness. As in analytic work, the material which is most new, most powerful, and most meaningful rises to the surface. The editors discuss the thematic patterns that emerge from these selected submissions. Much like an interpretation, the editorials work synthetically to articulate the global theme by weaving together each contributor's distinctive voice. In this way, each iteration of *ROOM* reflects a particular point in time. Over the last five years, *ROOM*'s website has become a living archive of a national and worldwide analytic process.

ROOM demystifies and promotes the value of psychoanalytic thinking by moving across writing styles, disciplinary perspectives, and theoretical points of view. In this way, our platform invites greater familiarity with psychoanalysis as an important lens for personal, cultural, and political discourse. The interdisciplinary aspect of the magazine leans upon the analytic principle that makes use of both verbal and nonverbal material as a means of communication. Through this refined understanding of conscious and unconscious communication, clinical psychoanalysis fosters space for individuals to connect to the more disconnected (or never experienced) aspects of their being in the service of transformation. By marrying digital technology with these central tenets of classical psychoanalysis' therapeutic action, *ROOM*, as an analytic space for connections within the community, emerges as a new digital art of social change.

It became clear to all the founders that the importance of maintaining and fostering an interdisciplinary vision for *ROOM* would serve several purposes moving forward. Broadly, the inclusion of other disciplinary perspectives in *ROOM*'s publication casts a wider net for potential submissions and readers than those if we were strictly addressing a psychoanalytic community. The space is explicitly open to diversity and intersectionality of voices, opinions, styles, and subjects. By including the voices of poets, artists, and other writers among those of psychoanalysts and other mental health practitioners, each iteration of *ROOM* encouraged a multi-approached experience of the global concept.

ROOM 6.21 (June 2021) illustrates how *ROOM*'s editorial mission encourages a variety of contributions and weaves a global theme. Psychoanalyst Susan Kassouf's (2021) article "A

New Thing Under the Sun," raises important questions about the implications of climate change on the psyche, and in turn, psychoanalytic practice. "There was no useful language to describe what I was sensing," Kassouf writes. So she creates the words she needs. While psychoanalysis traditionally emphasizes the primacy of the individual, Kassouf's writing aligns with *ROOM*'s mission to deepen community awareness of how our psyches affect our world and how the world we live in impacts our psychology. *ROOM* 6.21's editorial, "Close Up" describes how one by one, each essay brought the reader into close contact with the author's particular experiences of disillusionment, confusion, heartbreak, shame, fear, and guilt, while lightly gesturing to a more universal experience. In keeping with this, the graphic art, designed to resonate with the essays, was purposefully gestural throughout. The background to Koussouf's essay, for example, represents the environment through an earthy color palette and disrupted the scene with intentional graphic accidents.

Kassouf's article moved more than half a dozen other authors to submit a variety of contributions on climate change during the next submission cycle. In the next issue, *ROOM* 10.21, three essays were published that deepen the discussion Koussouf began. Scholar and analyst Patricia Clough's (2021) "Climate Change and Knowledge Production" explicitly expands on Kassouf's essay, considering the relationship between climate change and digital media/technologies. Clough argues digital data can help us understand climate change in ways that do not mirror a lived reality. Coming from a far more clinical place, Wendy Greenspun's (2021) "Climate Crisis: a Reckoning" considers Greenspun's emotional trajectory of awakening to the threats of the climate crisis, as well as that of one of her patients. Greenspun describes a widening out into the experience of others, which helps both her and her patient connect and mourn in the face of the seemingly impenetrable.

The conversation about climate change parallels the development of psychoanalytic work, in which one session builds and deepens onto another. The elaboration of the existential conversation which began in *ROOM* 2.21 became intrinsically connected to the global theme of *solastalgia* which characterizes *ROOM* 6.21. Solastalgia describes trauma precipitated by terror or despair when lands or communities undergo unwanted, adverse, or unforeseen environmental change. Eric Chasalow's (2021) orchestral work "Elegy and Observation: For Chorus and Electronics" and Katie Gentile and Kathleen Del Mar Miller's (2021) prose-poem-essay *An End of The World-as-We-Know-It: After da Silva* captures the nature of this crisis as only artists could. *ROOM* 10.21's theme of Solastalgia not only deepens the conversation Kassouf starts in her essay, but broadens it to include other submissions related to what the community was experiencing three months later. Along with the essays and art pertaining to the Climate crisis, *ROOM* 10.21 features work by Afghan mental health professionals trapped in Kabul, which was translated by *ROOM* from Dari, as well as essays about the impact of COVID-19. Two months after its publication, *ROOM* 10.21 was already read in over 40 countries, including Afghanistan, Turkey, Iran, Romania, Qatar, Nigeria, and more. Digital technology makes it possible for this new psychoanalytic space to reach places where the field of psychoanalysis has not had strong inroads.

Through the use of technology that did not exist two decades ago and through information design, *ROOM*'s analytic space fosters and promotes voices that, for a variety of reasons, have not had access to be heard. *ROOM* has published essays from mental health professionals describing particular experiences in their countries, including Venezuela, Syria, China, Turkey, Great Britain, Mexico, Israel, and Lebanon. Some of these authors have not had space or opportunity to speak up—either because of political limitations in their own countries or limitations related to other forms of access. Many of the issues these writers have been able to express resonate with our own in the United States.

The chance to open discussion within *ROOM*'s community continues to be an essential tenet of the project, combating the totalitarian aspects of mass communication and promoting the notion that understanding happens through conversation and connection. While the general principles of psychoanalysis provide a pillar of *ROOM*'s transformational power, the other pillar is the interdisciplinary connection to digital technology and design. *ROOM* leads with a recognition that the level of sophistication and thoughtfulness conveyed in writing can only be as useful as its legibility.

Note

ROOM: A Sketchbook for Analytic Action can be found at Analytic-room.com

References

Bishop, C. (2006). The Social Turn: Collaboration and its Discontents. *Artforum International*, 44(6), 178–183.

Chasalow, Eric (2021, October). Elegy and Observation: For Chorus and Electronics. *ROOM: A Sketchbook for Analytic Action*, 10.21, 44–45.

Clough, P.T. (2021) Climate change and knowledge production. *ROOM: A Sketchbook for Analytic Action*, 10.21, 10–12.

Freud, S. (1958). *Standard edition of the complete psychological works of Sigmund Freud, volume XII (1911–1913): The case of Schreber, papers on technique and other works* (J. Strachey, Trans.). New York, NY: W.W. Norton.

Gentile, K & Del Mar Miller K (2021, October). An End of the World-as-We-Know-It: After da Silva. *ROOM: A Sketchbook for Analytic Action*, 10.21, 34–43.

Greenspun, W (2021, October). Climate Crisis: A Reckoning. *ROOM: A Sketchbook for Analytic Action*, 10.21, 50–55.

Kassouf, S (2021, June). A New Thing Under the Sun. *ROOM: A Sketchbook for Analytic Action*, 6.21, 16–22.

Kris, E. (1941). The "Danger" of Propaganda. *American Imago*, 2(1), 3–42.

Myers, H. (2017, May). Making Room. *ROOM: A Sketchbook for Analytic Action*, 5.17, 1–2.

Myers, H. (2021, June). Close Up. *ROOM: A Sketchbook for Analytic Action*, 6.21, 7–9

Myers, H. (2021, October). Solastalgia. *ROOM: A Sketchbook for Analytic Action*, 10.21, 7–9, 43.

INDEX

Note: **Bold** page numbers refer to tables.

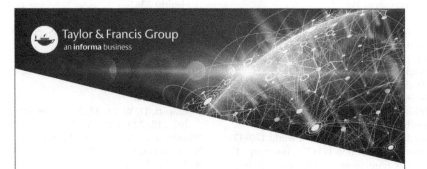

Taylor & Francis Group
an **informa** business

Taylor & Francis eBooks

www.taylorfrancis.com

A single destination for eBooks from Taylor & Francis
with increased functionality and an improved user
experience to meet the needs of our customers.

90,000+ eBooks of award-winning academic content in
Humanities, Social Science, Science, Technology, Engineering,
and Medical written by a global network of editors and authors.

TAYLOR & FRANCIS EBOOKS OFFERS:

A streamlined
experience for
our library
customers

A single point
of discovery
for all of our
eBook content

Improved
search and
discovery of
content at both
book and
chapter level

REQUEST A FREE TRIAL
support@taylorfrancis.com

 Routledge
Taylor & Francis Group

 CRC Press
Taylor & Francis Group